GLOBAL IKAT

Global Ikat: Roots and Routes of a Textile Technique
The David Paly Collection

Published by The Historic Textile Research Foundation in cooperation with Hali Publications Ltd.

Produced in the United Kingdom by Hali Publications Ltd., 6 Sylvester Path, London E8 1EN

British Library Cataloguing-in-Publication Data: a catalogue record for this book is available from the British Library

ISBN 9781898113904

Front cover: WCA25 velvet ikat panel and AF22 Dioula woman's strip-woven cloth

Back cover: WCA10 ikat fragment, AF27 tent panel, AM34 poncho, JP31 royal kimono fragment, EU04 *chiné à la branche* silk, IN28 *patola* sari with leaf design (*pan bhat*), IT05 *Tamago Basada* by Polly Barton, and MA01 shoulder cloth/shawl, *luka semba*

Pablo Picasso quote opposite Contents after Bedřich Forman, "Ikat, eine Erstaunliche und Geheimnisvolle Technik" in *Batik und Ikat: Textilkunst aus Indonesien* (Hanau: Verlag Wener Dausien, 1990). p. 118

Roots and Routes of a Textile Technique

GLOBAL IKAT

The David Paly Collection

Hali

If I didn't have so much to
do with ceramics, I might try
ikat—an amazing art form,
exciting and transcendental...

Pablo Picasso

CONTENTS

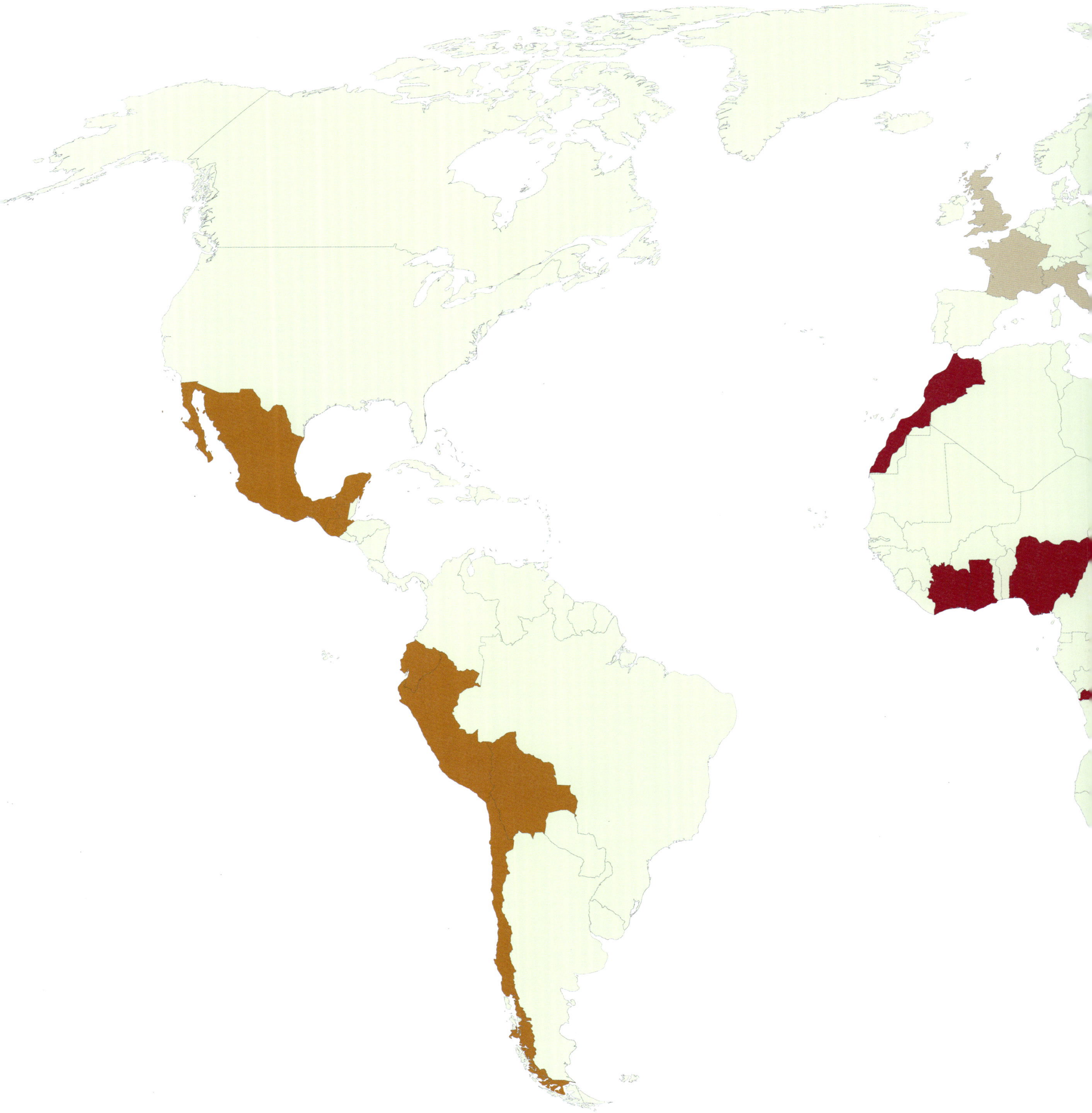

CHAPTERS

- Japan
- Monsoon Asia
- India
- West & Central Asia
- Africa
- Europe
- Americas

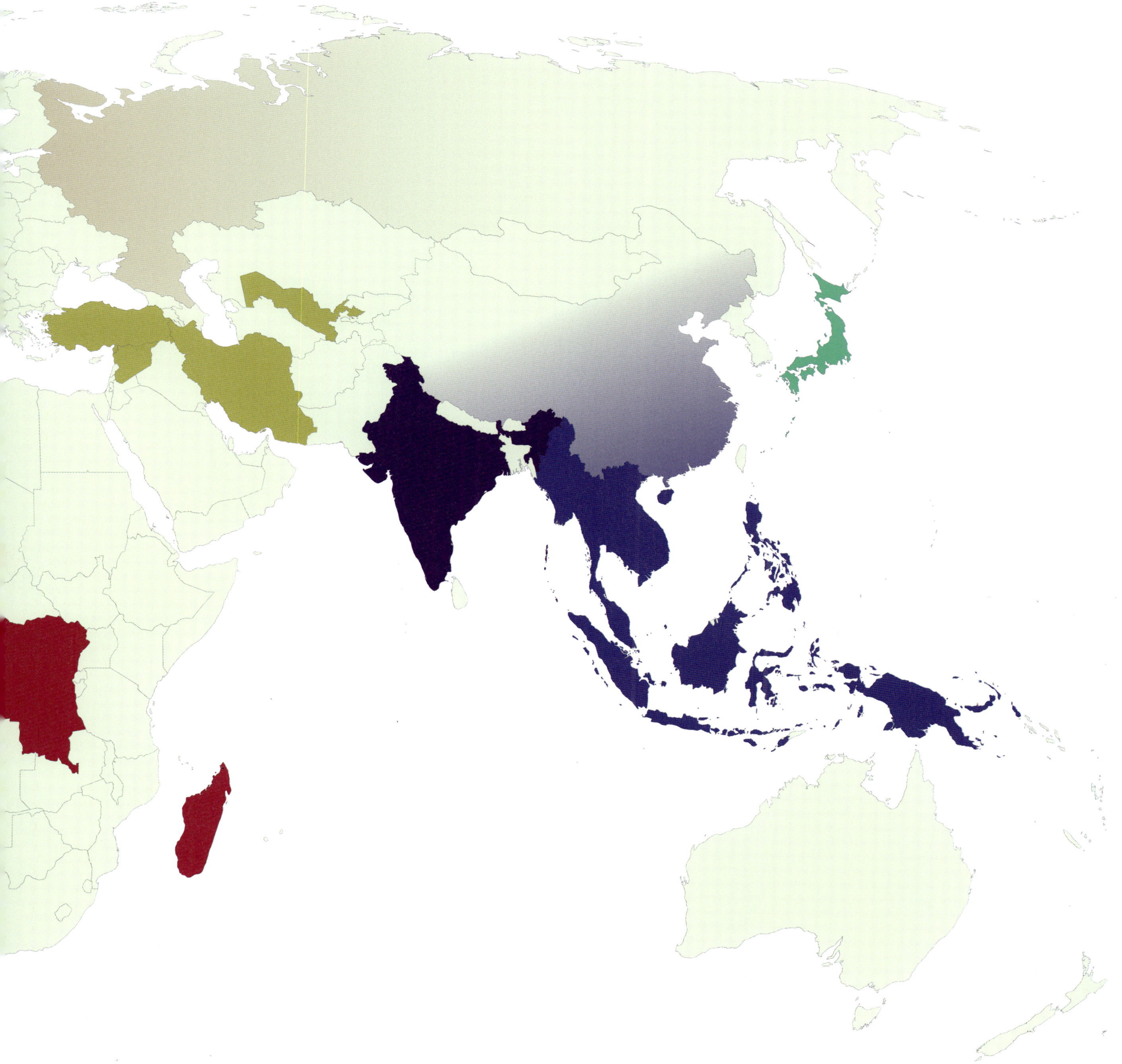

GLOBAL IKAT

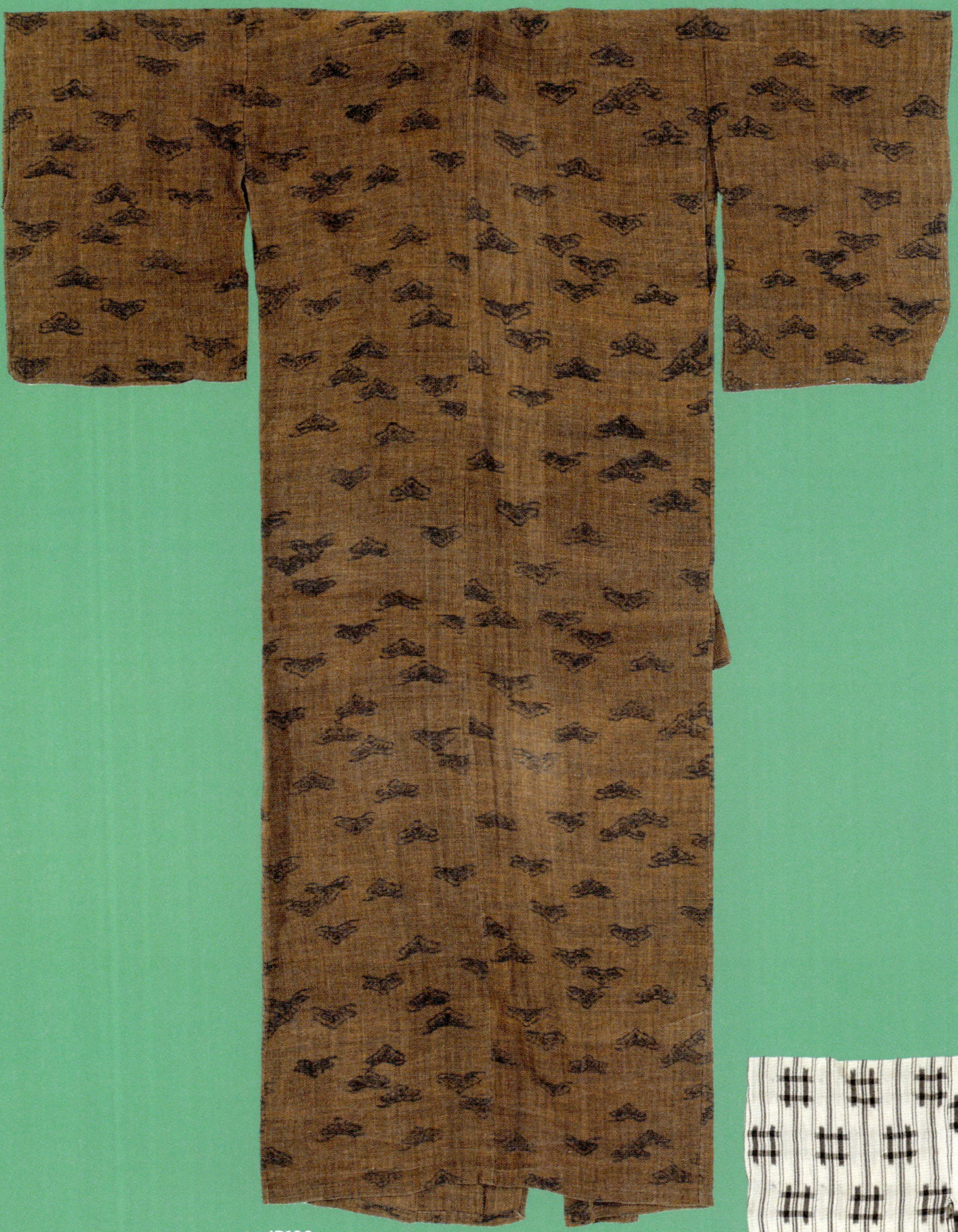

JP120

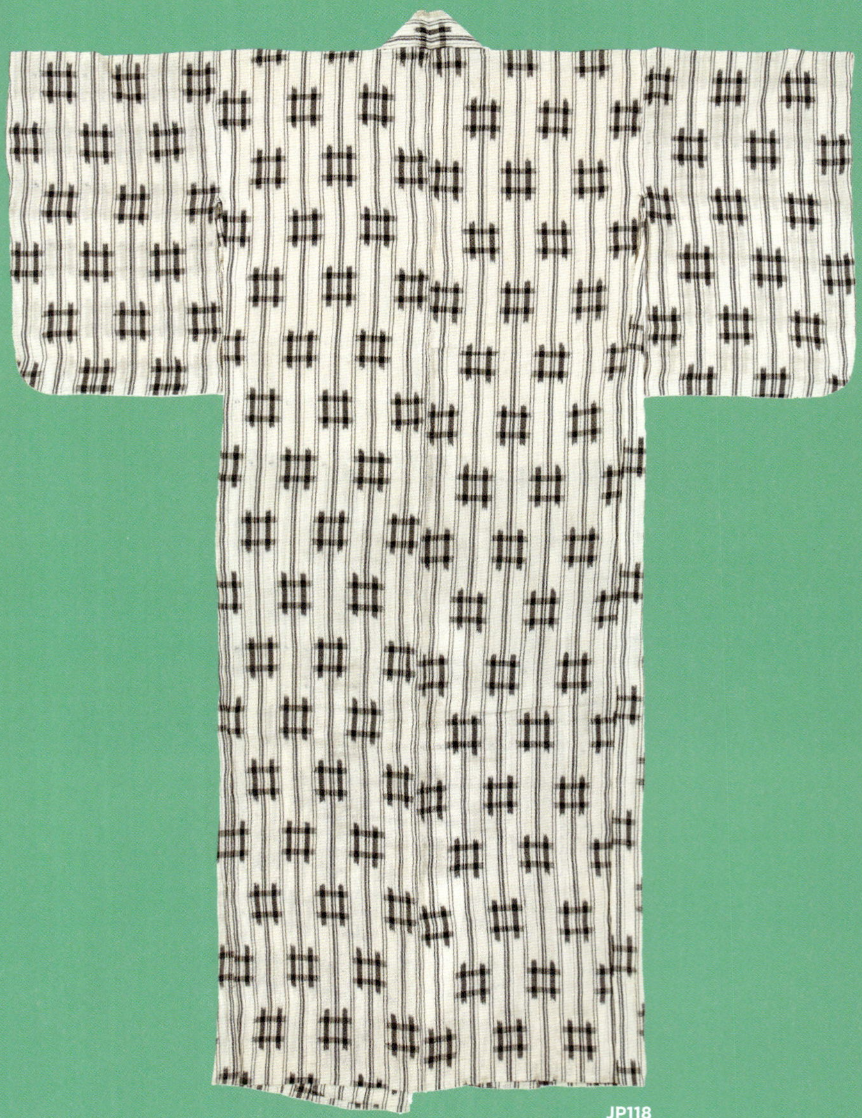

JP118

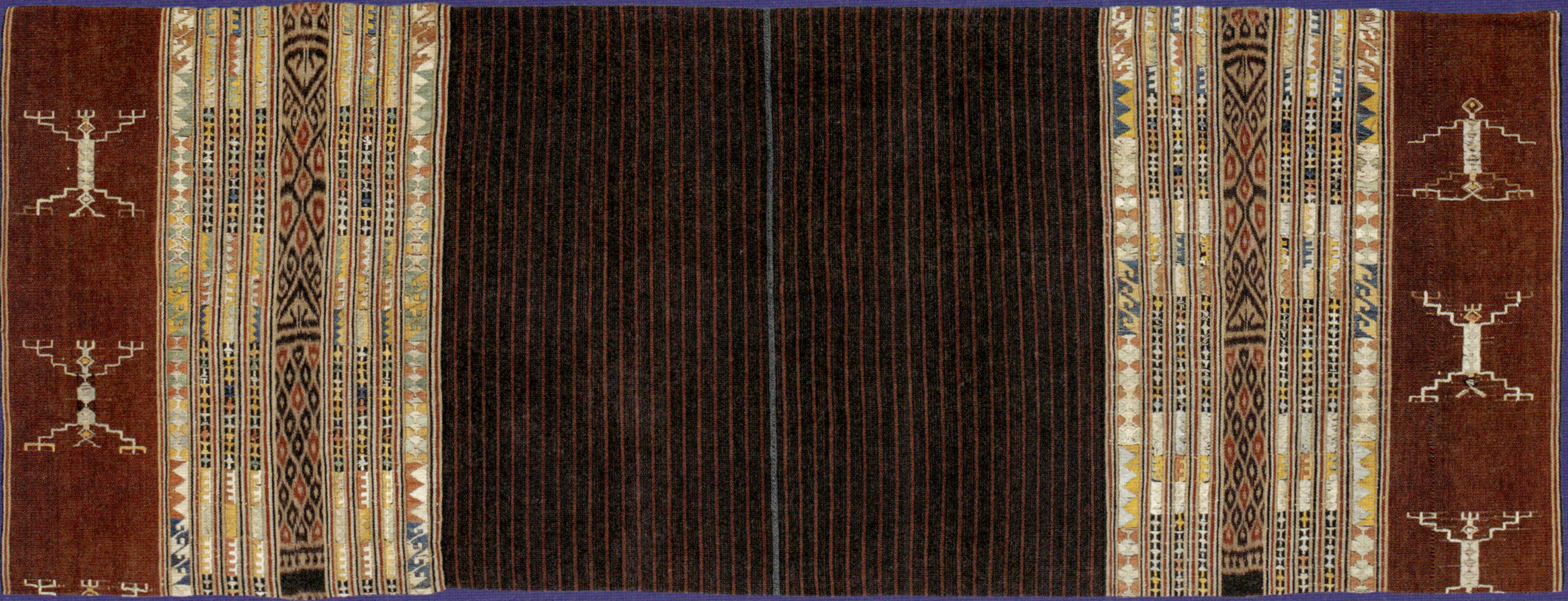

MA44

MA97

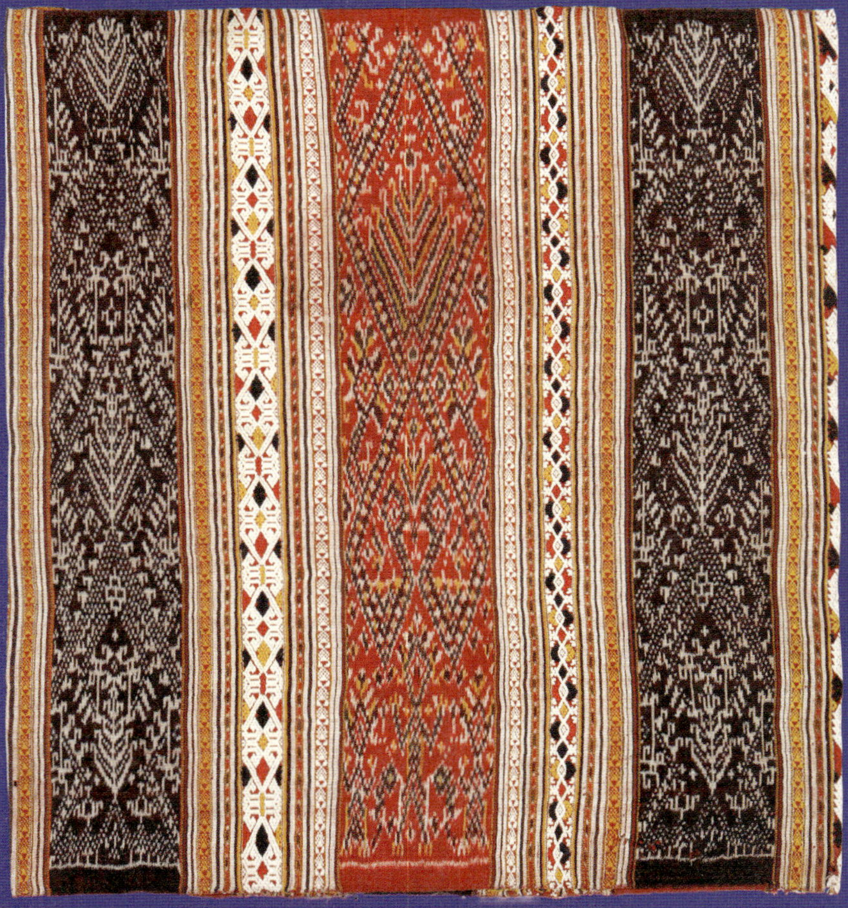

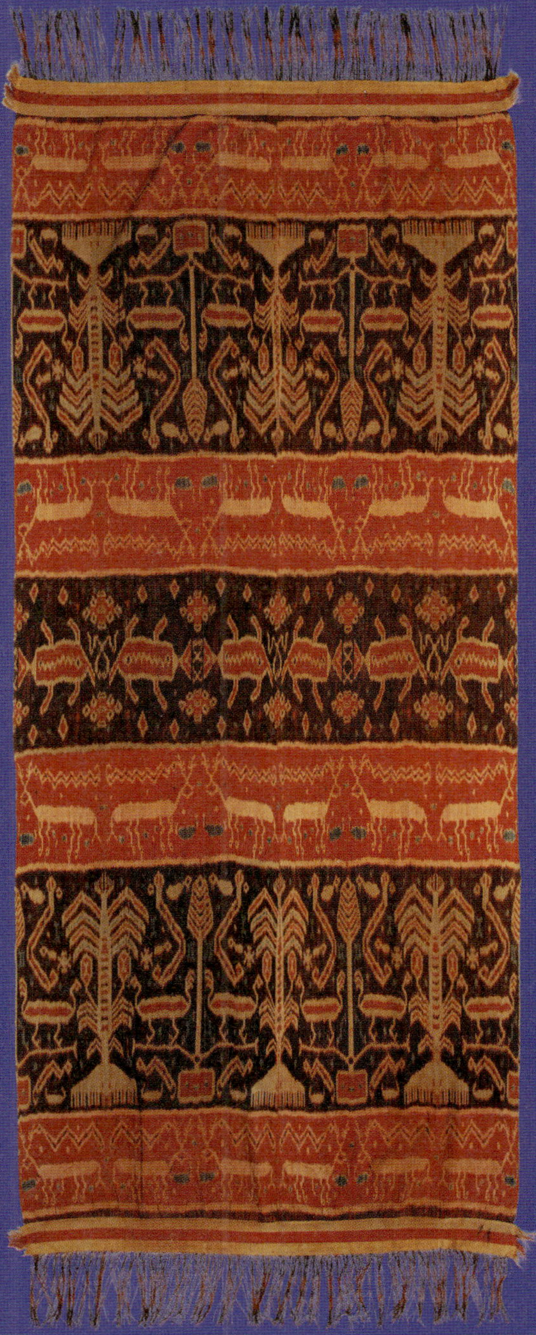

MA59

INDIA

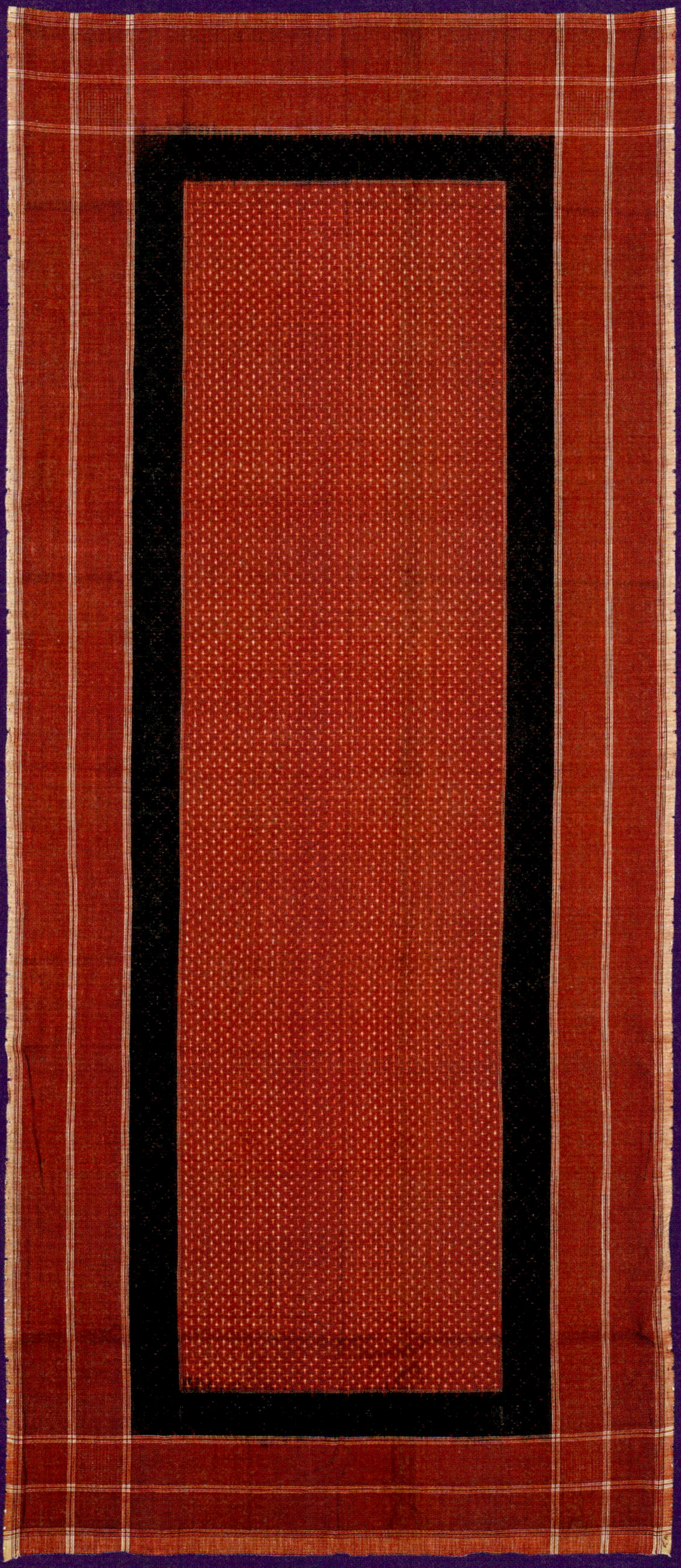

IN05

AMERICAS

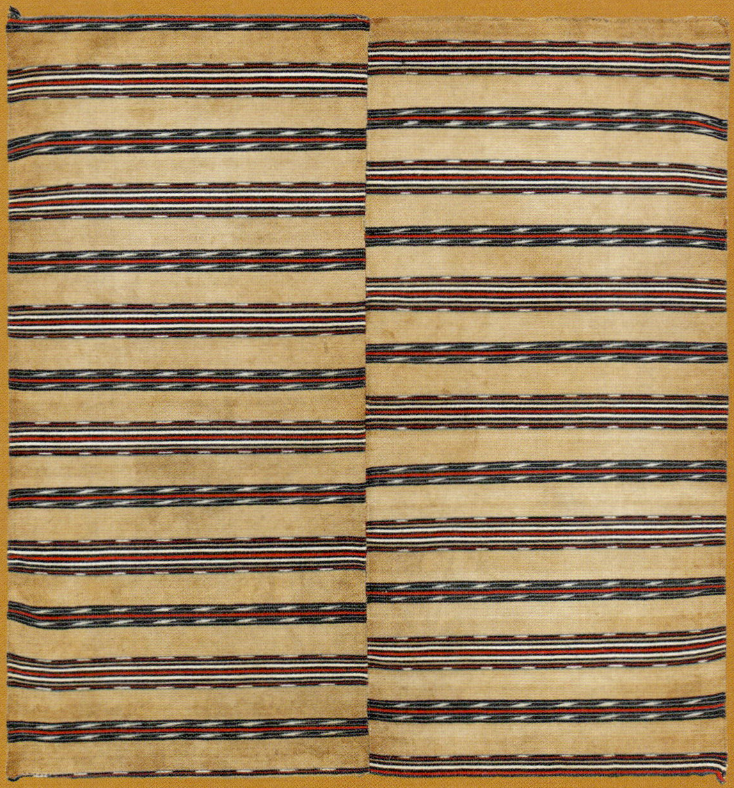

AM21

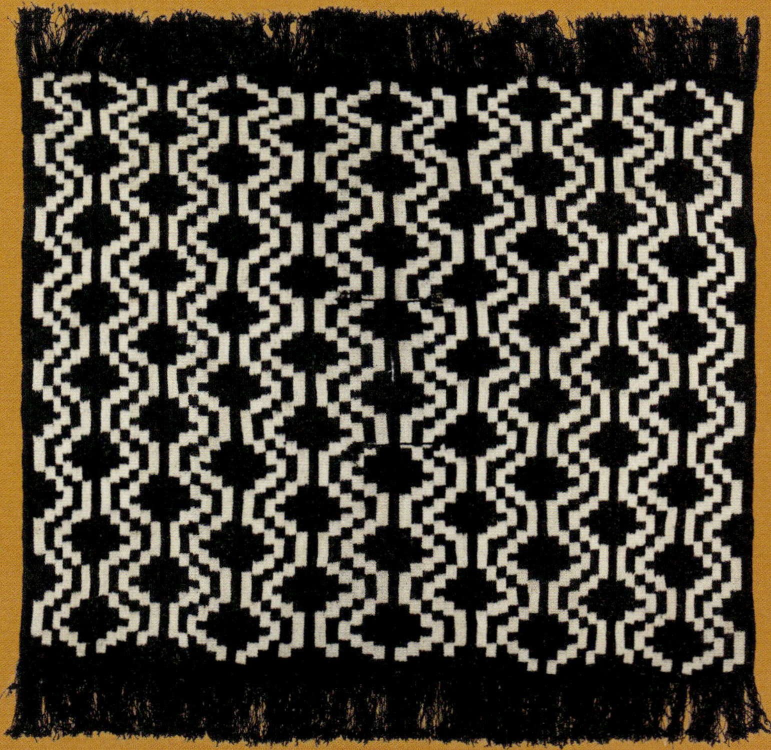

AM34

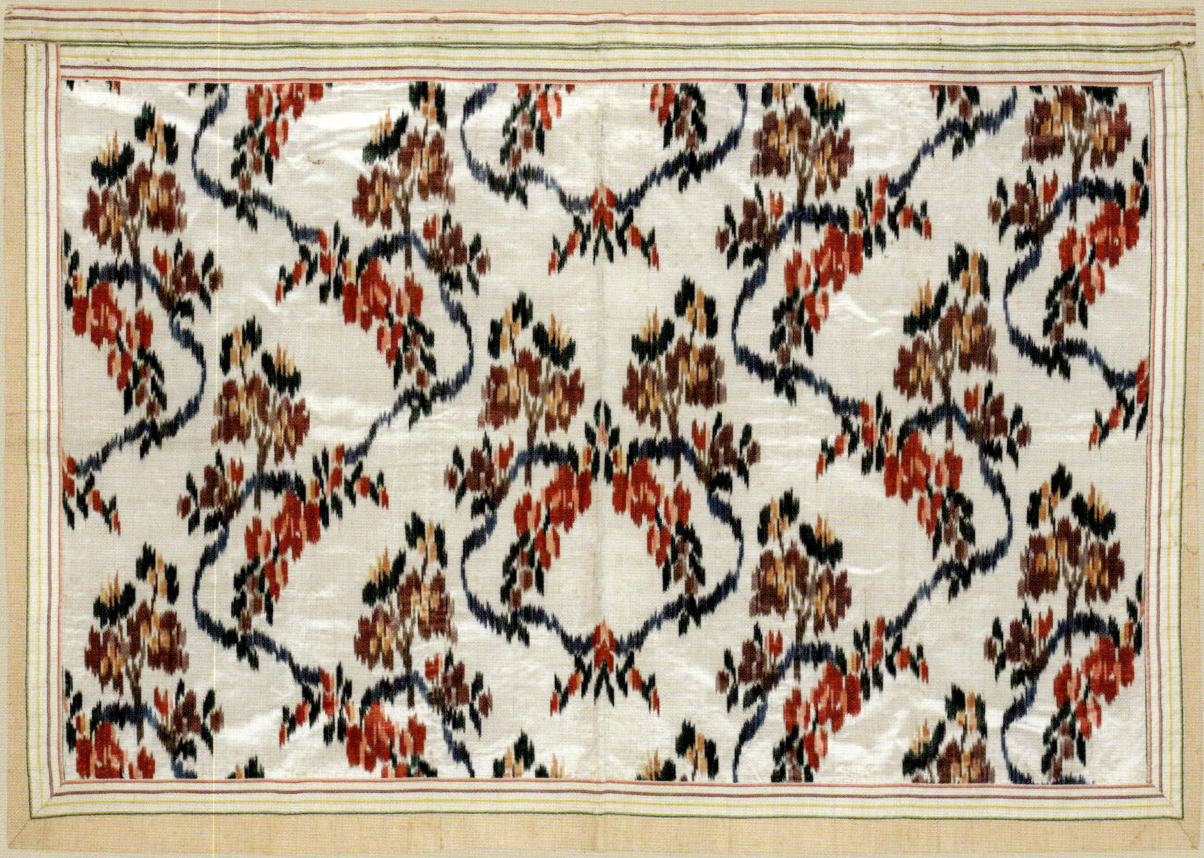

EU07

EUROPE

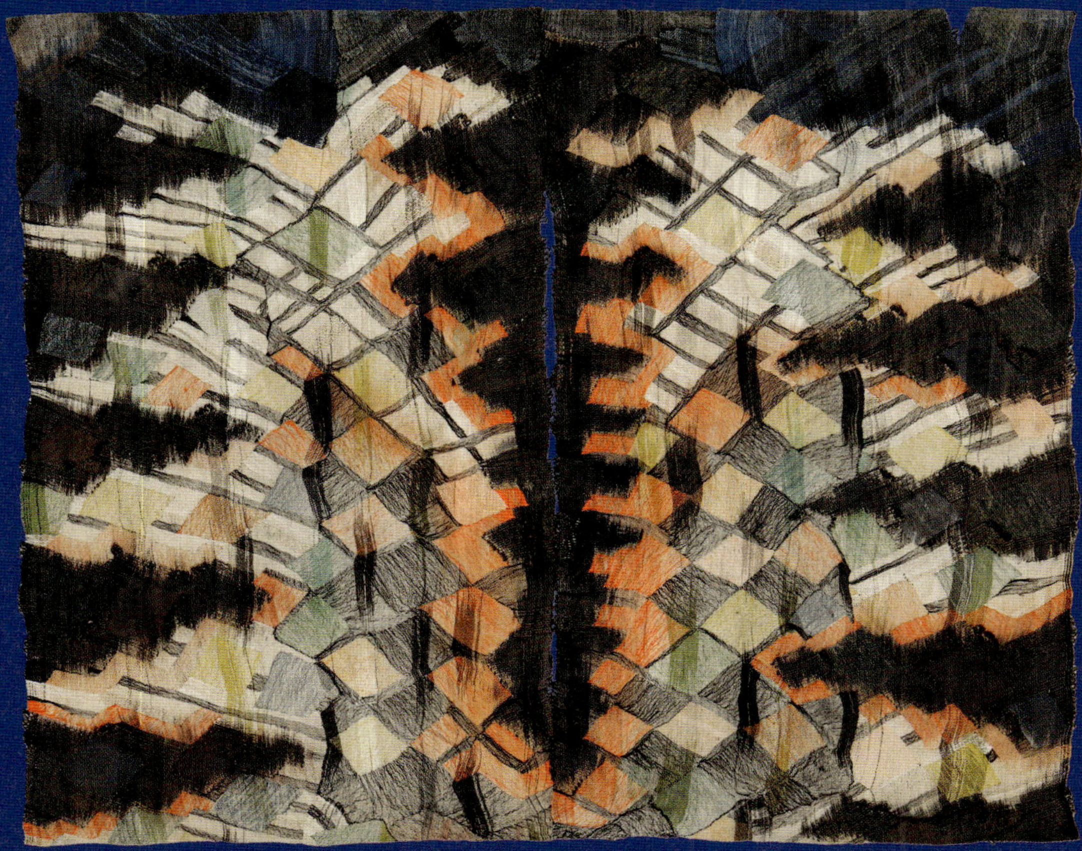

IT01

IKAT TODAY

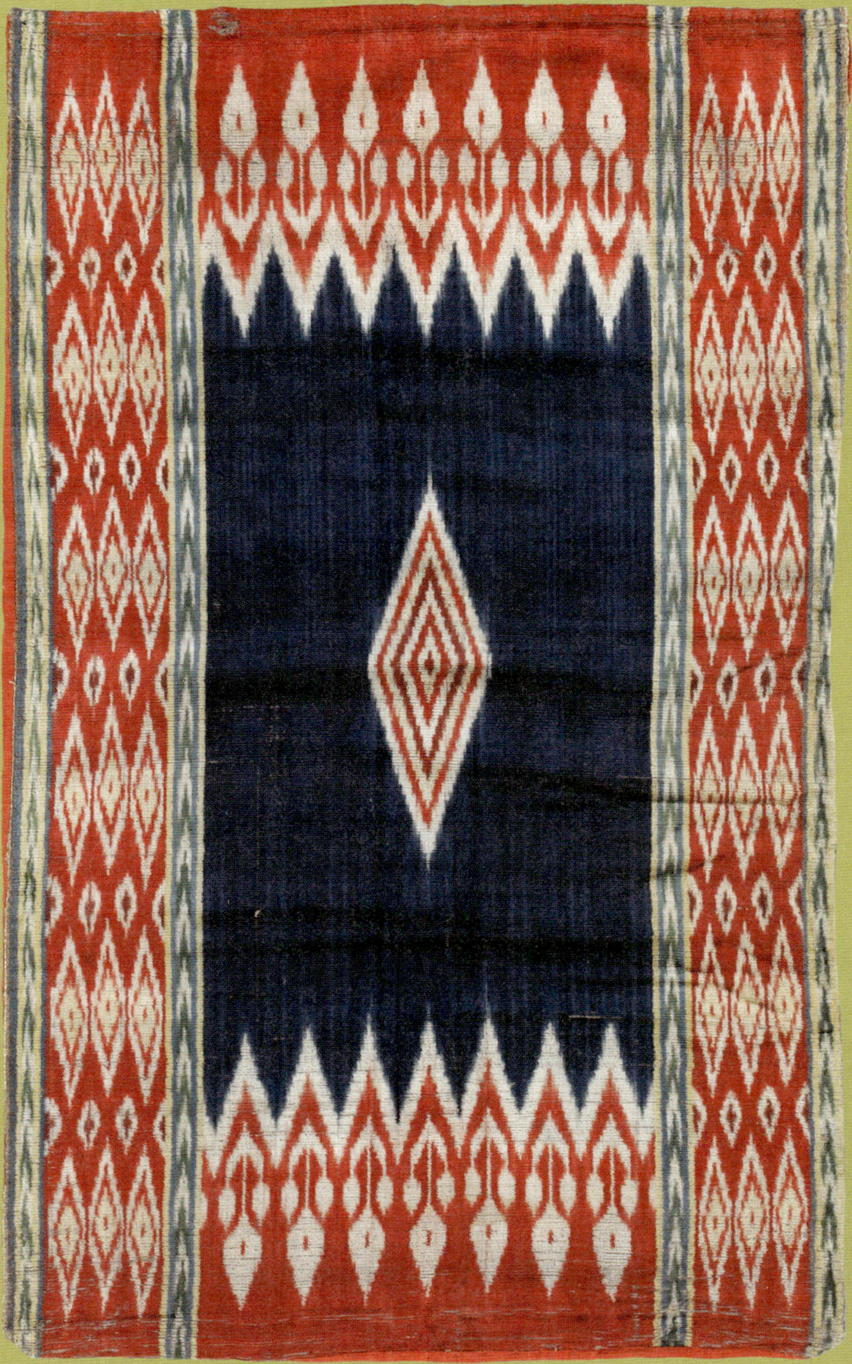

WCA39

WCA12

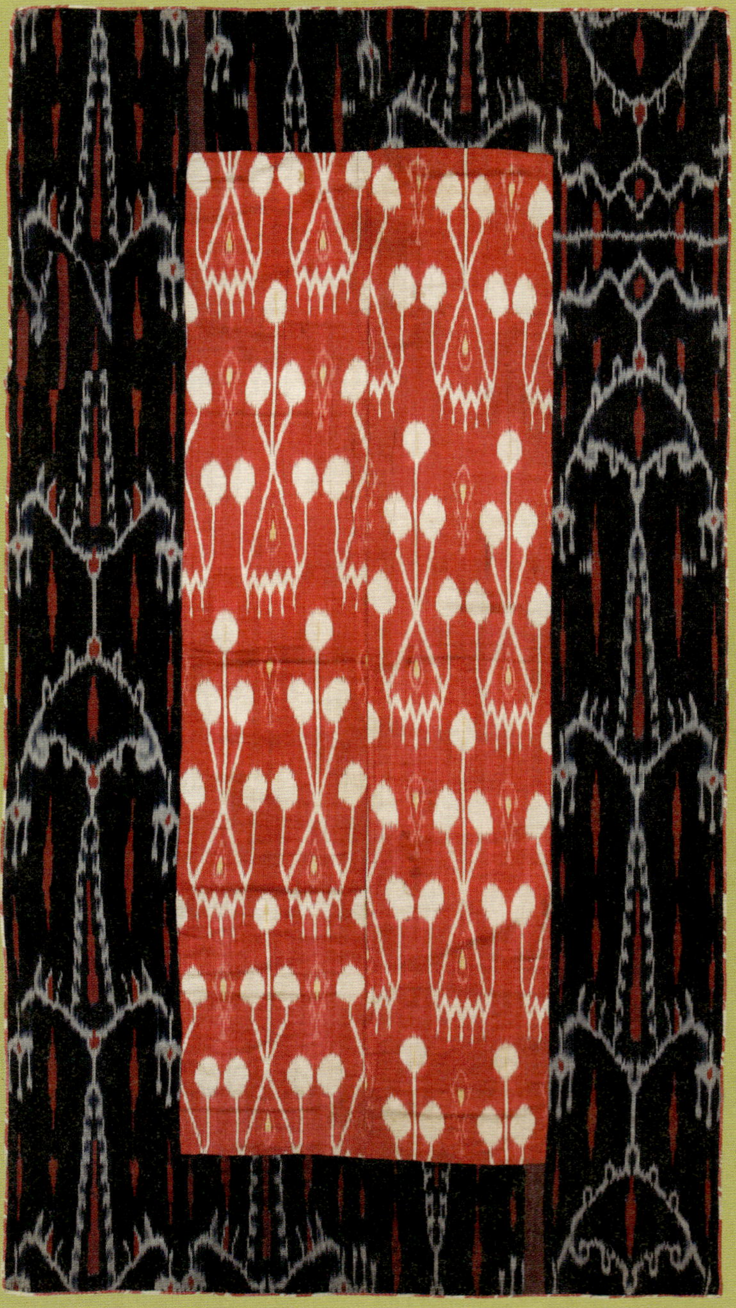

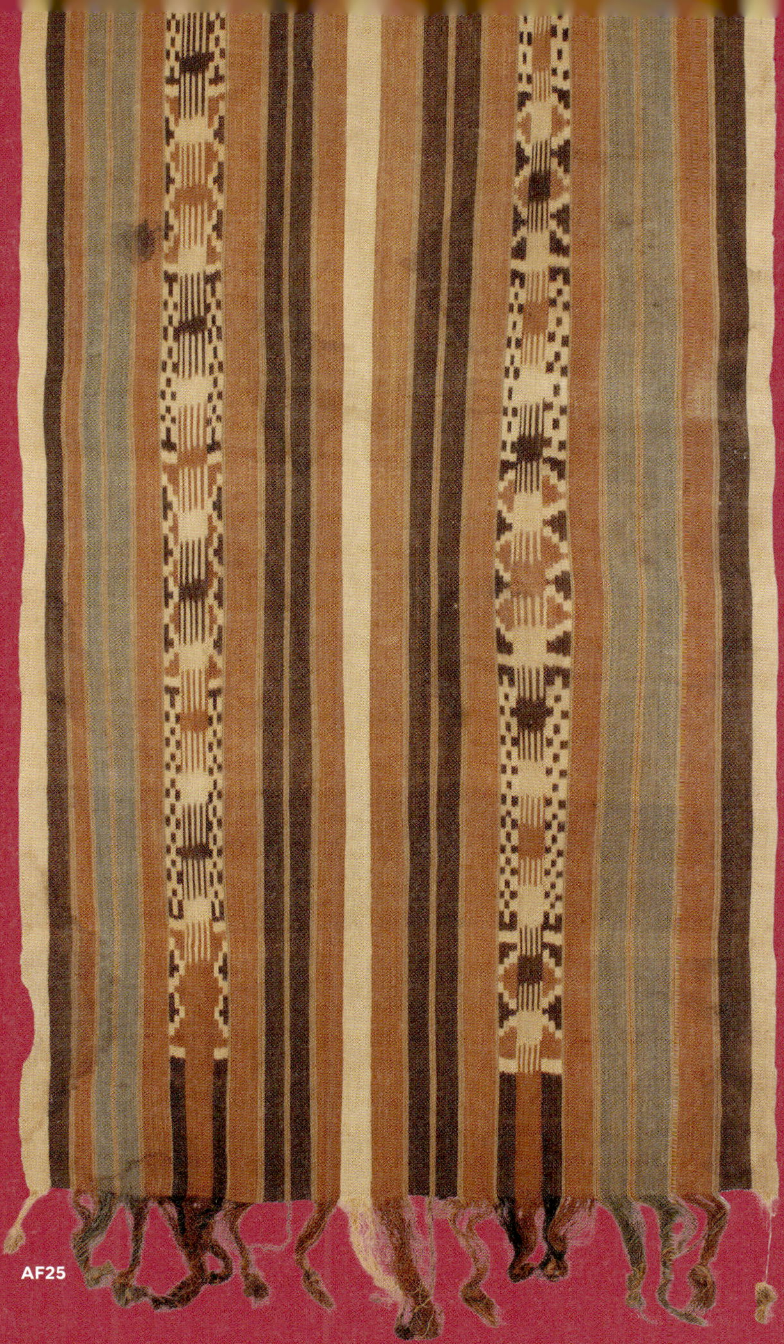

AF25

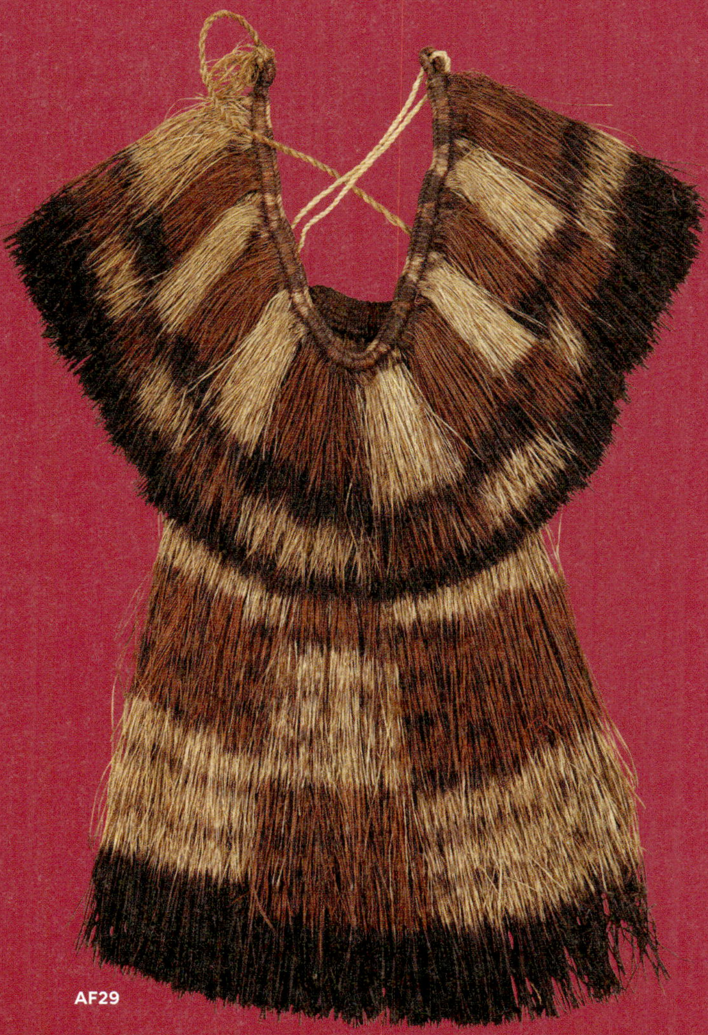

AF29

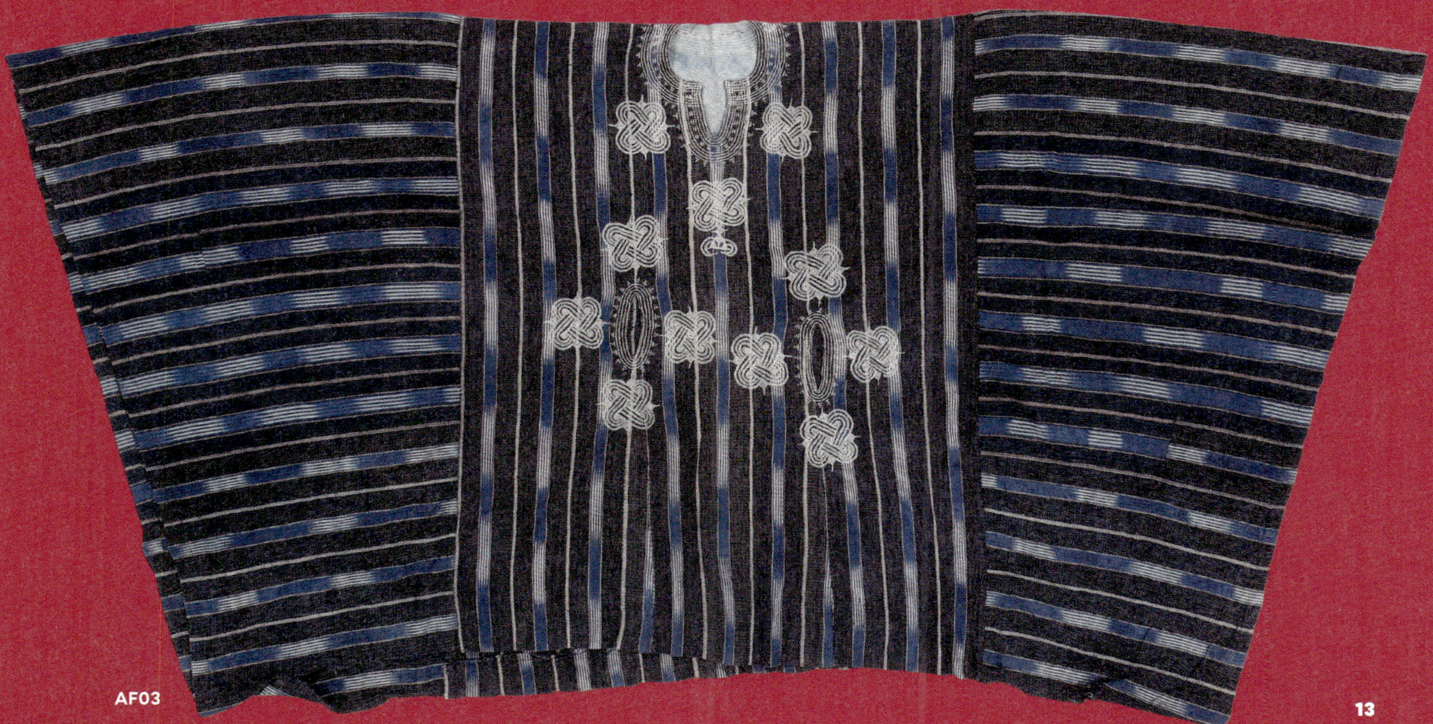

AF03

PREFACE

Let me preface this catalog with a disclaimer stating what I'm not: a textile scholar, historian, anthropologist, ethnographer, weaver, or dyer. I am a lifelong collector with a passion for curious and beautiful objects. Since childhood my fantasy has been to build a significant collection for my own amusement but with a purpose. My hope is that the grouping of ikat textiles presented here achieves this for others as it has for me. Lacking specific expertise, I hope any errors are forgiven and corrected.

Beyond the obsessive nature of the collecting impulse I need to answer, "why ikat?" Aside from the intellectual curiosity about the widespread geographical and cultural utility of the technique, I am fascinated by the fantastic difficulty of producing the exquisite beauty in the soft, blurring edges inherent in the resists. This effect is called *kasumi*, cloudlike, in Japanese, and it is cherished there and elsewhere. I have come to understand that ikat dominates in cultures where cloth is revered as a high artform but loom technology is not complex. As one way of producing pattern in a plain flatweave, in fact perhaps the most difficult way, ikat flourished in societies that could invest the time and multi-generational expertise to maintain this dyeing/weaving tradition. In these cultures the discipline and skill conveyed in cloth were generally appreciated as a mark of pride and prestige. As a person with no technical skill beyond my own profession I am still in awe of these artists, mostly women, and their creativity.

The biological concepts of confluence versus congruence reasonably define my view of the origins and spread of the ikat technique worldwide. Confluence describes the shared knowledge spread by travel, migration, and trade. Congruence denotes the separate evolution of a similar feature without common roots. Clearly both are at work in the global appearance of cloth, through the millennia, in which the fibers are dyed before weaving to produce a punctuated pattern. For the purposes of this catalog I use the term loosely to include any technique to pre-dye the warp or weft with pattern; it is not restricted to resist-dyed fibers.

Some of the shared influences are obvious, such as the widespread "Indian" designs in Southeast Asian cloth. Others are lost in antiquity, with few or no predecessors and the cloth remaining fully anonymous. The contributing scholars to this catalog are tasked with teasing out these loose threads, but I'm under no illusion that these questions are resolved. There is the known, the unknown, and the known unknown that may never be answered. Another scientific principle is that the absence of evidence is not the same as evidence of absence, so there is plenty of room for study and speculation. Hopefully this catalog will be a stimulus for furthering thought, and a small document for reference.

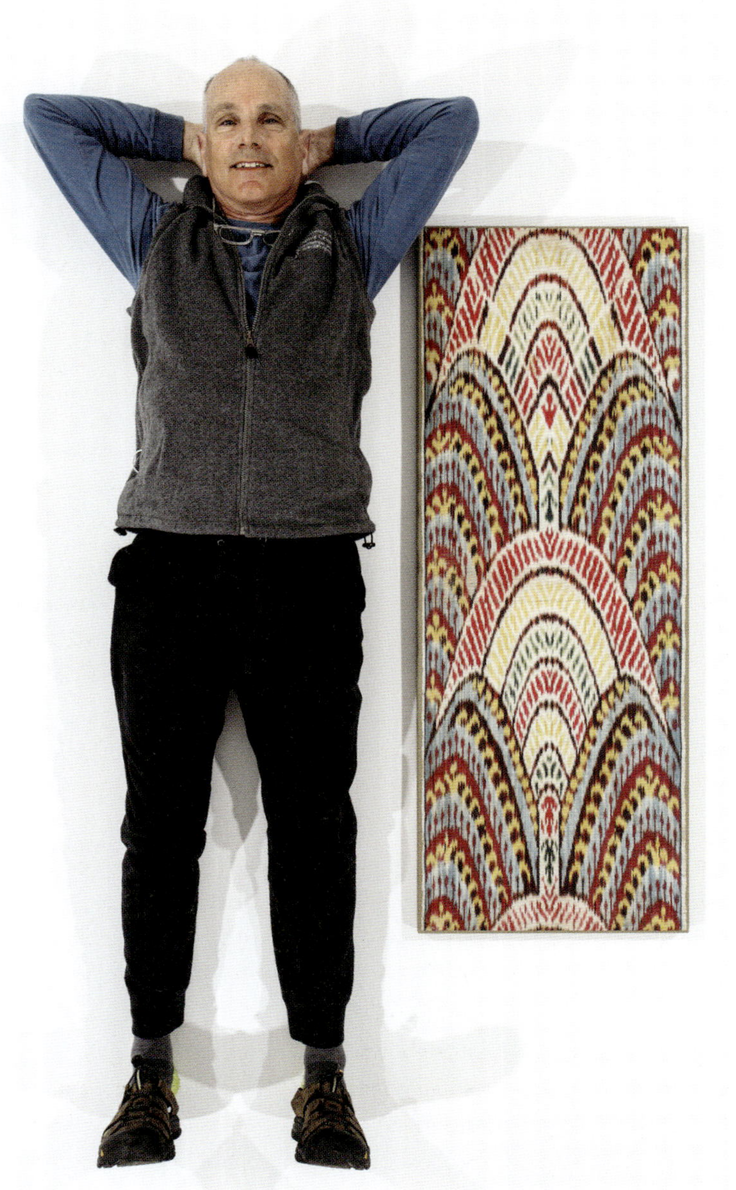

David Paly with WCA10, an ikat fragment from Uzbekistan

While I have attempted the Herculean task of finding great examples for this "comprehensive" assembly, I have been limited by market timing, sources, and funds. I acknowledge that concern for artistic quality, condition, age, and rarity was sometimes sacrificed in the pursuit of inclusivity. There are as many pieces that I regret buying as I regret missing over the years. To the extent that this is the document of a personal voyage, I am publishing the entire group, less-loved children included. There are many great stories attached to the objects–but that is for a different forum.

I only hope that this catalog does justice to the topic and serves as another testimony to our species' drive to create, wander, love, display, and wonder. *David Paly*

ACKNOWLEDGMENTS

First, let me blame my parents, Sidney Paly and Elisabeth Hilborn, for my collecting disorder. We were young New England transplants, and I accompanied them on forays to antique shops and auctions to decorate our homes. While neither took a disciplined approach to such pursuits I grew up around lovely old things and stacks of *Antiques*, *Connoisseur* and *Apollo* magazines which I devoured from an early age. My maternal grandmother, Peggy, was an artist and world traveler and I was also fascinated with her Manhattan apartment full of things. Perhaps my most formative drive toward the exotic was our proximity to the Peabody Museum (now PEM) in Salem, which had dusty cabinets of South Seas treasures with handwritten labels.

While not yet a teenager I apprenticed to a genteel Boston auctioneer on weekends and began buying and selling on my own, my wares including quilts and Navajo rugs. In a post-high-school gap year I worked as a "gofer" at Childs Gallery in Boston, where I was exposed to a wide variety of fine and decorative art, mostly American, and honed some aspects of connoisseurship. In college, I did a year's independent study at the Mead Art Museum at Amherst College, where I co-authored the Bicentennial catalog of the American Art Collection and acquired a scholarly research mindset.

As I finished college I had to decide between a career in the arts versus science/medicine. I decided that as a collector I could pursue the beauty inherent to the objects more than the informational aspects of scholarship or the monetary endpoints of art dealing. As I started traveling in South America I awakened to an intuitive love of textiles and pivoted away from Western fine and decorative art to the "ethnographic." The importance of cloth to so many world cultures, and the reverence shown to textiles, struck me as an underappreciated human aesthetic; more importantly, this evoked the rapture that great art brings. I have often said that I must have had a wandering rag picker as an ancestor, as the feel of fine cloth provokes an almost inborn delight.

I first encountered ikat in Riobamba, Ecuador, in 1976 in the form of an indigo cotton poncho. My next purchase was a Dayak *pua* in 1978. When I read *The Dyers Art: Ikat, Batik, Plangi* by Jack Lenor Larsen it opened my mind to the near universality of this mind-boggling, complex decorative technique. The disease of the collector is such that if you have two of anything you need to complete the set. Forty-five years later I am near enough that goal to want to present what I have accumulated.

As I pursued a career and built a home and family, the collecting became a surrogate for traveling and haunting local markets. I could not possibly have learned about and found these beautiful cloths without the dedicated coterie of dealers, too many to count, that have fed my obsession. Among them let me thank, first and foremost, Gail Martin and Vladimir Haustov whose Artweave Gallery was revolutionary in presenting non-Western and ancient cloth as fine art worthy of museum walls. More importantly, I met my

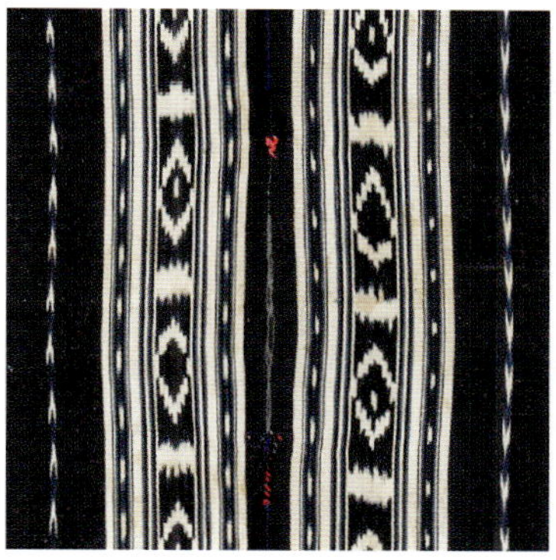

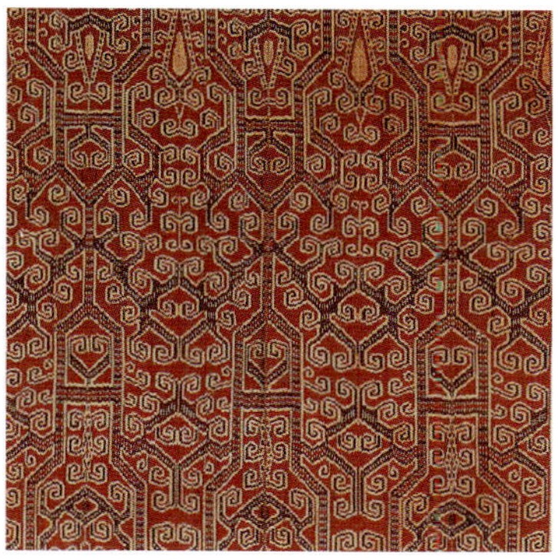

The first two ikat textiles in the series of over five hundred, AM35 and MA73

long-suffering wife, Marita Shimokawa Makabe, there, and we were married in the gallery. Andrés and Vanessa Moraga have provided some of my rarest and most esoteric pieces. Tom Murray has sold me a few great things but also served as support and a sounding board on issues of quality. Let me also thank Matt Polk and Amy Gould, indefatigable textile collectors, whose Historic Textile Research Foundation has helped support this catalog.

In addition to the above, I would like to credit in no particular order, with many not included, Diane Daniels, Mary Kahlenberg, Steve Berger, Don Tuttle, David Hamilton, Noriko Miyamoto, Haruko Watanabe, Ichiro Wada, Burton Holt, Vichai and Lee Chinalai, John Davis, Bruce Malcolm, Jonathan Hope, Rudolf Smend, Sim Tan, Titi Halle, Cora Ginsburg, Jack Lenor Larsen, Fifi White, Ali Istalifi, Mark Johnson, Doug Dawson, Kei Kawasaki, Duncan Clarke, Joss Graham, Gale Hoskins, David Lantz, Andrea Aranow, Linda S. McIntosh, Margaret Keith Clemson, Joe Gerena, Alan Kennedy, John and Kumi Ruddy, and the estate of Guido Goldman for sourcing the gems that grace these pages.

Let me also gratefully commend the contributing authors, Polly Barton, Shelley Burian, Duncan Clarke, Rosemary Crill, Martina D'Amato, Sumru Belger Krody, Linda S. McIntosh, and Lee Talbot, who helped advance this project; and the photographer of almost all the objects, Brian Parks. Lisa Mothersbaugh was a critical link helping break my tech-block with database help.

Lastly, thanks to my mother-in law "Bachi" Lidia Shimokawa Makabe who skillfully repaired, lined and sewed Velcro to nearly the entire collection. It is deeply appreciated.

The goal of this catalog is to draw some kind of a personal conclusion to the accumulation of 47 years which is intellectually satisfying and finite in its disposition. At the very least my two boys will have closet space. The objects will find new homes where they can be preserved, studied and displayed, starting with the Seattle Art Museum in 2023 and The Textile Museum in 2024. Hopefully the scholars who contribute critical essays can bring together the novel origins and interwoven paths that made ikat so widespread. If nothing else, I hope this serves as a source of wonder and pleasure for knowledgeable devotees and amateurs alike.

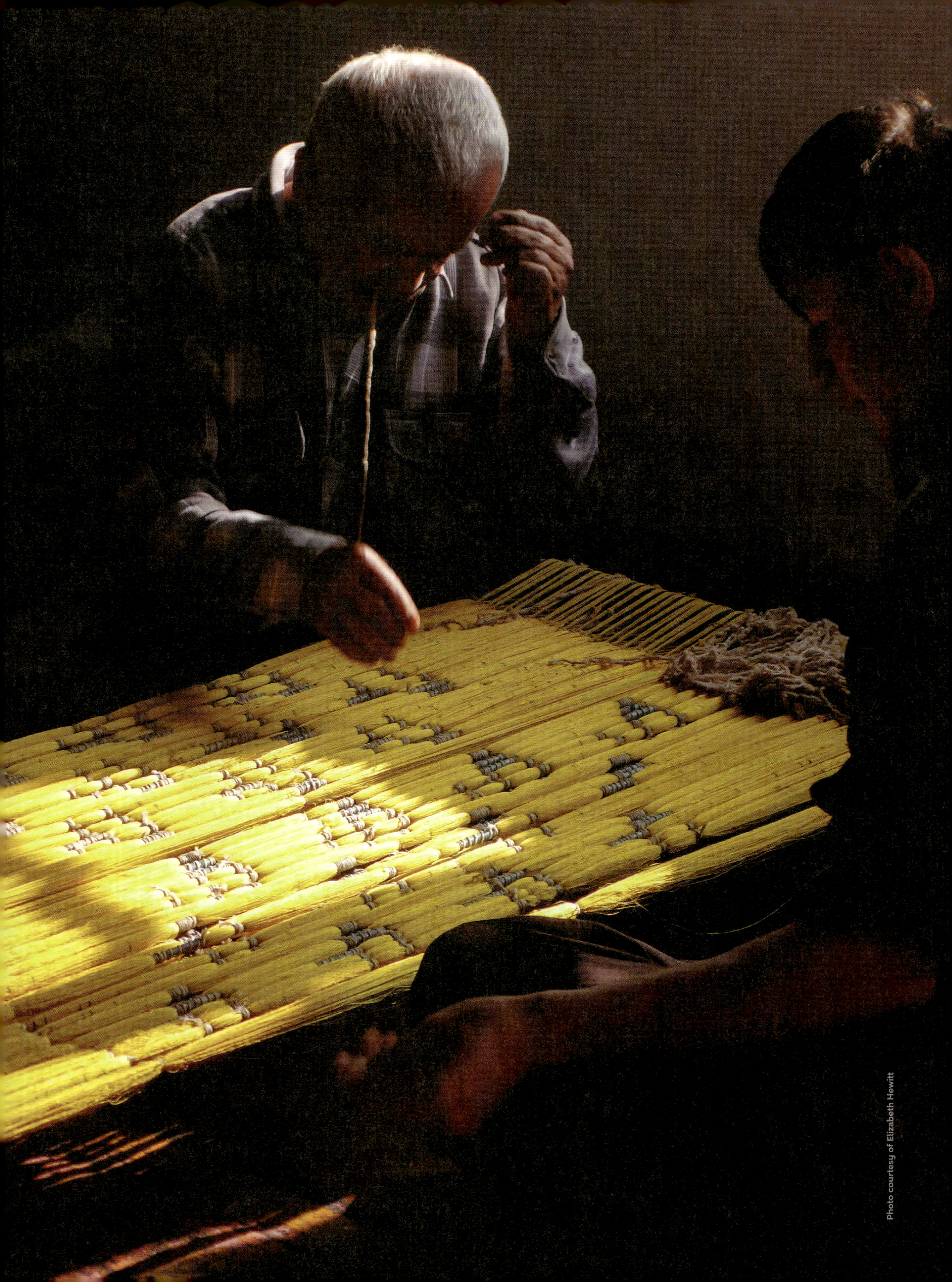
Photo courtesy of Elizabeth Hewitt

INTRODUCTION

by Rosemary Crill

A WORLD OF CLOUDED CLOTH

The distinctively blurred, feathered or jagged patterns of ikat-dyed textiles are found scattered across much of the world. Local names for ikat textiles invoke flames (German *Flammentuch*), clouds (Farsi *abr*) and English "clouded silks," variegated marble (Spanish *jaspe*) or speckled feathers (Yoruba *etu*), but the more prosaic Malay word "ikat" (from *mengikat*, to tie) has won out to become the internationally used default term for the technique.

The word "ikat" was first introduced to Western readers in 1890 by A. R. Hein in a book in German on the Dayaks of Borneo,[1] followed by G. P. Rouffaer's article in Dutch on ikats and other Indonesian textiles in 1901.[2] Fritz Iklé used the term as one of several names for the technique in his 1928 article "Über Flammentücher,"[3] but it was really through the work of the Swiss ethnologist Alfred Bühler (much of it in English) that the term gained greater currency and became the most widely used term for this form of the tie-resist technique.[4] A much broader audience was reached by Jack Lenor Larsen's seminal work (partly in collaboration with Bühler) *The Dyer's Art: Ikat, Batik, Plangi*, published in 1976. This richly illustrated volume was both visually appealing and scholarly: it brought global ikat and other resist-dyed textiles to the attention of designers and artists as well as textile scholars, and inspired a generation of makers and collectors.

Ikat-producing regions of the world stretch from Japan in the east to Central and South America in the west, with vast areas of Southeast Asia, India, Central Asia and the Middle East in between. The ikats made in some of these areas are strikingly similar to those made in distant regions, while others are vastly different. Some are made solely in warp ikat, others in weft ikat, and some in a combination of the two. Some use

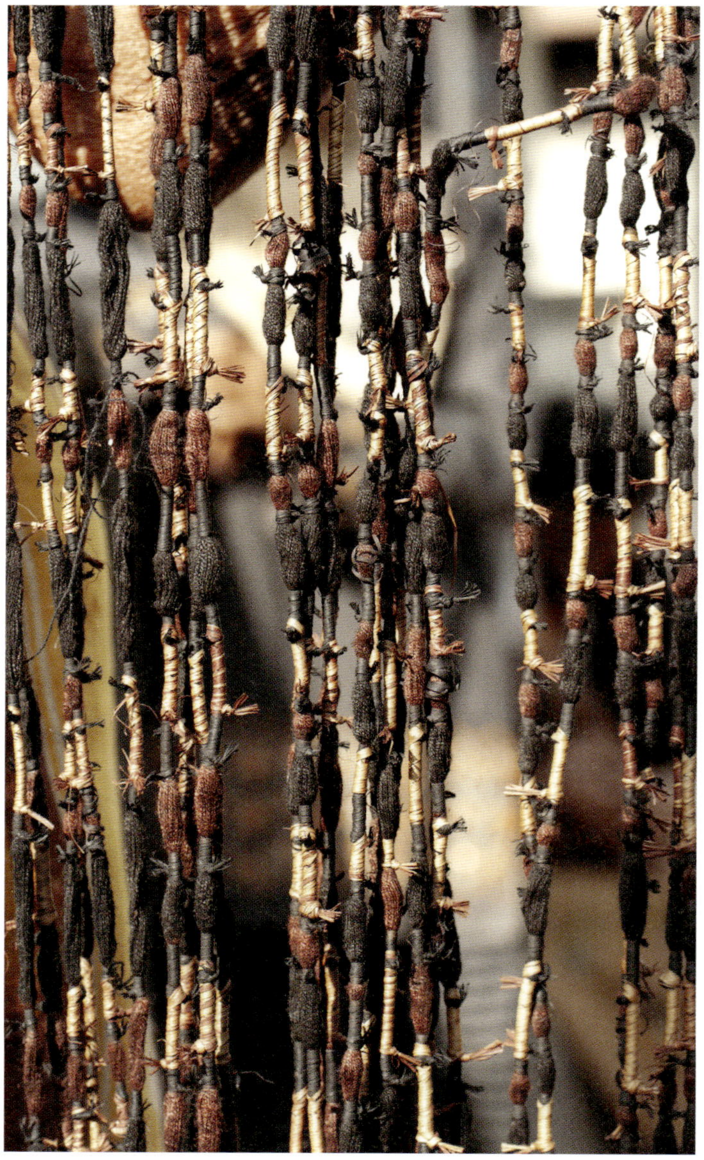

Photo courtesy of Chris Buckley

Fig.1

Opener, previous spread
Masters in the Ferghana Valley, Uzbekistan, tying the warp during the ikat-dyeing process, circa 2002

Fig.1
Partly dyed ikat yarns, Pulau Buayah, Indonesia

Fig.2
Weaving a warp-ikat textile in Sumba, Indonesia

Fig.3
IN21, Naga man's head decoration with "proto-ikat" dyed goat hair

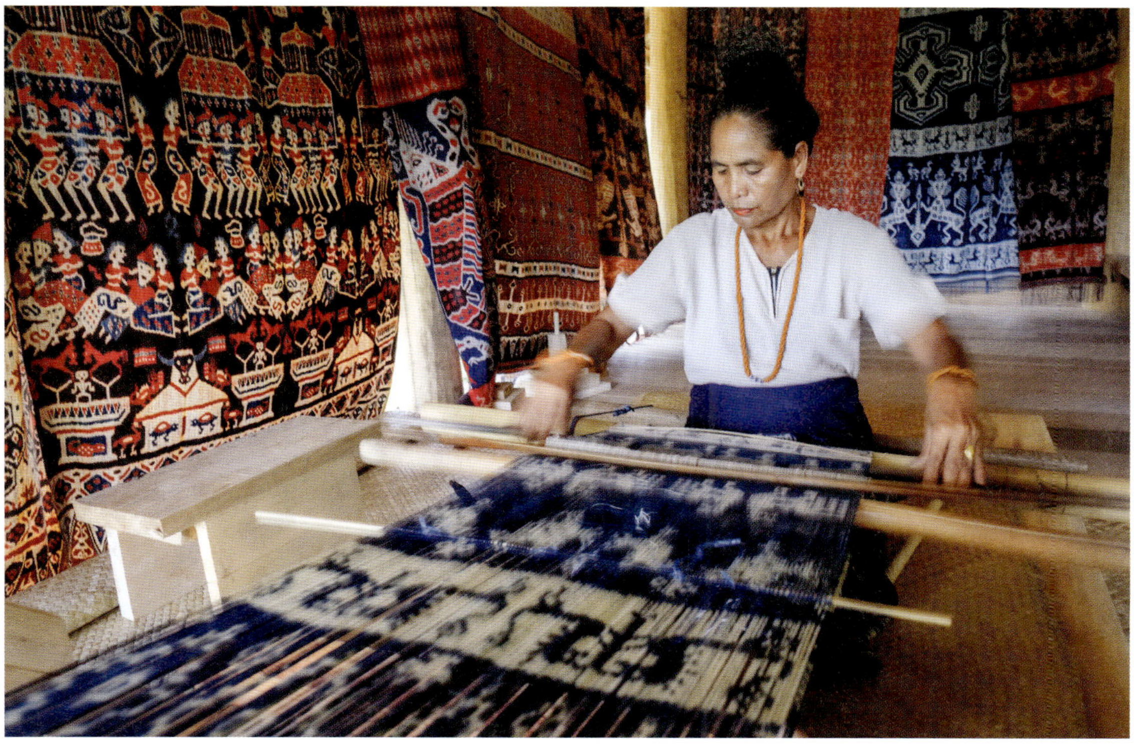
Anges van der Logt/Shutterstock.com

Fig.2

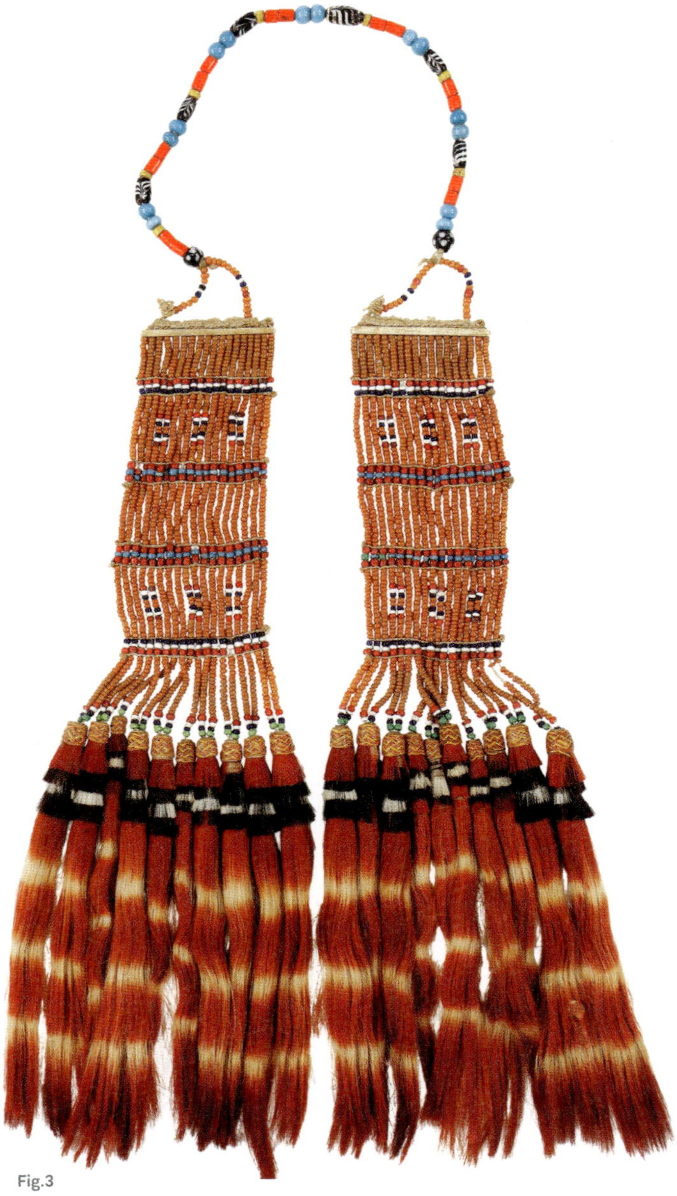
Fig.3

a limited palette, often of indigo and white, while others create a rainbow of color. The only apparent link between some diverse types of ikat textile is the technique itself of resist-dyeing yarn before weaving, which may be a relatively simple process if only a single color and a simple design is used, or an incredibly laborious and technically demanding operation involving many stages of resisting, dyeing, preparing the threads for weaving and, finally, weaving the patterned threads together to form a textile.

The ikat technique

Ikat is a simple idea which can be elaborated to an extraordinary degree. The basic premise is that a pattern is tie-resist-dyed onto warp and/or weft threads before the textile is woven (see Ikat: The Technique). In the finished textile, this pattern might be a simple streak or dash of white against a colored ground (Fig.6/IN06) or it could be a highly complex and multi-colored pattern (Fig.4/WCA05). A warp-ikat textile is generally simpler to produce than a weft-ikat one, as after dyeing the patterned warp threads are set up on the loom and the wefts simply passed through them to form the cloth (Fig.2). Weft ikat needs more planning before weaving, as the ikat-dyed patterns must be coordinated with the warps as the textile is woven to create the required design. Weft ikat is often associated with silk textiles: the setting up of ikat-dyed silk warps on the loom is more difficult than cotton, as they must be passed individually through a comb or reed to stop the threads becoming tangled. This process is made even more difficult if the warp threads have been ikat-dyed first, as they must be kept rigorously in place to maintain the pattern of the textile.

The blurred outline that gives ikat patterns their character is an intentional feature and is not, as is sometimes suggested, the result of a failure to match up the dyed and undyed yarns in the weaving process. The irregular seeping of dye beyond the resist material wrapping the yarns is almost unavoidable and is embraced as part of the textile's aesthetic (as it also is in the related technique of tie-dyeing a woven cloth). In some ikat textiles the jagged outline of the pattern motifs may be exaggerated by manipulating the warp threads while setting them up on the loom. In very few others, notably the double-ikat *patola*, the blurred outline is kept to a minimum, with the precise matching up of warp and weft ikat-dyed threads seen as desirable.

"Proto-ikat" is a term for a type of dyeing in which strands of fiber are resist-dyed in blocks of color but are not intended to be woven into cloth (Fig.3/IN21).[5] "Zone dyeing" is a simple form of ikat in which the warp and/or weft threads of a textile are ikat-dyed in a contrasting color to the borders (Fig.5/MA37)—this is a simpler way of achieving a different-colored field and borders than weaving, which would involve either manually tying the different-colored warp or weft threads together to enable the piece to be woven, or using a separate shuttle for the wefts of the side borders. This is not the only example of ikat being used as a simpler alternative to weaving a design: in South India, for example, weft-ikat dashes of white against a dark-blue ground are substituted for more laboriously woven brocaded motifs in the part of a sari that is less visible than the end.[6] It is possible that the elaborate figural patterns of the Gujarati *patola* (IN28) may similarly be derived from an elaborate woven pattern, and the striking Central Asian ikats with roundels (e.g. WCA01) may also be imitating earlier woven silks.[7]

Origins and spread of ikat

Ikat is such a widespread global phenomenon that it is likely to have arisen independently in at least three separate areas, probably South China, India, and Peru. From these disparate centers the technique spread out both to neighboring areas and far distant regions, but it is impossible to map a simple linear progression of ikat across its various zones of production. So far reaching were, first, the early migration of peoples and, later, the international textile trade that the lines of potential influence are in most cases impossible to disentangle fully. But it may be helpful to divide the main areas of ikat production into three broad regional zones.

Eastern Zone

(South China, eastern Southeast Asia, Japan, possibly Madagascar)

Warp-ikat dyeing in most of East and Southeast Asia is thought to have spread from South China across the region in the early period of Austronesian expansion (see Ikat in Monsoon Asia).

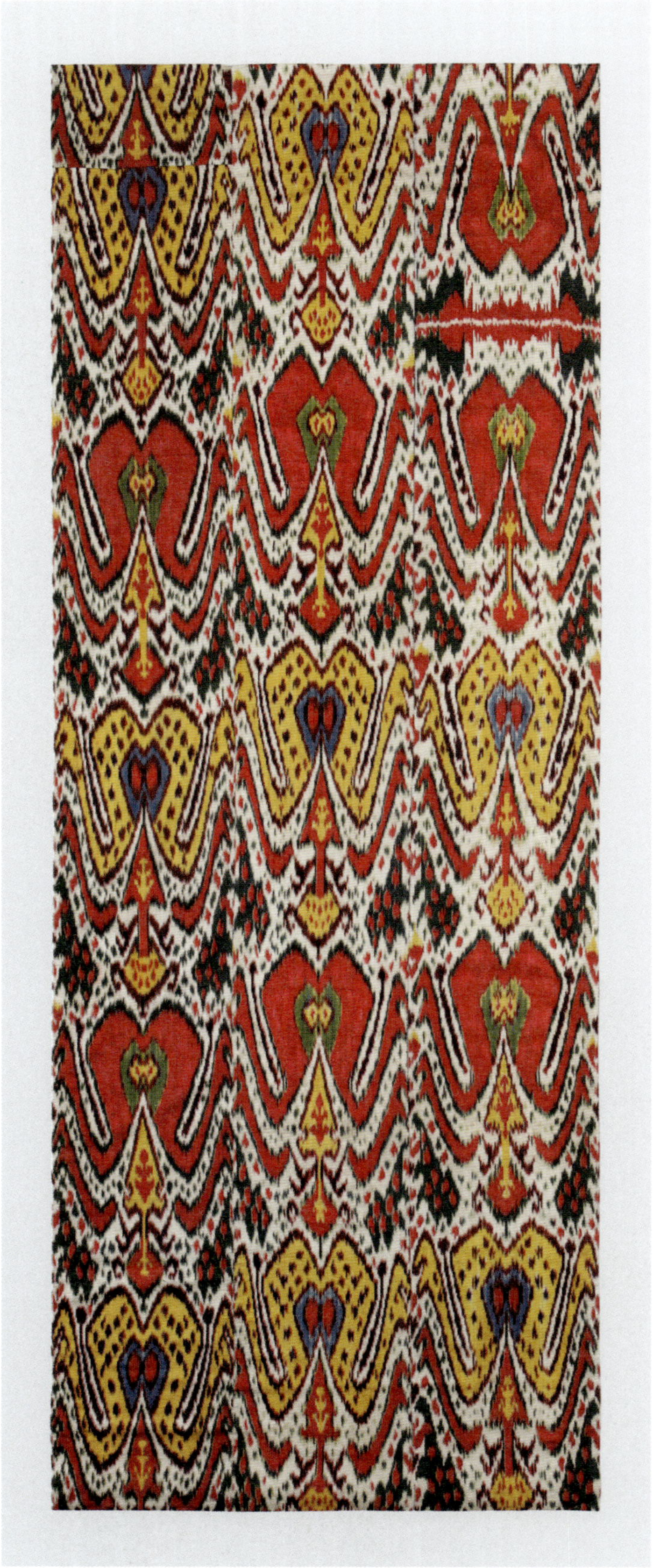

Fig.4

Fig.4
WCA05, hanging, *pardeh*

Fig.5
Detail of MA37, ritual cloth

Fig.6
Detail of IN06, *telia rumal*

Fig.5

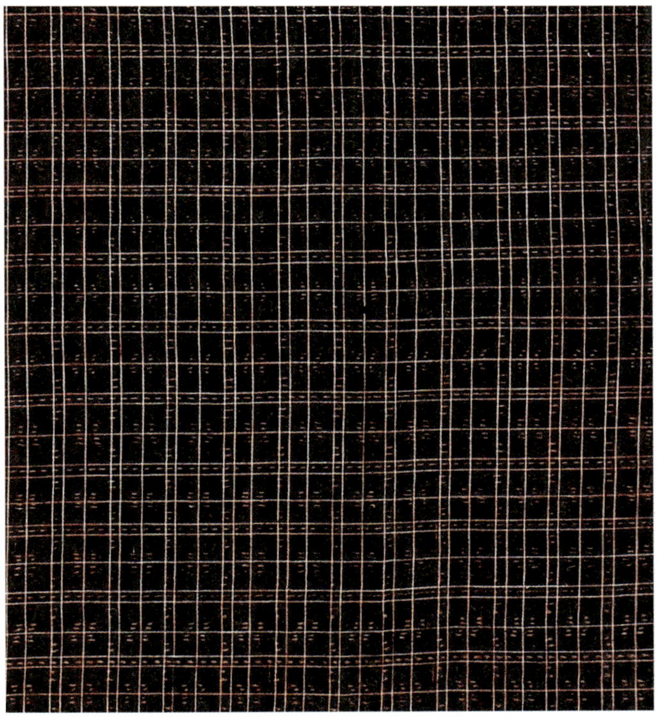

Fig.6

This huge ikat zone extends across Japan, insular Southeast Asia and possibly even as far west as Madagascar, although it is unknown when ikat first arrived on that island.[8] No very early textiles survive from the Eastern Zone, but perhaps the earliest example is a large, silk warp-ikat fragment excavated at Dulan in Qinghai Province, Northwest China, dating from the Tang period (7th–9th centuries), which may have been woven in southern China.[9] A similar aesthetic is visible in the ikat fragments dating to the 6th–7th century preserved in the Horyuji temple in Nara, Japan, but most likely imported from China (see Ikat in Japan, Fig.3).[10]

Warp ikat spread at an early period across the eastern part of insular Southeast Asia, and textile production was increased by the introduction of cotton around 1000 CE.[11] Christopher Buckley has convincingly suggested a division–the "ikat line"–roughly between the areas east and west of the center of the island of Flores: in the eastern sector, warp ikat was made on backstrap looms from a very early period, while the western sector, including mainland Southeast Asia, came under the influence of trade with India and developed a tradition of weft-patterned textiles (including weft ikat) and the use of silk on more rigid looms.[12] Extremely finely made silk ikat textiles, often incorporating metal-wrapped thread, were eventually adopted by ruling elites in Thailand, Cambodia, and Laos (see Ikat in Monsoon Asia). The ikat technique traveled to the Ryukyu Islands as part of the early migrations

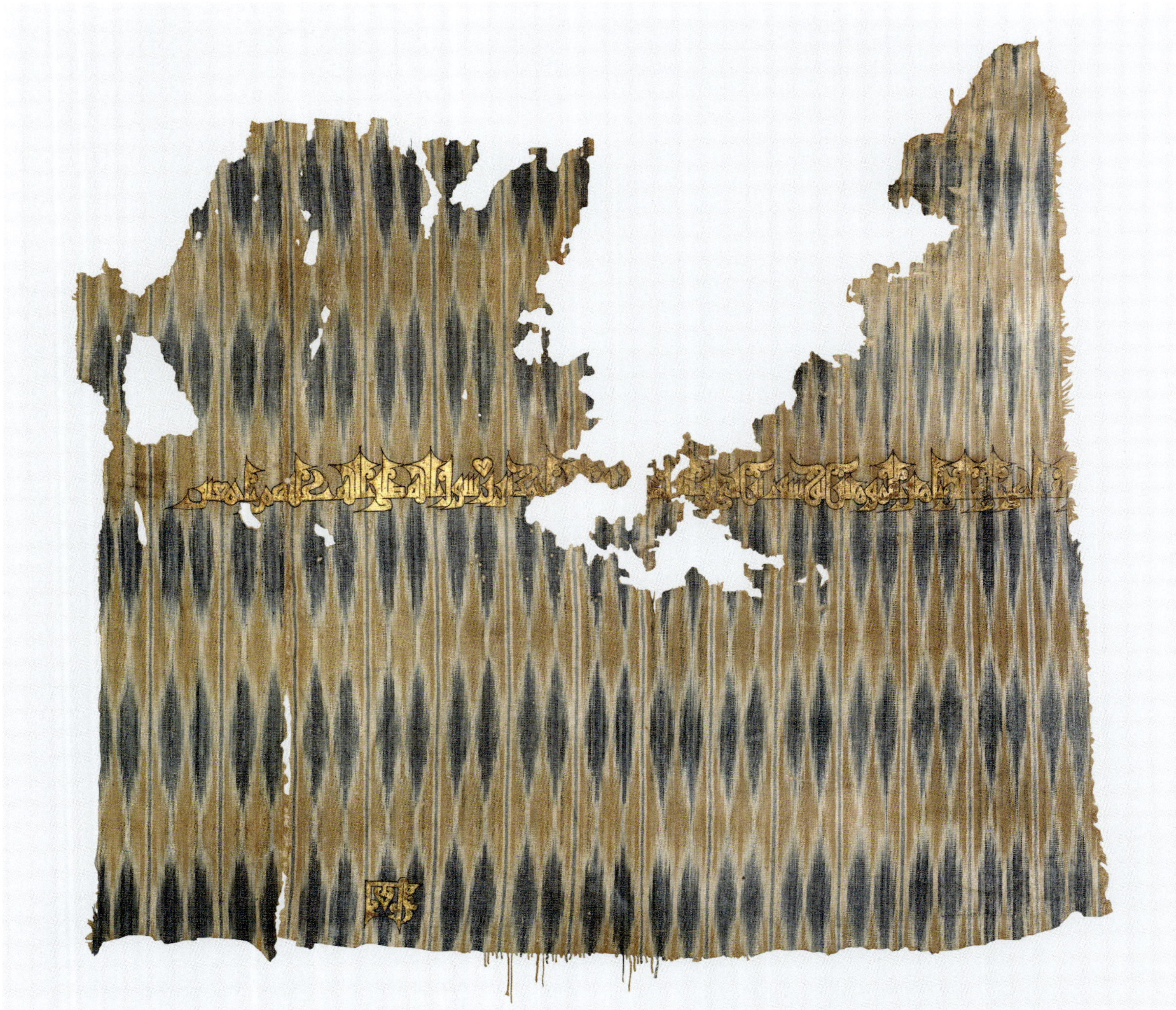

Fig.7

and thence to Japan, where it is known as *kasuri*, meaning blurred or scratched, although the term applies to textiles other than those using the ikat technique.[13] While the first *kasuri* textiles were based on abstract designs, pictorial ikats (*e-gasuri*) became popular in the 18th-19th centuries (see Ikat in Japan).

Central Zone

(India, Middle East, Europe, West Africa, Central Asia, western Southeast Asia)

Ikat was certainly in use in India by the 5th century CE, as it is clearly identifiable in the paintings from that date at the Ajanta caves in Maharashtra (see Ikat in India, Fig.2). Warp-ikat textile fragments dating to the 7th–8th centuries CE have been found in Israel and Jordan, the Israeli fragments of cotton, and those in Jordan of tasar silk, both fibers suggesting an Indian origin (see Ikat in India, note 2). Ikat, locally called *'asb*, was also being woven in Yemen by the late 6th century CE,[14] although most of the surviving examples date from the 9th–10th century (Fig.7) (see Ikat in West & Central Asia).[15] Although we know from the *Periplus of the Erythrean Sea* that Indian textiles were being traded to Muza in modern-day Yemen by the 1st century CE, it is impossible to say whether or not there is a direct link between Indian ikat textiles and those produced in Yemen.[16]

Textiles from Yemen were traded to other parts of the Middle East, and we have textual evidence from the 7th century for Yemeni fabrics being imported into Iran, which could very well have included ikats.[17] Ikat "in the style of Aden" was produced in Iran itself by the 14th century, notably at Rayy.[18] The spread of ikat through the Middle East seems to follow the rise of the Ottoman Empire: the Turks took Aden

Fig.7
Ikat *tiraz*, Yemen, 960–980. Cleveland Museum of Art, 1950.353, Purchase from the J. H. Wade Fund

Fig.8
Detail of AM11, shoulder cloth, *rebozo*

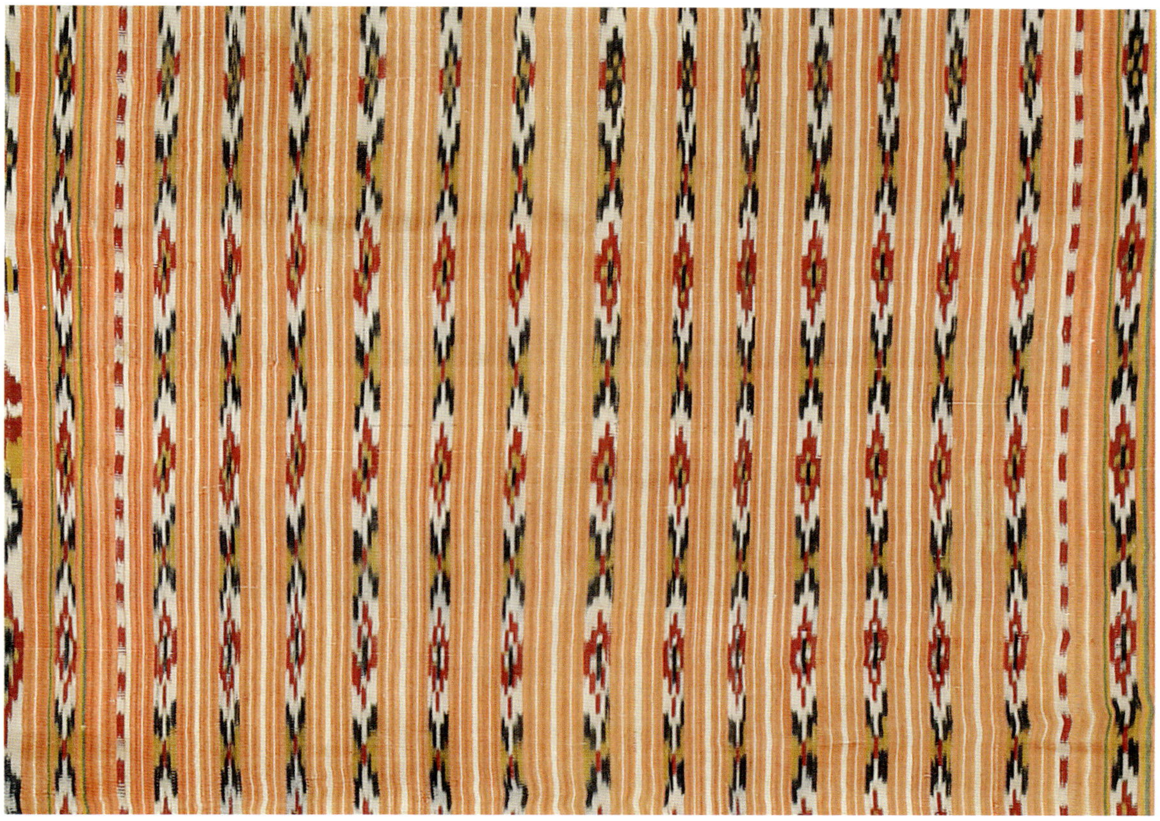

Fig.8

in 1547, and Indian as well as local textiles were brought to Istanbul. Yemeni *aladja*, a Turkish term meaning "multi-colored," is recorded as being imported into Bursa. It was likely the trade with the Islamic world that spread ikat to Italy, and thence to Greece, Mallorca, and France, and even to Britain and Scandinavia (see Ikat in Europe).

Ikat was probably introduced to West Africa by means of Indian textiles brought to the area by Portuguese, French, and British traders. Surprisingly, the flourishing maritime trade between western India and the eastern coast of Africa did not apparently include ikat textiles or ikat technology, and only Madagascar, off Africa's east coast, has any tradition of ikat weaving in the region.

To the east of India, India's trade with the western zone of Southeast Asia (i.e. west of Buckley's "ikat line") introduced weft ikat and double ikat to the region. Portuguese records emphasize how important Indian ikats (especially *patola*) were to the Southeast Asian trade, and they had a huge effect on local production. The broader transition from warp-patterned to weft-patterned textiles was also largely a result of this trade.

Western Zone

(Latin America)

A wide range of warp- (and sometimes weft-) resist techniques are found in Mexico and Guatemala in the north of the region and in Ecuador, Peru, Bolivia, Chile, and Argentina in South America. It is not known how old the tradition of ikat weaving is in Latin America, but some ikats excavated in Peru can be dated to the pre-Columbian and indeed pre-Incan (pre-1438) period, as can examples of the related tie-dye process.[19] It is possible that certain types of ikat textile (for example, those made in Mexico and Guatemala) developed later as a result of trade with Spain. The origins of the ikat *rebozo* (shawl) of Mexico (Fig.8/AM11) have been especially debated, with links to both India and Southeast Asia suggested (see Ikat in the Americas).

Ikat today

Ikat patterns still hold cultural relevance today in many of their traditional weaving areas, especially in parts of Indonesia and India, and continue to be dyed and woven in the traditional way, for local use. In South America, ikat textiles are still made in Peru, Bolivia, Ecuador, Chile, and Argentina. Other areas, such as Uzbekistan and Southeast Turkey, where ikats have largely fallen out of use locally, have broadened their markets and now cater mainly to foreign buyers or purveyors of "folkloric" costume. Textile artists and fashion designers in many countries have taken ikat in new directions, both drawing on traditional forms and palettes and diverging from them (see Ikat Today). The distinctive blurred and jagged outlines of ikat patterns appealed to 20th-century artists such as the fiber artist Ed Rossbach (IT02), who used dyeing as an alternative to painting to expand the possibilities of abstract art.

IKAT: THE TECHNIQUE

To create an ikat, warp or weft threads are separated into small bundles, the size of the bundle depending on the scale of the ikat design. The overall pattern is then drawn directly onto the threads. The threads are then prepared for the first dye bath: areas not to be dyed in the first color are tightly wrapped with a resist, which may be of any waterproof material including strips of rubber, treated string or plant fiber. After dyeing, the threads are dried and unbound and then re-bound so that different selected areas take the second color. This process of re-wrapping and dyeing the threads may be repeated as many times as the pattern requires.

1

Undyed threads are tightly bound for the first dye bath

2

Designated areas are bound, while others are exposed to the first dye

3

Bound areas resist the dye and remain undyed

4

Threads are bound for the second dye bath

5

Designated areas are exposed to the second dye

6

Bound areas resist the dye and keep their color

7

Threads are bound for the third dye bath

8

Designated areas are exposed to the third dye

9

Bound areas resist the dye and keep their color

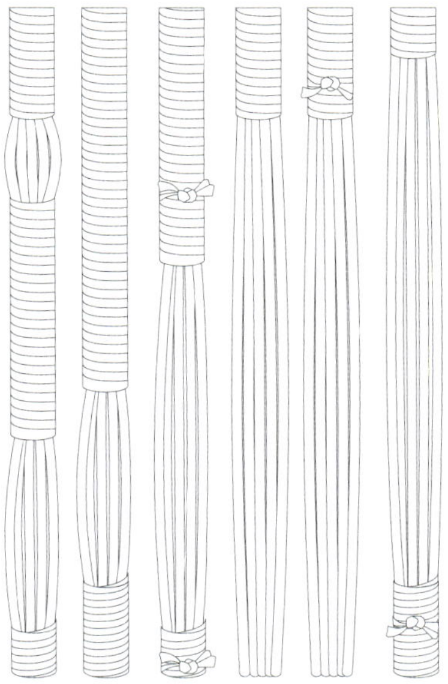

1

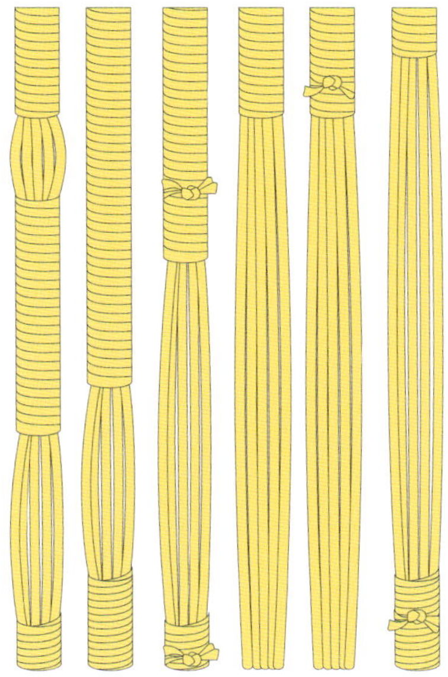

2

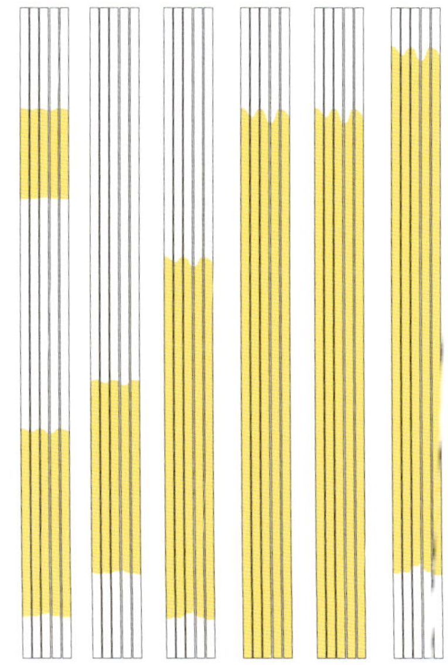

3

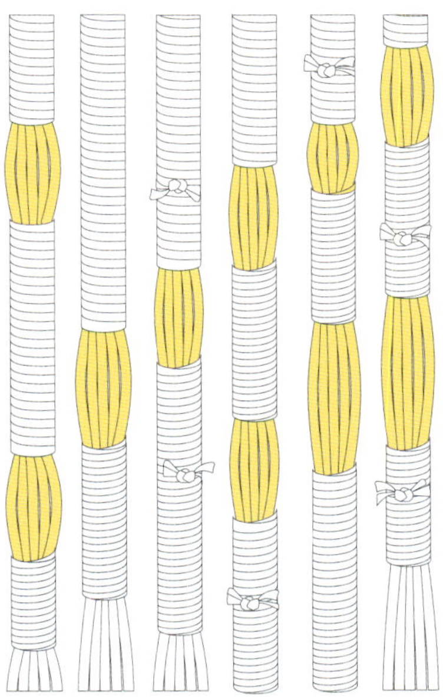

4

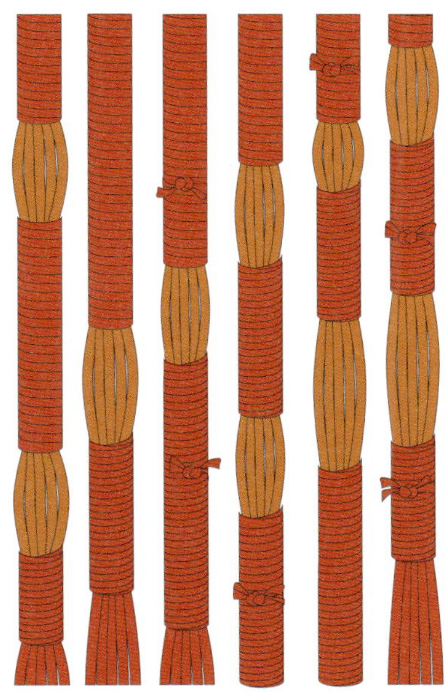

5

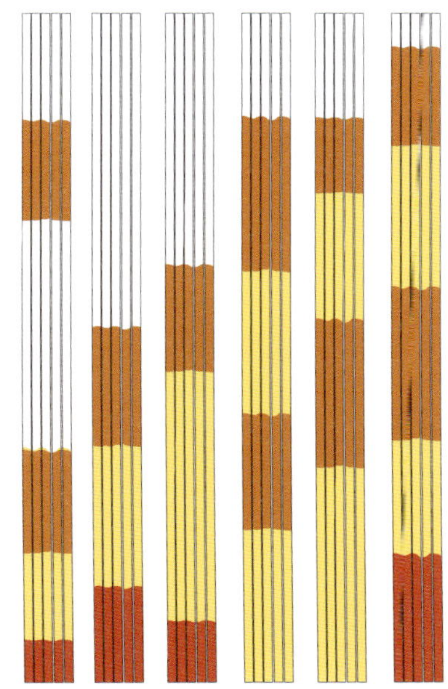

6

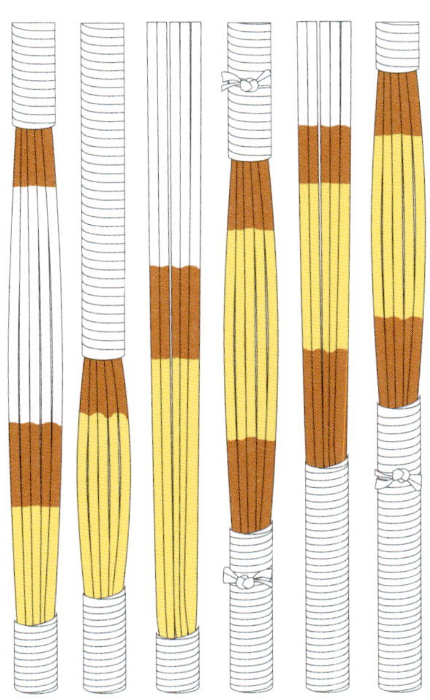

7

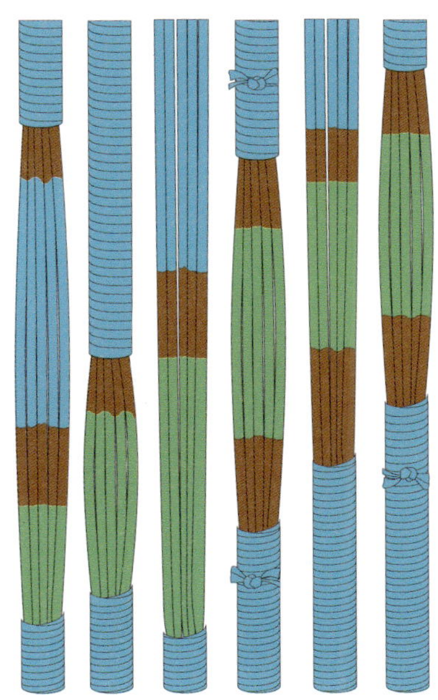

8

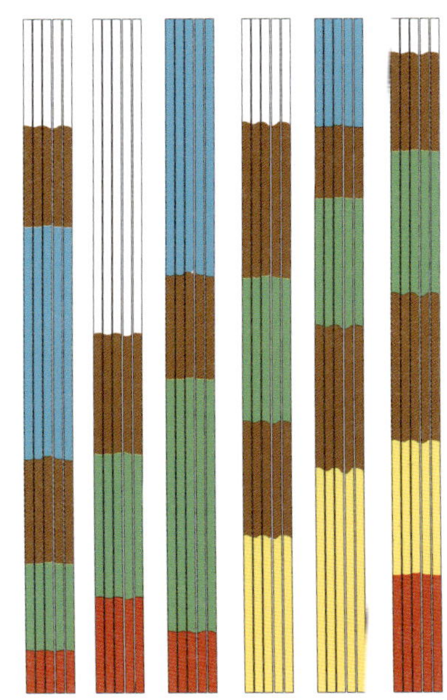

9

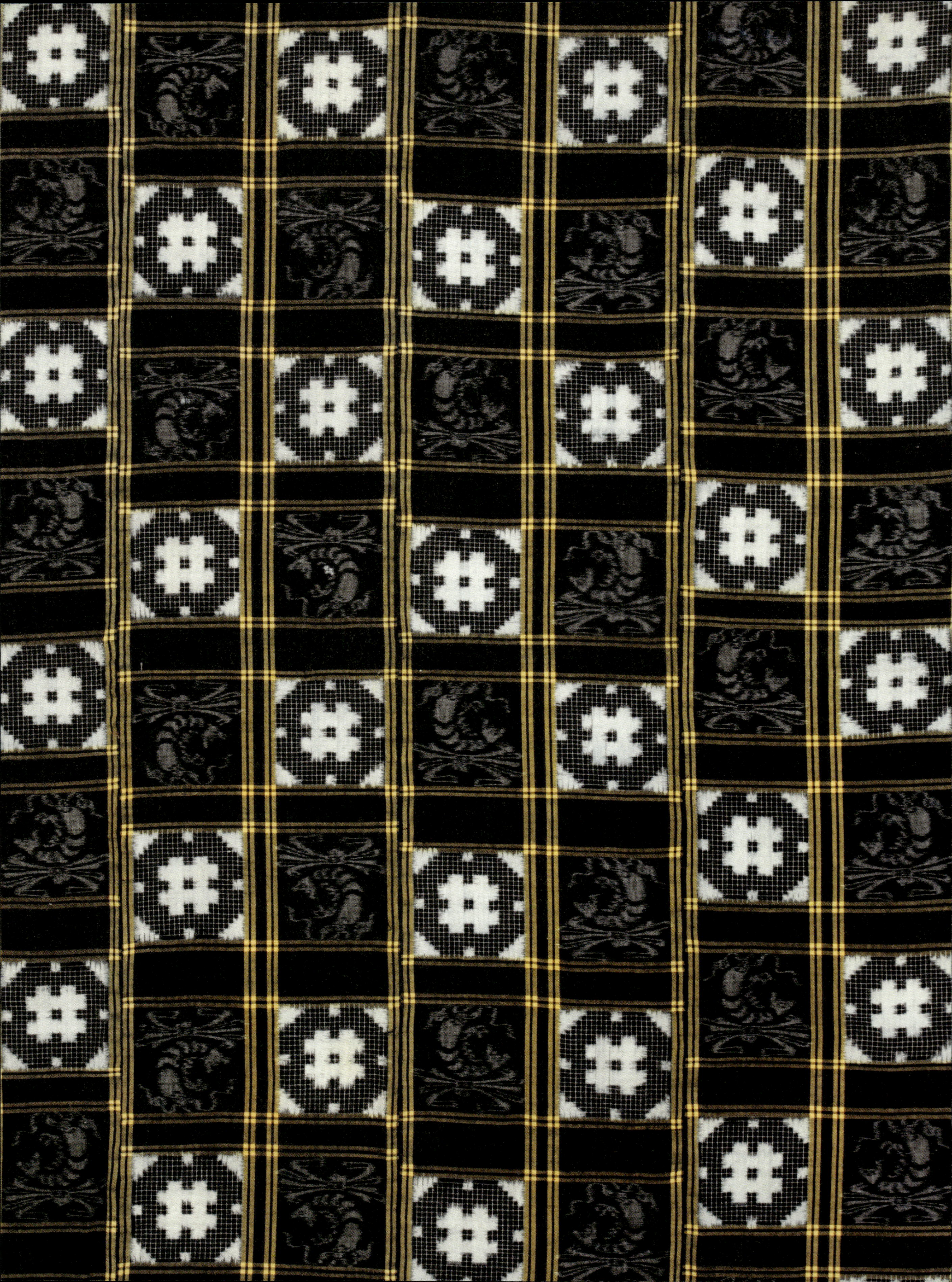

JAPAN

by Lee Talbot

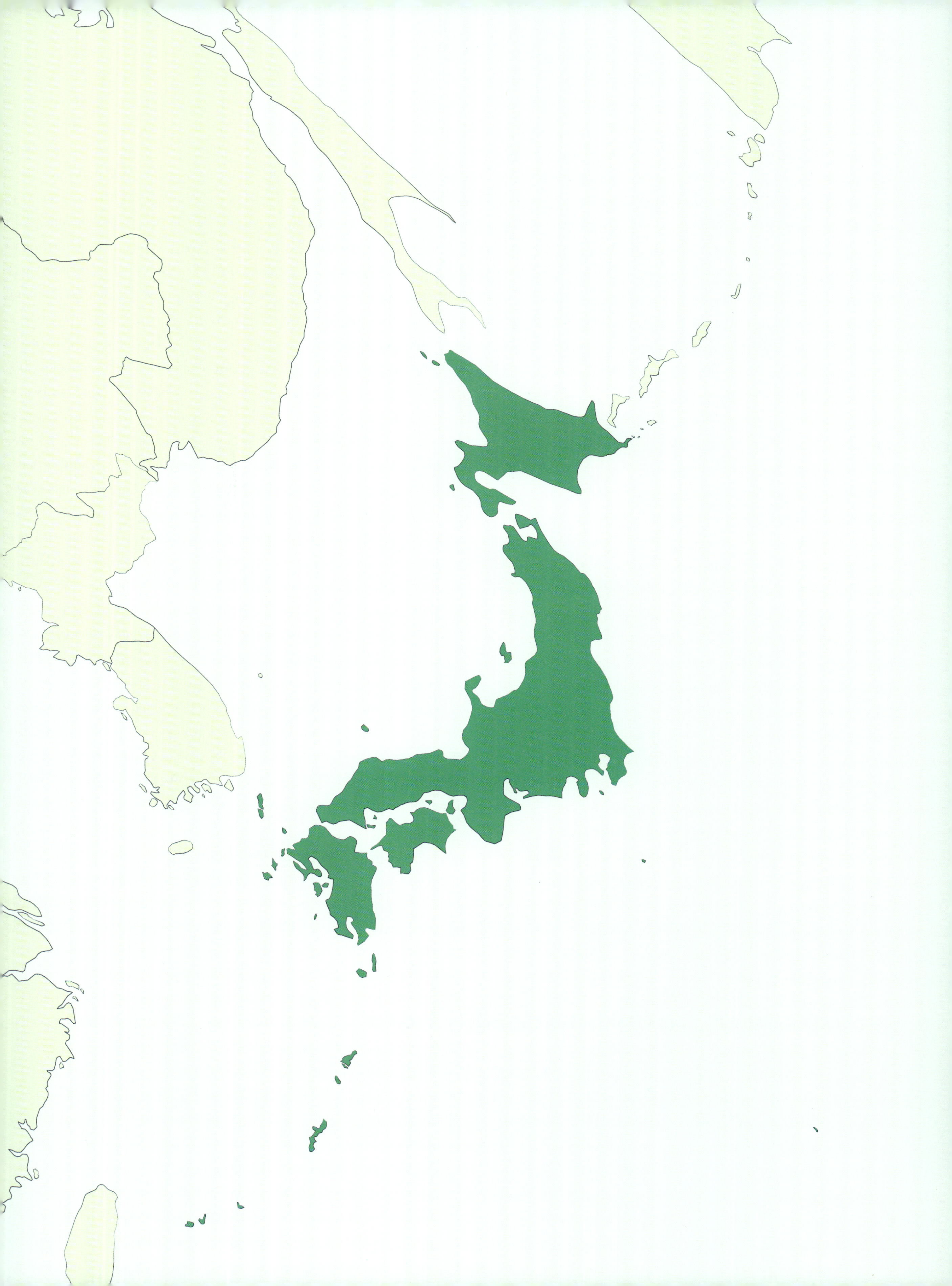

IKAT IN JAPAN

Japanese dyers and weavers have created one of the world's most vibrant and diverse ikat traditions. Acclaimed globally for their meticulous planning and execution, ongoing technical experimentation, and mastery of materials, artisans in Japan have developed a remarkable range of techniques for selectively dyeing yarns before weaving, all broadly categorized as *kasuri*. Colorful *kasuri* patterning appears in many different forms and contexts, from exquisite court and theater costumes to robust clothing for everyday wear. Technical and stylistic innovations have maintained *kasuri*'s popularity over several centuries, and hand dyeing and weaving continue alongside mechanized factory production. *Kasuri* textiles remain widely admired for their quintessentially Japanese beauty as well as the artistry, ingenuity, and cultural legacy that they embody.

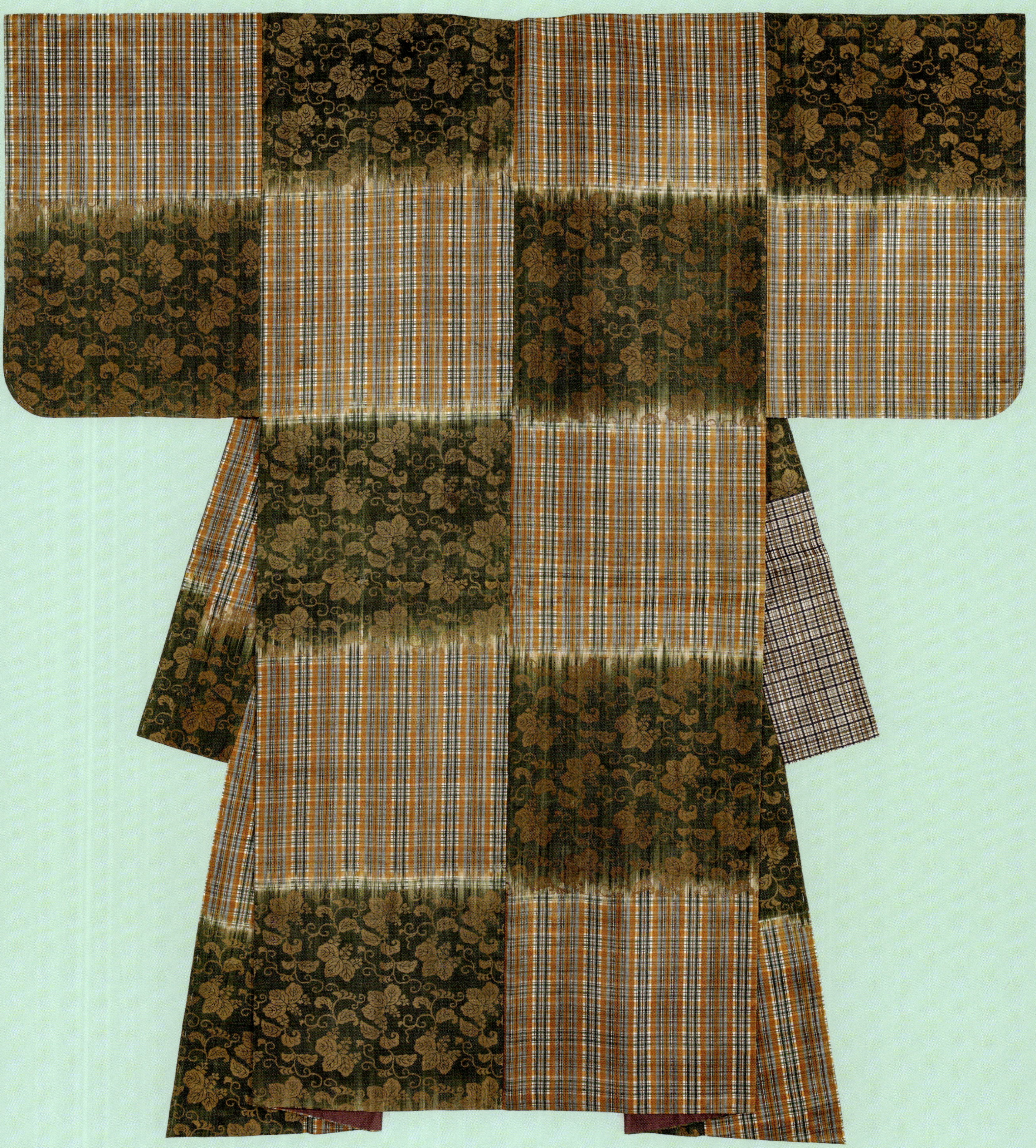

Fig.1
JP05, Noh robe

UNRAVELING KASURI

Japan maintains one of the world's richest and most diverse ikat traditions. Colorful ikat patterning appears in a variety of forms and contexts, from the resplendent costumes worn by courtiers and actors to sturdy work clothes for farmers and fishermen. Japanese artisans have developed a remarkable range of unique solutions for dyeing yarns before weaving, including techniques that do not involve binding but create visually similar results. Textiles made by these processes are broadly categorized as *kasuri*.[1] *Kasuri* dyers and weavers have achieved global recognition for their meticulous planning and execution, ongoing technical experimentation, and mastery of materials including cotton, silk, and various bast fibers. Technical and stylistic innovations have helped to maintain *kasuri*'s relevance and economic viability over several centuries, and time-consuming methods of hand weaving and dyeing continue alongside mechanized factory production in present-day Japan.

The earliest examples of ikat in Japan have survived in the repositories of two great Buddhist temples: Horyuji, built during the Asuka period (552–645), and Todaiji, dating to the Nara period (645–794). Each temple collection contains colorfully patterned warp-ikat silk fragments that likely formed part of banners used in Buddhist rituals during the 7th and 8th centuries (Fig.3). Coinciding with China's cosmopolitan Tang dynasty (618–907), this era witnessed the heyday of the so-called Silk Road, and luxury goods produced across Eurasia reached Japan via multiple trade routes. The warp-ikat fragments in the Horyuji and Todaiji collections traditionally have been referred to as *kanto-kin* ("Canton polychrome"), and scientific analyses of their fibers and dyes further suggest production in southern China.[2]

A sophisticated local tradition of yarn-resist silk textiles emerged in Kyoto, which became Japan's capital during the Heian period (794–1185). Heian aristocrats adopted many aspects of Tang Chinese court costume, including ceremonial sashes called *hirao*, which remain in use in certain court, ecclesiastical, and dance contexts. Using a technique called *karagumi* ("Chinese braiding"), a type of paired oblique twill interlacing, *hirao* are made of heavy silk cords that have been resist dyed to create large sections of contrasting color. During the Muromachi (1392–1573) and Momoyama (1568–1615) periods, Kyoto weavers achieved similar shifts in background color through *shimekiri*, in which warp yarns are resist dyed to create wide bands or blocks. Primarily used for high-end men's *kosode* (narrow sleeved garments), *shimekiri* production continued into the Edo period for the patterning of *noshime*, a type of inner *kosode*, as well as Noh theater costume (Fig.1/JP05, JP51).[3] In these Kyoto traditions, the silk yarns are resist dyed not as a means of creating representational motifs, but rather to create bold juxtapositions of color on the ground fabric, which sometimes is further embellished with embroidered or brocaded designs. While *shimekiri* relates to *karagumi hirao* technically and visually, artisans working in the *shimekiri* technique may also have drawn inspiration from imported Indian ikats that became increasingly available from the 17th century onwards.[4]

Kyoto's *shimekiri* and *karagumi hirao* silk-weaving traditions seem to have scarcely influenced the development of Japanese *kasuri* as it is known today, which arose primarily through interactions with the Ryukyu Kingdom (present-day Okinawa prefecture). From the 14th through the 16th centuries, the Ryukyu Kingdom was an important maritime trading center, and Ryukyuan ships regularly plied the seas between China, Japan, Korea, the Persian Gulf, and ports in nations now known as Indonesia, the Philippines, Thailand, and Malaysia. The *Rekidai Hōan*, a compilation of Ryukyuan court documents, confirms that ikat fabrics entered the kingdom via a far-reaching trade and tribute network from at least the 15th century.

Nonetheless, the absence of extant examples obscures understanding of the origins and development of a local *kasuri* weaving tradition within the Ryukyus. While ikat fabrics may have been produced before the advent of active maritime trade, local production likely was at least encouraged by exposure to imported fabrics as well as skills brought back by Ryukyuan sailors, whose reliance on monsoon winds required them to spend many months in Southeast Asian regions with longstanding ikat traditions. By the late 14th century, weavers in the Ryukyus were producing ikat fabrics prized as luxuries for royal court consumption and as valuable commodities for trade.[5]

The fabrics created by Ryukyuan weavers differed significantly from the Southeast Asian ikats that may have served as their inspiration. The most common fibers were *basho* (*Musa balbisiana var. liukiuensis*), a plant closely related to the edible

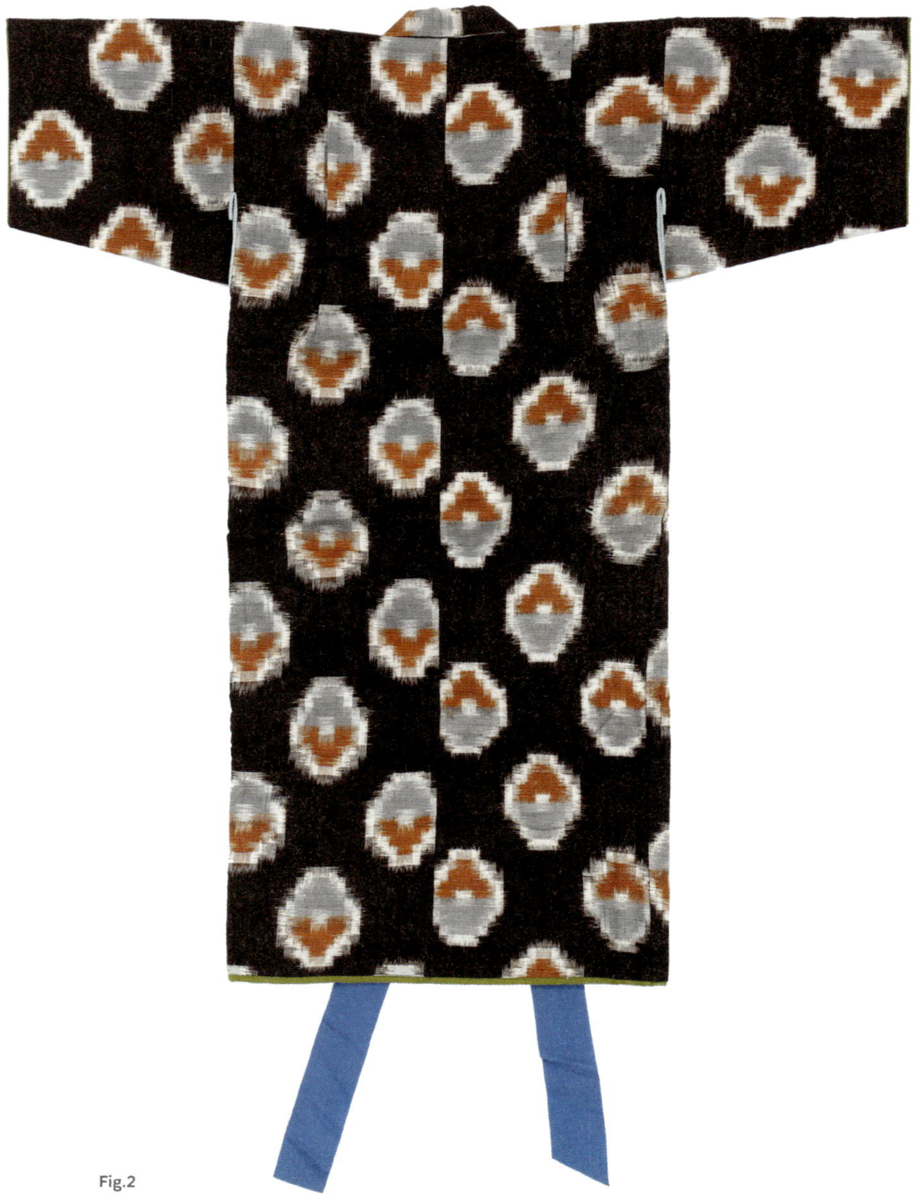

Fig.2

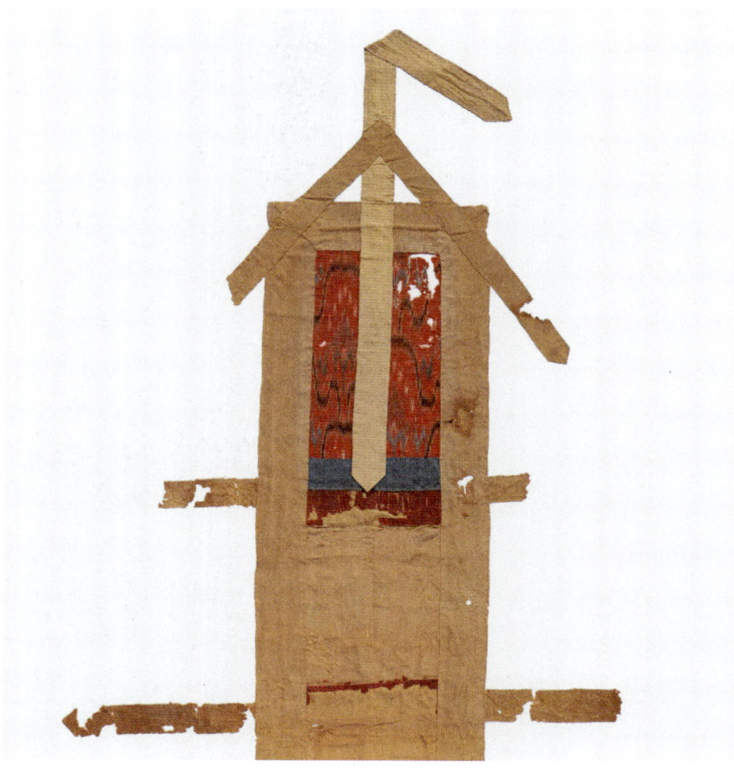

Source: ColBase (https://colbase.nich.go.jp/)

Fig.3

Fig.2
JP74, child's kimono

Fig.3
Detail of Buddhist ritual banner, *Kanton ban*, Japan, Asuka-Nara period, 7th–8th century. Silk, plain weave with warp ikat patterning. Tokyo National Museum, Horyu-ji collection

Fig.4
JP31, royal kimono fragment

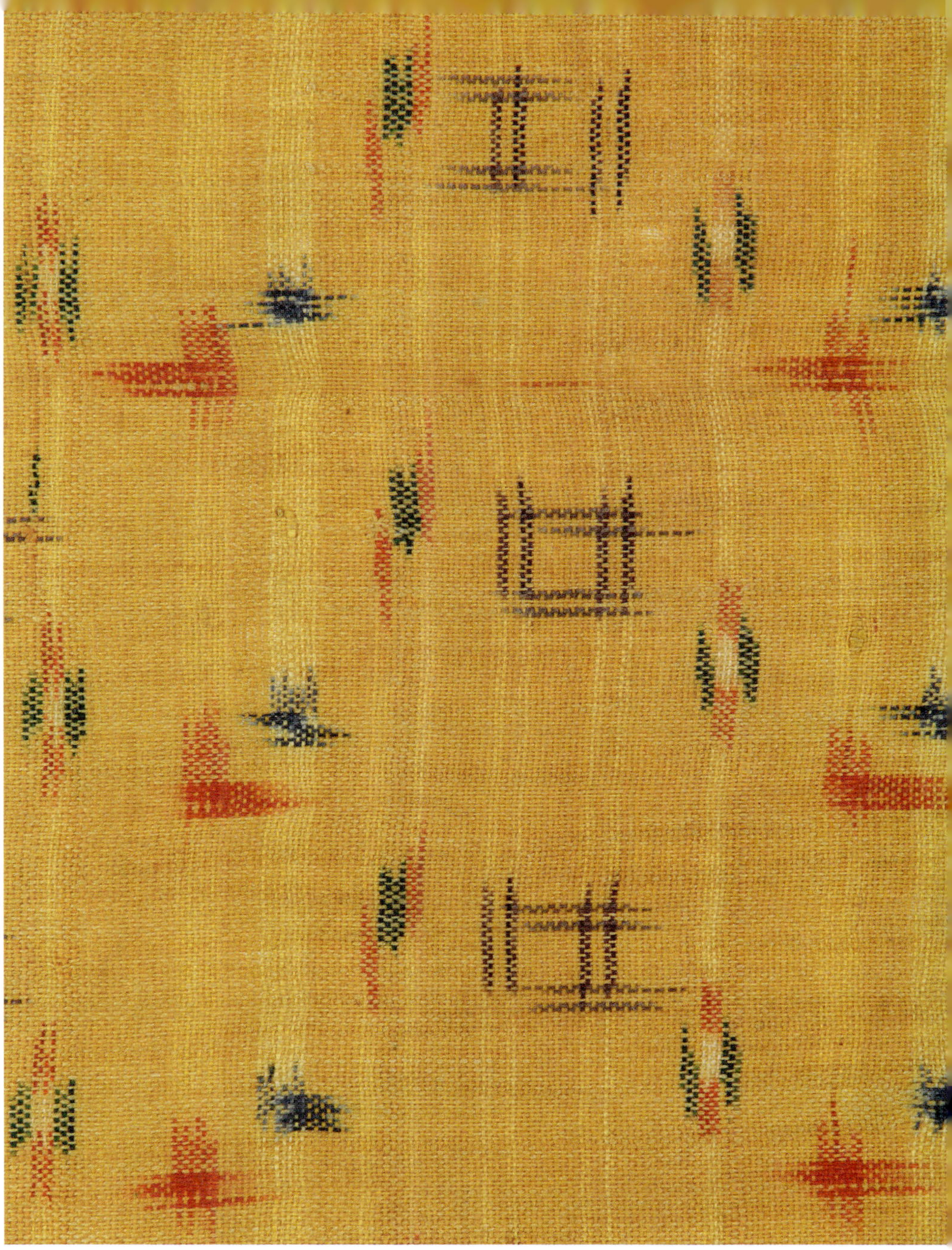

Fig.4

banana, and *choma* (ramie, *Boehmeria nivea*), a flowering plant in the nettle family. Although these fibers require laborious processing before weaving, they create lustrous, breathable fabrics suitable for wear in hot, humid weather. While most Southeast Asian ikats featured patterning only in the warp, Ryukyuan weavers fully exploited the technical potential of local looms—which included reeds that helped regulate the balance between warp and weft—to create warp, weft, and double-ikat patterning.[6] Warp patterns are relatively static once the warp yarns are attached to the loom, but wefts can be manipulated during the weaving process. By gently pulling the wefts left or right, Ryukyuan weavers could create diagonals and curves that allowed the formation of representational motifs including birds, clouds, and water.

Kasuri production expanded after 1611, when the Ryukyu Kingdom became a vassal state of the southern Japanese fiefdom of Satsuma. Required to present the lord of Satsuma with a heavy annual tribute, the Ryukyuan government levied new taxes on its citizens, payable in rice and textiles. On the island groups of Miyako and Yaeyama—primary centers of *kasuri* production—all women between the ages of fifteen and fifty were required to produce an annual quota of tax cloth to be used by the Ryukyuan royal court, for trade, and as tribute payment to Satsuma. Government officials strictly controlled all aspects of production, and court painters provided renderings of the desired patterns and colors.[7] This close supervision of *kasuri* manufacture heightened the quality of local production, and extant examples reveal the technical and aesthetic mastery achieved by Ryukyuan weavers (Fig.4/JP31, JP27).

The Ryukyuan *kasuri* textiles arriving in Japan via Satsuma appealed to the ruling samurai families, who began to wear them as *kosode*, *haori* (jackets), and other fashionable garments. The *sankin kotai*

Fig.5

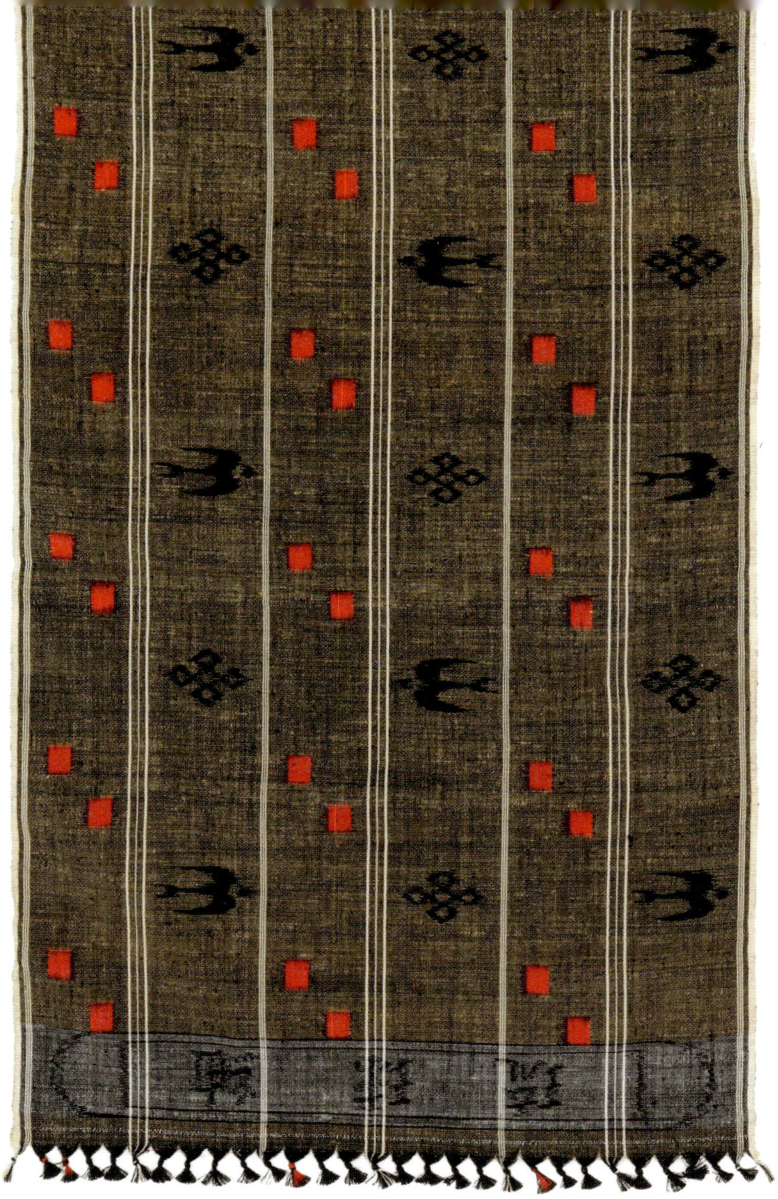

Fig.6

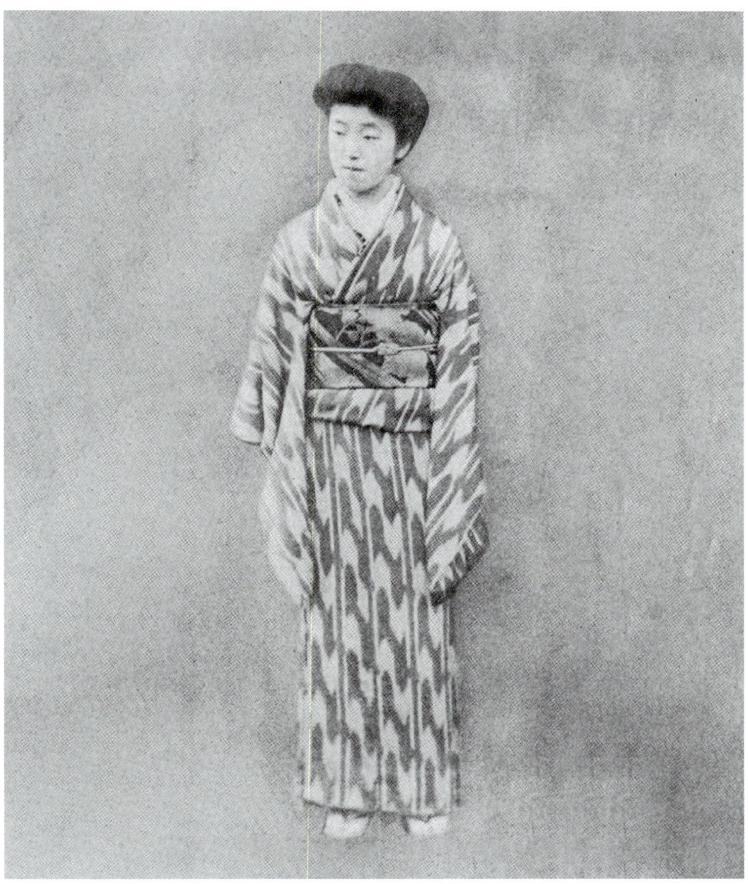

Fig.7

Fig.5
JP24, futon cover

Fig.6
Detail of JP39, loom length of cloth

Fig.7
Princess Nagako of Kuni wearing an ikat kimono, ca. 1920. *Osaka Mainichi Shimbun*, March 1, 1922

("alternate attendance") system, introduced in 1635, required *daimyo* (feudal lords) and their retainers to live alternately one year in their domains and one year in Edo, the capital. The *daimyo* typically brought their own artisans with them to Edo, where they maintained lavish lifestyles and socialized with their peers from other regions, so this policy served to introduce makers as well as consumers to new styles and techniques and to disseminate them across Japan. The political stability and economic prosperity of the Edo period (1603–1867) stimulated interregional trade, which further facilitated the spread of fashions and skills. Burgeoning market demand fueled local production and, although Japan seems to have manufactured few *kasuri* at the beginning of the 18th century, by the end of the century *kasuri* weaving was well established in many regions.

Although weavers attached to *daimyo* households probably created some *kasuri* fabrics, women working domestically in rural areas became the main producers. Primarily engaged in agriculture, these women and their families supplemented their incomes by cultivating fibers in summer and weaving them into saleable cloth during the winter. Textile production and family incomes expanded with the introduction of cotton, which became increasingly widespread through the 18th century. Cotton was not only warmer but also easier and faster to process and thus less expensive than the hemp and ramie fibers used previously. Cotton cultivation and weaving became integral to rural economies in many regions, and cotton clothing dyed in indigo with reserved white *kasuri* patterns became the archetypal costume of rural Japan (JP50).[8] Fabrics intricately dyed in

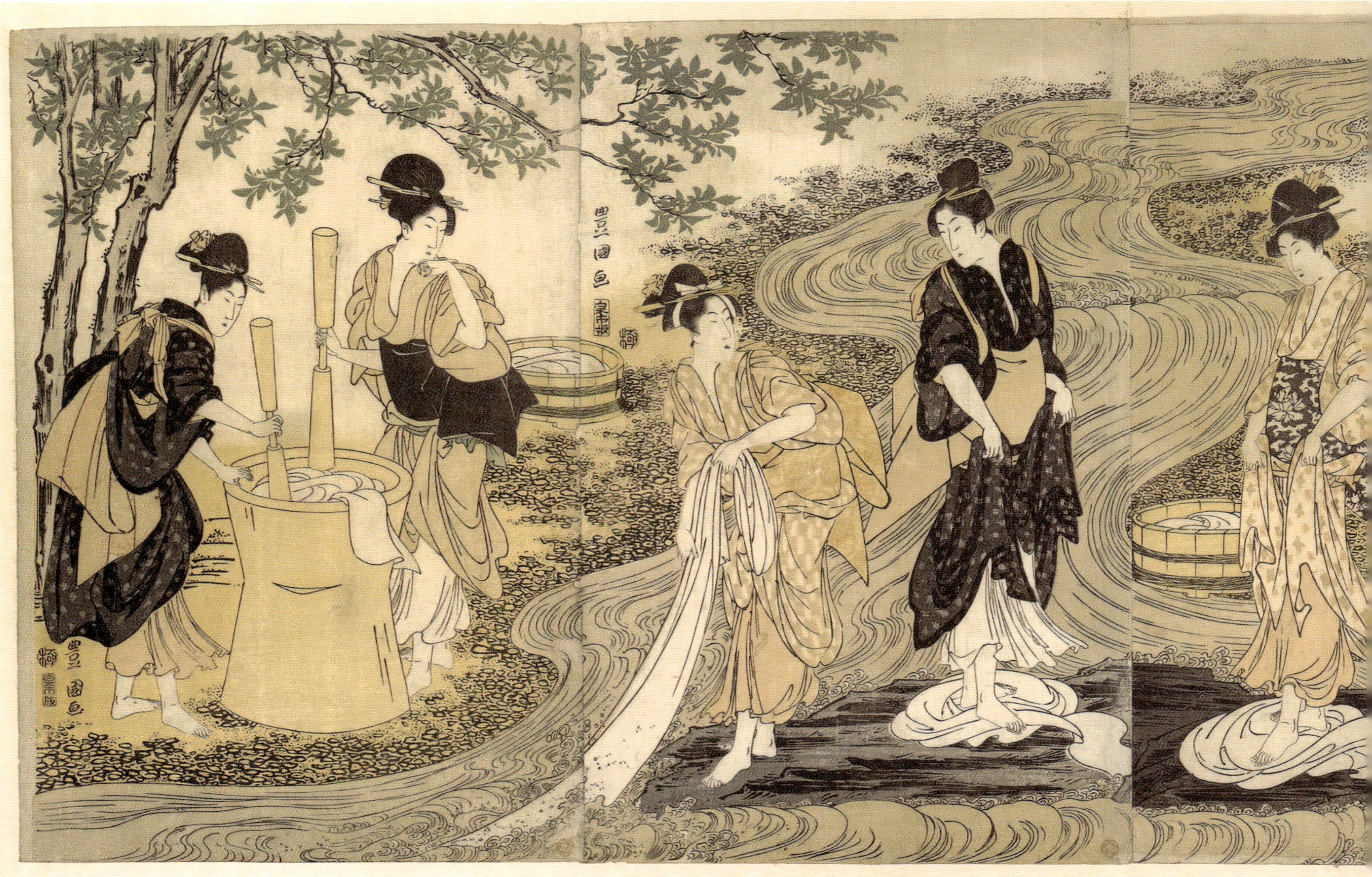

Fig.8

the *kasuri* technique also gained popularity in urban areas, especially since sumptuary laws restricted patterned silks to only the ruling classes. Woodblock prints from the late Edo period reveal the ongoing appeal of *kasuri*-patterned *kosode* among fashionable urbanites, from wealthy merchants to actors and courtesans (Fig.8).

Kasuri production proliferated as the economy expanded and more people could afford fabrics of this quality. With *kasuri*'s increased commercial importance in the late 18th and early 19th century, different regions began to develop their own distinctive designs as well as new techniques that allowed the creation of complex patterns and more efficient production. In the 19th century, for example, weavers in Kurume and along the San'in coast began to create elaborately patterned *e-gasuri* ("picture ikat") using a wooden frame known as an *e-dai* (picture stand) (Fig.5/JP24, JP19). Fitted with combs on two sides, an *e-dai* is constructed the same width as the cloth, plus an allowance for weaving take-up. A cotton guide thread is wound onto the frame to create a false weft, and the pattern is painted or stenciled onto it. The guide thread is unwound and laid parallel to the yarns to be used for weaving, which are bound according to the markings on the guide thread.[9] Weavers in Echigo and Omi began to employ a similar concept with *koba jogi*—a stack of thin, numbered boards painted on the side with the desired pattern. The boards are unstacked in numerical order and used to mark the yarn bundles for tying.[10] Both the *e-dai* and *koba jogi* facilitated the creation of larger, more precise pictorial designs.

The introduction of Western technologies—including machines for spinning cotton and reeling silk, as well as graph paper as a means of communication between designer and weaver—also enabled the creation of ever finer and more complex *kasuri* patterns. Other new methods eliminated the need to laboriously hand-tie the yarns. Using the *itajime* ("pressed board") technique, the yarns are pressed between two wooden blocks carved with mirror images of the pattern. The boards are clamped together and immersed in dye, which is resisted where the raised areas meet. In the *orijime* technique, the warp and/or weft yarns first are woven with a temporary binding warp. After dyeing, the cloth is unraveled and the temporary warp discarded. The areas where the yarns had been tightly interlaced resist the dye and create a pattern.[11] By the early 20th century, as techniques spread geographically and makers increasingly imitated patterns

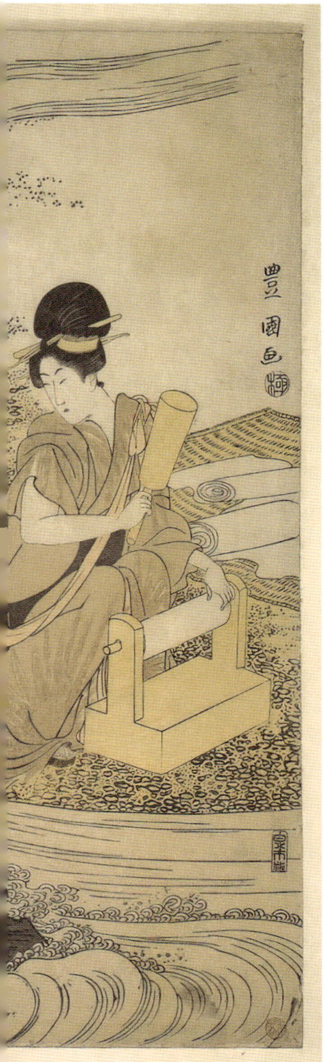

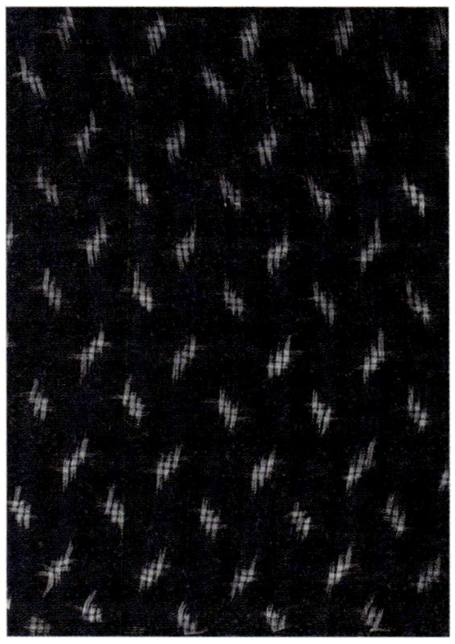

Fig.9

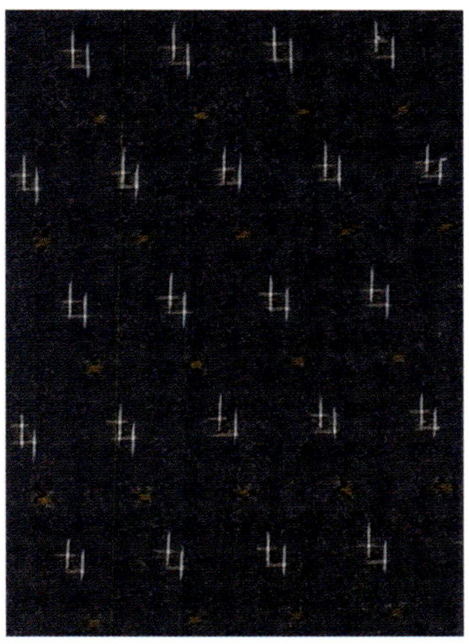

Fig.10

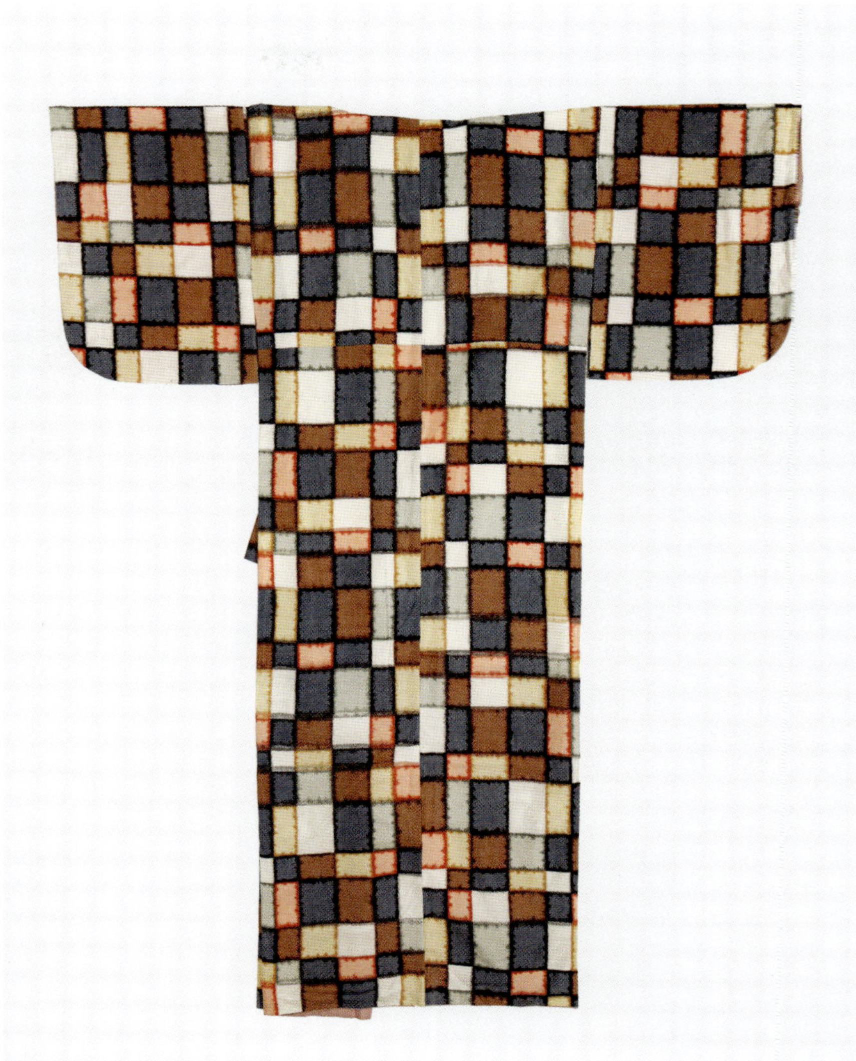

Fig.11

originating in other areas, regional differences in *kasuri* weaving had diminished significantly.

The flourishing of the *kasuri* market in the late 19th and early 20th century encouraged the establishment of many small, hand-industrial *kasuri* workshops across Japan. Through the 20th century, however, most small workshops gave way to large factories employing modern industrial techniques, such as the mechanized printing or stencil dyeing of warps and wefts and weaving on power looms (Fig.11/JP108). Nonetheless, factories never completely replaced small-scale household and workshop production. The last decades of the 20th century witnessed a resurgence of interest in hand techniques and the establishment of numerous makers' cooperatives and schools focused on *kasuri* weaving. Government initiatives—including subsidies for *kasuri* makers, the designation of certain *kasuri* traditions as "intangible cultural heritage," and the establishment of regional museums focused on local history—have helped enhance public understanding and appreciation of *kasuri*. Whether produced industrially or by hand, *kasuri* textiles remain widely admired for their quintessentially Japanese beauty as well as the artistry, ingenuity, and cultural legacy that they embody.

Fig.8
Tetsukuri no Tamagawa on the Musashino Plain, Utagawa Toyokuni I, ca. 1800. Metropolitan Museum of Art, JP665, The Francis Lathrop Collection, Purchase, Frederick C. Hewitt Fund, 1911. In this woodblock print, two figures wear dark kimonos with *kasuri* patterns

Fig.9
Detail of JP48, kimono

Fig.10
Detail of JP46, kimono

Fig.11
JP108, *Meisen* silk kimono

CATALOG

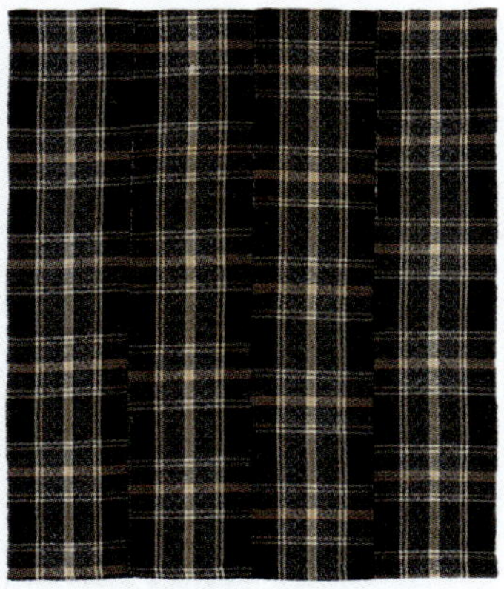

JP01 Futon cover, *tamba momen*
Tamba, Honshu, Japan, 19th century. Cotton compound ikat (sections of leftover *kasuri*). 62 in x 52 in

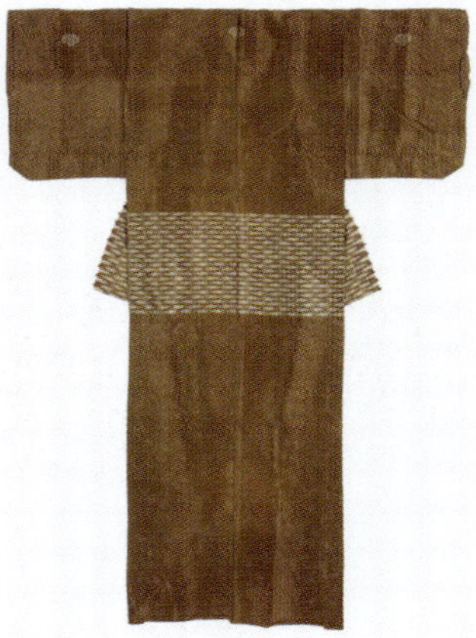

JP02 Man's court robe, *noshime*, for samurai
Probably Kyoto, Japan, early 19th century. Silk, warp ikat, field dyed; weft ikat; *shijira-ori* weaving technique. 60 in x 50 in. The Textile Museum, 2022.13.5

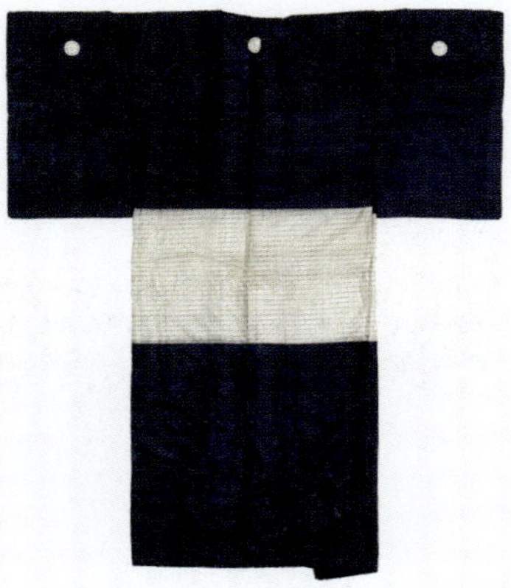

JP03 Man's court robe, *noshime*, for samurai
Probably Kyoto, Japan, early 19th century. Silk, warp ikat, field dyed; *shijira-ori* weaving technique. 54 in x 50 in

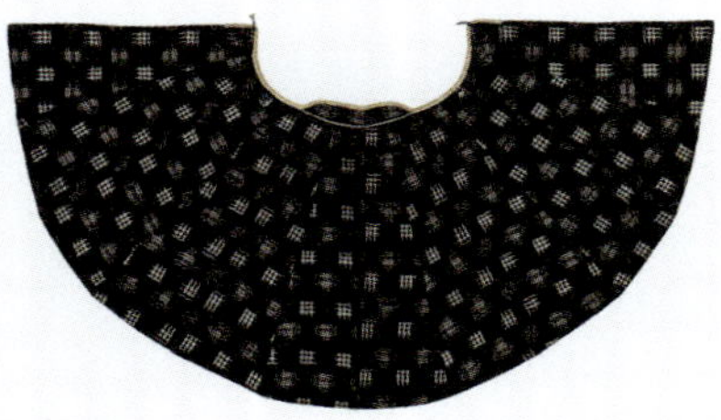

JP04 Child's *kappa*
Japan, mid-19th century. Warp and weft: cotton; double ikat, lined with mulberry paper. 62 in x 35 in

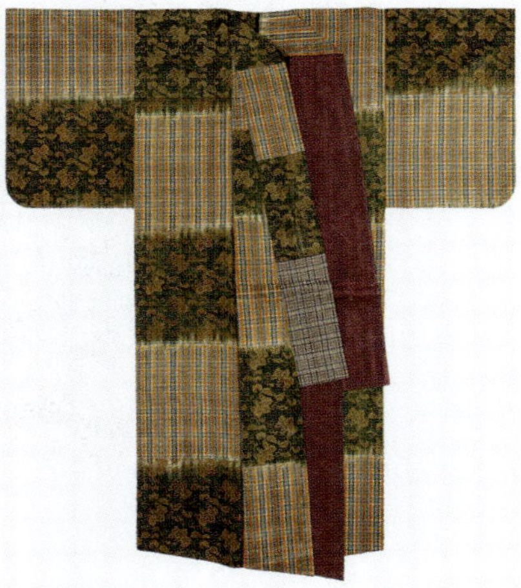

JP05 Noh robe
Nishijin, Kyoto, Japan, circa 1770–1780. *Atsuita karaori* technique; silk plaid, warp ikat and silk weft brocade; silk lining. 65 in x 55 in

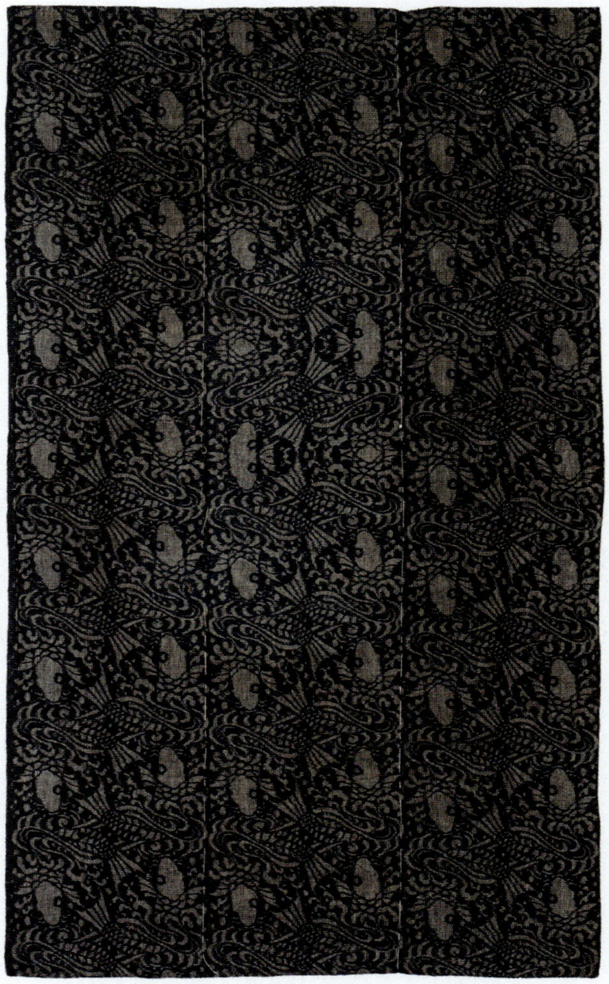

JP06 Boy's futon cover
Tottori, Honshu, Japan, mid-19th century. Cotton, weft ikat. 37 in x 61 in. The Textile Museum, 2022.13.9

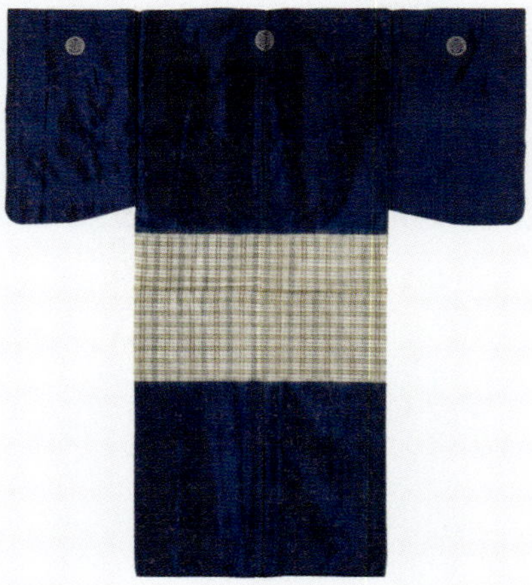

JP07 Man's court robe, *noshime*, for samurai
Probably Kyoto, Japan, early 19th century. Silk, warp ikat, field dyed. 58 in x 50 in. The Textile Museum, 2022.13.4

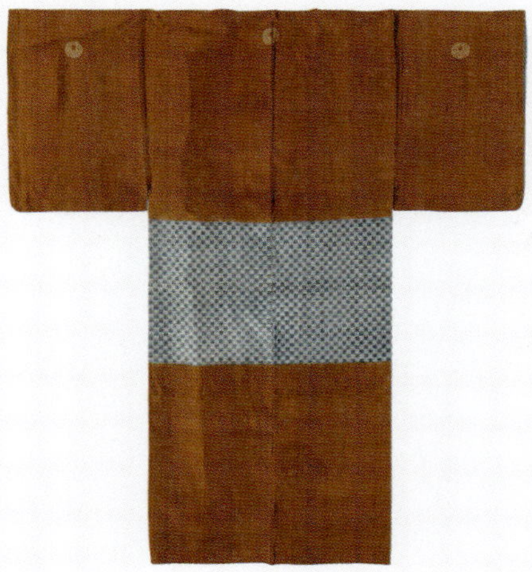

JP08 Man's court robe, *noshime*, for samurai
Probably Kyoto, Japan, early 19th century. Silk, warp ikat, zone dyed. 56 in x 50 in

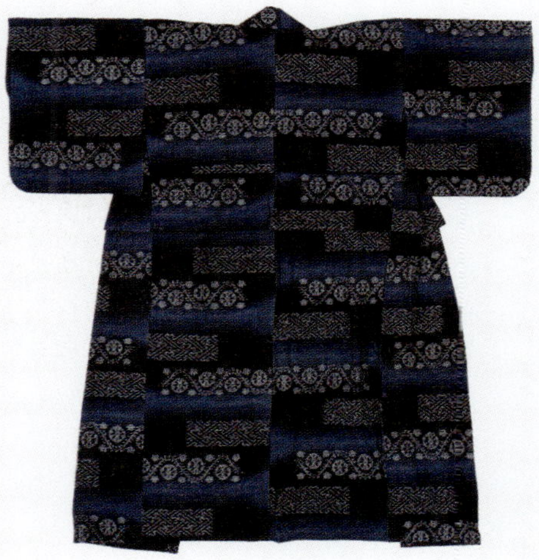

JP09 Kimono
Kurume, Kyushu, Japan, 20th century. Cotton, weft ikat, *e-gasuri*. 65 in x 52 in

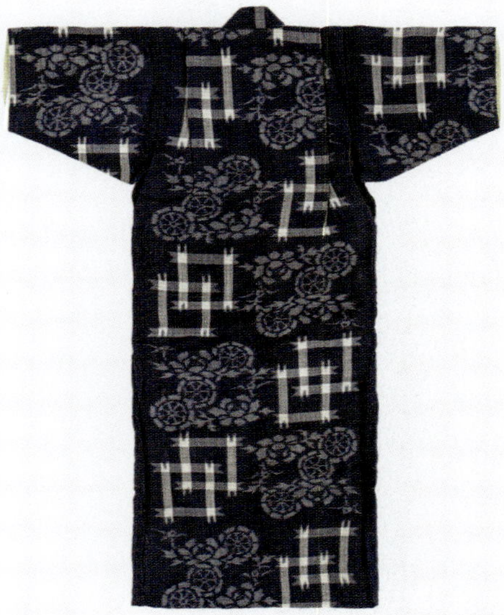

JP10 Child's kimono
Kurume, Kyushu, Japan, 20th century. Cotton, double ikat, *e-gasuri*. 36 in x 24 in

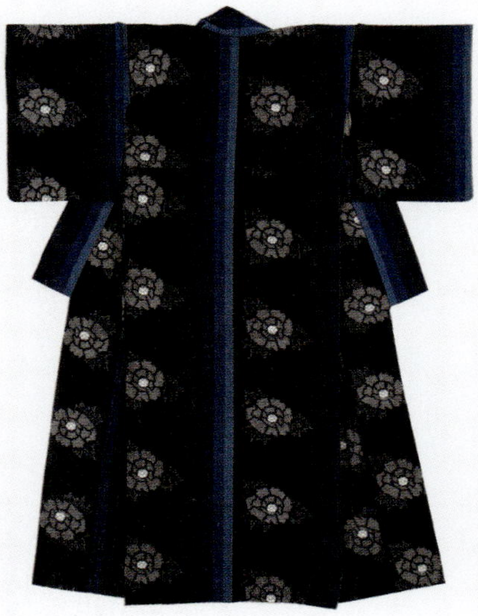

JP11 Kimono
Kurume, Kyushu, Japan, 20th century. Cotton, double ikat. 65 in x 50 in

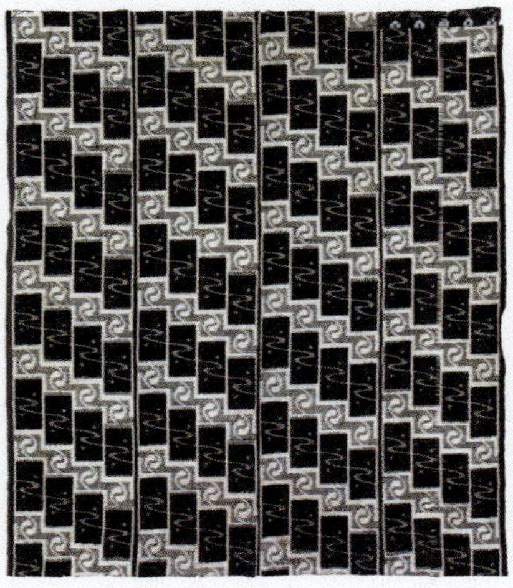

JP12 Futon cover
Kurume, Kyushu, Japan, early 20th century. Cotton, double ikat, *e-gasuri*. 65 in x 52 in

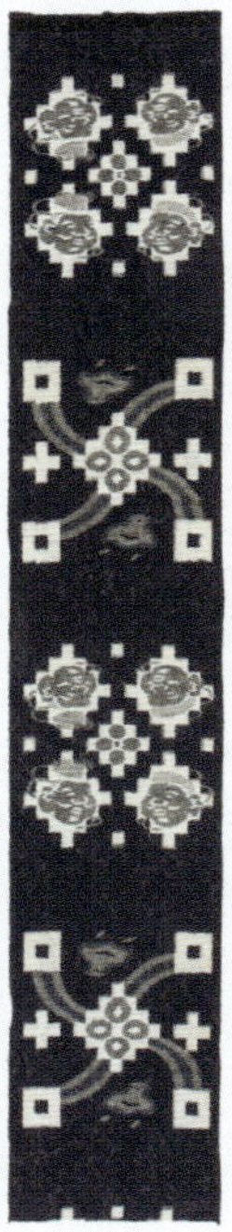

JP13 Futon cover panel
Kurume, Kyushu, Japan, early 20th century. Cotton, double ikat, *e-gasuri*. 65 x 52 in

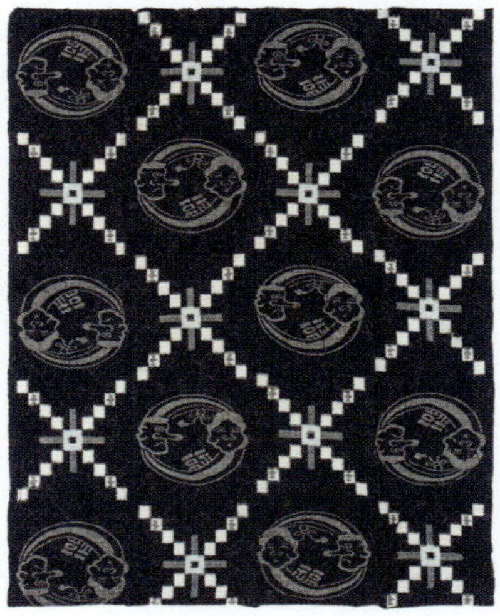

JP14 Futon cover
Japan, early 20th century. Cotton, double ikat, *e-gasuri*. 72 in x 52 in

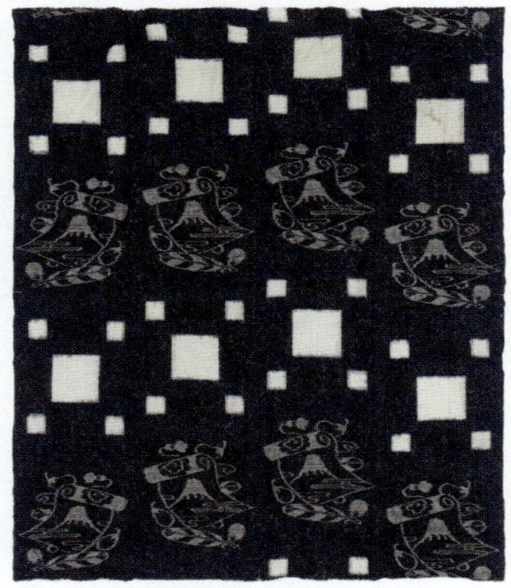

JP15 Futon cover
Kurume, Kyushu, Japan, early 20th century. Cotton, double ikat, *e-gasuri*. 70 in x 52 in

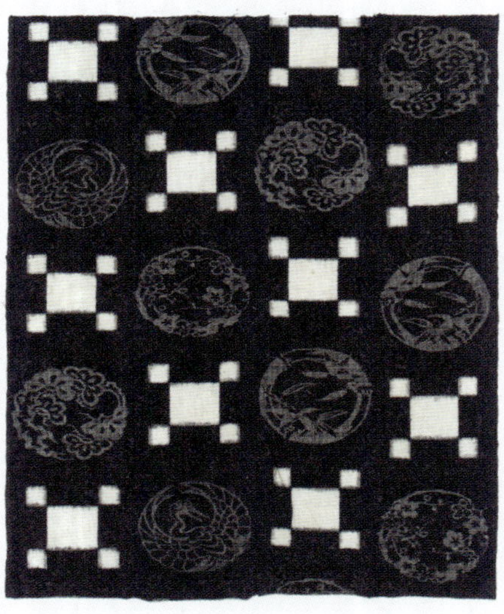

JP16 Futon cover
Kurume, Kyushu, Japan, early 20th century. Cotton, double ikat, *e-gasuri*. 68 in x 52 in

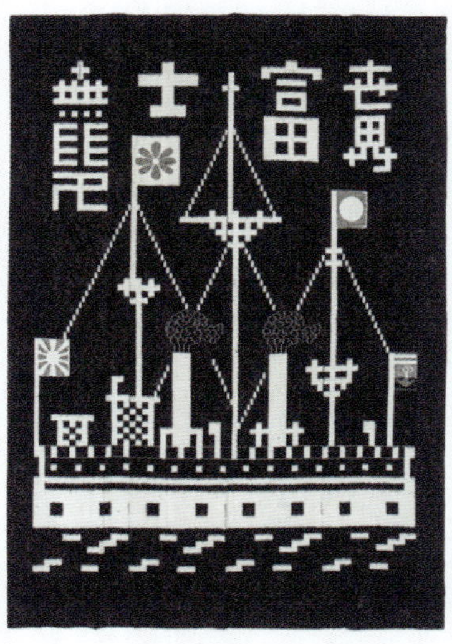

JP17 Futon cover
Kurume, Kyushu, Japan, late 19th century. Cotton, double ikat, *e-gasuri*. 90 in x 65 in

JP18 Futon cover
Kurume, Kyushu, Japan, early 20th century. Cotton, double ikat, *e-gasuri*. 80 in x 65 in. The Textile Museum, 2022.13.8

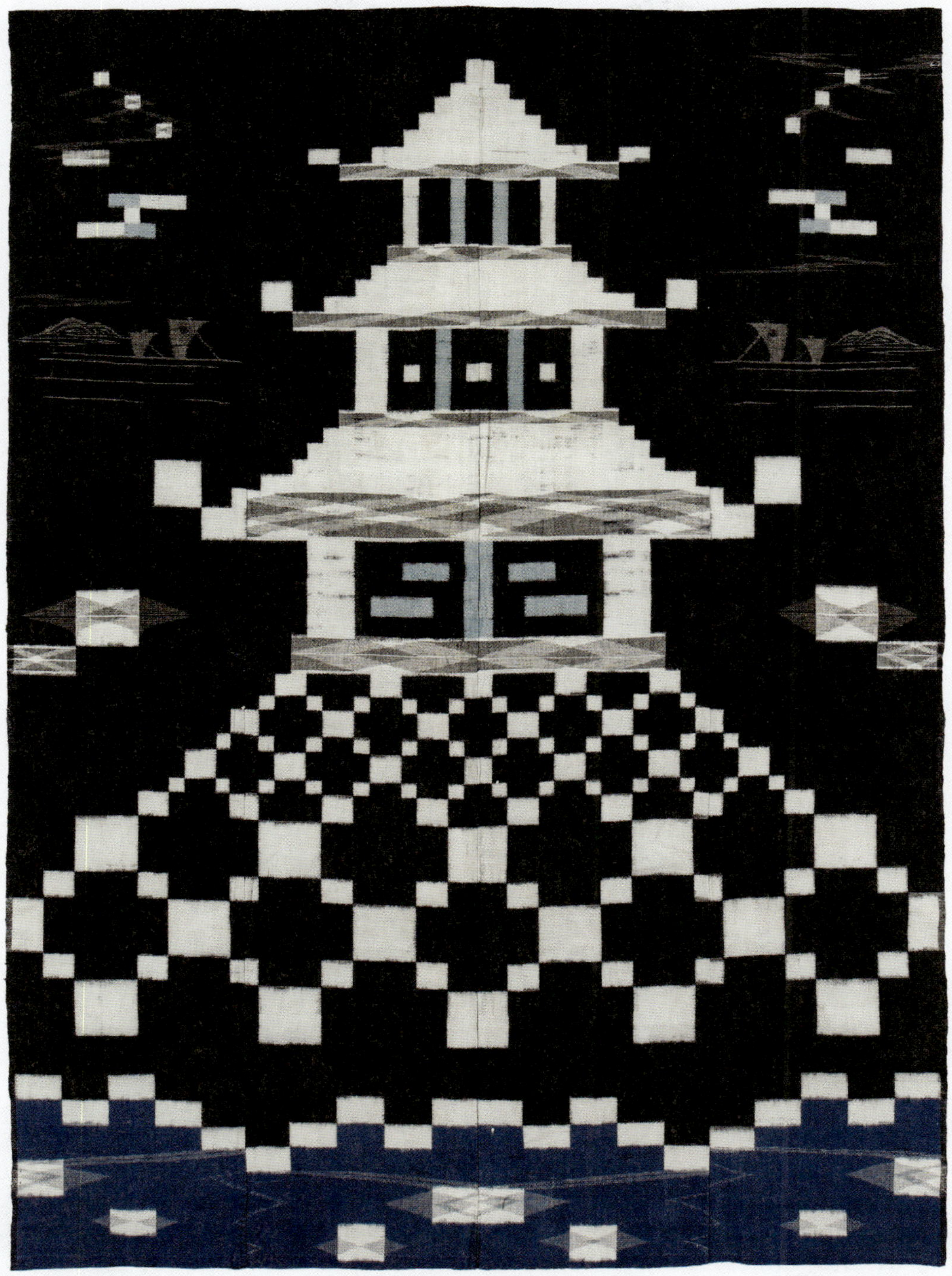

JP19 Futon cover, Kurume, Kyushu Island, Japan, ca. 1890. Cotton; plain weave with warp, weft, and double ikat. 68 in x 51 in. The Textile Museum, 2022.13.7

Made in the area around Kurume on the island of Kyushu, this futon cover likely was part of a wealthy bride's trousseau. Weavers in Kurume had been making *kasuri*-patterned textiles since the 18th century, but in the late 19th century they began to manufacture futon covers with large-scale pictorial images. Production of futon covers with continuous designs spread across four or five panels was a tour-de-force of planning and execution, requiring as many as thirty separate steps. Futon covers like this example were usually woven as one long bolt of cloth that was cut and sewn together. After determining the pattern, weavers typically used an *e-dai* ("picture stand") to create guide threads for tying the warp and weft yarn bundles. Tight control of the resisting, dyeing, and weaving created bright white areas of double ikat along with more subtle background imagery carried only in the weft. Creating two shades of blue required some areas to be painstakingly bound or unbound for additional submersions in the dye vat. In order to help preserve and transmit this craft tradition, the Japanese government designated Kurume *kasuri* as a *mukei bunkazai* ("important intangible cultural property") in 1957.

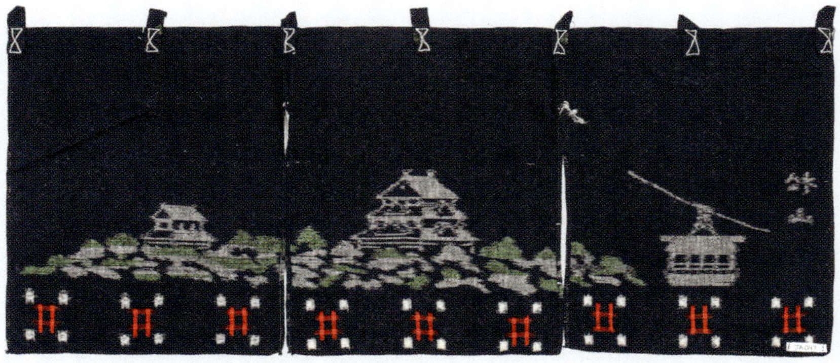

JP20 Door hanging, *noren*
Kurume, Kyushu, Japan, late 20th century. Cotton, double ikat, *e-gasuri*. 15 in x 40 in

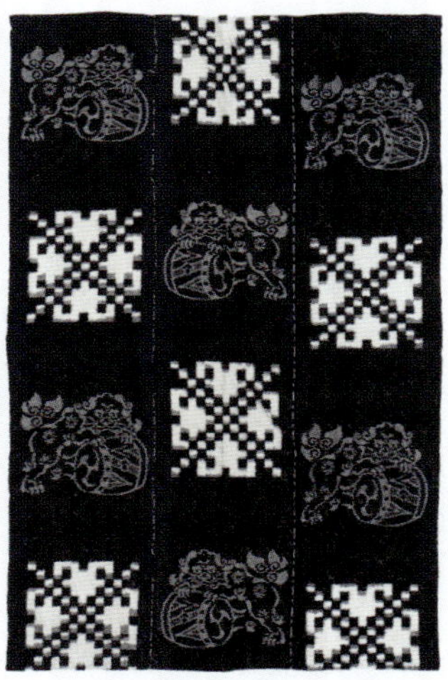

JP21 Futon cover
Kurume, Kyushu, Japan, 20th century. Cotton, double ikat, *e-gasuri*. 50 in x 39 in

JP22 Futon cover panel
Kurume, Kyushu, Japan, late 19th century. Cotton, double ikat, *e-gasuri*. 15 in x 13 in

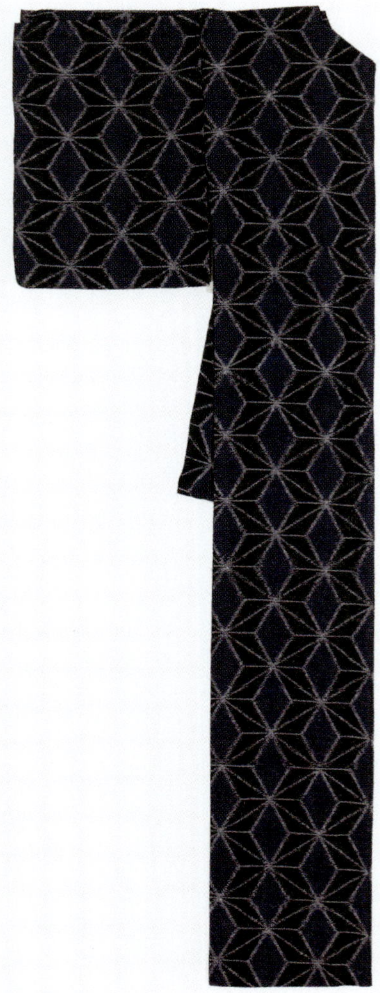

JP23 Kimono
Kurume, Kyushu, Japan, 20th century. Cotton, double ikat. 58 in x 48 in

JP24 Futon cover
Kurume, Kyushu, Japan, late 19th century. Cotton, double ikat, *e-gasuri*. 90 in x 65 in

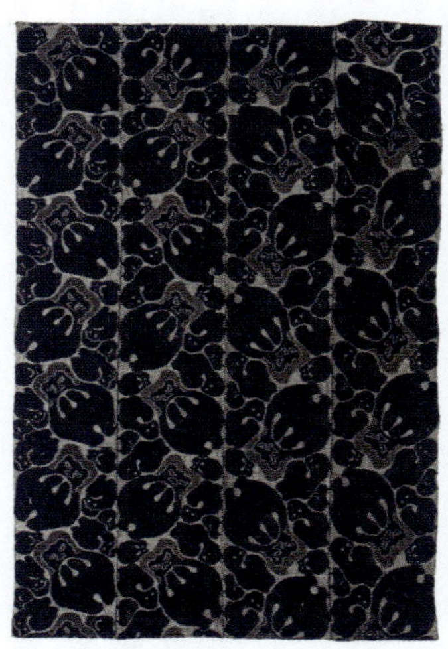

JP25 Futon cover
Kurume, Kyushu, Japan, 19th century. Cotton, weft ikat. 68 in x 48 in

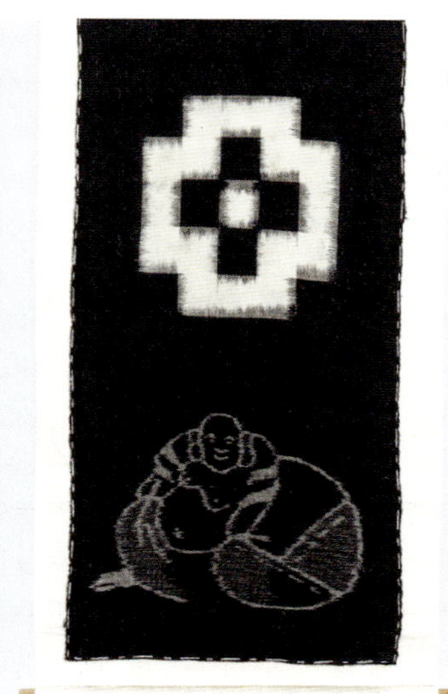

JP26 Futon cover panel
Kurume, Kyushu, Japan, late 19th century. Cotton, double ikat. 36 in x 13 in

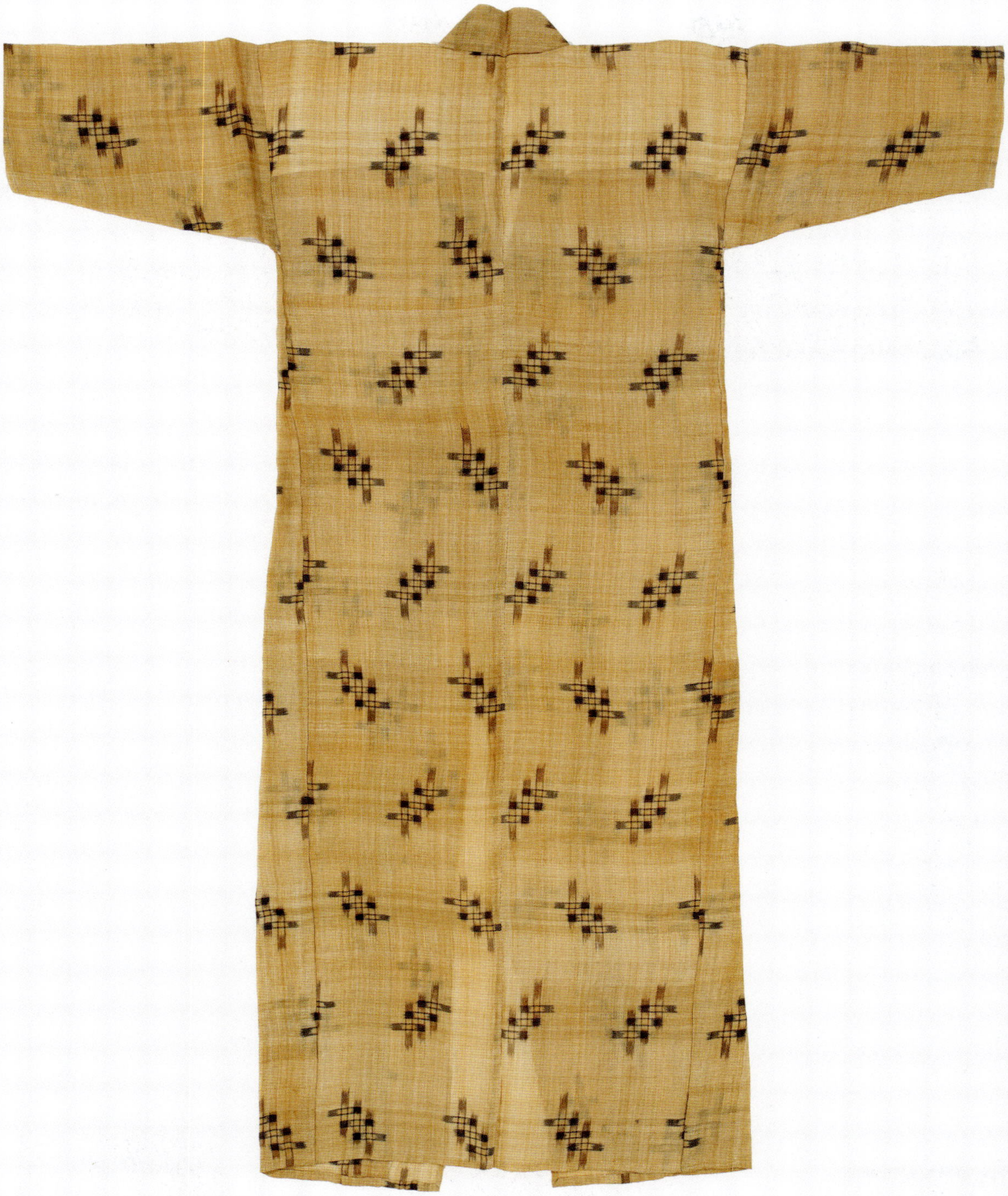

JP27 Summer robe, Miyako or Yaeyama, Ryukyu Islands, Japan, 19th century. *Basho-fu* (banana fiber), plain weave with warp, weft, and double ikat. 59 in x 50 in

Weavers in the Ryukyu Kingdom, an island chain largely corresponding to present-day Okinawa prefecture, developed remarkable skill in creating warp, weft, and double ikats. Ikat patterning traditionally indicated wealth and status, and aristocrats in the royal capital of Shuri reserved the right to wear large-scale designs like those on this robe. Garments with dark motifs on a light ground were particularly prestigious since all of the lighter area had to be laboriously hand tied to protect it from the dye. In creating robes for the ruling class, weavers often followed patterns painted by court artists. Most *kasuri* designs were abstracted representations of natural phenomena or everyday objects. On this garment, the brown-dyed warps and the black-dyed wefts combine to form a pattern called *kumi banjo*, or "joined carpenter's squares." Ryukyuan weavers typically worked with locally grown bast fibers. This garment is made from the inner fibers of *basho*, a type of wild banana introduced from southern China in the 13th or 14th century. By at least the middle of the 16th century, local artisans had perfected the many painstaking steps required to process and weave *basho*, which became closely associated with Ryukyuan textile arts and cultural identity.

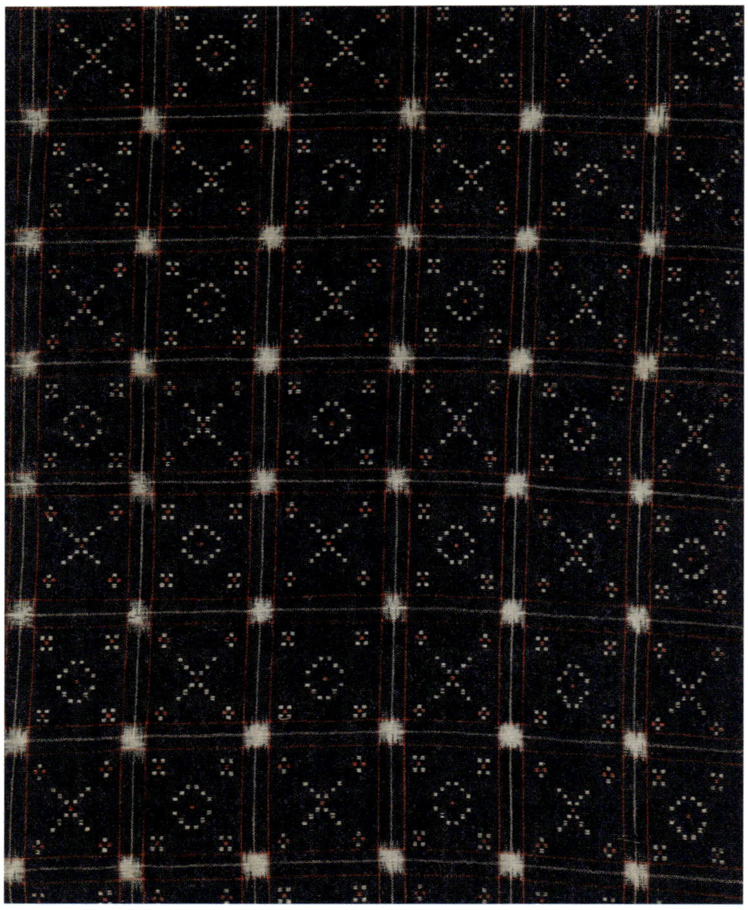

JP28 Kimono cloth (*hana-ui*) fragment
Yomitan, Okinawa, Ryukyu Islands, Japan, 19th century. Cotton, double ikat and weft brocade. 54 in x 13 in. The Textile Museum, 2021.19.18

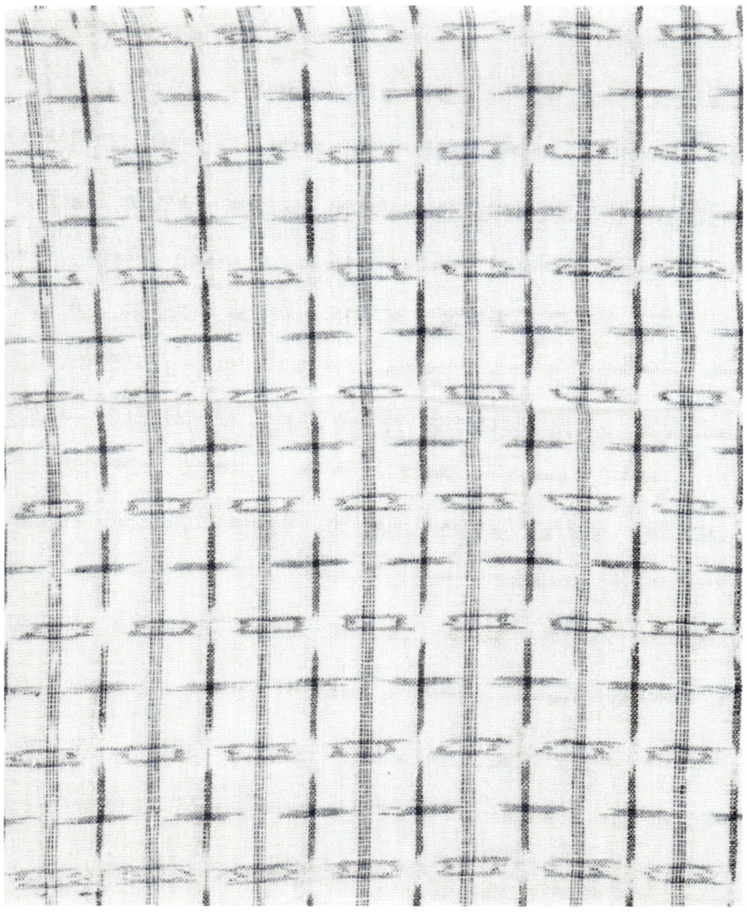

JP29 Kimono cloth fragment
Yomitan, Okinawa, Ryukyu Islands, Japan, 19th century. Cotton, double ikat. 14.5 in x 6.5 in. The Textile Museum, 2021.19.12

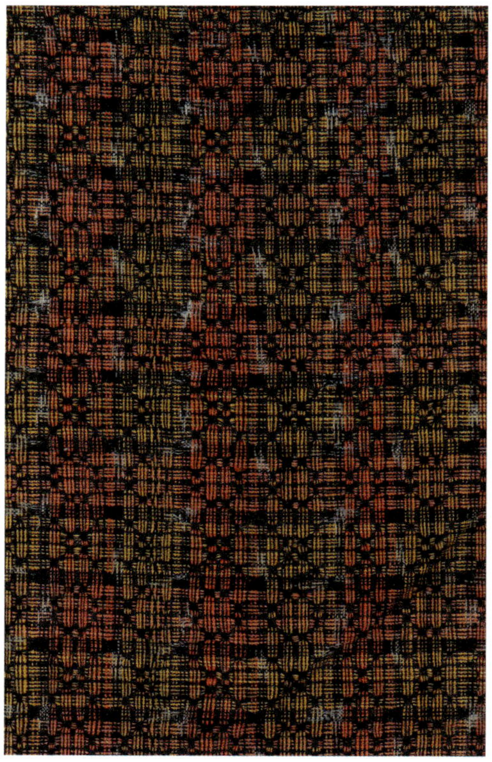

JP30 Cloth fragment
Shuri, Okinawa, Ryukyu Islands, Japan, early 19th century. Cotton, double ikat and possibly brocade. 11 in x 13 in. The Textile Museum, 2021.19.15

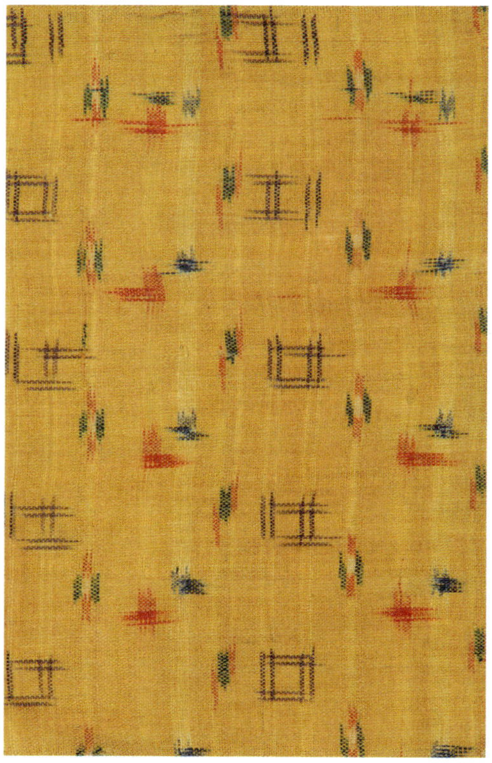

JP31 Royal kimono fragment
Shuri, Okinawa, Ryukyu Islands, Japan, early 19th century. Silk, double ikat. 7 in x 5 in. The Textile Museum, 2021.19.17

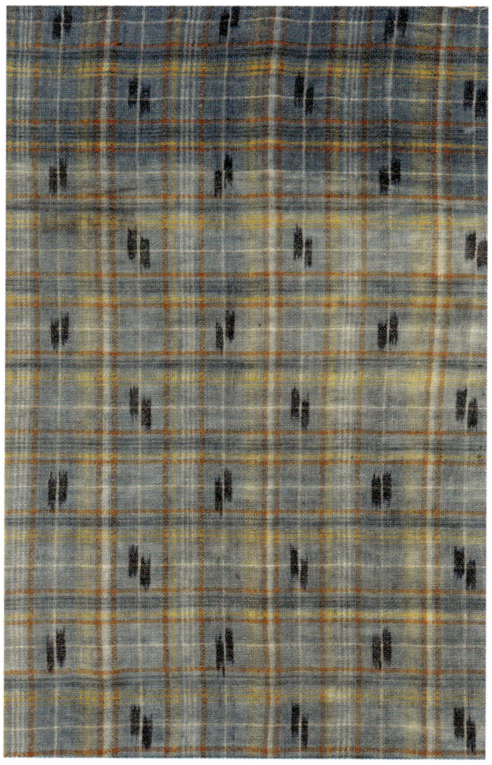

JP32 Royal kimono fragment
Shuri, Okinawa, Ryukyu Islands, Japan, 19th century. Silk, double ikat. 11.5 in x 10.5 in. The Textile Museum, 2021.19.13

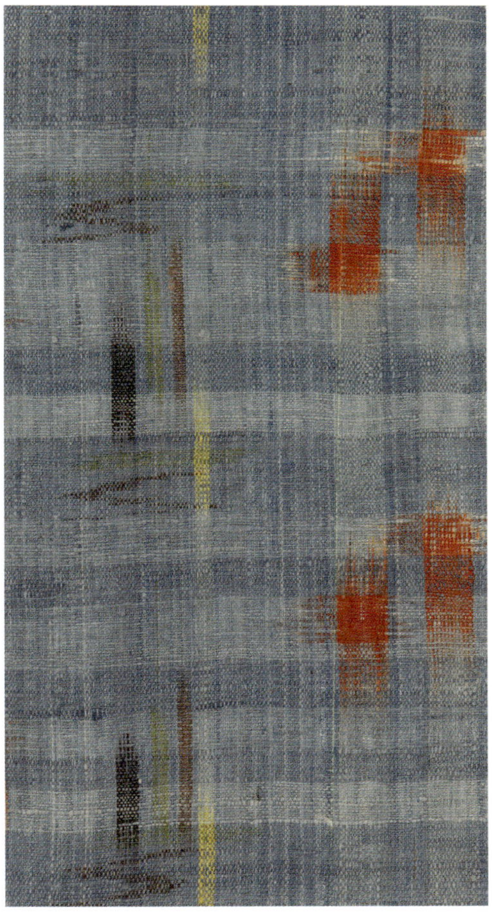

JP33 Royal kimono fragment
Shuri, Okinawa, Ryukyu Islands, Japan, early 19th century. Silk, double ikat. 11 in x 4.5 in. The Textile Museum, 2021.19.14

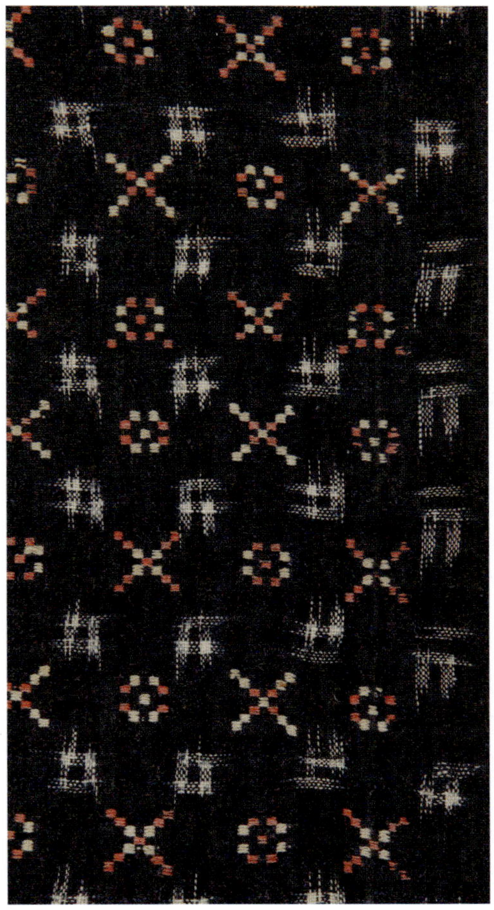

JP34 Cloth fragment
Yomitan, Okinawa, Ryukyu Islands, Japan, 19th century. Cotton, double ikat, weft brocade. 15 in x 13 in

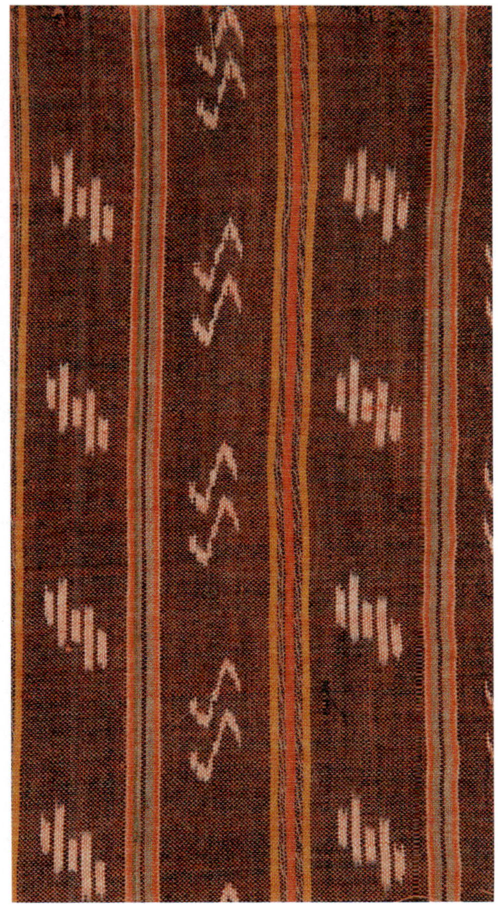

JP35 Cloth fragment
Shuri, Okinawa, Ryukyu Islands, Japan, 19th century. Silk, warp ikat. 8 in x 6 in

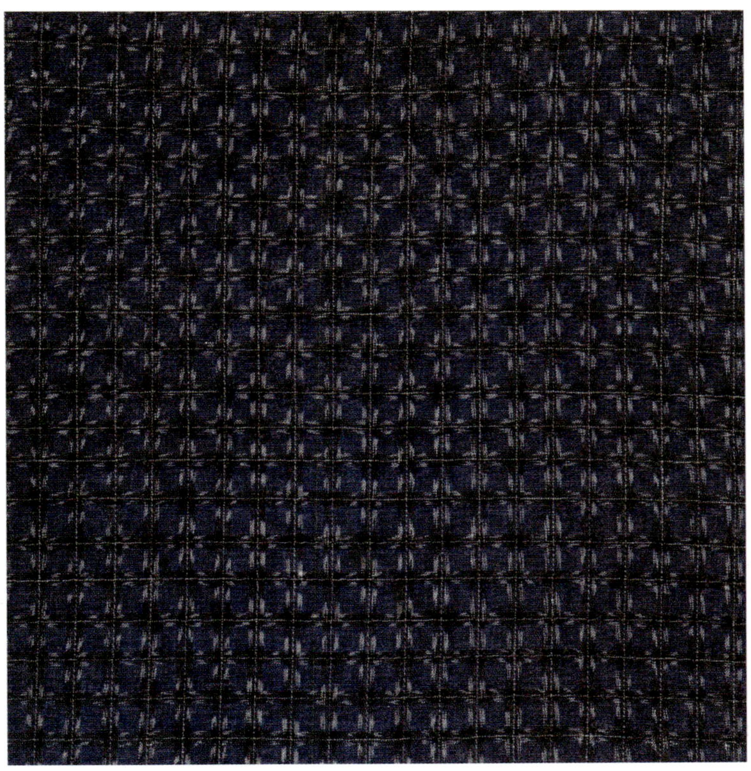

JP36 Cloth fragment
Yomitan, Okinawa, Ryukyu Islands, Japan, 19th century. Cotton, double ikat. 22.5 in x 13 in. The Textile Museum, 2021.19.16

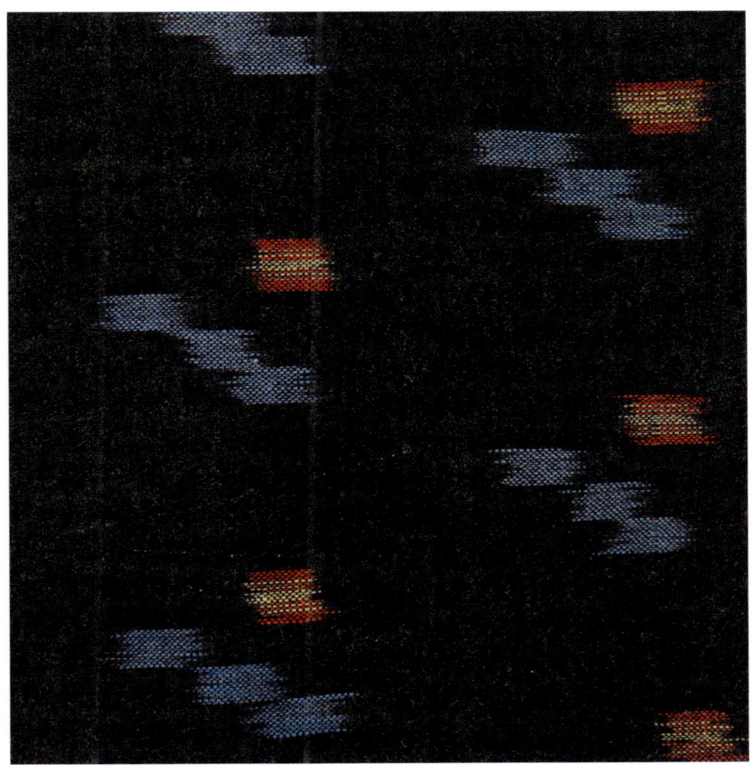

JP37 Cloth fragment
Okinawa, Ryukyu Islands, Japan, late 19th century. Cotton, warp ikat. 6 in < 8 in

CATALOG

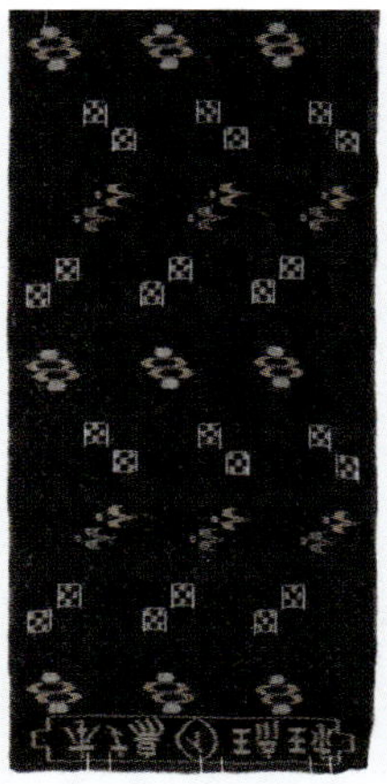

JP38 Loom length of cloth
Okinawa, Ryukyu Islands, Japan, 20th century. Cotton, double ikat. 108 in x 13 in

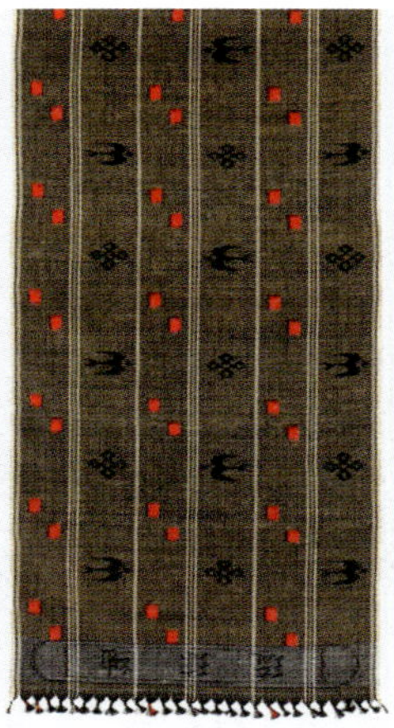

JP39 Loom length of cloth
Okinawa, Ryukyu Islands, Japan, early 20th century. Cotton, double ikat. 105 in x 13 in

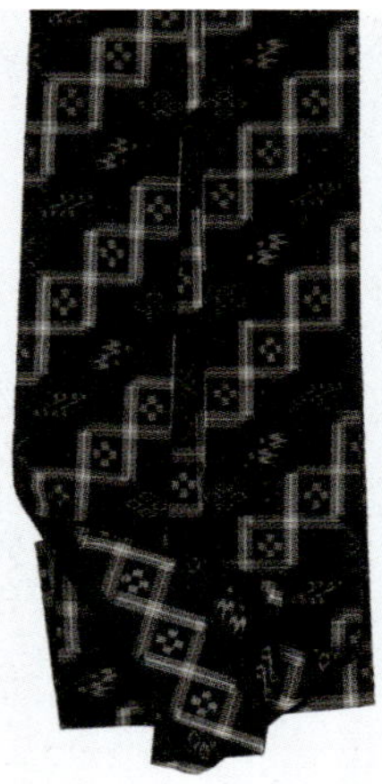

JP40 Length of cloth
Okinawa, Ryukyu Islands, Japan, 20th century. Cotton, double ikat. 84 in x 13 in

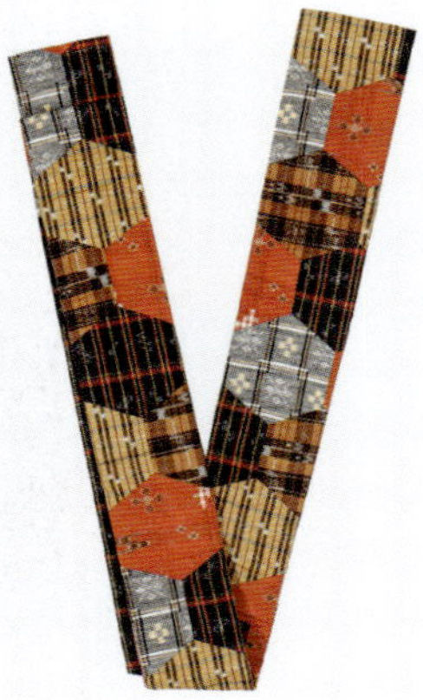

JP41 *Obi*
Okinawa, Ryukyu Islands, Japan, early 20th century. Silk and cotton, warp and double ikat, patchwork. 72 in x 14 in

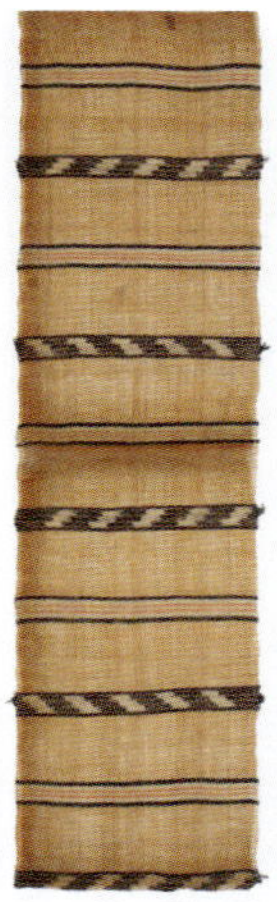

JP42 *Tisaji*
Okinawa, Ryukyu Islands, Japan, 19th century. *Basho-fu* warp and weft: inserted cotton weft ikat. 48 in x 14 in

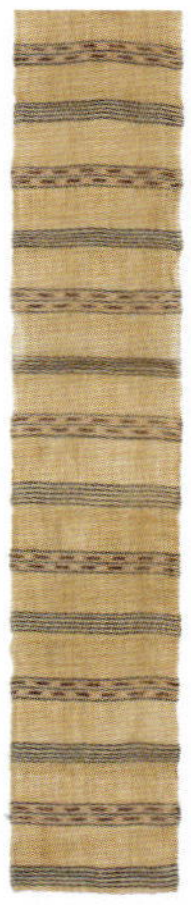

JP43 *Tisaji*
Okinawa, Ryukyu Islands, Japan, 19th century. *Basho-fu* warp and weft: inserted cotton weft ikat. 48 in x 14 in. The Textile Museum, 2021.19.19

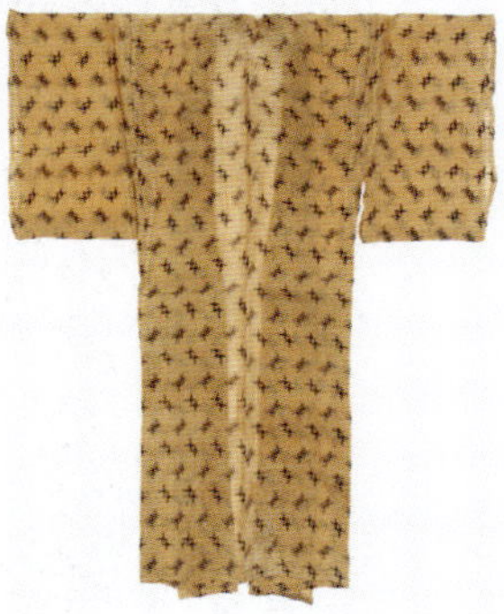

JP44 Kimono
Okinawa, Ryukyu Islands, Japan, 19th century. *Basho-fu*, double ikat. 50 in x 48 in. The Textile Museum, 2021.19.10

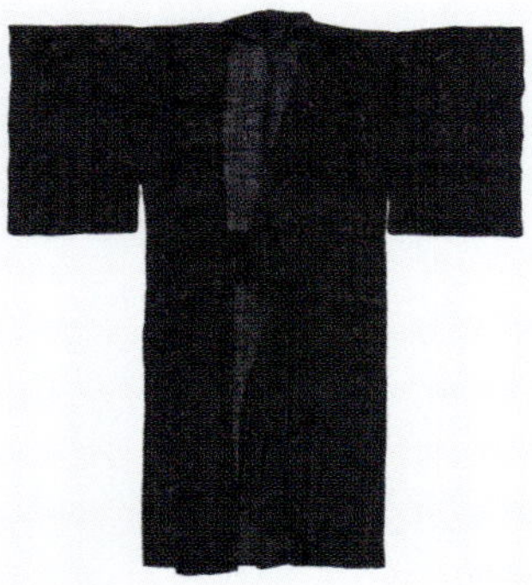

JP45 Kimono
Okinawa, Ryukyu Islands, Japan, 20th century. Ramie, double ikat. 55 in x 48 in. The Textile Museum, 2021.19.9

JP46 Kimono
Okinawa, Ryukyu Islands, Japan, 20th century. Ramie, double ikat. 56 in x 48 in

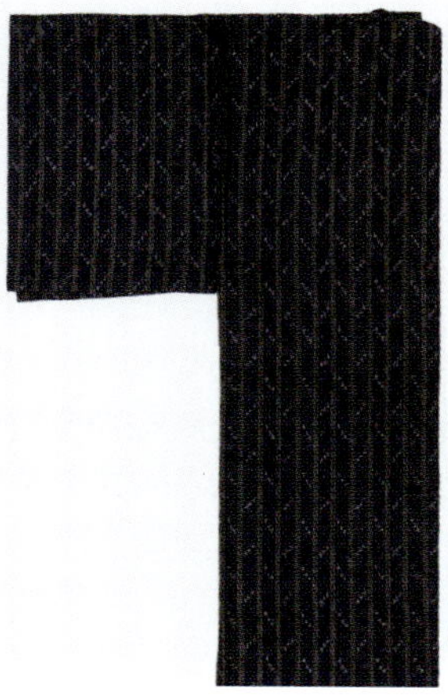

JP47 Kimono
Okinawa, Ryukyu Islands, Japan, 20th century. Handspun cotton, warp ikat. 52 in x 42 in. The Textile Museum, 2021.19.11

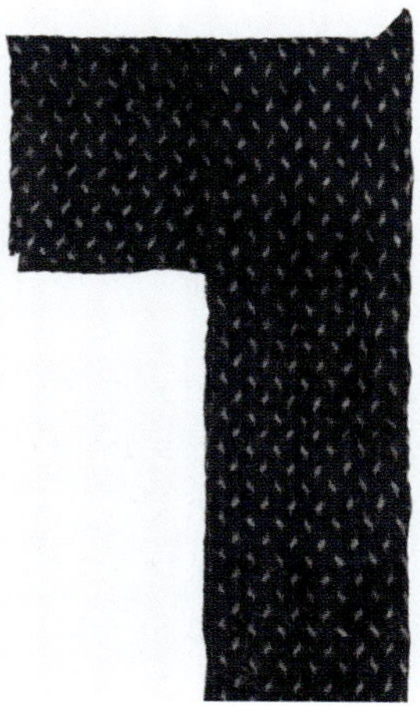

JP48 Kimono
Okinawa, Ryukyu Islands, Japan, possibly late 19th century. Ramie, double ikat. 54 in x 44 in

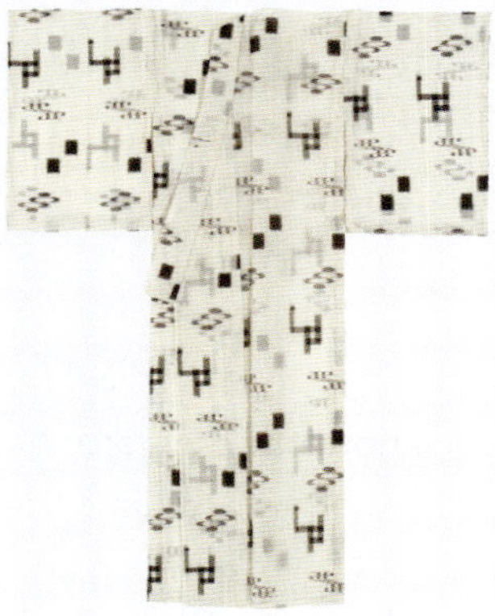

JP49 Kimono
Okinawa, Ryukyu Islands, Japan, 20th century. Silk, double ikat. 56 in x 50 in

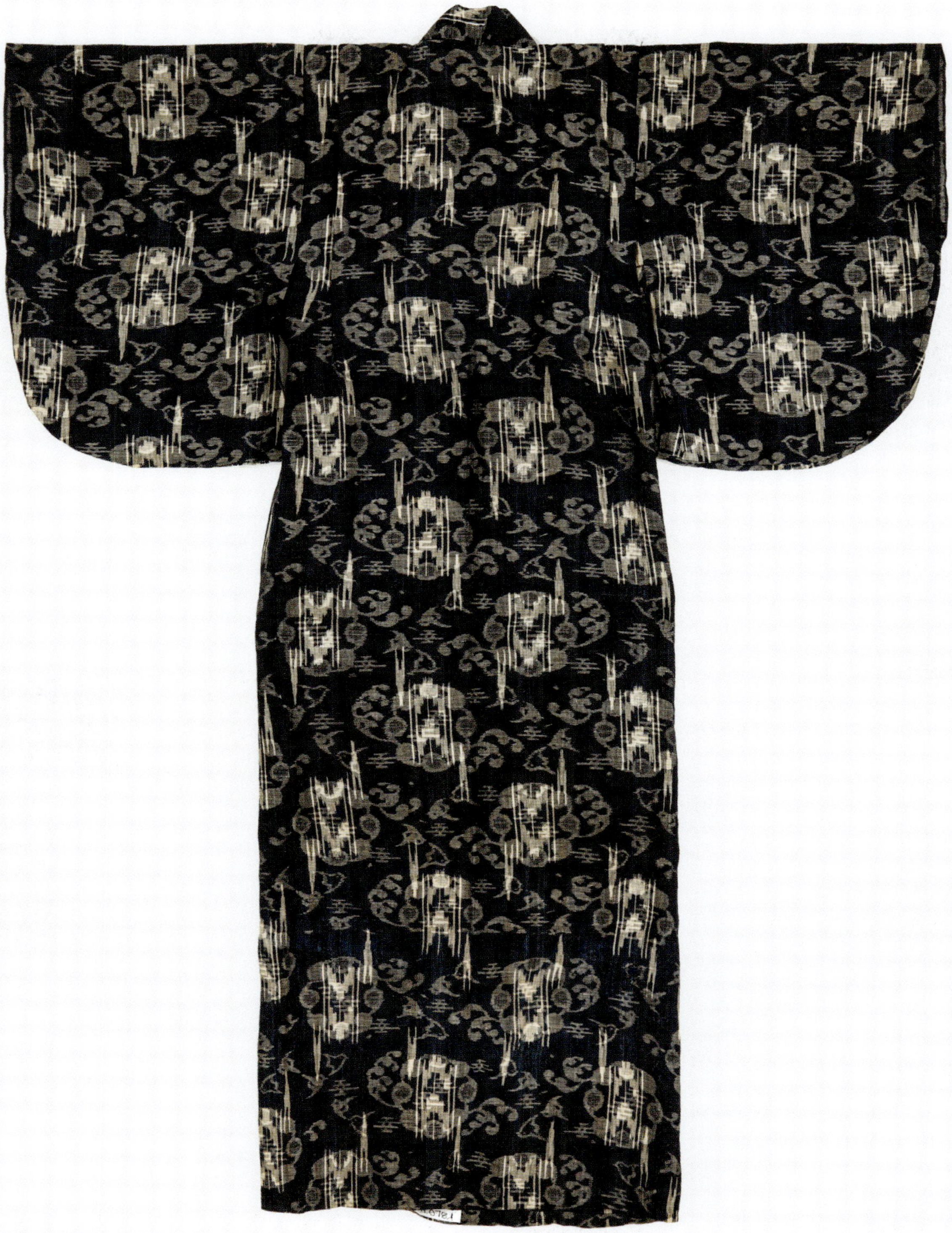

JP50 Child's kimono, Shiga prefecture, Japan, 19th century. Ramie; plain weave with warp, weft, and compound ikat. 20 in x 16 in

Likely worn by the child of a wealthy commoner or merchant family, this garment is made from a type of fine, plain-weave ramie fabric known as *omi-jofu*. Abundant water resources around the region of Omi, in present-day Shiga prefecture, render the area ideal for the cultivation and processing of ramie. Although farmers in Omi had grown ramie since medieval times, production expanded significantly during the 18th century under the close supervision of the local shogunate. Spurred by burgeoning demand in nearby urban centers such as Kyoto and Osaka, weavers began to create *omi-jofu* with *kasuri* patterning in the late 18th century. In order to weave *e-gasuri* ("picture ikat"), local weavers adopted a number of technical innovations. For this garment, the chevron patterns in the background likely were created by bundle-tying and dyeing the warp yarns, while the plovers and cloud patterns in the weft probably were achieved using a *koba jogi*, a device used for marking a guide thread or yarn bundles for tying. As different regions developed with their own distinctive designs, Omi became known for the combination of abstract and pictorial *kasuri*, a style well illustrated by this remarkable example.

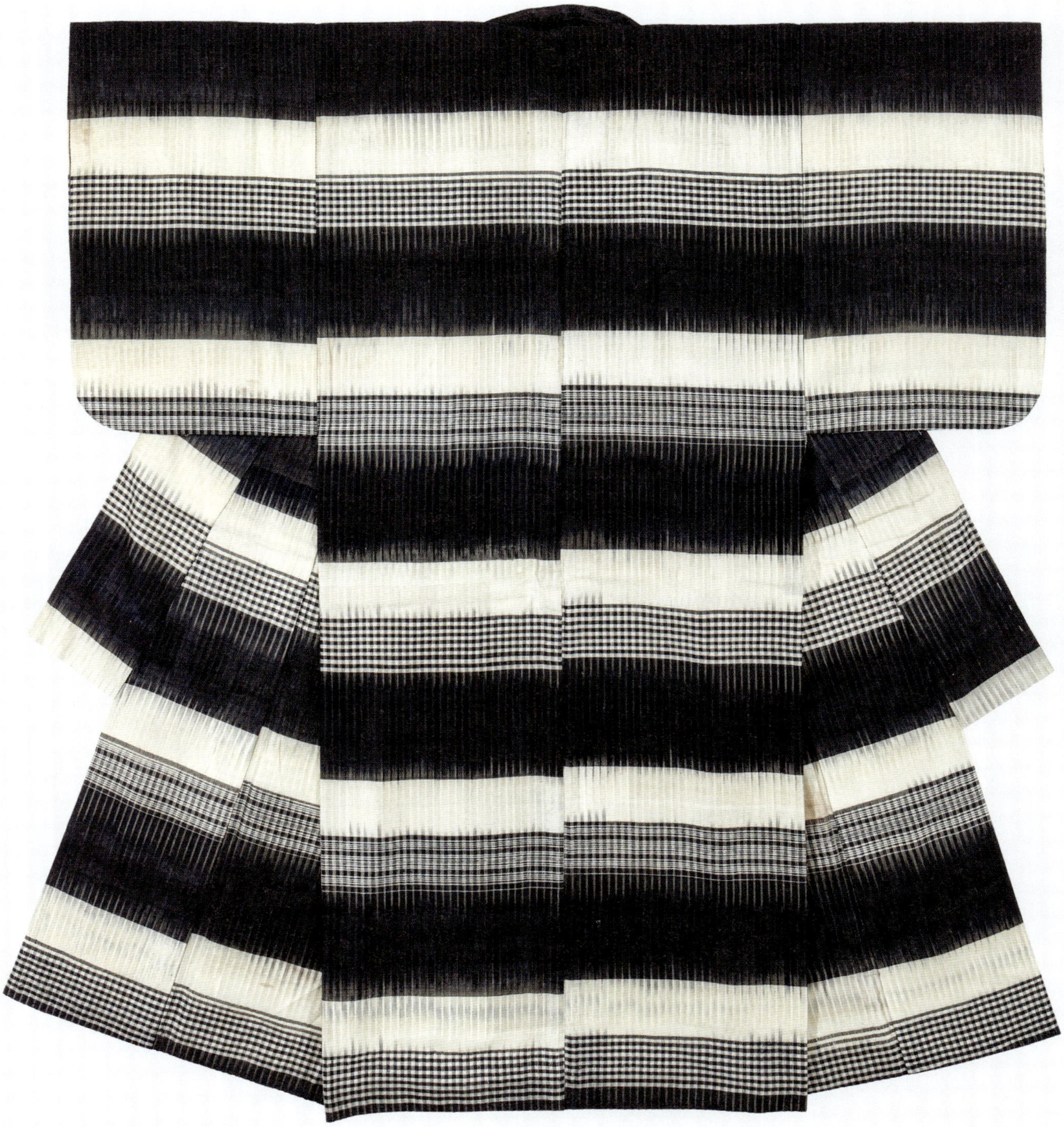

JP51 Noh costume, *noshime*, Kyoto, Japan, 18th century. Silk; plain weave with warp-ikat patterning. 60 in x 55 in. The Textile Museum, 2021.13.3

On this *noshime*, an inner robe worn for a male role in Noh theater, resist-dyed warps create dramatic shifts in the ground color. Weavers in Kyoto, where this example likely was made, sometimes exaggerate the diffused, feathered effect of *kasuri* by either hand-tying the yarn bundles to produce subtle pattern changes or by laboriously adjusting the warps when attaching them to the loom. The intentionally blurred contours of these designs recall the aesthetic of *bokashi* (shading), the hazy color transitions prized in printmaking and other arts. Warp-ikat robes seem to have been fashionable among men of the samurai class during the Muromachi and Momoyama periods. Samurai sometimes presented Noh players with their own garments as a token of appreciation, and their preferred styles were incorporated into and preserved in Noh and Kyogen costume. *Noshime* typically are only partly visible beneath a jacket and *hakama* (trousers), but on certain occasions the wearer may remove the jacket to showcase the finely patterned *noshime* underneath. In Noh and Kyogen theater, a striped and checked *noshime* like this example is worn by a low-ranking samurai character.

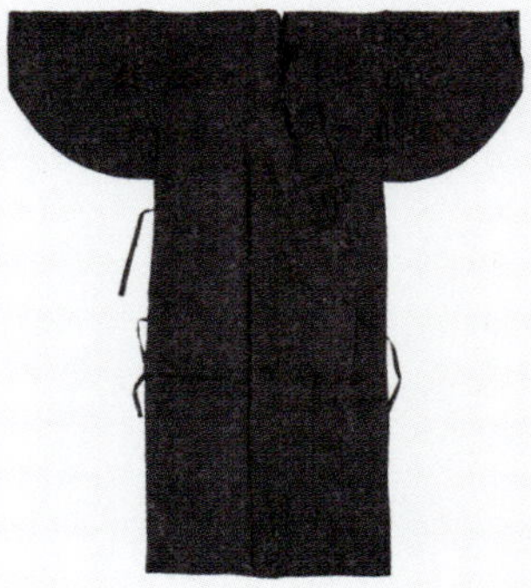

JP52 Kimono
Okinawa, Ryukyu Islands, Japan, 20th century. Ramie, double ikat. 52 in x 41 in

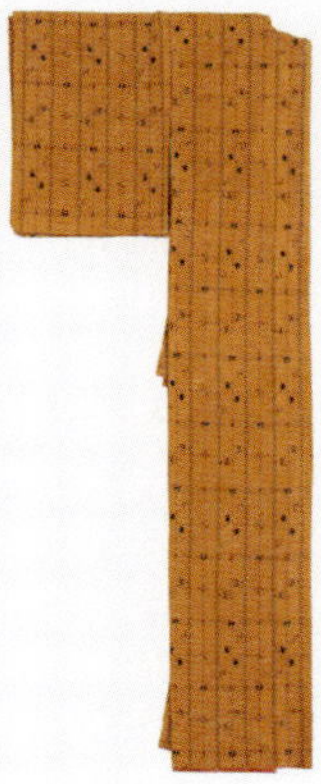

JP53 Woman's kimono
Possiby Okinawa, Ryukyu Islands, Japan, 20th century. Silk, double ikat. 58 in x 48 in

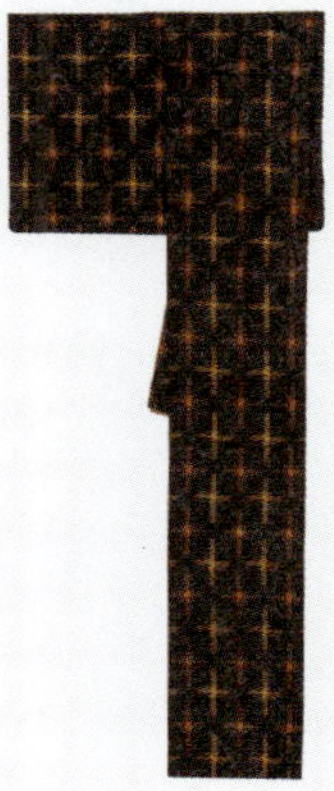

JP54 Kimono
Possibly Okinawa, Ryukyu Islands, Japan, 20th century. Cotton, double ikat. 60 in x 50 in

JP55 Kimono
Possibly Okinawa, Ryukyu Islands, Japan, 20th century. Handspun cotton, double ikat. 58 in x 50 in

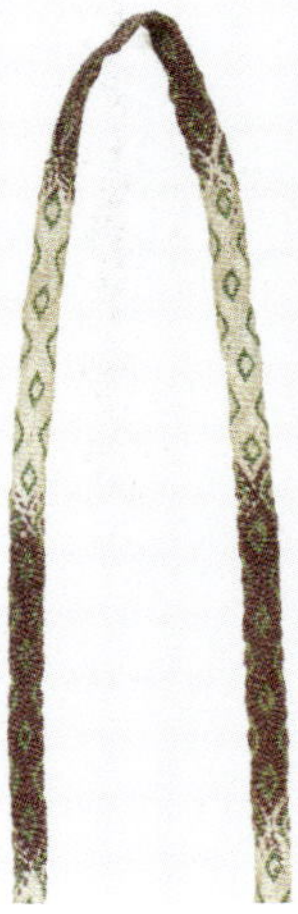

JP56 Man's sword tie, *karakumi hirao*
Japan, early 19th century. Silk, *kumihimo*, warp ikat. 0.5 in x 36 in. The Textile Museum, 2022.13.1

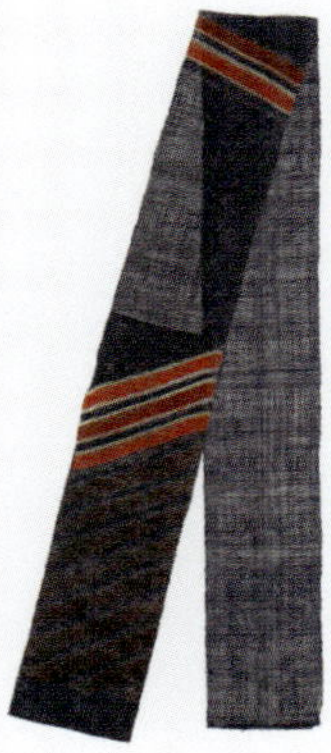

JP57 *Obi*
Japan, probably 20th century. Bast fiber, probably hemp, warp ikat. 144 in x 12 in

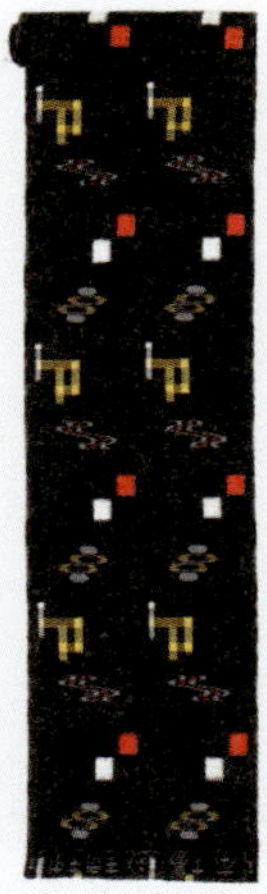

JP58 Loom length for kimono
Japan, 20th century. Cotton, double ikat. 104 in x 13 in

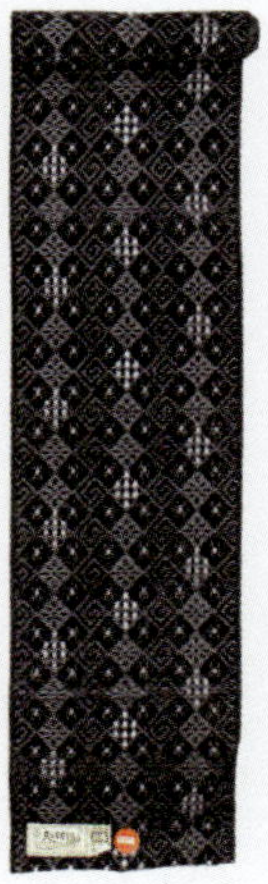

JP59 Loom length for kimono
Okinawa, Ryukyu Islands, Japan, 20th century. Cotton, double ikat. 104 in x 13 in

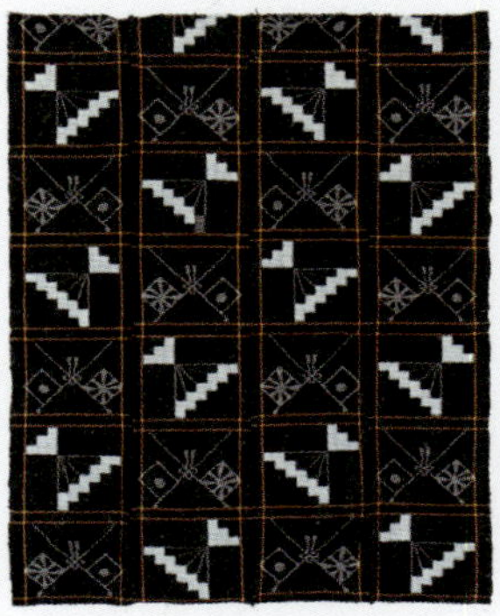

JP60 Futon cover
Japan, early 20th century. Cotton, double ikat, *e-gasuri*. 66 in x 52 in

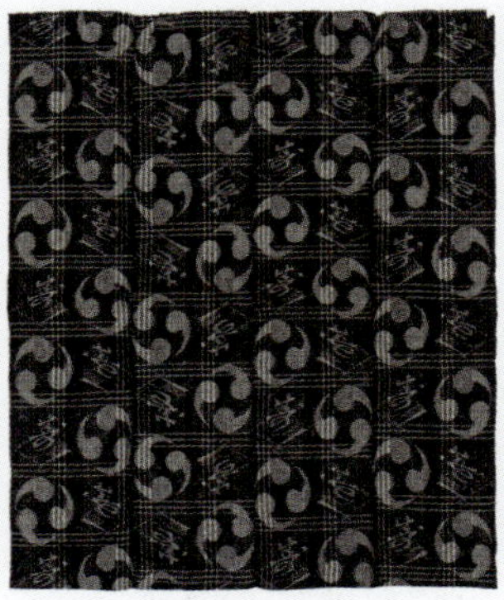

JP61 Futon cover
Japan, early 20th century. Cotton, double ikat, *e-gasuri*. 62 in x 52 in

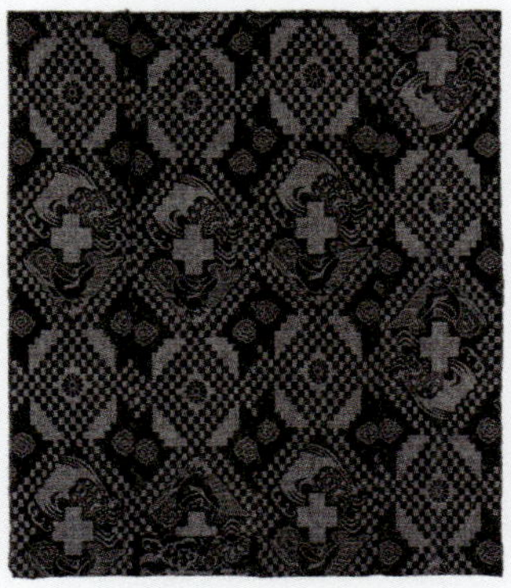

JP62 Futon cover
Japan, early 20th century. Cotton, double ikat, *e-gasuri*. 64 in x 52 in

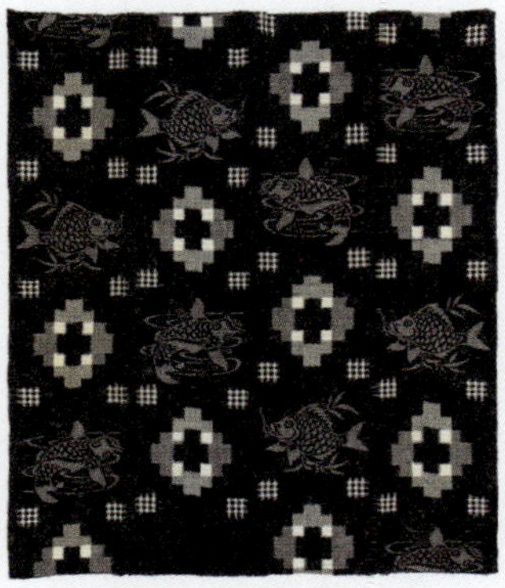

JP63 Futon cover
Japan, early 20th century. Cotton, double ikat, *e-gasuri*. 68 in x 52 in

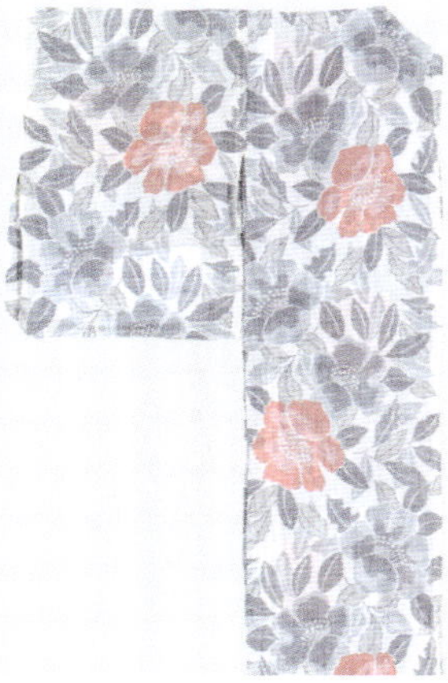

JP64 Kimono
Japan, mid-20th century. Cotton, weft ikat, *e-gasuri*. 62 in x 50 in

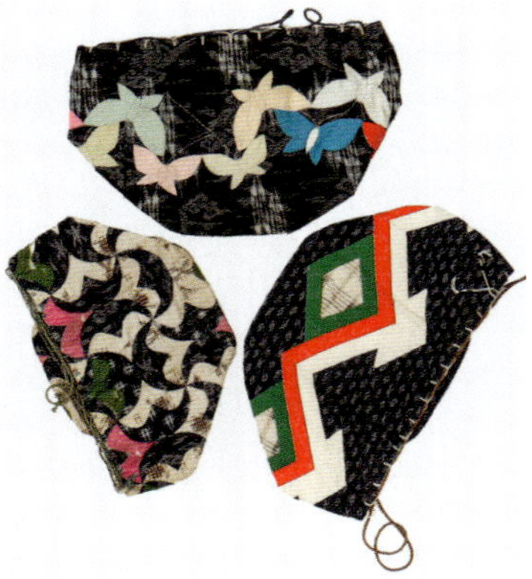

JP65 Ceremonial rice bags, *komebukuro*
Japan, early 20th century. Silk and ramie, double ikat, patchwork. 6 in x 5 in

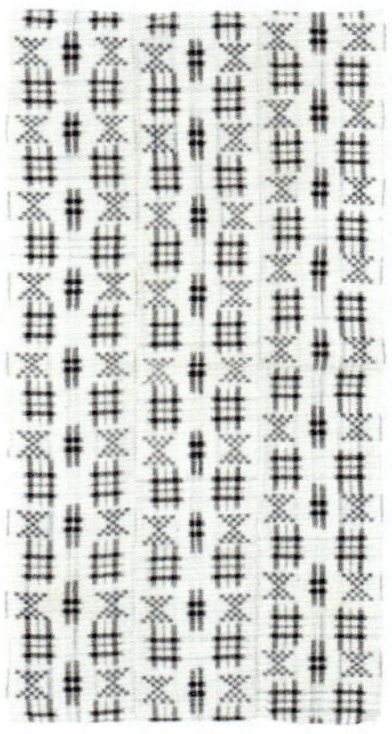

JP66 Futon cover
Japan, 19th century. Warp: cotton, weft: bast fiber, double ikat. 74 in x 40 in

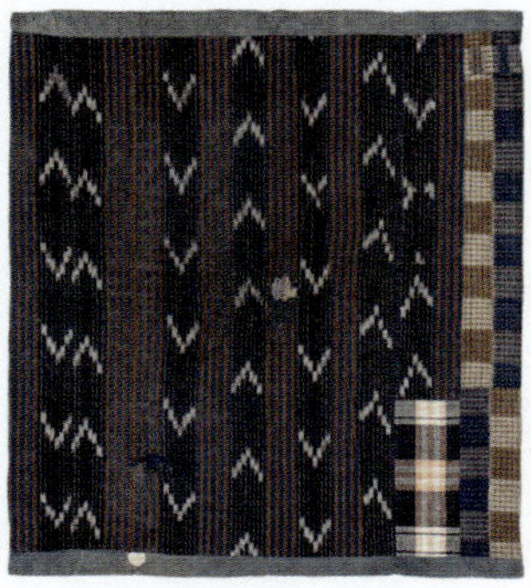

JP67 *Kotatsu* cover
Japan, 20th century. Cotton, warp ikat. 50 in x 52 in

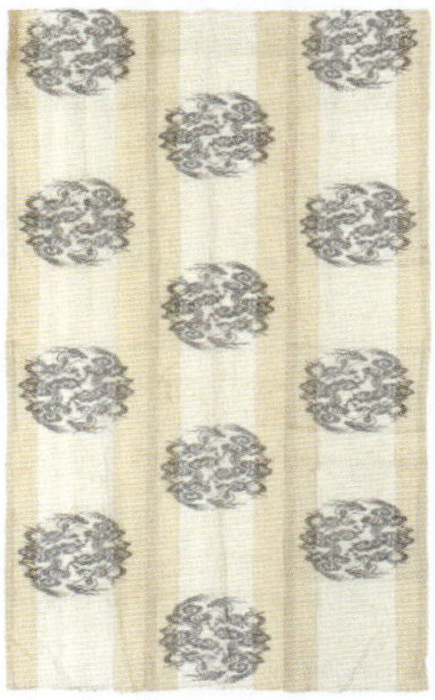

JP68 Child's futon cover
Omi, Honshu, Japan, 19th century. Ramie, weft-dyed ikat, *e-gasuri*. 58 in x 13 in. The Textile Museum, 2022.13.10

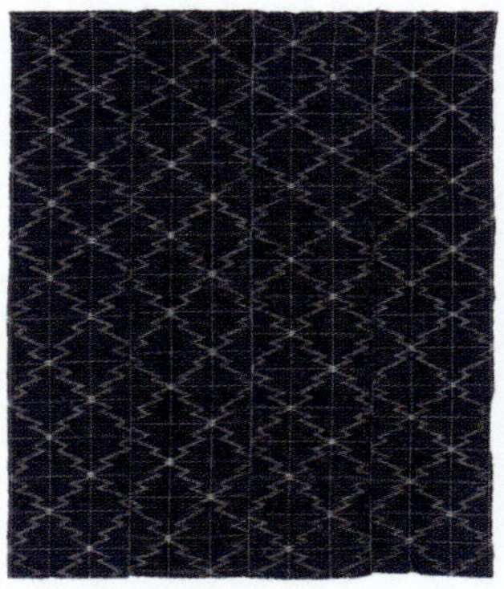

JP69 Futon cover
Japan, 19th century. Cotton, weft ikat, "pinebark" pattern (*matsukawa bishi*). 59 in x 52 in

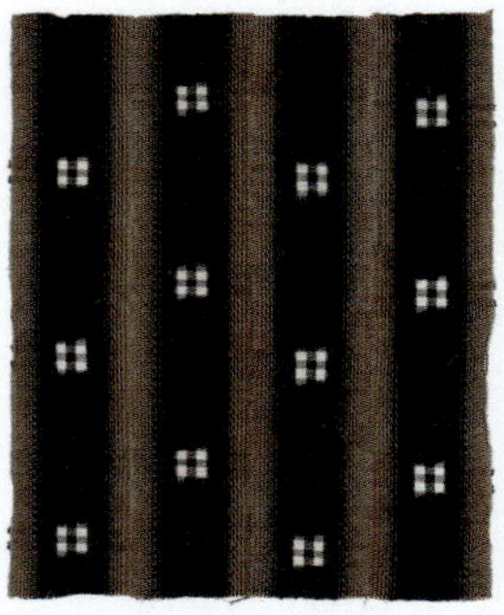

JP70 Futon cover
Japan, 19th or early 20th century. Cotton, double ikat. 52 in x 44 in

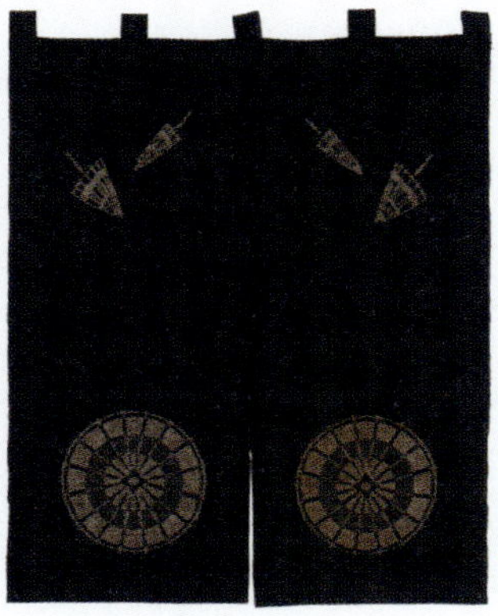

JP71 Door hanging, *noren*
Tottori, Honshu, Japan, 20th century. Cotton, weft ikat, *e-gasuri*. 30 in x 26 in

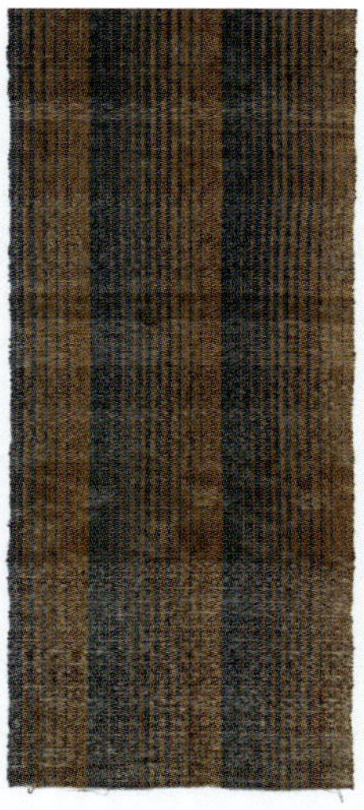

JP72 Futon cover panel
Japan, 19th century. Cotton, weft ikat. 44 in x 13 in

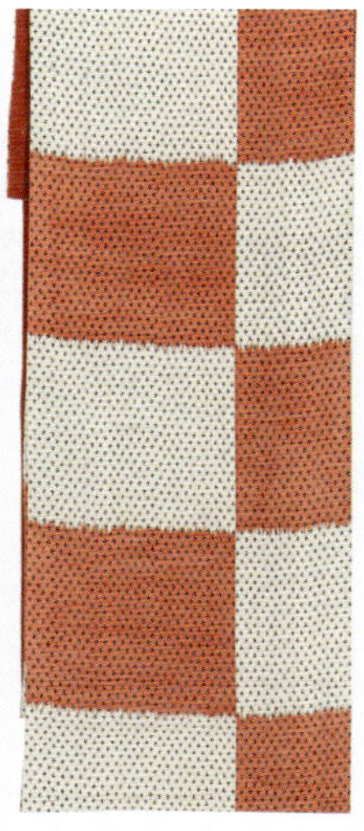

JP73 *Obi*
Japan, early 20th century. Silk, double ikat. 144 in x 12 in

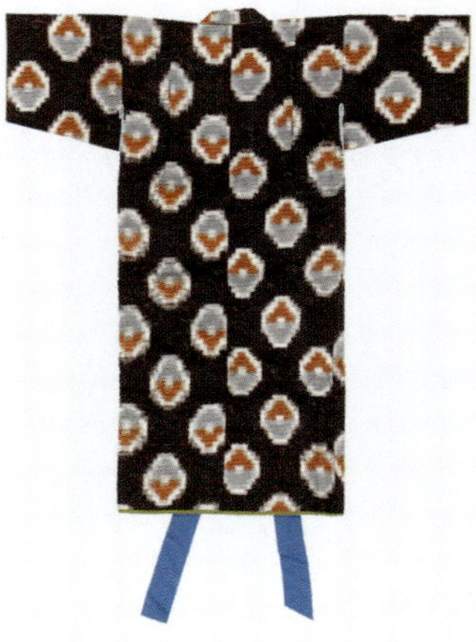

JP74 Child's kimono
Japan, 20th century. Cotton, double ikat. 32 in x 28 in. The Textile Museum, 2022.13.20

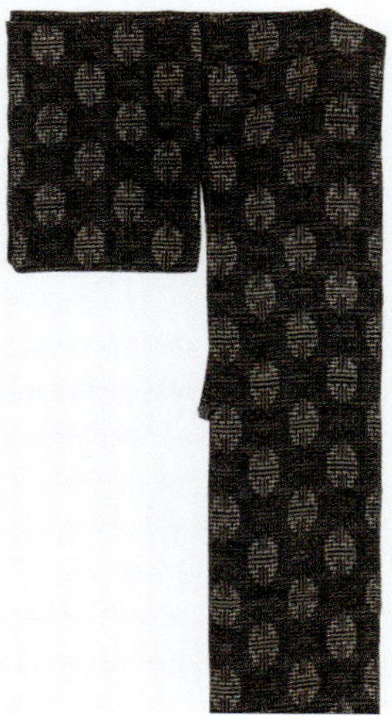

JP75 Woman's kimono
Japan, 20th century. *Asa* bast fiber, double ikat. 52 in x 46 in

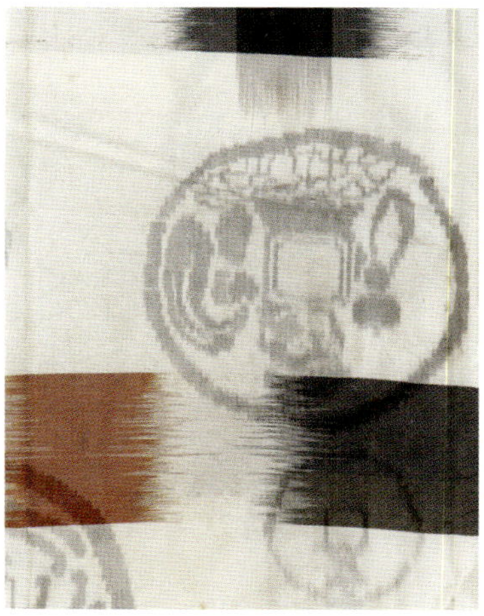

JP76 Textile fragment
Japan, 19th century. Silk, double ikat. 12 in x 9 in

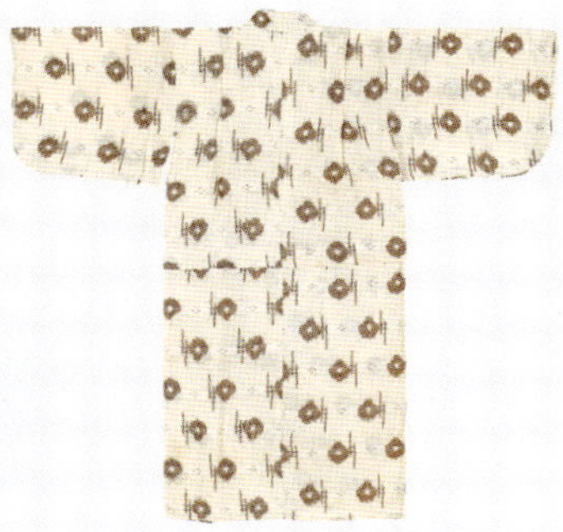

JP77 Child's kimono
Japan, possibly 19th century. Cotton, double ikat. 33 in x 28 in

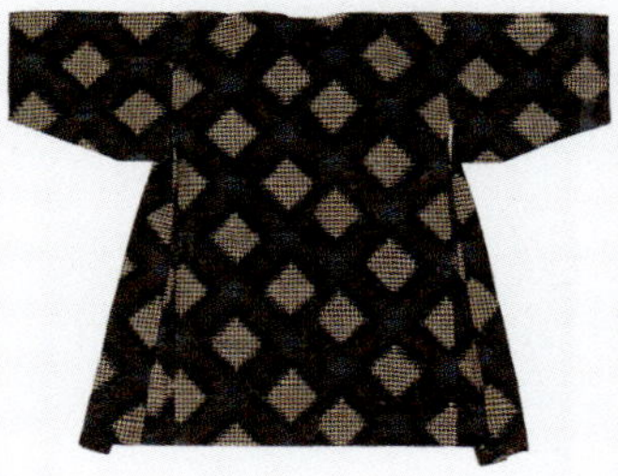

JP78 Child's kimono
Japan, 20th century. Silk, double ikat. 36 in x 30 in

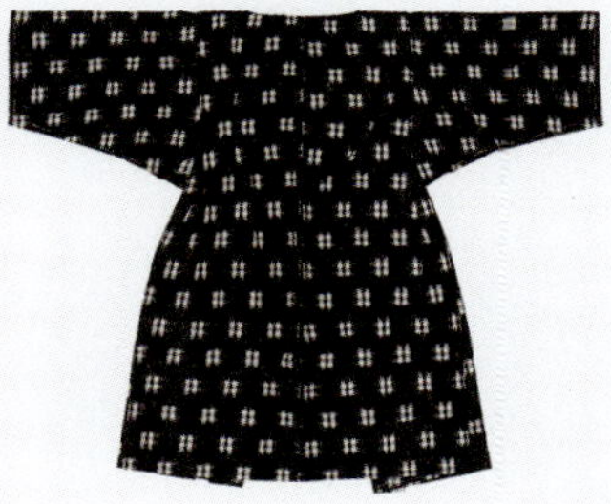

JP79 Child's kimono
Japan, 20th century. Cotton, double ikat. 30 in x 30 in

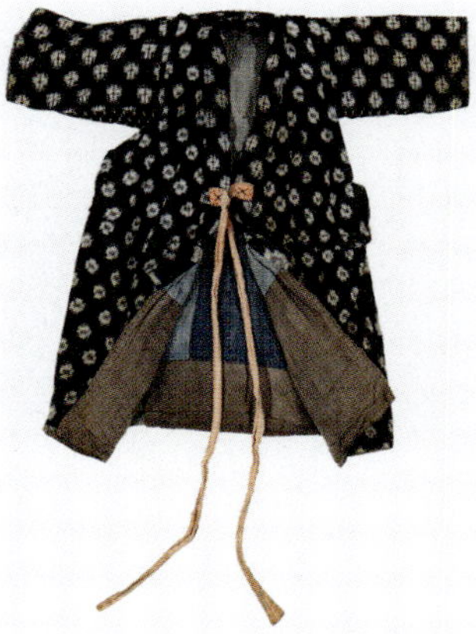

JP80 Child's kimono
Japan, 20th century. Cotton, double ikat, *bingo kasuri* technique, *boro* patchwork lining. 16 in x 15 in. The Textile Museum, 2022.13.23

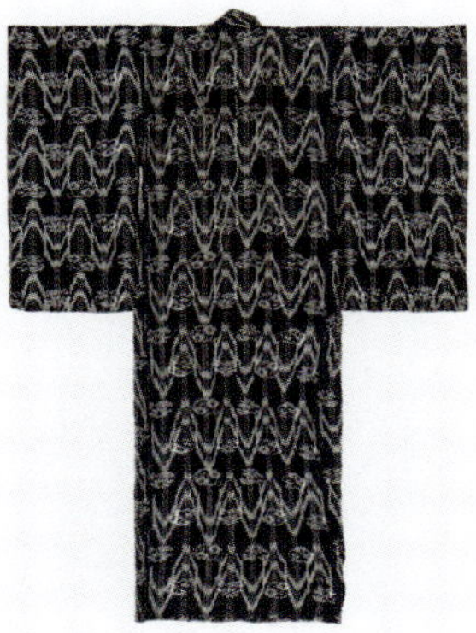

JP81 Child's kimono for the Miyamairi ceremony
Japan, late 19th century. Ramie, double ikat. 32 in x 22 in

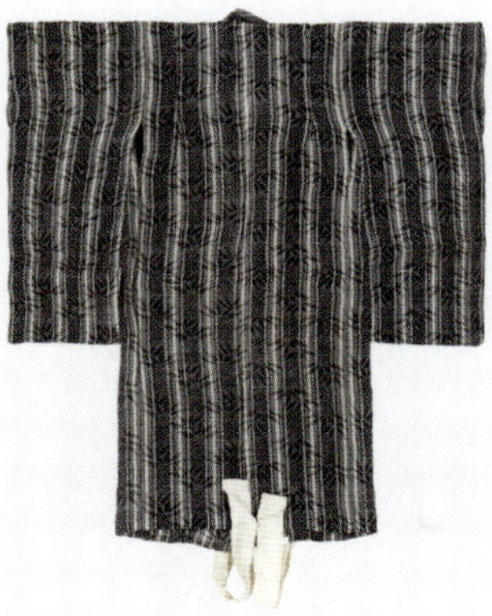

JP82 Child's kimono
Echigo, Honshu, Japan, early 20th century. Ramie, double ikat. 30 in x 28 in

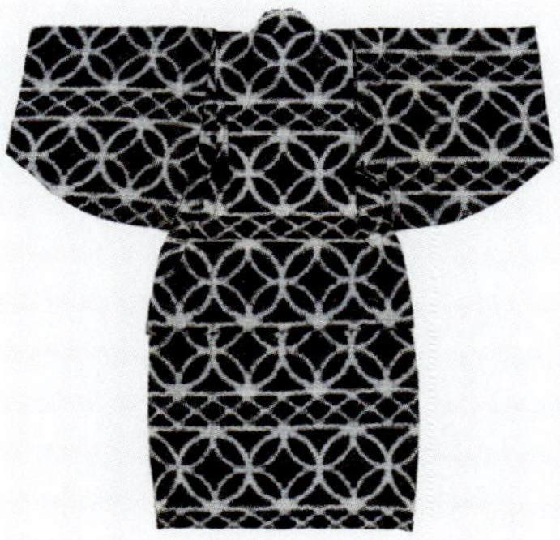

JP83 Child's kimono
Japan, 20th century. Cotton, double ikat. 32 in x 28 in

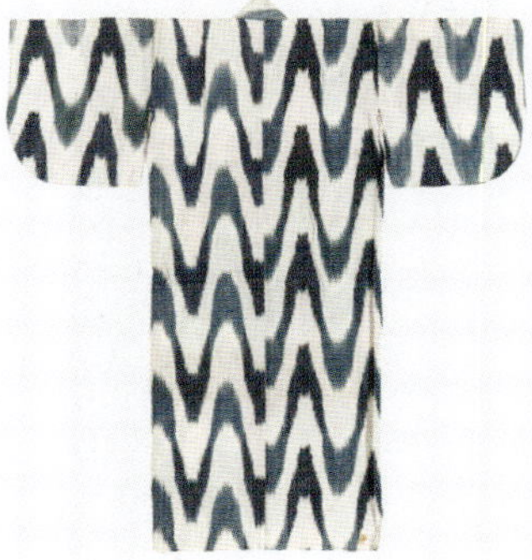

JP84 Child's kimono
Japan, 20th century. Cotton, warp ikat. 24 in x 20 in

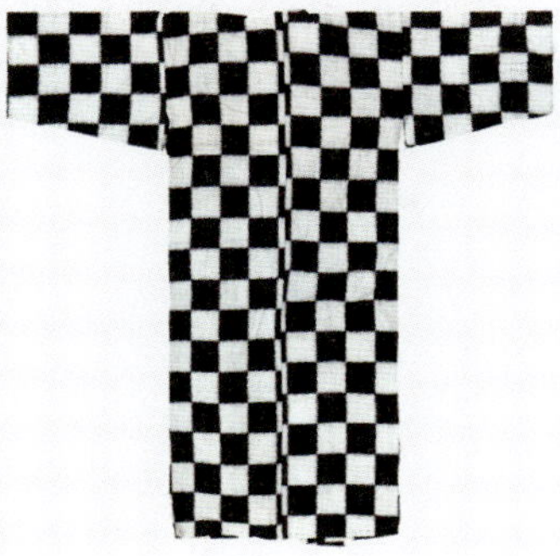

JP85 Child's kimono
Japan, 20th century. Cotton, double ikat. 32 in x 24 in

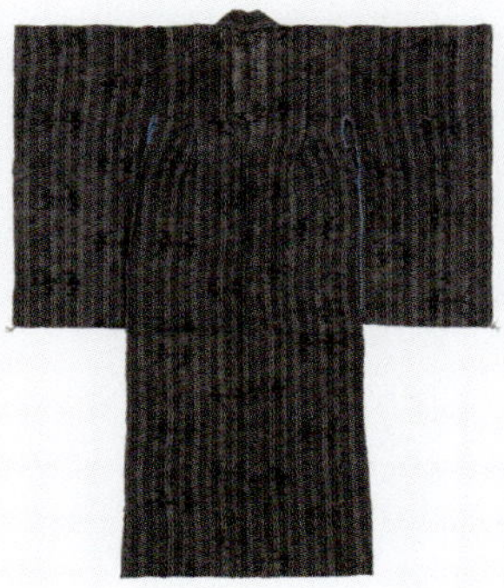

JP86 Child's kimono
Japan, late 19th century. Cotton, double ikat. 32 in x 24 in

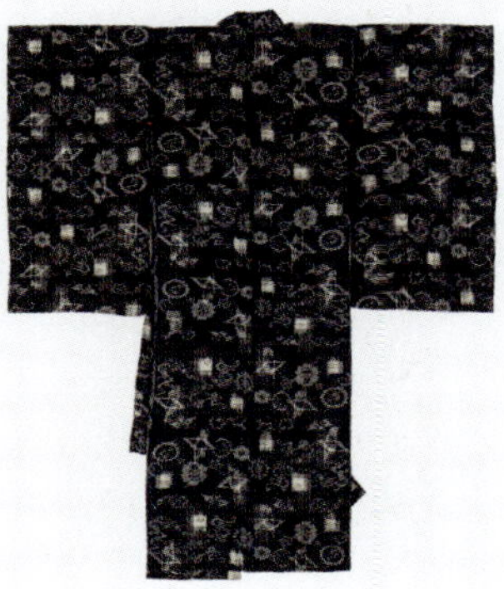

JP87 Child's kimono
Japan, late 19th century. Ramie, double ikat. 36 in x 30 in

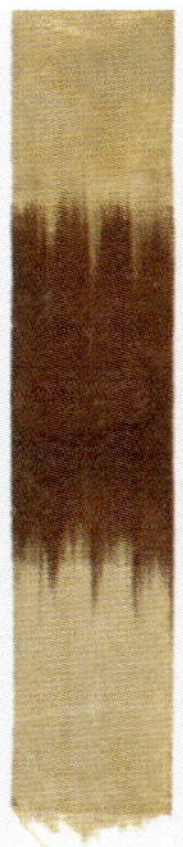

JP88 Aristocrat's ceremonial sash, *hirao*
Japan, Edo period, possibly 17th century. Silk, warp ikat. 14 in x 4 in. The Textile Museum, 2022.13.2

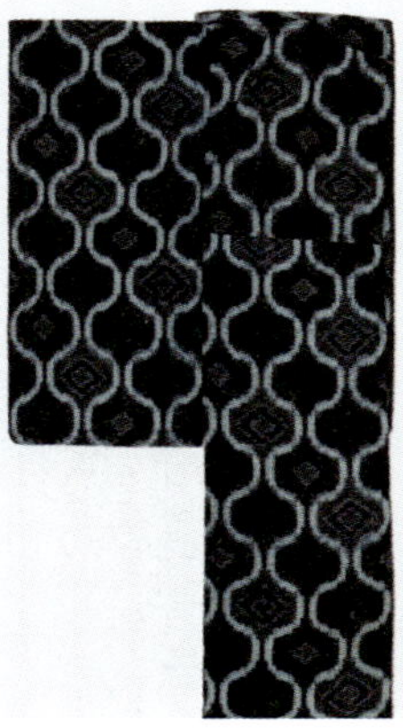

JP89 Woman's kimono
Japan, early 20th century. Cotton, printed double ikat, *bingo kasuri*. 44 in x 40 in

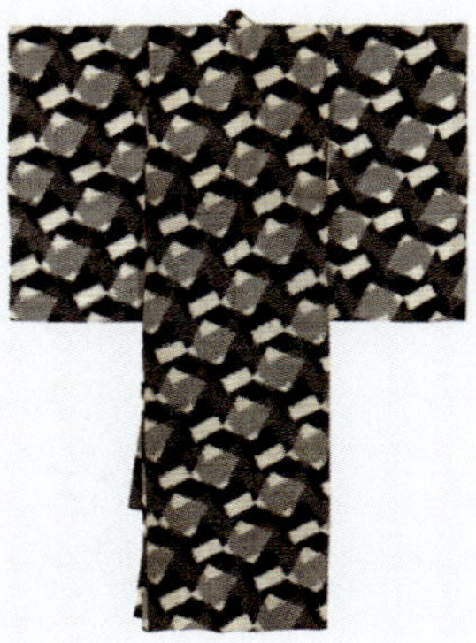

JP90 Child's kimono
Japan, early 20th century. *Meisen* silk, printed double ikat. 42 in x 36 in

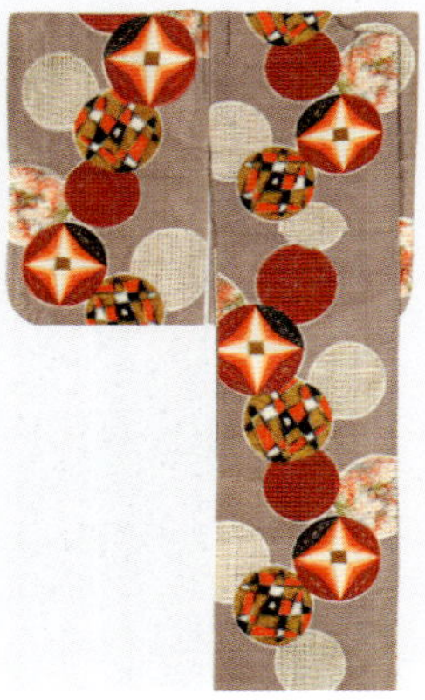

JP91 Woman's kimono
Japan, 1930s. *Meisen* silk, printed double ikat. 60 in x 50 in

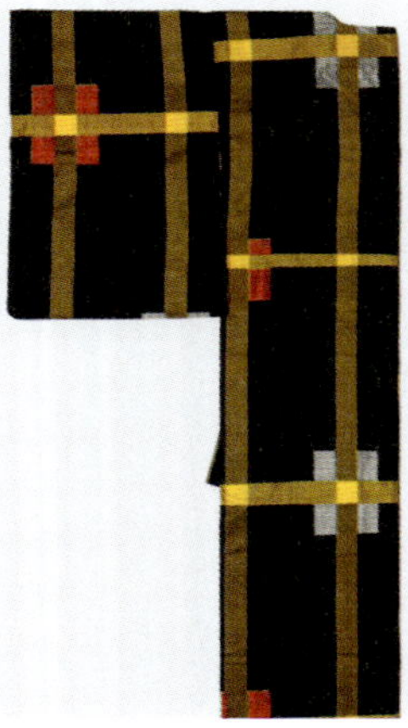

JP92 Woman's kimono
Japan, early 20th century. *Meisen* silk, printed double ikat. 58 in x 50 in

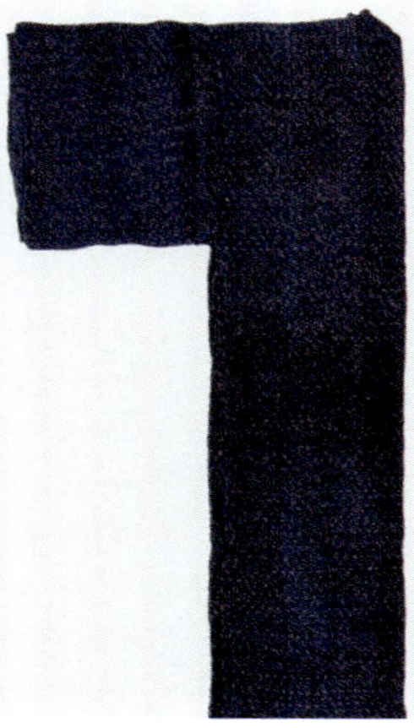

JP93 Woman's kimono
Japan, 20th century. *Asa* bast fiber, double ikat. 48 in x 42 in

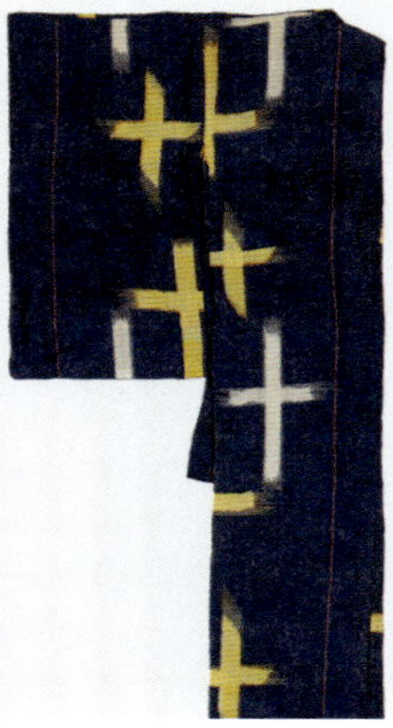

JP94 Woman's kimono
Japan, 20th century. Silk, double ikat. 60 in x 48 in

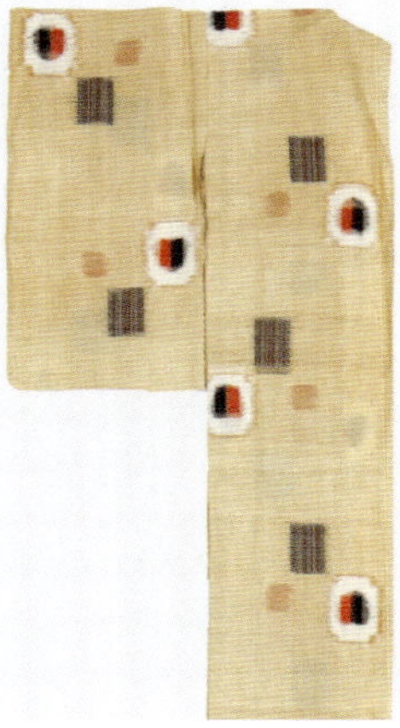

JP95 Woman's kimono
Japan, 1930s. *Meisen* silk, printed double ikat. 58 in x 50 in

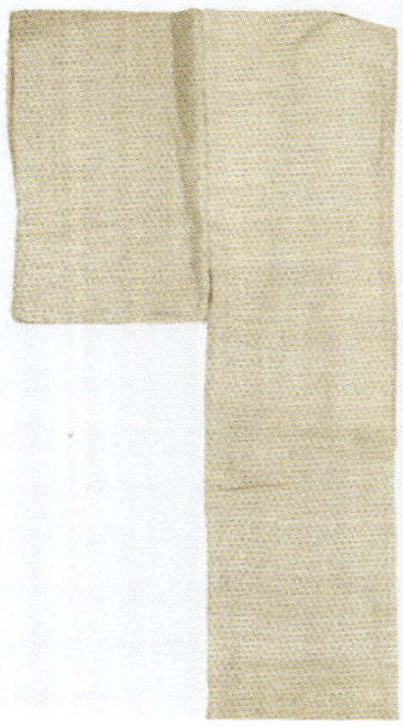

JP96 Kimono
Japan, late 19th century. Superfine *asa* bast fiber, double ikat. 52 in x 44 in

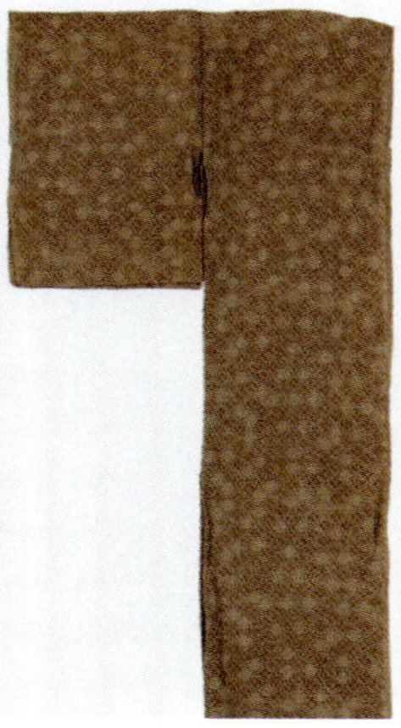

JP97 Kimono
Japan, late 19th century. Superfine *asa* bast fiber, double ikat. 55 in x 48 in

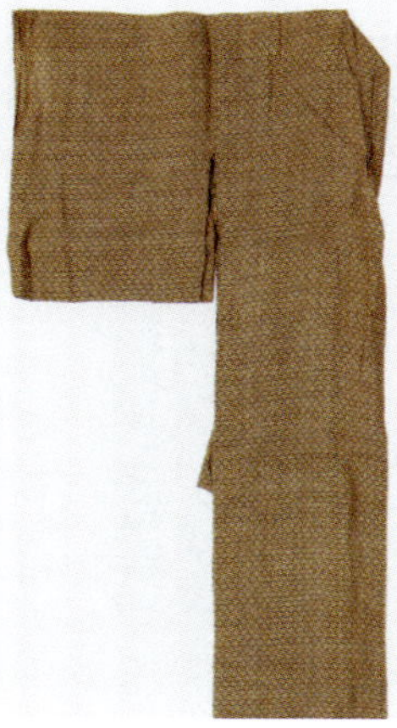

JP98 Kimono
Japan, late 19th century. Superfine *asa* bast fiber, double ikat. 55 in x 48 in

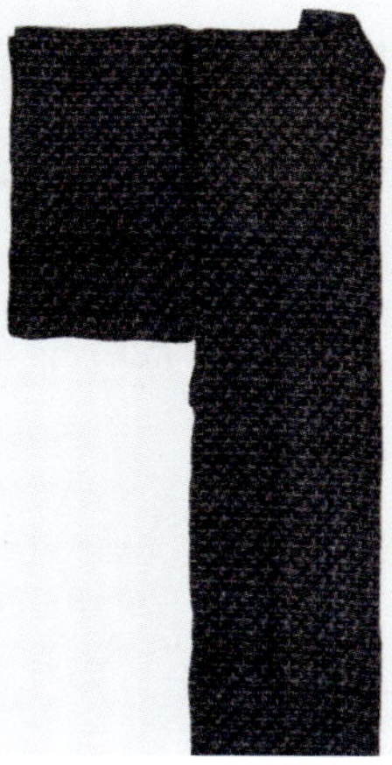

JP99 Kimono
Japan, late 19th century. Superfine *asa* bast fiber, double ikat. 58 in x 50 in

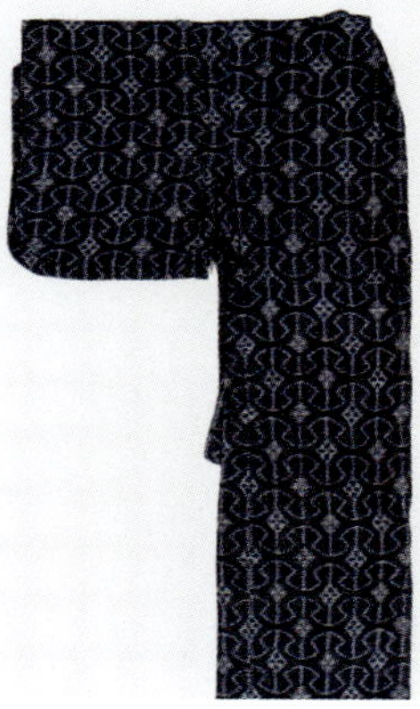

JP100 Kimono
Japan, early 20th century. Cotton, weft ikat. 52 in x 44 in

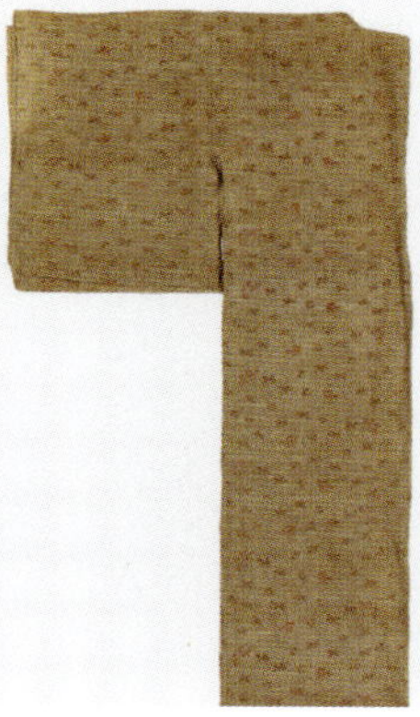

JP101 Kimono
Japan, 20th century. Hemp, weft ikat. 55 in x 48 in

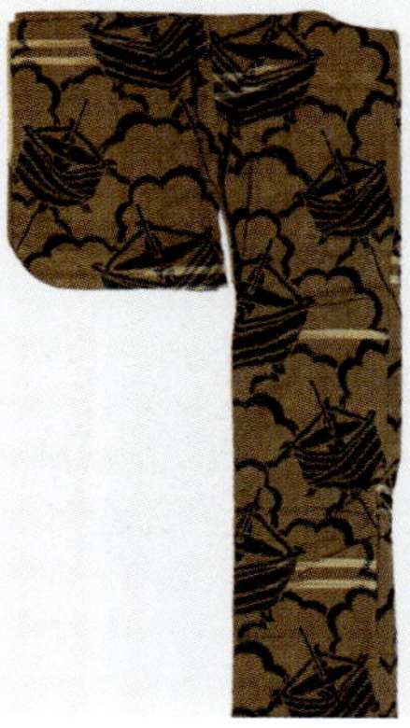

JP102 Kimono
Japan, early 20th century. *Meisen* silk, printed double ikat. 60 in x 50 in

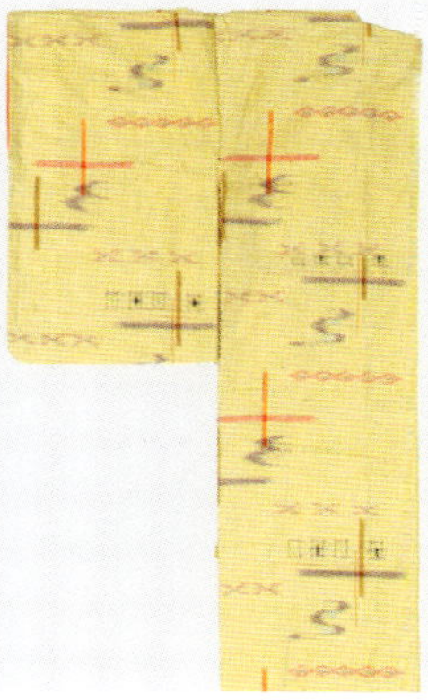

JP103 Kimono
Japan, 20th century. Silk, double ikat. 62 in x 50 in

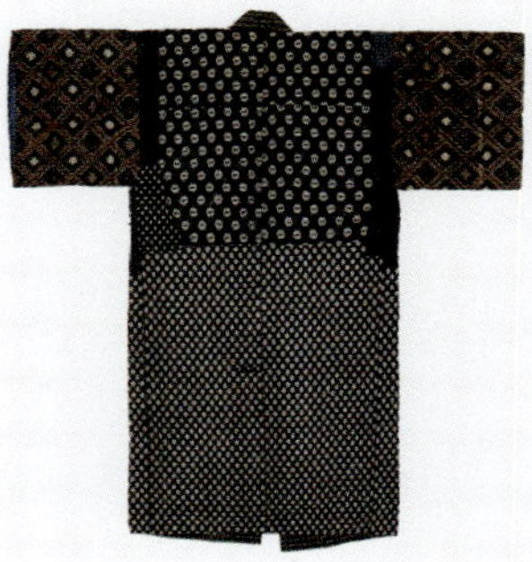

JP104 Child's kimono
Japan, 20th century. Cotton, double ikat, boro patchwork ikat. 30 in x 24 in

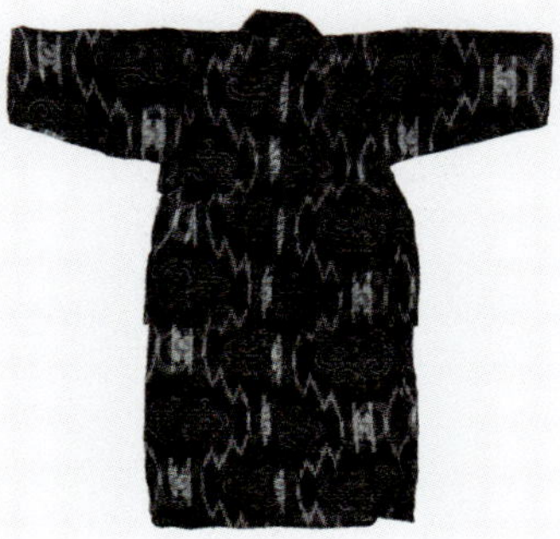

JP105 Child's kimono
Japan, early 20th century. Cotton, double ikat. 24 in x 22 in

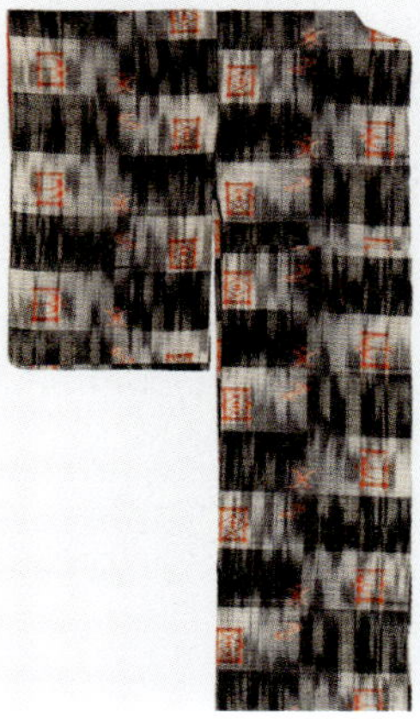

JP106 Kimono
Japan, 20th century. *Meisen* silk, printed double ikat. 60 in x 50 in

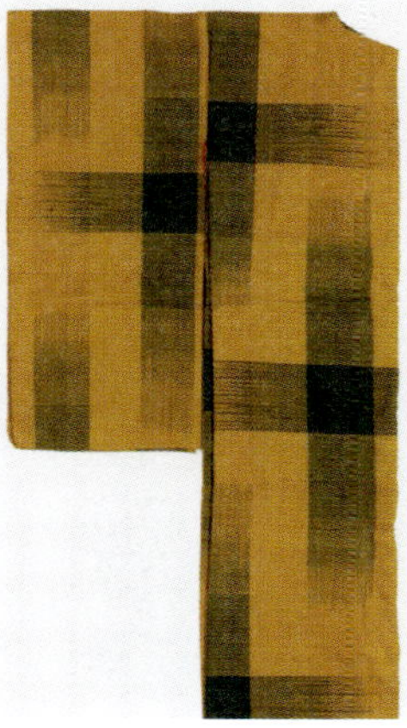

JP107 Kimono
Japan, 20th century. *Meisen* silk, printed double ikat. 58 in x 47 in

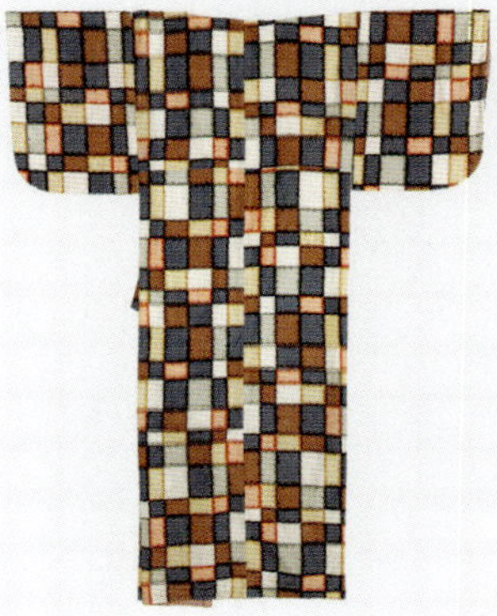

JP108 Kimono
Japan, 1930s. *Meisen* silk, printed double ikat. 60 in x 50 in

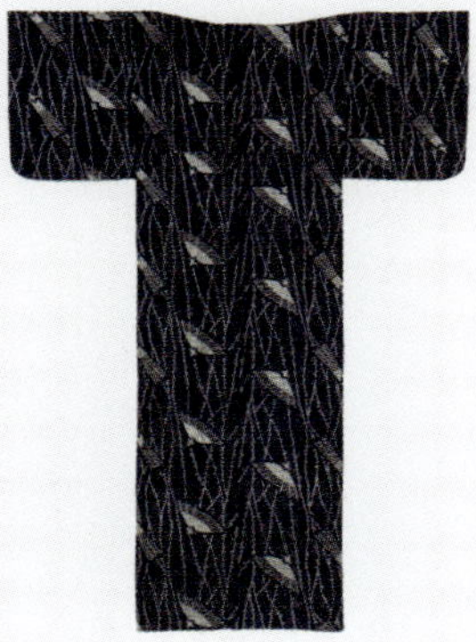

JP109 Kimono
Tottori, Honshu, Japan, 20th century. Cotton, weft ikat. 62 in x 50 in

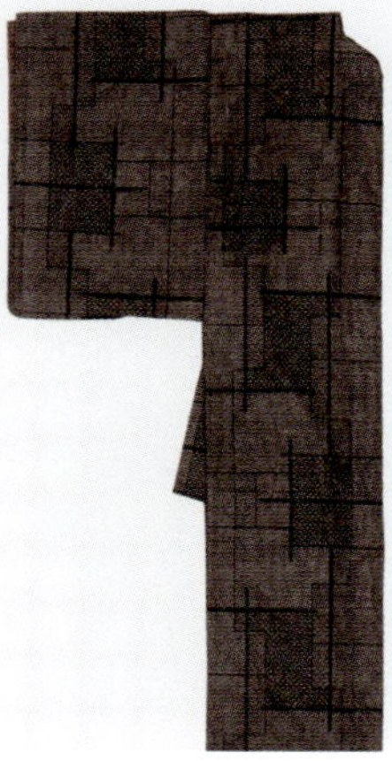

JP110 Kimono
Oshima Island, Japan, 20th century. Silk, double ikat, mud-resist dyed. 58 in x 48 in

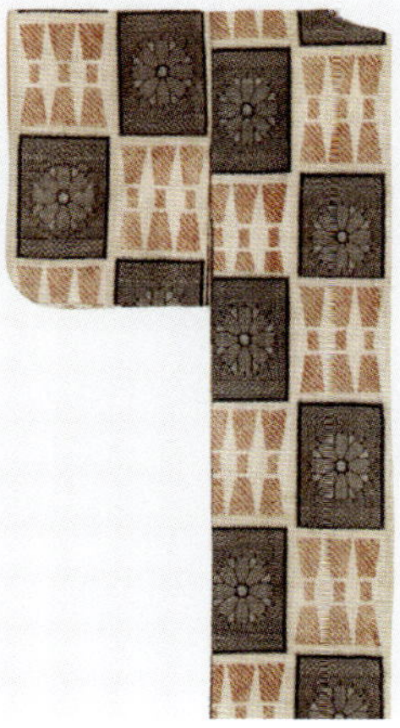

JP111 Kimono
Oshima Island, Japan, 20th century. Silk, double ikat. 56 in x 50 in

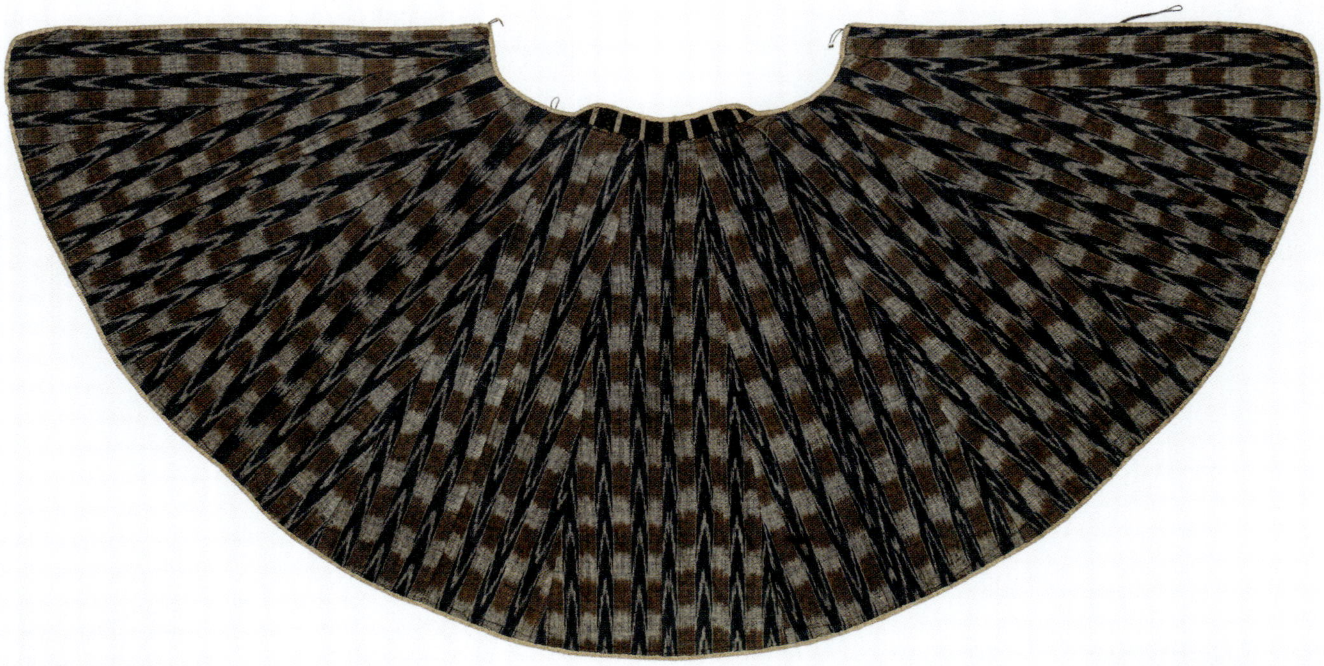

JP112 *Kappa*
Japan, mid-19th century. Cotton, warp ikat. 92 in x 45 in

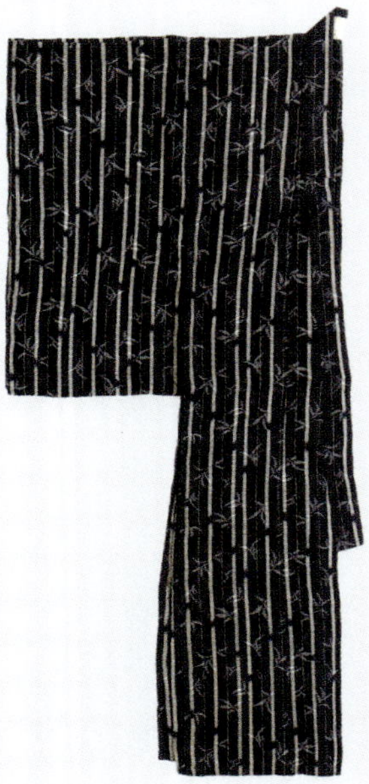

JP113 Kimono
Japan, late 19th century. *Asa* bast fiber, double ikat. 42 in x 36 in

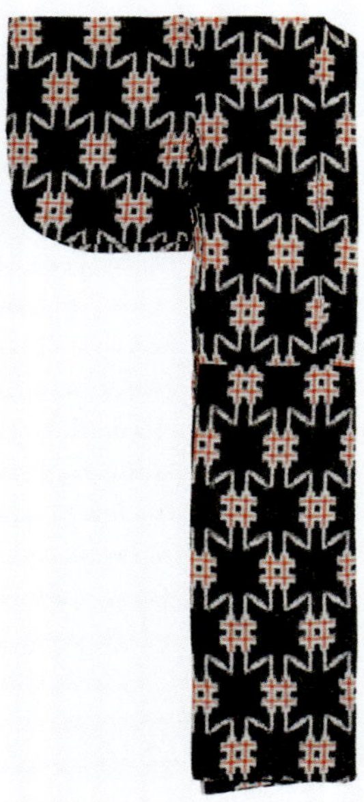

JP114 Kimono
Japan, probably late 19th century. Cotton, double ikat. 60 in x 50 in

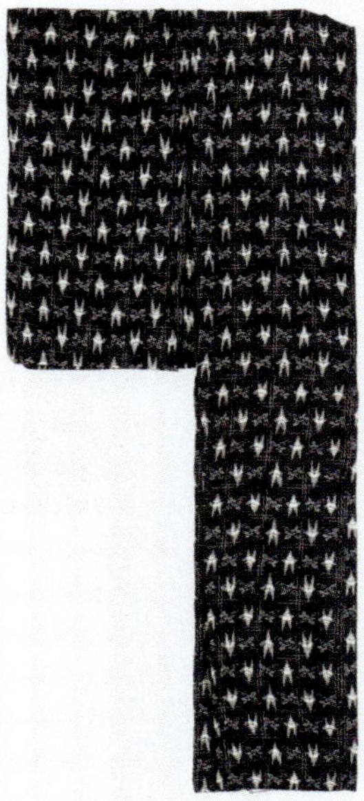

JP115 Kimono
Japan, late 19th century. *Asa* bast fiber, double ikat. 48 in x 40 in. The Textile Museum, 2022.13.17

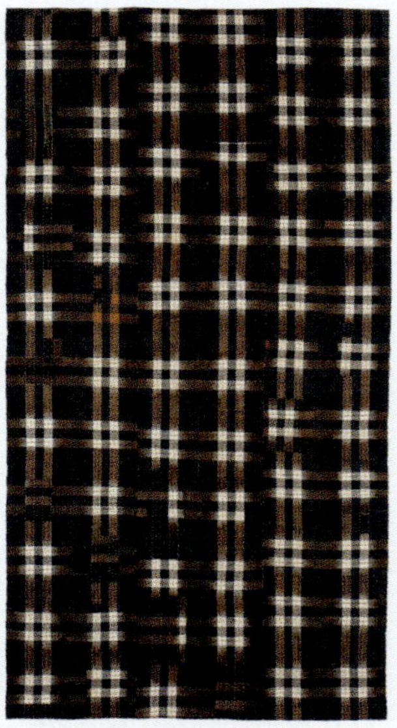

JP116 *Boro kotatsu* cover
Japan, 20th century. Cotton, double ikat. 79 in x 39 in

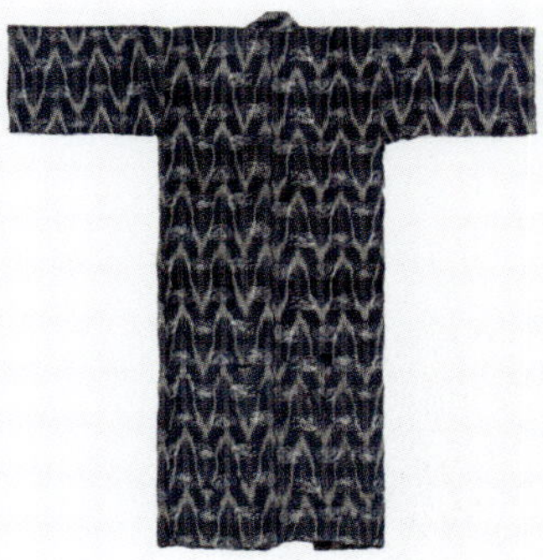

JP117 Child's kimono
Omi, Honshu, Japan, 19th century. Ramie warp and cotton weft, compound ikat, *e-gasuri*. 32 in x 28 in

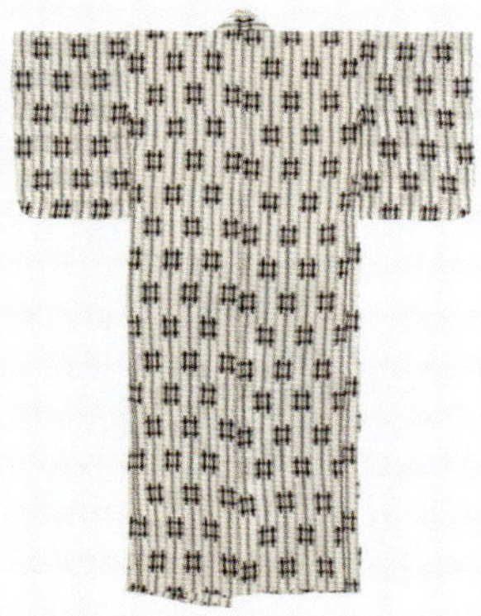

JP118 Kimono
Niigata, Honshu, Japan, 19th century. Snow bleached ramie (*choma*) double ikat; "wellhead" design. 60 in x 50 in. The Textile Museum, 2022.13.14

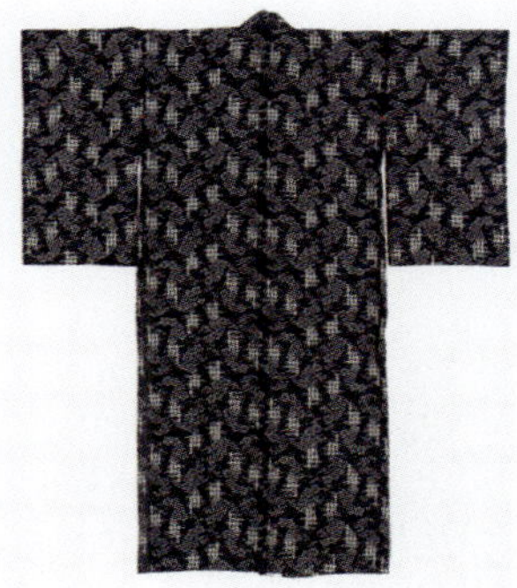

JP119 Kimono
Omi, Honshu, Japan, 19th century. Ramie, double ikat, *e-gasuri*. 55 in x 48 in. The Textile Museum, 2022.13.13

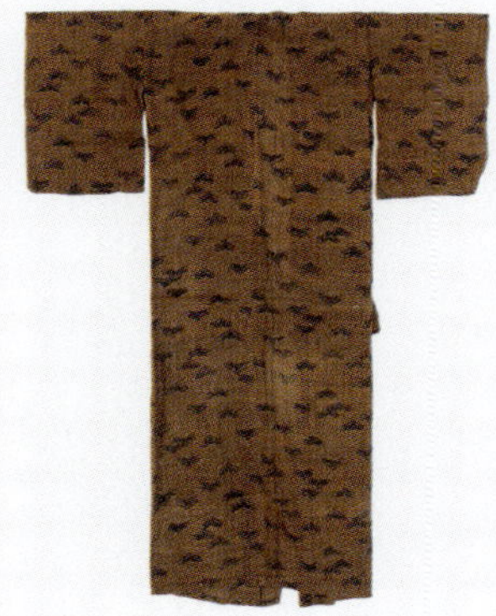

JP120 Kimono
Japan, 19th century. *Tsumugi* si k warp, cotton weft ikat. 54 in x 48 in

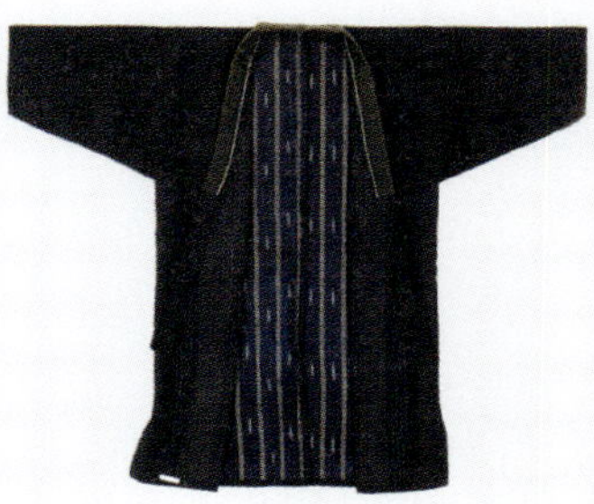

JP121 Farmer's coat, *noragi*
Japan, early 20th century. Cotton, warp ikat; heavy cotton embroidery. 42 x 40 in

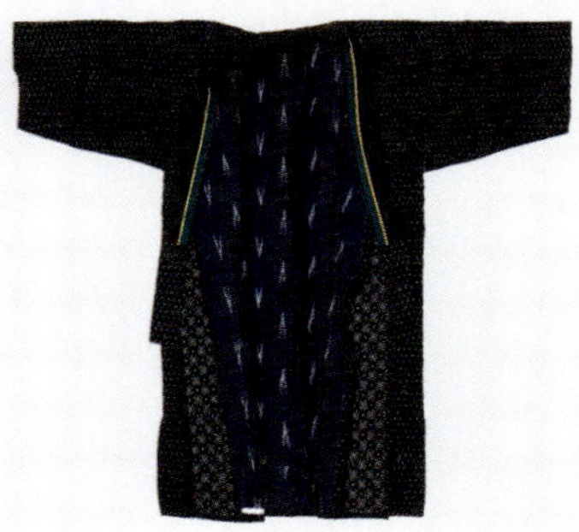

JP122 Farmer's coat, *noragi*
Japan, early 20th century. Cotton, warp ikat, patchwork of various ikat textiles, heavy cotton embroidery. 44 in x 40 in

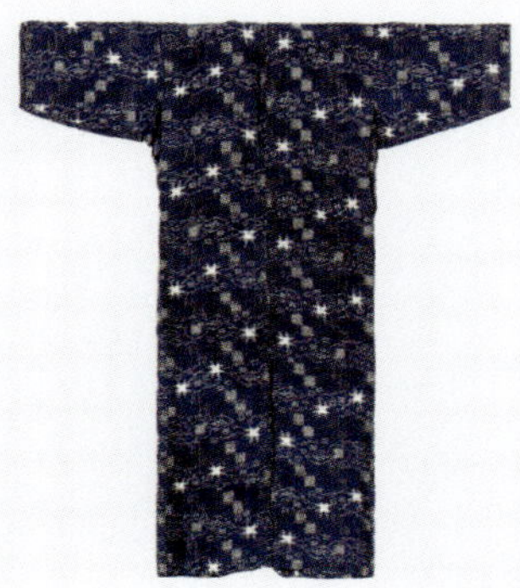

JP123 Child's kimono
Omi, Honshu, Japan, 19th century. *Asa* bast fiber warp and weft, double ikat. 48 in x 40 in

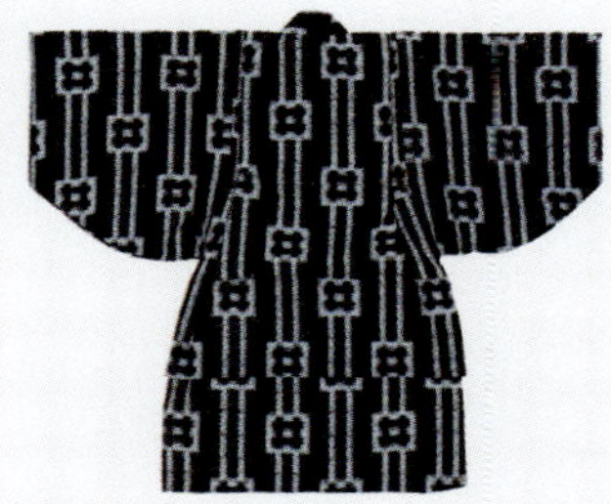

JP124 Child's kimono
Omi, Honshu, Japan, 20th century. Cotton, double ikat. 30 in x 28 in

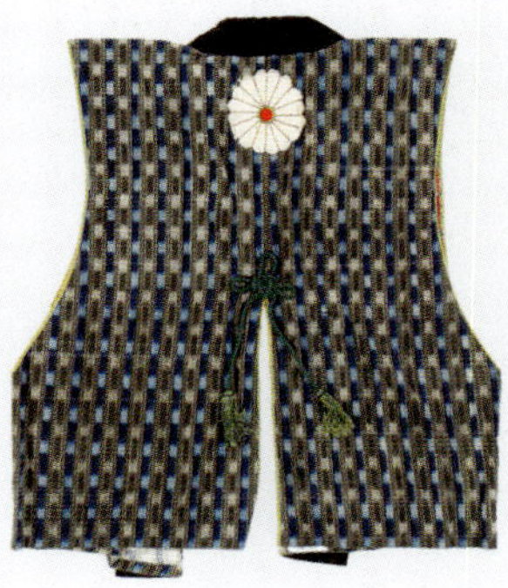

JP125 Samurai vest, *jinbaori*
Japan, mid-19th century. Printed faux ikat pattern on European velvet. 25 in x 23 in

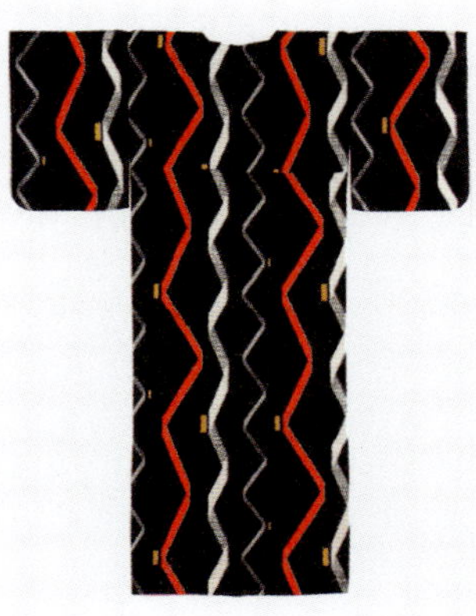

JP126 Woman's kimono
Japan, mid-20th century. Printed silk warp and weft ikat. 60 in x 50 in. The Textile Museum, 2022.13.19

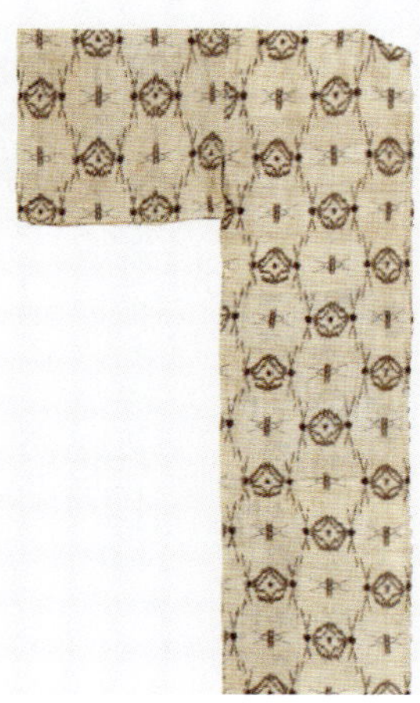

JP127 Kimono
Echigo, Honshu, Japan, 19th century. *Asa* bast fiber, double ikat. 58 in x 48 in

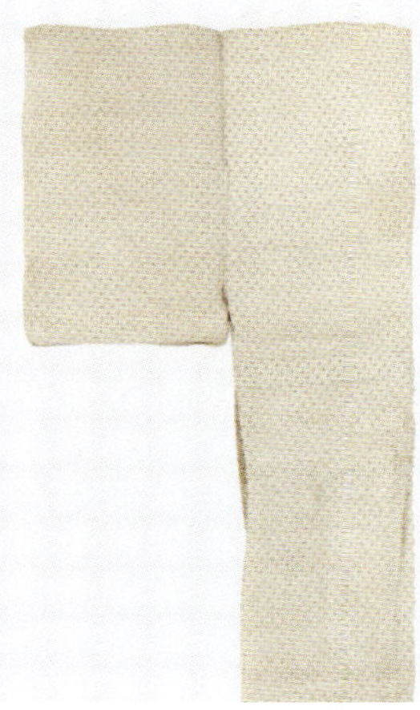

JP128 Kimono
Japan, 19th century. *Asa* bast fiber, double ikat. 54 in x 48 in. The Textile Museum, 2022.13.15

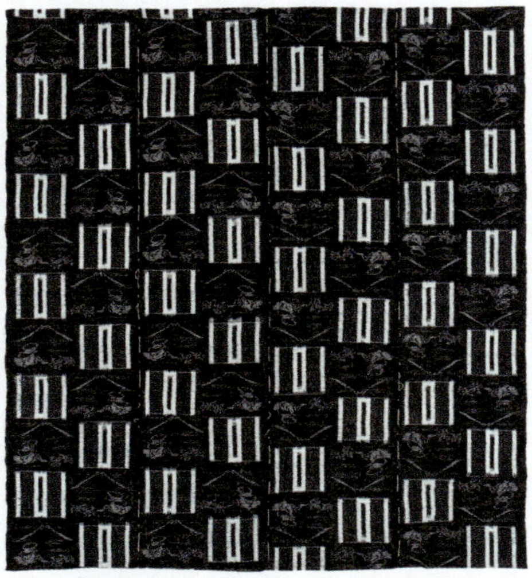

JP129 Futon cover
Japan, 19th century. Combination of weft *kasuri* and double ikat. 54 in x 50 in

JP130 Boy's futon cover
Japan, ca. 1890s. Cotton, compound ikat. 58 in x 52 in

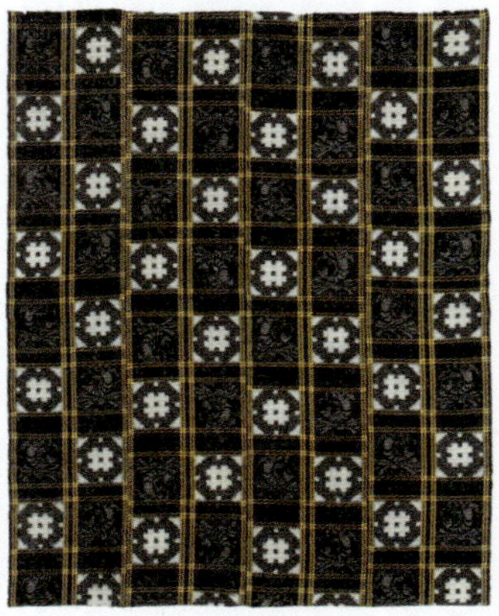

JP131 Futon cover
Japan, Taisho period (1912–26). Combination of weft ikat and double ikat. 61 in x 50 in

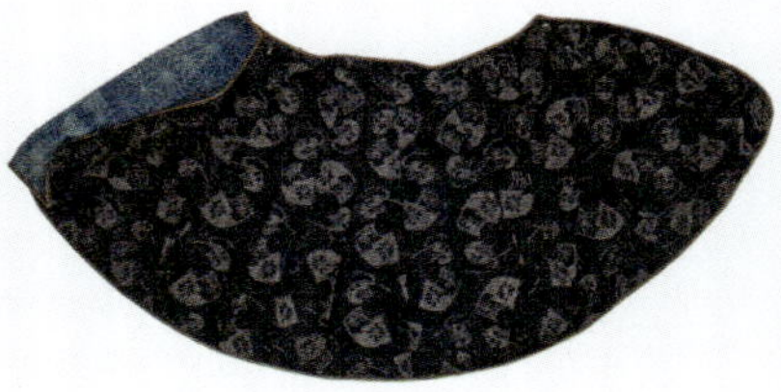

JP132 *Kappa*
Japan, 19th century. Cotton, weft ikat. 86 in x 44 in

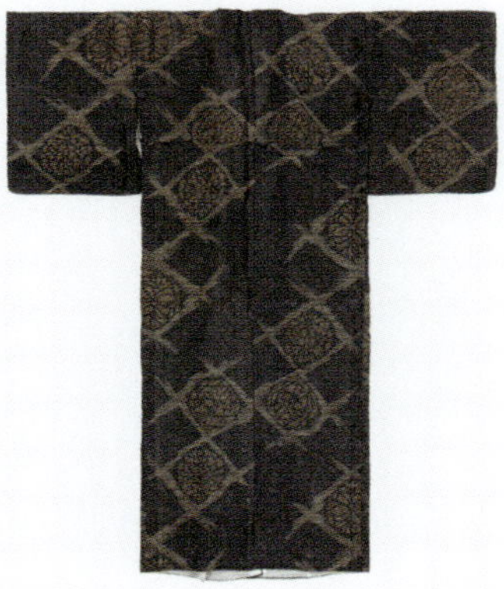

JP133 Kimono
Japan, possibly first quarter 19th century. Superfine *ro* silk, clamp-resist weft ikat. 54 in x 46 in

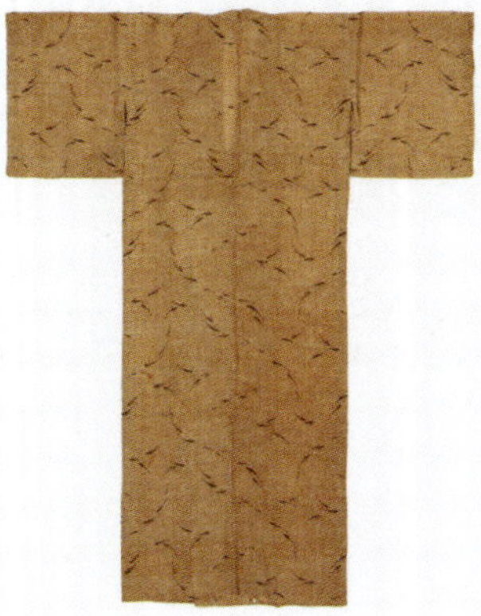

JP134 Kimono
Japan, 20th century. Hemp, weft ikat. 54 in x 46 in

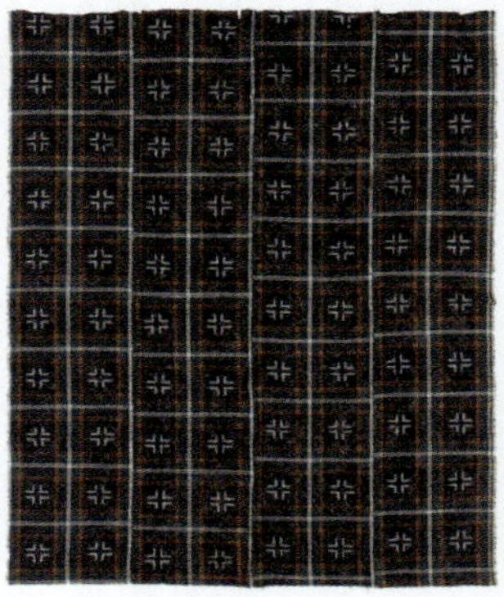

JP135 Futon cover
Japan, 20th century. Cotton, double ikat. 59 in x 51 in

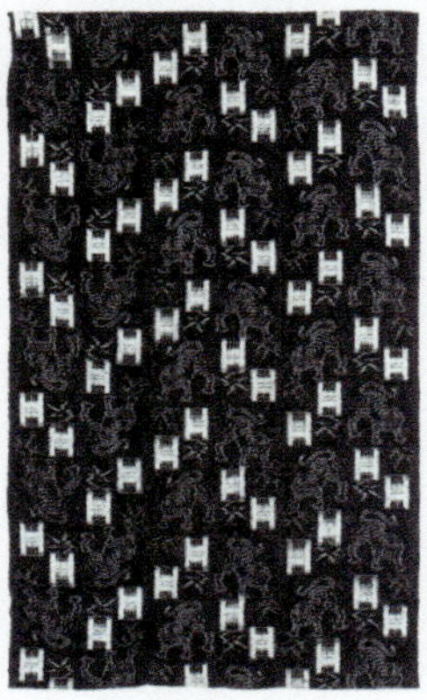

JP136 Child's futon cover
Japan, late 19th century. Combination of weft *kasuri* and double ikat. 60 in x 37 in

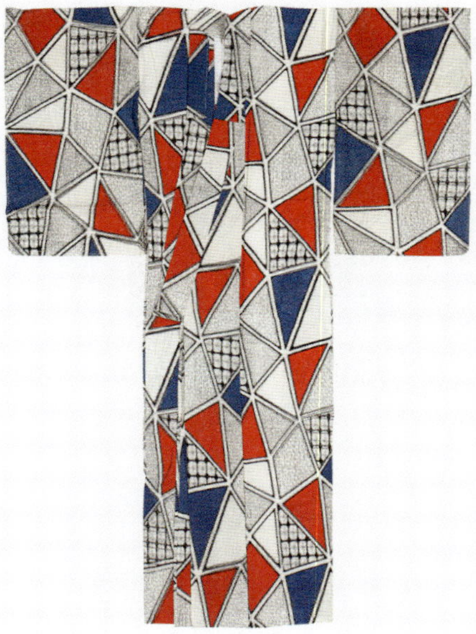

JP137 Kimono
Japan, 20th century. *Meisen* silk, printed warp and weft ikat. 58 in x 44 in

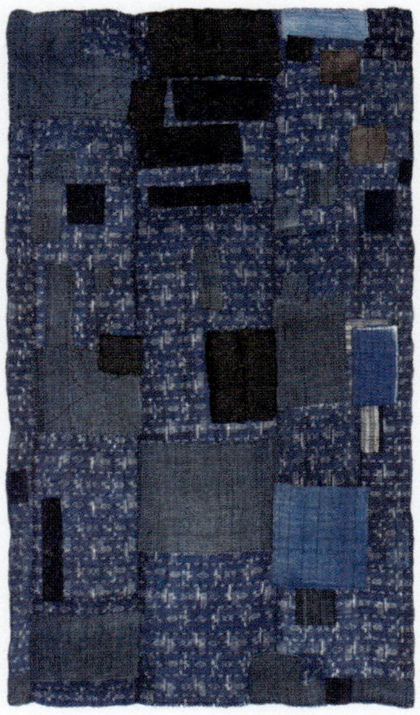

JP138 *Boro* futon cover
Japan, 20th century. Cotton, double ikat, patchwork. 62 in x 38 in

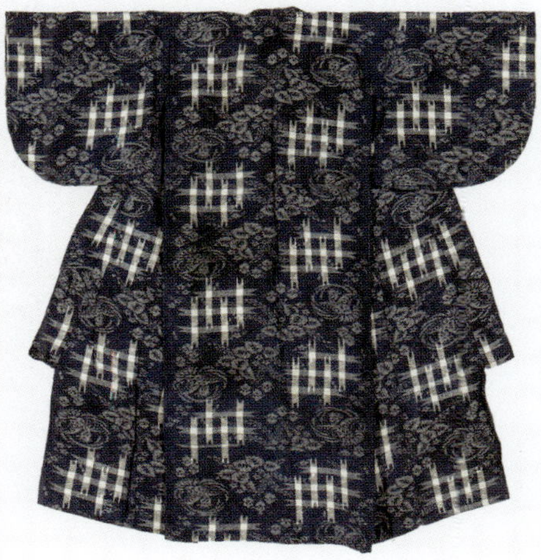

JP139 Child's kimono
Omi, Honshu, Japan, 19th century. Ramie, double ikat. 36 in x 32 in. The Textile Museum, 2022.13.12

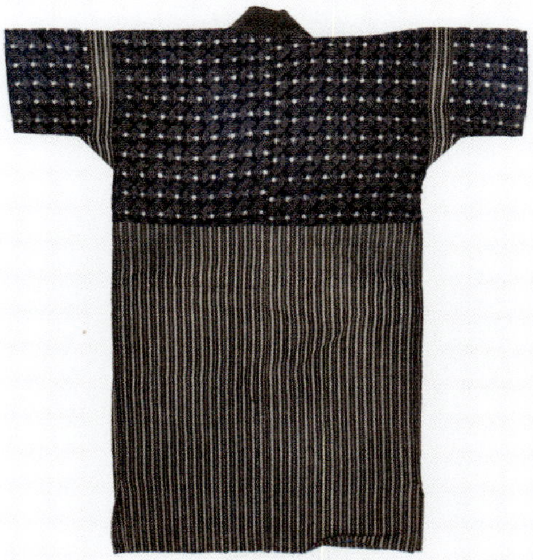

JP140 Child's kimono
Japan, 20th century. Cotton, double ikat. 26 in x 22 in. The Textile Museum, 2022.13.22

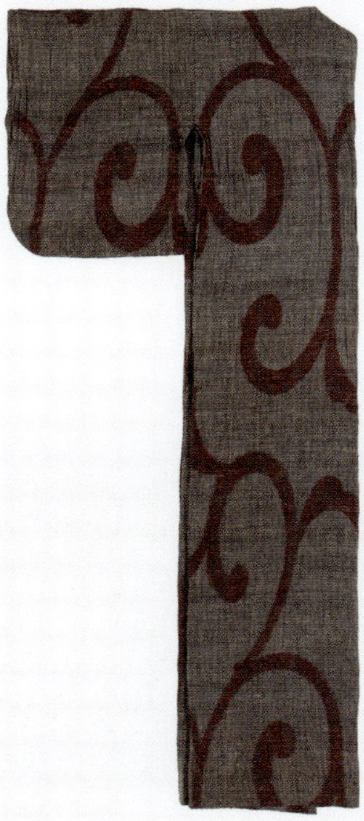

JP141 Kimono
Japan, probably 20th century. Cotton weft ikat and *asa* bast-fiber warp. 60 in x 50 in. The Textile Museum, 2022.13.16

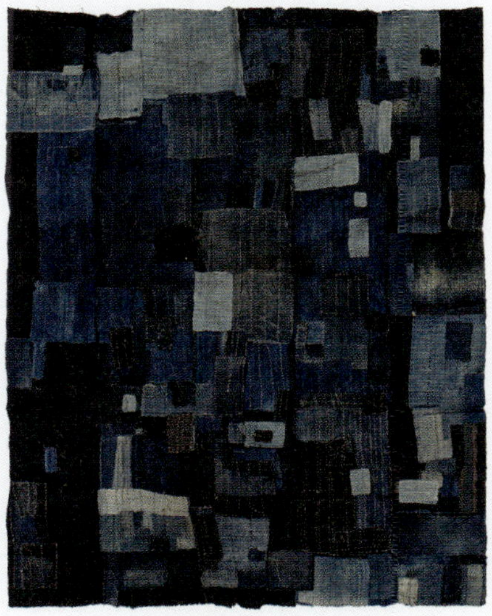

JP142 *Boro* futon cover
Japan, 19th–early 20th century. Stripe and plain weave cotton, fragments of *kasuri*, *asa sashiko* reinforced embroidery. 96 in x 76 in

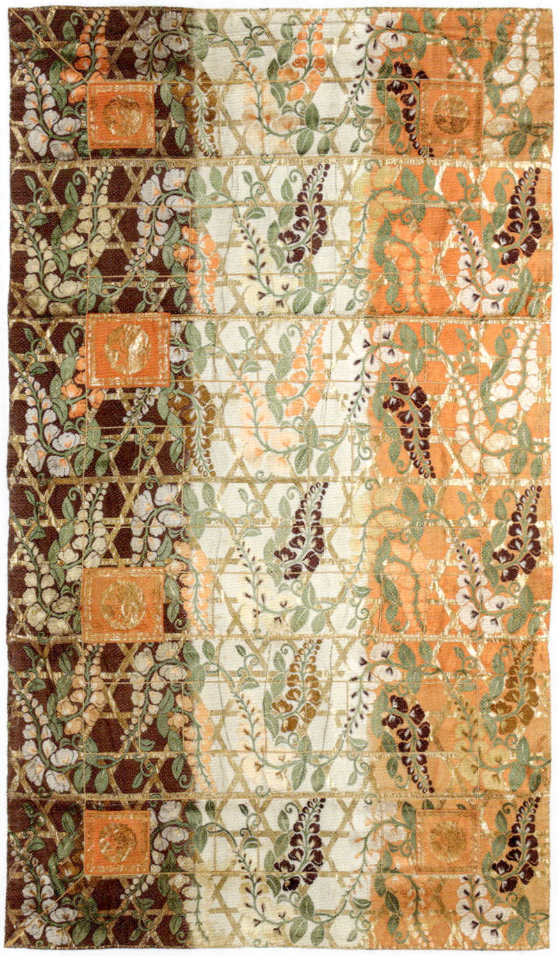

JP143 Buddhist monk's robe, *kesa*
Kyoto, Japan, late 19th century. Silk warp ikat and metallic weft brocade (*atsuita karaori*), natural dyes. 45 in x 77 in. The Textile Museum, 2022.13.6

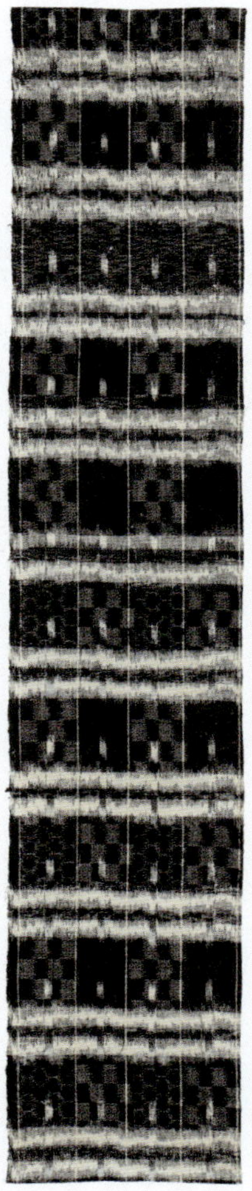

JP144 Futon cover (*zanshi-ori*) panel
Japan, 20th century. Cotton, double ikat. 60 in x 13 in

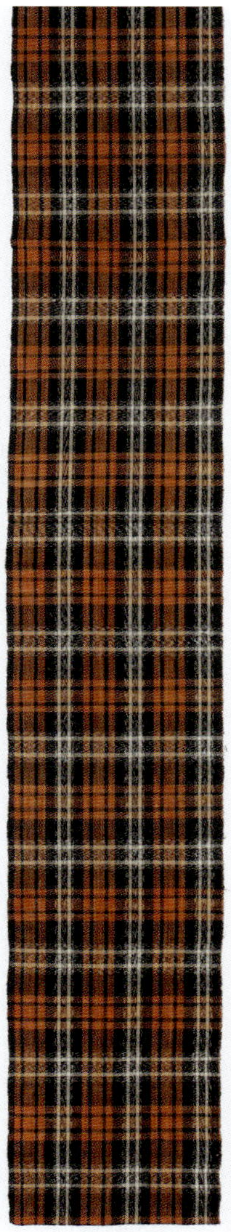

JP145 Futon cover panel
Japan, 19th century. Cotton, compound ikat. 77 in x 13 in

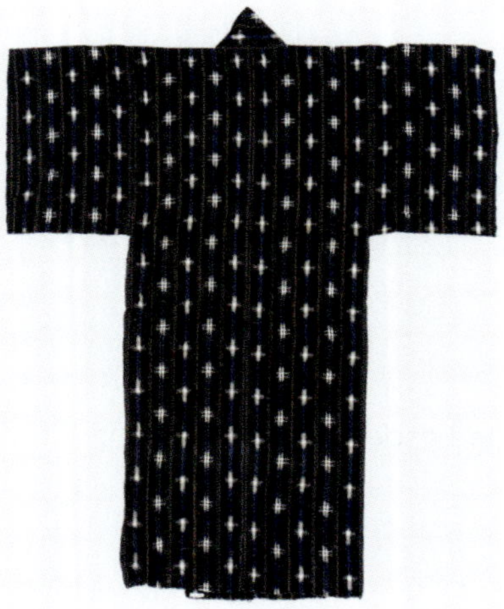

JP146 Kimono-shaped sleeping futon, *yogi*
Japan, 19th century. Cotton, double ikat. 68 in x 72 in

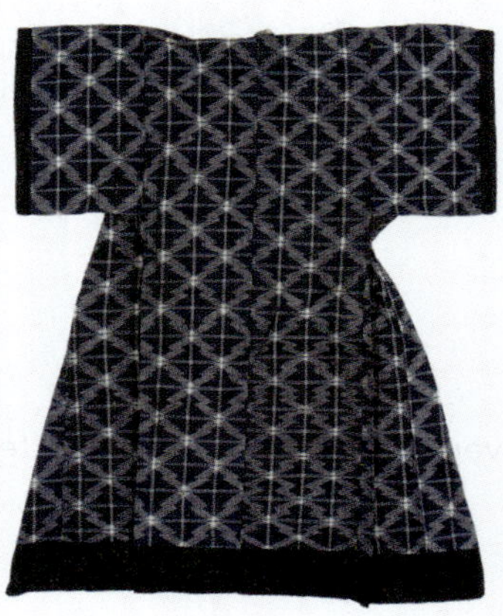

JP147 Kimono-shaped sleeping futon, *yogi*
Japan, 19th century. Cotton, double ikat. 78 in x 54 in

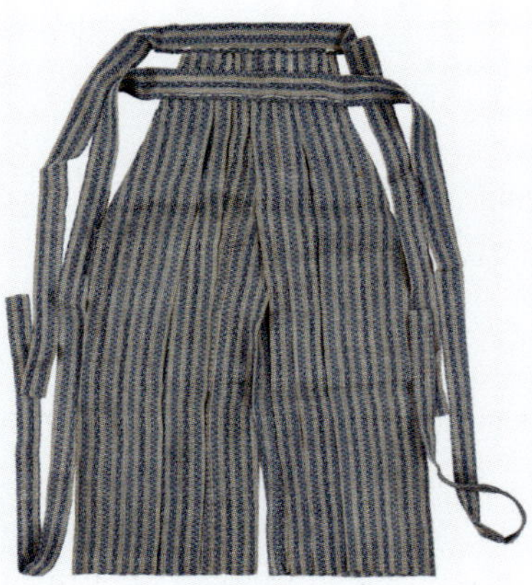

JP148 *Hakama* pants
Probably Omi, Honshu, Japan, 19th century. Ramie, warp ikat. 36 in x 24 in. The Textile Museum, 2022.13.11

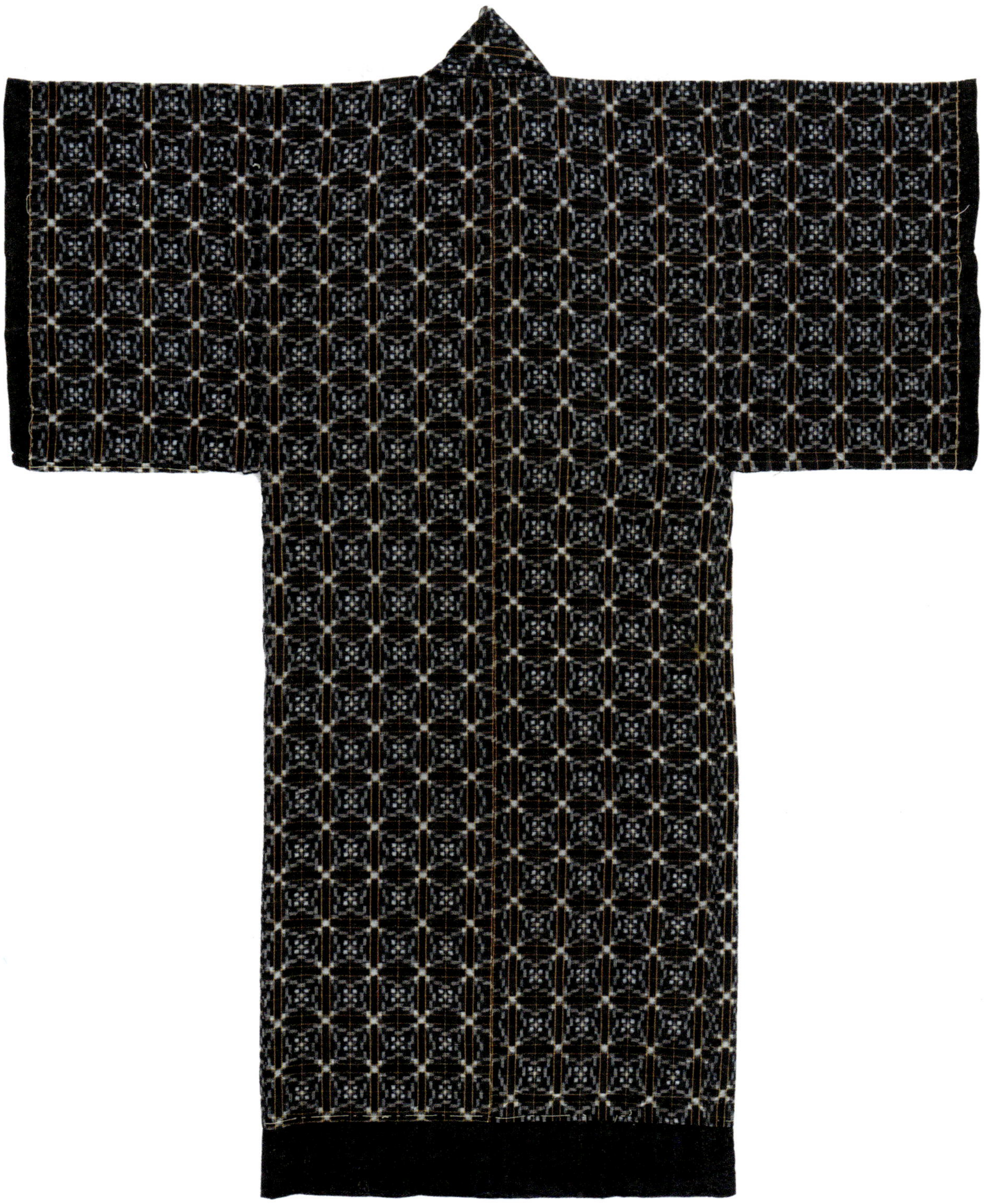

JP149 Kimono-shaped coverlet, *yogi*, Japan, 19th century. Cotton, double ikat. 78 in x 82 in. The Textile Museum, 2022.13.21

In Edo- and Meiji-period Japan, wealthy families typically provided their daughters with trousseaux that included bedding forms such as *futons* and *yogi*–kimono-shaped coverlets like this example. Often commissioned especially for weddings, these costly furnishings were displayed publicly in colorful, festive processions from the bride's home to the groom's. Likely stemming from the earlier custom of using garments as bed covers, *yogi* are constructed much larger than kimono and usually comprise an upper and lower layer of fabric filled with cotton or silk batting. The topmost layer often features auspicious motifs that augured well for the newly married couple's future. This *yogi* is patterned with an interlocked circle design called *shippo* ("seven treasures"), referencing the so-called "seven treasures" of Buddhism. In a tour de force of craftsmanship, the circles align perfectly to form squares of bright white double ikat where they overlap. After the first few days of marriage, such fine *yogi* typically were stored carefully and brought out only for special occasions.

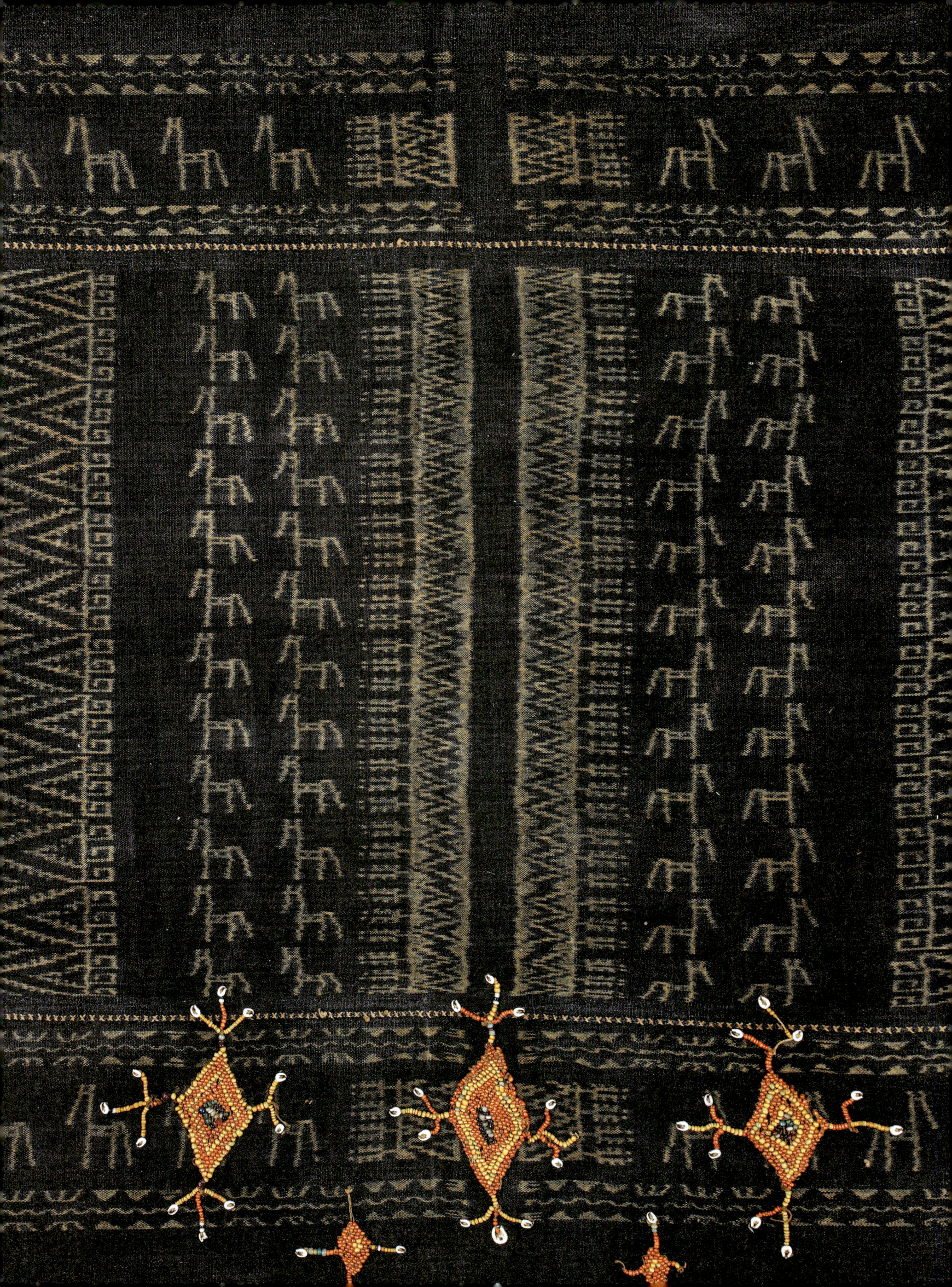

MONSOON ASIA

by Linda S. McIntosh

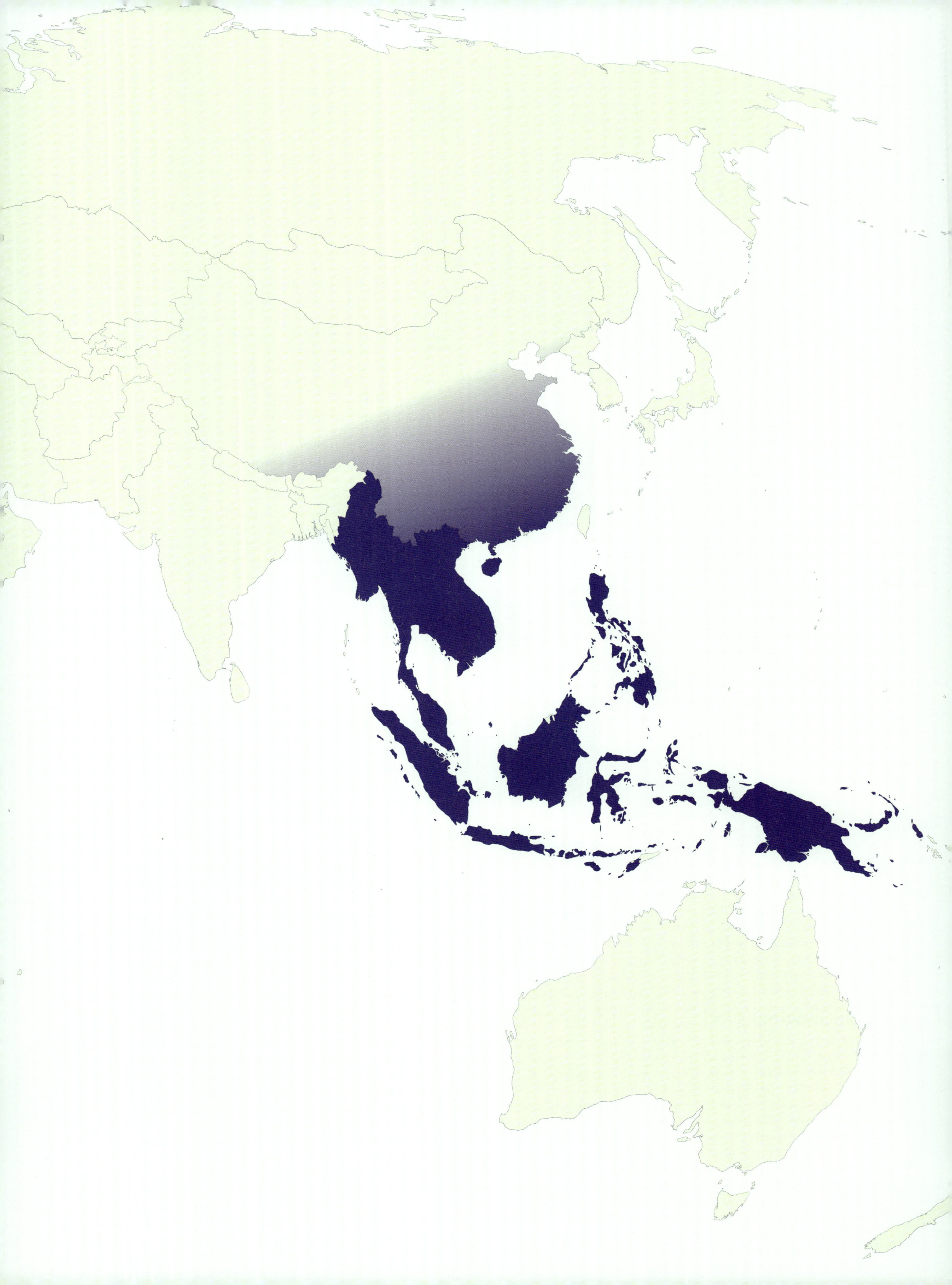

IKAT IN MONSOON ASIA

Monsoon Asia, or the region between China and India encompassing Mainland and Insular Southeast Asia and adjacent areas, possesses the richest and most diverse resist-dye textile traditions in the world. Warp ikat and weft ikat are the main resist-dye techniques used in the region, while one village in Bali, Indonesia, utilizes double-ikat technique. Zone-dyeing and the tie-dye decorative methods of *plangi* and *tritik* are rare but still exist in small pockets of Monsoon Asia. Weavers from different cultures, primarily women, have developed ikat textiles that serve as markers of ethnic identity, marital status, and status in society. Inspiration for the resist-dye patterns originates from the weavers' immediate social and natural environments and from imported goods held in high regard in each community. The combination of overall design layout, techniques, and motifs creates distinctive textiles identifying these communities.

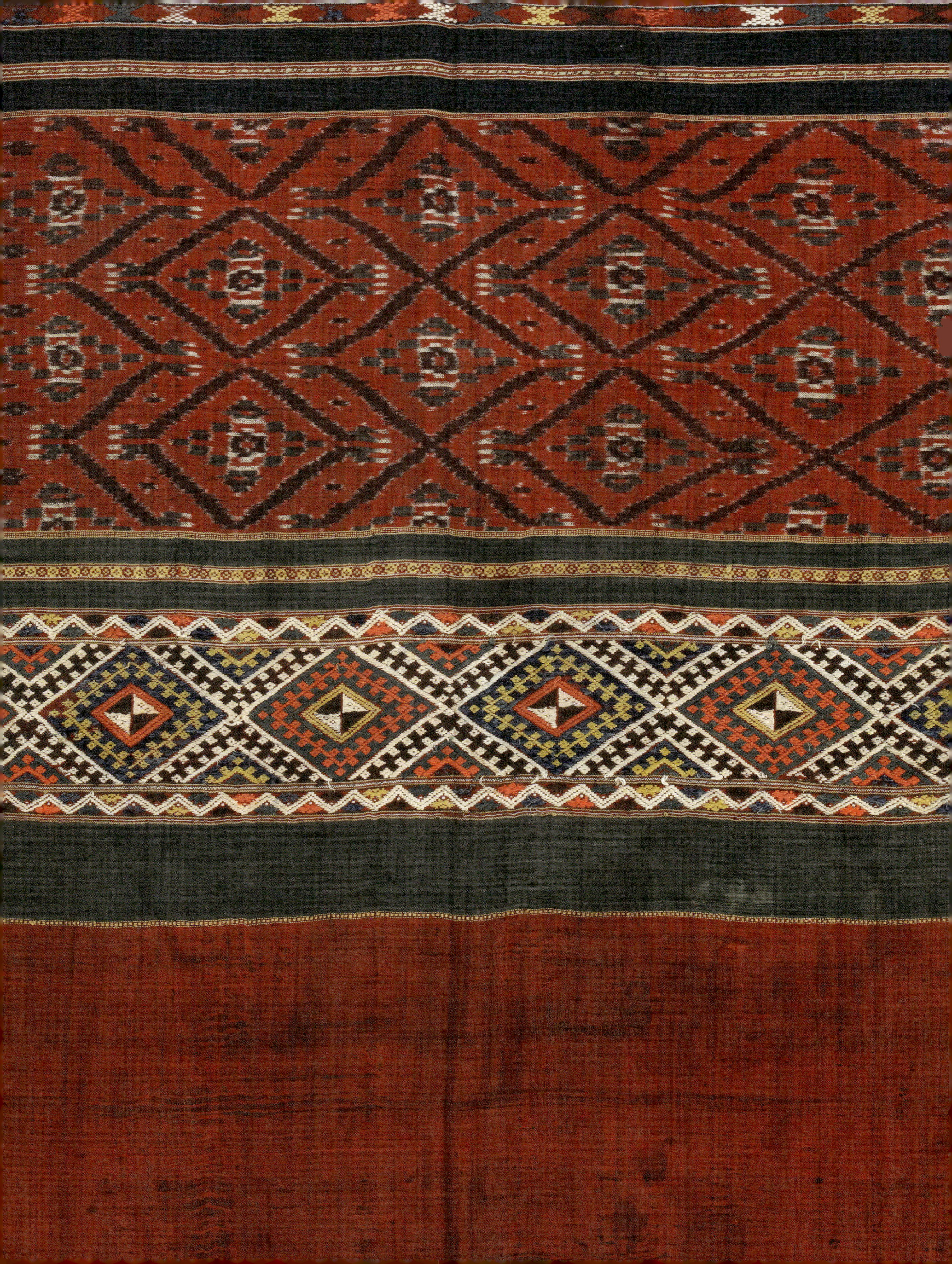

Fig.1
Detail of MA138, Lao women's ceremonial skirt, *sin mii*

TEXTILES BELOW THE WINDS

The seas surrounding the landmasses known as Southeast Asia separated settlements but led to the development of distinct groups of people and independent polities. These groups developed identifying characteristics including language, descent, and religious beliefs. Women, regardless of ethnicity, were and continue to be the primary producers of textiles in Monsoon Asia. Weavers apply an array of techniques to decorate handwoven cloth including a variety of resist-dye techniques, such as warp and weft ikat.

The waterways also allowed people to move from one area to another, whether for permanent or temporary settlement, pilgrimage, or trade. Anthony Reid aptly called Southeast Asia "the land below the winds."[1] Monsoon winds facilitated traveling throughout Southeast Asia and beyond. The winds blew in one direction for half of the year and the opposite direction during the other half. The monsoon also brought rain, which was vital for life and sustenance. These winds were essential for regional maritime trade, and interactions as a result of commerce affected the polities of Monsoon Asia to varying degrees. Traders and others, such as religious men, brought textiles, glass beads, and other goods that became symbols of prestige for the different groups of people inhabiting this region.

Chris Buckley's "Ikat Line" designates approximately the areas of Monsoon Asia that primarily created weft-ikat textiles and warp-ikat-decorated cloth on different types of body-tension looms.[2] When applied to Indonesia, the ethnic groups of West Indonesia, West Flores Island, and the coastal areas of South Sulawesi and Borneo Islands primarily weave weft-ikat textiles. Weft-ikat production in Mainland Southeast Asia occurs in coastal and lowland areas. The application of warp ikat occurs via weavers living in highland areas of West Indonesia and Mainland Southeast Asia and throughout East Indonesia. The Bali Aga community of Tenganan Pegeringsingan, Bali, Indonesia, is the only locale where the double-ikat technique is used.

The older, indigenous textile design format, whether warp or weft ikat, consists of bands of various sizes. Weavers of ethnic groups of polities directly involved in regional trade began to assimilate layouts of imported cloth, especially a central field with each side flanked by bands of patterning.[3] Women living in highland or remote areas

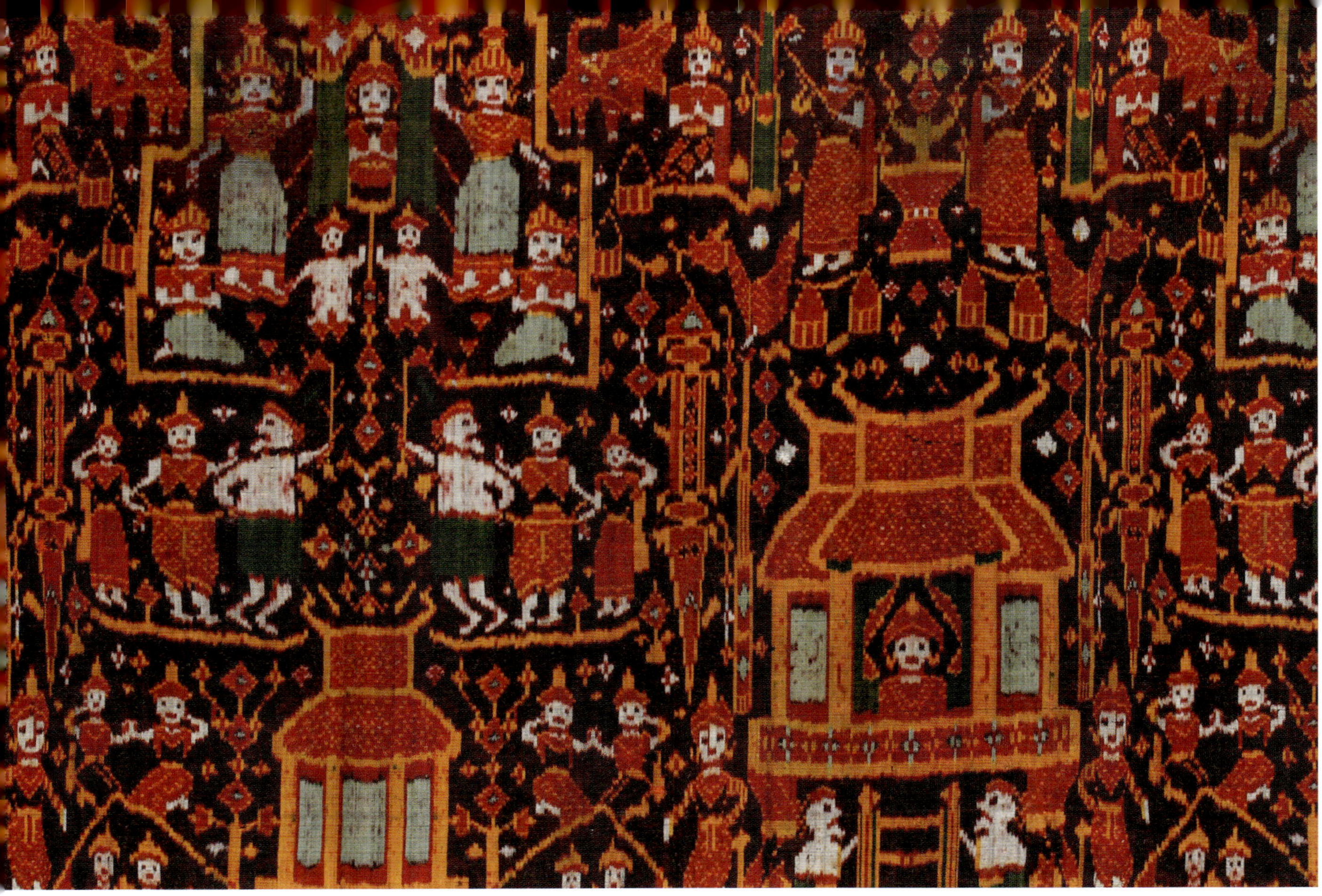

Fig.2

incorporated elements of the imported fabrics, such as motifs, into their production of textiles. Merchants brought different types of weavings to gift and sell to local rulers. The monarchs, such as the Thai monarch of Ayutthaya, also commissioned specific textiles from South Asia.[4] The imported textiles became items of prestige, and locally woven versions also were held in high regard.

Mainland Monsoon Asia and Neighboring China

The breadth of textiles decorated with ikat and other resist-dye techniques reflects the diversity of the ethnic groups residing in Mainland Monsoon Asia and adjacent areas of China, including Hainan Island, whether produced by groups living in the mountainous interior or lowland areas. Both similarities and differences can be observed in this array of resist-dyed cloth.

Concerning resist-dye techniques: Textiles woven on backstrap looms generally feature warp-ikat patterns, and weft ikat dominates the resist-dye designs decorating cloth created on frame looms in Mainland Southeast Asia.[5] However, some types of frame-loom weaving by the Tai of Northeast Laos and adjacent areas of North Vietnam feature warp ikat. Both warp and weft techniques are applied to a single cloth by some Tai weavers in Northeast Laos, and by Khmer and Kui weavers in Southeast Thailand, but the patterning composed of white dashes lacks complexity. The weft-ikat textiles made by groups living in the lowland areas of Mainland Southeast Asia, including Lao, Khmer, and Cham, are the opposite of simple: intricate in terms of design and the number of dyes applied to create different-colored sections of a pattern.

The warp-ikat designs on body-tension-woven textiles made by groups living in the region's highland areas, including the Asho Chin of Northwest Myanmar and Pakoh of Southern Laos or the Central Highlands of Vietnam, are generally minimal, consisting of dashes, geometric shapes, and simple lattices (Fig.5/MA148).[6] An exception is the Meifu subgroup of the Li ethnic group residing on Hainan Island, China, which produces complex warp-ikat designs. The Lua weavers of North Thailand organize short and long dashes to create a rippling effect resembling python skin. Generally, one type of dye, such as indigo, is used to create two-color ikat patterns (MA137).

The Li ethnic group of Hainan Island, China, belongs to the Tai-Kadai ethnolinguistic family and is distantly related to the Tai peoples. Li women continue to weave cloth on a foot-braced backstrap loom, one of the oldest loom types. The fabric produced on this loom is narrow, and four to six panels are joined together to form a ceremonial tubular skirt. The Meifu Li is the only Li subgroup that continues to create complex warp-ikat patterns (MA121,

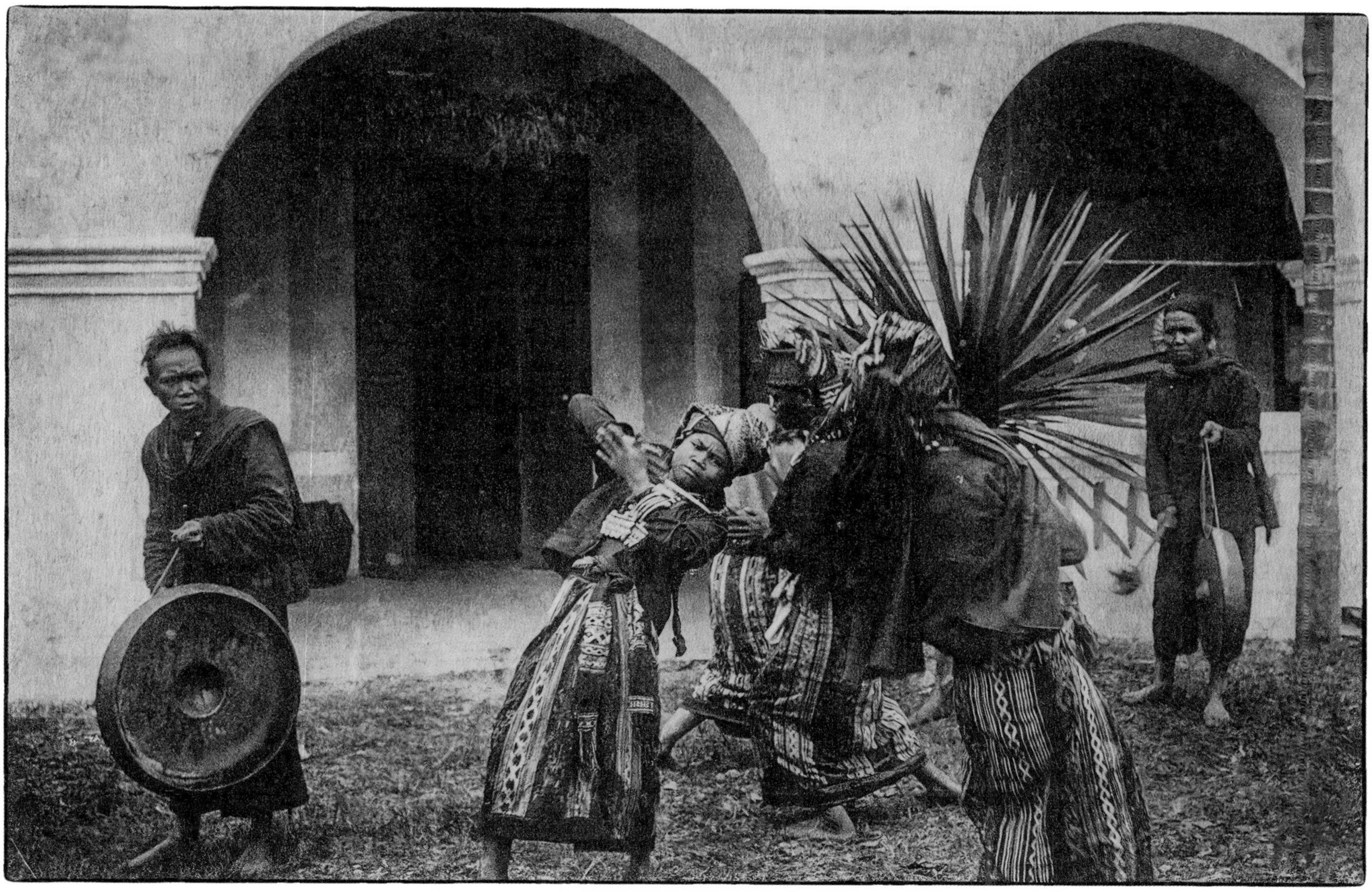

Fig.3

MA126).[7] Meifu Li warp-ikat patterning is intricate, consisting of numerous small dots organized into geometric shapes and zigzag lines (Fig.4/MA118). Warp-ikat-decorated skirts that also have a panel of supplementary-weft-decorated cloth are worn by unmarried Meifu Li women (MA114).

The Tai ethnic groups, including the Lao, Tai Dam, Tai Daeng, Tai Khoen, and Tai Lue, are spread across the Mainland Southeast Asian region spilling into adjacent areas of Southwest China and Northeast India. Tai women weave on frame looms and thus rely on weft ikat instead of warp ikat as a decorative method. However, the warp-ikat technique is still in use among some Tai groups residing in present-day Northeast Laos and adjacent areas of Northwest Vietnam such as the Tai Daeng and Tai Dam (modern political borders divide the area where these groups live). The weavers apply this decorative method to create dashes on the warp threads, which may be the sole decoration or combined with supplementary warp designs (MA103). Ceremonial skirts produced in this area incorporate warp ikat with weft ikat, supplementary warp, and discontinuous weft designs.[8]

The Tai peoples generally use weft-ikat-decorated textiles as lower garments or coffin covers rather than for covering the upper body. However,

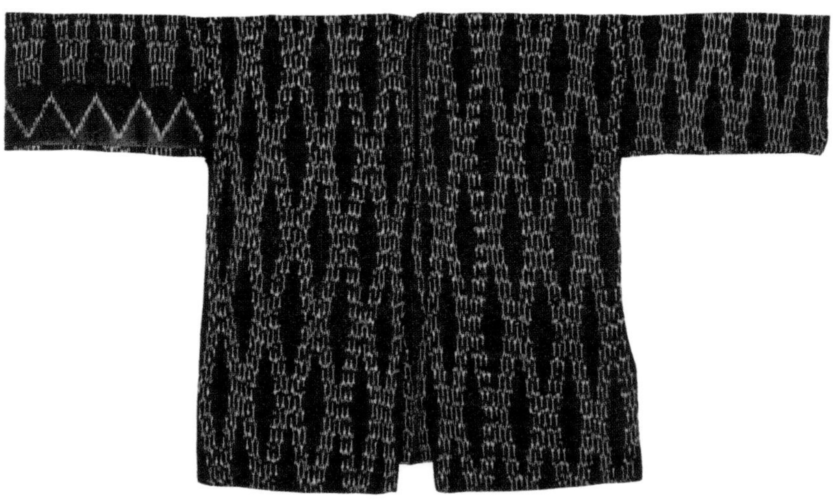

Fig.4

Fig.2
Detail of MA92, Khmer ceremonial hanging, *pidan*

Fig.3
Dans des Khas Kmous (Hou Pahn), Hua Phan Province, Laos, photograph by Alfred Raquez, early 1900s. The Khmu do not weave but acquired handwoven textiles from neighboring ethnic groups such as the Tai Daeng. Male shamans are wearing weft-ikat-decorated skirts woven by Tai Daeng women

Fig.4
MA118, Meifu Li man's jacket

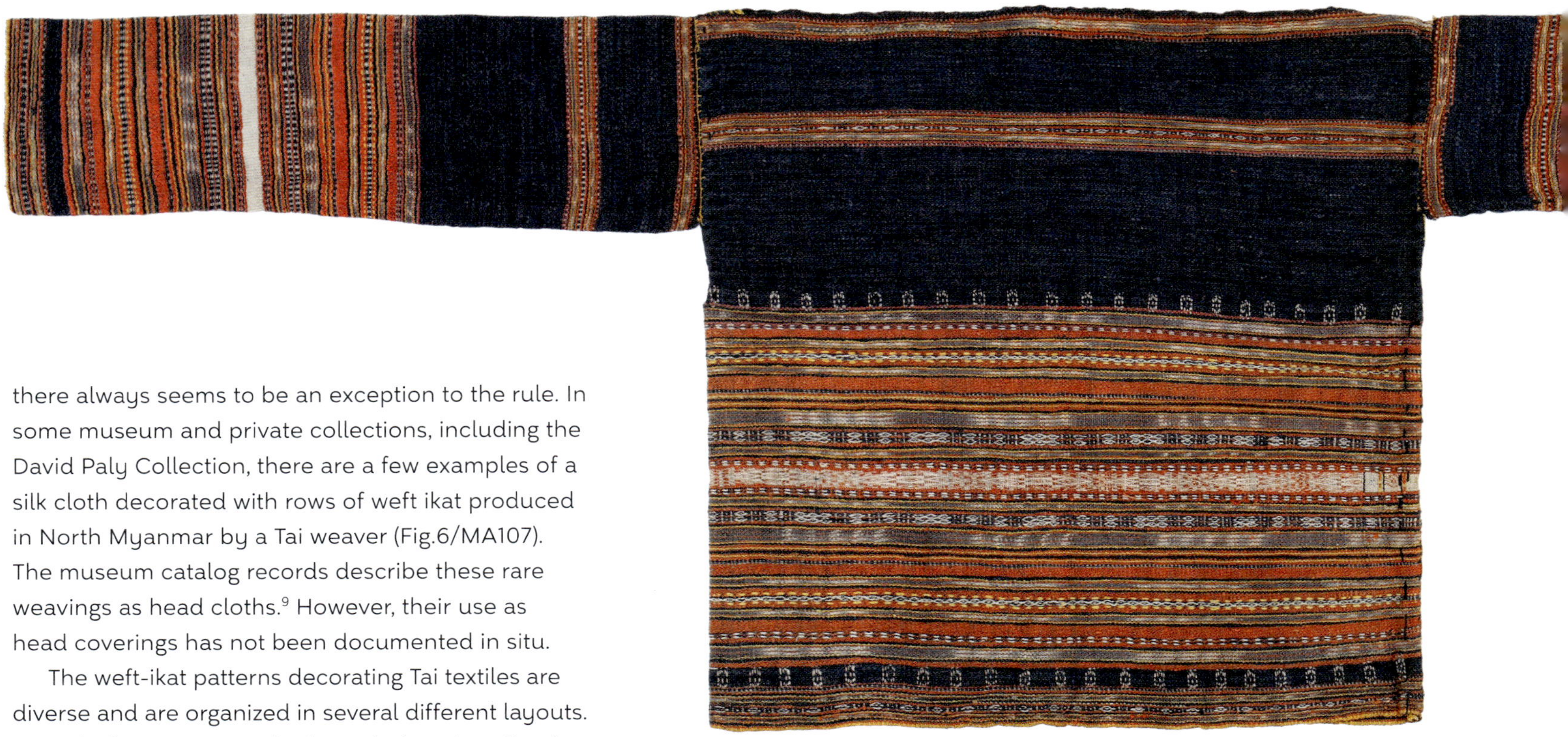

there always seems to be an exception to the rule. In some museum and private collections, including the David Paly Collection, there are a few examples of a silk cloth decorated with rows of weft ikat produced in North Myanmar by a Tai weaver (Fig.6/MA107). The museum catalog records describe these rare weavings as head cloths.[9] However, their use as head coverings has not been documented in situ.

The weft-ikat patterns decorating Tai textiles are diverse and are organized in several different layouts. Mattiebelle Gittinger and other scholars describe the arrangement of designs into rows as being an older form than a full field of ikat, with the latter format assimilated from Indian trade textiles.[10] Generally, weavings made by women from Tai groups originating from North Laos and adjacent areas of Northwest Vietnam, and thus far from the plains of the Mekong River Basin, alternate bands of weft ikat with weft stripes and rows of supplementary-weft patterning (Fig.3). When used as a skirt's midsection for a Tai Daeng or Tai Dam woman, for example, the orientation of the bands is vertical (MA95 and MA97). Some Tai Lue subgroups, especially those residing in present-day Northwest Laos and adjacent areas of North Thailand, also apply the weft-ikat technique to fabric that serves as skirt midsections, but the orientation of the bands of patterning is horizontal. Two panels of material form a Tai Lue woman's midsection, resulting in two seams instead of one.[11]

An exception to this categorization is a skirt with two side seams and a midsection covered with weft-ikat patterning. Lao women residing in east Uttaradit Province, North Thailand, near the Mekong River, weave this distinct skirt style (Fig.1/MA138).[12] Regional trade was active along the Mekong River, and the Nam Pat/Fak Tha area was a trade center; its community was ethnically diverse with Lao, Tai Lue, Tai Yuan, and other groups residing here. Lao weavers in this area have combined characteristics of skirts produced by these groups into one design layout, including having weft-ikat patterning covering the entire midsection.

Lao, Phuthai, and Tai Phuan women living on both sides of the Mekong River produce skirt material

Fig.5

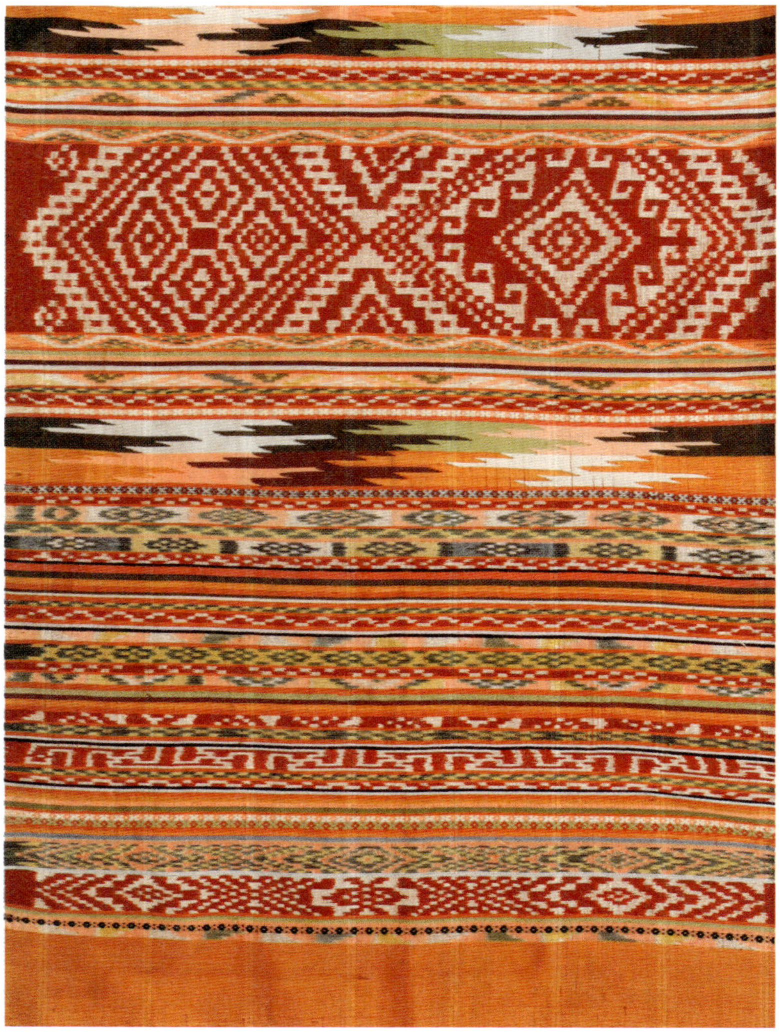

Fig.6

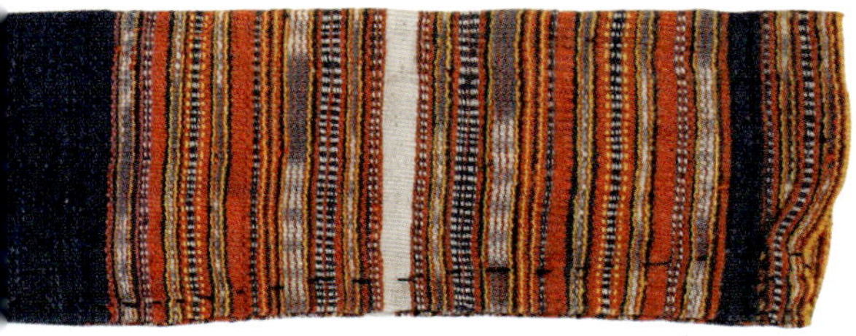

Fig.7

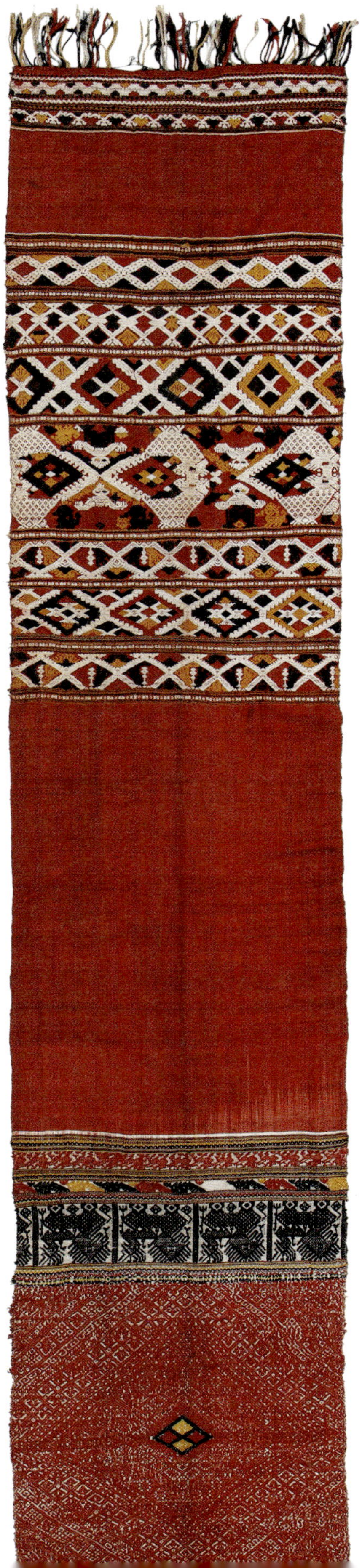

decorated with weft-ikat patterns arranged into two layouts.[13] The older layout resembles the format of skirts described above with thin weft stripes alternating with narrow bands of weft-ikat designs. The design consisting of two-colored weft-ikat dashes symbolizing the tip of sugarcane plants alternating with stripes is associated with Luang Prabang, the former royal center of Laos. This pattern is replicated by the Lao and related Tai groups living along the Mekong River and its tributaries.

The other design layout of skirts woven by Lao and Tai women features weft ikat decorating a cloth's entire surface, a trait considered to have been inspired by the central fields of Indian trade textiles (MA141, MA142 and MA143). The lattice is a recurring pattern that has been customized to have meaning in the weaver's culture. Bodies of intertwining mythical snakes that were confined to bands are expanded to compose a lattice, and hooked appendages radiating from this grid symbolize the snakes' crested heads. Serpent deities have roles as guardians and founders of some Tai groups.

The format of Indian trade textiles is evident in weft-ikat-decorated silk hip wrappers approximately one meter wide and several meters long, acquired by Thai royalty during the Ayutthaya and early Rattanakosin periods. The Thai court ordered *kalamkari* fabrics from India customized with motifs relevant to Thai culture.[14] The layout of the imported textiles was transferred to silks produced by Lao, Khmer, and related groups in present-day Northeast Thailand and Khmer and Cham in Cambodia (MA91 and MA104).[15] Tai weavers in the periphery regions, such as the Tai Daeng, created their versions of these large silks that were reserved for ritual use, for example funerals. The cloth they produced is narrow; thus, a long panel was cut or folded over and sewn together along one side to create a wider textile (MA94 and MA105).[16]

Khmer and Cham women of Cambodia have become accomplished creators of weft-ikat-decorated silk textiles woven in 2:1 twill weave (MA89). As for clothing, this material serves as women's tubular skirts and as hip wrappers for both men and women. Some of these weavings have other purposes. During an ordination ceremony, an applicant to the Buddhist monkhood may wear a hip wrapper decorated with mythical snake patterns. A similarly patterned weaving is hung during this and other rites. Other ceremonial hangings feature the floating offering motif whose shape symbolizes Mount Meru from Buddhist cosmology (MA90). Khmer weavers are also accomplished at creating Buddhist narrative

Fig.5
MA148, Bahnar woman's blouse

Fig.6
Detail of MA107, Tai accessory

Fig.7
Detail of MA101, Tai Daeng shoulder or healing cloth

weavings called *pidan* using the weft-ikat technique and 2:1 twill weave (Fig.2/MA92). These ceremonial cloths serve as canopies over a Buddha statue or as hangings in the interior or exterior of a temple.[17]

A ceremonial textile attributed to Cham production features a unique decoration of resist dyeing of continuous supplementary-weft threads (MA88).[18] Different sections of these threads are dyed a specific color. In the obverse of the textile, different colored, continuous supplementary-weft designs mimicking discontinuous supplementary-weft patterning fill the central area. The reverse side reveals continuous weft floats. This uniquely decorated weaving has ceremonial roles such as a coffin cover or hanging.

The Malay polities of South Thailand, including Pattani, and adjacent states of North Malaysia, such as Kelantan and Terengganu, were active in trade, attracting visitors from the Old and New World. Malay weavers from this area produce distinctive weft-ikat silk textiles that sometimes include zone dyeing (MA82, MA83 and MA84).[19] Whether the weft-ikat designs are organized into bands or spread across a textile's midsection, the long columns of patterning that flank the central fields of imported Indian textiles are absent in these Malay weavings. Rows of weft ikat designs are adjacent to the top and bottom ends of the midsection. The textiles from these three Malay principalities, now states or provinces, are similar, but weavings from Terengganu are darker than cloths produced in Kelantan and Pattani (MA71).

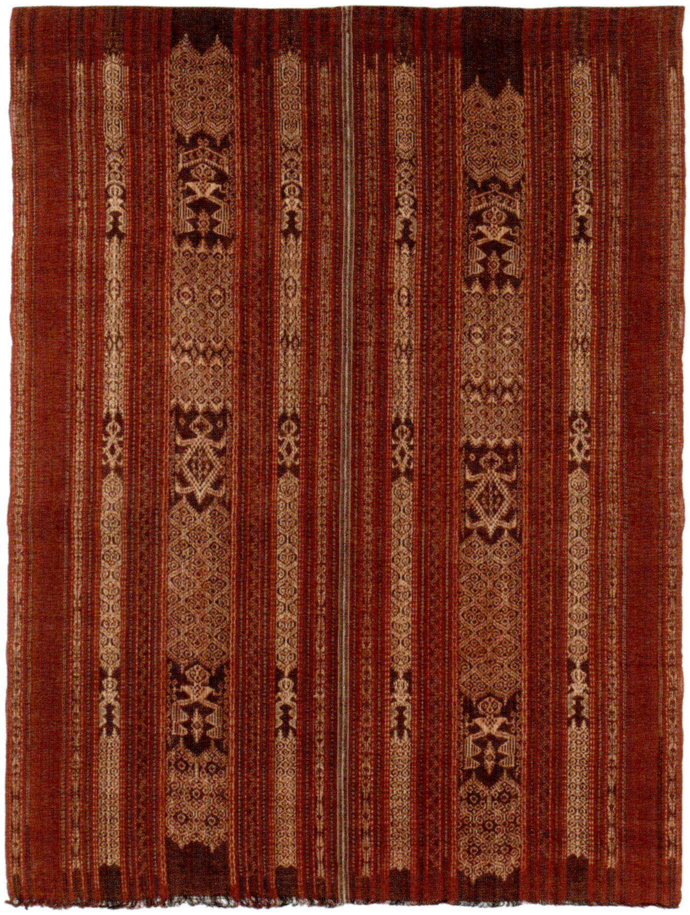

Fig.8

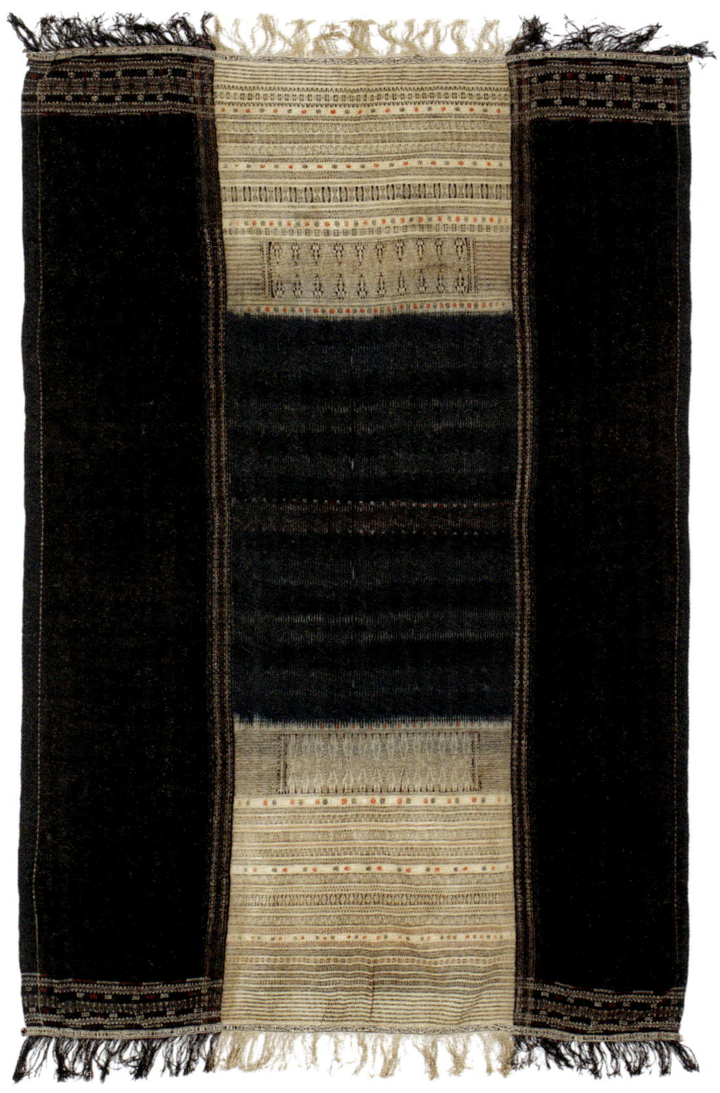

Fig.9

Insular Monsoon Asia

The majority of the peoples of Insular Monsoon Asia speak an Austronesian language, and the use of warp ikat is widespread among ethnic groups from the Malayo-Polynesian branch of this ethnolinguistic family. The application of this technique occurred on bast fibers before the introduction of cotton to Island Southeast Asia. Some ethnic groups in the Philippines, such as the Bagobo, Blaan, and Tboli, continue to apply this technique to abaca or threads made from banana plants. The Bagobo people consider warp-ikat-decorated abaca to be the most appropriate material for ceremonial clothing and ritual gifts, positioning these textiles as high-status items (MA127).[20]

The use of various resist-dye techniques occurs throughout the Philippines. Textiles of the Ifugao from the Cordillera region in the north and Bagobo, Blaan, and Tboli of Mindanao Island in the south, feature bands of warp-ikat patterning. The weavers' social and natural environments inspire patterning. The horse motif recurs in Ifugao warp ikat (MA134) while the crocodile is a popular pattern among the Blaan, Bagobo, Mandaya, and Tboli (Fig.8/MA131). Women from these three ethnic groups also apply *plangi* and *tritik* resist-dye techniques to decorate abaca cloth. The Maranao people who also reside on Mindanao Island were active in regional trade, and women wove silk textiles decorated with weft ikat, sometimes with supplementary-weft patterning. Indian *patola*, such as the

Fig.8
MA131, Mandaya woman's sarong

Fig.9
MA31, Toba Batak ritual cloth, *ulos*

Fig.10
Welcome party, Lamaholot people, Pamakayo Village, Solor Island, Indonesia, photograph by Linda S. McIntosh, 2019

Fig.11
Detail of MA86, Iban ritual textile, *pua kumbu*

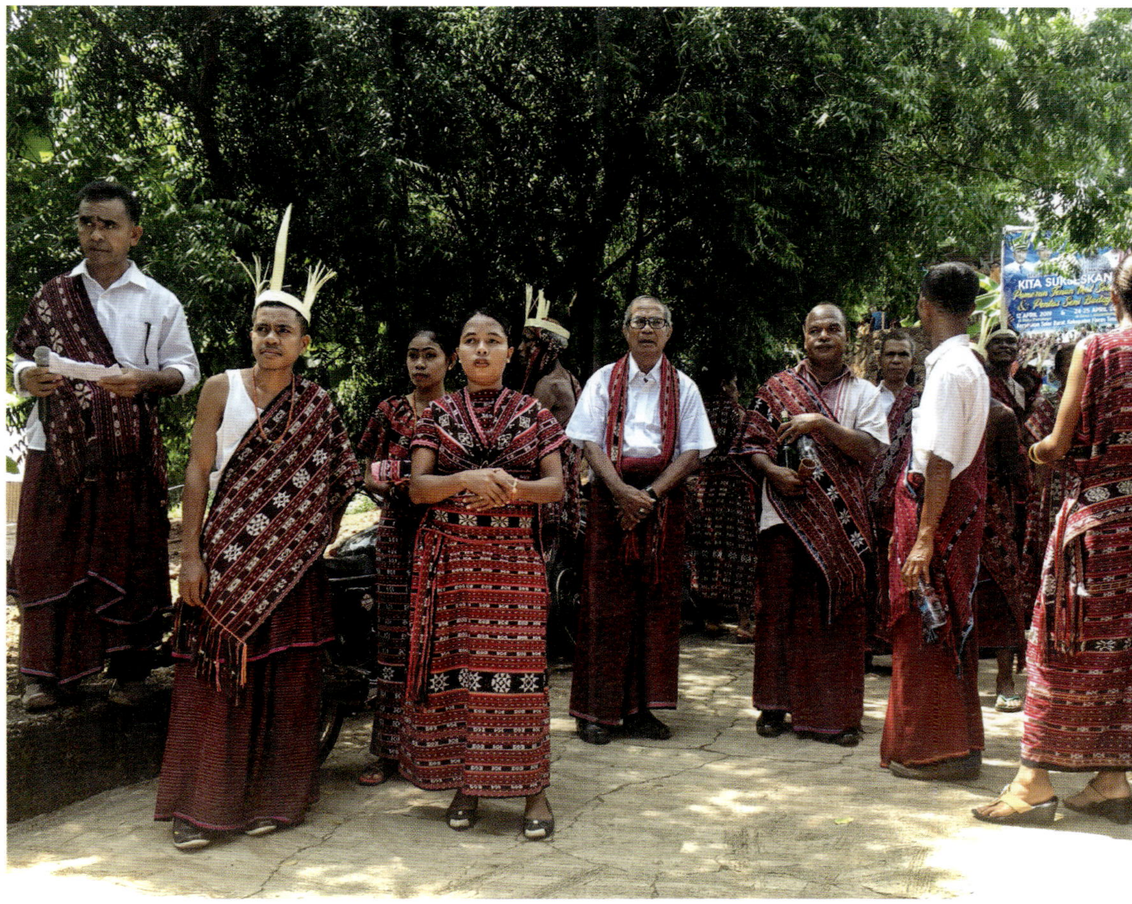

Fig.10

Fig.11

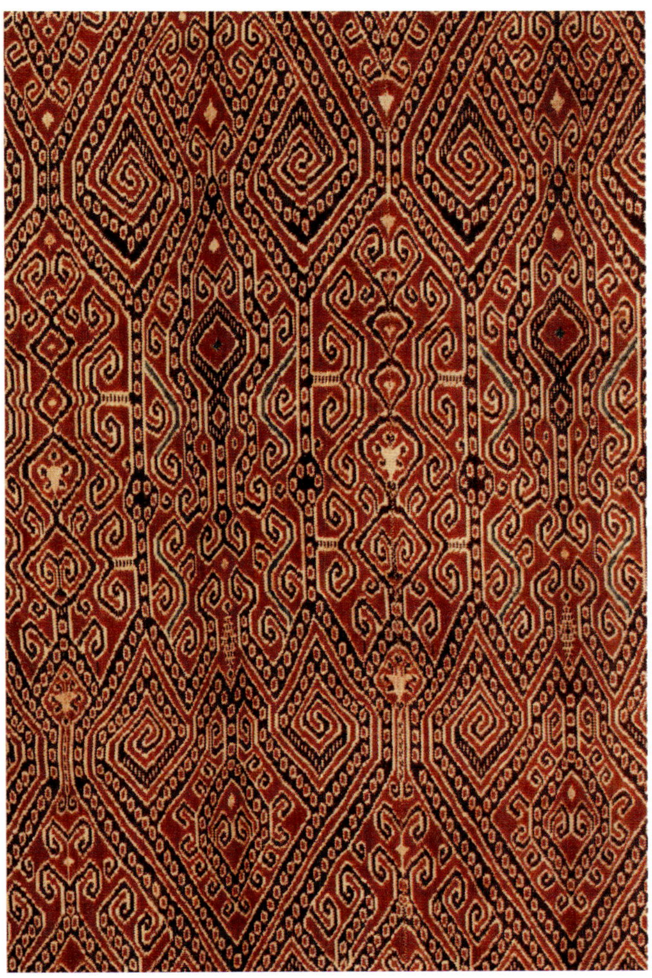

patolu chabadi bhat, provided some inspiration for designs decorating ceremonial skirts (MA128 and MA129).[21]

Borneo Island, which composes the territory of three countries, possesses a similar dichotomy in the textiles produced by groups living in coastal lowlands and the uplands of the interior. The warp-ikat-decorated cotton weavings of the Iban of the interior of Sarawak, Malaysia, and the related Kantu' or Kantuk of the highlands of West Kalimantan, Indonesia, serve as ritual items and attire (Fig.11/MA86). The advanced skills of a woman from one of these Ibanic subgroups creating the ritual weavings are compared to the prowess of a warrior (MA72).[22] New weavers and veteran weavers resting after producing a spiritually powerful textile create skirt material whose patterning lacks supernatural potency (MA70).

Buckley's "Ikat Line" delineates the use of various loom types and ikat techniques in Indonesia.[23] Indonesia's western region is dominated by weft ikat woven on backstrap looms. These weavings are composed of cotton, silk, and previously bast fiber. The addition of a reed allows silk to be woven on a body-tension loom. Ethnic groups falling in the Malay cultural sphere of Sumatra, the Indonesian part of Borneo, and neighboring islands such as Riau weave weft-ikat silks that serve as both upper and lower garments. Untailored textiles function as upper garments including shawls, shoulder cloths, and head coverings (MA27). A rectangular cloth may also be worn as a hip wrapper or sewn into a tubular skirt. The layout

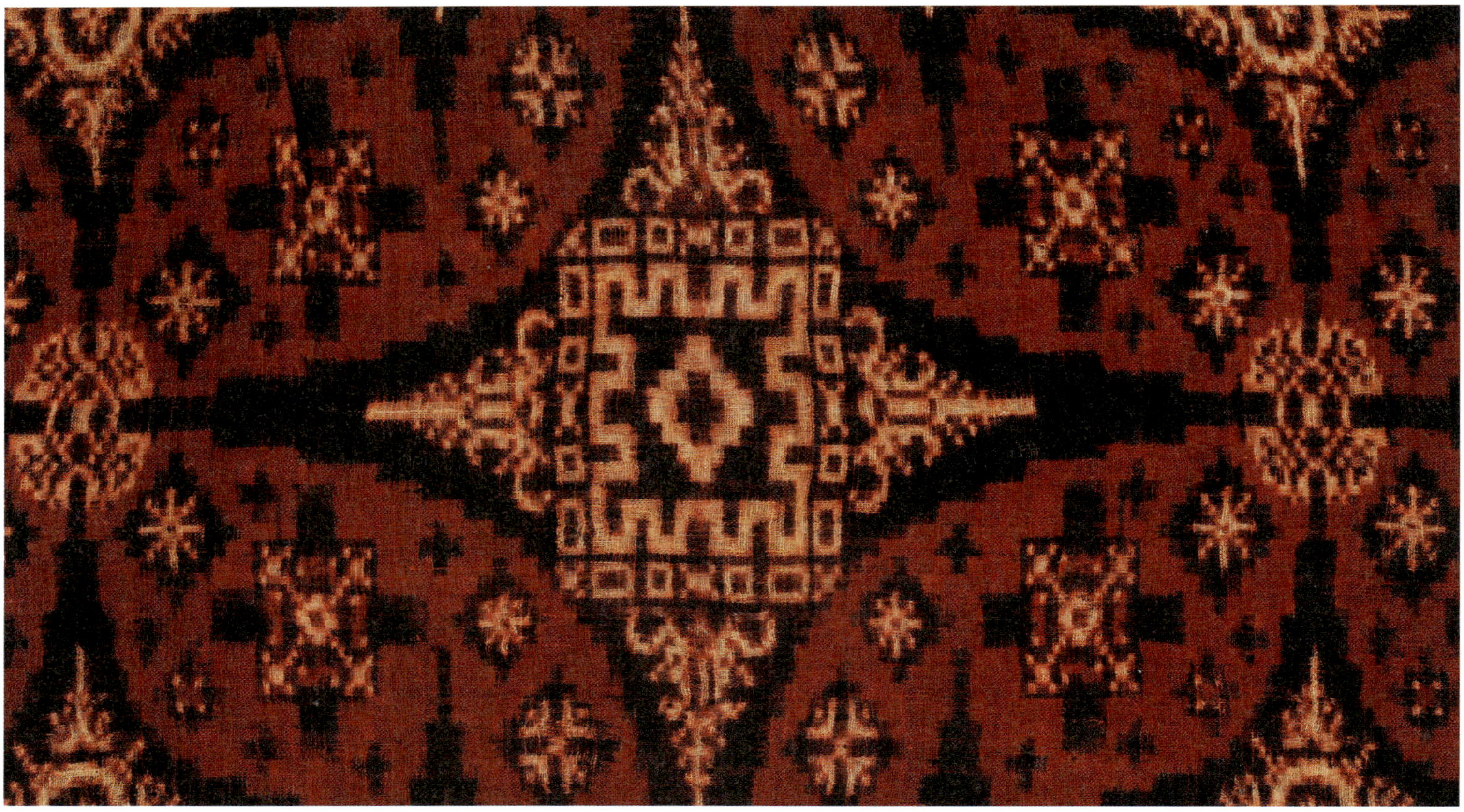

Fig.12

of a central field surrounded by bands of patterning recurs on the textiles made in Palembang and Komering of South Sumatra and nearby areas such as Bangka Island (MA17).

Weft-ikat-decorated cloth or *endek* has become an identifying cultural marker of the Balinese (Fig.13/MA11).[24] This material was reserved for royalty and nobility until Bali became part of the Dutch East Indies colony in the early 20th century. Hindu iconography joins designs inspired by Indian trade textiles, especially *patola*, on Balinese *endek* (MA11 and MA12). The Balinese consider *patola* and locally woven, ritual textiles decorated with weft-ikat patterns inspired by *patola*, or *cepuk*, to possess healing powers. Both types of textile were preserved as heirlooms and worn as ceremonial attire at court. *Cepuk* woven in Bali were primarily composed of silk, but examples produced in the small island of Nusa Penida off the south coast of Bali were woven in cotton (MA08 and MA10).

The Bali Aga village Tenganan Pegeringsingan is the only locale in Bali and the entirety of Indonesia that produces a cotton textile decorated with the double-ikat technique or the *geringsing* (Fig.12/MA13). Different categories of this loosely woven cloth exist, and criteria include designs and size of the woven fabric. *Geringsing* weavings serve as ceremonial attire of the Bali Aga people and as components of ritual offerings. Some examples presented to the former Balinese courts in the past have embroidered ends. This embellishment was added after the textiles arrived at one of these courts (MA16).

The older design format consisting of ikat designs confined to bands is found in the highland areas of West Indonesia such as in North Sumatra. Toba Batak women excel at textile production (Fig.9/MA31) for use within their group and to trade with other Batak subgroups. Warp-ikat designs fill columns decorating different types of *ulos* or fringed weavings serving as men's and women's clothing and ritual gifts. This format is absent in some textiles woven in the interior of South Sumatra such as Pasemah or Komering.[25] The midsection of textiles from this area may be covered with weft-ikat designs without columns of patterning flanking the selvages (MA26), or the weft-ikat patterns are arranged in rows.

The layout of different-sized bands of warp-ikat designs on cotton permeates throughout the eastern islands of Indonesia or Nusa Tenggara Timur and Maluku (MA64 and MA65). Both the seas and the geography of the islands (including volcanos and mountain chains) separated the settlements on these islands. The seas, however, also connected people residing on these islands and brought others originating from afar to their shores. Many of these outsiders were traders who supplied glass beads, metal items, and textiles to exchange for the region's natural resources, such as spices, sandalwood, and marine life.

Both the Ngada and Lio peoples live in the central region of Flores Island, but they have developed distinct cultural traits including language and textiles. Ngada textiles feature two-color warp ikat in dark, almost black, indigo and white (MA07). The horse is a symbol of wealth and prestige, and its likeness decorates both Ngada and Lio textiles.[26] Weavings made by Lio women also feature motifs inspired by their natural and social environments, and some weavers have incorporated designs originating from Indian trade textiles. Although elephants do not exist in Flores, their form is represented as a Lio warp-ikat pattern. The *chabadi bhat* motif from *patola* decorates textiles worn by high-status Lio

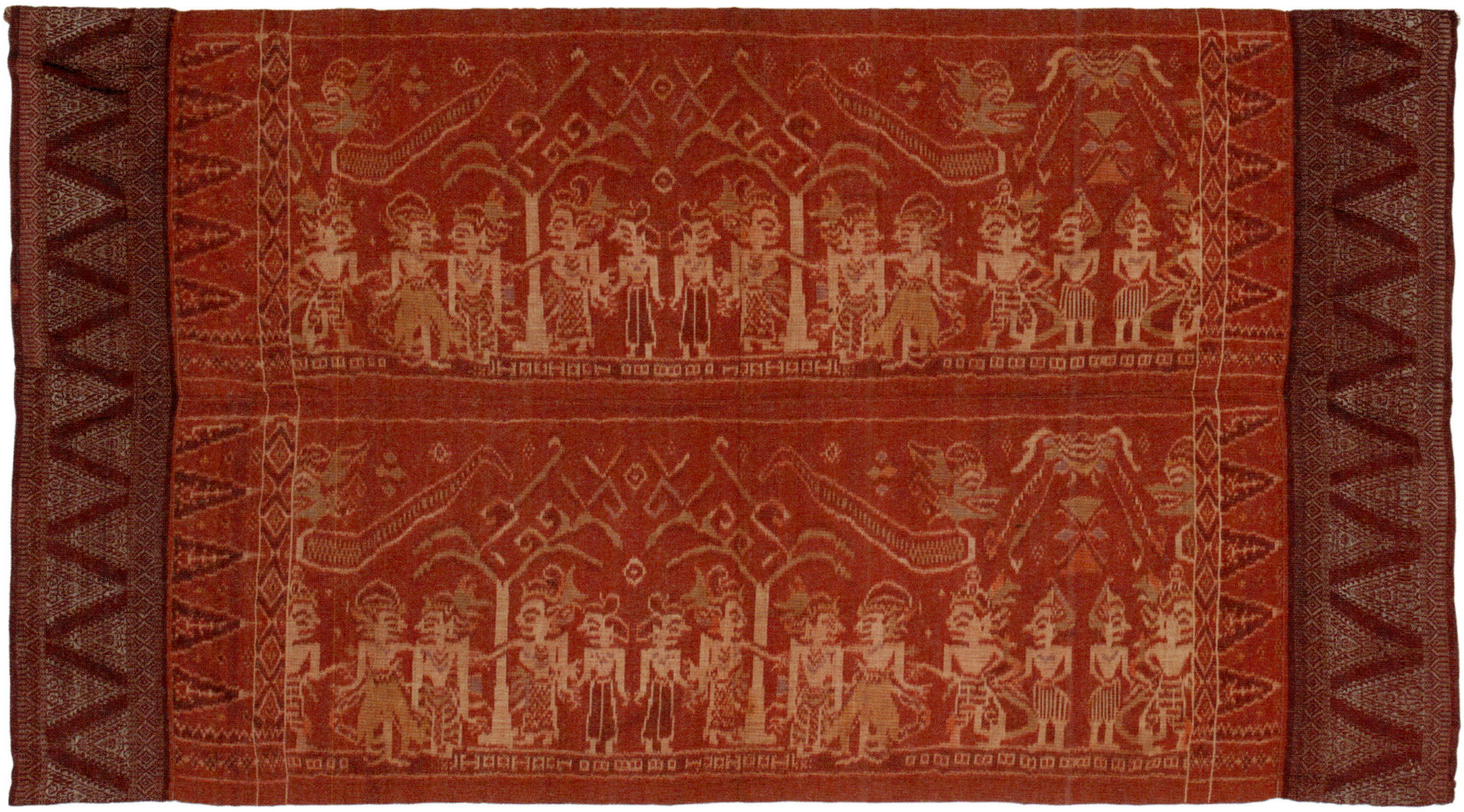

Fig.13

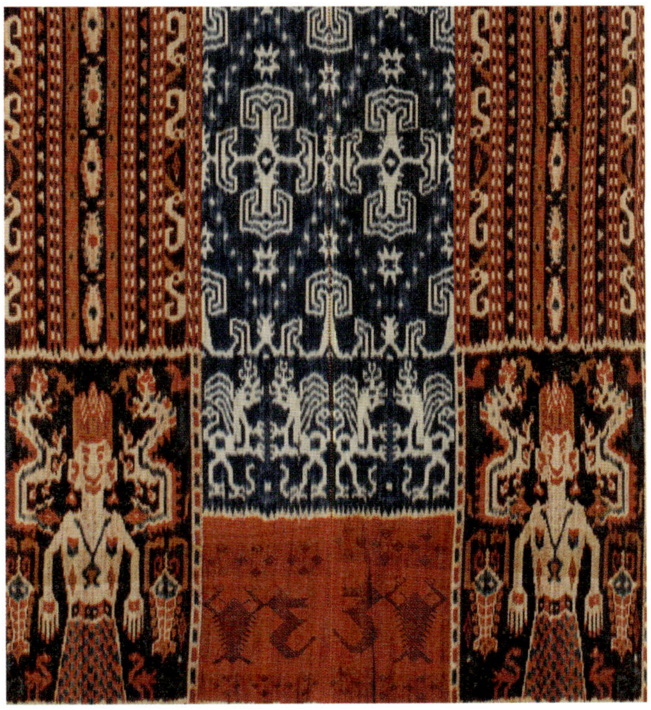

Fig.14

Fig.12
Detail of MA13, Bali Aga ritual cloth, *geringsing*

Fig.13
MA11, Man's outer hip wrapper, *saput endek*

Fig.14
Detail of MA60, man's shawl or hip wrapper, *hinggi kombu*

men and women. The *luka semba* shawl worn by esteemed Lio males also features this prestigious motif in a central field surrounded by rows and bands of other warp-ikat patterns (MA01, MA05 and MA06).[27] Both cultures preserve examples of weavings with high-status designs as sacred heirlooms.

Textiles produced by other ethnic groups in Eastern Indonesia also combine indigenous patterns of hooked lozenges, reptiles, and aquatic life with imported ones (Fig.14/MA60). Weavers have produced new design layouts to create their versions of central fields flanked by bands of patterning. Some two- and three-paneled skirts consist of a midsection decorated with a repeating pattern such as different forms of lattices that decorate the central field of *patola* (MA46 and MA69). Designs originating from these and other imported textiles also fill some of the bands. Shawls woven by Rotenese women consist of two types: one with columns of warp-ikat patterning and another featuring the central field of a repeating pattern such as flowering scrolls or the *chabadi bhat* motif.

Local production of textiles resembling Indian trade textiles, whether in design layout or designs, expanded when access to these was limited. The communities also held these locally woven fabrics in high regard. Textiles woven in the older format, or bands filled with motifs inspired by a weaver's immediate social and natural environment, still have value in the community (Fig.10). Both types can exist in one ethnic group's textile repertoire, while in another one kind dominates, sometimes completely.

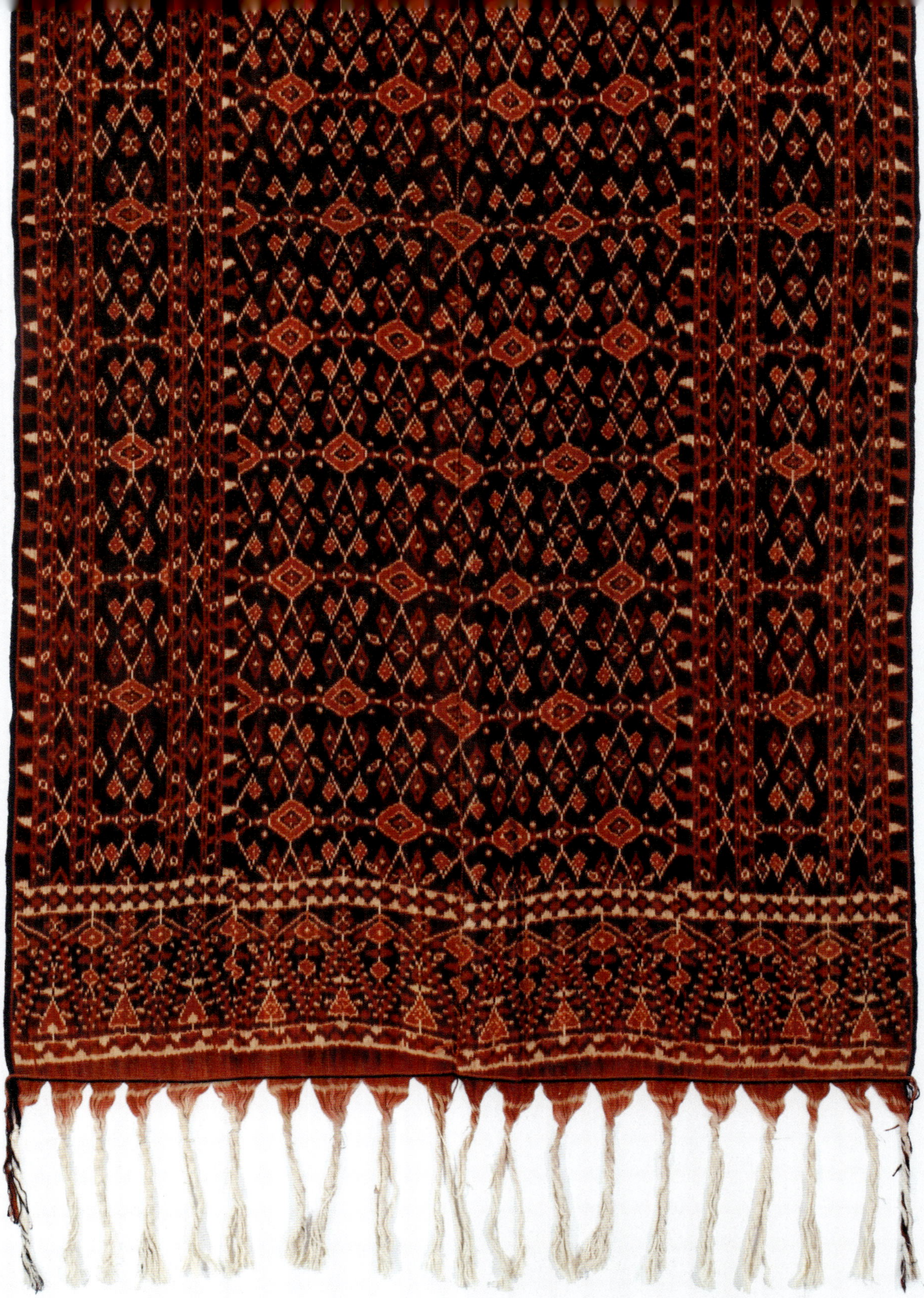

MA01 Shoulder cloth/shawl, *luka semba*, Lio ethnic group, Flores, Indonesia, 20th century. Cotton, warp ikat. 84 in x 31 in

The use of this garment was the prerogative of a respected Lio man, usually an elder sitting on a village's council. Some settlements have preserved examples as sacred heirlooms after the weavings were presented as offerings to guardian or ancestor spirits. According to traditional societal rules, Lio women residing in coastal settlements are able to weave, but Lio women living inland are forbidden to weave. Lio weavers utilize a backstrap loom to produce cloth, which is typical for Insular Indonesia. The dark-brown shade was produced from multiple rounds of dyeing with morinda roots, and black was created from overdyeing indigo with morinda. It could take years to achieve these rich colors. The repeating motif in its central field was inspired by patterns decorating the same section of the *patolu chabadi bhat* originating from Gujarat, India. Another design also found at the ends of *patola* comprises the triangular shapes decorating this textile's ends. The overall design format was inspired by Indian trade textiles with a central field and bands of ikat in varying sizes flanking each of its sides.

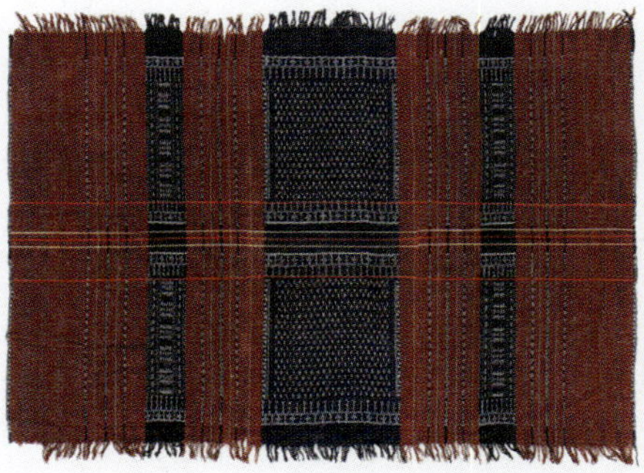

MA02 Nage Keo woman's sarong, *hoba pojo*
Flores, Indonesia, 20th century. Cotton, warp ikat.
45 in x 82 in

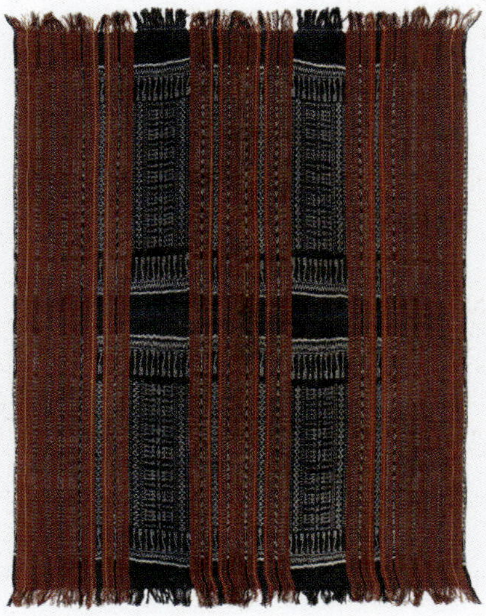

MA03 Nage Keo woman's sarong, *hoba pojo*
Flores, Indonesia, 20th century. Cotton, warp ikat.
72 in x 56 in

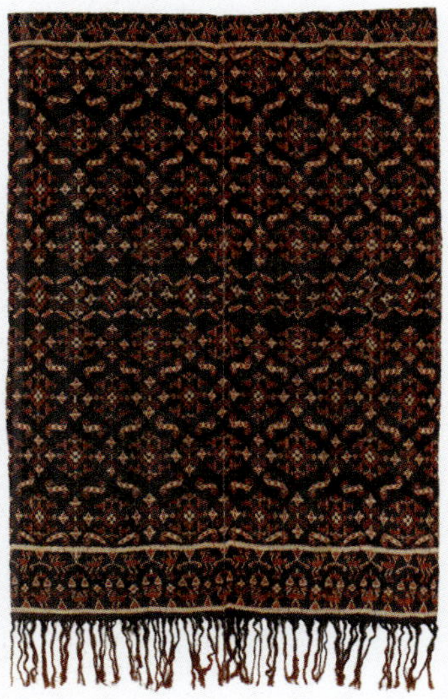

MA04 Endeh man's shawl
Flores, Indonesia, 20th century. Cotton, warp ikat.
72 in x 44 in

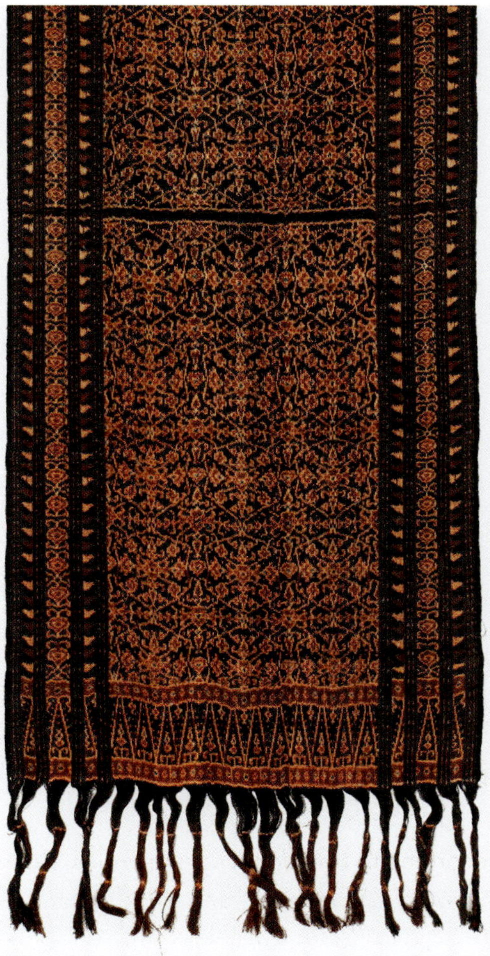

MA05 Lio man's shawl, *luka semba*
Flores, Indonesia, 20th century. Cotton, warp ikat. 80 in x 27 in

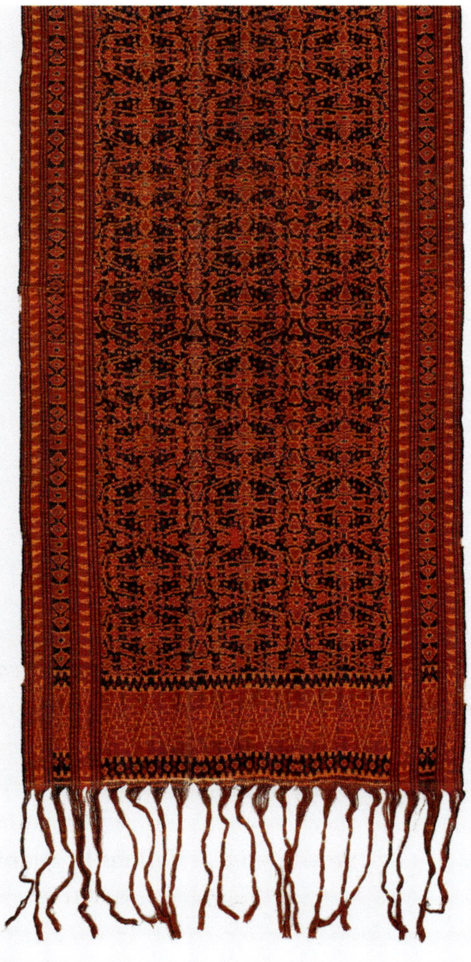

MA06 Lio man's shawl, *luka semba*
Flores, Indonesia, 20th century. Cotton, warp ikat. 84 in x 31 in

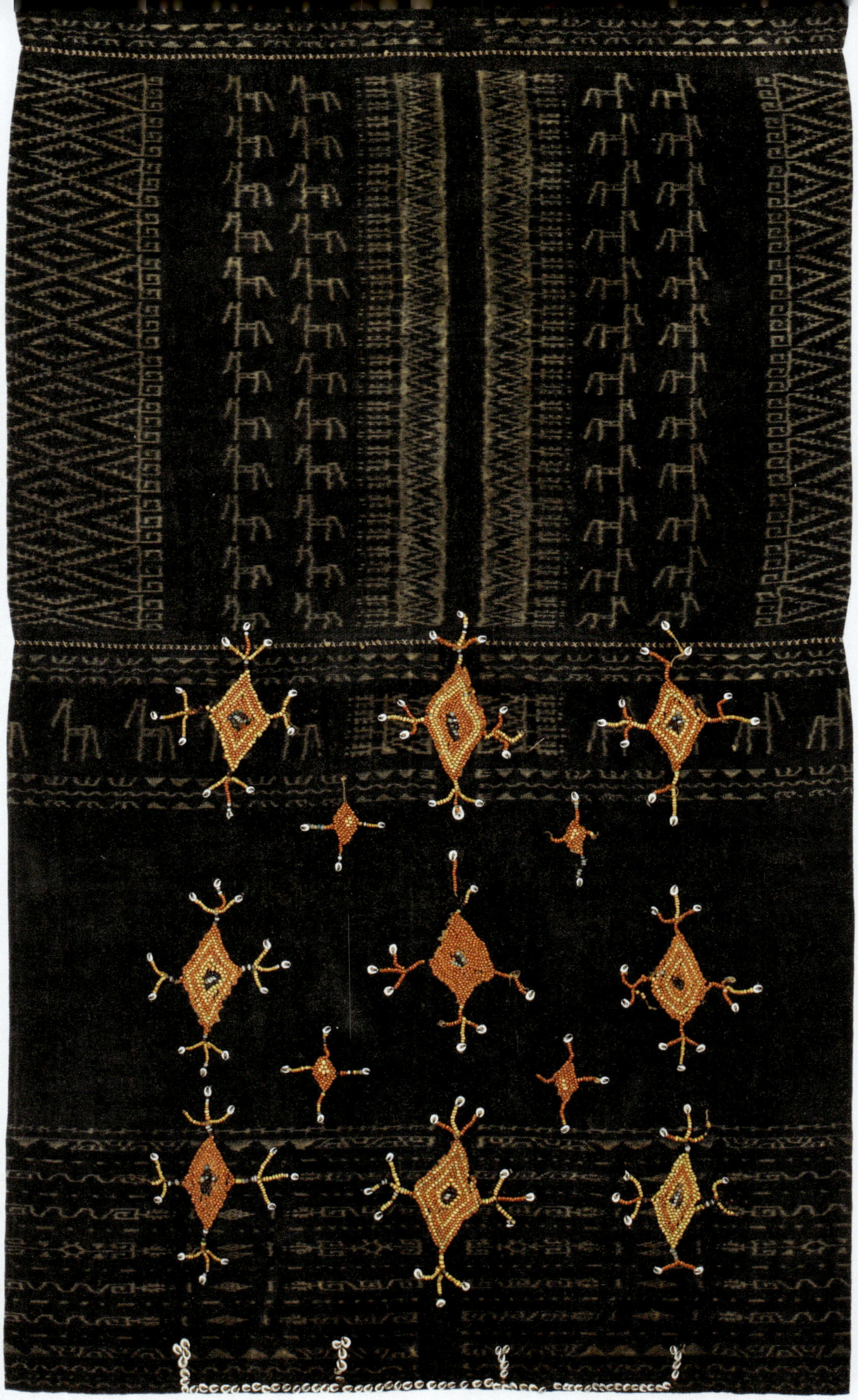

MA07 Woman's ceremonial skirt and sacred heirloom, *lawo butu*, Ngada ethnic group, Flores, Indonesia, 19th century. Cotton, glass beads, seashells, warp ikat, appliqué. 72 in x 31 in

The cotton textiles of the Ngada people living in the interior of Central Flores are dyed multiple times with indigo to create a deep blue, almost black, color. The top and bottom of this *lawo butu* have the same warp-ikat patterning confined to narrow rows. The most prominent band of warp ikat, located near the sides abutting the central section, contains designs of horses (*jara*), a form of wealth in local society. Connecting diamond shapes, which to some signify women's gold earrings, join the patterns of horses in the middle section. The bottom end is embellished with the appliqué of imported glass beads and seashells. A high-status Ngada woman, a woman who was of mature age and had helped her husband sponsor specific ceremonies or feasts of merit, wore this garment for the most sacred rituals. Some *lawo butu* were produced specifically to serve as heirlooms and not to be worn.

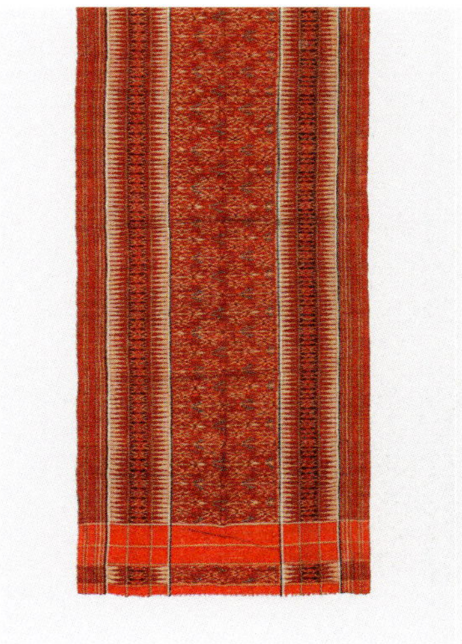

MA08 Ritual cloth, *cepuk*
Nusa Penida, Bali, Indonesia, 20th century. Cotton, weft ikat. 88 in x 31 in

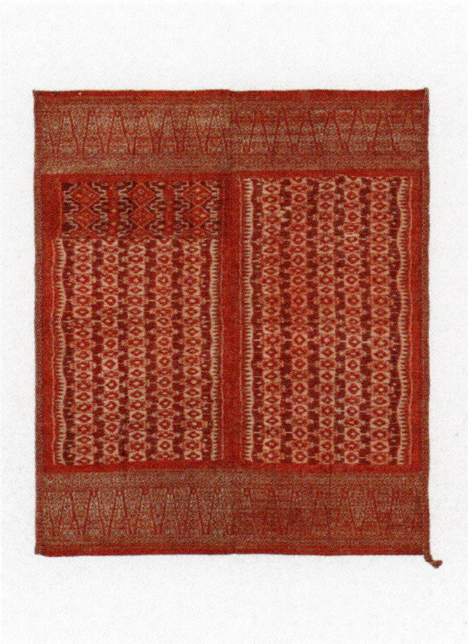

MA09 Man's outer hip wrapper, *saput endek*
Bali, Indonesia, early 20th century. Silk, weft ikat, metallic continuous supplementary weft. 56 in x 50 in

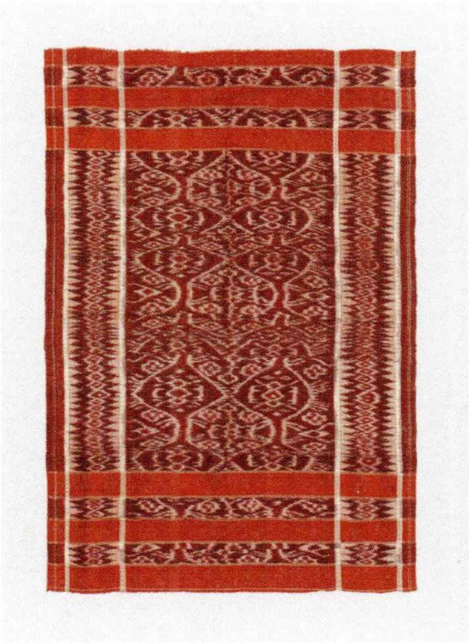

MA10 Ritual cloth, *cepuk*
Nusa Penida, Bali, Indonesia, 20th century. Cotton, weft ikat. 44 in x 30 in

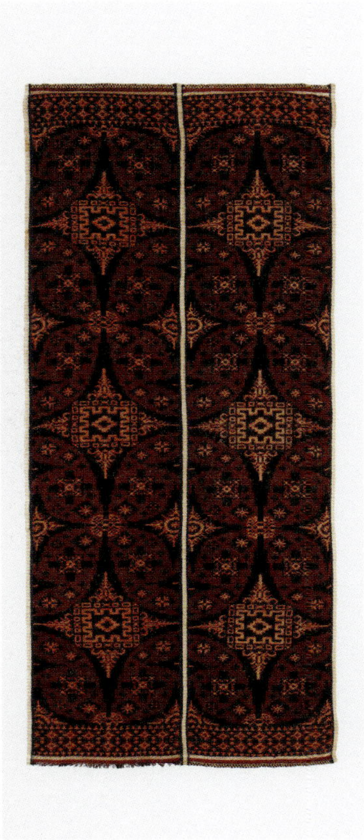

MA13 Bali Aga ritual cloth, *geringsing*
Tenganan Pegringsingan, Bali, Indonesia, early 20th century. Cotton, double ikat. 73 in x 31 in

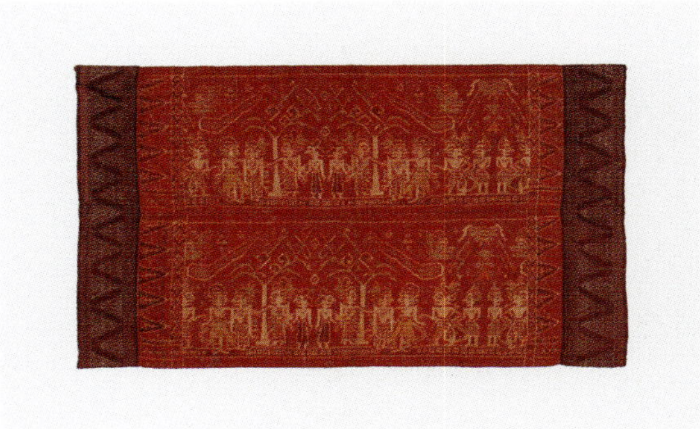

MA11 Man's outer hip wrapper, *saput endek*
Bali, Indonesia, late 19th or early 20th century. Silk, weft ikat, metallic supplementary weft. 77 in x 42 in

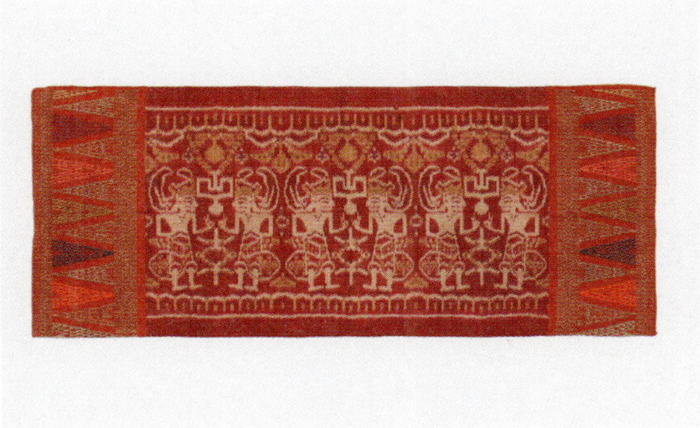

MA12 Man's outer hip wrapper, *saput endek*
Bali, Indonesia, early 20th century. Silk, weft ikat, metallic supplementary weft. 50 in x 20 in

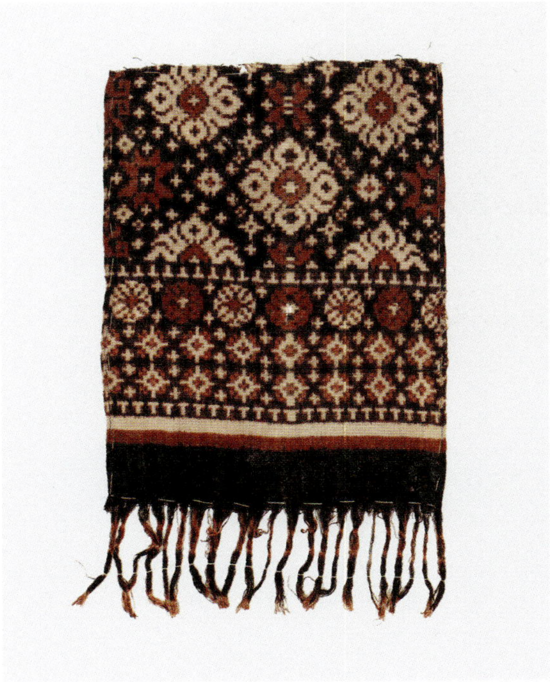

MA14 Bali Aga ritual cloth (*geringsing*) fragment
Tenganan Pegringsingan, Bali, Indonesia, early 20th century. Cotton, double ikat. 11 in x 17 in

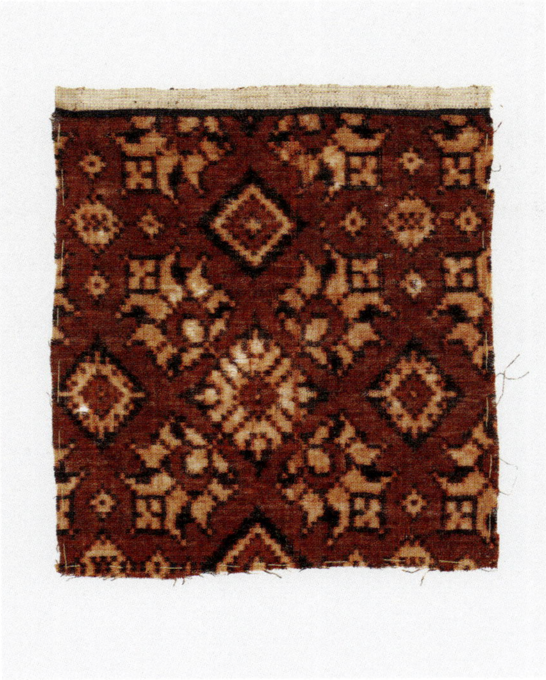

MA15 Bali Aga ritual cloth (*geringsing*) fragment
Tenganan Pegringsingan, Bali, Indonesia, early 20th century. Cotton, double ikat. 11 in x 12 in

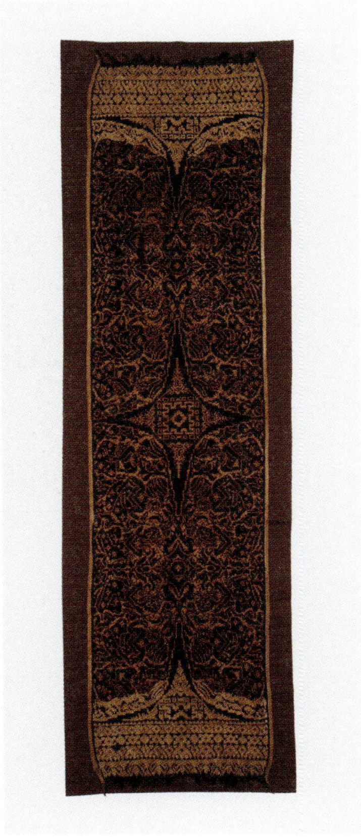

MA16 Bali Aga ritual cloth, *geringsing wayang*
Tenganan Pegringsingan, Bali, Indonesia, 19th century. Cotton, double ikat, metallic supplementary weft. 80 in x 20 in

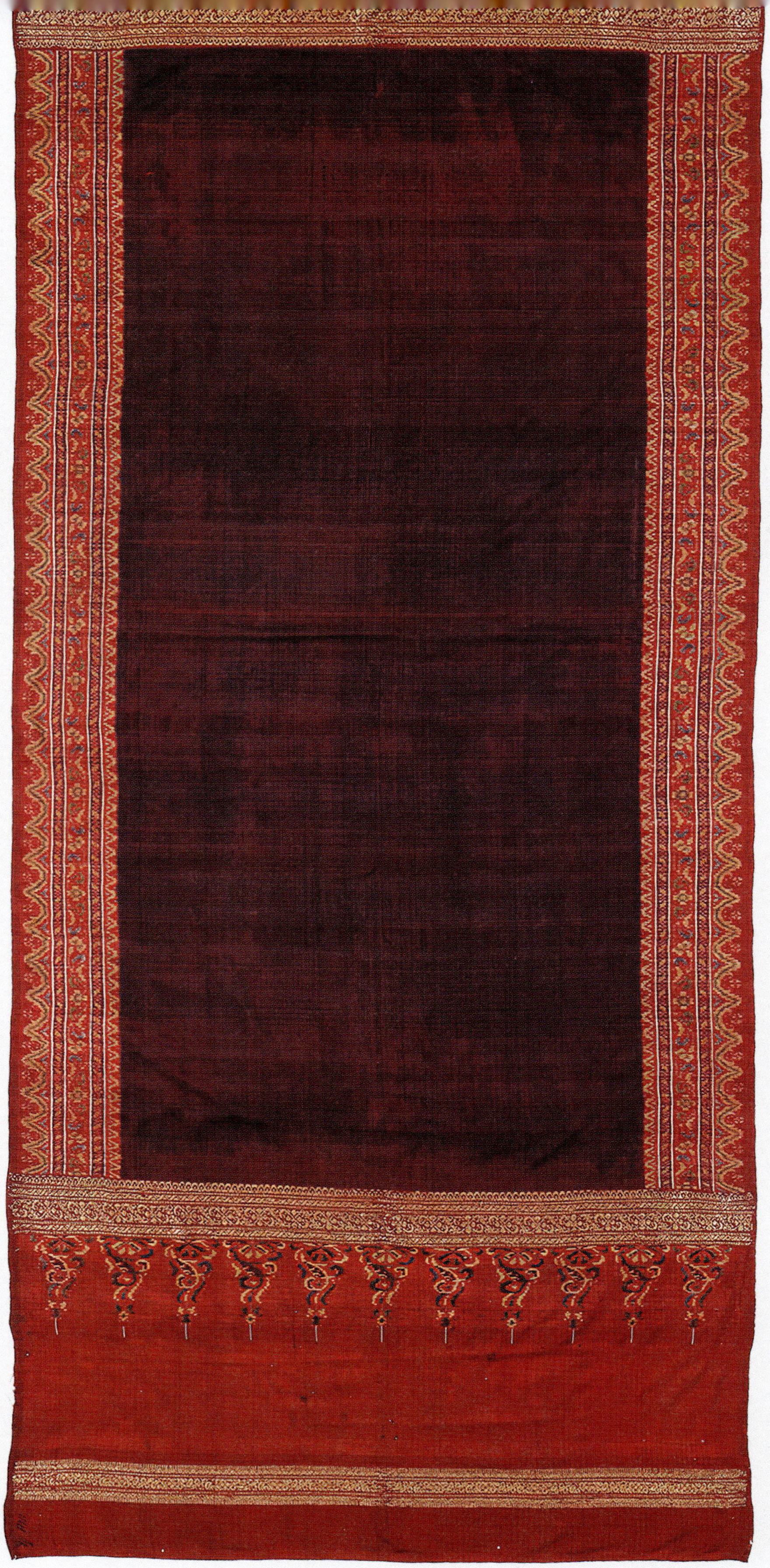

MA17 Shawl/head cloth, *selendang janda beraes*, Malay ethnic group, South Sumatra, Indonesia, 19th century. Silk, gold metal-wrapped threads, weft ikat, continuous supplementary weft. 84 in x 35 in

Malay weft-ikat textiles generally feature a design layout of a central field surrounded by bands of ikat patterns on all four sides that is similar to the design format of Indian trade textiles. The center section usually contains a repeating design, but this textile's middle area is a solid color lacking any distinctive patterning. The weaver applied weft-ikat technique to create this "plain" section and the designs of the bands parallel to the selvages. A row of continuous supplementary weft in gold metal threads or *songket* flanks the middle section's top and bottom ends. A row of triangular-shaped weft-ikat patterns fills a row on the other side of the *songket* band. Some publications state that a central field bereft of designs indicated that the wearer was a widow coming out of mourning.

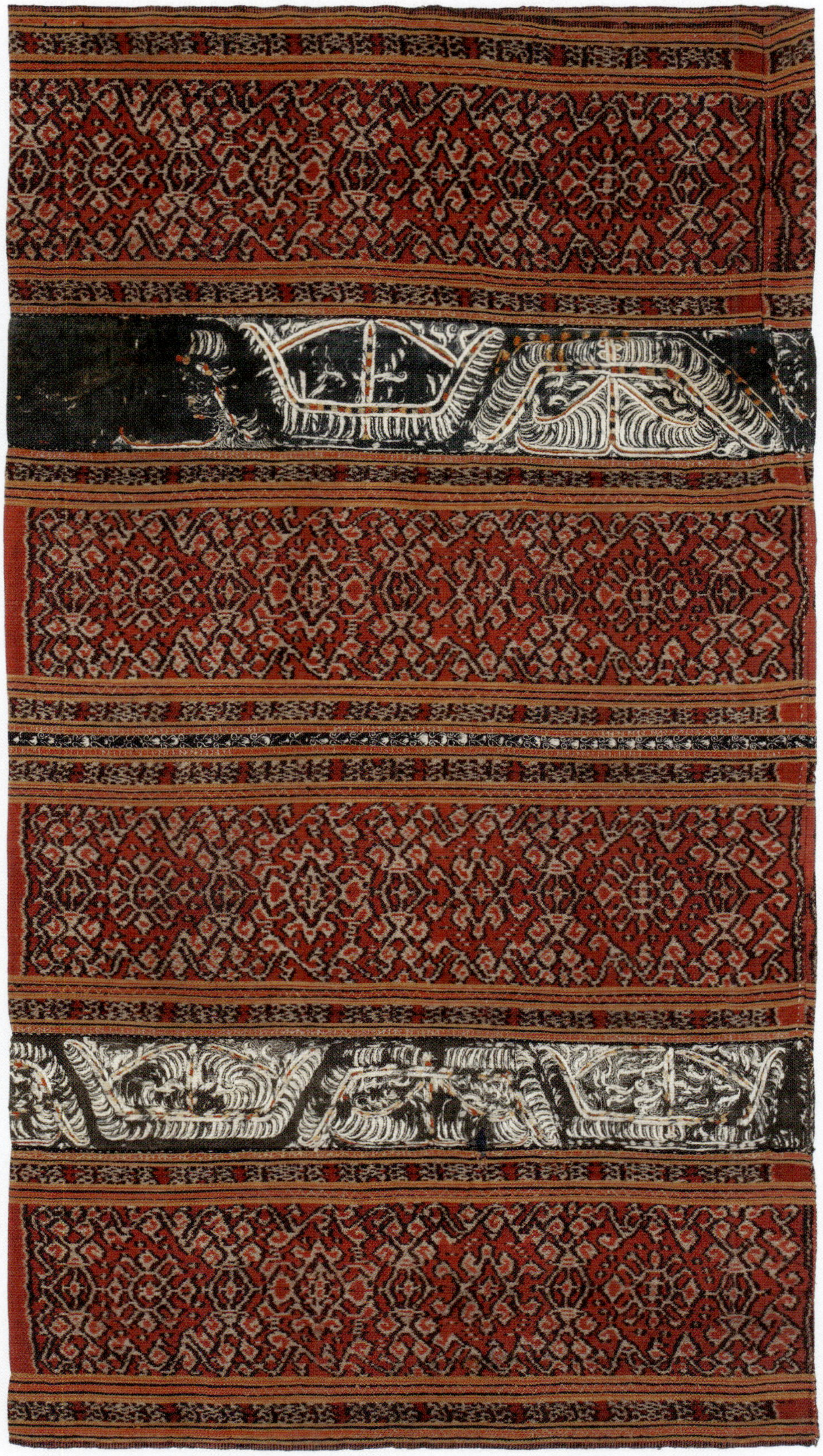

MA18 Woman's ceremonial skirt, *tapis merah*, Paminggir or Komering ethnic group, Lampung, South Sumatra, Indonesia, 18th century. Cotton, silk, warp ikat, embroidery. 45 in x 26 in

The Paminggir founded their settlements along the coast of the southern tip of Sumatra Island, and their location on a maritime route led to exposure to different cultures as religious men and traders sailed past between South and East Asia. This *tapis merah*, literally red skirt, is composed of several panels of warp-ikat-decorated cloth and two panels embroidered with imported silk. The embroidery is worn, but the imagery resembles ceremonial structures on boats or raft-like platforms. Different types of patterning decorate *tapis merah*, but this garment's warp ikat designs emulate Indian trade textile patterns. The motif has been likened to the *geringsing lubang* double-ikat-decorated textile from Bali.

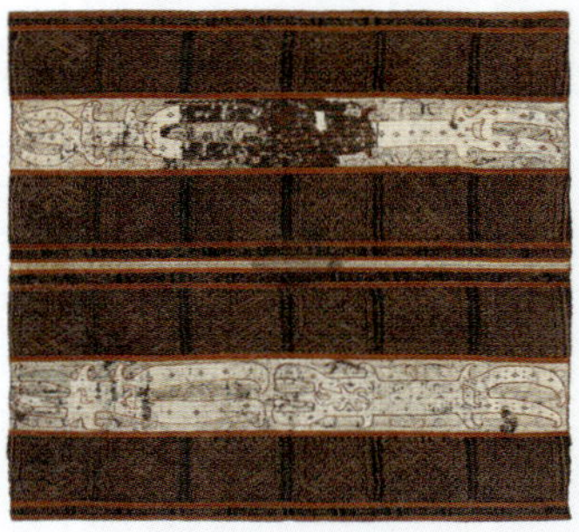

MA19 Woman's sarong, *tapis inuh* Lampung, South Sumatra, Indonesia, early 19th century. Cotton, silk, warp ikat, embroidery. 49 in x 44 in

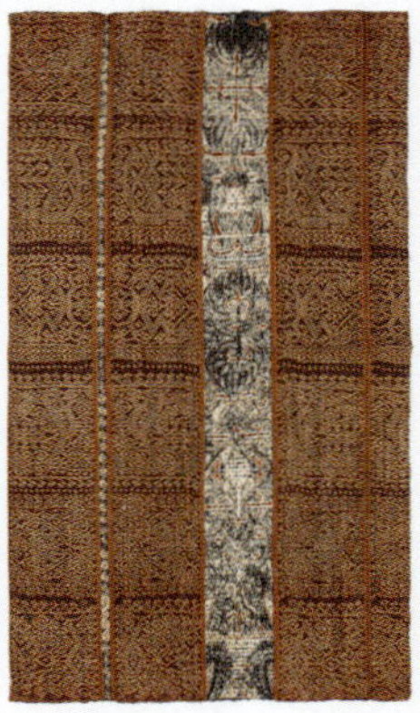

MA20 Fragment of woman's sarong, *tapis merah* Lampung, South Sumatra, Indonesia, late 18th or early 19th century. Cotton, silk, warp ikat, embroidery. 51 in x 30 in

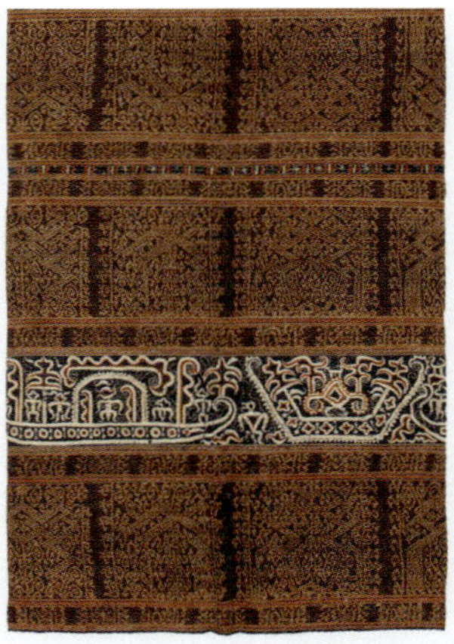

MA21 Woman's sarong, *tapis merah* Lampung, South Sumatra, Indonesia, 19th century. Cotton, silk, warp ikat, embroidery. 51 in x 25 in

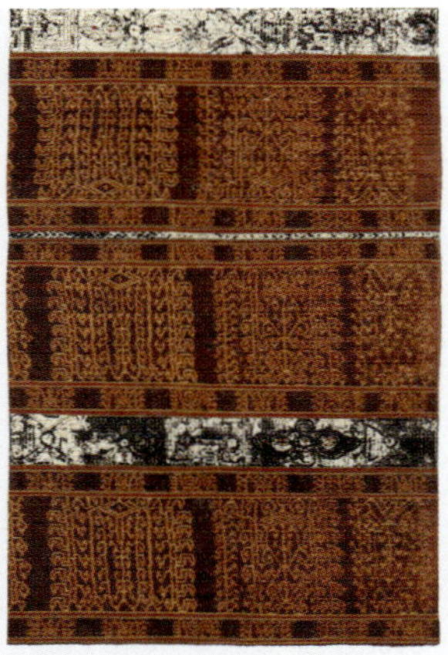

MA22 Woman's sarong, *tapis merah* Lampung, South Sumatra, Indonesia, early 19th century. Cotton, silk, warp ikat, embroidery. 48 in x 26 in

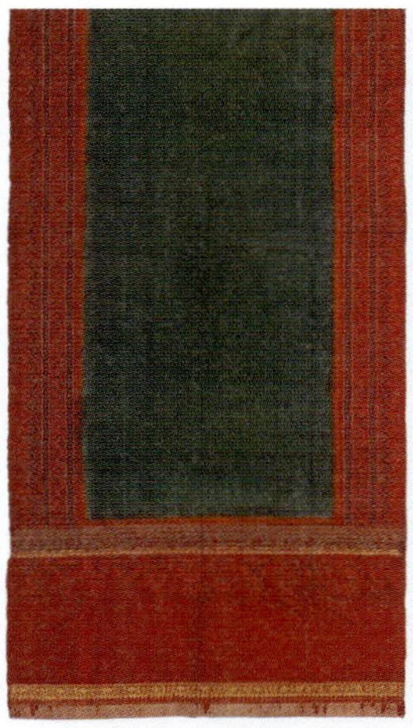

MA23 Malay shoulder cloth, *selendang* Palembang, South Sumatra, Indonesia, 19th century. Silk, weft ikat, *plangi*, metallic supplementary weft. 77 in x 32 in

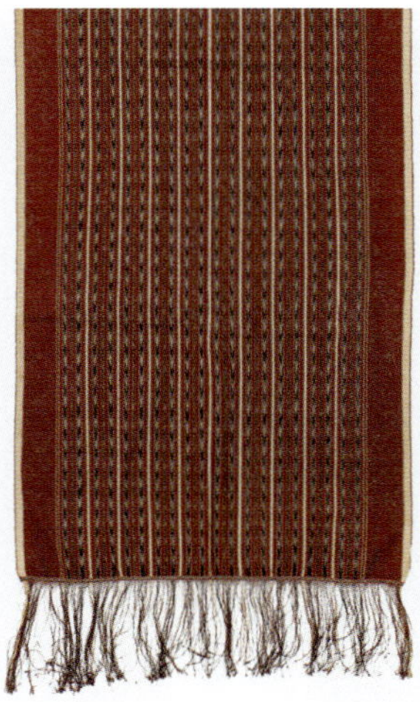

MA24 Batak ritual cloth North Sumatra, Indonesia, 20th century. Cotton, warp ikat, weft twining. 87 in x 31 in

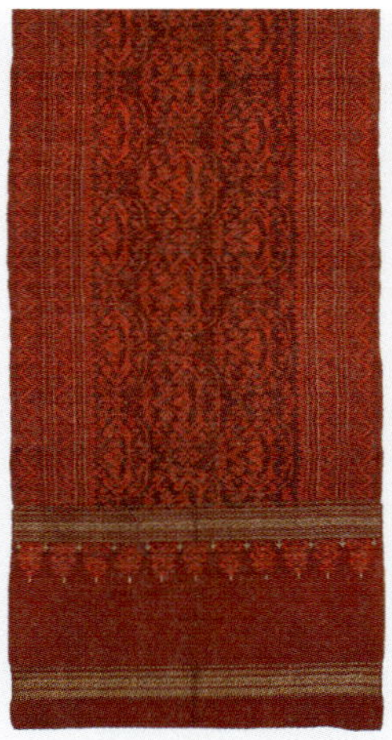

MA25 Malay shoulder cloth, *selendang* Palembang, South Sumatra, Indonesia, early 20th century. Silk, weft ikat, zone dyeing, metallic supplementary weft. 81 in x 31 in

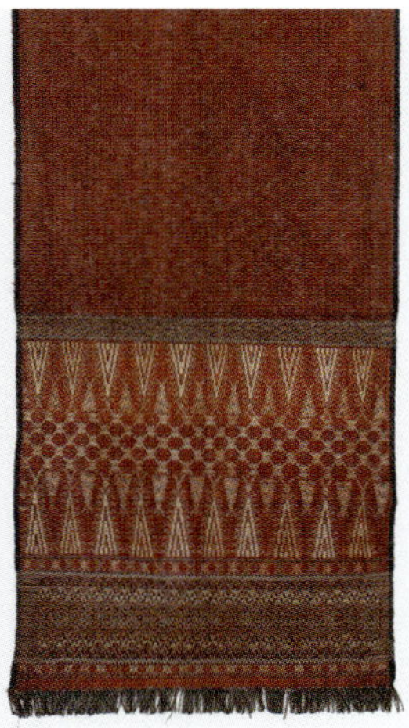

MA26 Pasemah shoulder cloth, *kain bidak* Sumatra, Indonesia, 19th century. Cotton, weft ikat, continuous supplementary weft, fringe decorated with tin. 81 in x 21 in

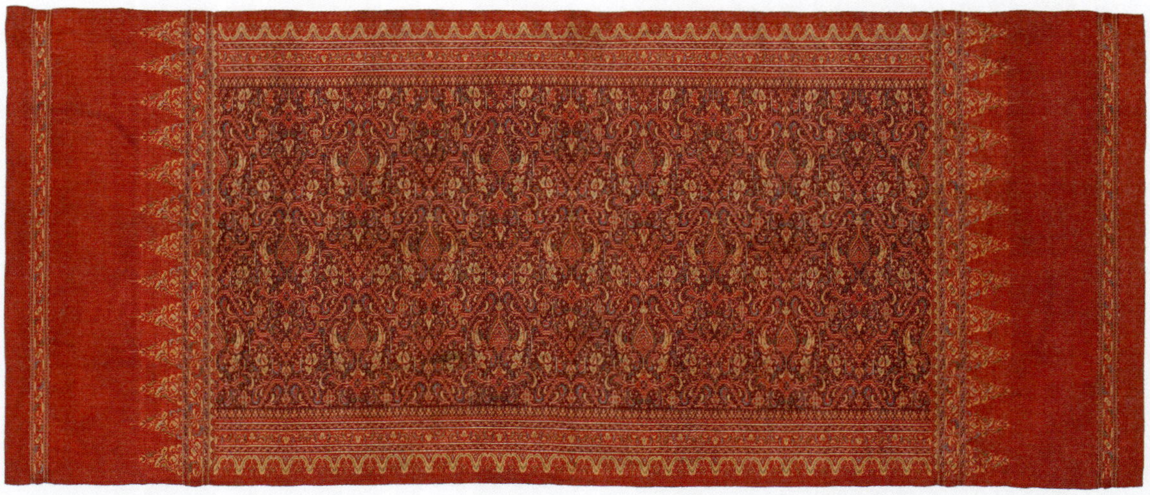

MA27 Malay shoulder cloth, *selendang* Bangka, South Sumatra, Indonesia, 19th century. Silk, weft ikat, zone dyeing. 85 in x 35 in

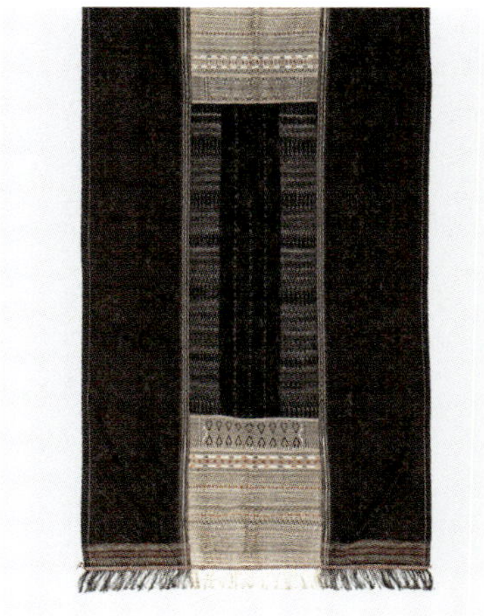

MA28 Toba Batak ritual cloth, *ulos ragidup*
North Sumatra, Indonesia, 19th century. Cotton, warp ikat, supplementary weft, weft twining. 90 in x 54 in

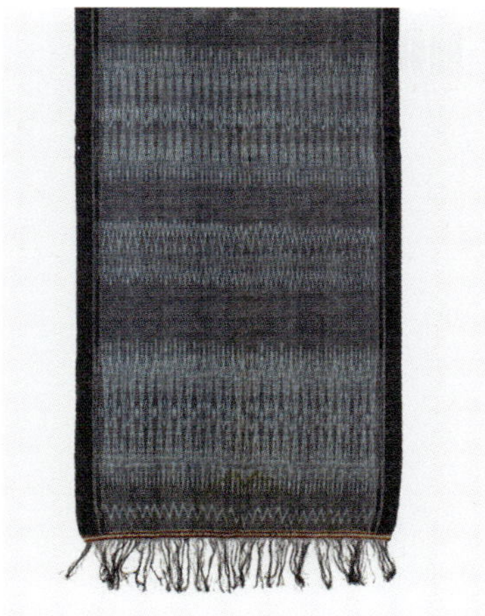

MA29 Toba Batak ritual cloth, *ulos*
North Sumatra, Indonesia, 19th century. Cotton, warp ikat, weft twining. 96 in x 40 in

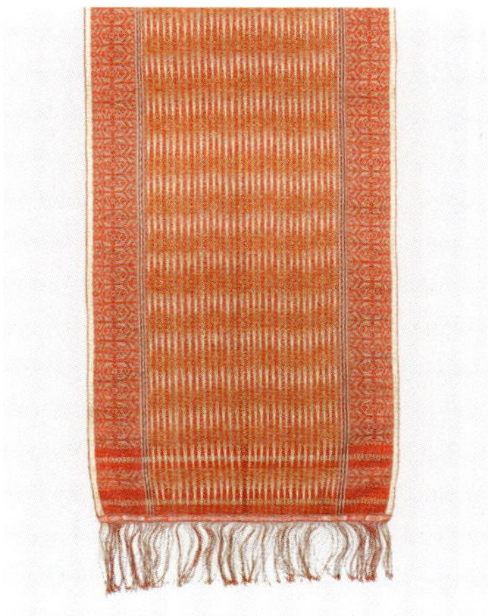

MA30 Karo Batak shoulder cloth
North Sumatra, Indonesia, 19th century. Cotton, warp ikat, supplementary weft, weft twining. 72 in x 23 in

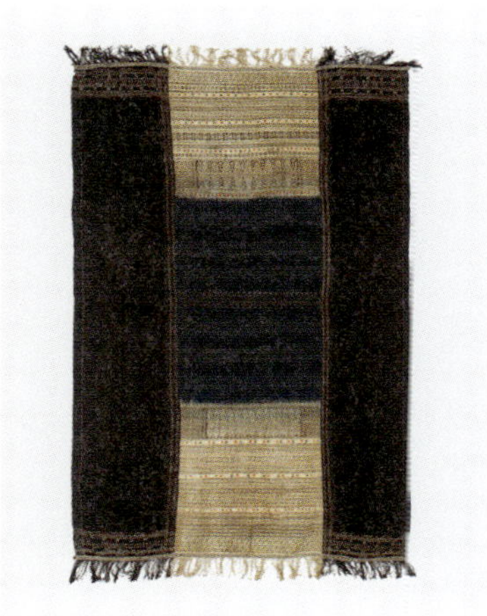

MA31 Toba Batak ritual cloth, *ulos*
North Sumatra, Indonesia, 19th century. Cotton, warp ikat, warp float, supplementary weft, weft twining. 78 in x 55 in

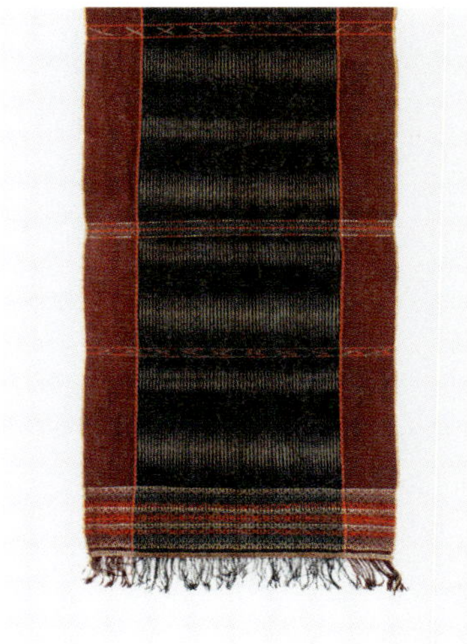

MA32 Toba Batak ritual cloth, *ulos*
North Sumatra, Indonesia, 20th century. Cotton, warp ikat, supplementary weft, weft twining. 60 in x 30 in

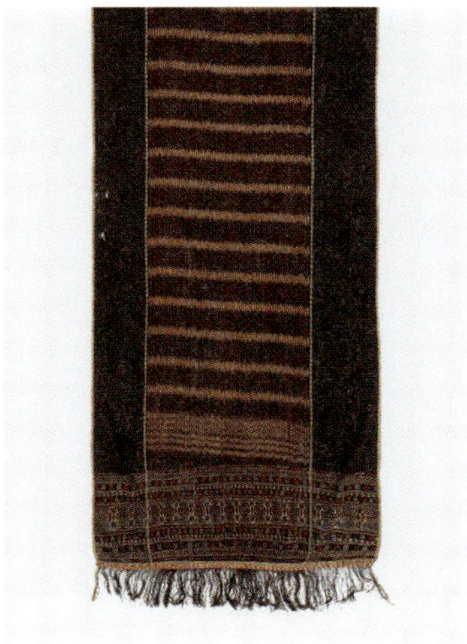

MA33 Toba Batak ritual cloth, *ulos ragidup*
North Sumatra, Indonesia, 19th century. Cotton, warp ikat, warp float, supplementary weft, weft twining. 80 in x 32 in

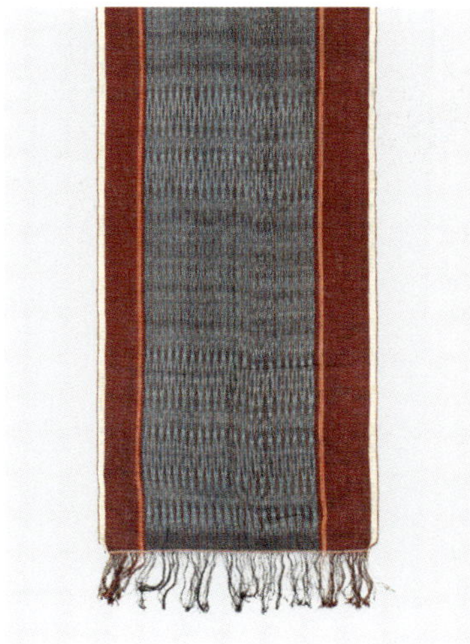

MA34 Toba Batak ritual cloth, *ulos ragidup*
North Sumatra, Indonesia, 20th century. Cotton, warp ikat. 92 in x 32 in

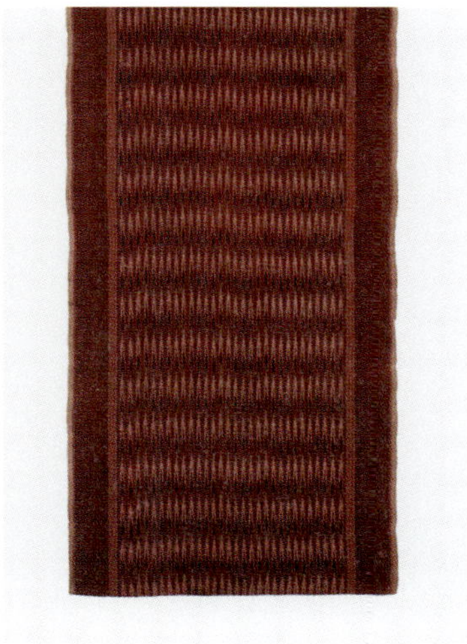

MA35 Acehnese hip wrapper, *ija panggang*
North Sumatra, Indonesia, 19th century. Silk, warp ikat. 75 in x 31 in

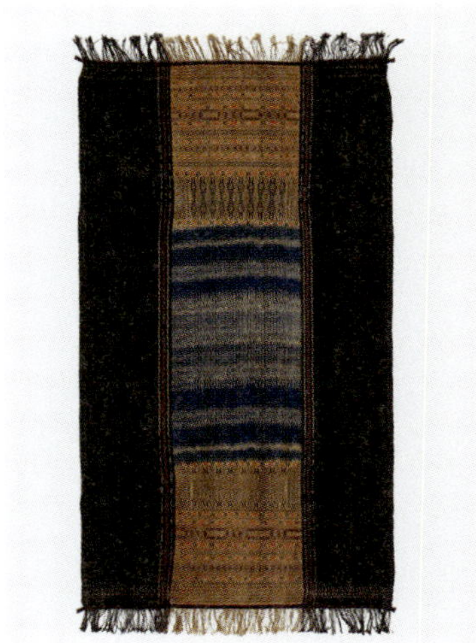

MA36 Toba Batak ritual cloth, *ulos*
North Sumatra, Indonesia, early 20th century. Cotton, warp ikat, supplemental weft, supplementary warp. 75 in x 44 in

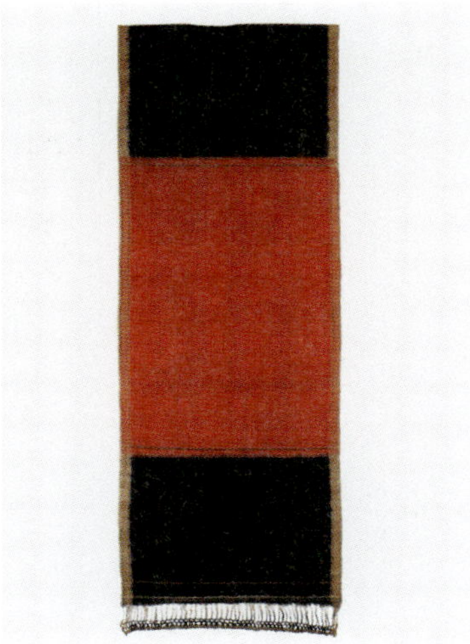

MA37 Ritual cloth
Sumatra (?), Indonesia, 17th century. Cotton, double ikat. 94 in x 33 in

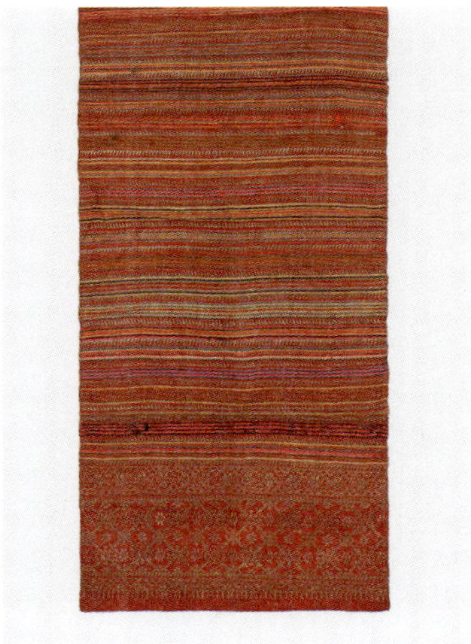

MA38 Woman's skirt cloth
Minangkabau, Southwest Sumatra, Indonesia, 20th century. Silk, weft ikat, metallic supplementary weft. 53 in x 20 in

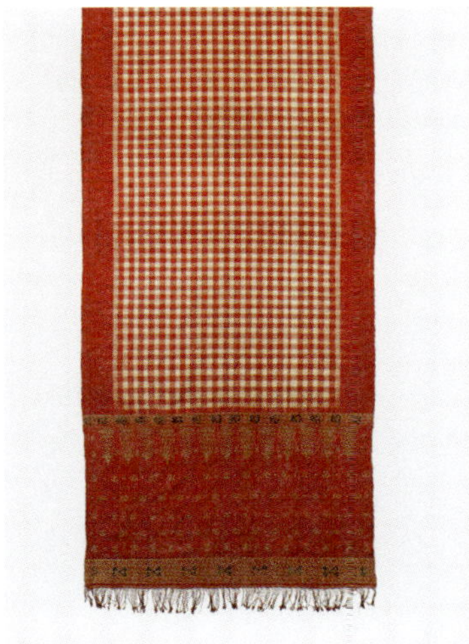

MA39 Malay shoulder cloth, *selendang*
Palembang, South Sumatra, Indonesia, 19th century. Silk, double ikat, metallic supplementary weft. 97 in x 33 in

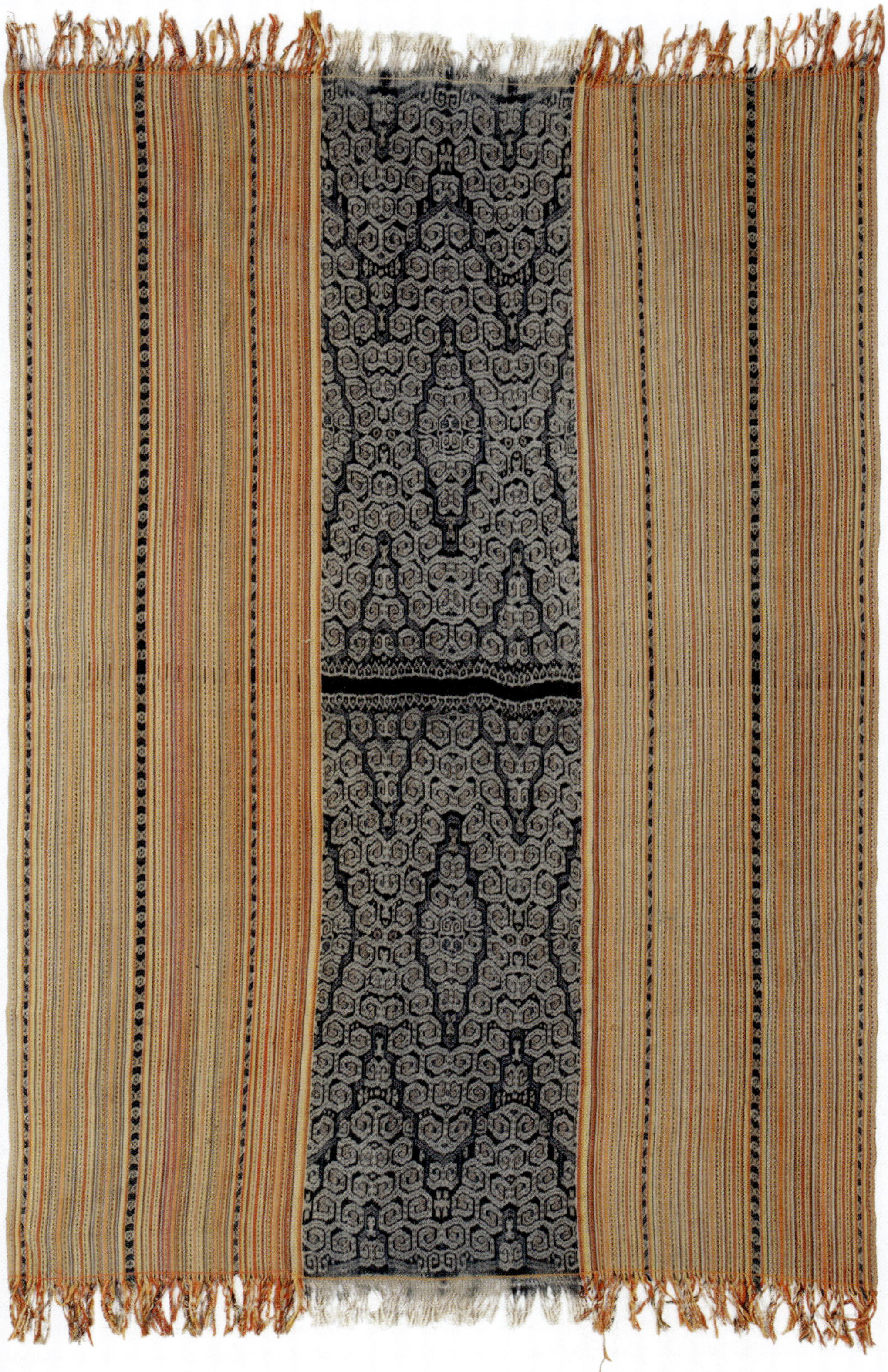

MA40 Man's wrap, *beti naek*, Atoin Meto ethnic group, Miomafo, West Timor, Indonesia, 20th century. Cotton, warp ikat, weft twining. 71 in x 48 in

Three panels of cloth compose this man's cloth, which could be worn as a hip wrapper or a shawl. Backstrap looms produce narrow textiles, and two or more panels are joined together to form a wide textile. This man's wrap consists of two identical side panels flanking the middle panel decorated with warp ikat or *futus*. The center section is decorated with repeating warp ikat designs of hooked lozenges (*maikaif* or *kaif*). This motif signifies ancestors to some and crocodiles to others. Some small patterns that represent small reptiles or anthropomorphic figures also appear among the diamond shapes. The crocodile is considered the founding ancestor of the people of Timor, and legend describes the island of Timor formed by this animal. The greater the number of hooks radiating from the rhombus's sides, the higher the status of the wearer.

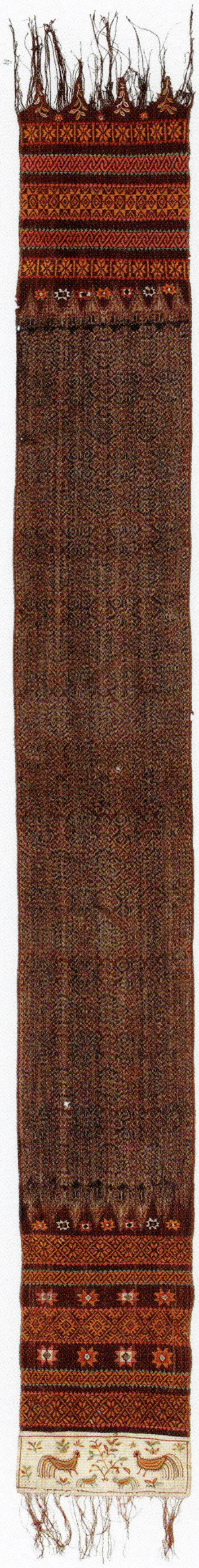

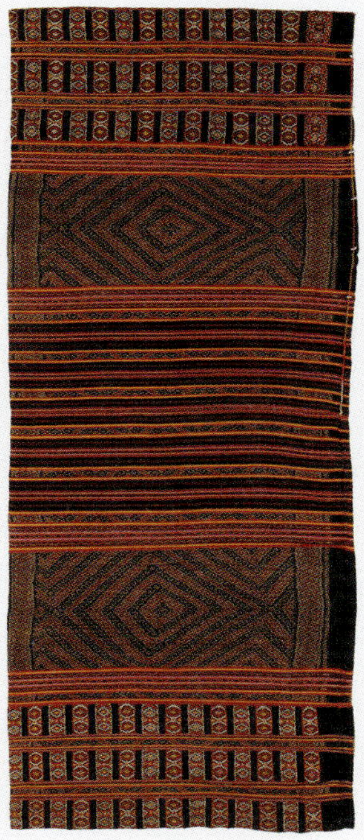

MA42 Woman's sarong, *tais*
Malaka, West Timor, Indonesia, mid-20th century. Cotton, warp ikat, supplementary weft wrapping. 60 in x 24 in

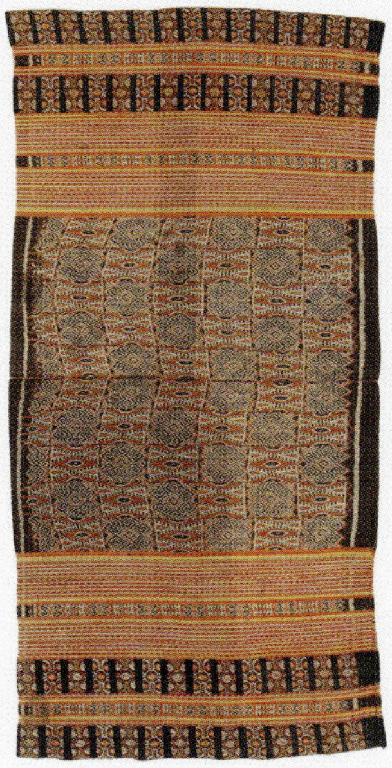

MA43 Atoin Meto woman's sarong, *tais*
West Timor, Indonesia, mid-20th century. Cotton, silk, warp ikat, supplementary weft wrapping. 42 in x 21 in

MA44 Tetun woman's sarong, *tais feto*
Malaka, West Timor, Indonesia, 19th century. Cotton, silk, warp ikat, embroidery. 55 in x 21 in

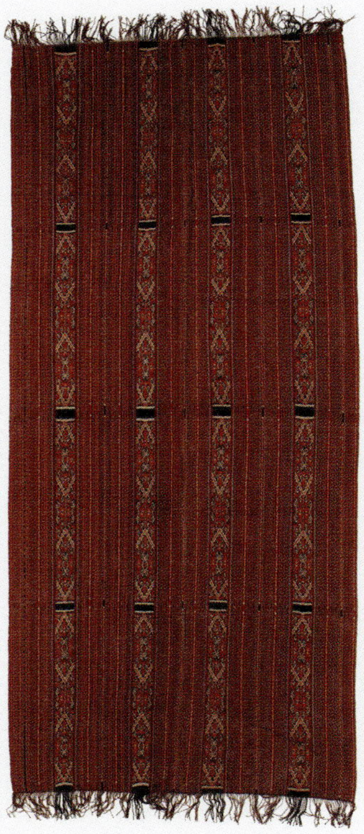

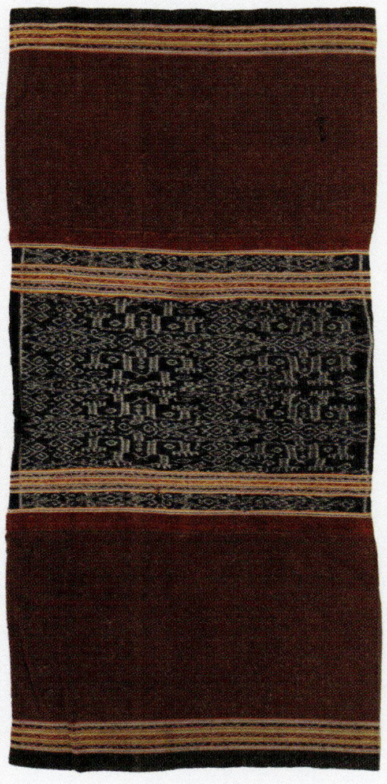

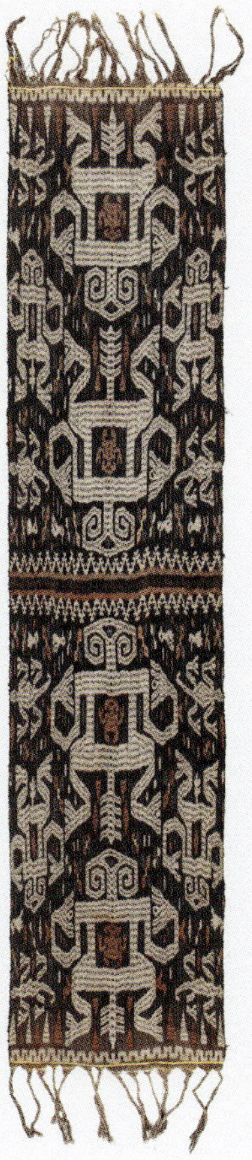

MA41 Man's sash
Timor, 20th century. Cotton, warp ikat, supplementary weft, embroidery. 92 in x 12 in

MA45 Atoin Meto man's shawl or hip wrapper, *beti*
West Timor, Indonesia, 20th century. Cotton, warp ikat. 76 in x 42 in

MA46 Belu woman's sarong, *tais feto*
West Timor, Indonesia, mid-20th century. Cotton, warp ikat. 53 in x 40 in

MA47 Atoin Meto man's shawl, *beti*, central panel
West Timor, Indonesia, 20th century. Cotton, warp ikat, weft twining. 82 in x 16 in

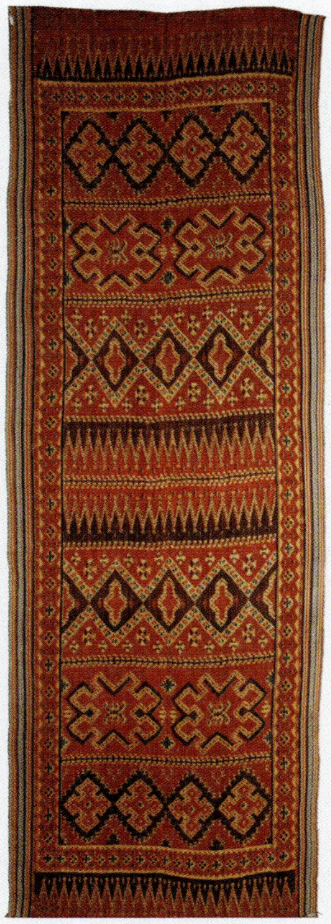

MA48 Toraja ritual cloth, *pori lonjong*
South Sulawesi, Indonesia, 20th century. Cotton, warp ikat. 155 in x 52 in

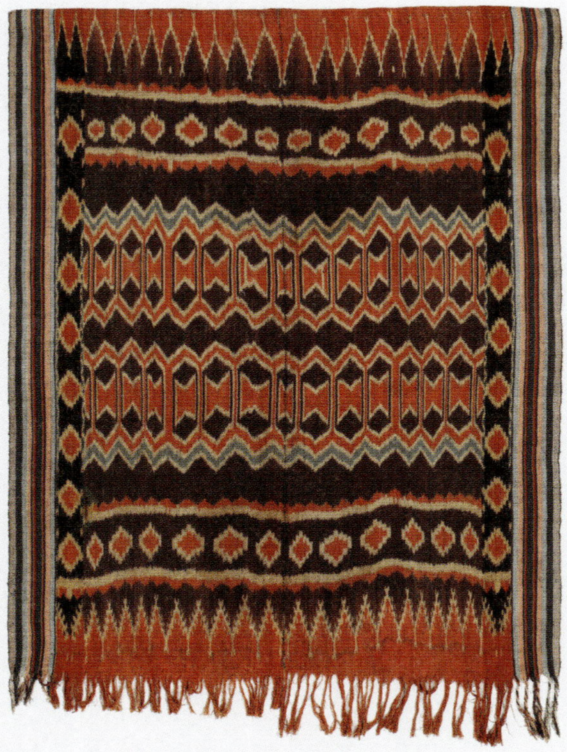

MA49 Toraja ritual cloth, *papori tonoling*
South Sulawesi, Indonesia, 20th century. Cotton, warp ikat. 58 in x 43 in

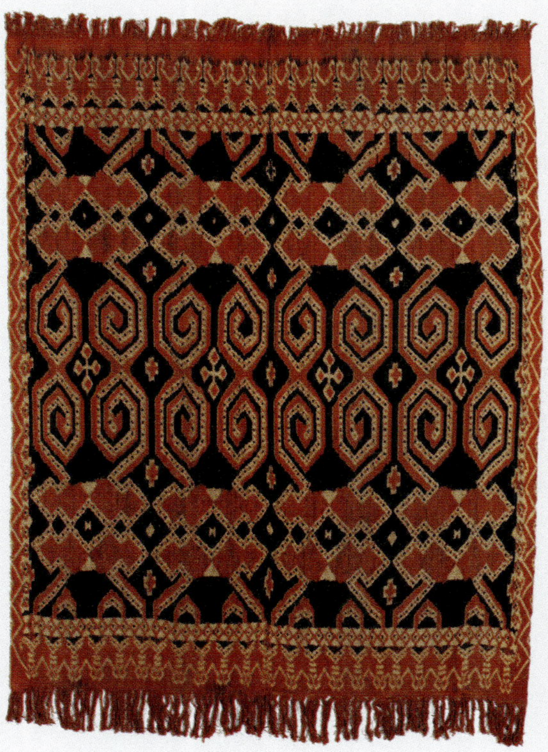

MA50 Toraja ritual textile, *sekomandi*
South Sulawesi, Indonesia, late 20th century. Cotton, warp ikat. 88 in x 54 in

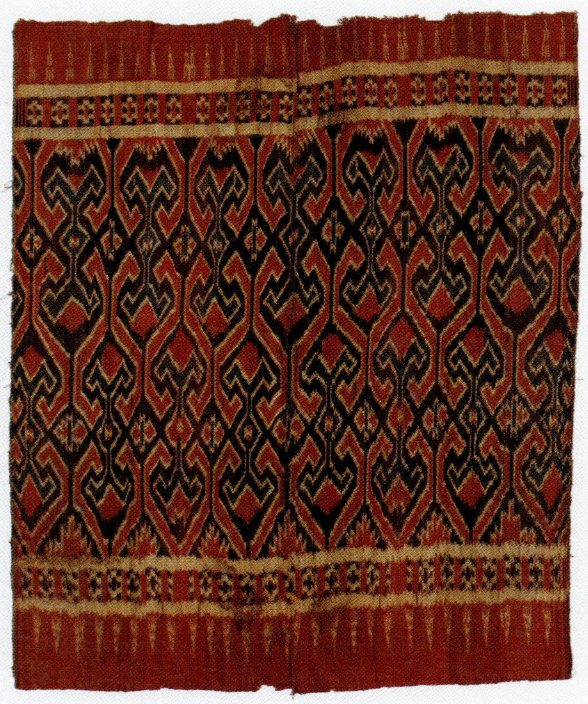

MA51 Toraja ritual textile, *sekomandi*
Galumpang, South Sulawesi, Indonesia, 20th century. Cotton, warp ikat. 66 in x 60 in

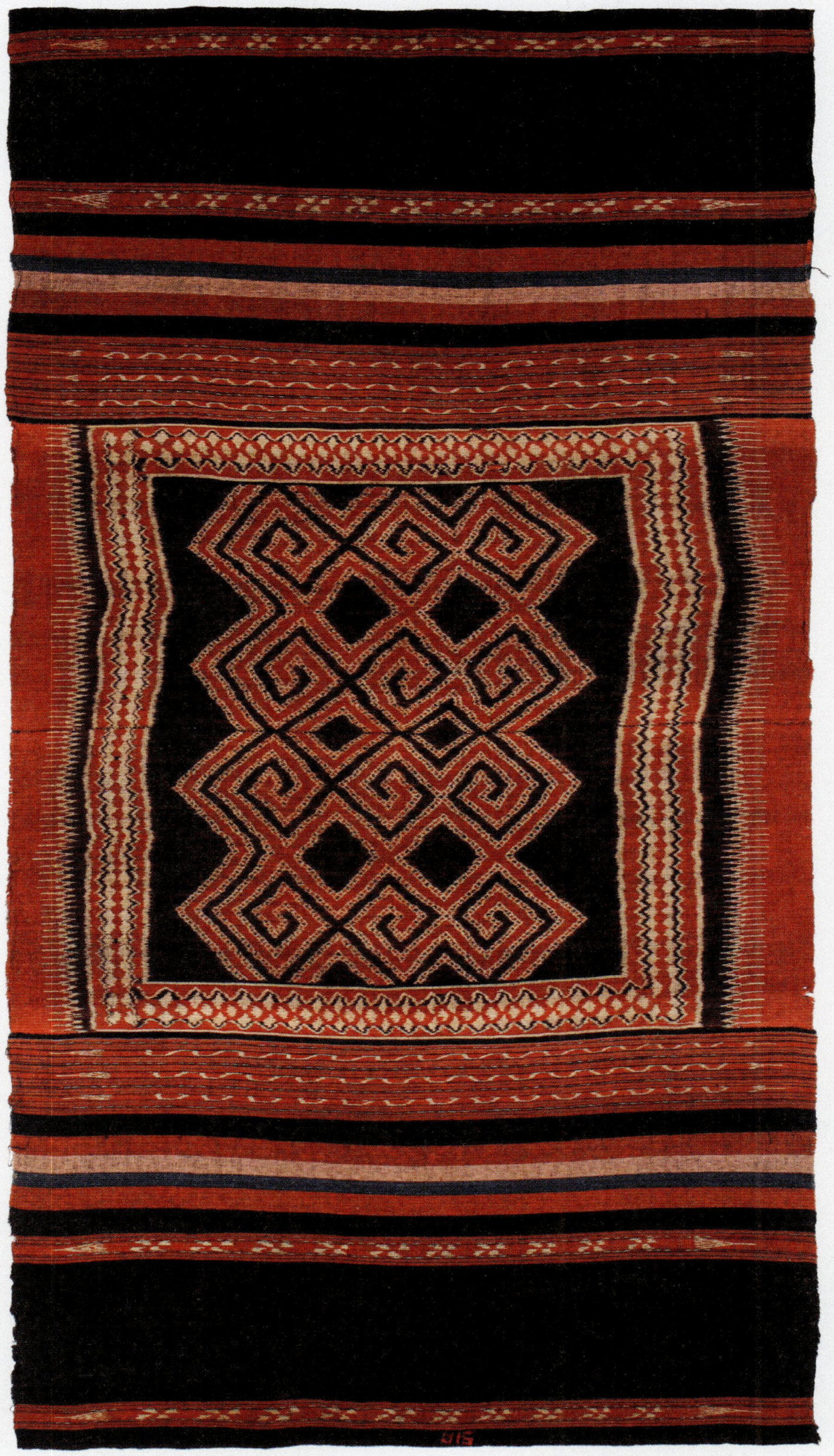

MA52 Toraja ceremonial textile, *pori situtu*, Rongkong, Sulawesi, Indonesia, early 20th century. Cotton, warp ikat. 105 in x 55 in

Toraja is the Bugis term referring to related but different groups of people living in upland areas in the interior. Two main areas of warp ikat production by the Toraja people are Rongkong and Kalumpang. Textiles from Rongkong are less densely woven compared with Kalumpang textiles, and recurring colors of Rongkong weavings are red, blue, and dark blue/almost black. Women from both areas create large warp-ikat weavings used within their own communities and by others in neighboring areas. This large warp-ikat-decorated weaving is called *pori situtu* (*pori*–to bind) and is used as a shroud by the Rongkong. Other Toraja groups use it as a hanging during rites.

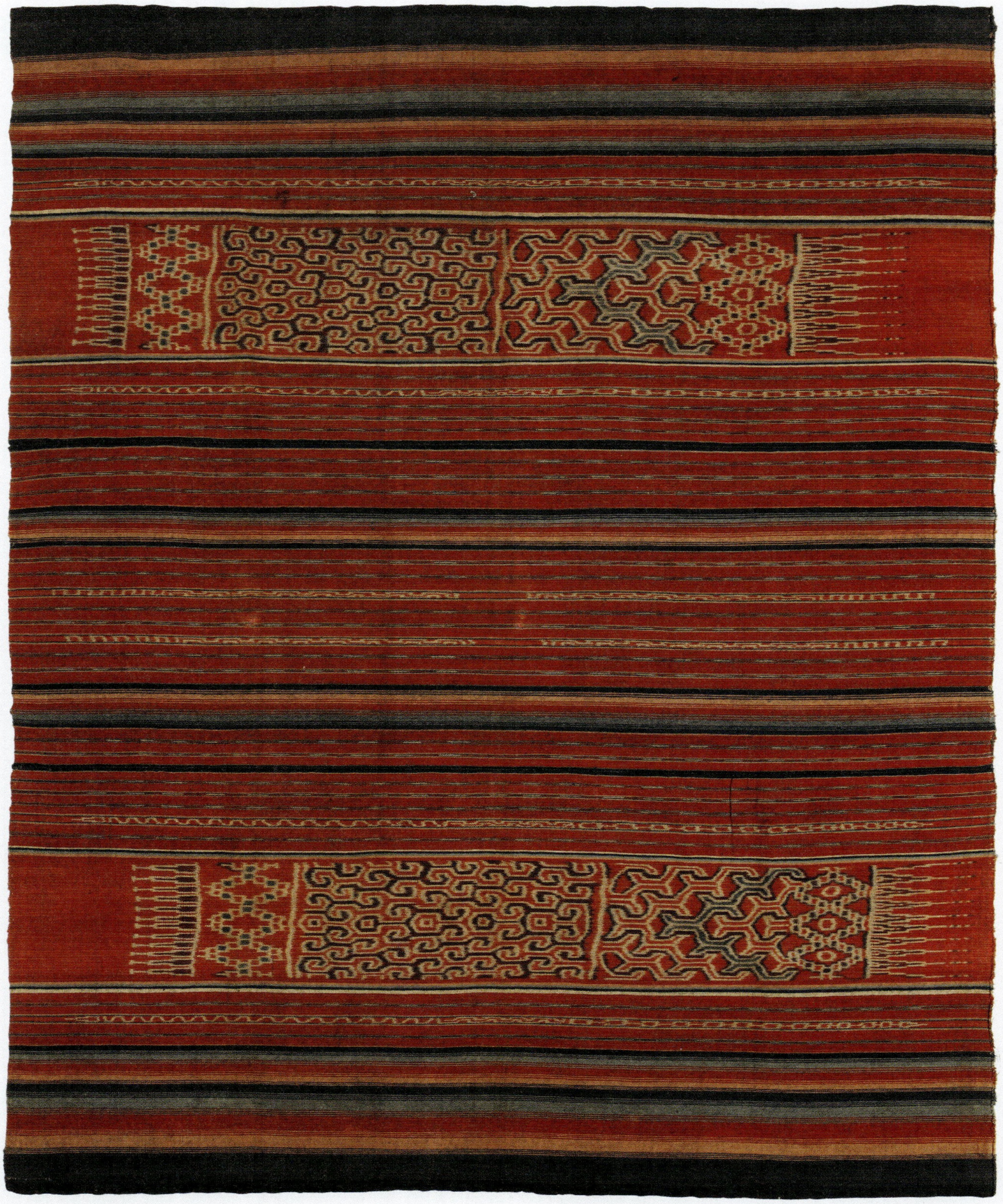

MA53 Toraja ceremonial textile or women's skirt material, Palu or Kalumpang, Sulawesi, Indonesia, 19th century. Cotton, warp ikat. 60 in x 70 in

Two panels of cloth are decorated with warp stripes and rows of warp-ikat patterning. Similar textiles are used as a shroud by the Kalumpung. Women of Palu tailored warp-ikat-decorated textiles from Kalumpang into skirts. Warp-ikat production in Palu ceased some centuries ago. The main bands are filled with warp-ikat designs of interlocking hooks, stepped squares, and narrow triangular shapes. A distinctive detail is found in the dark outlines around the exterior of the main designs.

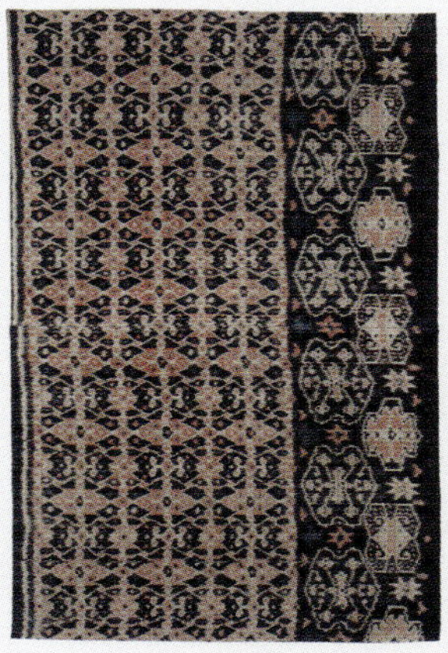

MA54 Woman's sarong, *lau*
East Sumba, Indonesia, 20th century. Cotton, warp ikat. 65 in x 45 in

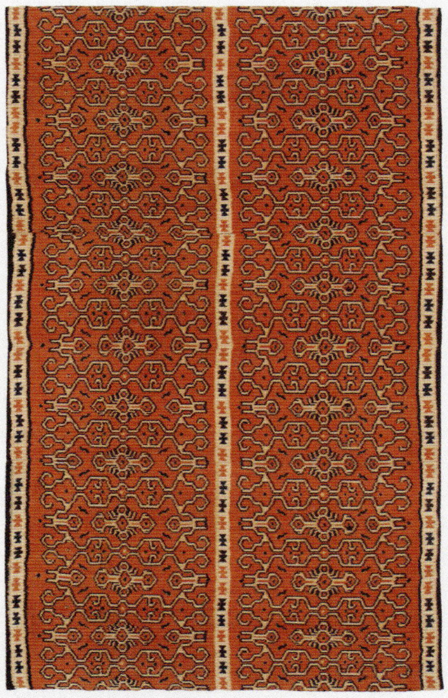

MA55 Woman's sarong (*lau*),
East Sumba, Indonesia, 20th century. Cotton, warp ikat. 45 x 71 in

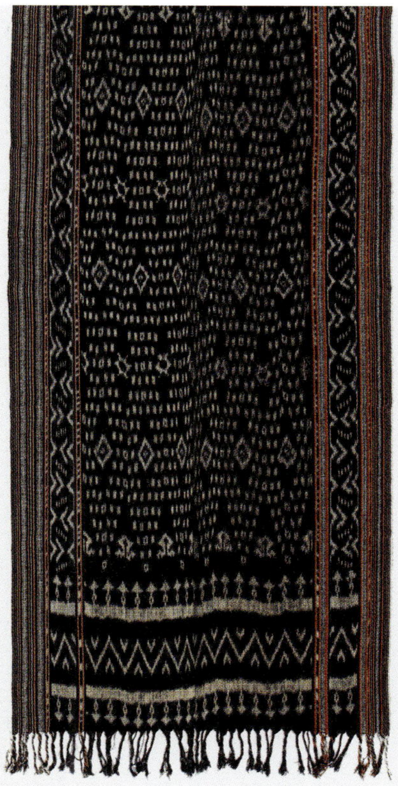

MA56 Kodi man's wrap or coffin cover, *hanggi ngoko* or *hanggi wolo remba*
Sumba, Indonesia, early 20th century. Cotton, warp ikat 105 in x 60 in

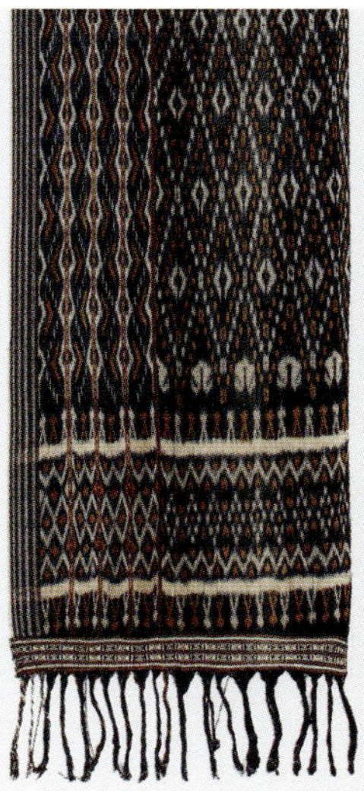

MA57 Kodi man's wrap or coffin cover, *hanggi ngoko* or *hanggi wolo remba*
Sumba, Indonesia, early 20th century. Cotton, warp ikat. 110 in x 29 in

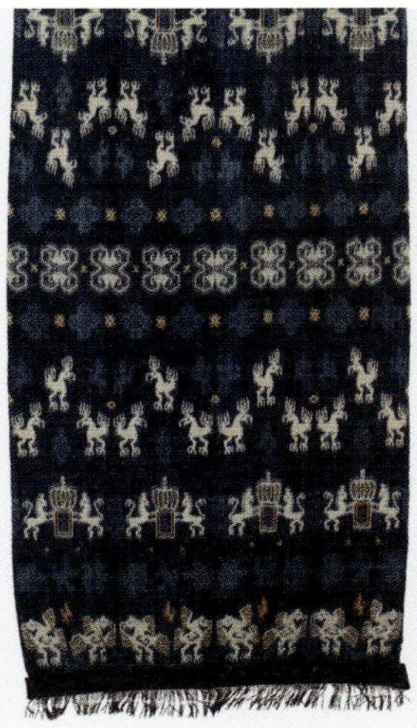

MA58 Man's shawl or hip wrapper, *hinggi kawuru*
East Sumba, Indonesia, first half 20th century. Cotton, warp ikat. 100 in x 42 in

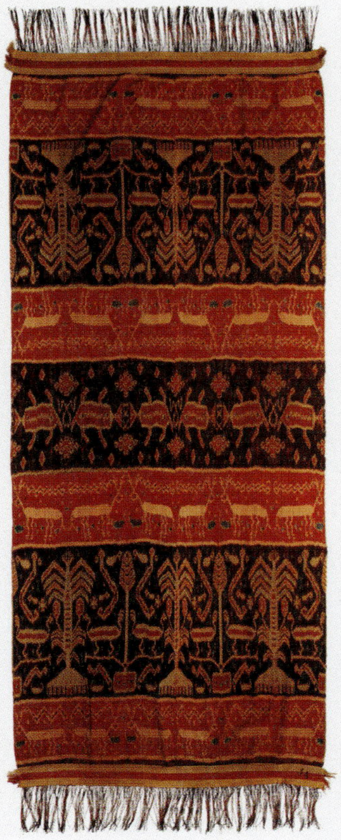

MA59 Man's shawl or hip wrapper, *hinggi kombu*
East Sumba, Indonesia, 19th or early 20th century. Cotton, warp ikat. 104 in x 45 in

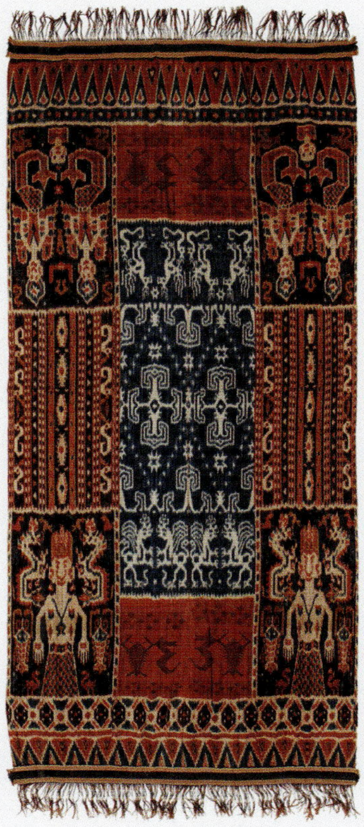

MA60 Man's shawl or hip wrapper, *hinggi kombu*
East Sumba, Indonesia, one of a pair woven in 1947 by a queen in the region. Cotton, warp ikat. 105 in x 66 in

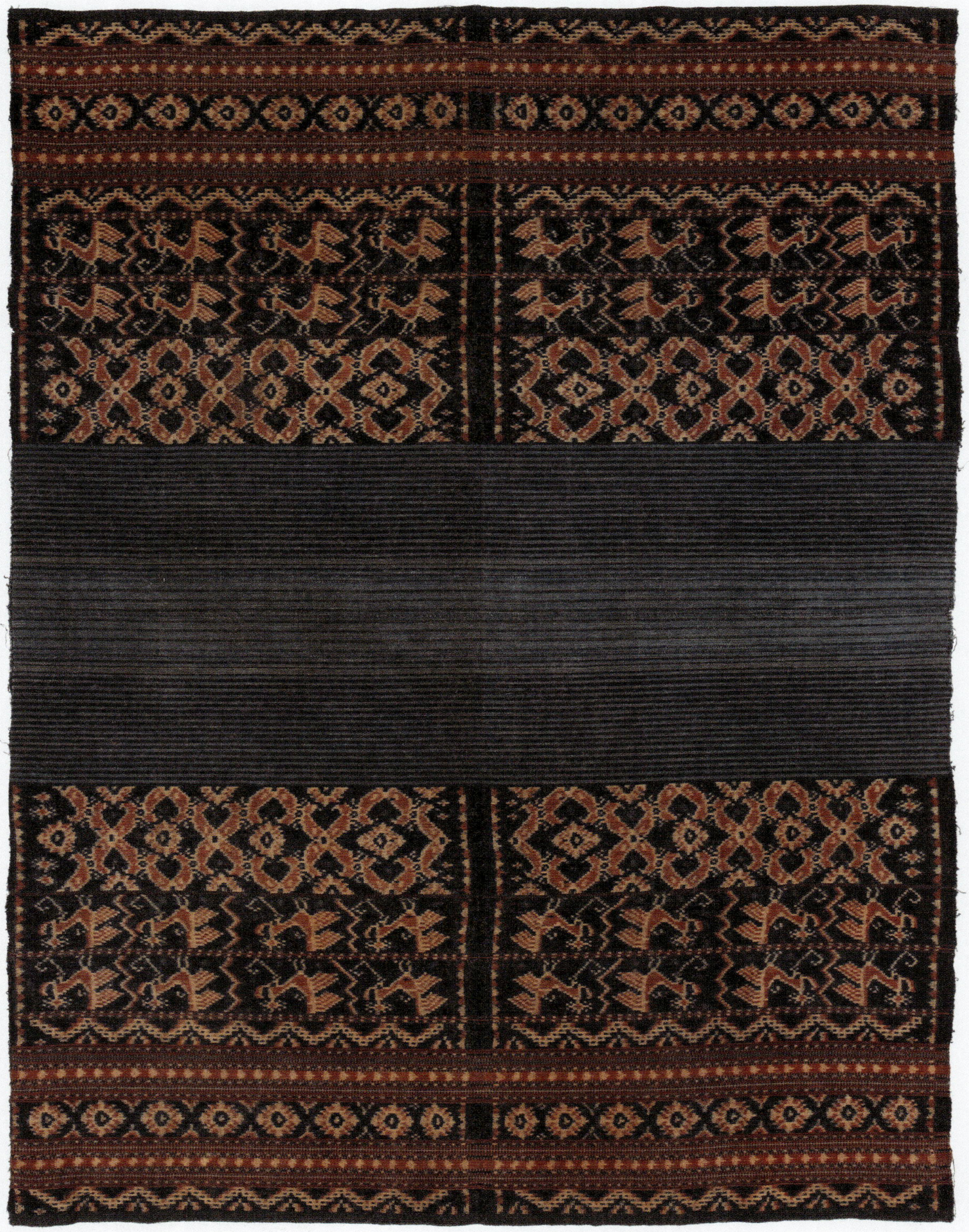

MA61 Rotenese *sarong* or *pou* (opened), Rote, Indonesia, early 20th century. Cotton, warp ikat. 57 in x 45 in

Most Rotenese textiles are dominated by indigo blue. The rulers of Rote's domains required schools to be founded as part of the trade agreements they signed with the Dutch East India Company. The educated Rotenese rose quickly in the Dutch colonial administration leading to their relocation to Kupang, Timor Island. Their indigo-dyed attire distinguished the Rotenese from others. The warp-ikat designs are arranged in bands in the upper and lower thirds of this woman's skirt while the middle is composed of light and dark indigo stripes. Some motifs represent elements from ancestral beliefs such as the undulating line symbolizing a snake. Birds, including roosters, have crucial roles in these beliefs, with their ability to fly. Fowl also constitute a sacrificial offering used for auguries. Patterning in the innermost rows resembles designs decorating Indian trade textiles such as *patola*. Rulers and their family members owned Indian trade textiles, and patterns inspired by these prestigious goods on locally woven cloth were also the prerogative of this elite class.

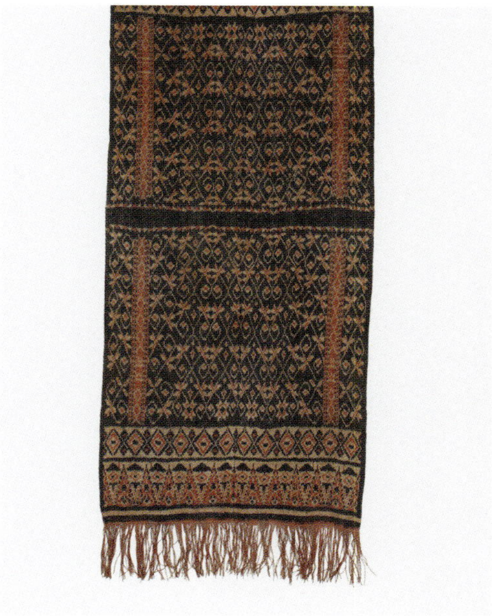

MA62 Shawl, ***lafa***
Roti, Indonesia, mid-20th century. Cotton, warp ikat. 77 in x 30 in

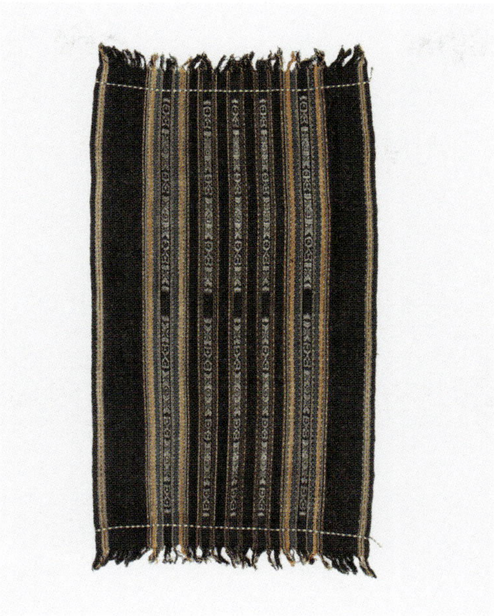

MA63 Shawl, ***tais marin***
Maluku, Tanimbar Archipelago, Indonesia, 20th century. Cotton, warp ikat, weft twining. 48 in x 29 in

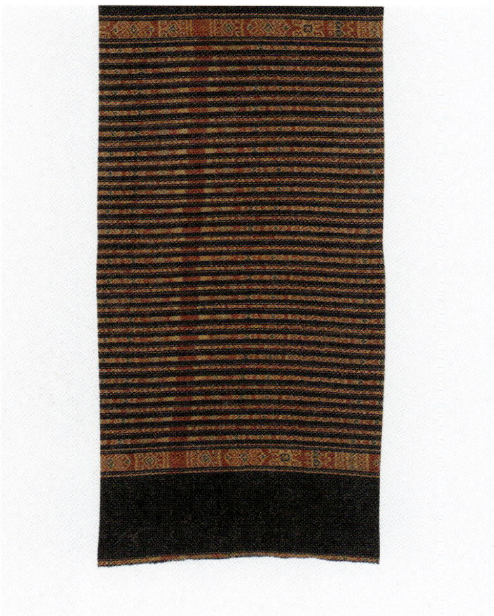

MA64 Woman's sarong, ***bakan***
Maluku, Tanimbar Archipelago, Indonesia, 19th century. Cotton, warp ikat. 60 in x 27 in

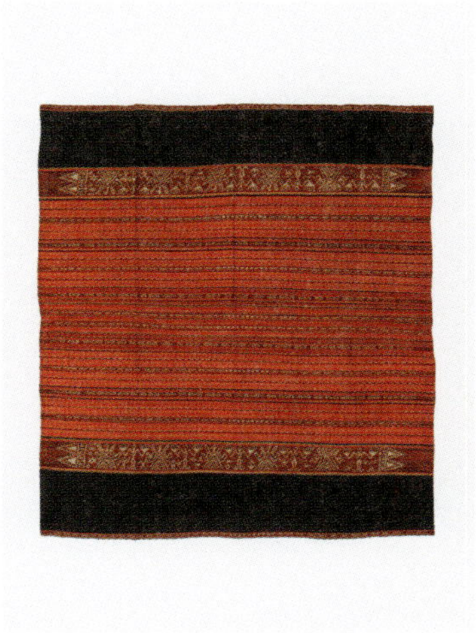

MA65 Woman's sarong, ***hom nom***
Kisar, Indonesia, mid-20th century. Cotton, warp ikat. 42 in x 56 in

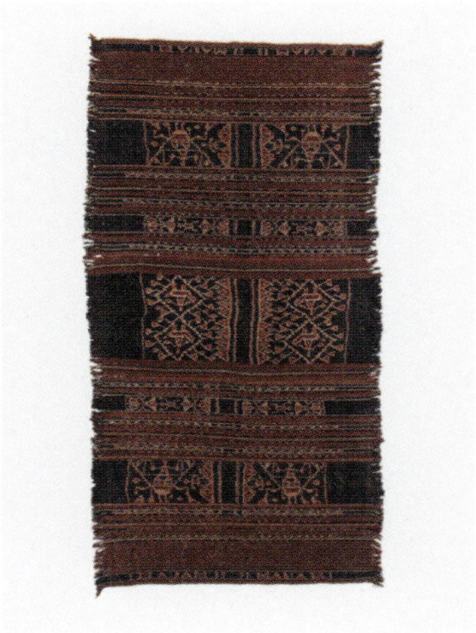

MA66 Lamaholot bride wealth cloth, ***kewatek nai telo***
Lembata, Indonesia, 20th century. Cotton, warp ikat. 84 in x 44 in

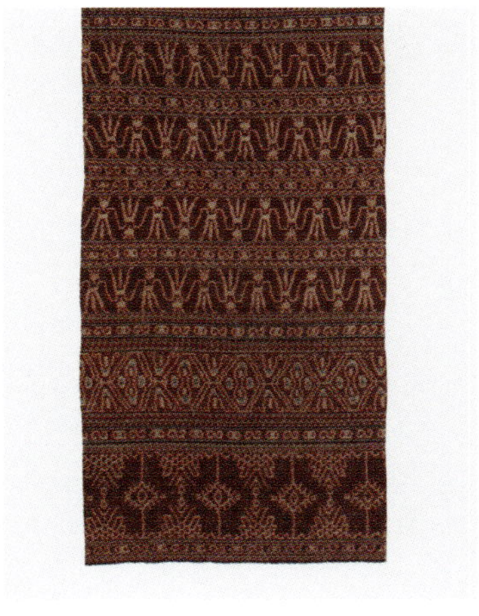

MA67 Woman's sarong
Sammur, Indonesia, 20th century (?). Cotton, warp ikat. 61 in x 24 in

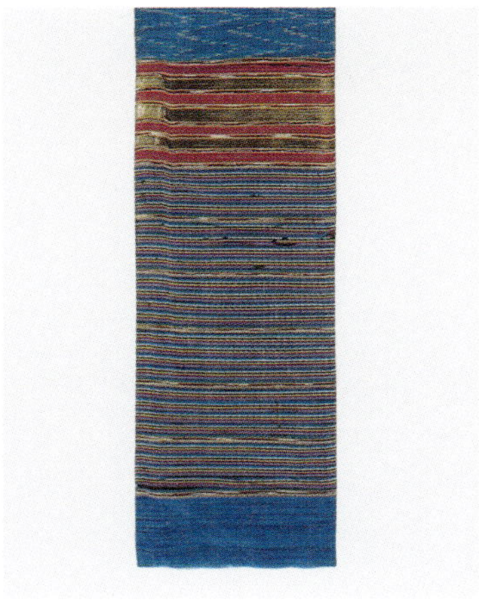

MA68 Man's sash
Yogyakarta, Java, Indonesia, 19th century. Silk, weft ikat. 86 in x 5 in

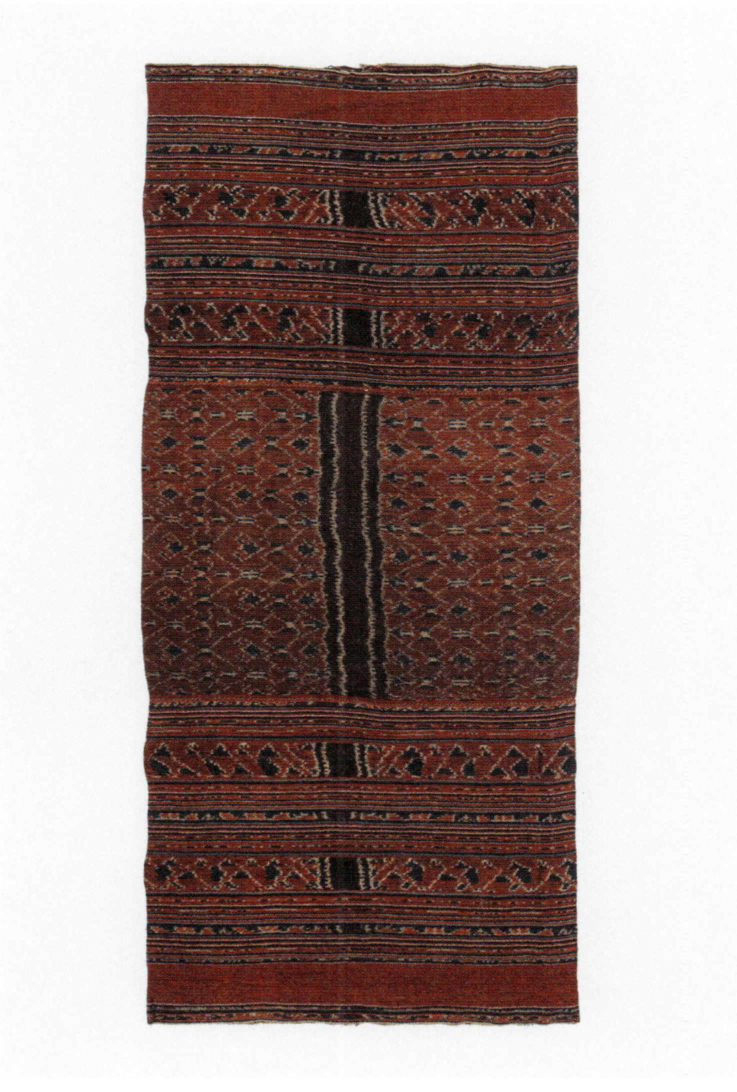

MA69 Lamaholot bride wealth cloth, ***kewatek nai telo***
Lembata, Indonesia, 20th century. Cotton, warp ikat. 68 in x 31 in

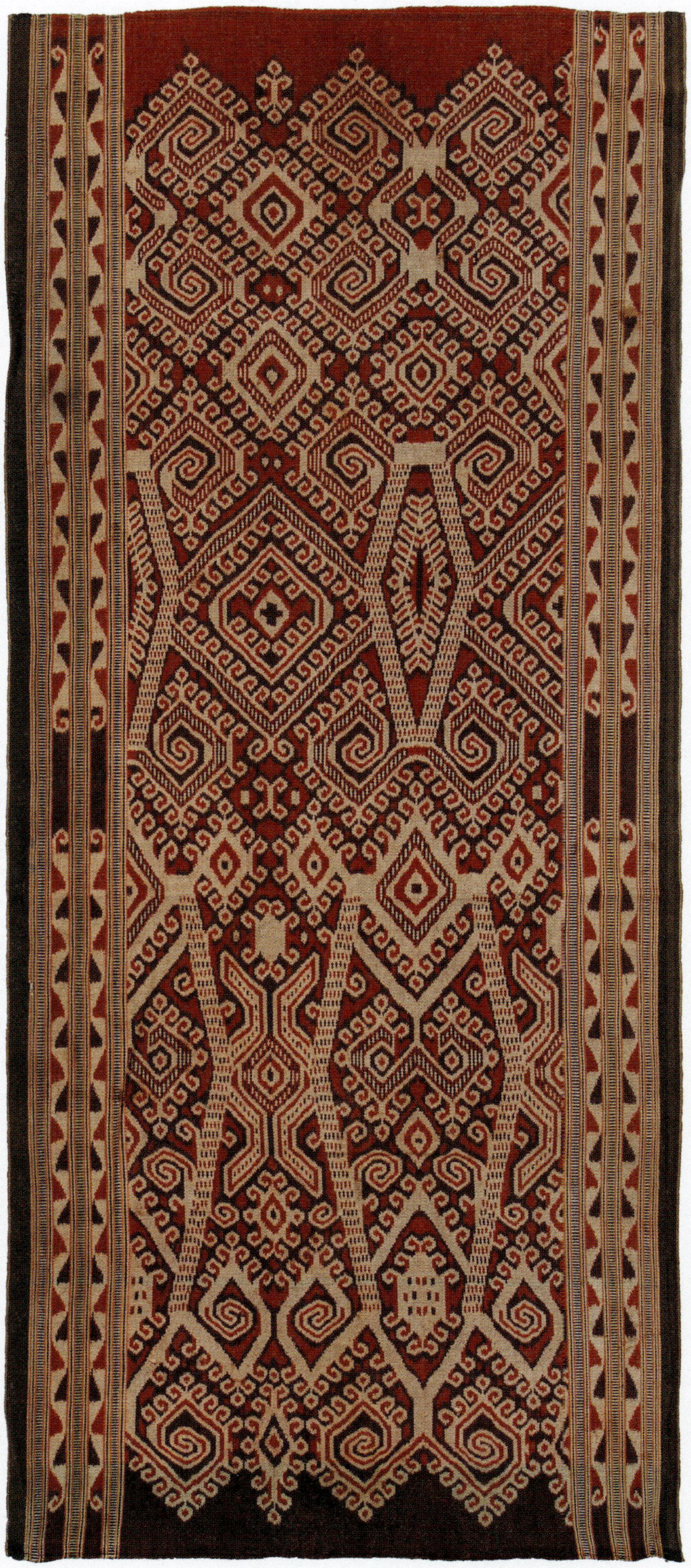

MA70 Kantuk or Kantu' skirt panel, *kain kebat*, West Borneo, Indonesia, late 19th or early 20th century. Cotton, warp ikat. 46 in x 21 in

The Kantuk people are related to the Iban but reside in the Indonesian part of Borneo. Motifs adorning women's skirts lack supernatural power. A young woman learning how to weave begins making skirts before attempting to create a spiritually powerful ritual textile such as a *pua*. A master weaver also alternates making supernaturally powerful textiles such as a *pua* with a *kain kebat*. The designs of women's skirts consist of numerous hooks and angles that signify flora and fauna. Kantuk warp-ikat patterning is distinct, especially if compared with Iban warp ikats. One distinguishing characteristic is the number of undyed sections in the patterns. Binding these areas tightly, so that the dye doesn't seep in when the warp threads are submerged in a vat, requires skill. Popular motifs include deer, birds, shrews, insects, reptiles, amphibians, bamboo, ferns, gingers, gourds, and rattans.

MA71 Malay hip wrapper, *kain limar*, Terengganu, Malaysia, 19th century. Silk-weft ikat, warp-zone dyeing. 92 in x 32 in

The northernmost states on the eastern coast of present-day Malaysia produce distinctive silk textiles decorated with weft ikat. Malay ruling families controlled the commerce in their ports located on a regional maritime trade route. They consumed Indian trade textiles and other items considered valuable and prestigious. Weavers of Kelantan, Pattani (located in present-day Thailand), and Terengganu assimilated motifs and design formats of *patola* and other Indian textiles into local production. The design format of the weft-ikat silks from this area consists of a center section with rows abutting its ends. The patterning may repeat throughout the area or be organized into rows. However, columns parallel to the selvages and flanking the central field are absent. The textiles from Terengganu are darker, such as the black central field with white weft-ikat designs, compared with similar weavings made in Pattani and Kelantan.

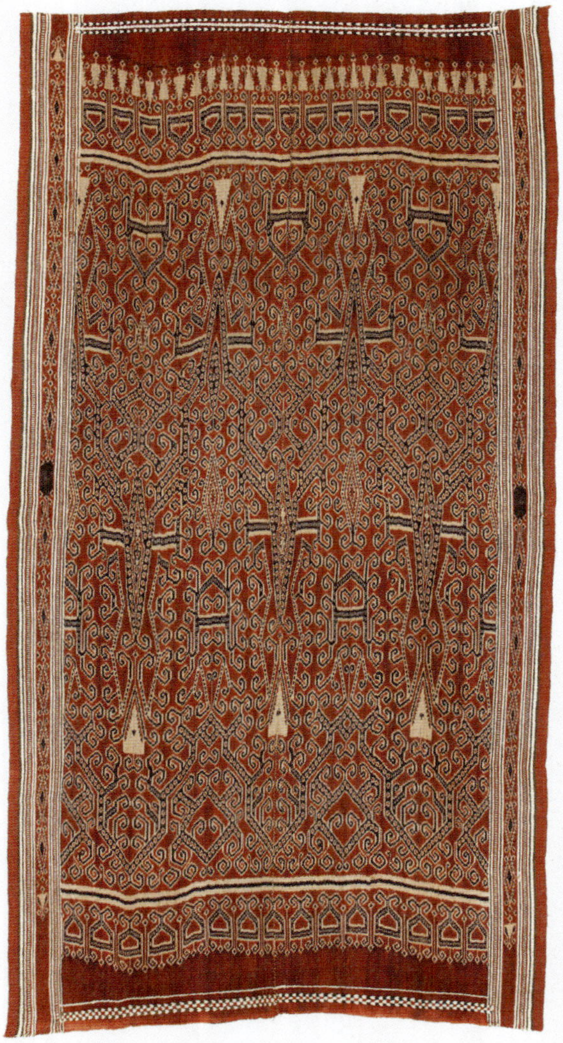

MA72 Iban ritual textile, *pua kumbu* Sarawak, Borneo, Malaysia, late 19th or early 20th century. Cotton, warp ikat. 89 in x 54 in

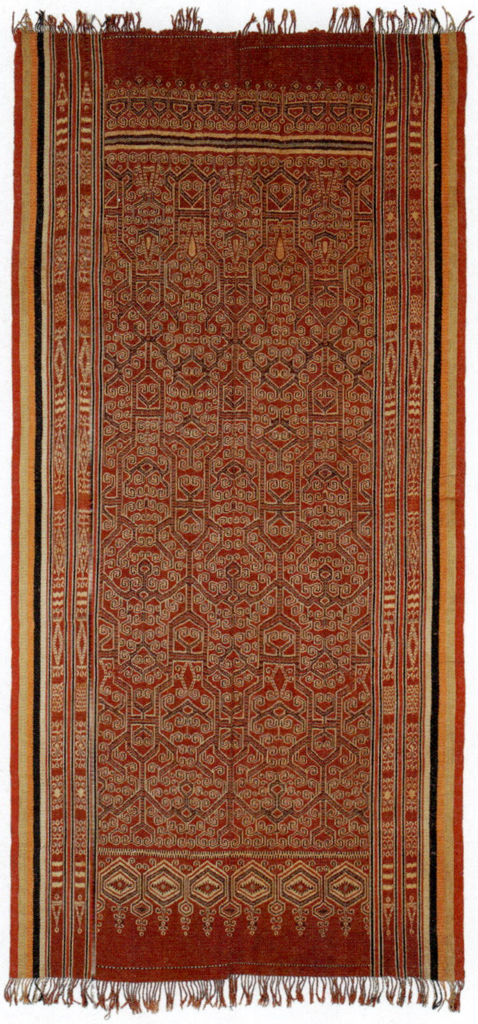

MA73 Iban ritual textile, *pua kumbu* Sarawak, Borneo, Malaysia, late 19th or early 20th century. Cotton, warp ikat. 89 in x 39 in

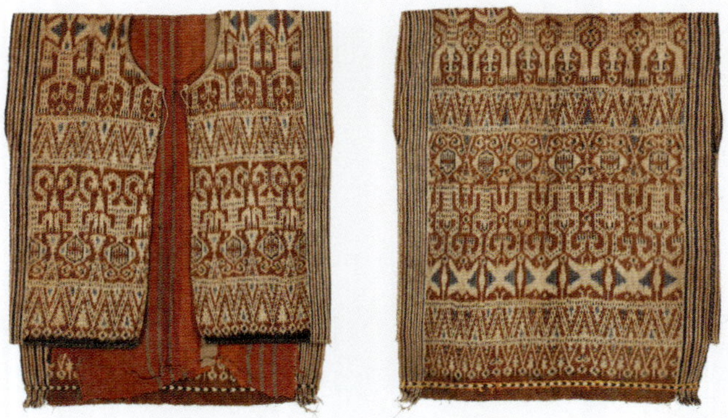

MA74 Iban man's vest (front and back)
Sarawak, Borneo, Malaysia, early 20th century. Cotton, warp ikat, weft twining. 22 in x 19 in

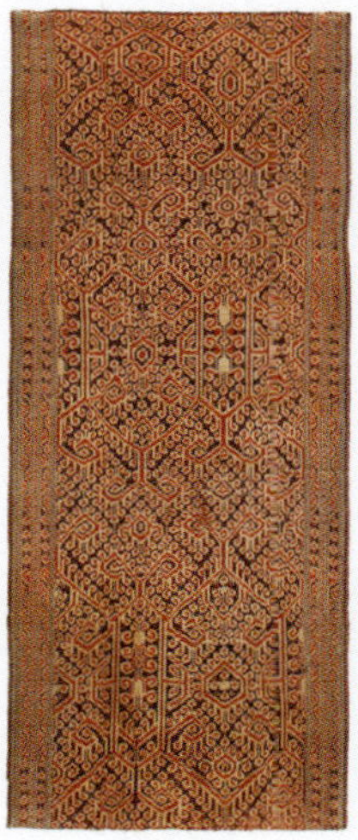

MA75 Iban woman's sarong, *kain kebat*
Sarawak, Borneo, Malaysia, 20th century. Cotton, warp ikat. 43 in x 18 in

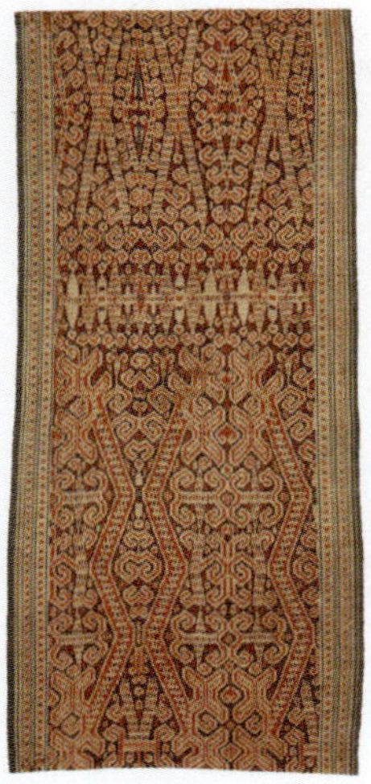

MA76 Iban woman's sarong, *kain kebat*
Sarawak, Borneo, Malaysia, mid-20th century. Cotton, warp ikat. 36 in x 21 in

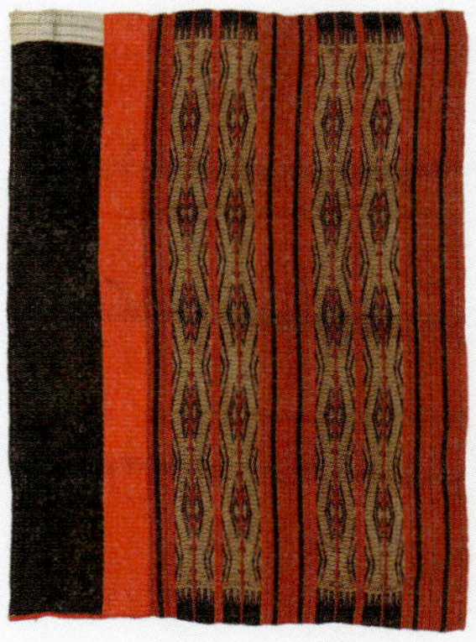

MA77 Benuaq woman's skirt
Sarawak, Borneo, Malaysia, first half 20th century. Lemba (*Curculigo latifolia*), warp ikat. Side panels composed of cotton trade cloth. 30 in x 21 in

MA78 Malay shawl, head cloth or hip wrapper, *kain limar*
Northeast coast, Malaysia, 19th century. Silk, weft ikat. 90 in x 30 in

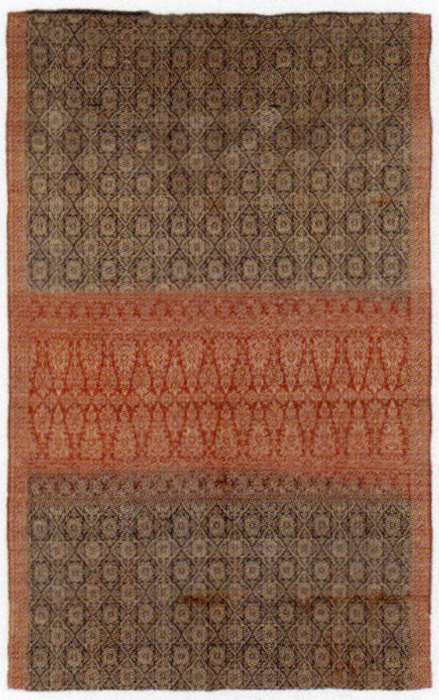

MA79 Malay woman's sarong, *sarung songket*
Peninsular Malaysia, 19th century. Silk, zone-dyed warp, metallic continuous supplementary weft. 65 in x 32 in

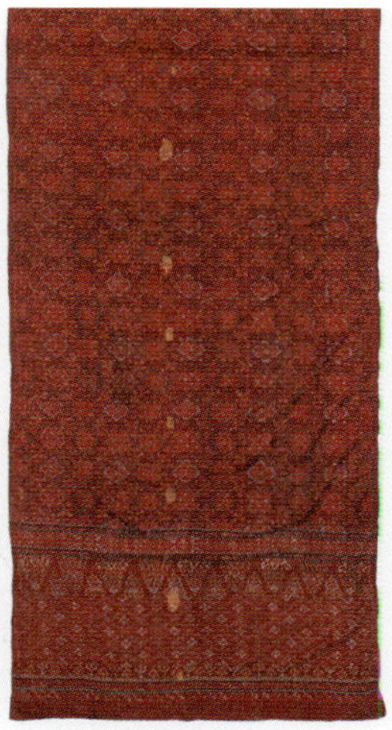

MA80 Malay shawl, head cloth or hip wrapper, *kain limar*
Northeast coast, Malaysia, 19th century. Silk, weft ikat. 90 in x 31 in

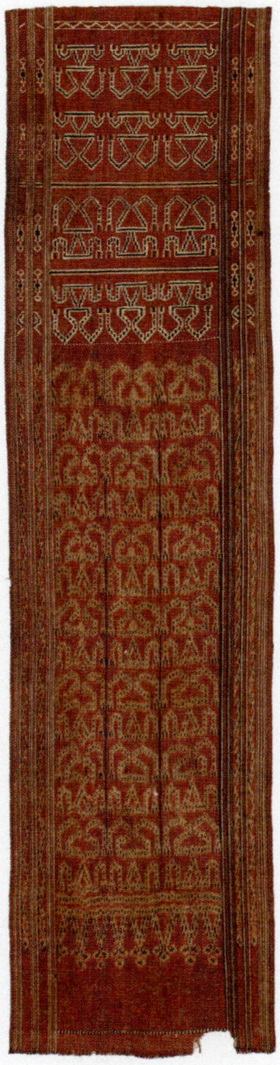

MA81 Iban ritual cloth, *kain sungkit*
Sarawak, Borneo, Malaysia, early 20th century. Cotton, warp ikat, discontinuous supplementary weft wrapping. 62 in x 17 in

MA82 Malay shawl, head cloth or hip wrapper, *kain limar*
Northeast coast, Malaysia, 19th century. Silk, weft ikat, zone dyeing. 92 in x 31 in

MA83 Malay shawl, head cloth or hip wrapper, *kain limar*
Northeast coast, Malaysia, 19th century. Silk, weft ikat, zone dyeing. 90 in x 30 in

MA84 Malay shawl, head cloth or hip wrapper, *kain limar*
Northeast coast, Malaysia, 19th century. Silk, weft ikat, zone dyeing. 90 in x 30 in

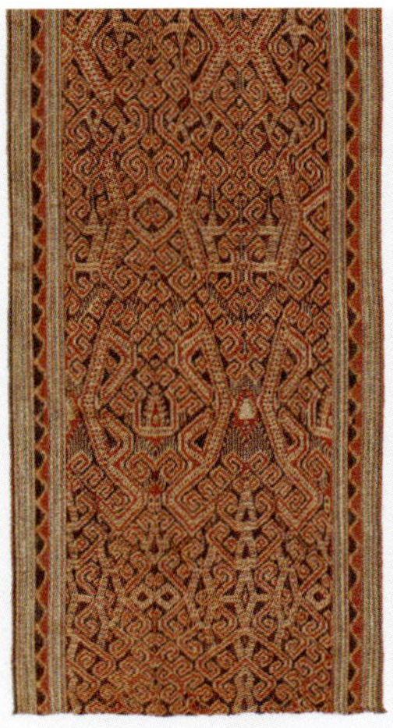

MA85 Iban woman's sarong, *kain kebat*
Sarawak, Borneo, Malaysia, 20th century. Cotton, warp ikat. 43 in x 18 in

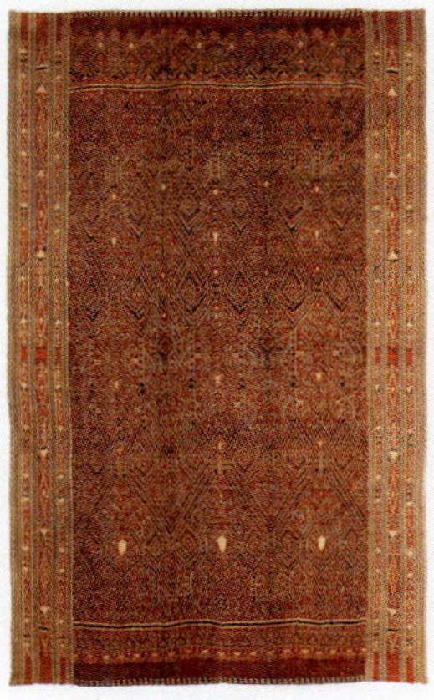

MA86 Iban ritual textile, *pua kumbu*
Sarawak, Borneo, Malaysia, 19th century. Cotton, warp ikat. 112 in x 67 in

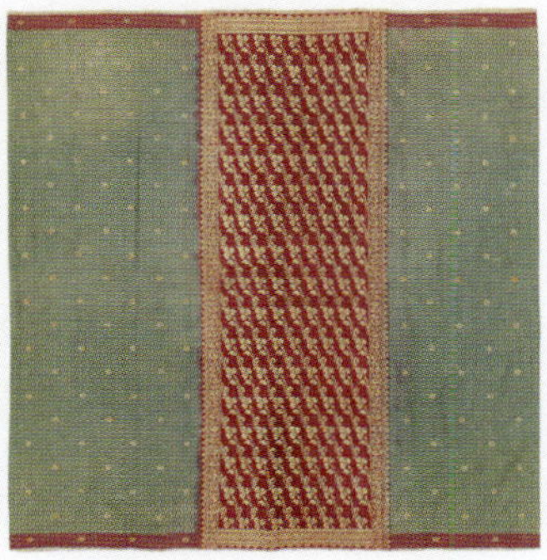

MA87 Malay woman's sarong, *sarung*
Malaysia, 19th century. Silk, zone dyeing, metallic continuous supplementary weft. 40 in x 41 in

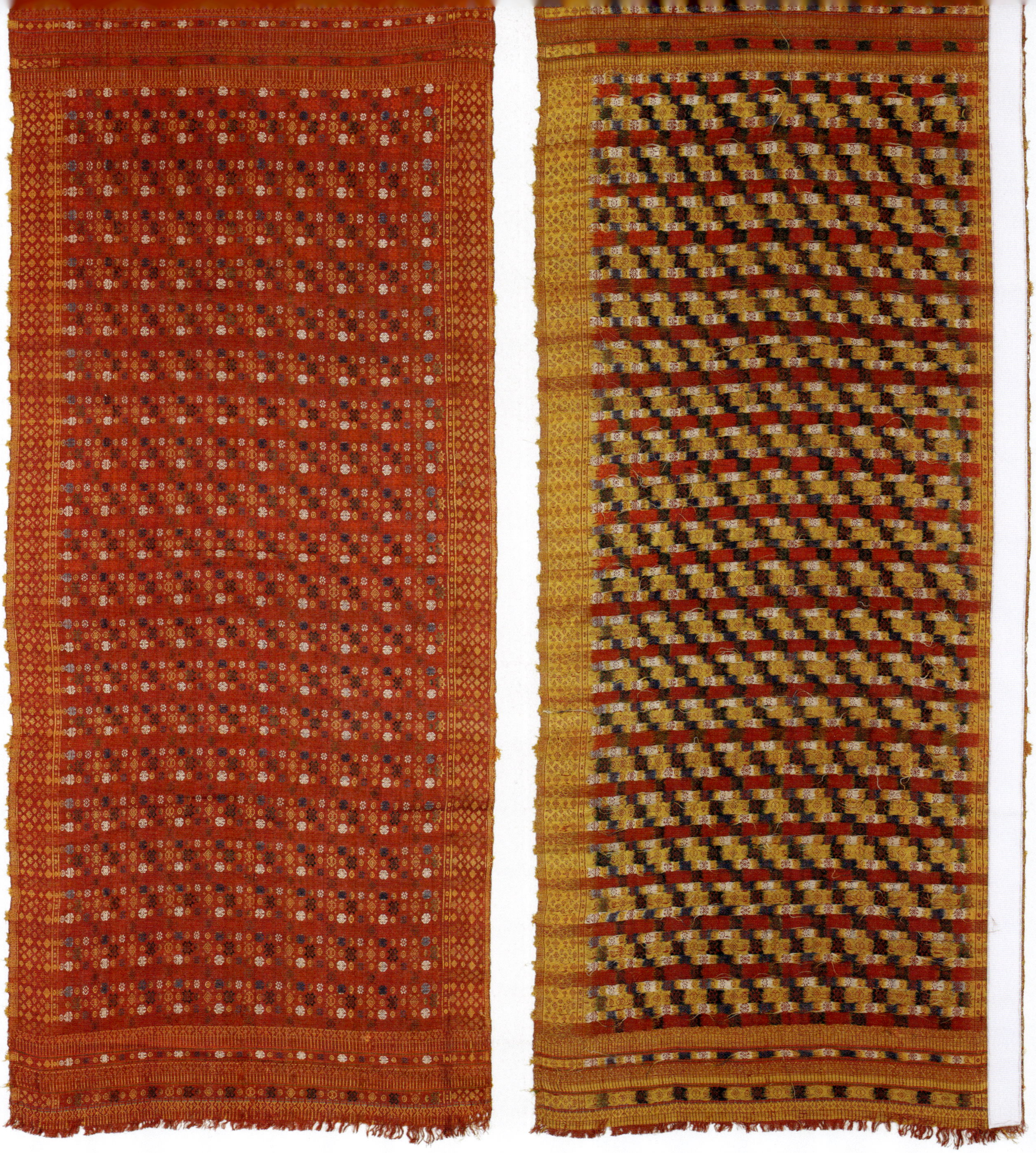

MA88 Cham ceremonial textile, Cambodia, 19th century. Silk, resist dye, continuous supplementary weft. 69 in x 29.5 in

The weaver of this ceremonial cloth applied a resist-dye technique other than ikat to color different sections of the threads forming the continuous supplementary-weft patterning. The results resemble different-colored discontinuous supplementary-weft designs in the textile's central field, but weft floats occur on the reverse. Continuous supplementary-weft patterning (*rbauk*) is generally in one color per shed, as in the rows of single-colored designs at the top and bottom ends of this ritual cloth. This textile's use was reserved for ceremonial occasions including as a coffin cover or as a canopy. A border of plain silk once flanked each side of the textile, but it is no longer present. Textiles similar in size and material and decorated only with continuous supplementary technique and not this resist-dye method serve as hip wrappers and are called *sampot rbauk*.

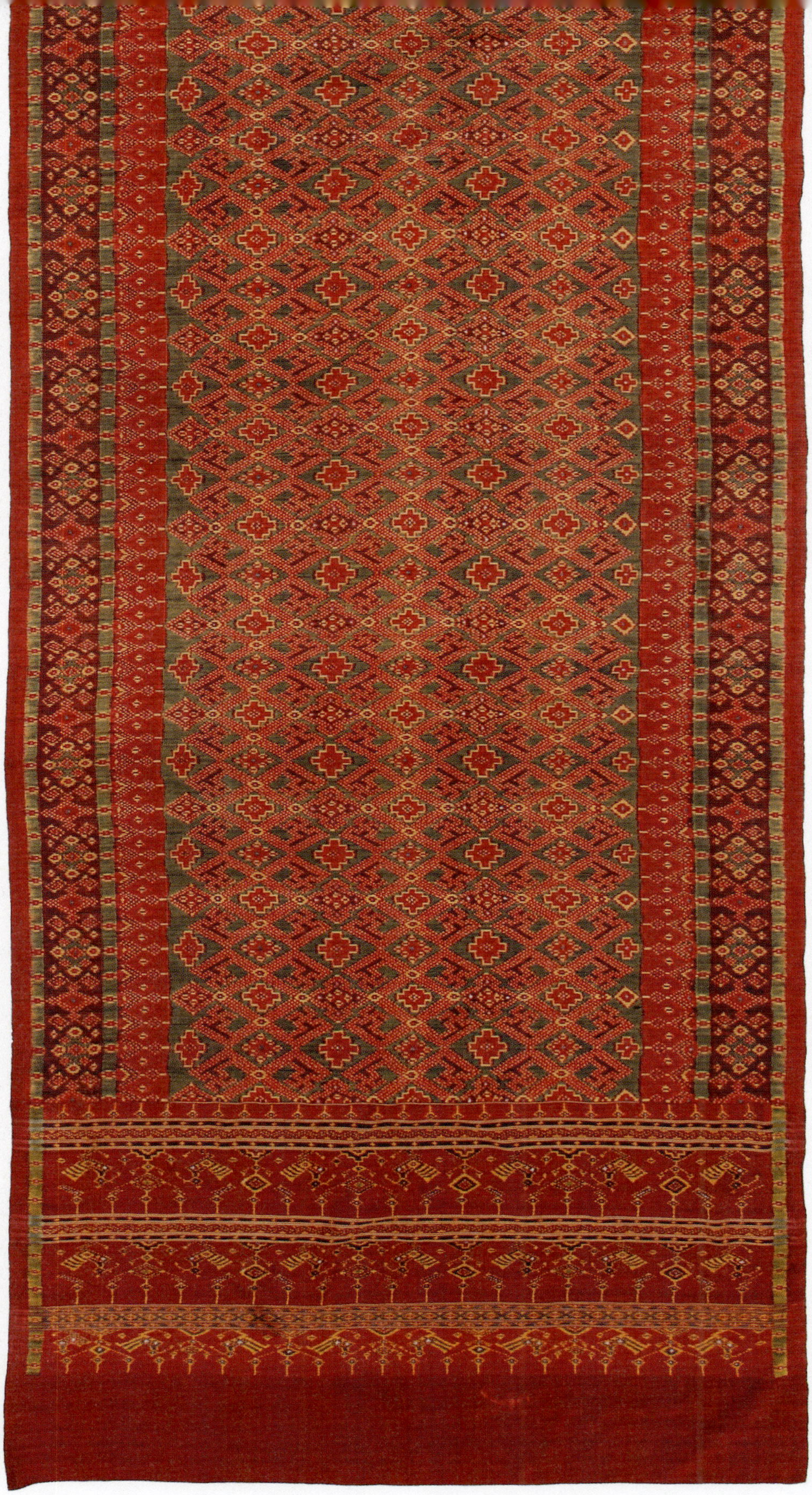

MA89 Hip wrapper, *sampot hol*, Cham or Khmer ethnic group, Cambodia, 19th century. Silk, weft ikat, 2:1 twill. 132 in x 36 in

Weavers of both Cham and Khmer descent wove weft-ikat-decorated silk textiles in a 2:1 twill weave in Cambodia. The combination of these two techniques also occurs in southern Northeast Thailand where there is a population of Khmer and related groups such as Kui. The central field of a hip wrapper generally consists of a repeating weft-ikat design of a lattice flanked by columns containing different ikat patterning. Stepped squares fill the lattice decorating this hip wrapper. These longitudinal bands are the same length as the center section. Both ends are decorated with three large bands of ikat patterns separated by smaller, contrasting rows of ikat dashes and roundels. The green background of the central field is often attributed to production by a Cham woman.

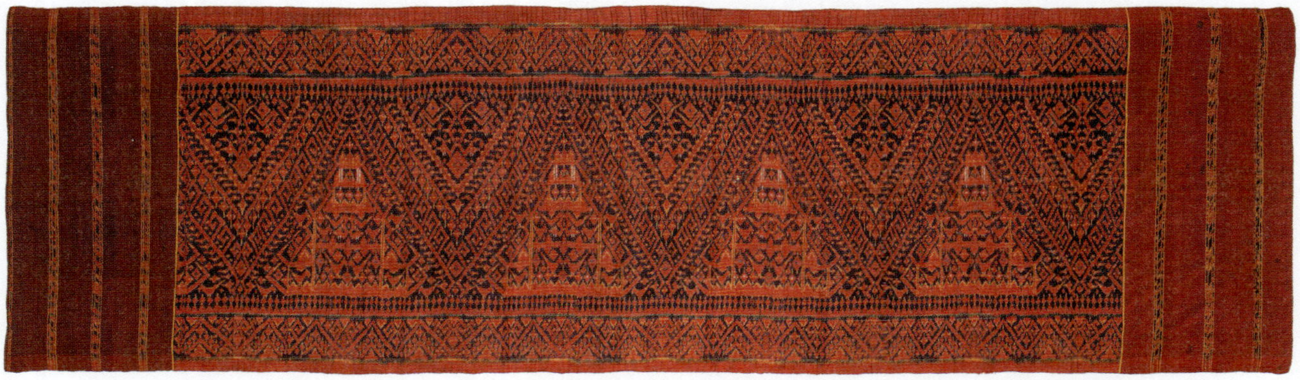

MA90 Khmer ceremonial hanging, *pidan* Cambodia, late 19th or early 20th century. Silk, weft ikat, 2:1 twill. 109 in x 32 in

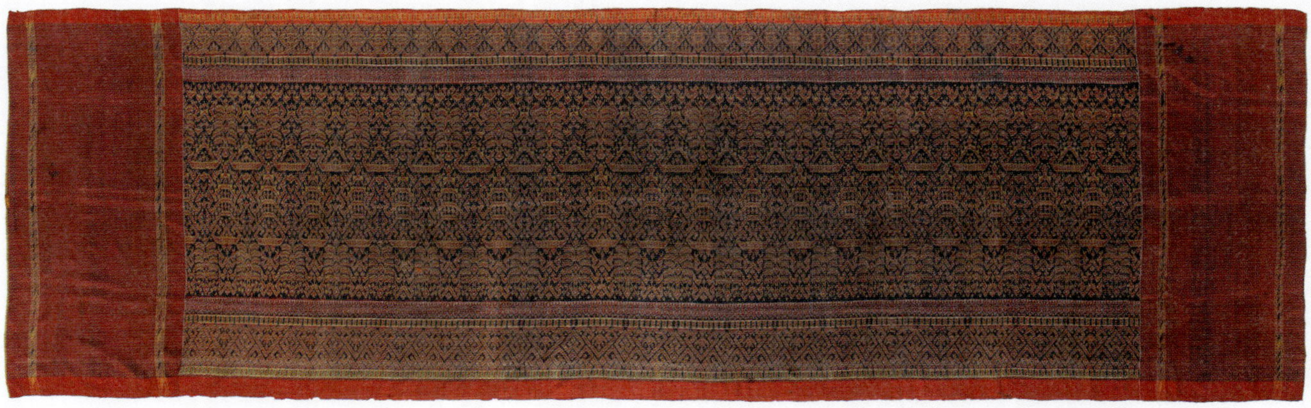

MA91 Hip wrapper, *sampot hol chang kben* Cambodia, 19th century. Silk, weft ikat, zone dyeing, 2:1 twill. 116 in x 36 in

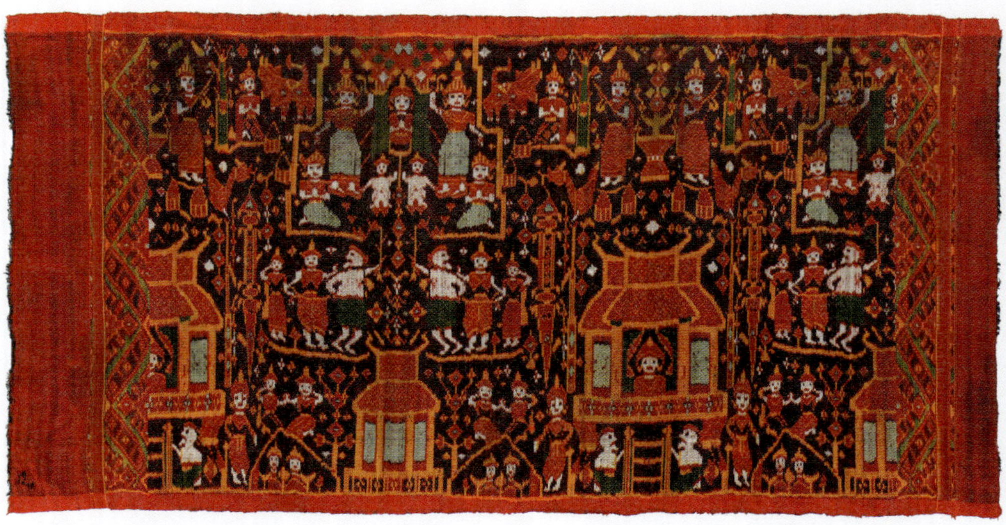

MA92 Khmer ceremonial hanging, *pidan* Cambodia, early 20th century. Silk, weft ikat, 2:1 twill. 31.5 in x 61 in

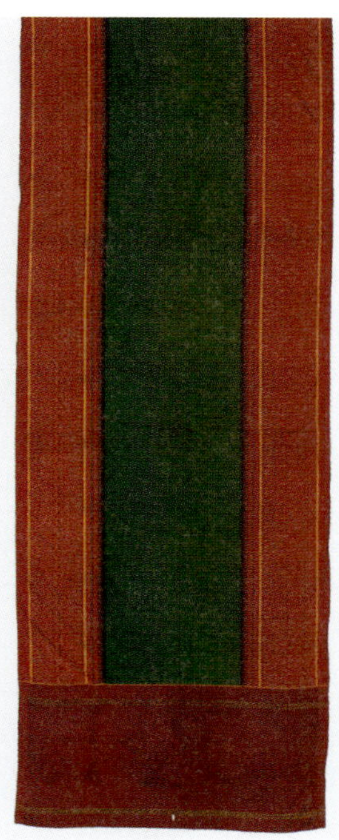

MA93 Hip wrapper, *sampot hol chang kben*
Cambodia, 19th century. Silk, weft ikat, zone dyeing, 2:1 twill. 118 in x 35 in

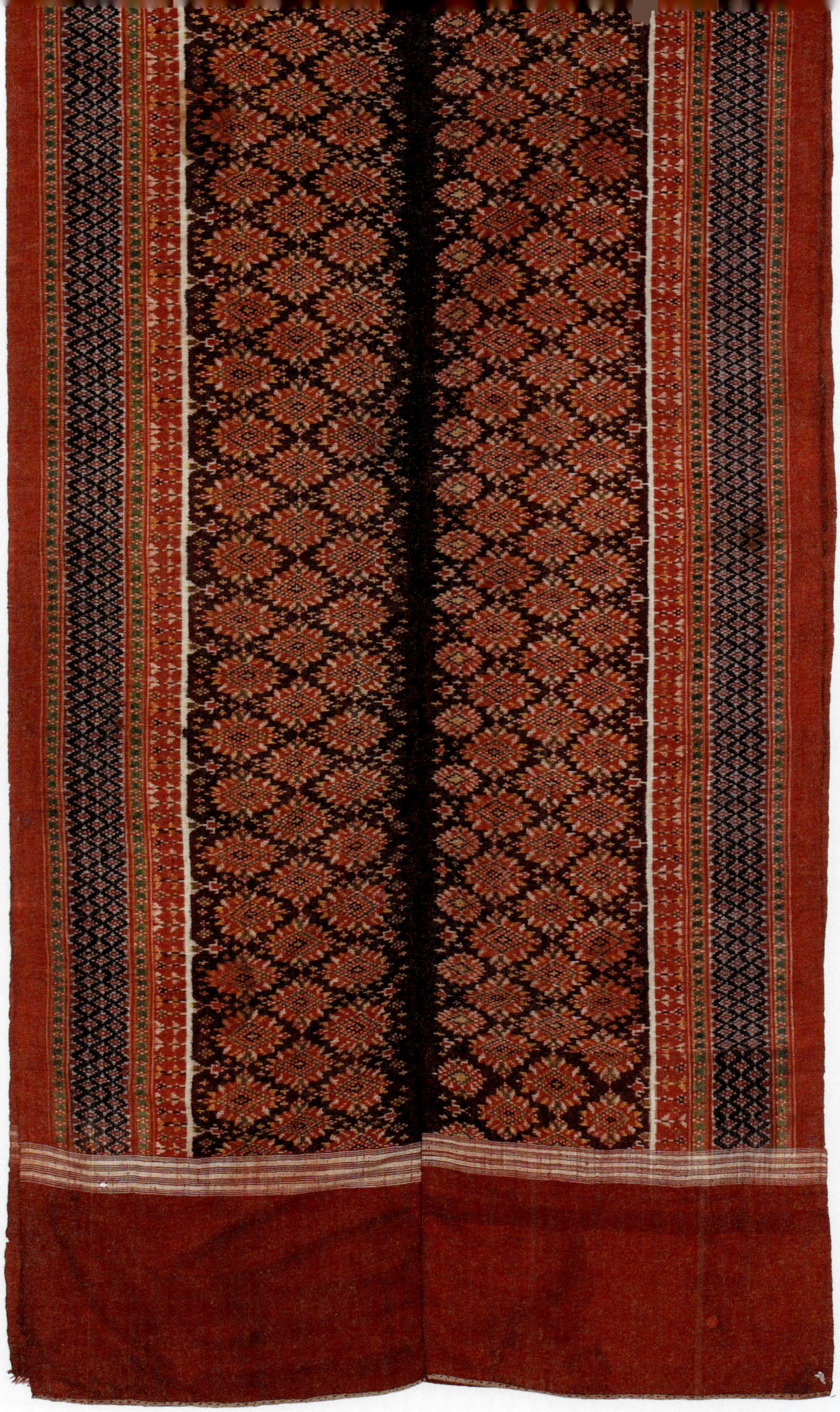

MA94 Tai Daeng ceremonial textile, *phaa viang long*, Northeast Laos, 19th century. Silk, weft ikat, zone dyeing. 144 in x 35 in

The design layout and patterning of this two-paneled ceremonial textile resemble *patola* or double-ikat silk textiles from Gujarat, India. There are no written records of these, or other types of Indian trade textile, reaching the remote mountain valleys where the Tai Daeng resided. *Patola* silks are not mentioned in the historical records about the types of textile brought to present-day Laos. The exposure was most likely indirect via exposure to weft-ikat silk textiles from present-day Cambodia or Thailand that were inspired by Indian trade textiles. Traditional Tai frame looms produced narrow textiles, and the weaver of this rare ceremonial cloth wove one panel that she cut in half and joined together along one side to form a wide cloth. Tai weavers utilized weft ikat instead of double ikat and applied zone dyeing to produce the solid red ends. This precious textile served as a coffin cover among the non-Buddhist Tai and was not worn.

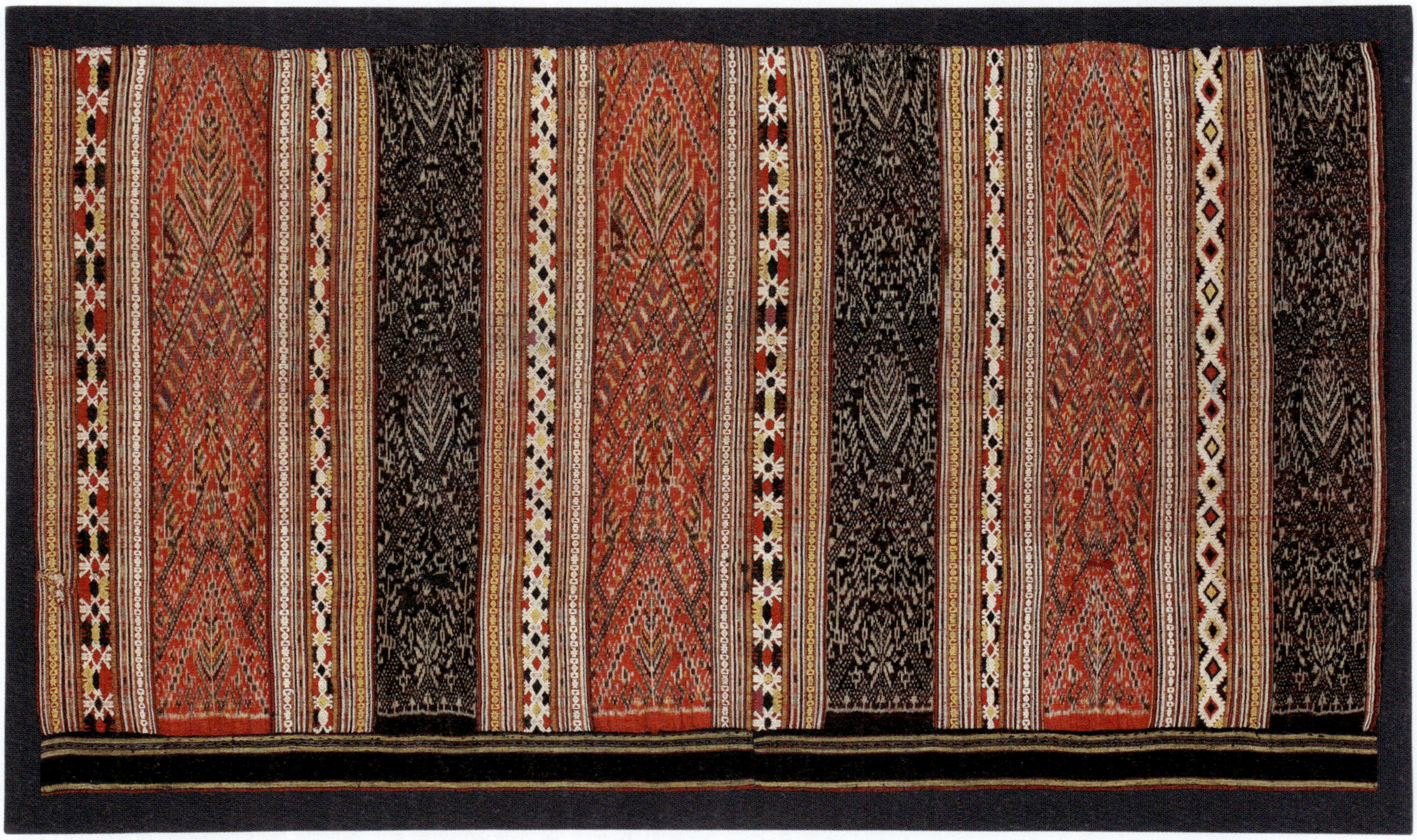

MA95 Tai (Tai Daeng or Tai Neua) woman's or shaman's ceremonial skirt, *sin mii taa* or *sin mor phi/sin phi*, Hua Phan Province, Northeast Laos, late 19th or early 20th century. Silk, cotton, weft ikat, continuous and discontinuous supplementary weft. 28 in x 51 in

Women belonging to non-Buddhist Tai groups such as Tai Daeng and Tai Neua wear a specific type of skirt decorated with bands of weft-ikat patterning when attending the funerals of their in-laws. These groups are patrilineal, and a woman joins her husband's lineage upon marriage. Her mother-in-law gifts her a skirt decorated with bands of weft ikat and supplementary-weft designs. A specific motif must be present in the weft-ikat patterning for the garment to be worn for a woman's in-law's funeral or by a shaman when conducting a rite. This motif is triangular, representing the gable to the house-like structure placed on a grave (deceased non-Buddhist Tai are buried, not cremated). Heads of the *naak* mythical serpent decorate each side of the roof gable.

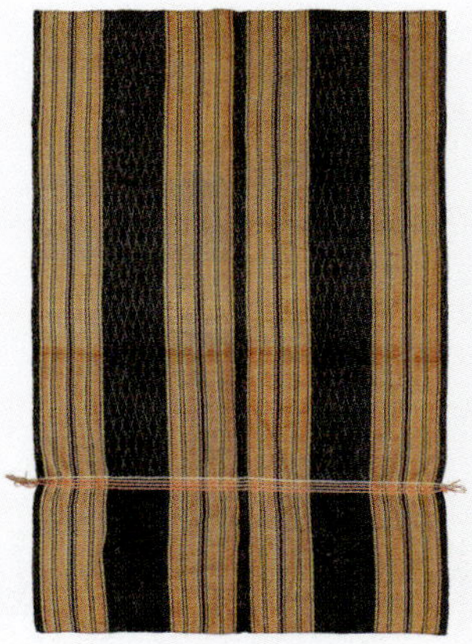

MA96 Pakoh blanket
South Laos, early 20th century. Cotton, warp ikat, weft twining. 81 in x 54 in

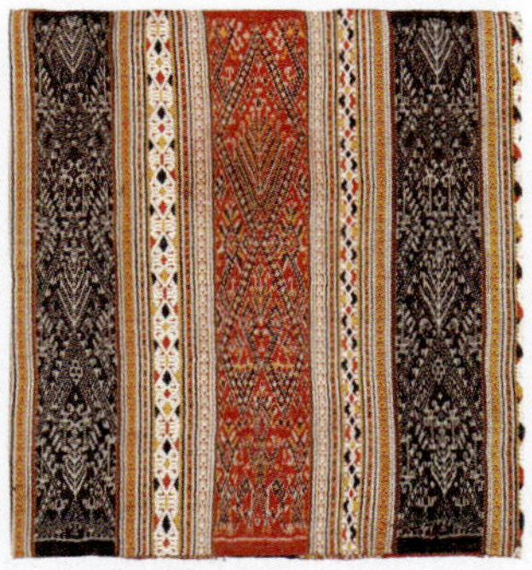

MA97 Tai Daeng woman's sarong, *sin mii taa*
Northeast Laos, early 20th century. Silk, cotton, weft ikat, continuous and discontinuous supplementary weft. 28 in x 27 in

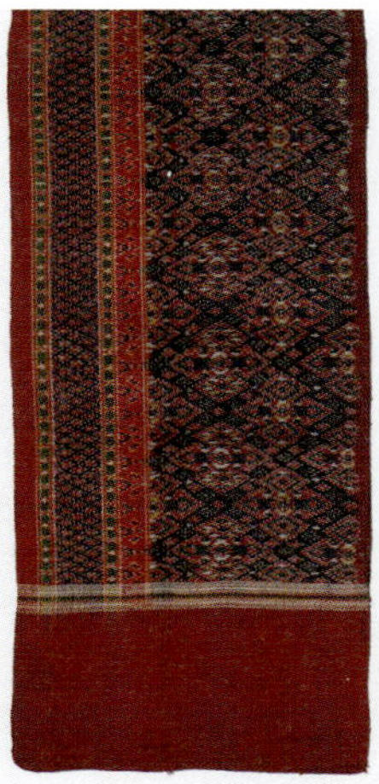

MA98 Tai Daeng funerary cloth or coffin cover fragment
Northeast Laos, 19th century. Silk, weft ikat, warp zone dyeing. 44 in x 18.5 in

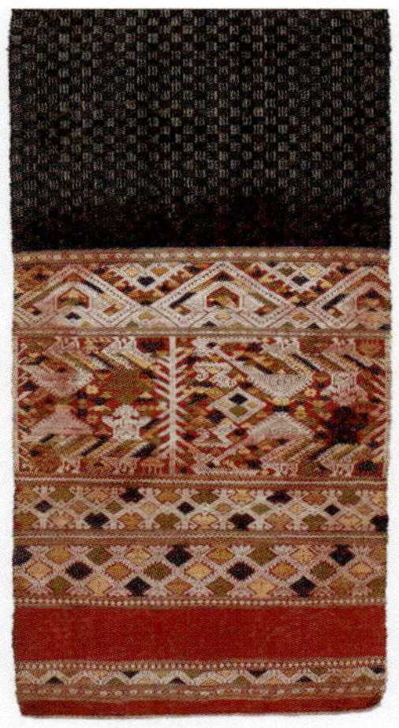

MA99 Tai Neua shawl (*phaa thum*) panel
Northeast Laos, early 20th century. Silk, cotton, zone dyeing, continuous and discontinuous supplementary weft. 66 in x 17 in

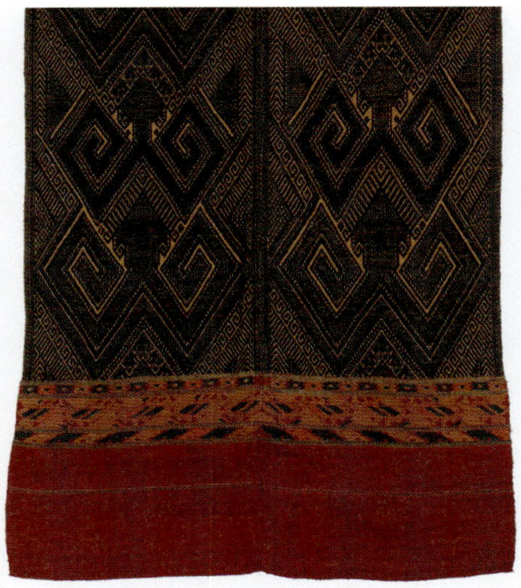

MA100 Tai Neua shawl, *phaa thum*
Northeast Laos, 20th century. Silk, cotton, zone dyeing, continuous and discontinuous supplementary weft. 75 in x 25.5 in

MA101 Tai Daeng shoulder or healing cloth
Northeast Laos, 19th century. Silk, cotton, zone dyeing, continuous and discontinuous supplementary weft. 85 in x 15.5 in

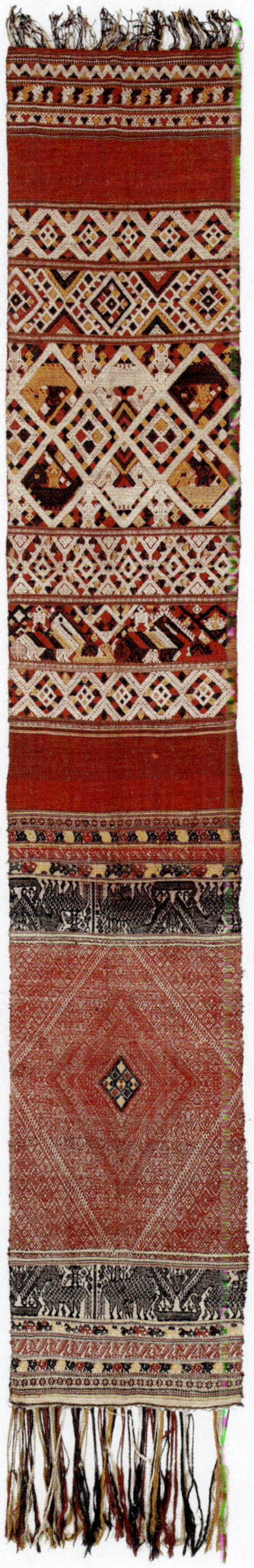

MA102 Tai Neua shoulder or shaman's cloth
Northeast Laos, 19th century. Silk, cotton, zone dyeing, continuous and discontinuous supplementary weft. 87 in x 14.5 in

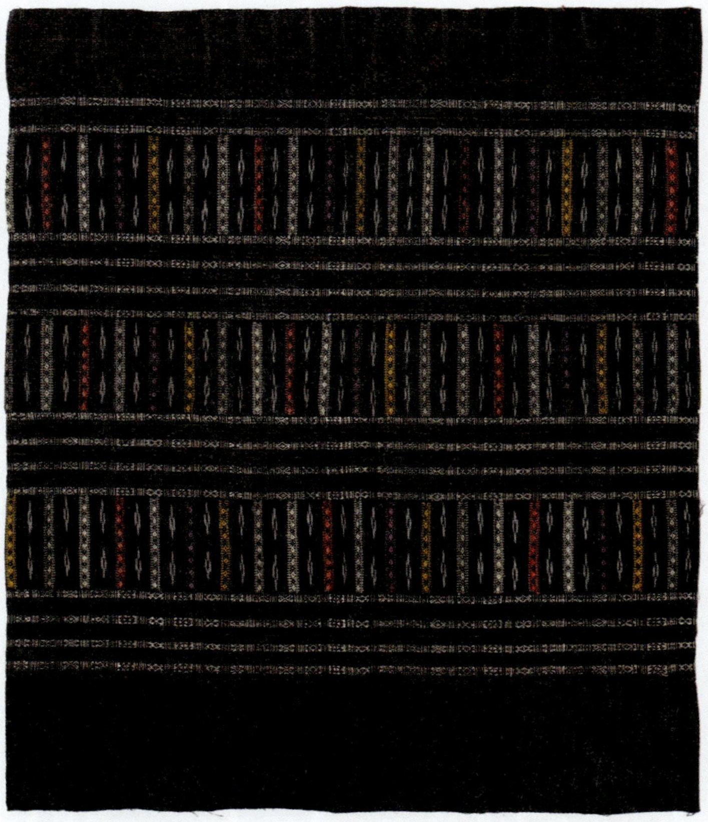

MA103 Tai Daeng woman's sarong, *sin mii muk koh* Northeast Laos, 20th century. Cotton, silk, warp ikat, weft ikat, discontinuous supplementary weft, supplementary warp. 30.5 in x 26 in

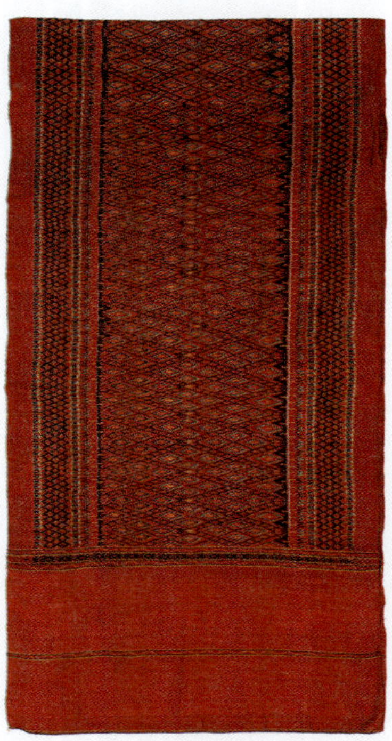

MA104 Tai Phuan funerary cloth or hip wrapper
Northeast Laos, 20th century. Silk, weft ikat, warp-zone dyeing. 128 in x 32 in

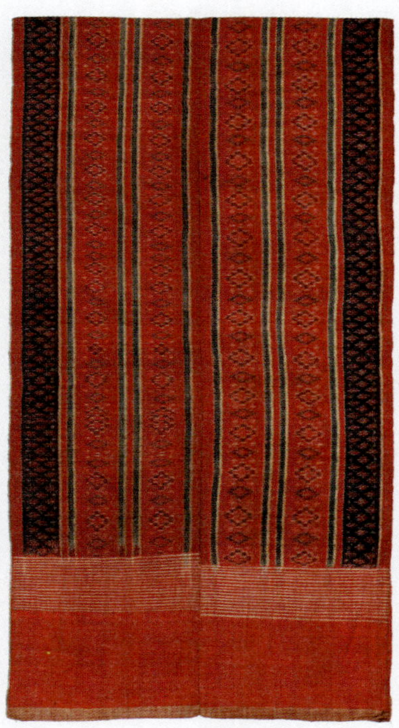

MA105 Tai funerary cloth or coffin cover
Laos, 19th century. Silk, weft ikat, zone dyeing. 132 in x 35 in

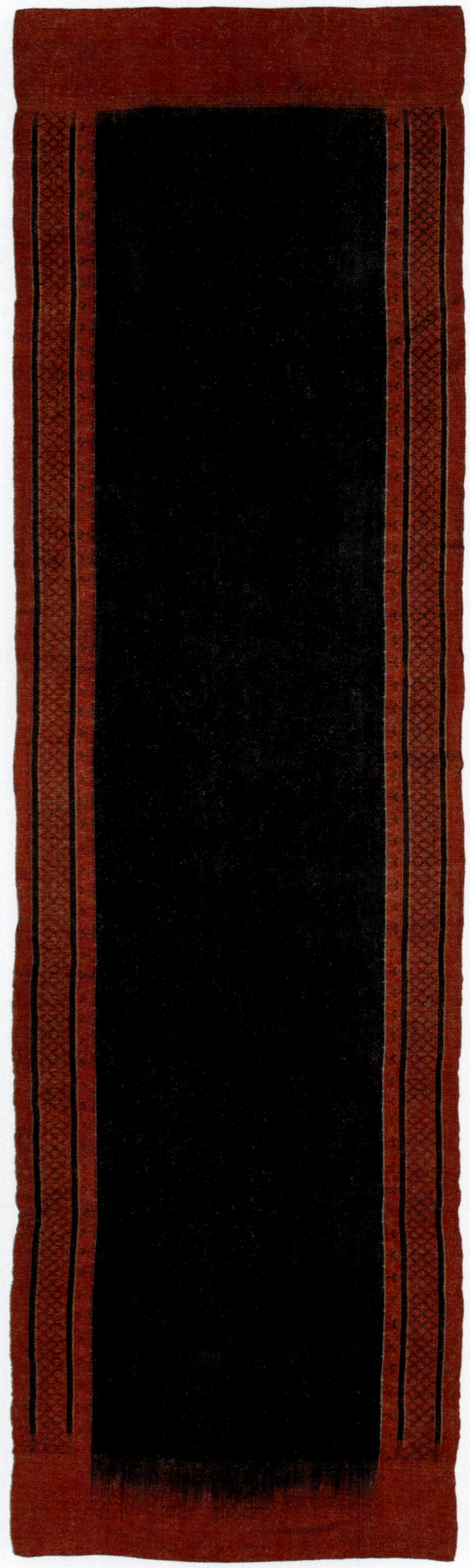

MA106 Tai funerary cloth or coffin cover
Laos, 19th century. Silk, weft ikat, zone dyeing. 113 in x 32 in

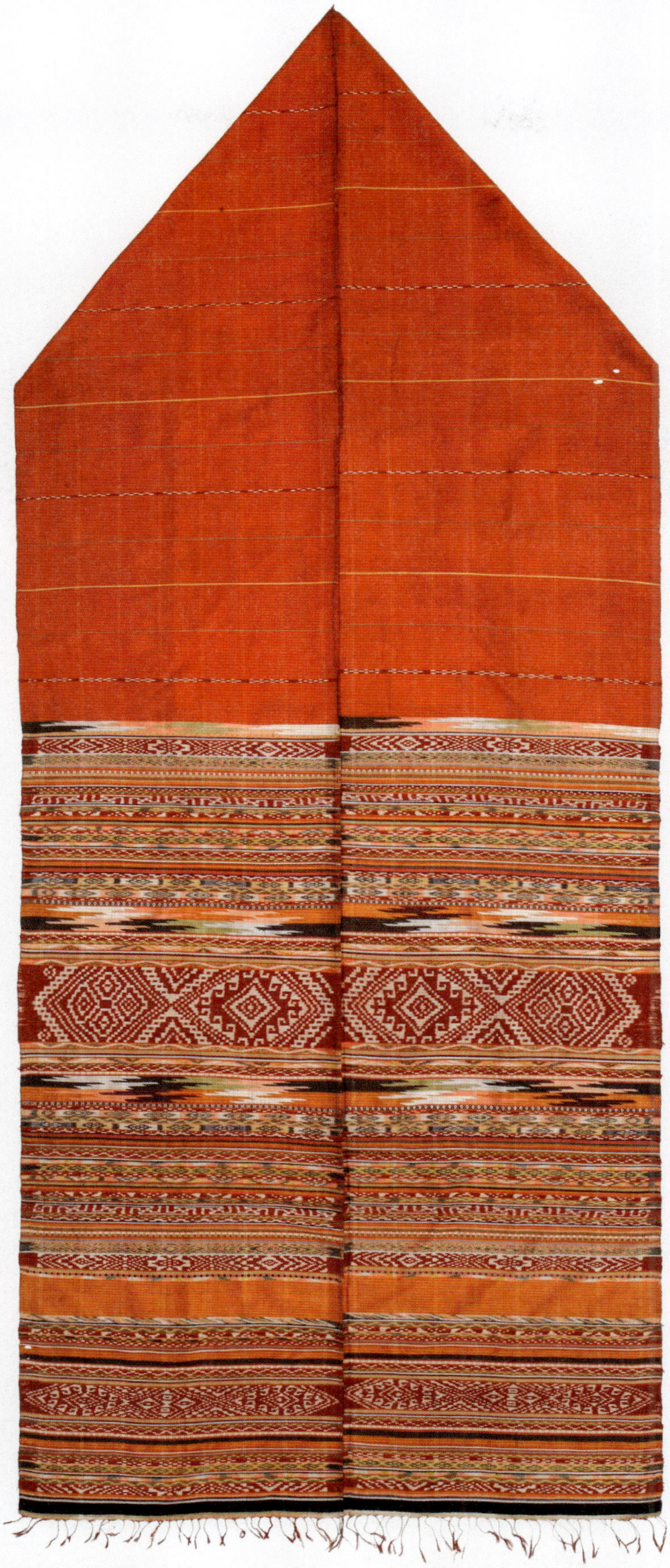

MA107 Tai accessory, Northeast Myanmar or adjacent Southwest China, 19th century. Silk, weft ikat, dovetail tapestry, continuous supplementary weft. 79 in x 34 in

The overall layout consists of various-sized rows of designs created primarily with weft ikat and dovetail tapestry techniques. This textile is one of a handful of extant weavings known of this type. Textiles produced by the Tai Khoen and related Tai Lue and Tai Neua generally do not contain weft-ikat patterning, but this rare example features a large row of red-and-white hooked rhombs and stepped squares as well as smaller bands of geometric patterning. The combination of techniques also occurs in skirts of some Tai Lue subgroups, especially among communities in the vicinity of the Mekong River which was a major regional trade route. The wearer was a person of wealth and high status since the textile is made entirely of imported silk.

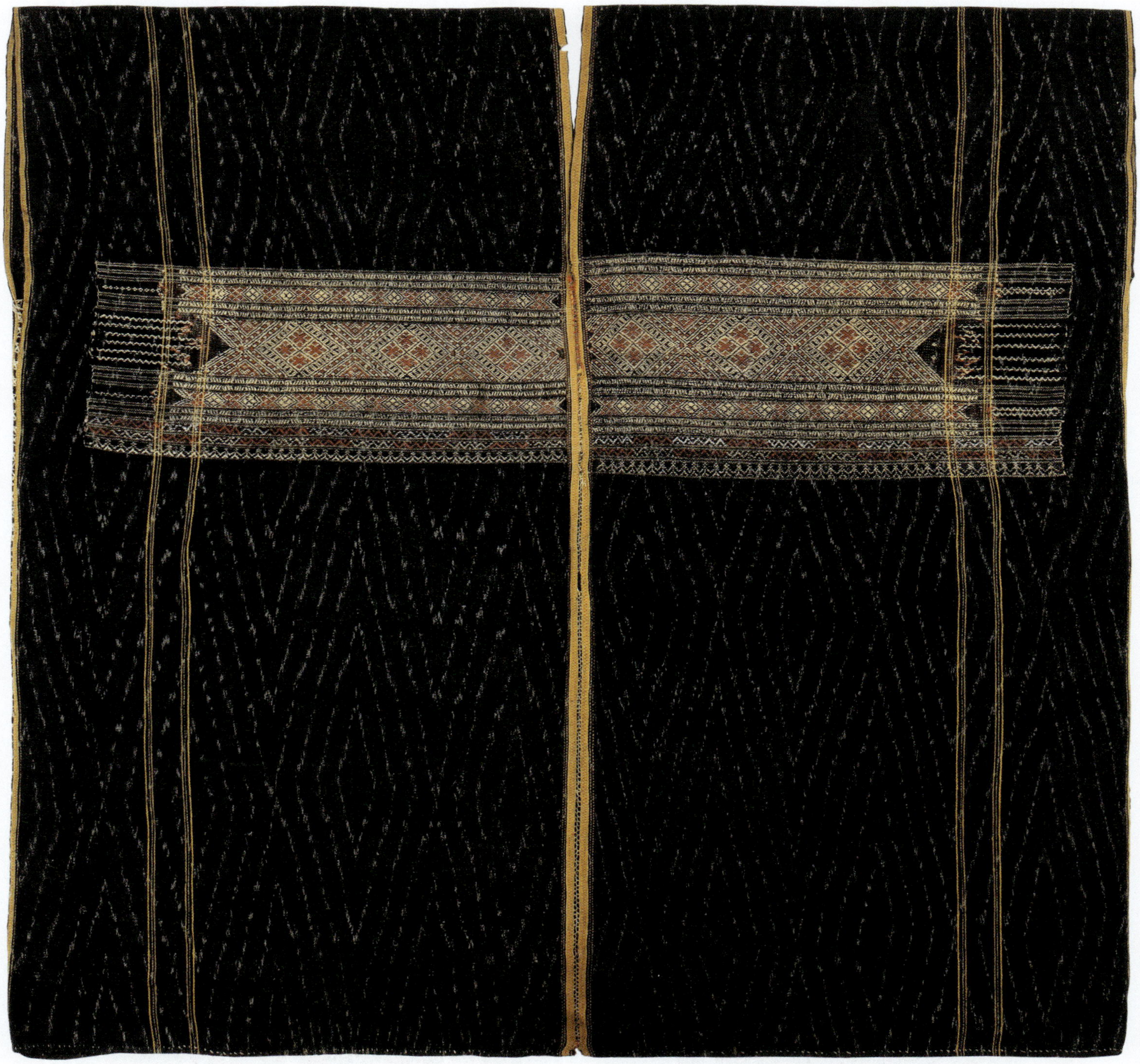

MA108 Asho Chin tunic or *phyang*, Myanmar, 19th century. Cotton, silk, warp ikat, continuous and discontinuous supplementary weft. 38 in x 35 in

Warp-ikat designs created on textiles woven on a backstrap loom are presently not complex in mainland Southeast Asia. These patterns consist of two colors: the color of the warp threads before applying the ikat technique and one type of dye that is often indigo. This tunic is composed of two panels primarily decorated with warp ikat in indigo and white, and yellow and red warp stripes provide contrast. The garment's top section contains several bands of silk supplementary-weft designs of layered diamonds and zigzags. Asho Chin weavers acquired the silk via trade with China, Bangladesh, or Northeast India. The Asho Chin consists of several subgroups. The group that produces this textile type is sometimes called Khamau, but ethnic Chin interlocuters find this term derogatory.

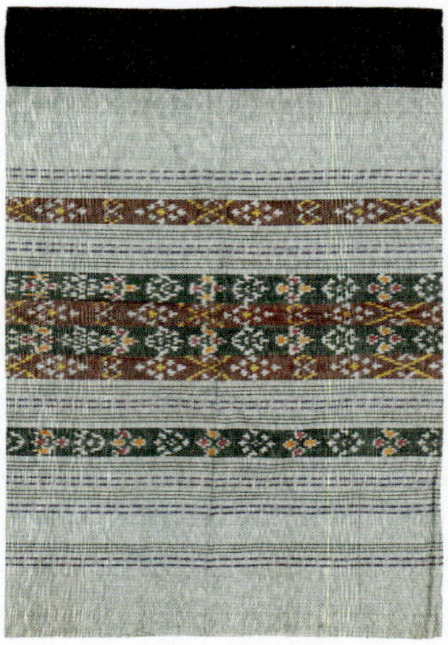

MA109 Shan or Tai Yai woman's sarong
Inle Lake, Myanmar, 20th century. Silk, warp ikat, cotton waistband. 43 in x 32 in

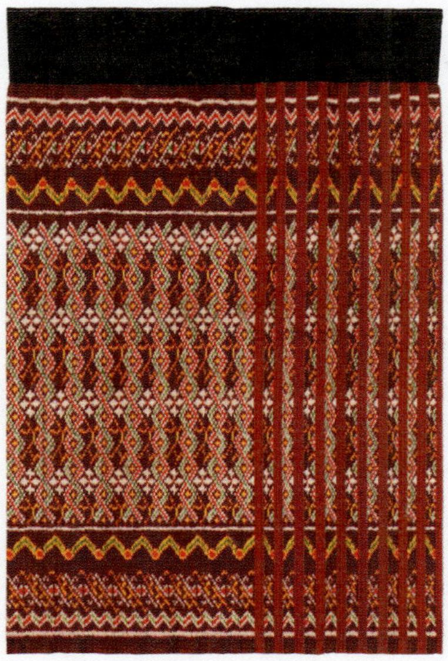

MA110 Intha woman's sarong
Inle Lake, Myanmar, 20th century. Silk, weft ikat, 2:1 twill, cotton waistband. 43 in x 44 in

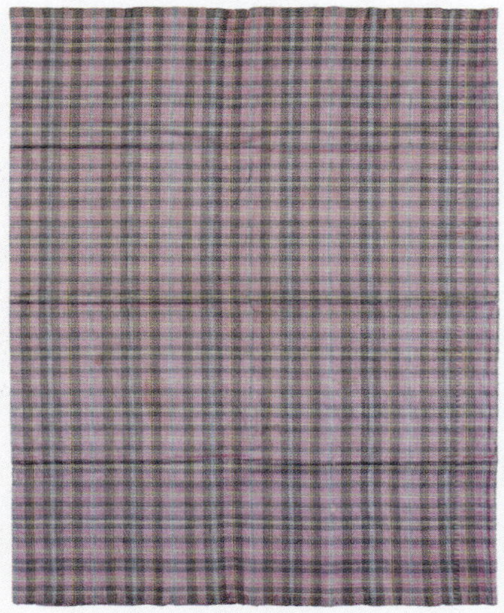

MA111 Man's sarong, *longyi*
Myanmar, 20th century. Silk, weft ikat. 43 in x 35 in

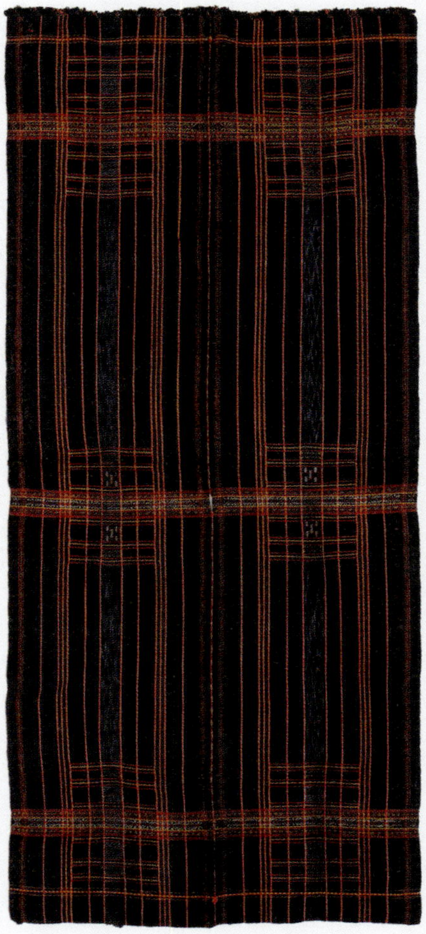

MA112 Asho Chin shawl or mantle
Myanmar, 20th century. Cotton, silk, warp ikat, supplementary weft. 61.5 in x 14.5 in

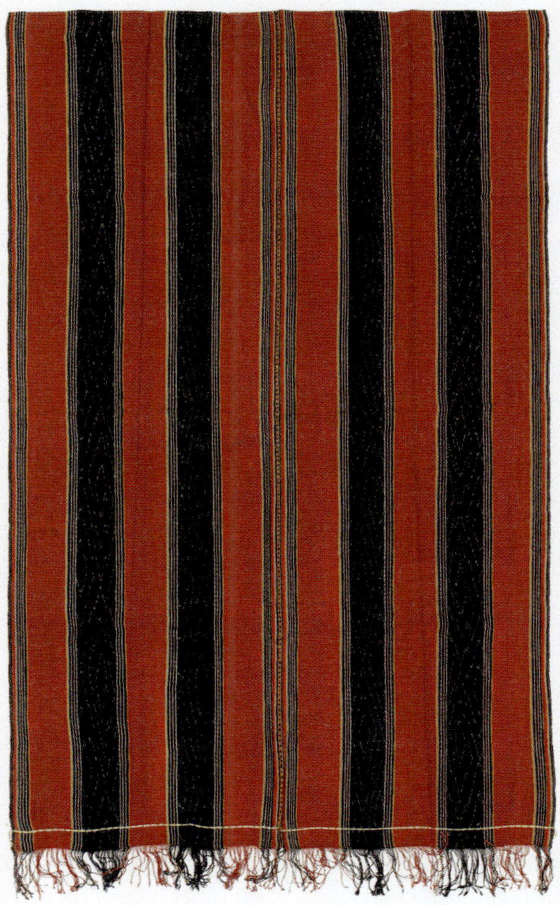

MA113 Asho Chin man's shawl or mantle
Myanmar, early 20th century. Cotton, warp ikat, weft twining. 77 in x 44 in

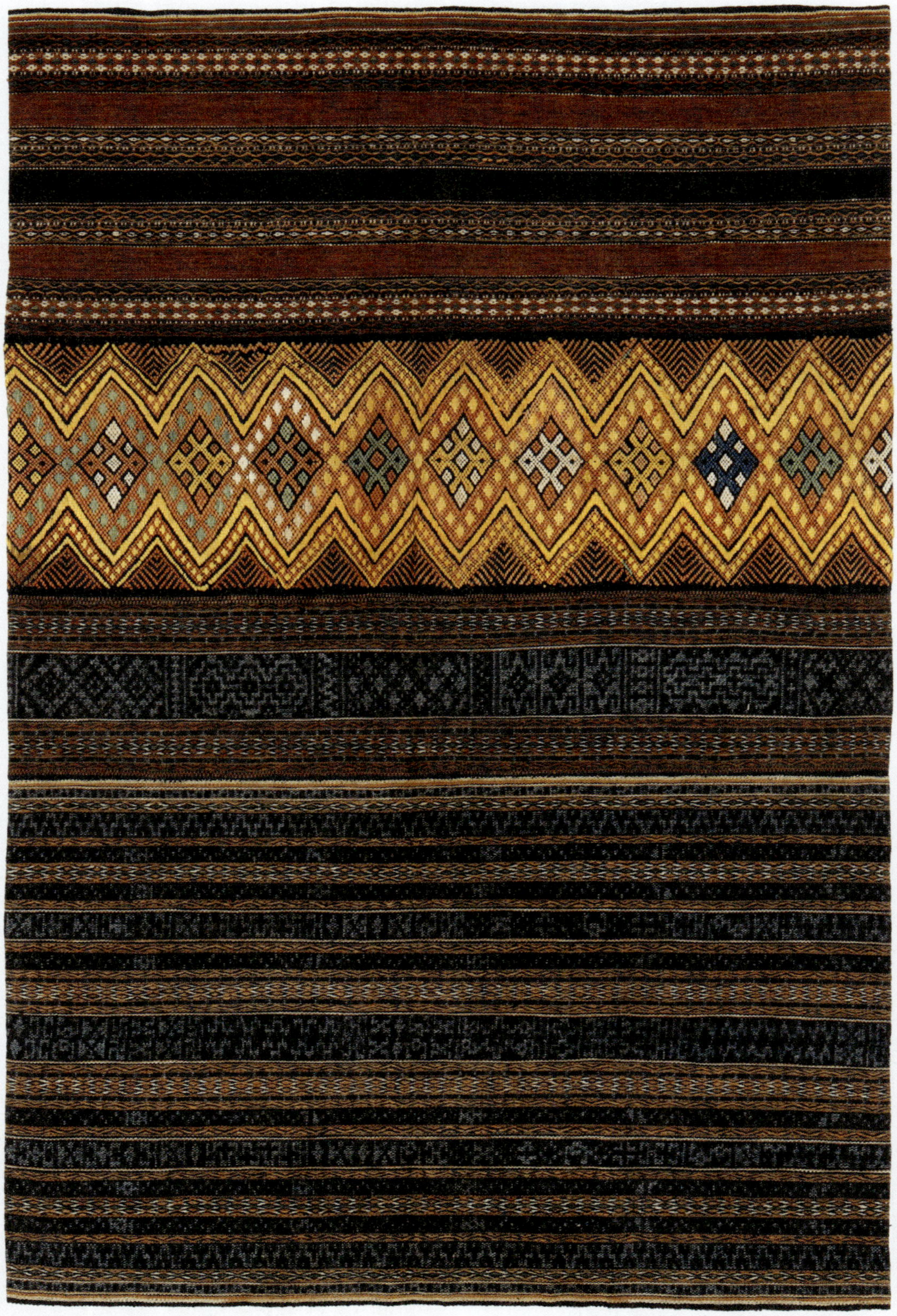

MA114 Meifu Li women's ceremonial skirt, Hainan, China, first half 20th century. Cotton, silk, warp ikat, discontinuous supplementary weft, warp float. 33 in x 22 in

Li women weave on a foot-braced, backstrap loom, an ancient type of equipment whose use continues in a few areas of Asia. The textiles produced on the Li loom are narrow, and this garment consists of a panel decorated with silk supplementary-weft patterning and several panels featuring clear warp-ikat designs in indigo blue and white and warp-float patterns. Unmarried women would wear skirts with a panel of silk supplementary-weft patterning, such as this example, for ceremonial occasions. The Li form a Daic group, belonging to the Tai-Kadai ethnolinguistic family and related to the Tai peoples of Mainland Southeast Asia and Southwest China. The Meifu Li tradition of complex warp-ikat designs is the sole surviving example of this tradition among the Daic groups.

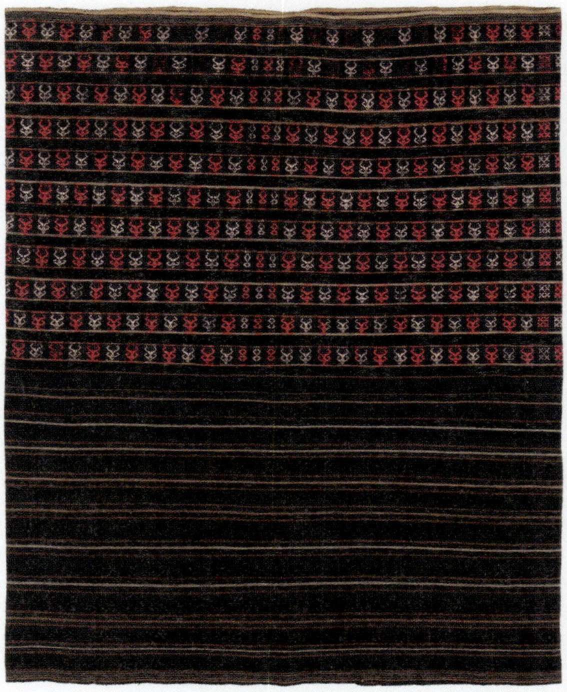

MA115 Li woman's skirt Hainan, China, first half 20th century. Cotton, silk, warp ikat, discontinuous supplementary weft, embroidery. 33 in x 28 in

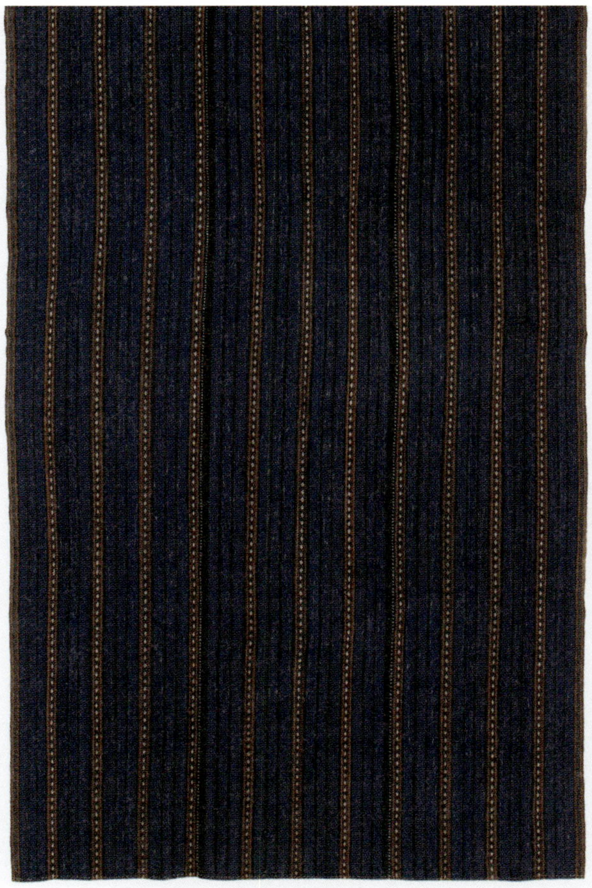

MA116 Li blanket Hainan, China, first half 20th century. Cotton, warp ikat, supplementary warp. 65 in x 35 in. The Textile Museum, 2020.7.16

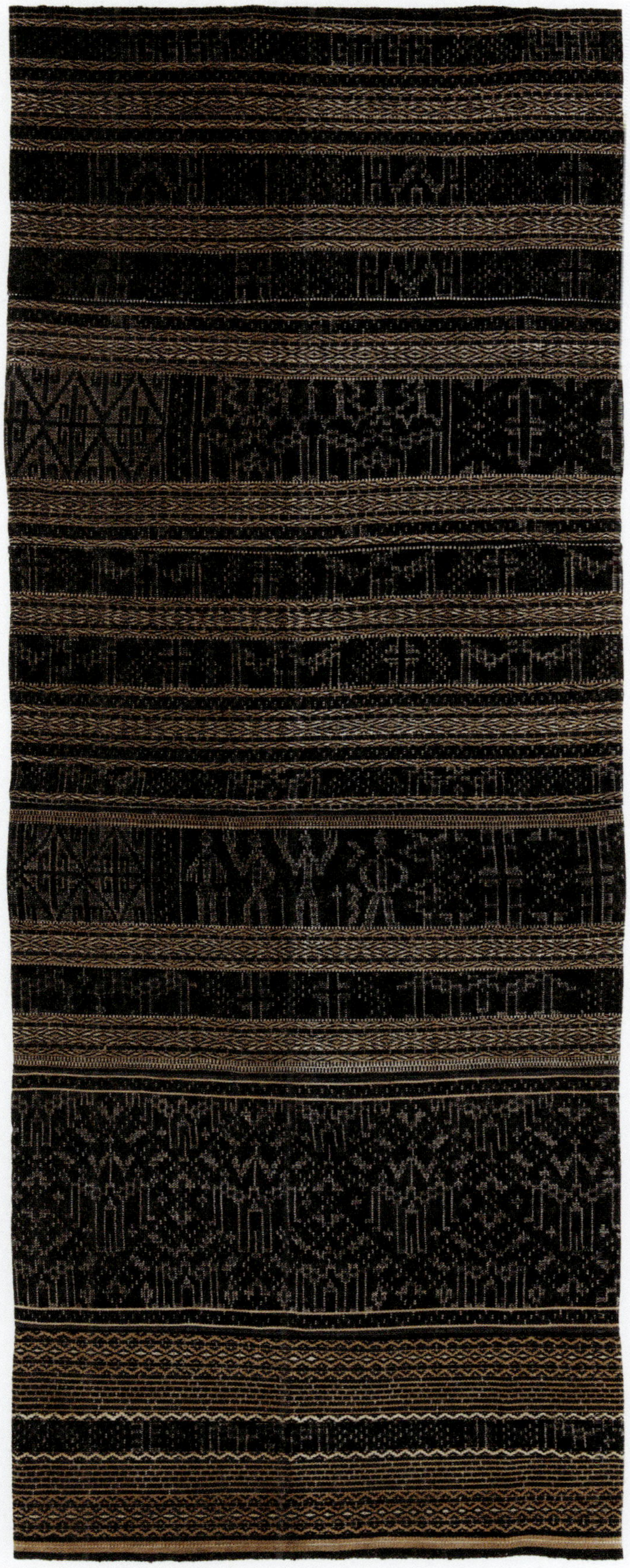

MA117 Meifu Li woman's sarong Hainan, China, first half 20th century. Cotton, warp ikat, supplementary warp. 65 in x 35 in. The Textile Museum, 2020.7.3

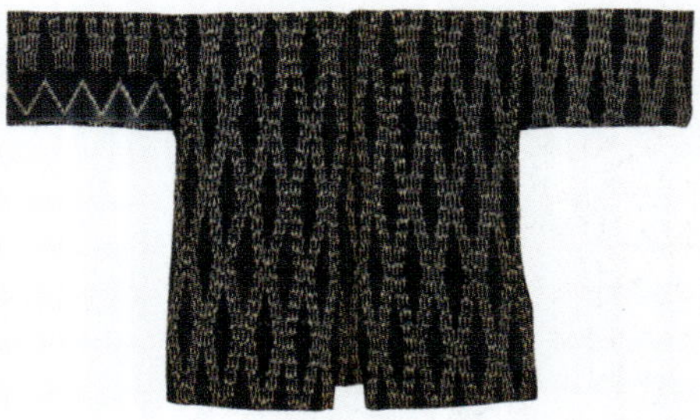

MA118 Meifu Li man's jacket Hainan, China, early 20th century. Cotton, warp ikat. 44 in x 36 in. The Textile Museum, 2020.7.15

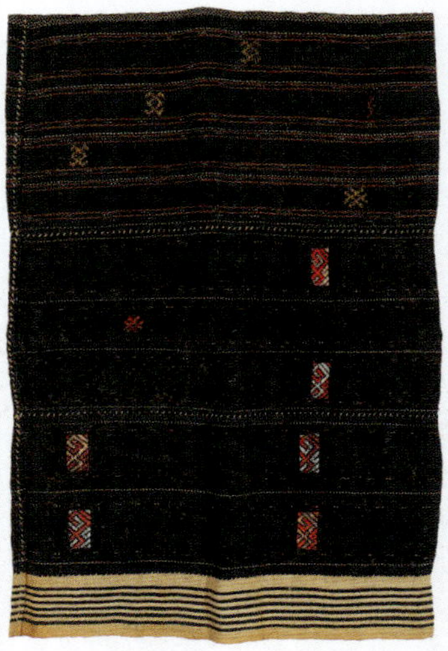

MA119 Qi Li woman's sarong
Hainan, China, first half 20th century. Bast fiber, silk, warp ikat, discontinuous supplementary weft. 32 in x 22 in

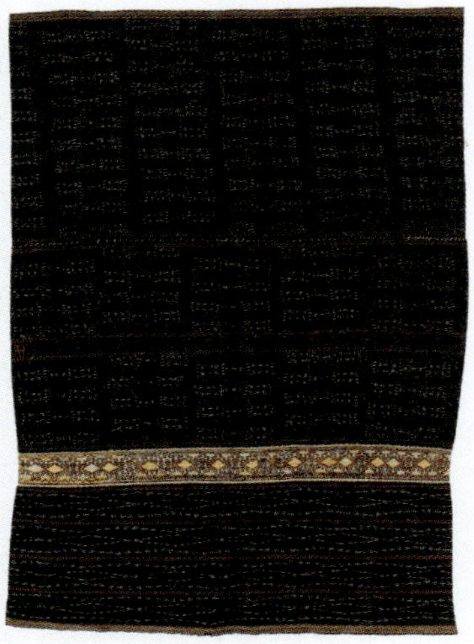

MA120 Meifu Li woman's sarong
Hainan, China, early 20th century. Cotton, warp ikat, supplementary warp. 36 in x 24 in. The Textile Museum, 2020.7.12

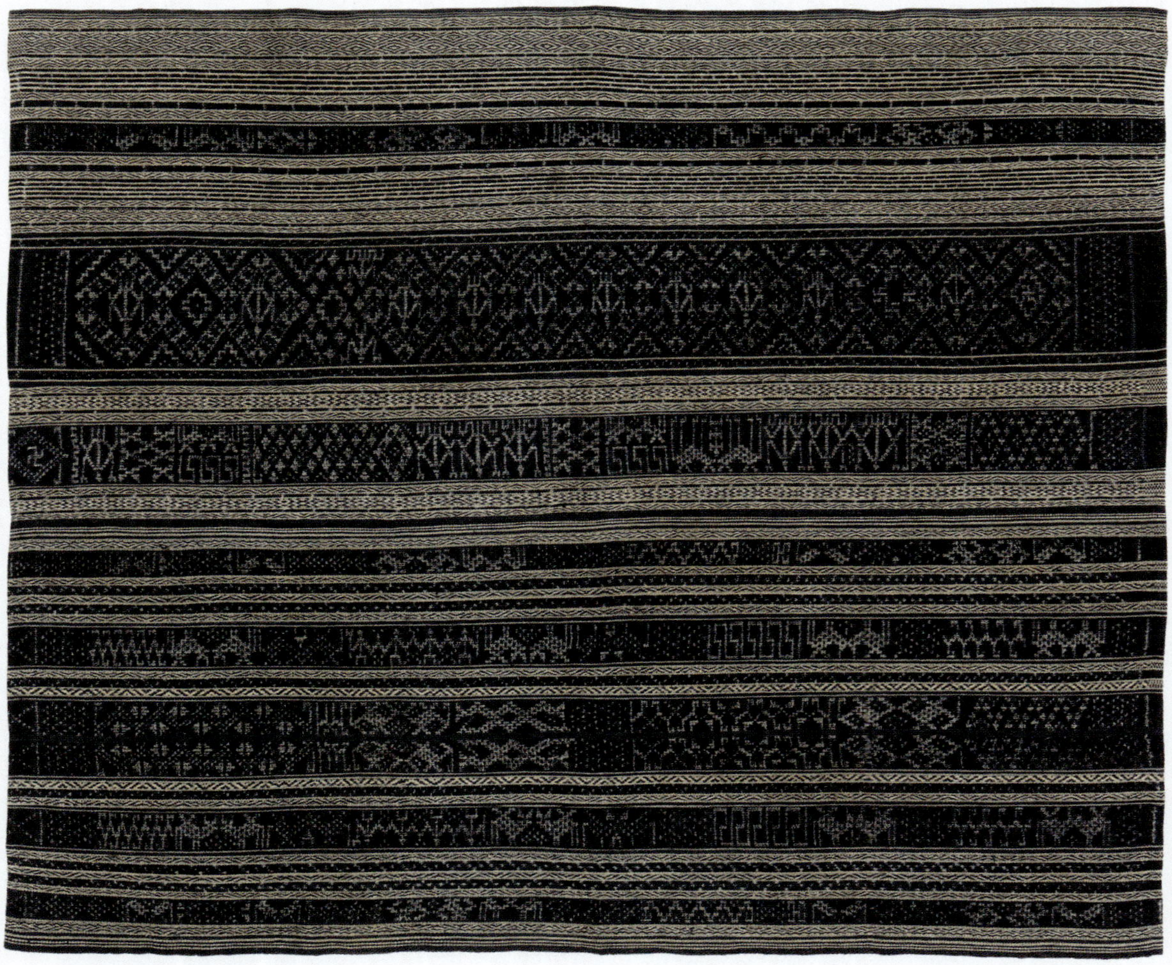

MA121 Meifu Li woman's sarong
Hainan, China, early 20th century. Cotton, warp ikat, supplementary warp. 24 in x 44 in. The Textile Museum, 2020.7.13=

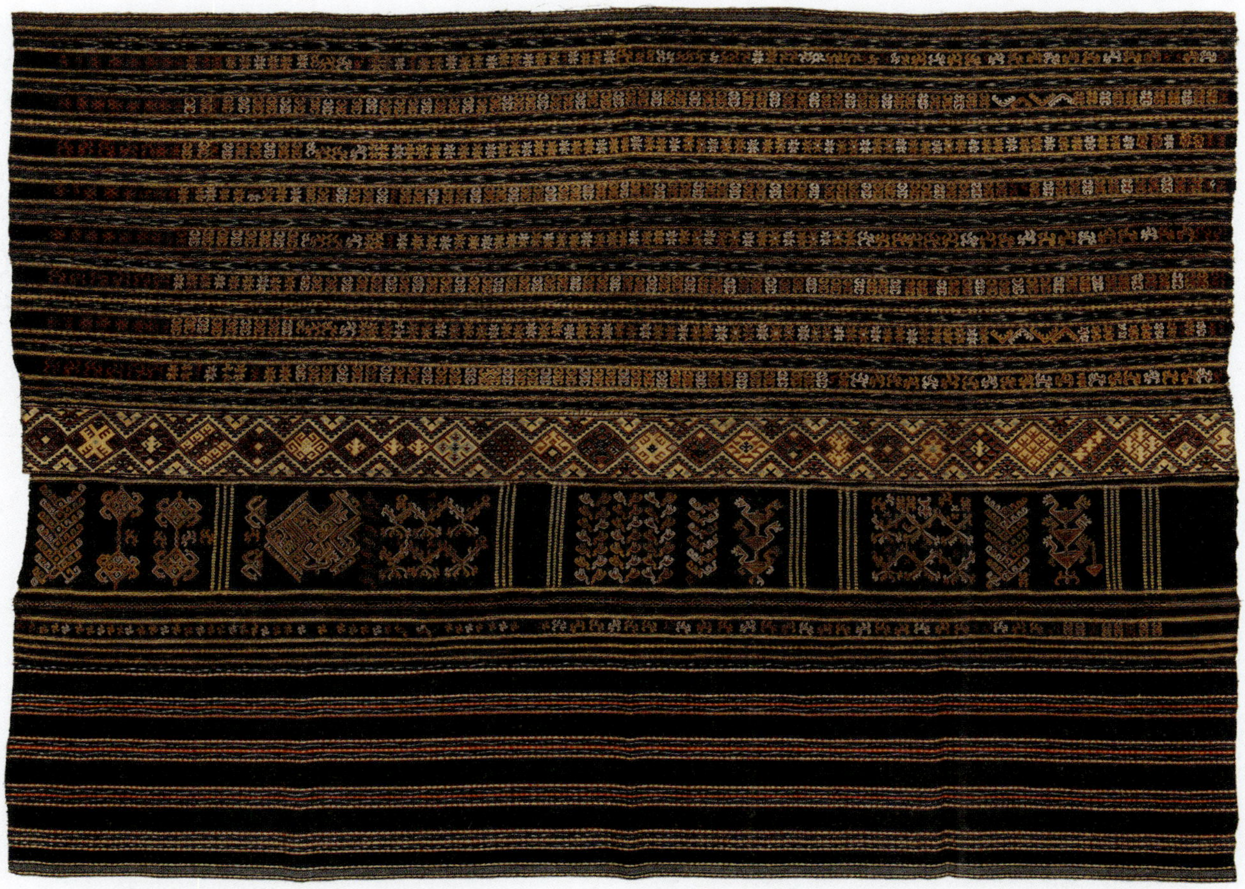

MA122 Ha Li woman's sarong
Hainan, China, probably late 19th century. Cotton, silk, warp ikat, discontinuous supplementary weft, complementary warp, embroidery. 36 in x 54 in

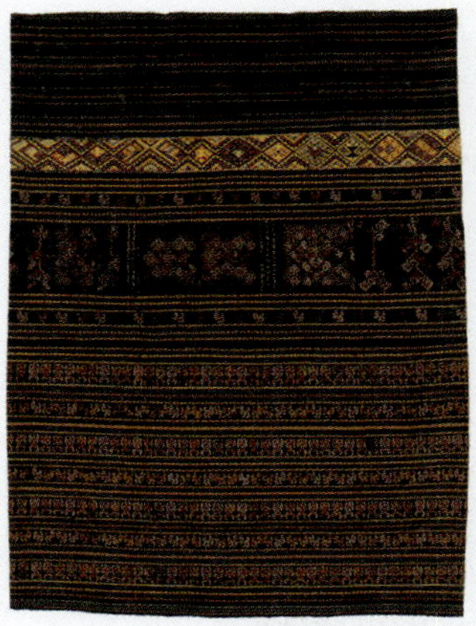

MA123 Ha Li woman's sarong
Hainan, China, late 19th century. Cotton, silk, warp ikat, discontinuous supplementary weft, complementary warp, embroidery. 36 in x 28 in

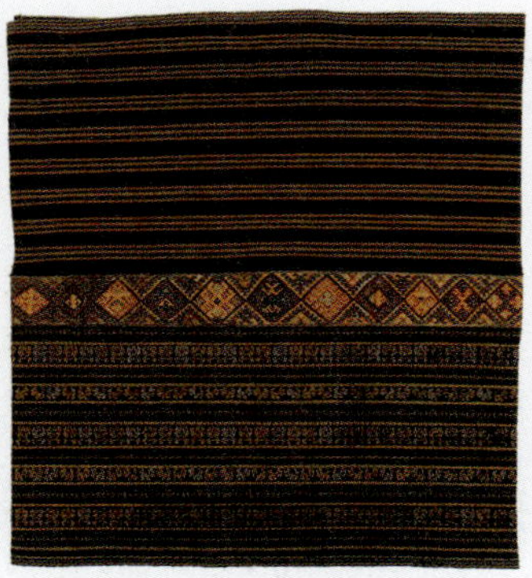

MA124 Meifu Li woman's sarong
Hainan, China, early 20th century. Woven in four panels, cotton, warp ikat, supplementary warp. 36 in x 28 in. The Textile Museum, 2020.7.11

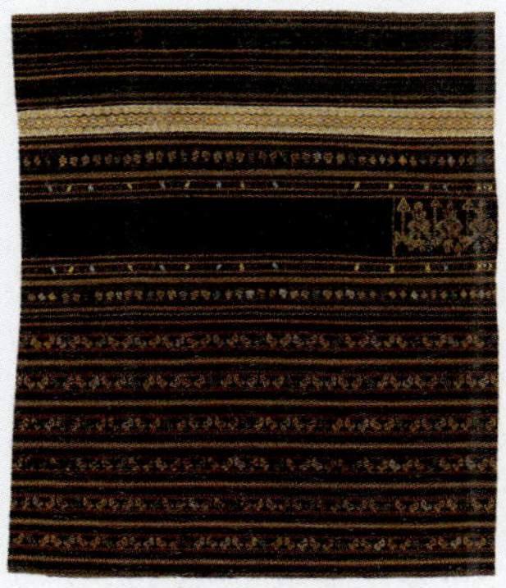

MA125 Ha Li woman's sarong
Hainan, China, probably early 20th century. Cotton, silk, warp ikat, discontinuous supplementary weft, complementary warp, embroidery. 36 in x 28 in

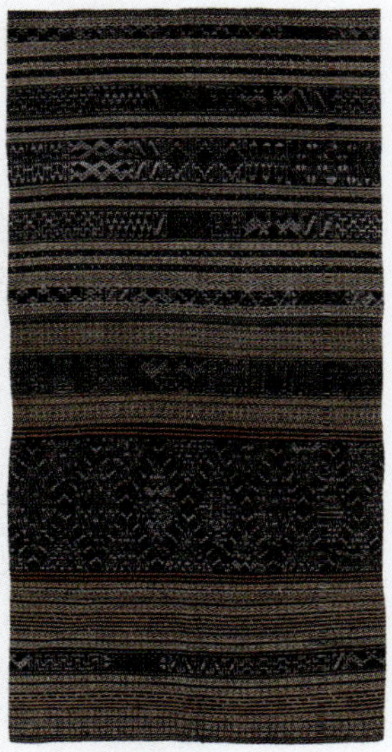

MA126 Meifu Li woman's sarong
Hainan, China, first half 20th century. Cotton, silk, warp ikat, supplementary warp. 43 in x 24 in

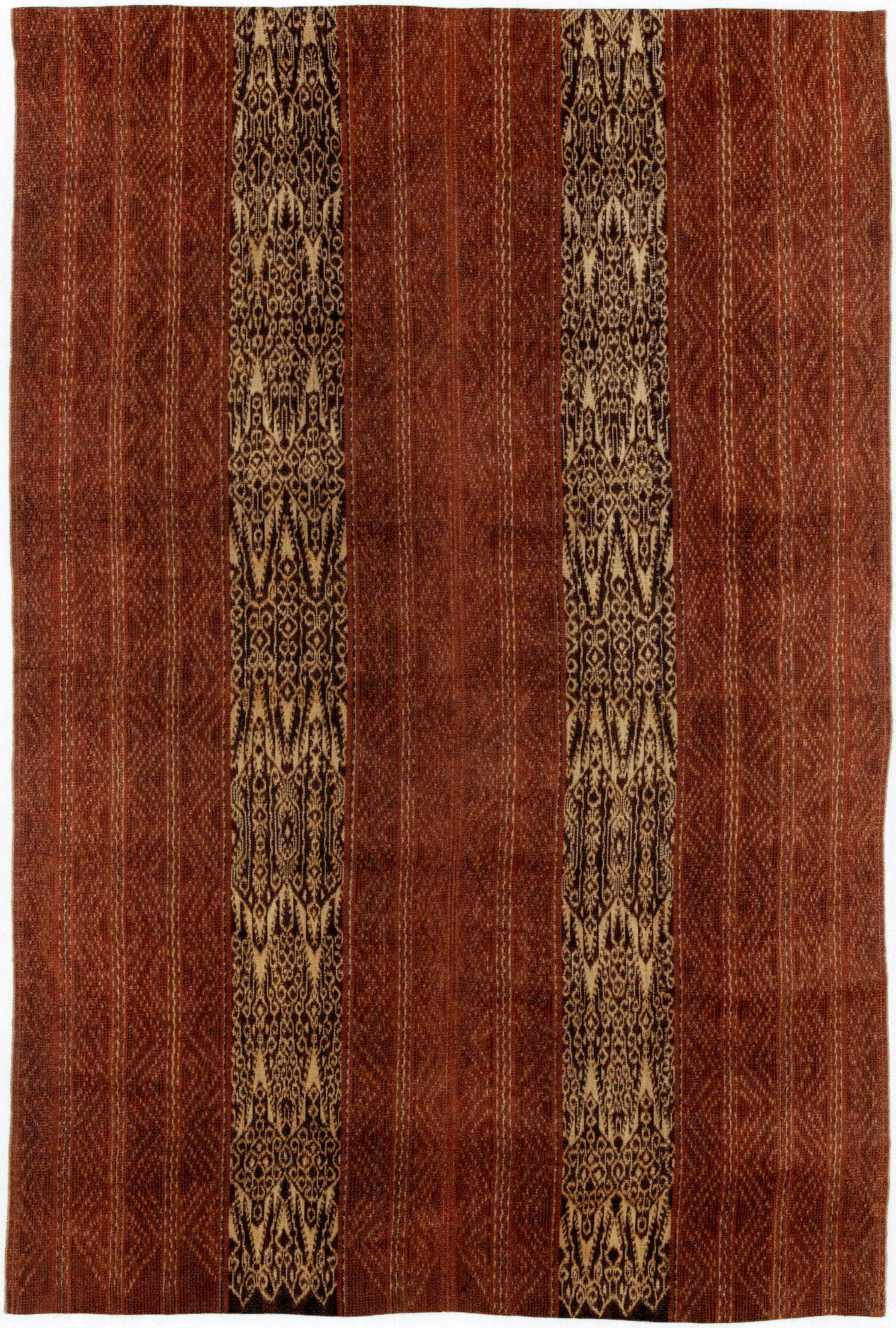

MA127 Bagobo women's ceremonial skirt (opened), Mindanao, South Philippines, early 20th century. Abaca, warp ikat. 49 in x 34 in

Weavers from several ethnic groups in the South Philippines utilize abaca or threads made from stalks of a banana species (*Musa textilis*) to weave into cloth, and the Bagobo call abaca or banana fabric *inabal*. The Bagobo people consider *inabal* to have high status and use it for ceremonial dress and gifting. A hierarchy in the quality of warp-ikat skirts exists, and examples composed of three panels with the middle one covered in ikat patterning are the most valuable. The names of the skirt types vary depending on the Bagobo subgroup. Weavers of the Bagobo subgroups also use *plangi* and *tritik*, other resist-dye techniques, to decorate cloth. This skirt is composed of two panels, and the crocodile or *buwaya* motif fills a band on each panel. Red, associated with the warrior class, is produced from morinda, and black is created from ebony or *Diospyros*.

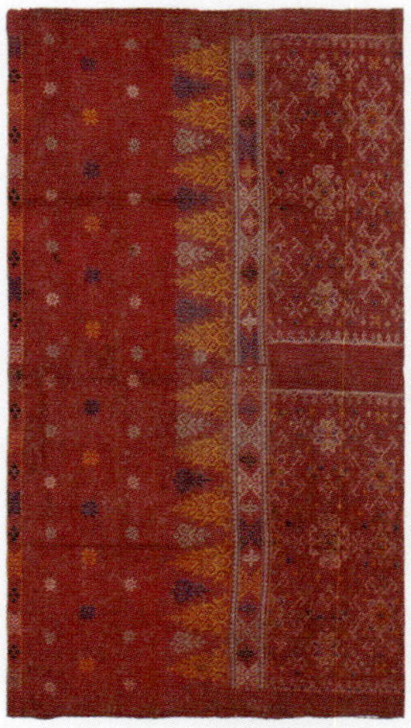

MA128 Maranao woman's sarong, *malong a andon*
Mindanao, Philippines, 20th century. Silk, weft ikat.
59 in x 32 in

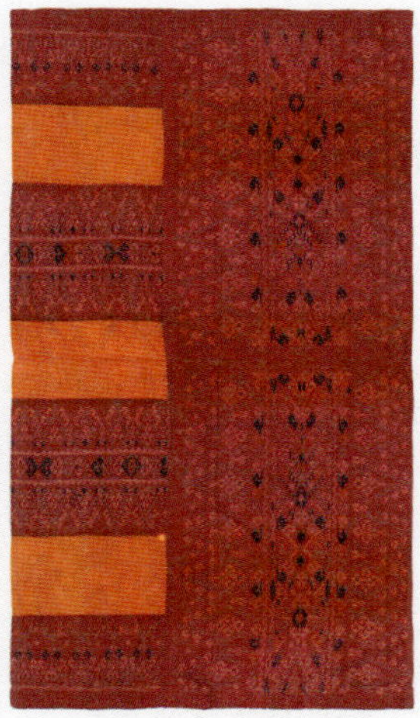

MA129 Maranao woman's sarong, *malong a andon*
Mindanao, Philippines, 20th century. Silk, weft ikat.
62 in x 36 in

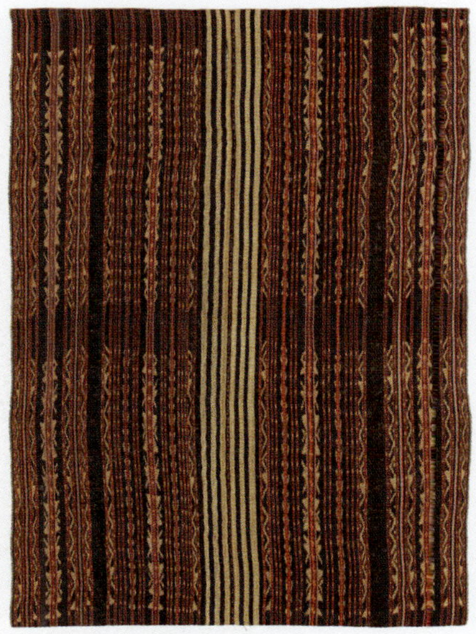

MA133 Subanen sarong
Mindanao, Philippines, early 20th century. Abaca, warp ikat. 41 in x 31 in

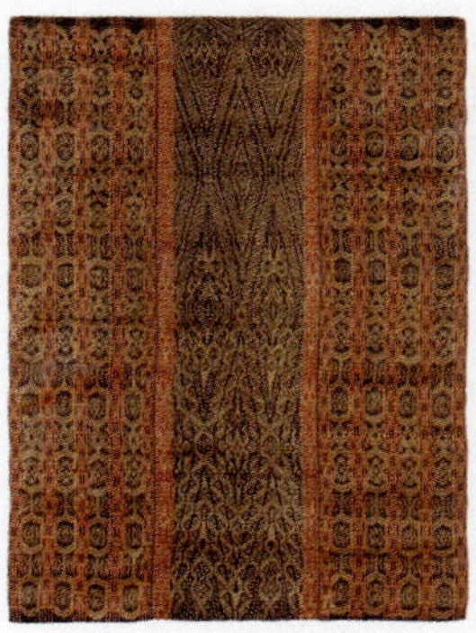

MA130 Bagobo or B'laan woman's sarong
Mindanao, Philippines, early 20th century. Abaca, warp ikat. 51 in x 39 in

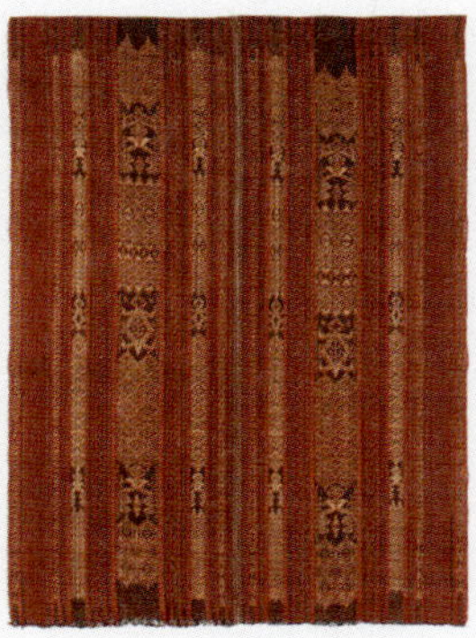

MA131 Mandaya woman's sarong
Mindanao, Philippines, early 20th century. Abaca, warp ikat.
75 in x 56 in

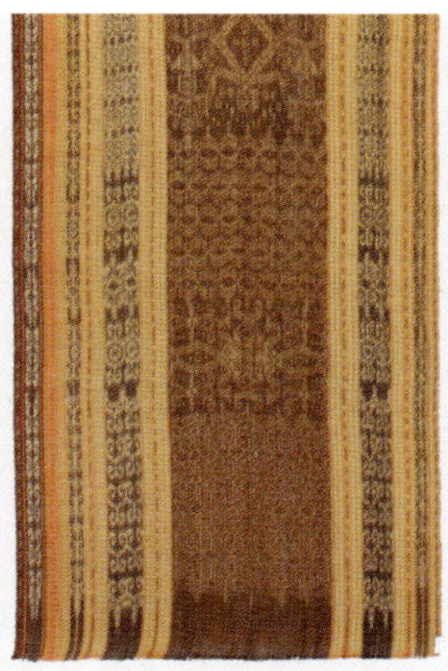

MA132 Mandaya sarong panel (?)
Mindanao, Philippines, 20th century. Abaca, warp ikat.
75 in x 29 in

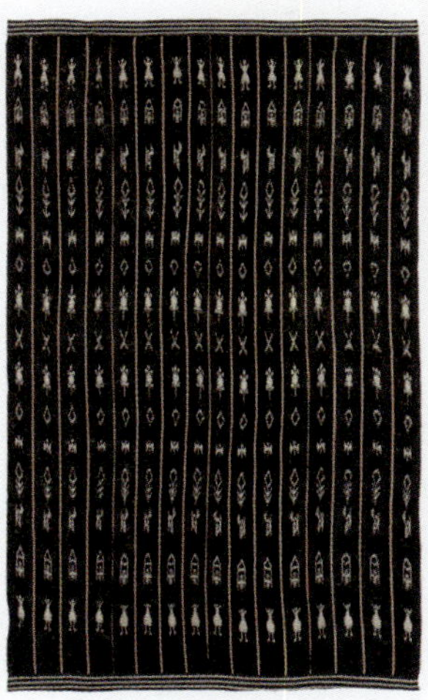

MA134 Ifugao blanket
Luzon, Philippines, late 20th century. Cotton, warp ikat.
105 in x 88 in

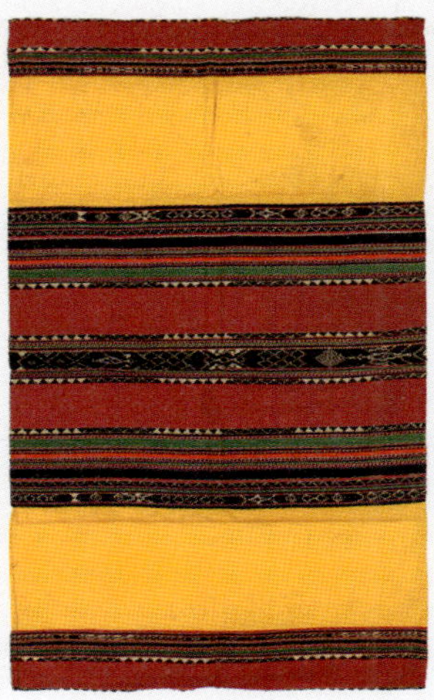

MA135 Maguindanao woman's sarong
Mindanao, Philippines, 20th century. Cotton, silk, warp ikat. 52 in x 34 in

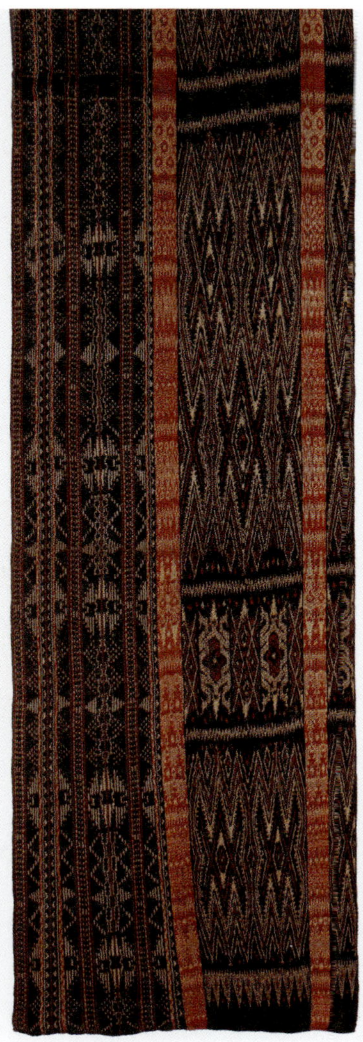

MA136 T'boli ritual cloth, *t'nalak*
Bagobo, Mindanao, Philippines, 20th century. Abaca, warp ikat. 51 in x 39 in

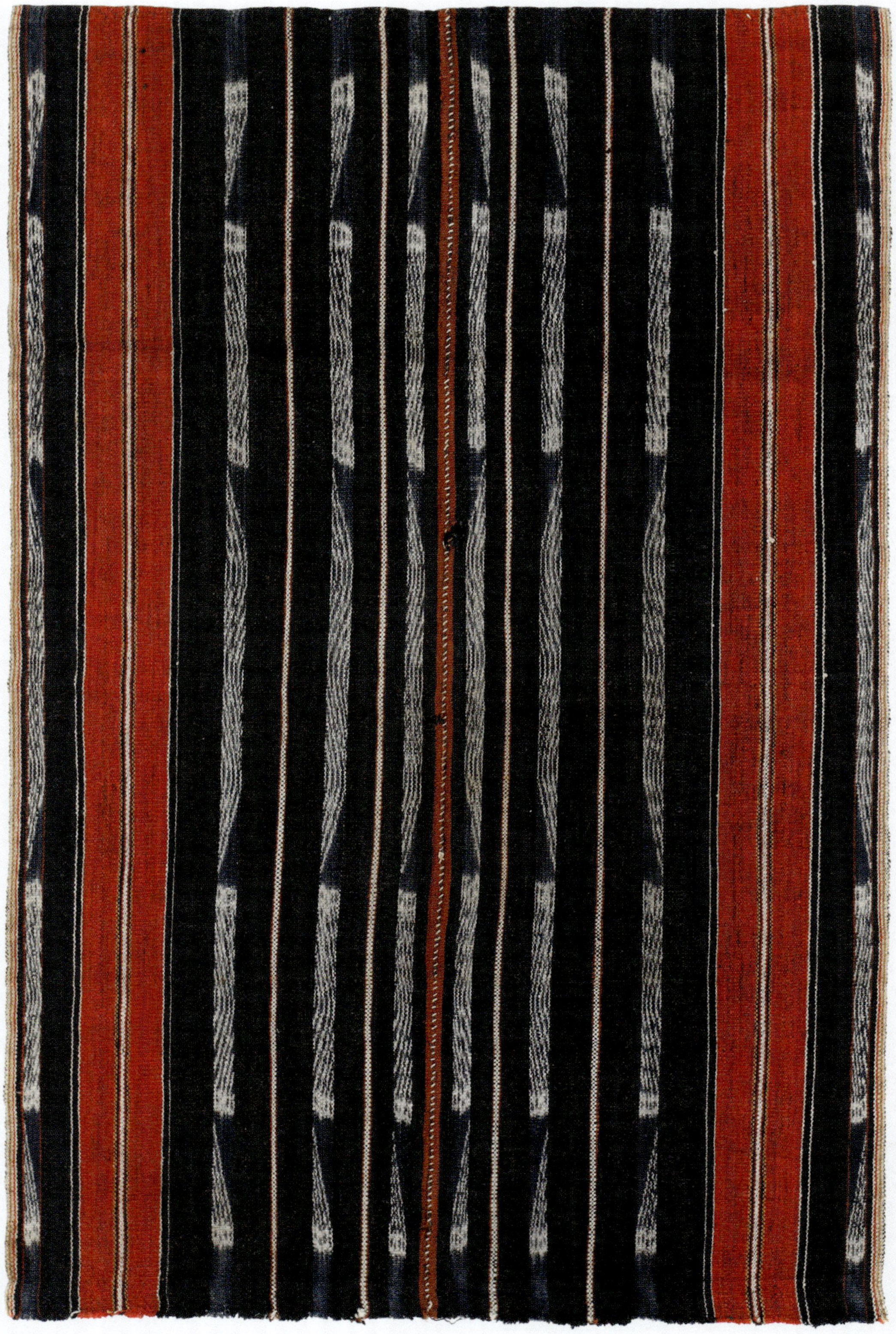

MA137 Lua or Lawa skirt panel, Chiang Mai Province, North Thailand, 20th century. Cotton, warp ikat. 35 in x 24 in

The Lua, also called Lawa, group belongs to the Palaungic sub-branch in the Austro-Asiatic ethnolinguistic family. The Lua lived in North Thailand before various Tai groups settled in the area. When the Tai arrived, the Lua were forced into the uplands. The Lua is one of a few Austro-Asiatic groups that continue to produce warp ikat on a backstrap loom and is the sole Palaungic group to utilize the warp-ikat technique. Designs are organized in bands that are horizontal when a cloth is made into a skirt. Lua weavers create warp-ikat patterns of staggered lines that resemble python skin in two colors: the color indigo and white or the undyed sections of the cotton thread.

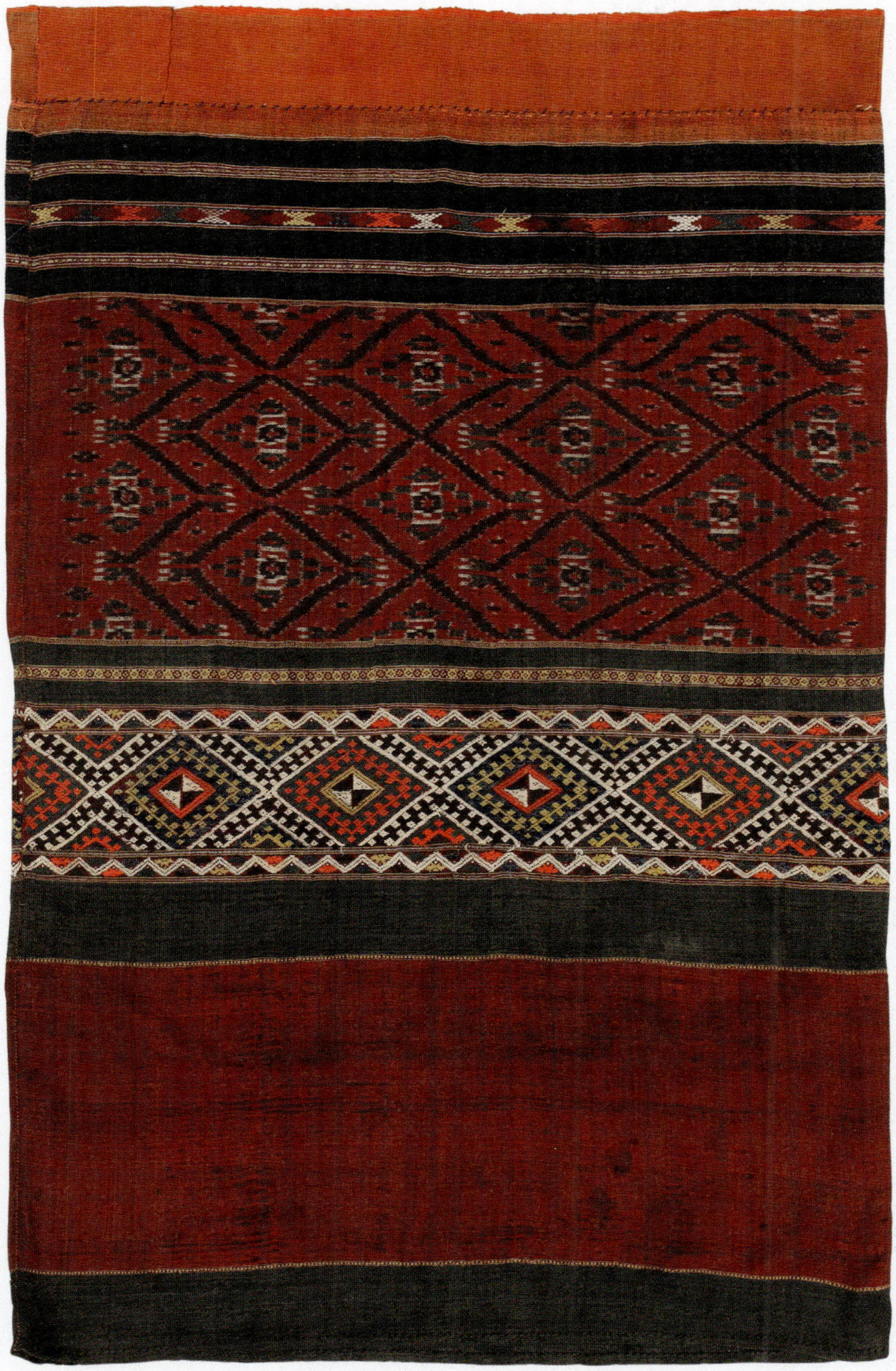

MA138 Lao women's ceremonial skirt, *sin mii*, Fak Tha/Nam Pat District, Uttaradit Province, North Thailand, 20th century. Silk, cotton, weft ikat, discontinuous supplementary weft. 36 in x 23 in

The eastern part of Uttaradit abuts the right bank of the Mekong River, and the river was a major mode of transport of goods traded throughout Mainland Southeast Asia, China, and afar. People from numerous ethnic groups including the Lao, Tai Lue, and Tai Yuan settled here. Lao women combined different elements from their own textile repertoire with characteristics of other people's textiles. Lao women are adept at weft ikat, and the repeating pattern decorating this skirt's midsection is assimilated from Indian trade textiles. The large, plain border resembles Tai Lue skirt borders although Tai Lue borders are typically indigo blue instead of red. The bottom section of Tai Yuan skirt borders tends to be red with supplementary-weft designs adorning the top. The Lao weaver of this garment incorporated these elements into one garment.

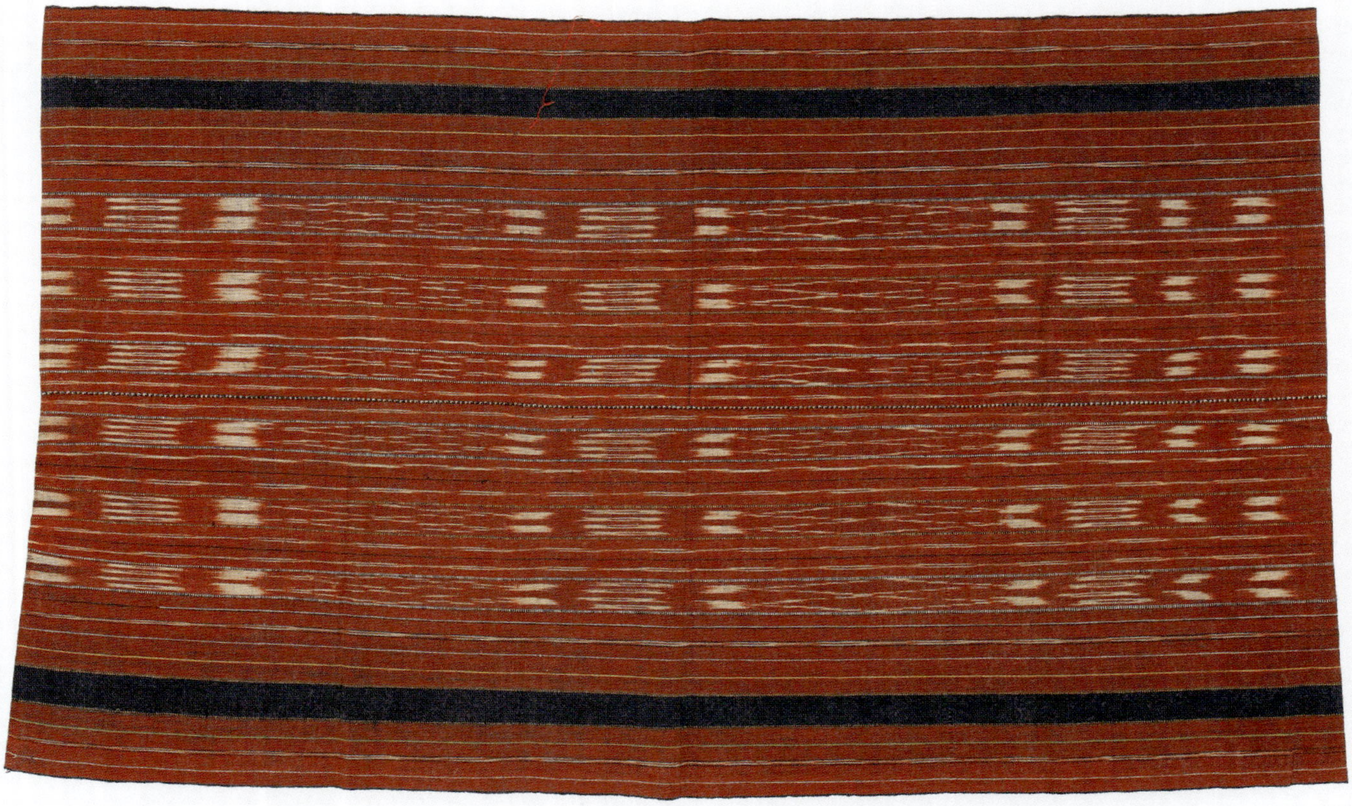

MA139 Karen woman's sarong North Thailand, mid-20th century. cotton, warp ikat. 54 in x 32 in

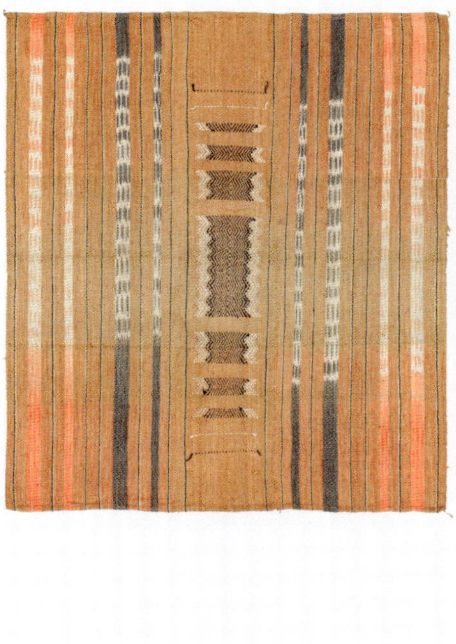

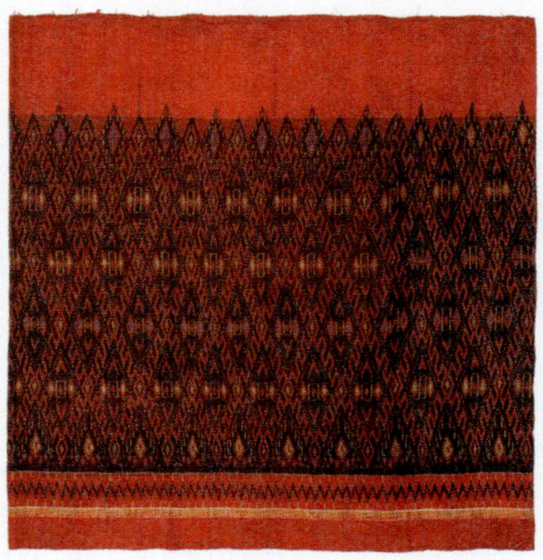

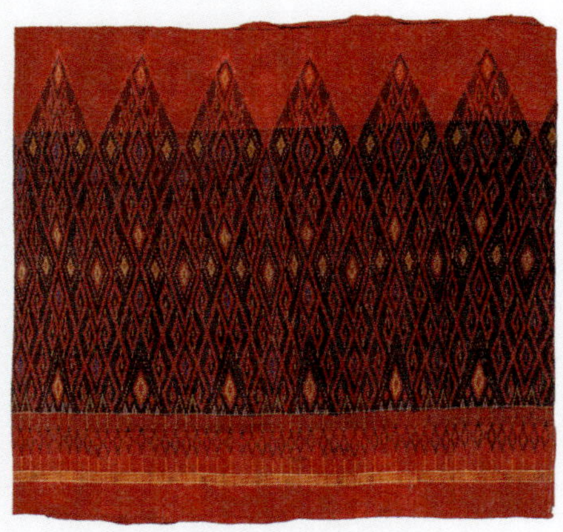

MA140 Lawa blanket
North Thailand, 20th century. Cotton, warp ikat, discontinuous supplementary weft. 41 in x 37 in

MA141 Kui woman's sarong, *sin mii*
Northeast Thailand, 20th century. Silk, weft ikat. 33 in x 34 in

MA142 Kui woman's sarong, *sin mii*
Northeast Thailand, 20th century. Silk, weft ikat. 31 in x 34 in

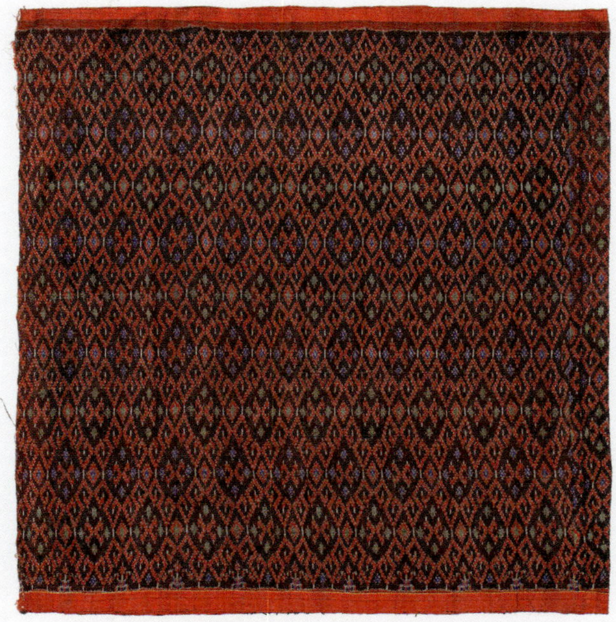

MA143 Tai Phuan woman's sarong, *sin mii*
Northeast Thailand, 20th century. Silk, weft ikat. 33 in x 33 in

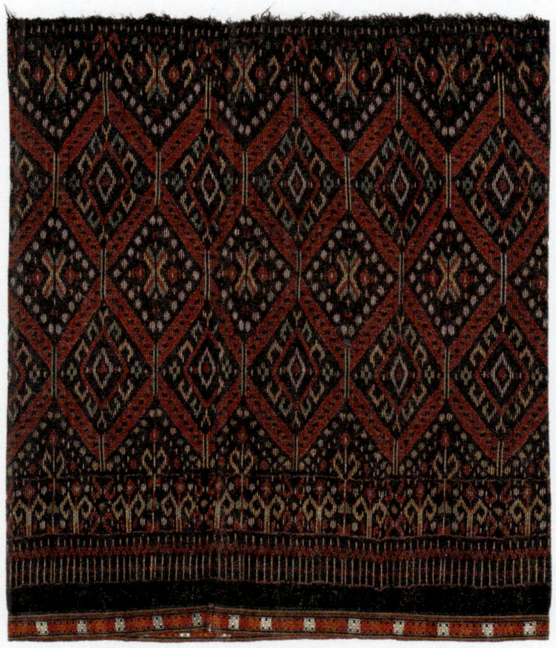

MA144 Phuthai woman's sarong, *sin mii*
Northeast Thailand, 20th century. Silk, weft ikat. Border silk, discontinuous supplementary weft. 34 in x 29 in

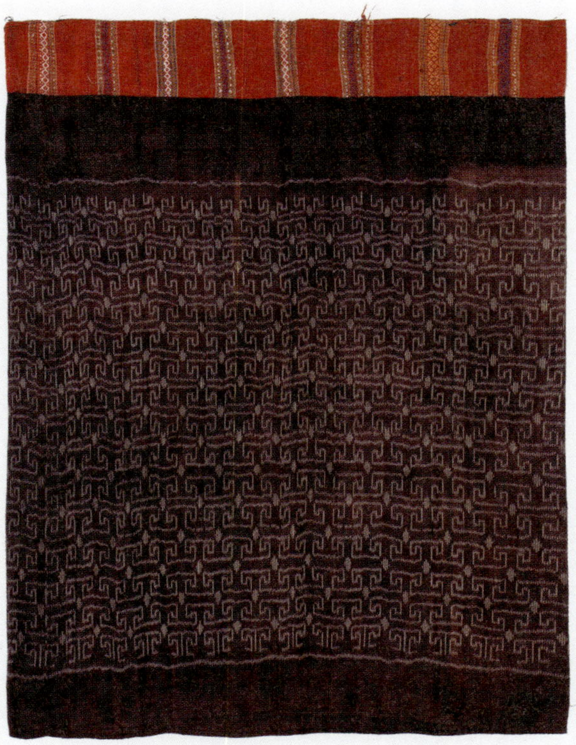

MA145 Lao woman's sarong, *sin mii*
Northeast Thailand, 20th century. Silk, weft ikat. Waistband silk, continuous supplementary weft. 37 in x 30 in

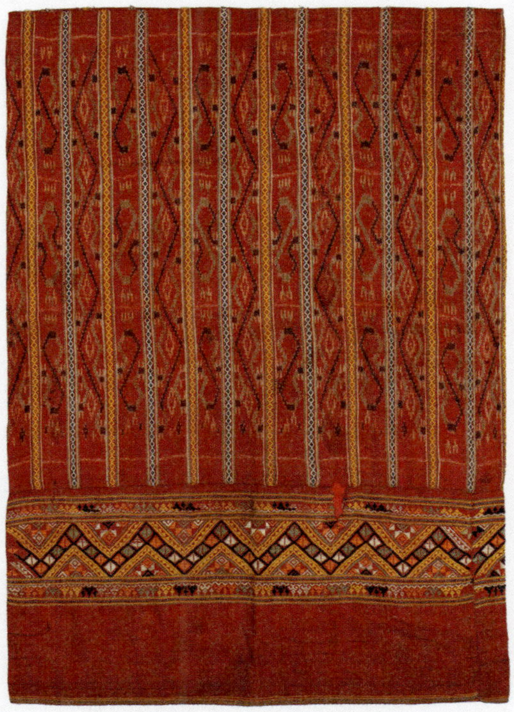

MA146 Tai Khang woman's sarong, *sin mii*
Central Thailand, 20th century. Silk, weft ikat, continuous and discontinuous supplementary weft. 34 in x 29 in

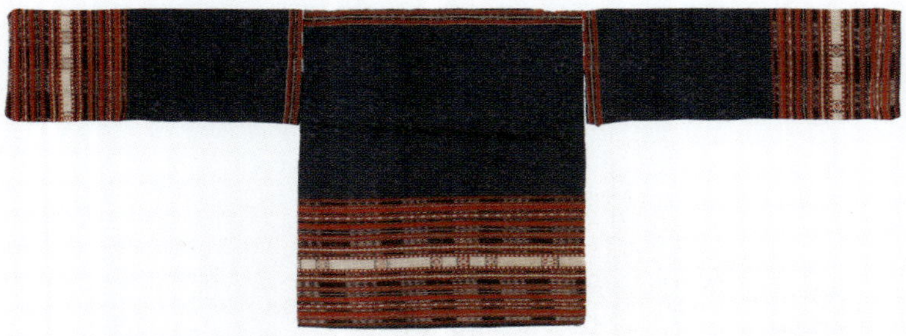

MA147 Bahnar woman's blouse
Central or South Vietnam, 20th century. Cotton, warp ikat, discontinuous supplementary weft, supplementary warp. 17 in x 50 in

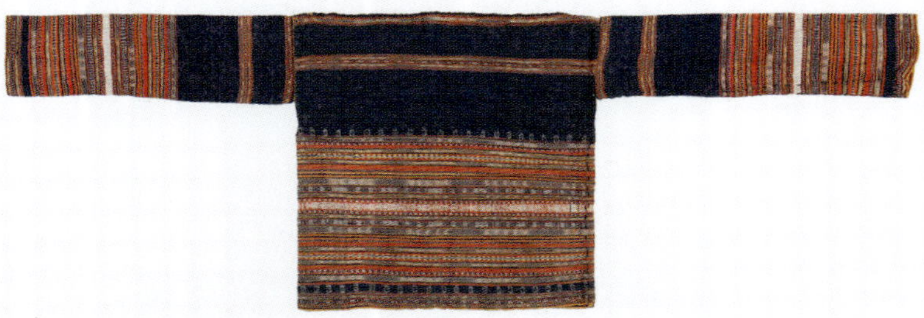

MA148 Bahnar woman's blouse
Central or South Vietnam, 20th century. Cotton, warp ikat, discontinuous supplementary weft, supplementary warp. 15 in x 47 in

MA149 Cham (?) shawl
South Vietnam, probably late 19th or early 20th century. Silk, cotton, warp ikat, twill. 76 in x 33 in

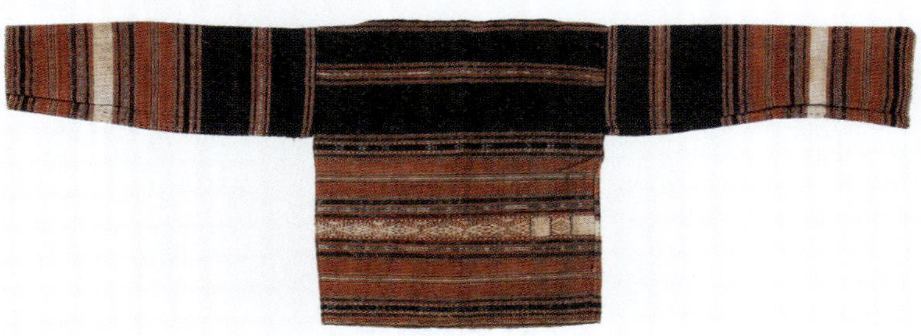

MA150 Bahnar woman's blouse
Central or South Vietnam, 20th century. Cotton, warp ikat, discontinuous supplementary weft, supplementary warp. 15.5 in x 48 in

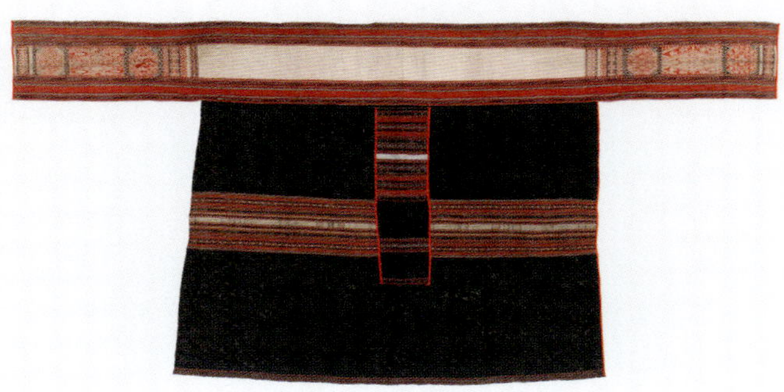

MA151 Bahnar woman's apron, *hban*
Central or South Vietnam, 20th century. Cotton, warp ikat, discontinuous supplementary weft, supplementary warp. 34 in x 72 in

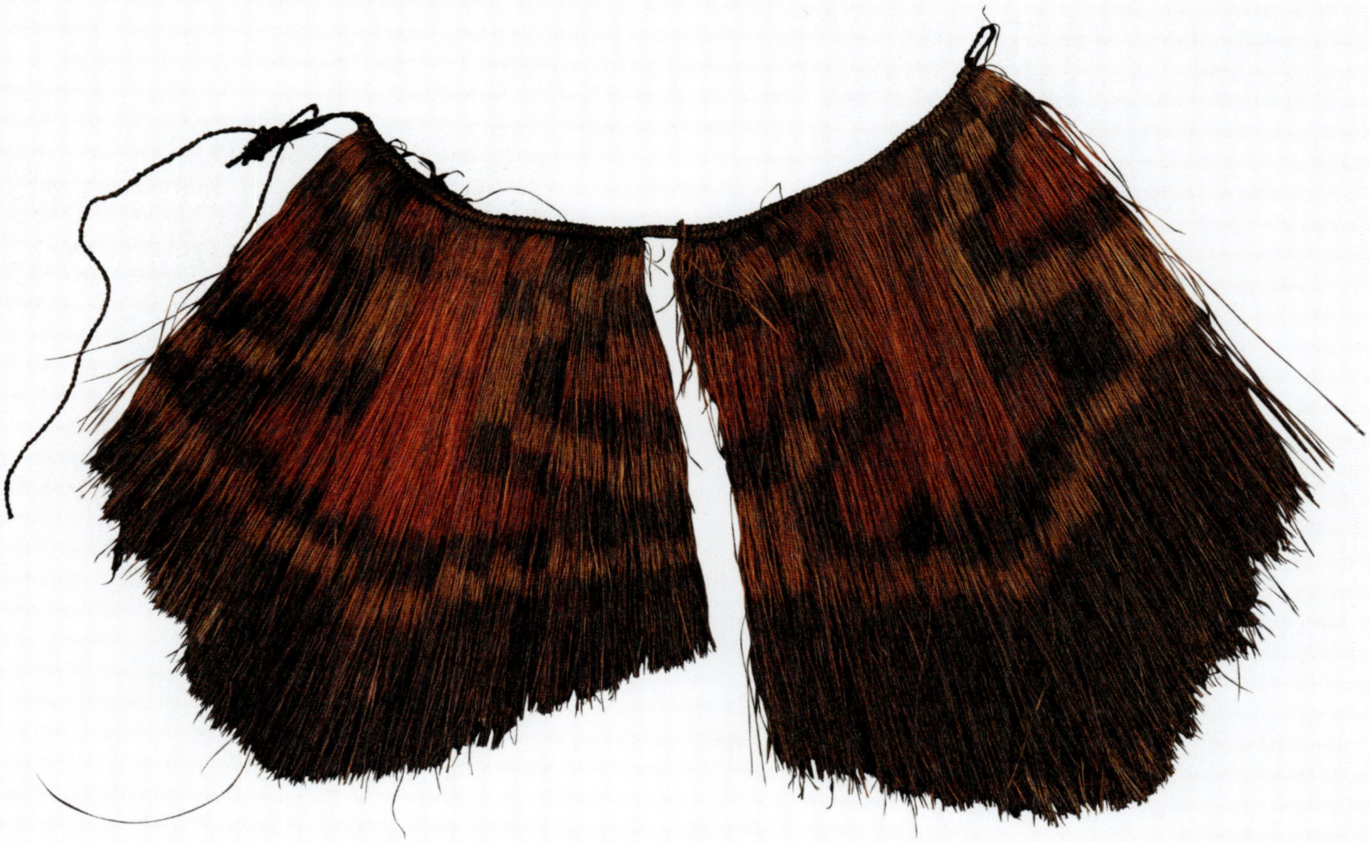

MA152 Woman's dance skirt Sepik River region, Papua New Guinea, 1920s. Grass, proto-ikat. 30 in x 24 in

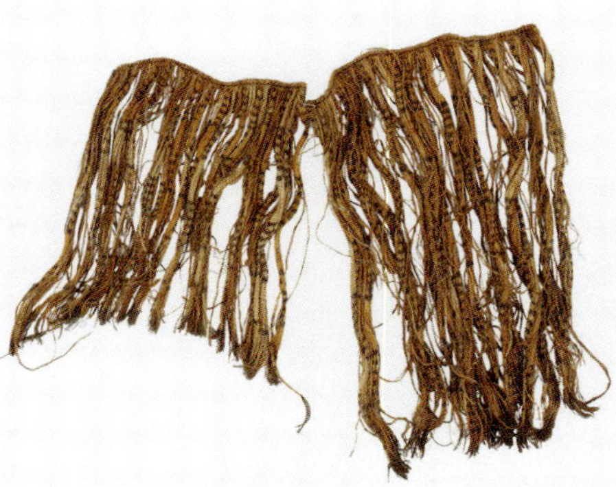

MA153 Skirt
Sepik River region, Papua New Guinea, 1920s. Grass, proto-ikat. 20 in x 25 in

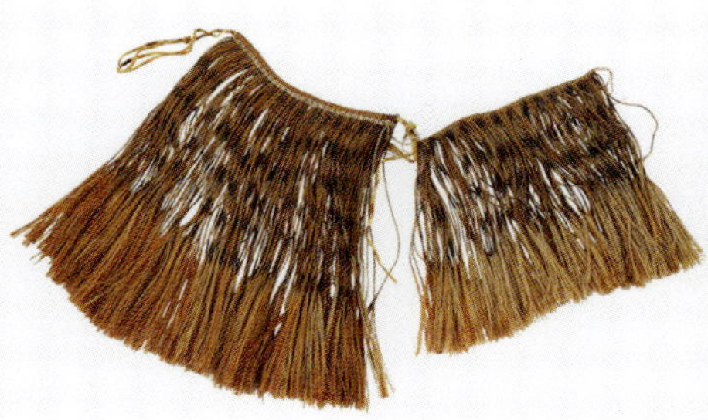

MA154 Woman's dance skirt
Sepik River region, Papua New Guinea, 1920s. Grass, proto-ikat. 30 in x 24 in

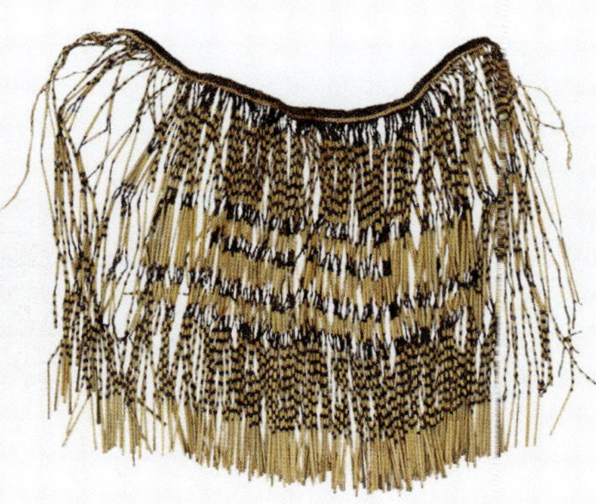

MA155 Maori woman's dance skirt
New Zealand, early 20th century. Flax, protɔ-ikat. 28 in x 36 in

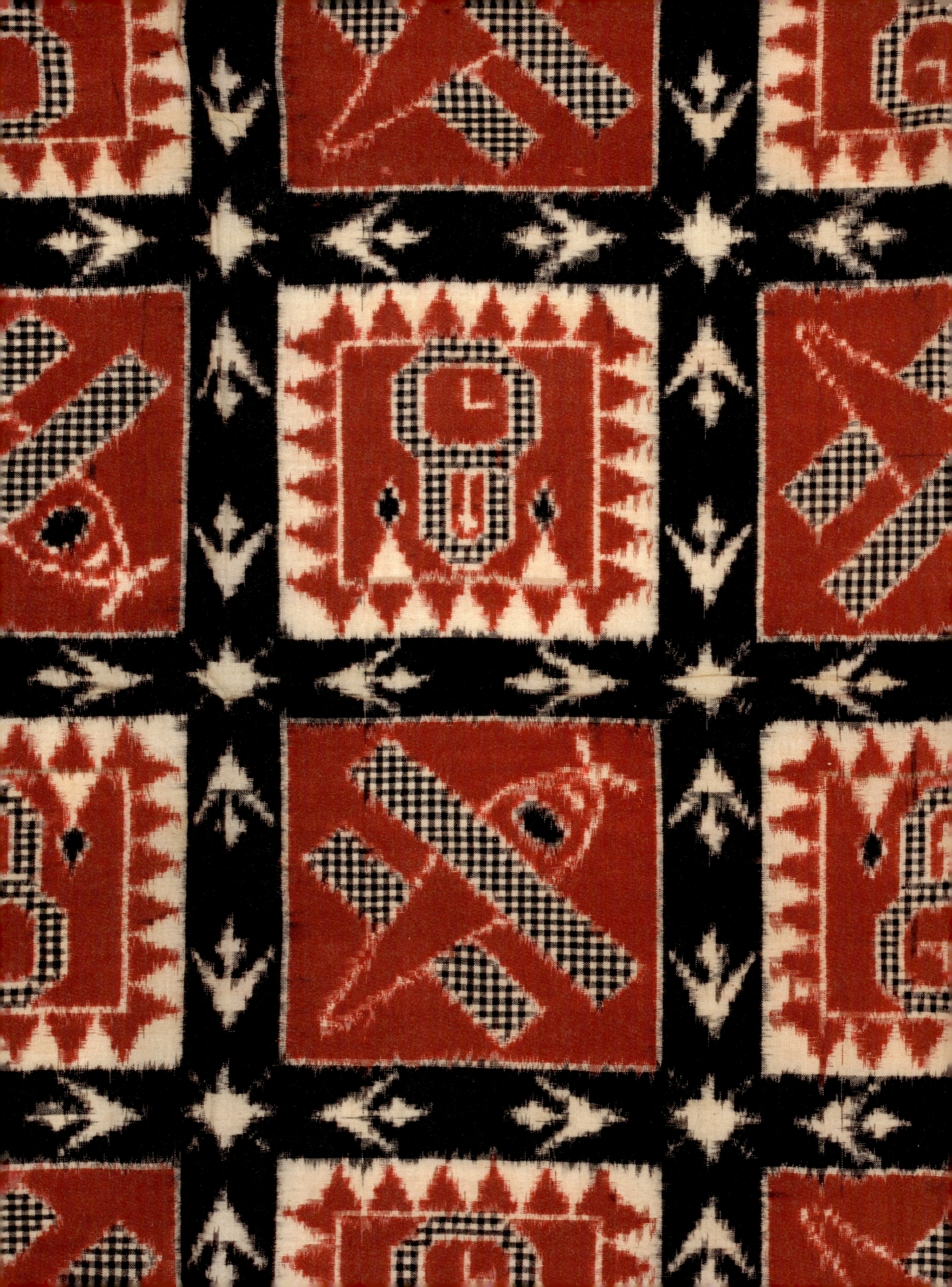

INDIA

by Rosemary Crill

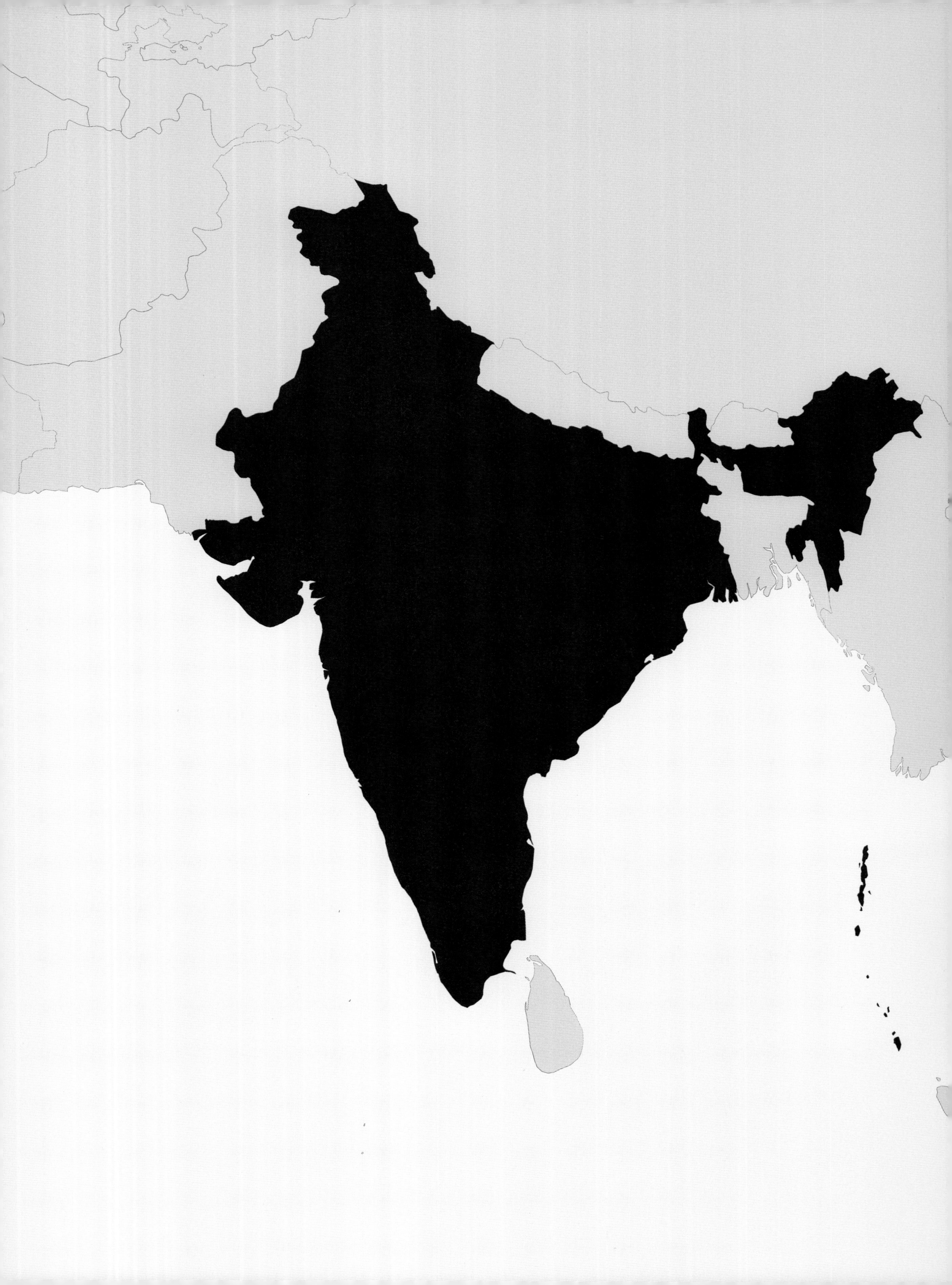

IKAT IN INDIA

India's ikat textiles range from the extremely labor-intensive double-ikat *patola* to simple ikat border patterns for saris. In between lie the squared *telia rumals*, saris from Odisha with checkerboard and animal patterns, and satin *mashru* with arrowhead and chevron designs. Many areas of India (and elsewhere) use ikat for "zone-dyeing," a widespread and pragmatic way of using ikat-dyed warp or weft threads to allow different colors to be used in the field and borders of a sari without the need for warp or weft substitution. The rich variety of ikats made in India reflects the wide range of patronage, tradition, and technical expertise across this huge area over many centuries.

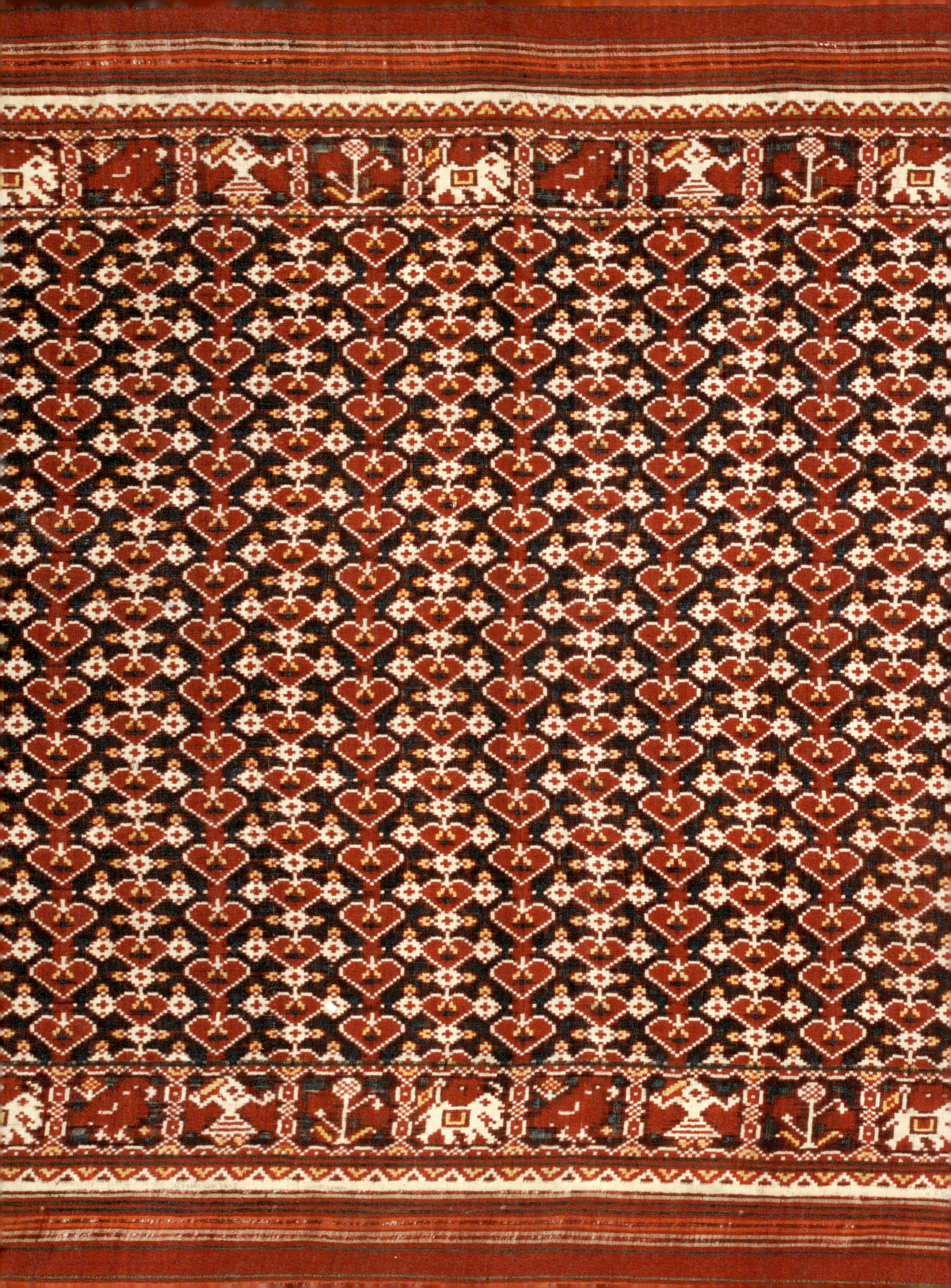

Fig.1
Detail of IN28, *patola* sari with leaf design (*pan bhat*)

THE MANY FACES OF INDIAN IKAT

The making, trading, and use of Indian ikat has an immeasurably long history. Ikat textiles have certainly been made and used in India since at least the 5th century CE, when they are clearly identifiable in the wall paintings in the Ajanta caves, executed around 462–80 CE (Fig.2).[1] Fragments of Indian warp-ikat textiles in both cotton and tussar silk, dating from the 7th–8th centuries CE, have been excavated in Israel and Jordan respectively.[2] These small, scattered historic fragments, together with the appearance of ikat textiles in the Ajanta paintings, constitute our only reliable evidence for the early history of ikat in India, as no textiles of any kind have survived in India itself from such early periods.

Written documents of the medieval period provide evidence for textile manufacture, possibly including ikat, in south India and the Deccan, but these are often hard to identify from texts alone.[3] Later on, striking visual evidence for the use of ikat textiles in the 17th century can be found in manuscript illustrations such as Fig.6. The ikat fabric in this painting is likely have been made in the Deccan, in southern India. A great many surviving paintings document the imperial Mughal court at this time, often depicting textiles and garments in great detail; it is worth noting that none of these shows any ikat textiles in use at the Mughal courts of Agra, Lahore, and Delhi, much further north.

These visual and literary references suggest that India's ikat tradition may have arisen in the Deccan, from where its predominantly geometric chevron and squared designs spread south to present-day Tamil Nadu, Karnataka, Telangana, and Andhra Pradesh, and eastwards to Odisha. While the ikat saris of Odisha continued to develop into floral, calligraphic, and figurative designs and are still produced today, the ikats of Tamil Nadu and several other southern states sadly died out some time after the end of the 19th century. The colorful weft-ikat blouse pieces of Bellary and Narayanpet, the subtly patterned ikat saris of Madurai, and the vibrant chevron-patterned *mashru* fabrics of Tamil Nadu are now found only in private and museum collections.[4]

Telia rumal

A type of ikat textile that survived into the 20th century but which is also now defunct in its traditional form is the *telia rumal* (literally "oily kerchief," so called because the yarn is steeped in gingelly oil or til); this understated but beautiful everyday cloth was formerly made in Chirala in coastal Andhra Pradesh. A more decorative variant of the mass-produced "Madras handkerchief," with its simple format of checked ground and wide, plain borders, the *telia rumal* was traditionally made with plain red borders and an ikat-patterned field in dark shades of red, blue, or black (Fig.3/IN04, IN02, IN06), or sometimes with an undyed field with dark cross pattern in ikat.[5]

These *rumals* had a wide range of uses: single squares could be wrapped around the head, while double pieces were used as *lungis* by men and *dupattas* or wrapped garments by women. As well as supplying a large domestic market in India itself, they were traded to the Middle East, Southeast Asia, and East Africa, where they were put to the same uses. In the early 20th century, their designs became more elaborate and figurative, with modern motifs such as gramophones, airplanes, and clocks starting to appear (IN01), sometimes in combination with animals, birds, and flowers (Fig.9/IN03). This type was especially popular in the Arabian Gulf, and was sometimes overdyed with a synthetic pink dye to make examples more appealing to this market. The early 20th century saw the heyday of the *telia rumal*, with over 500 looms involved in their production in Chirala. By 1959, the number had dropped to fifty, and today there are none.[6]

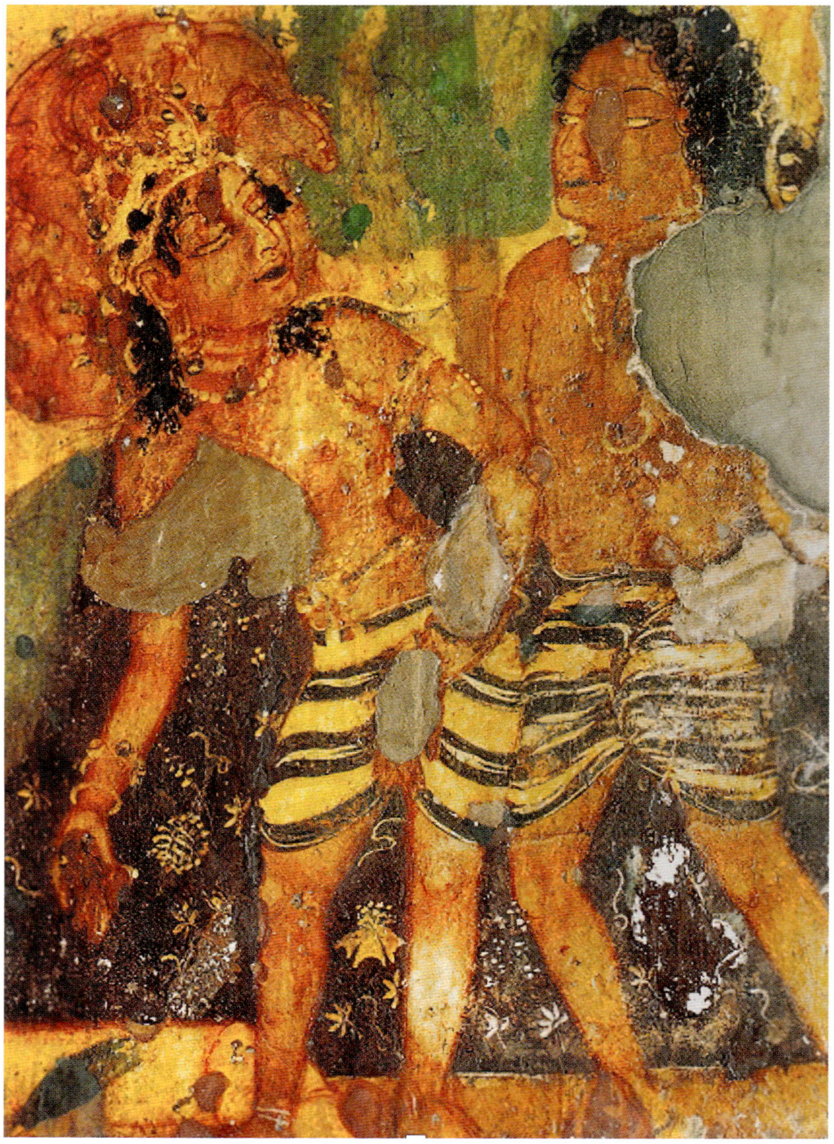

After Behl, Benoy, *The Ajanta Caves*. Thames & Hudson, London and New York, 1998

Fig.2

Fig.2
Wall-painting showing ikat textiles in use, Ajanta, Maharashtra, India, ca. 462–480 CE.

Fig.3
IN04, *telia rumal*

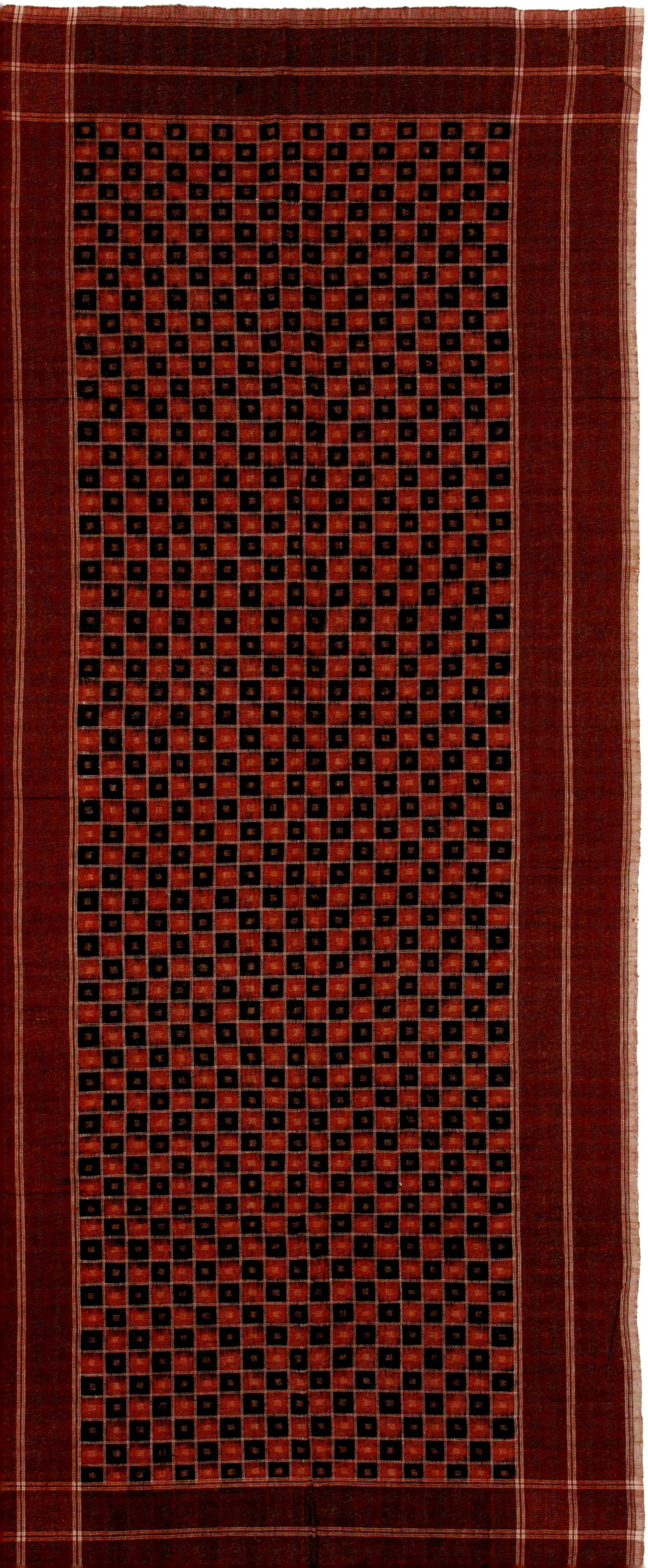

Fig.3

Although *telia rumals* are no longer made in Chirala, weavers from villages such as Pochampalli, Koyyalagudem, and Puttapaka in Andhra and Telengana have taken up ikat weaving and are now supplying both the domestic and foreign markets with fabrics for dress and furnishing. While some of these have squared designs based on *telia rumals*, many others have patterns derived from Japanese *kasuri* ikat that appeal to an international market. Other ikat textiles are exported to the Middle East, especially ikat *lungis* made to the format of Indonesian sarongs.[7]

Odisha

Similar squared designs to those on the *telia rumal* are also found on the cotton ikats of inland Odisha (formerly Orissa) in eastern India.[8] Known as *saktapar* saris, these are often combined with ikat-patterned figurative patterns of fish, ducks, and flowers, and in recent times other elements like airplanes and temples.[9] Other exclusively Odishan ikat textiles, both made in the coastal Nuapatna area, include the calligraphic shawls made for presentation to the Jagannath temple at Pur ,[10] and the decorative *khandua*, worn by women on ceremonial occasions (IN31).

Patola of Gujarat

In spite of the long and varied history of ikat-making in the Deccan and South India, by far the best known and most prestigious type of Indian ikat comes from the other side of the subcontinent: this is the double-ikat *patola* sari from Gujarat in the northwest (Fig.1/IN28). Wrapped garments with basic ikat patterns are also known from Gujarat, such as the simple but elegant saris of Ahmedabad which have plain cotton fields and warp-ikat silk borders,[11] and the coarse cotton multi-purpose wraps made for the rural Chodhri community near Surat,[12] but the *patola* clearly spring from another, more sophisticated tradition.

How the manufacture of the fantastically intricate, labor-intensive and prohibitively expensive double-ikat silk *patolu* (plural: *patola*) arose in Gujarat is not yet fully understood. Several ambiguous terms that may or may not refer to double-ikat *patola* have been recorded from the 10th century onwards, but the first reliable mention of such as textile seems to date from as late as 1676, when the French traveler Jean-Baptiste Tavernier described "patoles" as "stuffs of silk, very soft, decorated all over with

Fig.4
Detail of IN26, export *patola*

Fig.5
Page from an album showing dancers and musicians, Thanjavur, Tamil Nadu, India, ca. 1830. Victoria and Albert Museum, IS 39-1987, f. 24. Two of the men wear *mashru* trousers, one with an ikat pattern, and the two women on the right wear ikat *mashru* skirts

Fig.6
A prince dressed as an ascetic, wearing an ikat robe, probably Deccan, India, ca. 1660. British Library, Johnson Album 19, No. 2

Fig.4

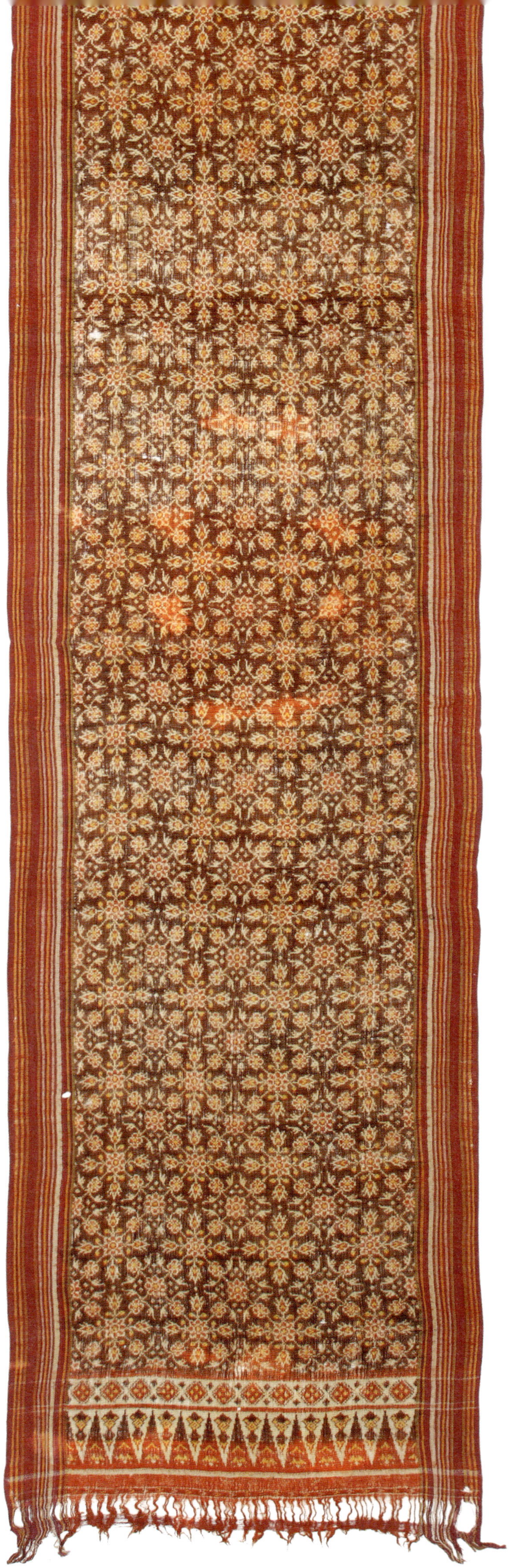

flowers of different colours … manufactured at Ahmedabad."[13] He also notes that they are frequently bought by Dutch merchants and exported to "the Philippines, Borneo, Java, Sumatra and other neighbouring countries." *Patola* were (and still are) woven by male weavers of the Salvi community who supplied specific patterns to the various merchant and Brahmin communities of Gujarat, which included Muslim, Jain, and Hindu groups.

Each group traditionally preferred certain design types for its rituals and ceremonies: *patola* with a plain yellow field and figurative borders (IN14) were reportedly favored by Jain communities of northern Gujarat;[14] those with a floral trellis pattern (IN29) were appropriate for several communities and were also widely exported to Southeast Asia;[15] the popular leaf pattern (Fig.1/IN28) was widely used by Brahmin and Jain communities in Gujarat, and seems not to have been exported;[16] the "basket" pattern, with floral motifs forming repeating circles, was reputedly popular with the Brahmin community of Surat, as well as being exported to Southeast Asia; the trellis pattern (IN29) was favored especially by Vohra Muslims, hence its name Vohra *gaji bhat*, and was also a popular export type. Complex figurative patterns with elephants, flowers, and parrots within a trellis are associated with the Brahmin communities of northern Gujarat.[17] Such was the spiritual status of the *patola* that less-wealthy communities, unable to afford whole pieces, used scraps of old *patola* as auspicious adornments to wedding outfits:

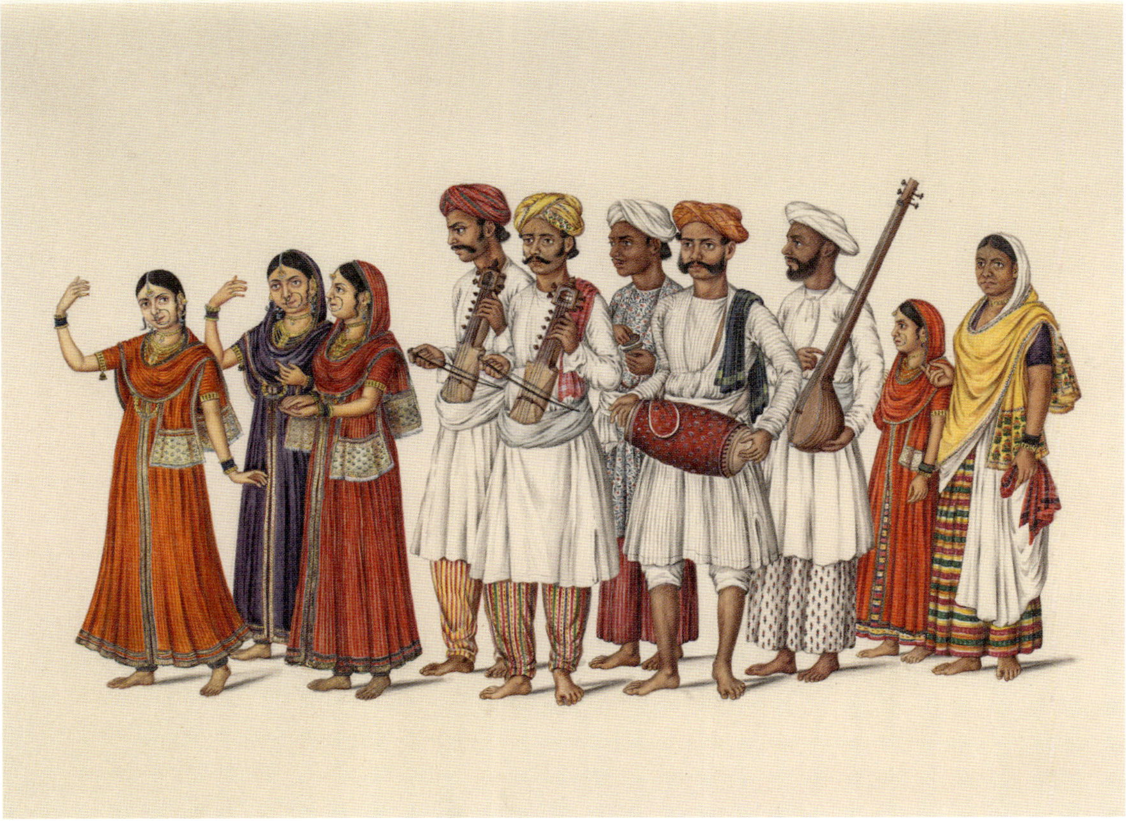

© Victoria and Albert Museum, London

Fig.5

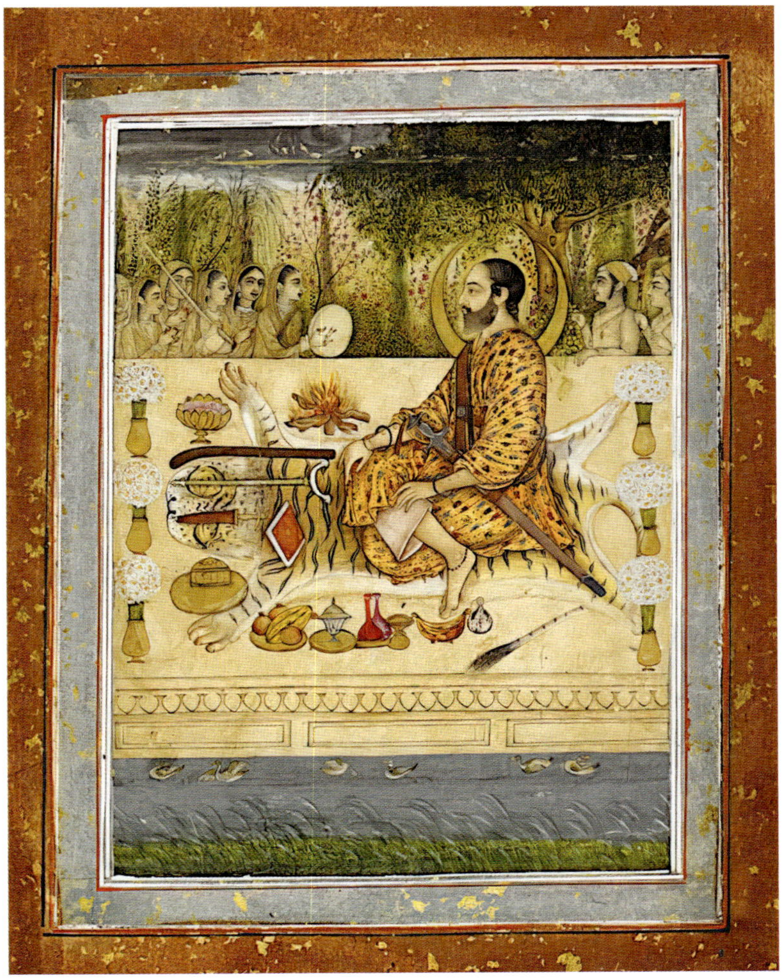

Fig.6

the Salvi *patola*-weavers of Patan reported that members of the Hindu oil- and ghee-sellers' communities would ask them for scraps of old pieces for their weddings, and that they would accept any design, even those favored by Muslim communities.[18]

While some *patola* types were evidently appropriate to both the domestic and export markets, others were produced exclusively for export to Southeast Asia (Fig.4/IN26). These are usually not only in different designs from those made for use in India but are also in formats different from the sari-size pieces made for home consumption. One of the most frequently found of these export types is a floral trellis pattern (IN16), usually produced in relatively small formats for use as shoulder cloths or sashes in the islands of Indonesia.[19] While some export *patola* of this type are made to a fairly high standard of weaving and dyeing,[20] others, like IN16, are more loosely woven, less deeply dyed and have cotton rather than silk warps in the borders, reflecting the different standards that were applied to some export pieces. Geometrically patterned export *patola* were also imitated in block-printed cotton in Gujarat for more affordable versions.[21] Rarer and more prestigious export *patola* have large-

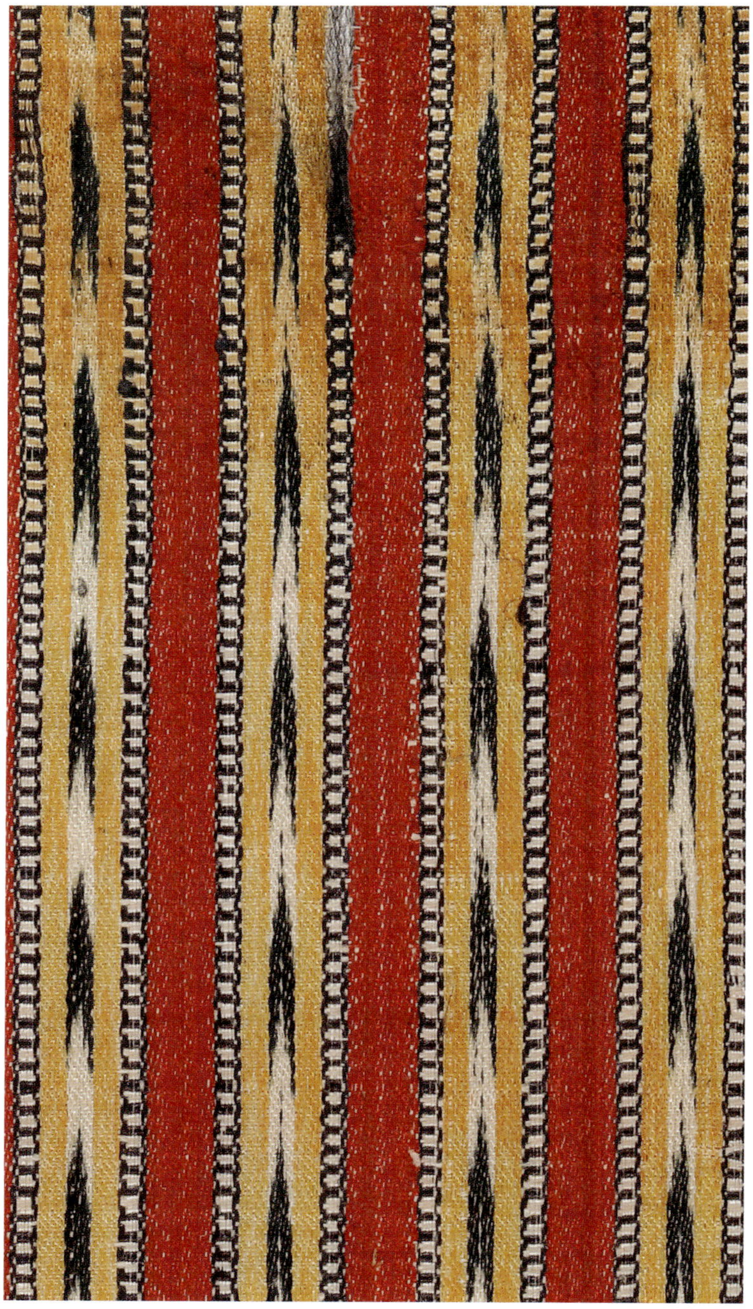

Fig.7

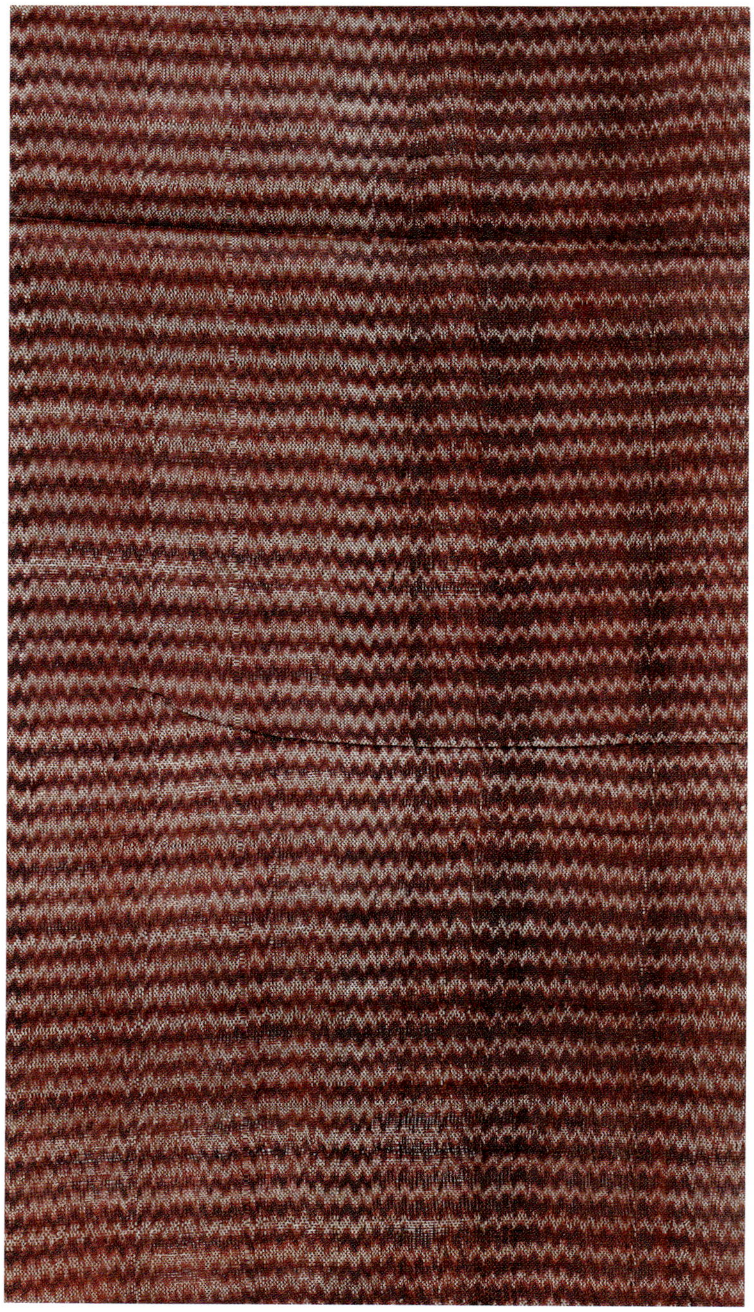

Fig.8

scale elephant designs (IN27) or trellis patterns with elephants and tigers.[22] Trellis patterns like that of IN09 and IN29 and the "basket" pattern of IN26 (called *jlamprang* in Java)[23] had a dramatic impact on local textiles, whether in ikat or other techniques such as batik. Repeating trellis patterns are to be found all over Southeast Asia, their ubiquity a testament to the popularity of the imported patterns (see Monsoon Asia).

Mashru

Another type of ikat textile that has traveled across Asia is the satin-woven fabric known in India as *mashru* (Fig.7/IN25, Fig.8/IN11 and Fig.10/IN22). The word is Arabic in origin and means "permitted," specifically "in accordance with Shari'a law." Wearing pure silk next to the skin was not permitted to Muslim men; *mashru* however has silk warps and cotton wefts and the warp-faced satin weave means that only the cotton wefts on the back of the fabric are against the wearer's skin, and hence the fabric is "permitted." Ikat patterning is not a prerequisite for *mashru*, and it is often found in plain colors, in contrasting stripes or with woven rosettes,[24] but its satin weave lends itself very well to warp-ikat patterns, especially those with chevron or "dagger" (*khanjari*) designs (Fig.7/IN25 and Fig.8/IN11). Ikat *mashru* was formerly made in both Gujarat and South India; while some *mashru* (without ikat) is still being made in Gujarat today, it has totally fallen out of production in South India.[25] *Mashru* is a relatively thick fabric and was often used for furnishing, either in its own right or as a decorative lining for window blinds, floor spreads, and saddlecloths.[26] It was also popular for trousers and skirts in both North and South India, both in its ikat and plain-striped form: in Kutch, Gujarat, full

Fig.7
Detail of IN25, *mashru* fragment

Fig.8
Detail of IN11, *mashru* fragment

Fig.9
Detail of IN03

Fig.10
IN22, *mashru* skirt

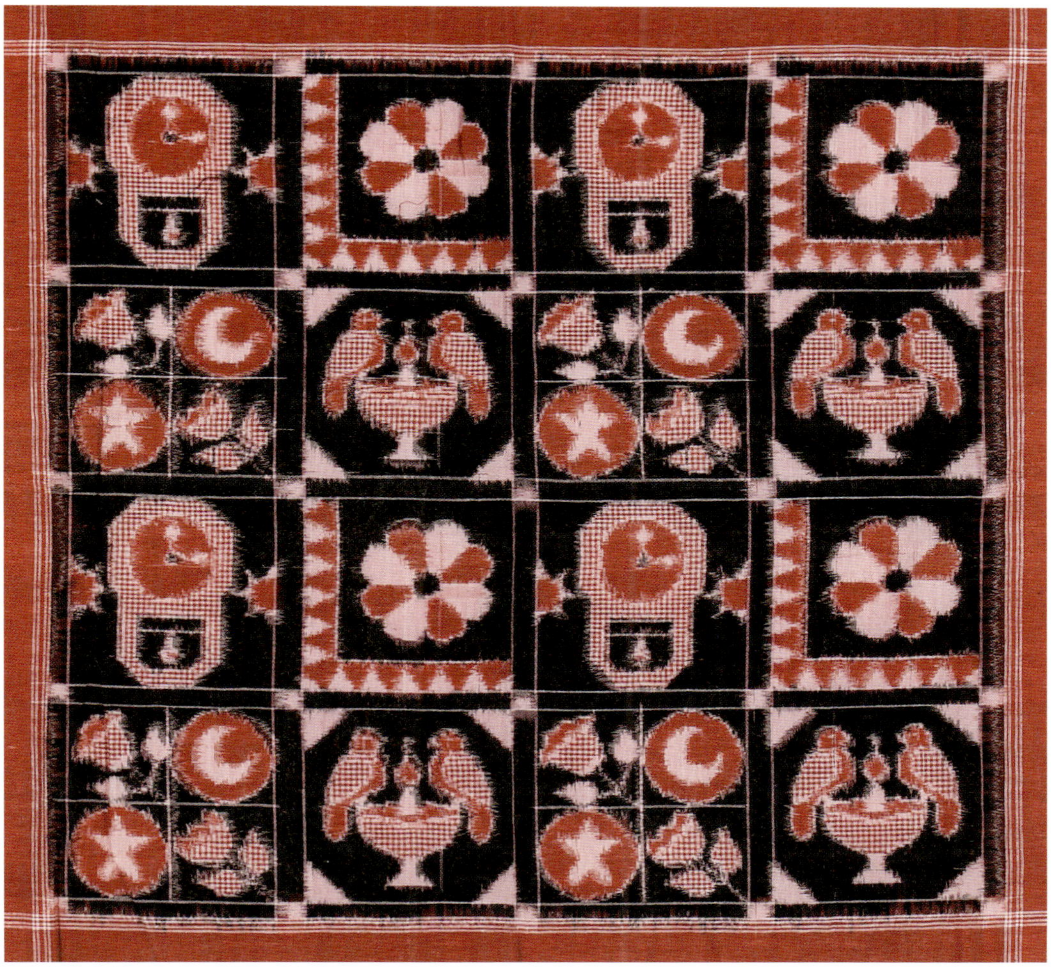

Fig.9

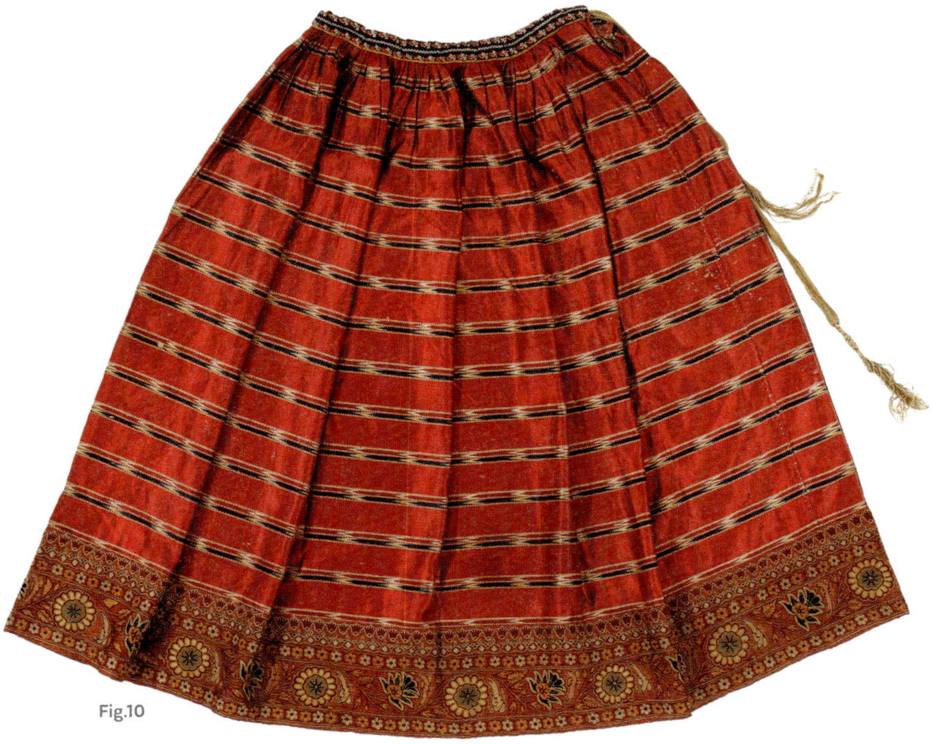

Fig.10

skirts of *mashru* fabric often had added borders of the fine local chain-stitch embroidery,[27] while 19th-century paintings from South India show men in *mashru* trousers and women in horizontally striped *mashru* skirts (Fig.5).[28]

Velvet

Ikat velvet appears in a small number of luxury furnishings. This extremely time-consuming technique done in expensive silk would be available only to royal patrons, and two documented pieces are still in Rajput royal palaces in Jodhpur and Jaipur, although it is likely that the pieces were made in Gujarat.[29] Ikat velvet is more usually associated with Iran than India, although the few surviving Indian examples do have sufficiently different designs that they may be attributed to Indian royal workshops rather than being imported from Iran.[30] While Iranian ikat velvets usually favor large-scale tree patterns (see West and Central Asia), the surviving Indian versions show smaller repeating patterns of chevrons, small trees, or diamond patterns in blue and red, perhaps echoing the geometric designs of the prestigious *patola*.[31]

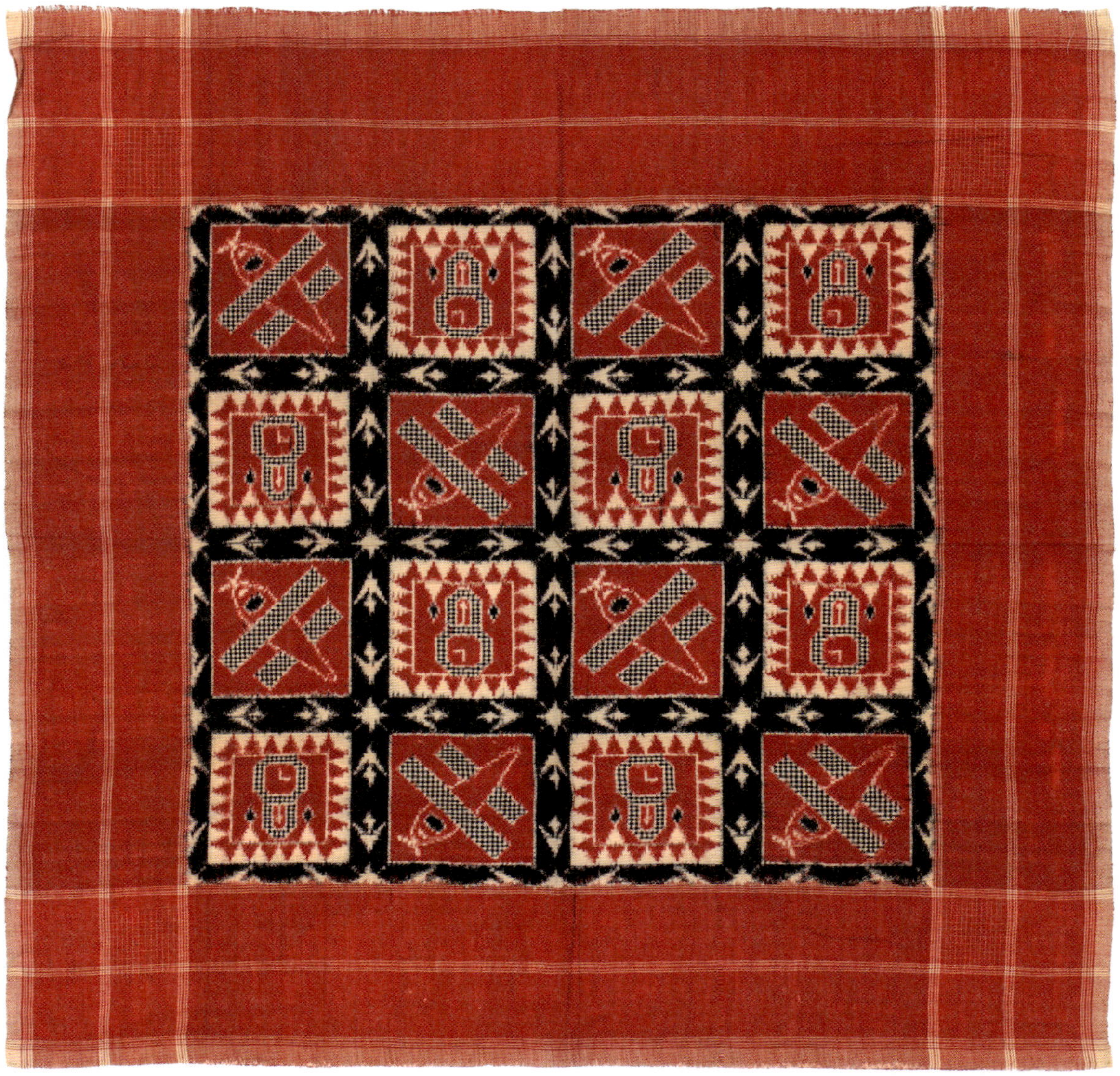

IN01 *Telia rumal* with airplane and clock design, Chirala, Andhra Pradesh, India, ca. 1930–40. Cotton, weft ikat with warp ikat used for the transition between the field and borders and in the corner squares. 39 in x 42 in

Figurative designs started to be used in *telia rumals* in the early 20th century, and were intended mainly for export to the Middle East. Wall clocks and airplanes, as in this piece, were popular designs, along with lions, peacocks, and flowers, all fitting into the traditional square format that was ultimately derived from South Indian handkerchiefs.

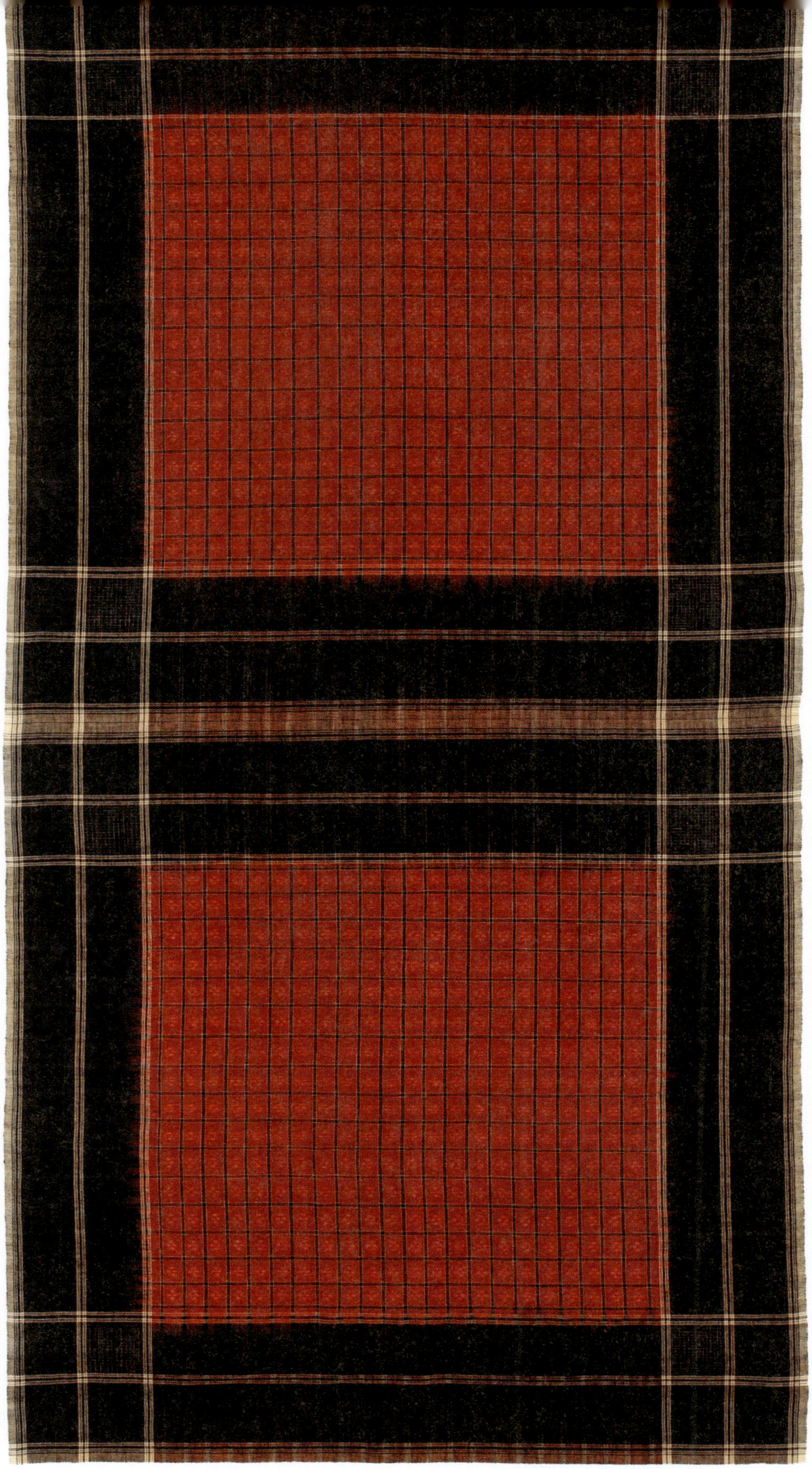

IN02 Pair of *telia rumals*, Chirala, Andhra Pradesh, India, early 20th century. Cotton, weft ikat with warp ikat used for the transition between the field and borders and in the corner squares. 81 in x 44 in

Telia rumals (literally "oily kerchiefs") are a more decorative variation of the simple South Indian checked cotton handkerchief. Like them, *telia rumals* were woven in lengths of eight squares, which could be cut from the length as required. This pair could have been used as a head cover, shoulder cloth or all-purpose carrying cloth, while longer lengths were used as complete wrapped garments. Unlike simple checked cotton handkerchiefs, *telia rumals* were patterned in weft ikat (with warp ikat used for zone-dyeing the transition from field to border) and were prepared by steeping the yarn in til or gingelly (sesame) oil. This was originally done as part of the pre-dyeing process, but the distinctive smell and feel it gave to the cloth became part of its appeal and buyers would reject any imitation.

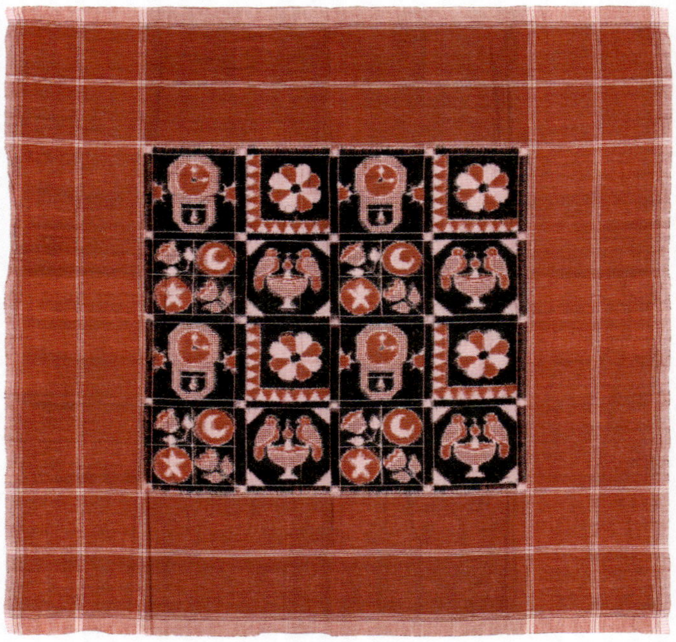

IN03 ***Telia rumal***
Andhra Pradesh, first quarter 20th century. Cotton, double ikat. 39 in x 42 in

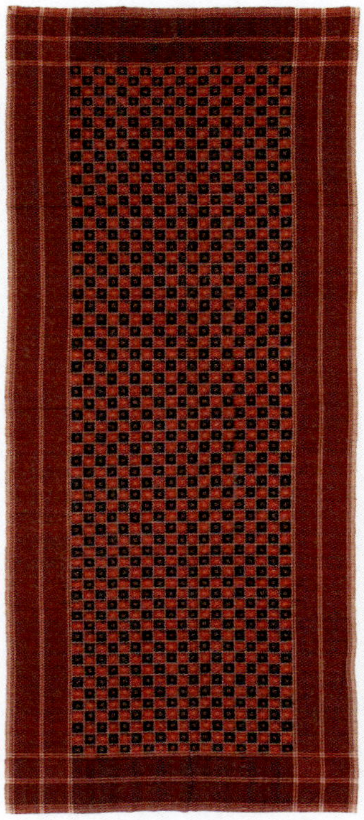

IN04 ***Telia rumal***
Andhra Pradesh, India, third quarter of the 19th century. Cotton, double ikat. 100 in x 44 in

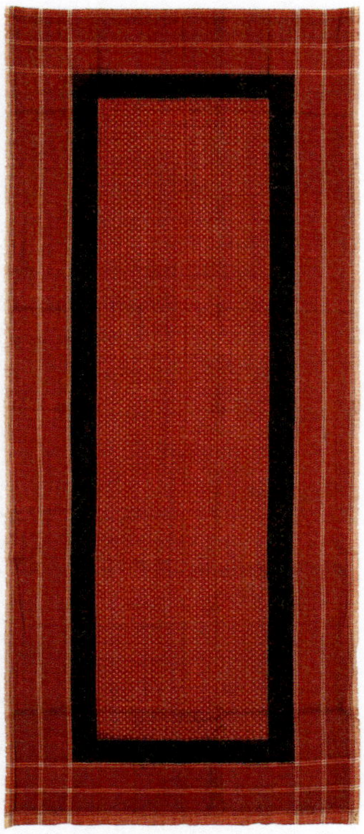

IN05 ***Telia rumal***
Andhra Pradesh, India, 19th century. Cotton, double ikat. 102 in x 43 in

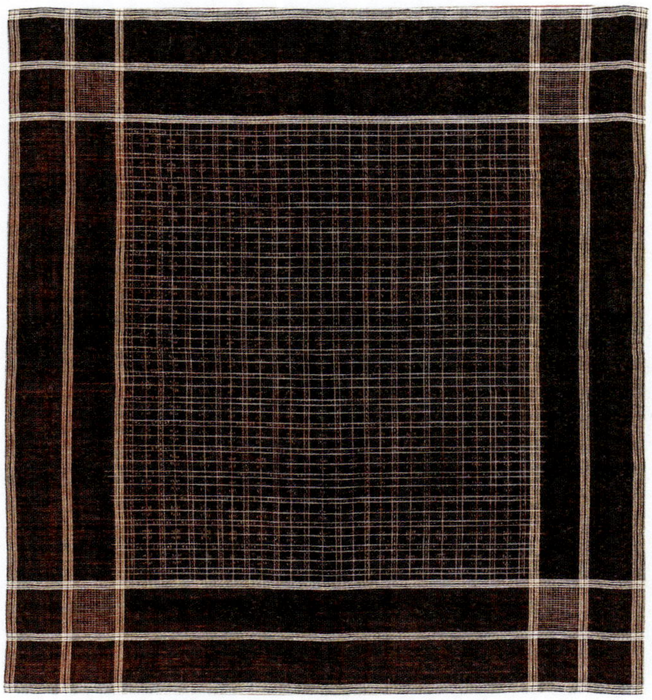

IN06 ***Telia rumal***
Andhra Pradesh, India, first quarter 20th century. Cotton, double ikat. 43 in x 41 in

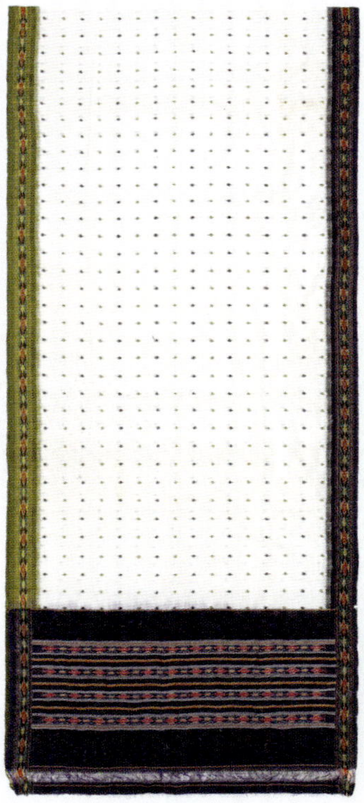

IN07 Sari
Andhra Pradesh, India, ca. 1950–60s. Silk, warp and weft ikat. 152 in x 47 in

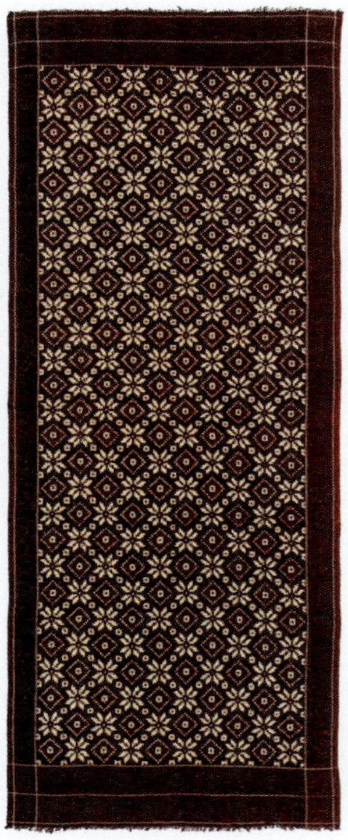

IN08 ***Telia rumal***
Andhra Pradesh, India, first quarter 20th century. Cotton, double ikat. 82 in x 34 in

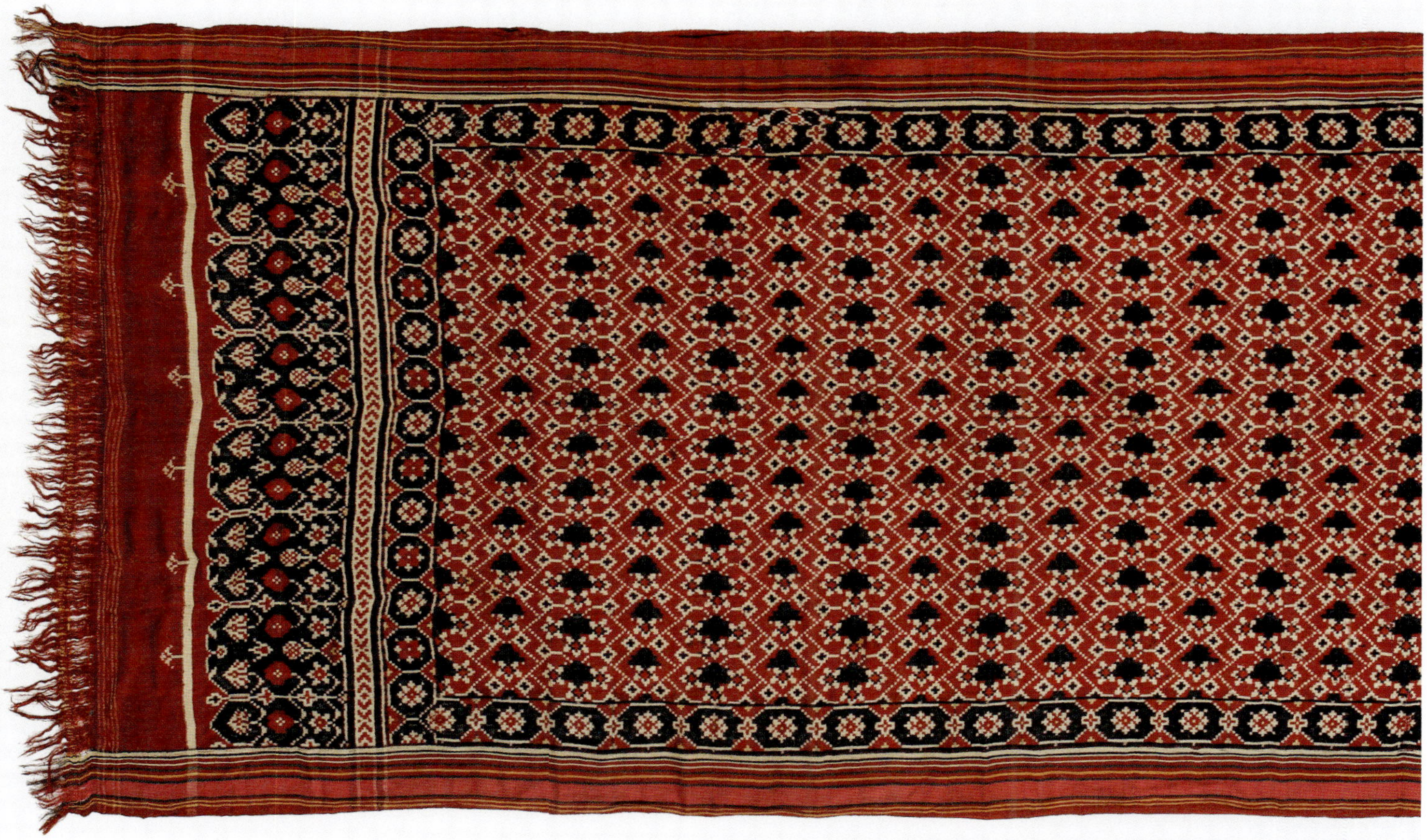

IN09 ***Patola*** **sari (*tran phul bhat*)**
Gujarat, India, 19th century. Silk, double ikat. 180 in x 40 in

IN10 ***Mashru*** **fragment**
Gujarat, India, 19th century. From the Kotah Treasury, Rajasthan. Silk and cotton, warp ikat. 10 in x 12 in

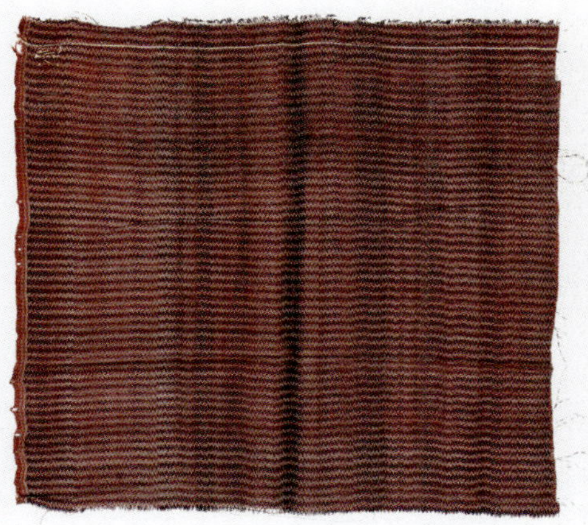

IN11 ***Mashru*** **fragment**
Gujarat, India, 19th century. From the Kotah Treasury, Rajasthan. Silk and cotton, warp ikat. 15 in x 13 in

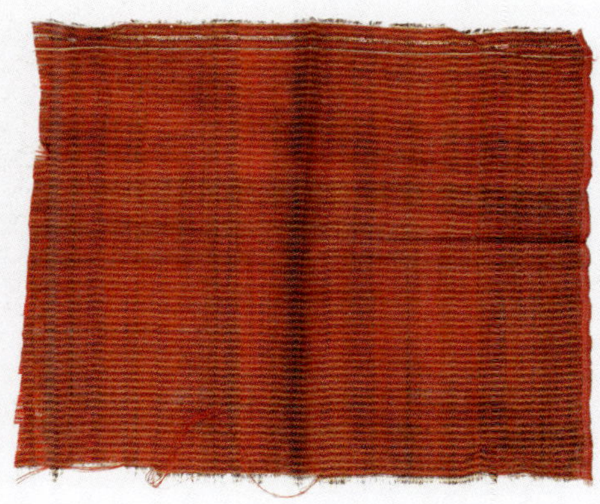

IN12 ***Mashru*** **fragment**
Gujarat, India, 19th century. From the Kotah Treasury, Rajasthan. Silk and cotton, warp ikat. 21 in x 12 in

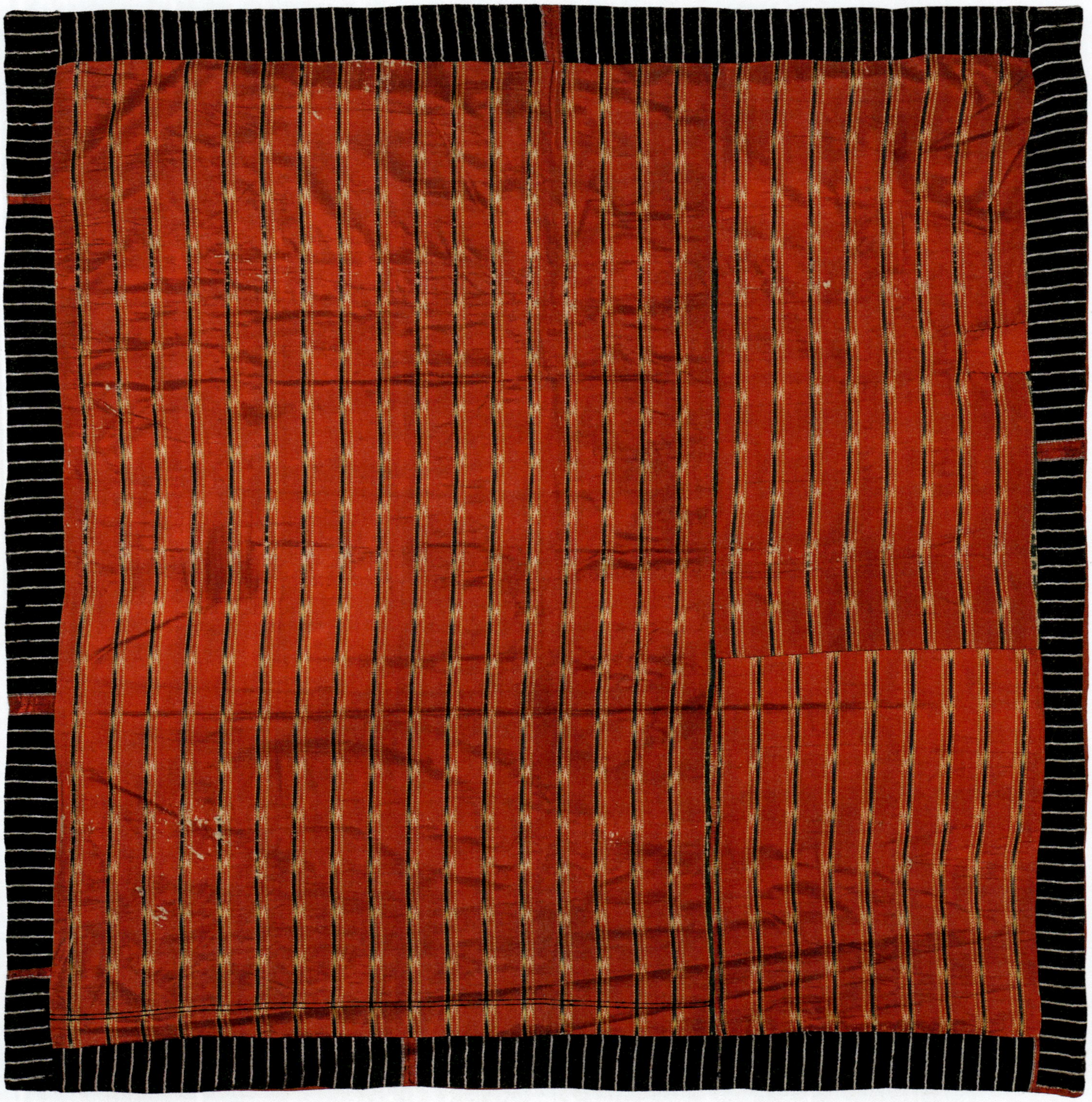

IN13 Canopy, Gujarat, India, late 19th century. *Mashru*: satin weave with silk warps and cotton wefts; warp-ikat chevron pattern. 52 in x 52 in

This canopy is made of *mashru*—a mixed fabric of satin weave with satin warps and cotton wefts—and the main field is patterned with warp-ikat chevrons, known in India as *khanjar* or *katardar* design, both meaning "dagger." *Mashru* was not always made with ikat patterns: it could also be plain-colored or striped (like the edging fabric on this piece), but warp-ikat designs like those on this canopy work very successfully with the satin weave. As *mashru* is a relatively robust fabric, it was traditionally used for furnishings like this canopy, or for covering cushions, but was also used for men's trousers and robes as well as women's gathered skirts. The expert dyeing of both the ikat design and the deep lac-red field show that this was a piece of high quality possibly intended for a royal household.

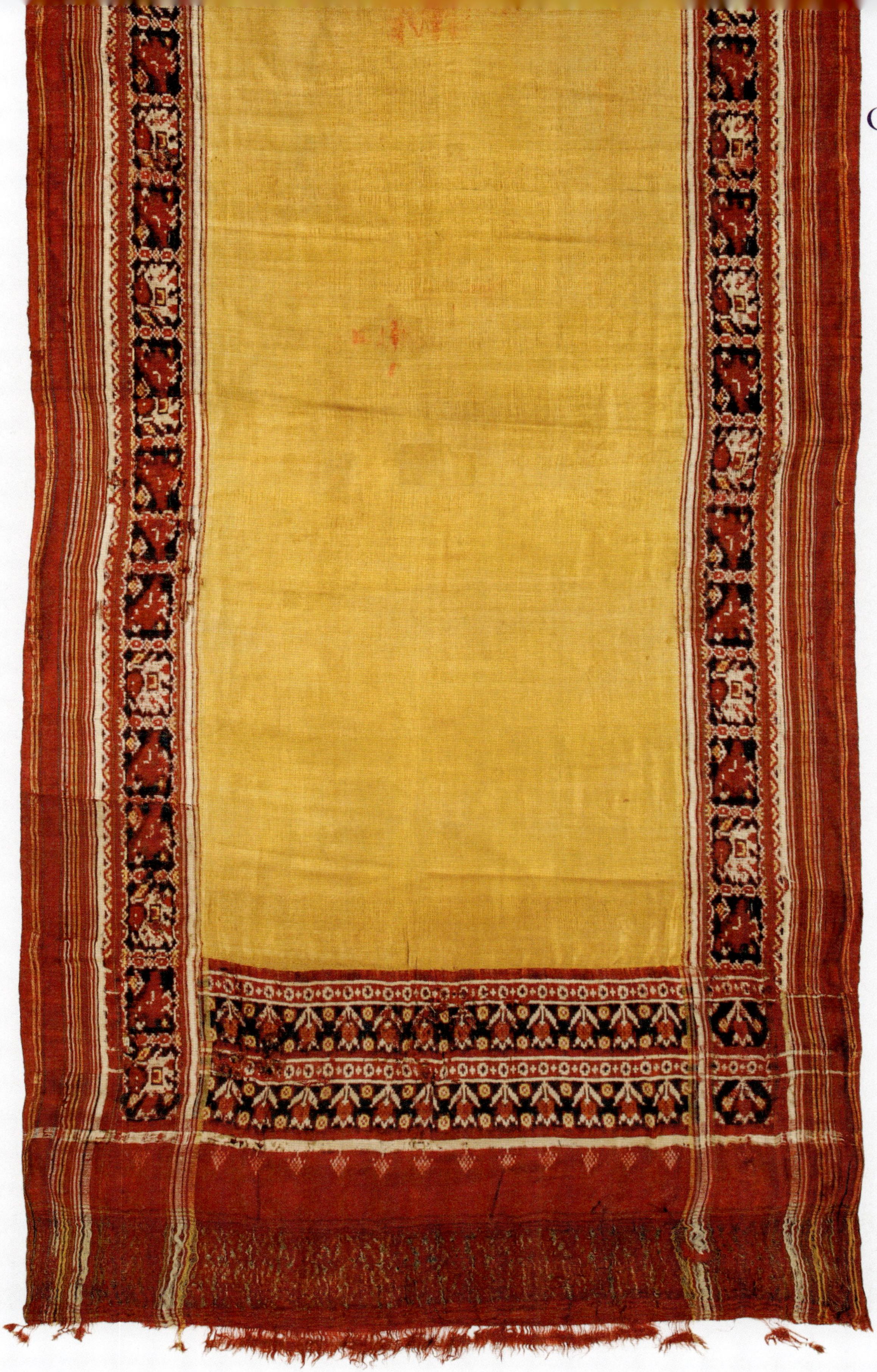

IN14 *Patola* shawl with plain yellow ground (*gala vali bhat*), probably Patan, Gujarat, India, late 19th–early 20th century. Silk, double ikat with metal-wrapped thread wefts at one end. 112 in x 48 in

Patola with plain fields are less expensive than those completely patterned with double ikat, but they still approach something of the status of their more elaborate equivalents. This type of *patola* was reportedly popular among the Jain communities of northern Gujarat. The field is almost always dyed a deep yellow, either with turmeric or pomegranate rind, but some variants have vertically striped fields. The side borders show the popular parrot and elephant motifs that appear in several other *patola* types, and both end borders have a double row of standing flowers.

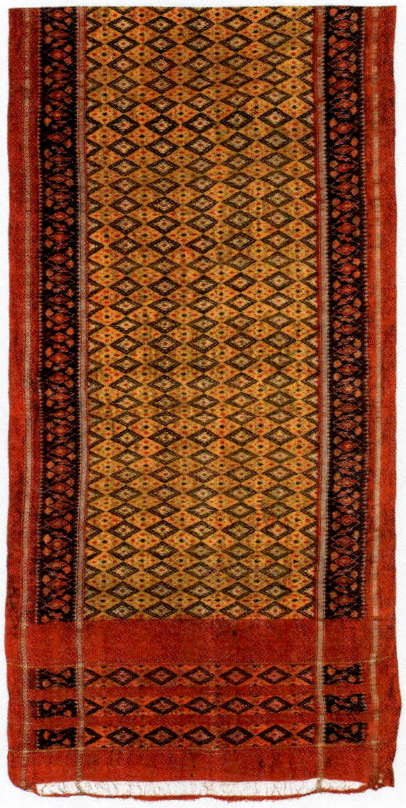

IN15 Sari
Odisha, India, mid-20th century. Silk and metallic threads, weft ikat. 184 in x 44 in

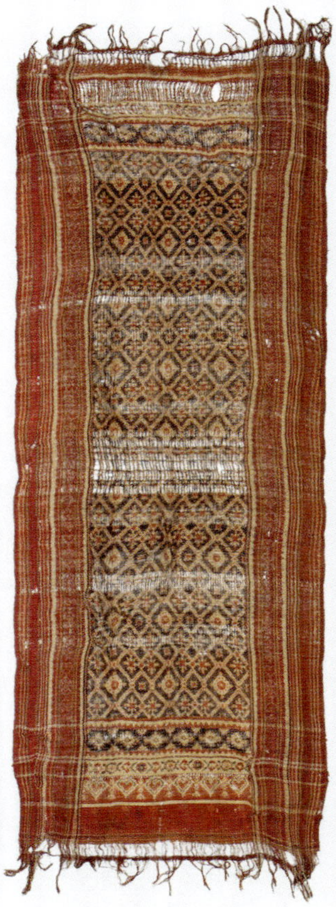

IN16 Export *patola*
Gujarat, India, 19th century. Silk, double ikat. 80 in x 30 in

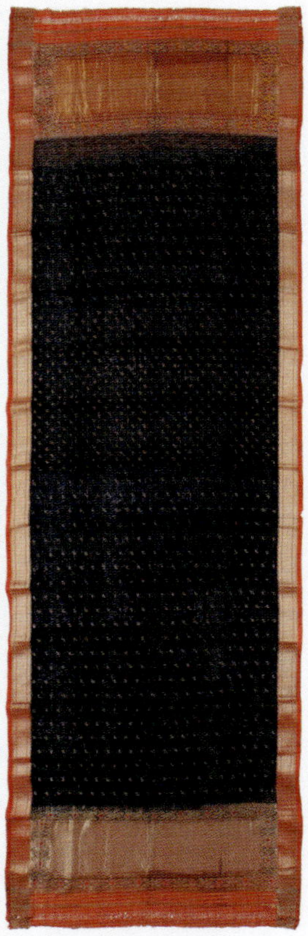

IN17 Sari
Paithan, Maharashtra, India, 20th century. Cotton, warp ikat, silk metallic weft brocade. 148 in x 47 in

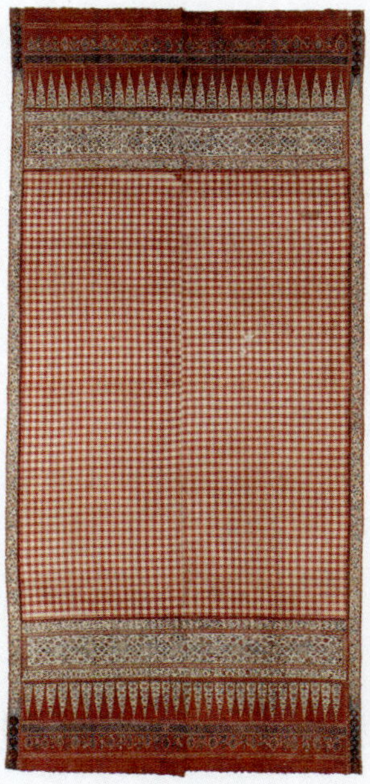

IN18 Trade cloth
Coromandel Coast, India, late 18th century. Cotton, mordant-resist-dyed block-printed ends, warp and weft ikat. 160 in x 62 in

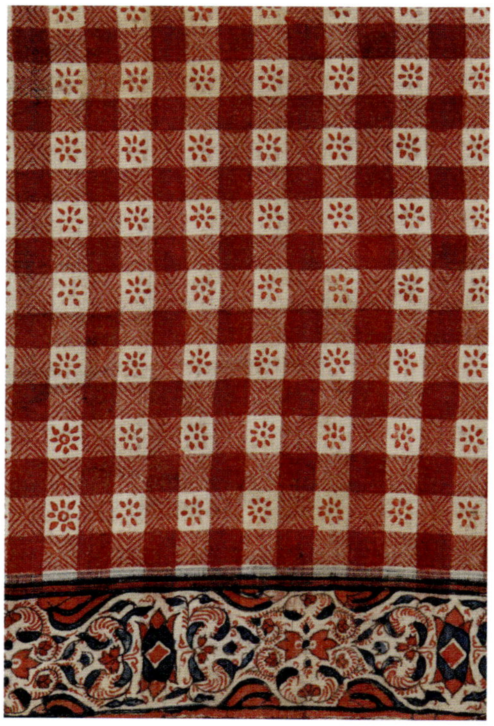

IN19 *Sarasa* fragment
Coromandel Coast, India, late 18th century. Made for the Sri Lankan market, probably traded by the Dutch. Cotton double ikat, stamped and handpainted resist. 12 in x 18 in

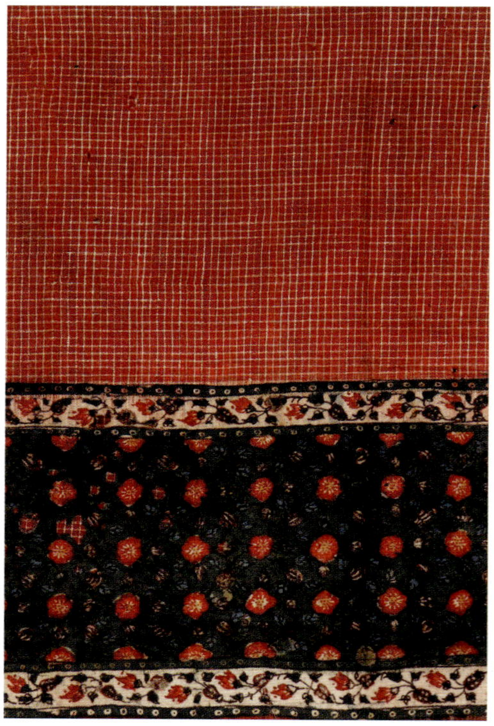

IN20 *Sarasa* fragment
Coromandel Coast, India, late 18th century. Made for the Sri Lankan market, traded by the Dutch. Cotton zone-dyed warp ikat, block printed. 6 in x 9 in

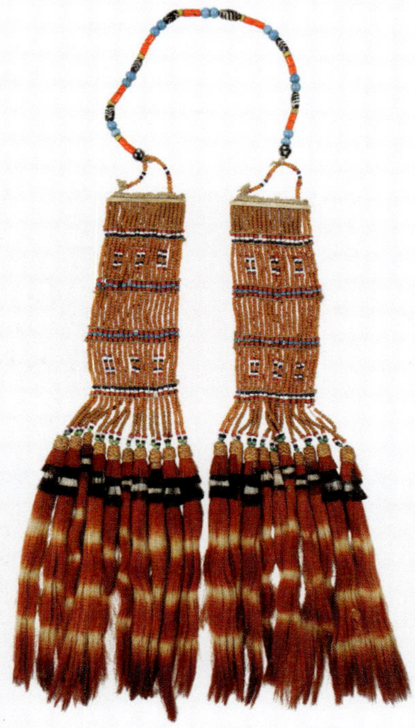

IN21 Naga man's head decoration Nagaland, India, early 20th century. Goat's hair, proto-ikat, glass beadwork. 21 in x 13 in

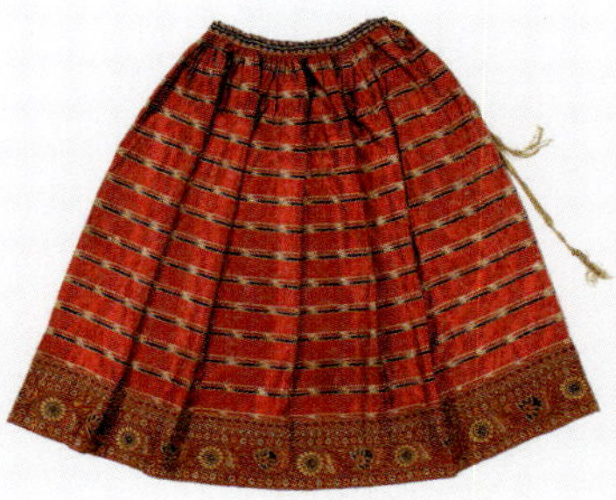

IN22 *Mashru* skirt
Gujarat, India, 19th century, Silk and cotton, warp ikat, silk embroidery. 36 in x 46 in

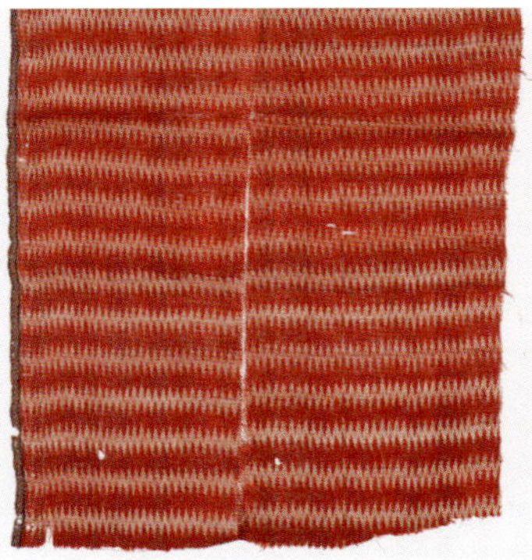

IN23 *Mashru* fragment
Gujarat, India, 19th century. From the Kotah Treasury, Rajasthan. Silk and cotton, warp ikat. 16 in x 12 in

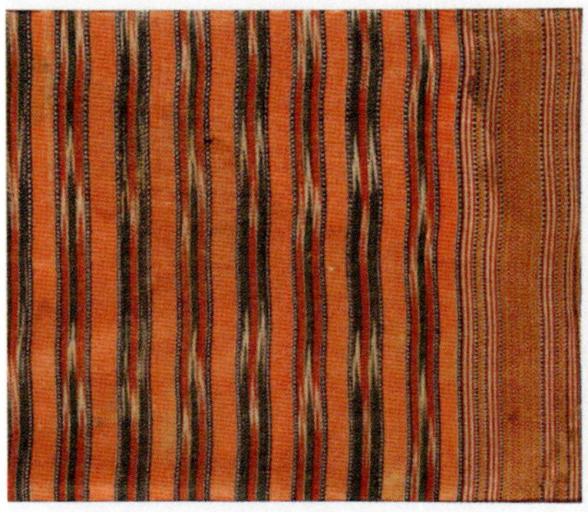

IN24 *Mashru* fragment
Gujarat, India, possibly 18th century. From the Kotah Treasury, Rajasthan. Silk and cotton, warp ikat. 12 in x 8 in

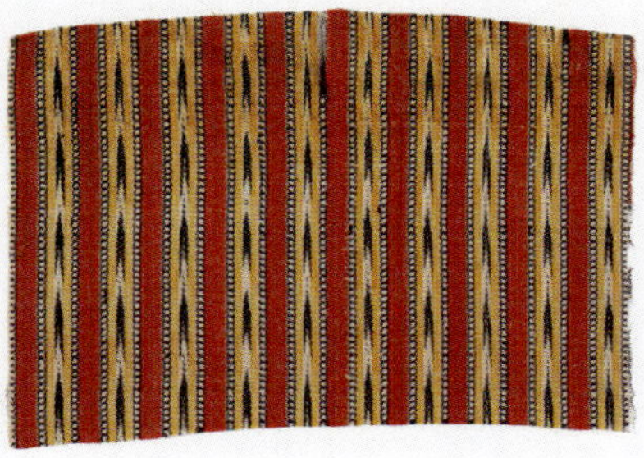

IN25 *Mashru* fragment
Gujarat, India, possibly 18th century. From the Kotah Treasury, Rajasthan. Silk and cotton, warp ikat. 6 in x 3.5 in

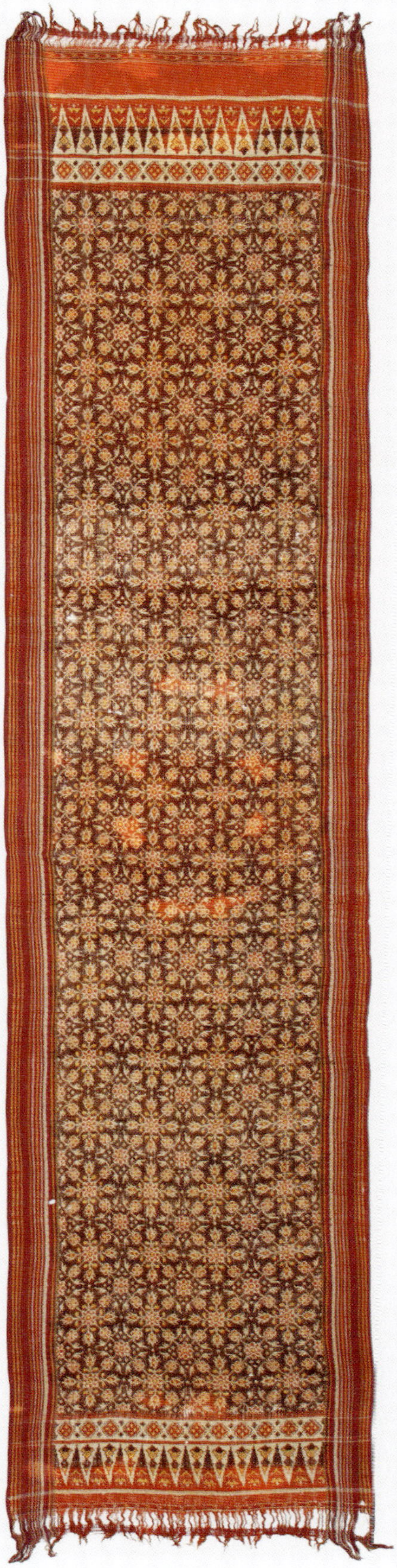

IN26 Export *patola*
Gujarat, India, 19th century. Silk, double ikat. 144 in x 35 in

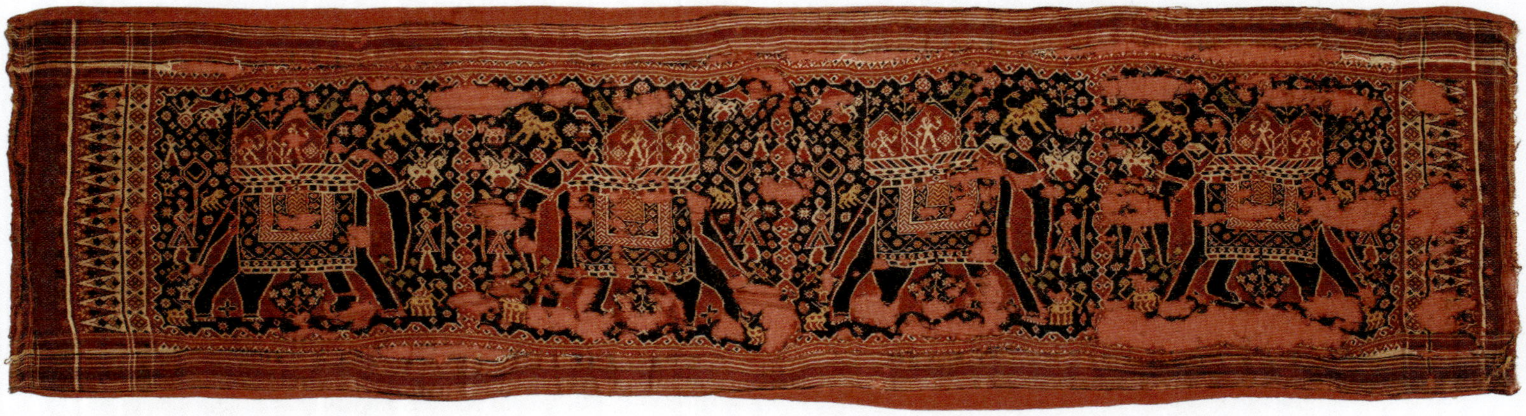

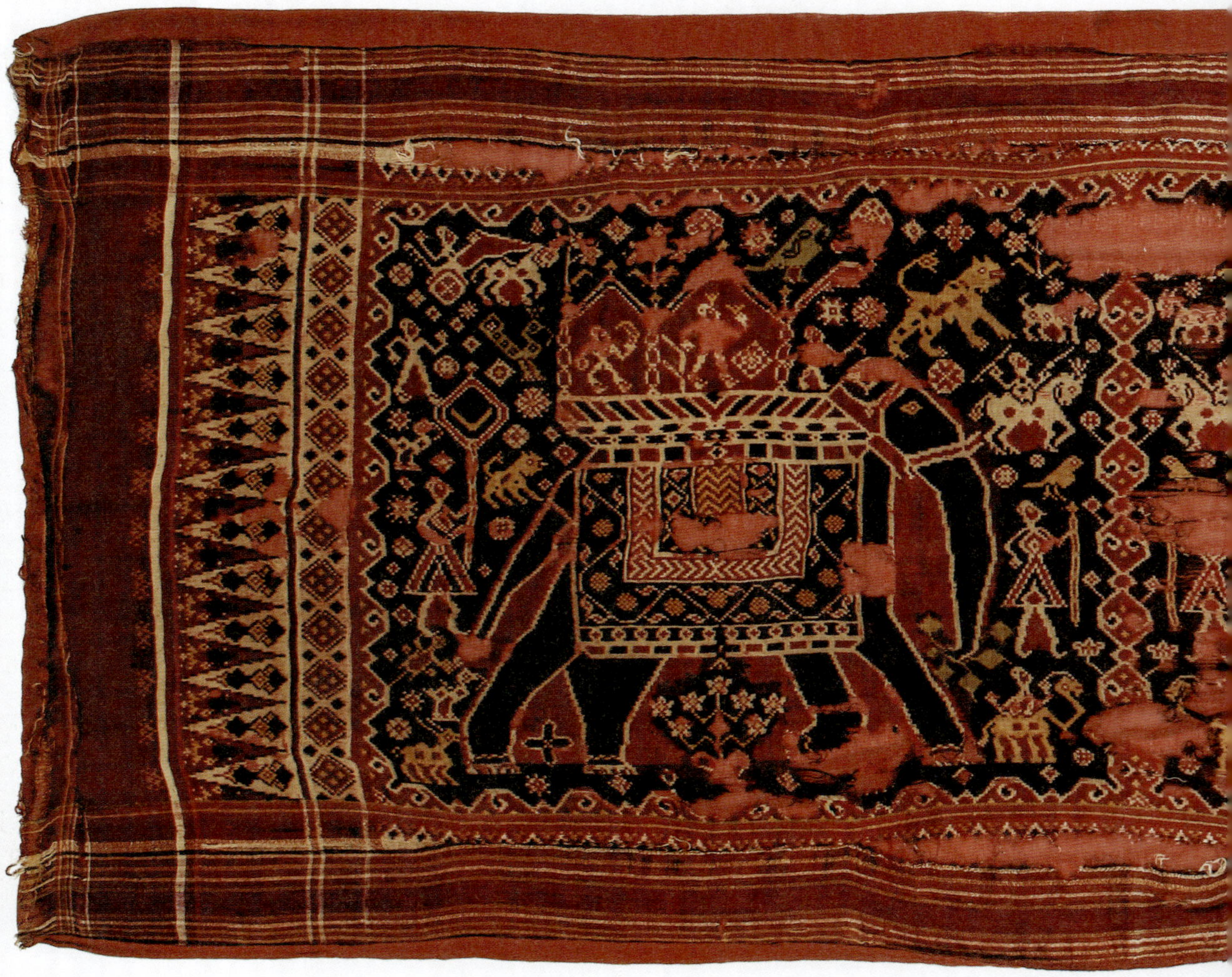

IN27 Export *patola* with large elephant design, Gujarat, India, probably 19th century. Silk, double ikat. 166 in x 36 in

The elephant *patola* is the most prestigious of the many kinds of textile exported from Incia to Indonesia. The large-scale pattern of two pairs of facing elephants bearing *howdahs* with rulers and a *mahout* on their backs, and with tigers and standard-bearers between them, is not used in India itself, but was produced solely for export to insular Southeast Asia, where such pieces were used ceremonially as hangings and canopies. Most of the surviving examples have been collected in the Lesser Sunda Islands of Indonesia, where they seem to have been part of the personal wealth of local rulers. Exoort *patola* with smaller designs of elephants and tigers, and of hunting scenes, were also produced for the Southeast Asian trade: while cheaper, printed imitations of those patterns were also traded, the large elephant *patola* do not seem to have been imitated in this way, perhaps because of their exceptionally high status and exclusive use.

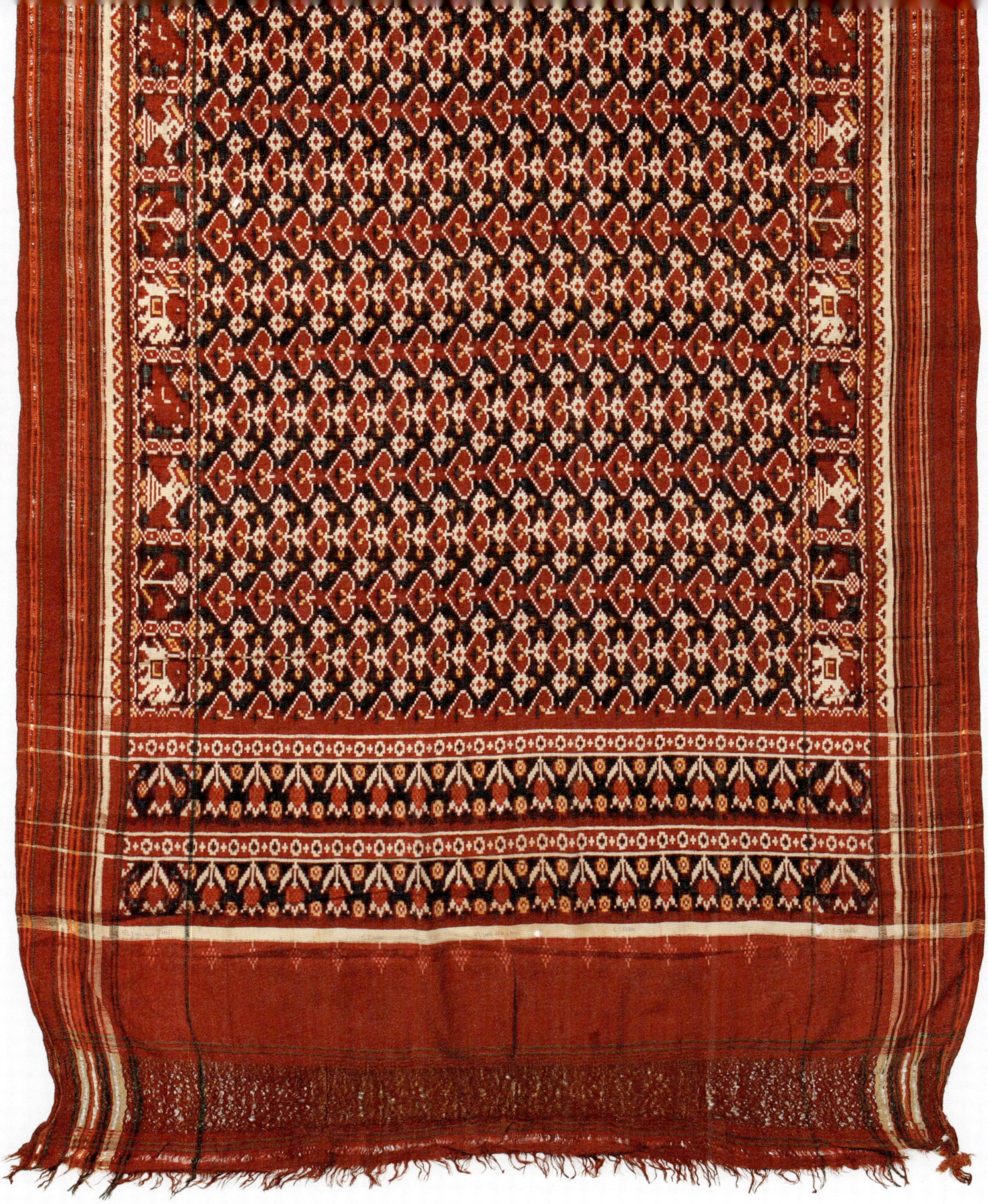

IN28 *Patola* sari with leaf design (*pan bhat*), probably Patan, Gujarat, India, late 19th–early 20th century. Silk, double ikat. 144 in x 40 in

This type of *patola*, with leaf designs in the field and a sequence of female figures, parrots, elephants, and flowers in the side borders, is one of the most popular and most widely found in collections. They were made mainly for a variety of Hindu patrons in Gujarat, especially the Nagar Brahmans of Junagadh, Anavil Brahmans from Surat, Bhatias from Kutch, and Lohanas from Saurashtra, as well as for the Jain Kapol Vanias. *Patola* of this design were not usually traded to Indonesia, although one such had reportedly been found in south Sumatra.

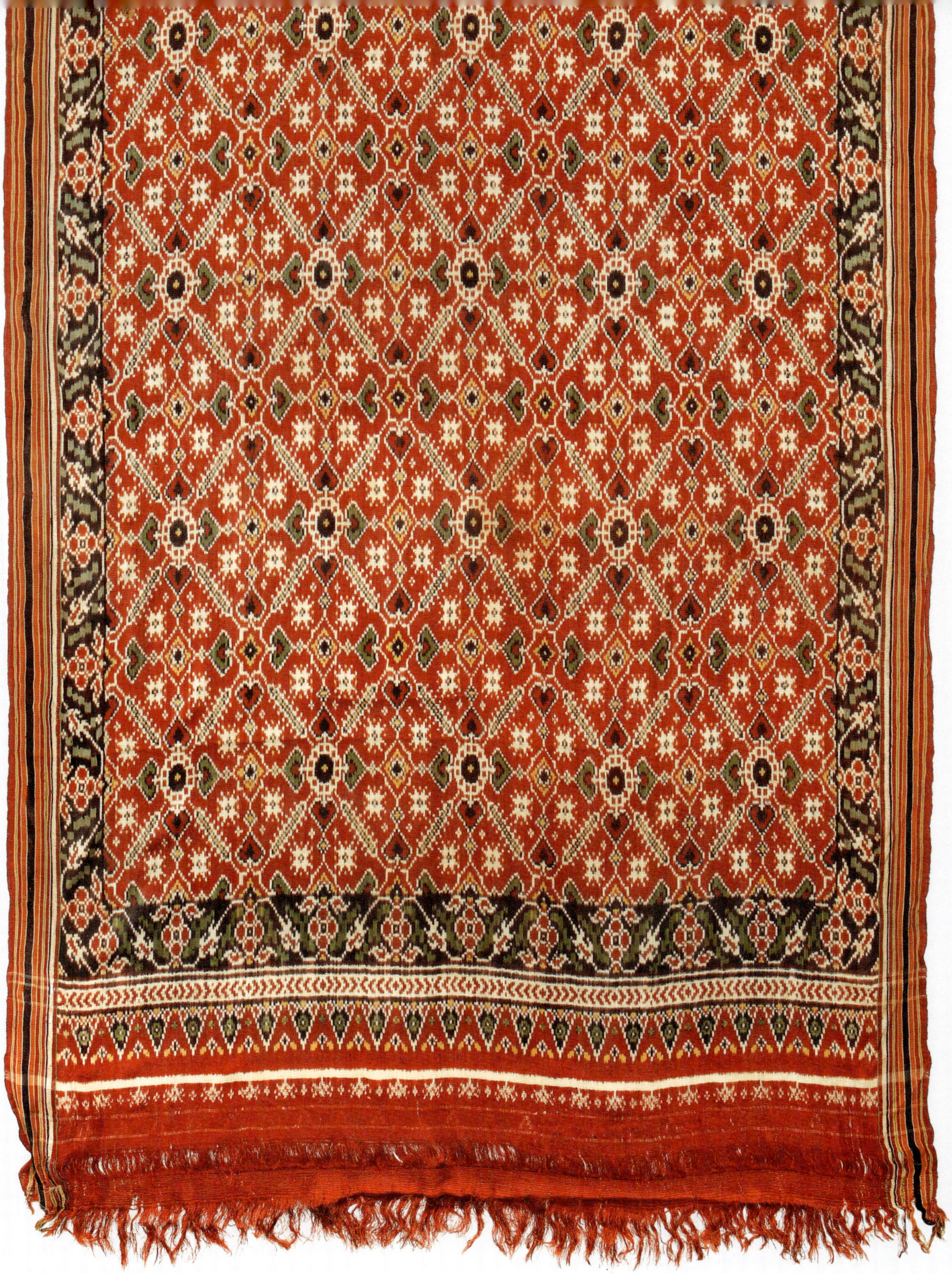

IN29 *Patola* sari with trellis design (Vohra *gaji bhat*), probably Patan, Gujarat, India, late 19th–early 20th century. Silk, double ikat. 125 in x 36 in

Patola saris with geometric trellis designs like this one were made predominantly for the Muslim Vohra trading community, who give their name to the design. *Patola* of this design were traditionally worn by the bride and other members of the bride and groom's family at weddings and on other auspicious occasions. Abstract patterns are favored by Muslim patrons as figurative designs are discouraged in Islamic tradition. Like other types of *patola*, they may once have been produced in several towns in Gujarat: one 19th-century account links this type in particular to Surat, but it was certainly used in Ahmedabad and other centers. In spite of the presence of triangular *tumpal*-like designs at the ends, this type of *patola* does not seem to have been exported to Southeast Asia.

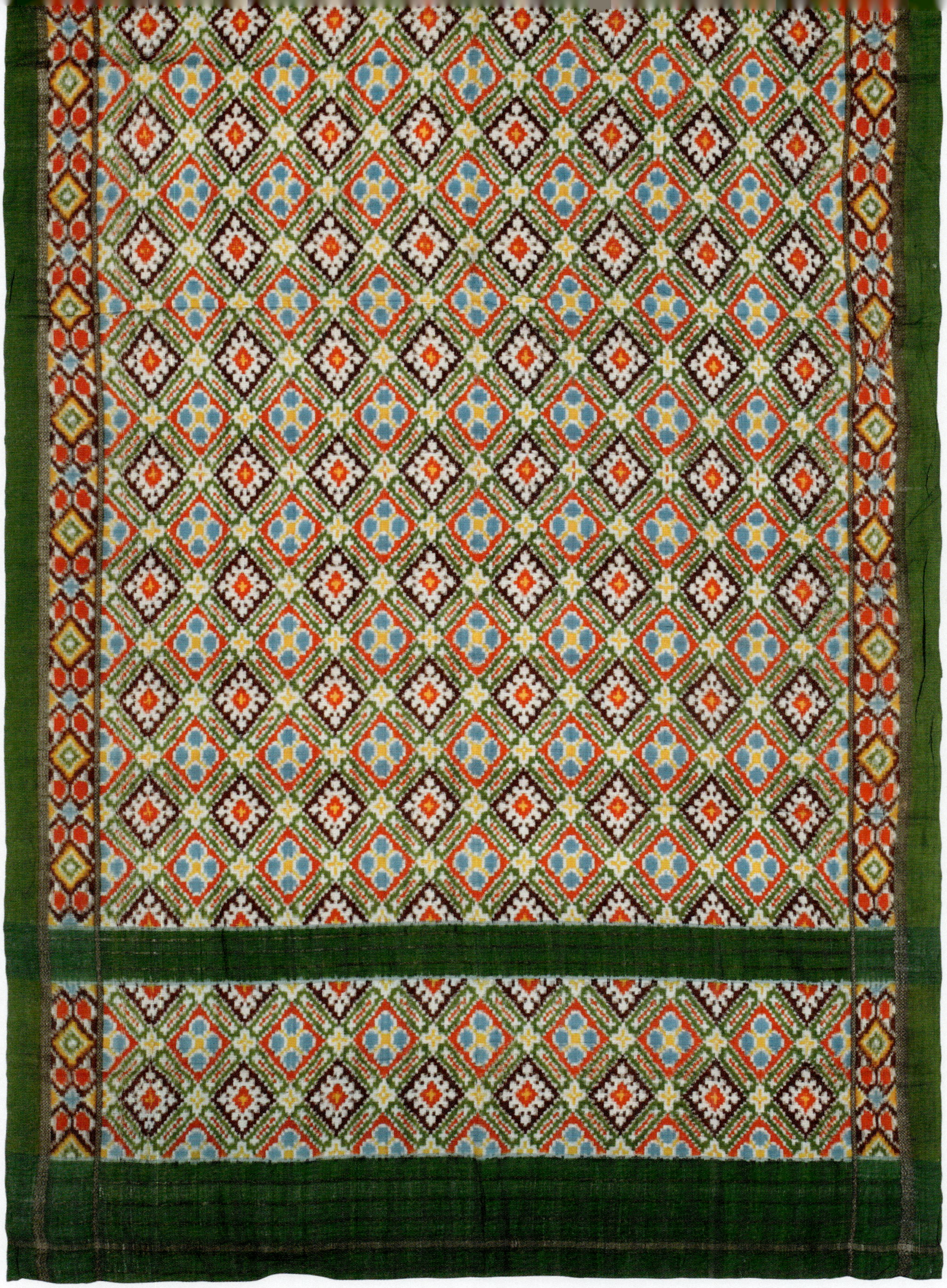

IN30 Sari, Pochampalli, Andhra Pradesh, India, ca. 1970s. Silk, double ikat. 188 in x 47 in

This silk double-ikat sari from South India combines inspiration from both the traditional squared *telia rumal* of the local area and also from the much more luxurious silk double-ikat *patola* of Gujarat. Several centers beyond the traditional *patola*-weaving city of Patan in Gujarat started producing their own versions of these prestigious saris, providing high-end, hand-woven ikat saris to local patrons who would not normally buy or wear Gujarati *patola*. Ikat-weaving in Andhra Pradesh is traditionally associated with the *telia rumals* of Chirala, but from the mid-20th century several expert weavers have taken up other styles, as seen in this vibrant sari.

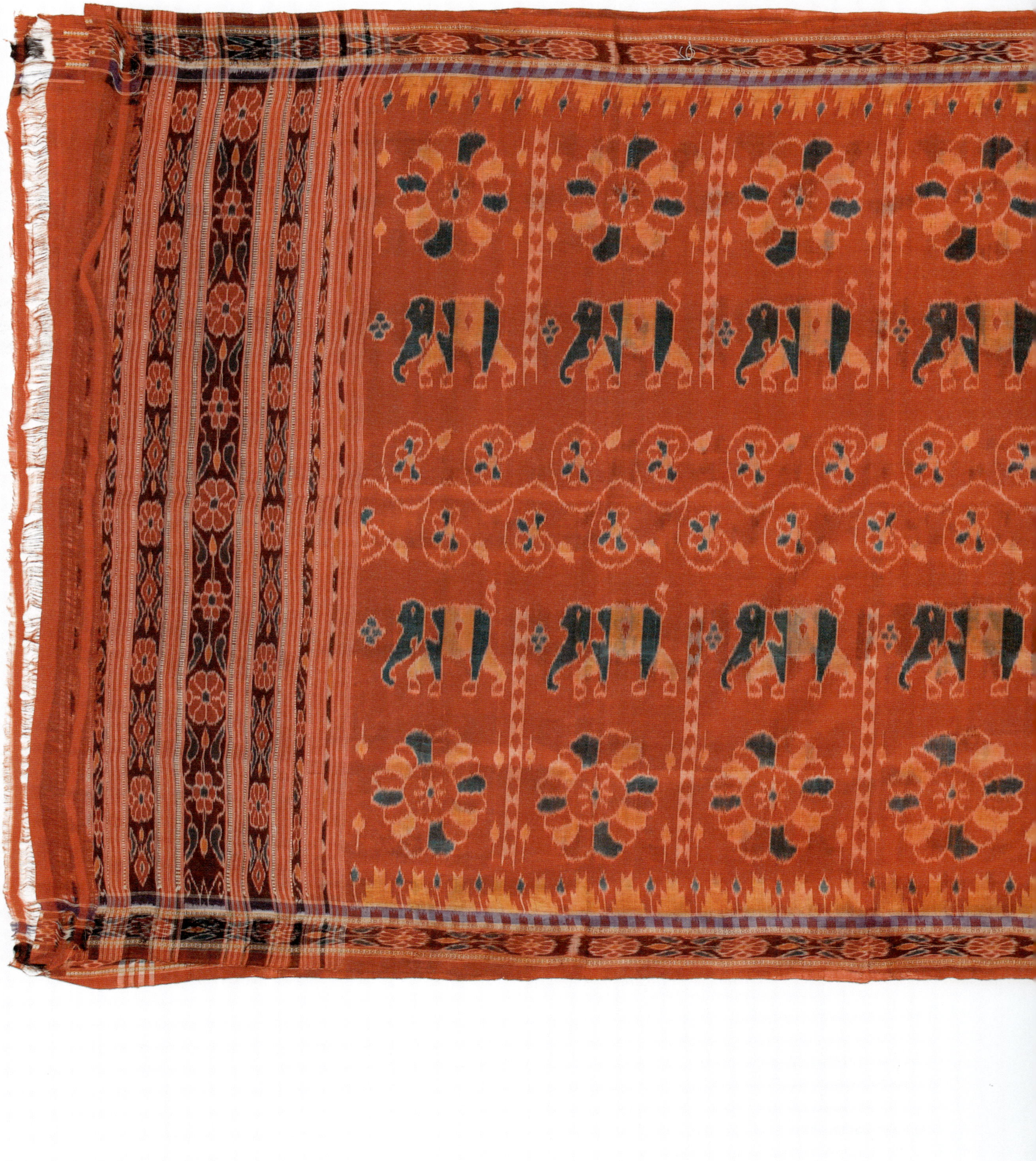

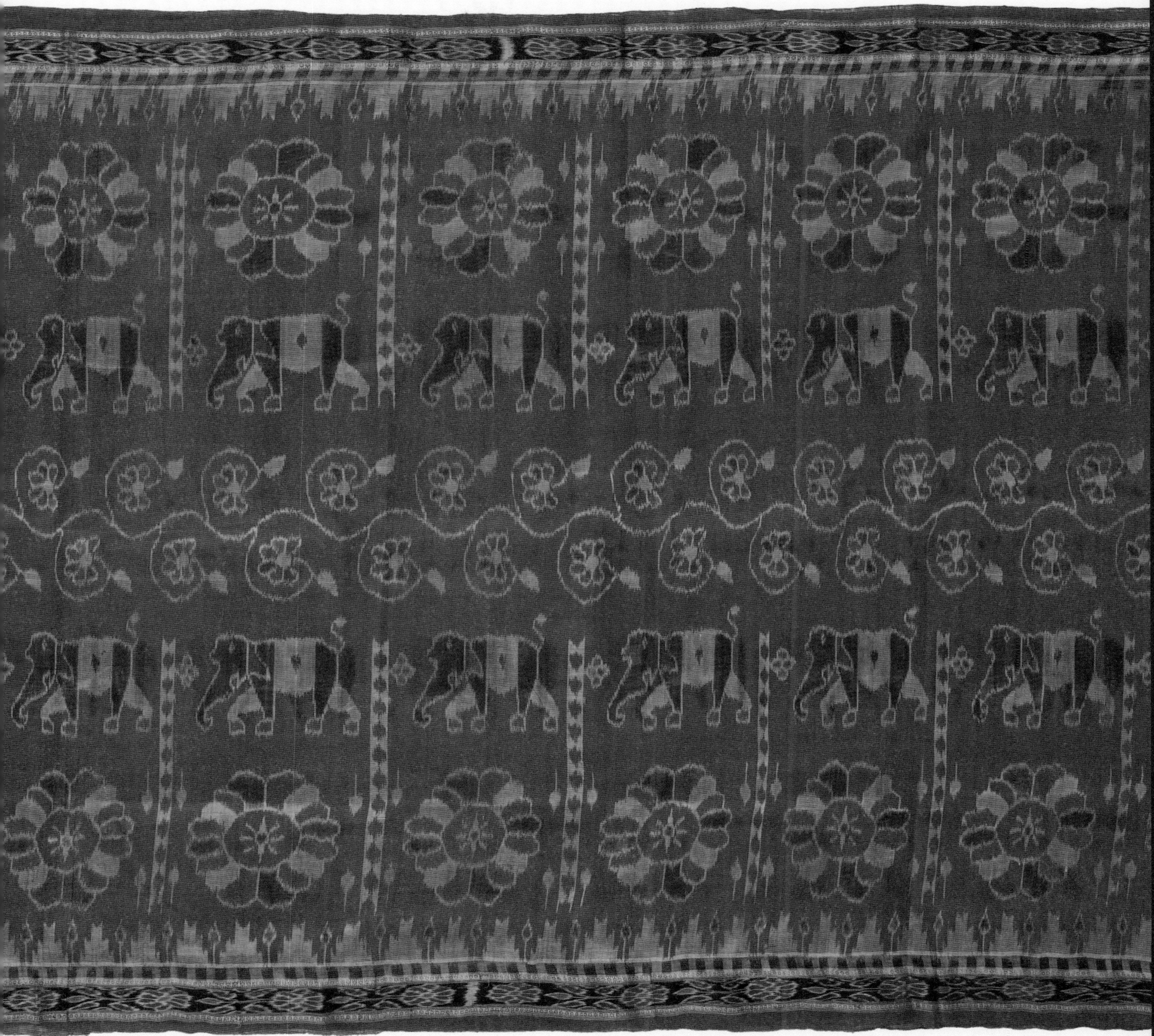

IN31 Sari (*khandua*), Nuapatna, Odisha, India, 20th century. Silk compound ikat, weft ikat in the field and warp ikat in the borders. 204 in x 45 in

Odisha in eastern India is known for its weft-ikat saris, with different parts of the region producing their own designs. It is one of the few parts of India where locally made ikat is still a popular fabric for saris and women's tailored garments and scarves (*dupatta*). While inland towns such as Sambalpur traditionally make saris with checkerboard patterns in the field and figurative designs in the borders, this decorative sari is one of the typical products of the coastal town of Nuapatna. Originally intended to be worn at weddings and other ceremonies, the *khandua* design has now been absorbed into saris for regular use.

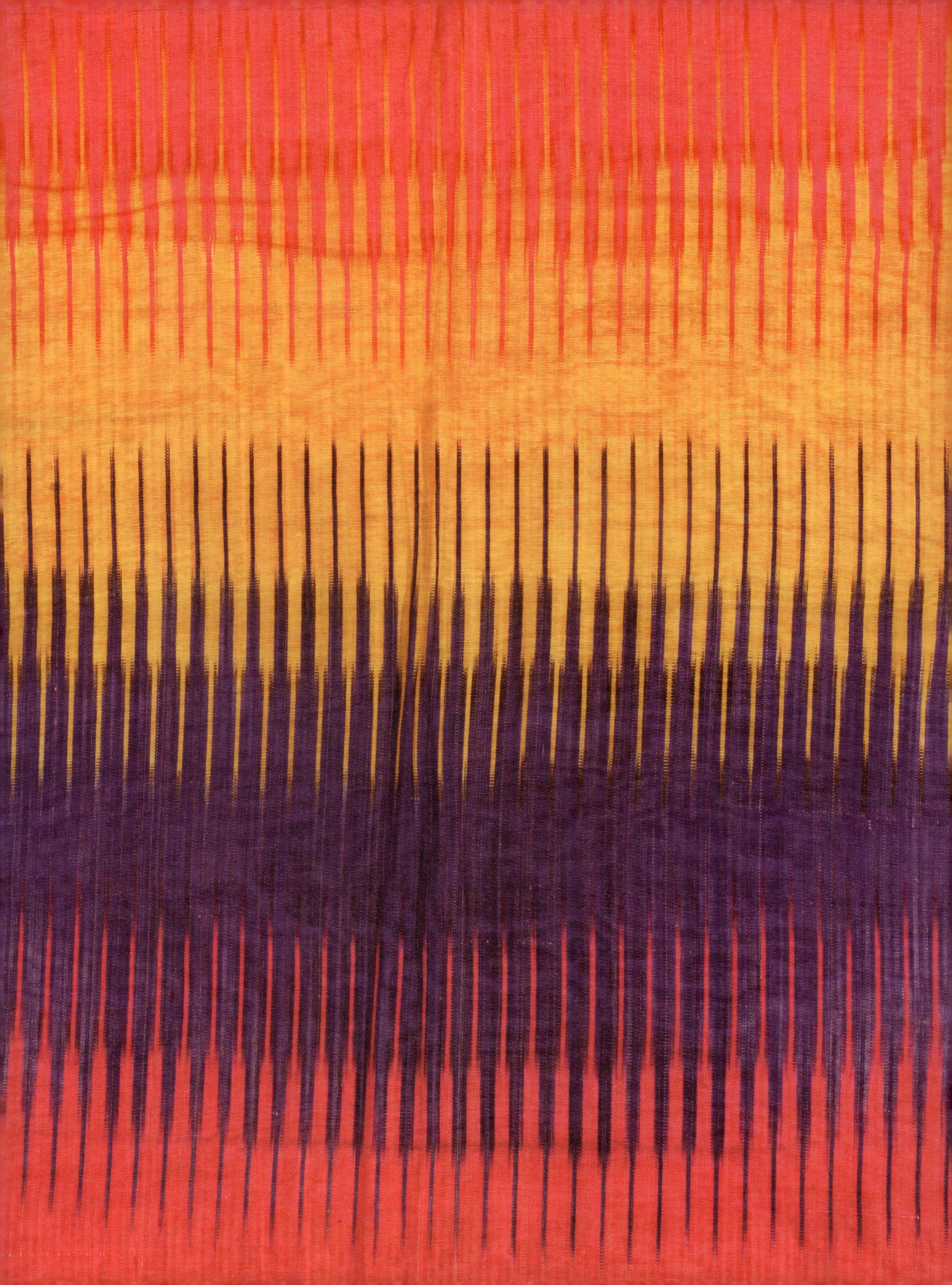

WEST & CENTRAL ASIA

by Sumru Belger Krody

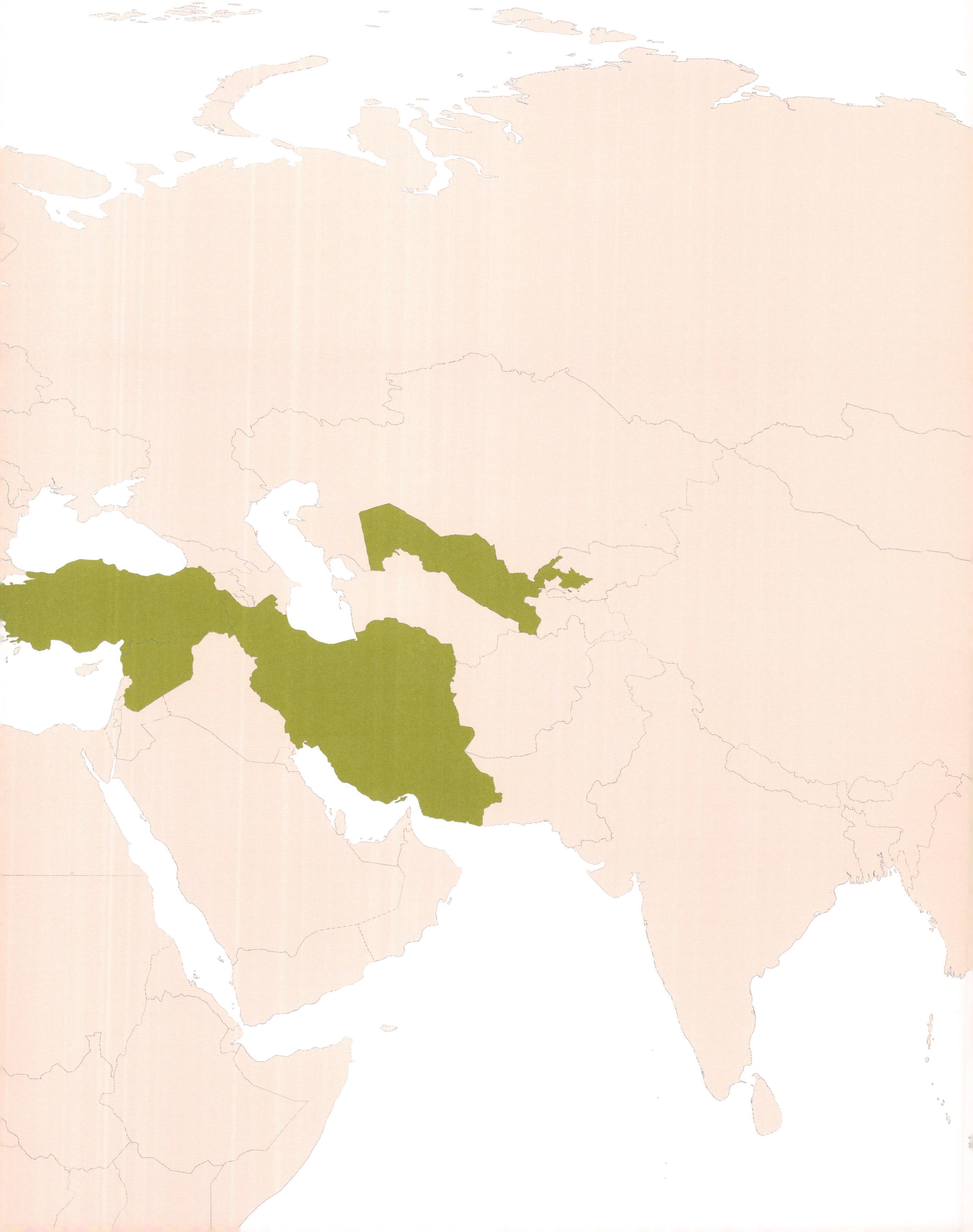

IKAT IN WEST & CENTRAL ASIA

Ikat fabrics were considered precious and prestigious in any culture that produced them in West and Central Asia. They were light, made with expensive materials, required sophisticated and costly labor to produce, and did not lose their value. Furthermore, we can posit that wearing one's wealth was a lingering vestige of a nomadic past among long-settled societies of the region. Ikat in this part of the world has a long history, going from medieval textiles to contemporary applications of the tradition.

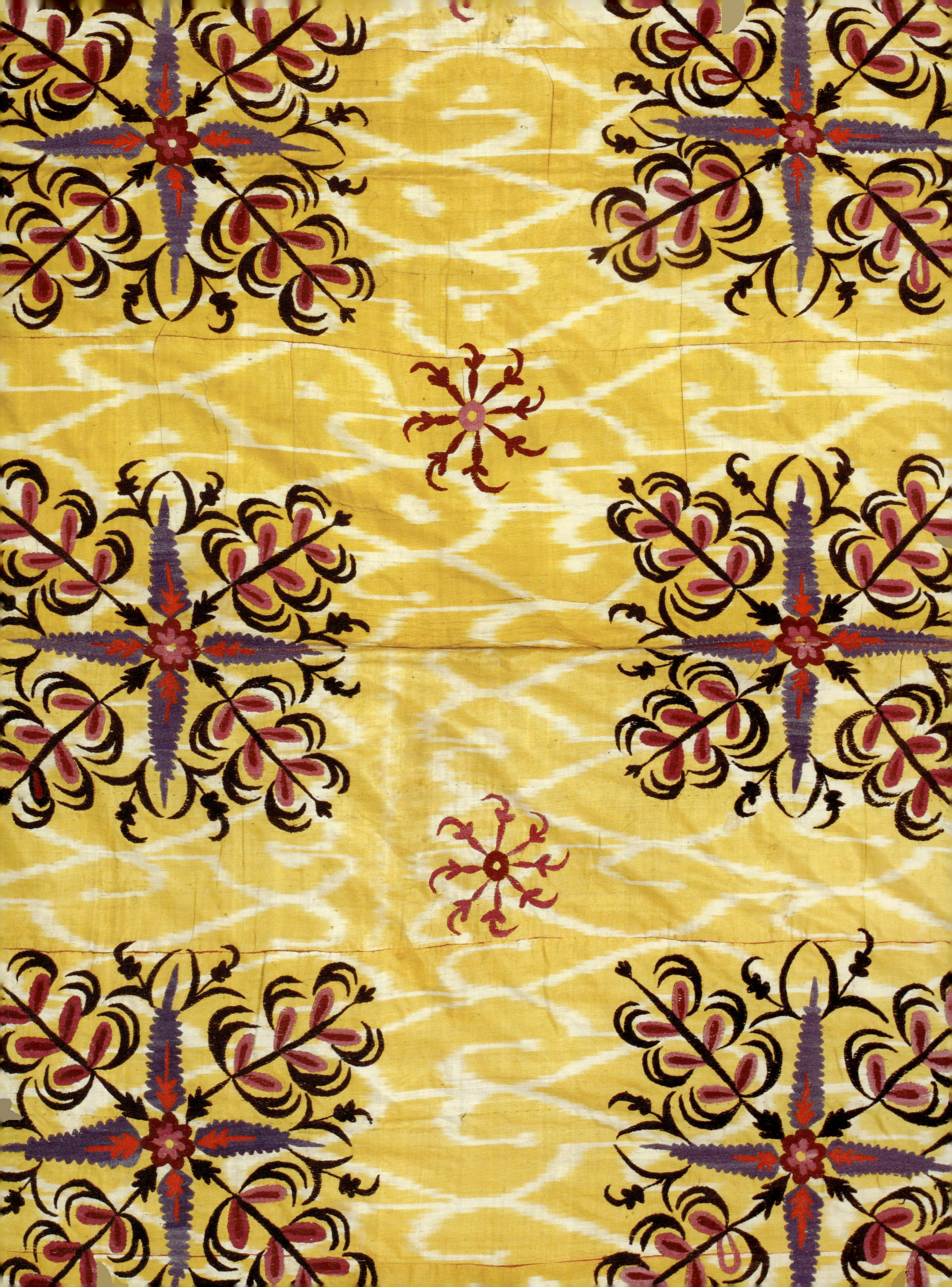

Fig.1
Detail of WCA16, cover, *suzani*

BOUND BY ART: IKAT ON THE WESTERN SILK ROAD

Fascinating and varied forces shaped the ikat traditions around the globe, making the writing of its extensive history impossible within the confines of a few pages or even a book. The myriad surviving ikat fabrics attest to the preciousness of these textiles and the glorious civilizations that produced them. This timeless art form varied from one culture to another. Understanding of each different ikat tradition requires studying the complex picture of shared culture among the designers, dyers, weavers, finishers, tailors, and consumers in each tradition. The following few paragraphs are a very short summary of various ikat traditions in West and Central Asia, examining their differences and similarities, from the earliest surviving examples to more contemporary applications of the tradition.

Fine ikat motifs of arrowheads and diamonds arranged in strips to form a vertical pattern are characteristic of Western Asia ikat traditions, where surviving ikat-making traditions cluster in Syria and Central Iran. The earliest-known ikat textiles from the early Islamic period, however, are from Yemen, and were found in Egypt, pointing to an active trade between these two regions. Yemeni striped-cotton textiles with inscriptions were sought after far and wide during the period when the Islamic empire stretched from Central Asia to Spain, with Baghdad serving as its capital.[1] The fabric used for these textiles was patterned on the warp by resist dyeing, and then embellished with embroidery or decorative Arabic scripts executed in ink with gold leaf (Fig.3). Based on the style of Arabic script, and historical inscriptions that name rulers and the city of Sana'a, they are attributed to 9th- and 10th-century Yemen. The weavers would have manipulated the already resist-dyed, finely spun cotton warp yarns stretched on their looms to create chevrons and lozenges as the fabric emerged. The favored weave structure was warp-faced plain weave, permitting the resist-dyed warp yarns to predominate the surface of the fabric, allowing the pattern to show.

Similar design aesthetics, and dyeing and weaving techniques using stripes with chevrons and lozenges, are also apparent in the surviving Syrian ikat tradition—our knowledge of which dates to 19th- and 20th-century production.[2]

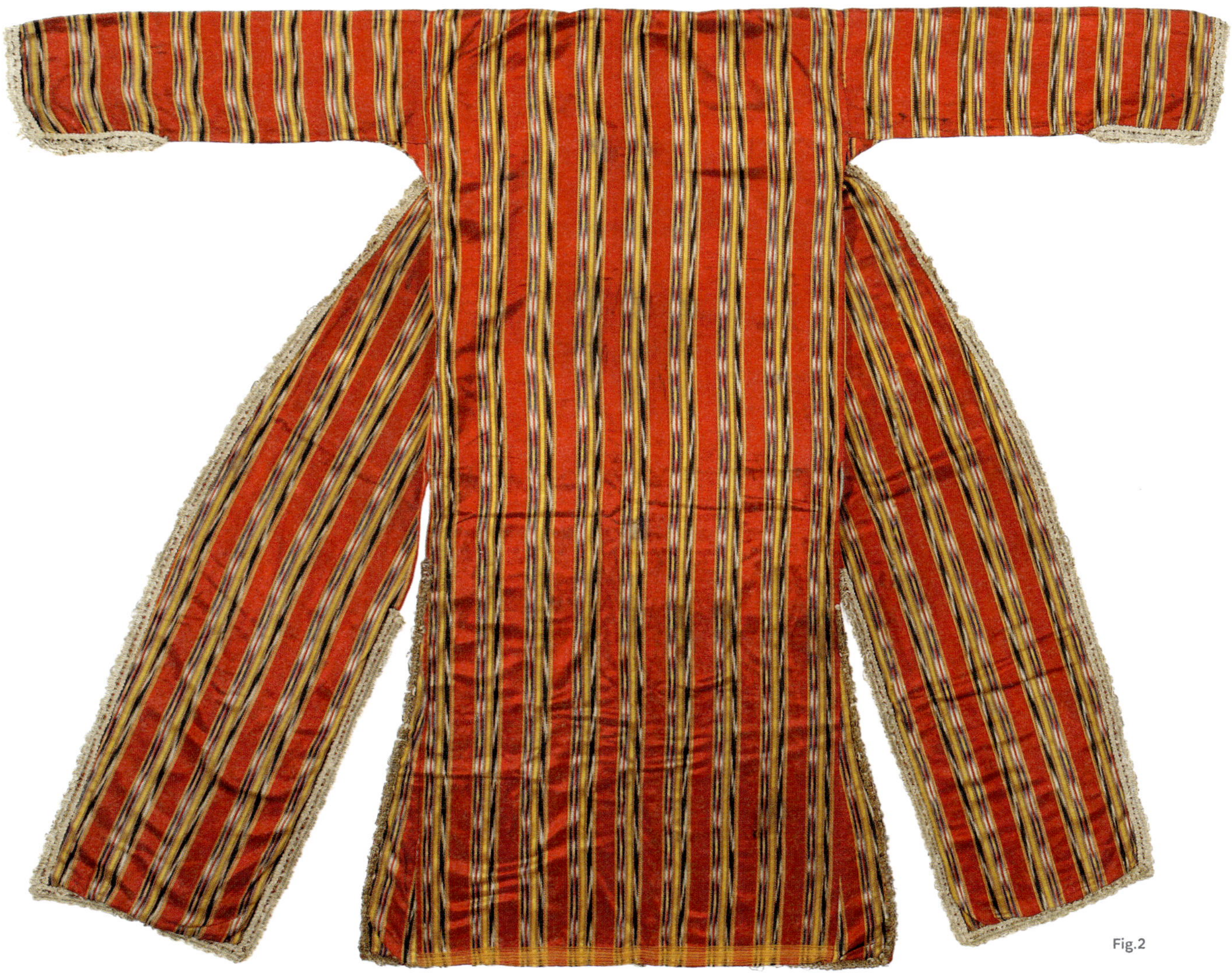

Fig.2

Among Syrian cities, Aleppo and Damascus were the most active centers of textile weaving, where over millennia weavers produced luxury textiles using expensive silk yarns and complex dyeing—the resist-dyeing technique being one of them—and weaving techniques.[3] The textiles produced in these centers were made available to consumers at the far corners of the Ottoman Empire from the early modern period into the early 20th century, among them *aladja* or *qutni*, silk-and-cotton-mixture striped fabrics containing resist-dyed, ikat stripes.

Knowledge of silk cultivation possibly arrived in the Eastern Mediterranean during the Sasanian period sometime between the 3rd and 6th centuries. On the other hand, it is harder to speculate when and from where ikat dyeing arrived in the region, owing to a lack of surviving evidence. Ikat might have reached the Eastern Mediterranean region from India through Islamic trade networks in the Indian Ocean, as evidenced by the surviving Yemeni ikats. Alternatively, it might have come from the East via Iran from Central Asia and beyond, as this region was the terminus of the Silk Road in the West. The arrival of ikat might have been as late as in the early Islamic period when the Islamic armies reached into Central Asia. But all these hypotheses await actual surviving examples as evidence to direct further research.

Sericulture in Syria has most likely been continually practiced since its arrival in the eastern coastal regions to the west of the Orontes River and in the foothills of the Alawite and the Anti-Lebanon Mountains.[4] Silk yarns from these regions, most likely supplemented by imports, were woven into striped fabrics that were turned into clothing, especially women's clothing (Fig.2/WCA35). Because the fabrics were sold as yard goods, they were easily incorporated into numerous other uses.

Ikat in Syria is known as *tarbit*, meaning "to tie or attach with several links or in several places."[5] It is the warp yarns that were resist dyed; thus

Fig.2
WCA35, woman's robe

Fig.3
Turban end, Yemen, 9th century. Cotton, warp-predominant plain weave with ikat warp. 21 in x 15 in. The Textile Museum Collection, 73.59, acquired by George Hewitt Myers in 1931

Fig.4
Detail of WCA34, shawl

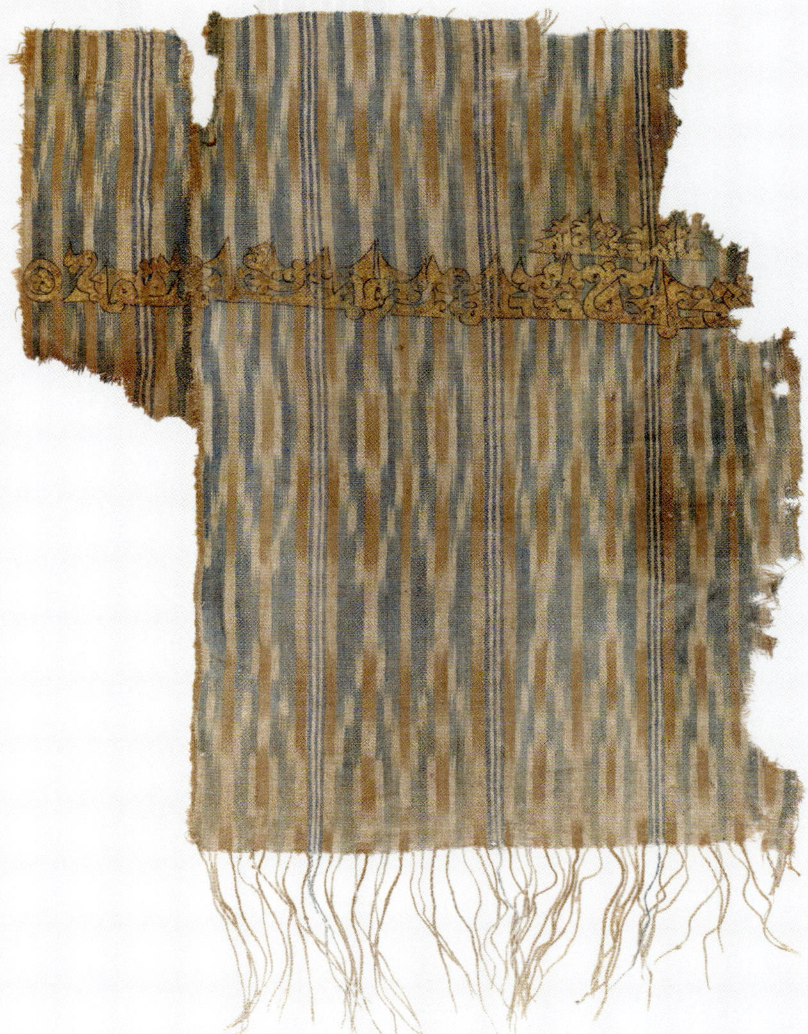

Photography by Breton Littlehales

Fig.3

Fig.4

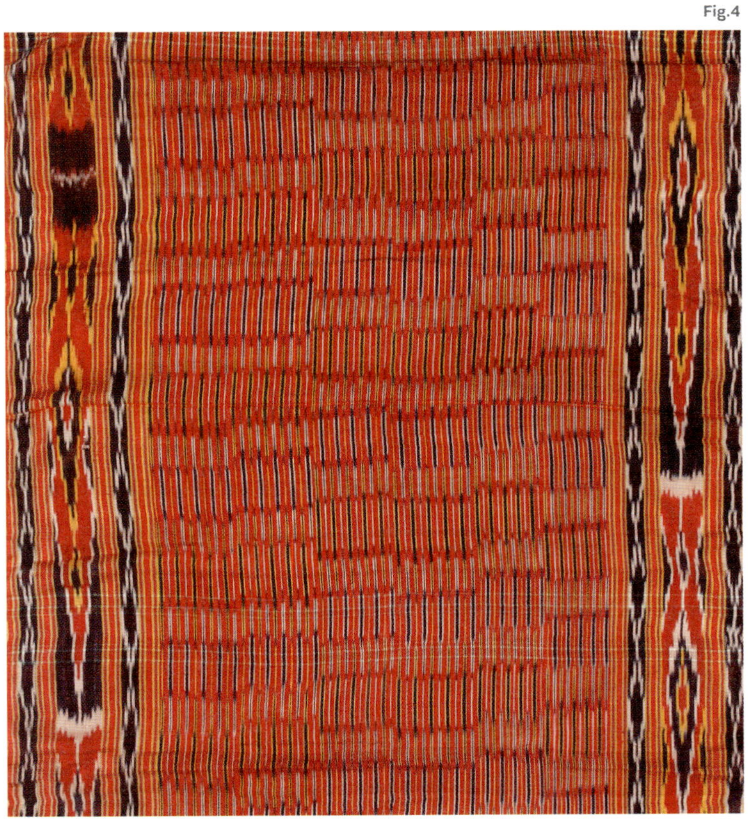

Syrian weavers always use warp-faced, plain-weave structures with silk-warp yarns and silk- or cotton-weft yarns to emphasize the pattern on the warp. The region's long-established textile production, in general, and Syria's specifically, has produced results that are diverse in technique and pattern. Thus even a single type of fabric woven in the region has been endowed with many different names over a millennium. *Aladja* and *qutni* are two fabrics that incorporate silk-ikat-warp yarns and have been known and appreciated in the region for centuries. *Aladja* had a warp-faced plain-weave structure with a silk warp and silk or cotton weft, and striped designs where some of the stripes could include resist-dyed warp yarns. Damascus was the largest center of production for this textile in the 18th and 19th centuries; in the 20th century Aleppo took over as the production center.[6] On the other hand, *qutni* appeared to have resist-dyed warp yarns, but it was woven using silk warp and cotton weft yarns in satin weave.[7] In the fourth quarter

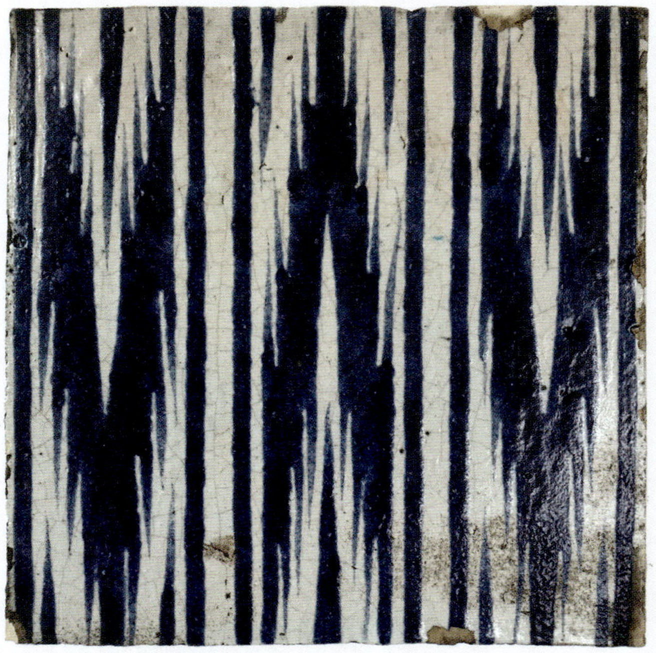

Fig.5

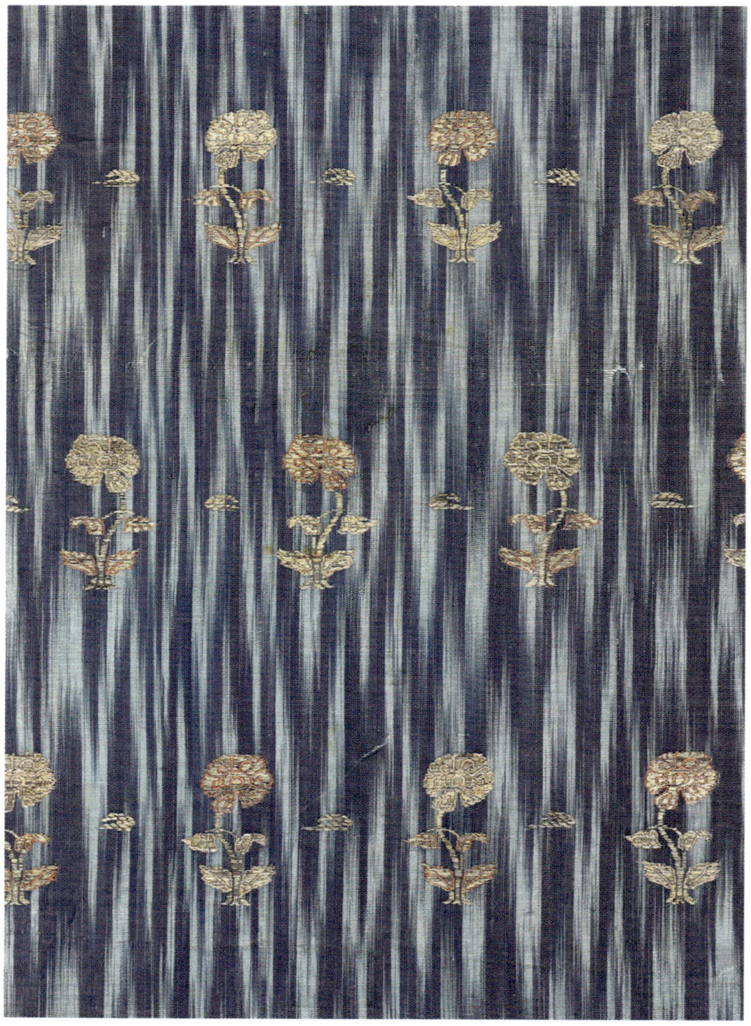

Photography by Breton Littlehales

Fig.6

of the 19th century, fabrics woven entirely of cotton became available (WCA35).

One group of ikat textiles said to have been produced in Syria was composed of rectangular, all-silk ikat fabrics that were used as wrapping cloths to store belongings, or as wrappers around bathers' hips in the baths (WCA38). They were known as *ajami* (designating Iranian) towels (*Futa ajamiye*).[8] Their weave structure differs slightly from the *aladja* or *qutni* by being warp-predominant plain weave. This structure allows multi-color silk weft yarns to appear on the surface and contribute to the design as horizontal bands, giving it a more contained and square appearance. Further, in-depth research on both Iranian and Syrian ikat traditions and textile trade between the two countries may reveal why these covers are called *ajami* and if they were produced in Iran for the Syrian market, in Syria for the Iranian market, or if this is a shared tradition.

The Iranian textile tradition is millennia old and known for its high artistic and technical innovations. Ikat production was one among myriad textile productions that Iranians honed to perfection. Ikat dyeing in Iran has been centered on Yazd in Central Iran for centuries, although the city of Kashan also produced ikat fabrics.[9] In Iran and far into Central Asia, ikat textiles are termed *abr*. The ikat fabric dyed and woven in Yazd, however, is referred to as *dara'i*.[10] A few examples can be dated as early as late 18th century, but most surviving Iranian ikat textiles date from the 19th and early 20th centuries, indicating that production of *dara'i* fabrics was booming in the second half of the 19th century. On the other hand, a small number of rare Iranian ikats go as far back as the 17th century and to the Safavid period. In these surviving Safavid ikats, the subtle flame-like ikat pattern serves as a background for motifs introduced in supplementary-weft patterning using gold- or silver-wrapped silk thread (Fig.6).

Persian weavers produced ikat textiles in two structures: warp-faced plain weave and velvet. In both cases, the resist dyeing was applied to the warp yarns, as is the case with all West Asian ikat traditions (Fig.7/WCA37 and WCA39). Among the velvets, one type had a directional design, which contained an arch, cypress trees, and birds. The execution of this design on various velvet textiles closely resembling each other indicates a possible single source for this design (Fig.7/WCA37). It appears

Fig.5
Tehran floor tile imitating ikat-patterned silk, Iran, 1850–60. Victoria and Albert Museum, 1531:56-1876

Fig.6
Textile fragment (detail), Iran, 17th century. Silk, warp-faced plain weave with ikat warp, supplementary-weft patterning with gold-wrapped thread. 17 in x 11 in. The Textile Museum Collection, 3.103A, acquired by George Hewitt Myers in 1931

Fig.7
Detail of WCA37, prayer cloth

that, starting in the early 19th century, myriad weaving workshops adapted this format in their design inventory, possibly because it was popular among consumers.[11]

Syrian and Iranian ikat traditions share the same kind of resist-dyeing technique and similar decorative styles; in both cases we find materials with multi-color stripes in which only the yarns of the warp are resist dyed, and where motifs are arranged in vertical alignment, often in well-delineated stripes. This indicates a similar method of preparing the yarns for dyeing and weaving, which may also indicate a single point in time and place for the introduction of ikat dyeing to West Asia. The technique and aesthetic, of course, might have been further cultivated because of a common preference for striped fabrics in the region, which this technique suited.

During the 19th century, the oasis towns of modern-day Uzbekistan were centers of high artistic innovation, most notably in the art of creating very bold and colorful designs for ikat fabrics. Even today, these textiles are appreciated for their remarkable visual impact. Produced for both urban and rural consumption and made into utilitarian objects, ikat was a commercially manufactured fabric that reflected society's evolving taste.

Fig.7

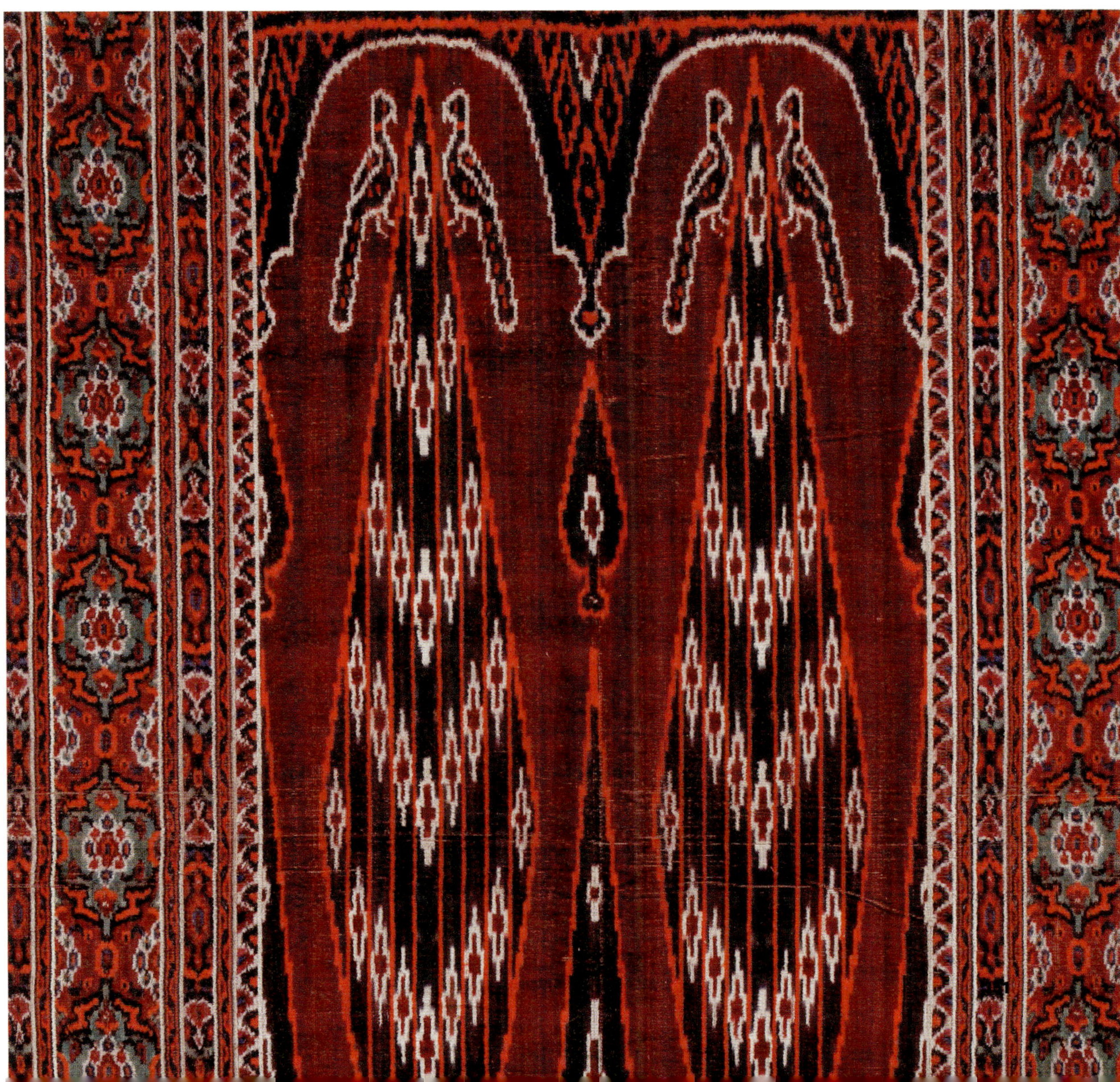

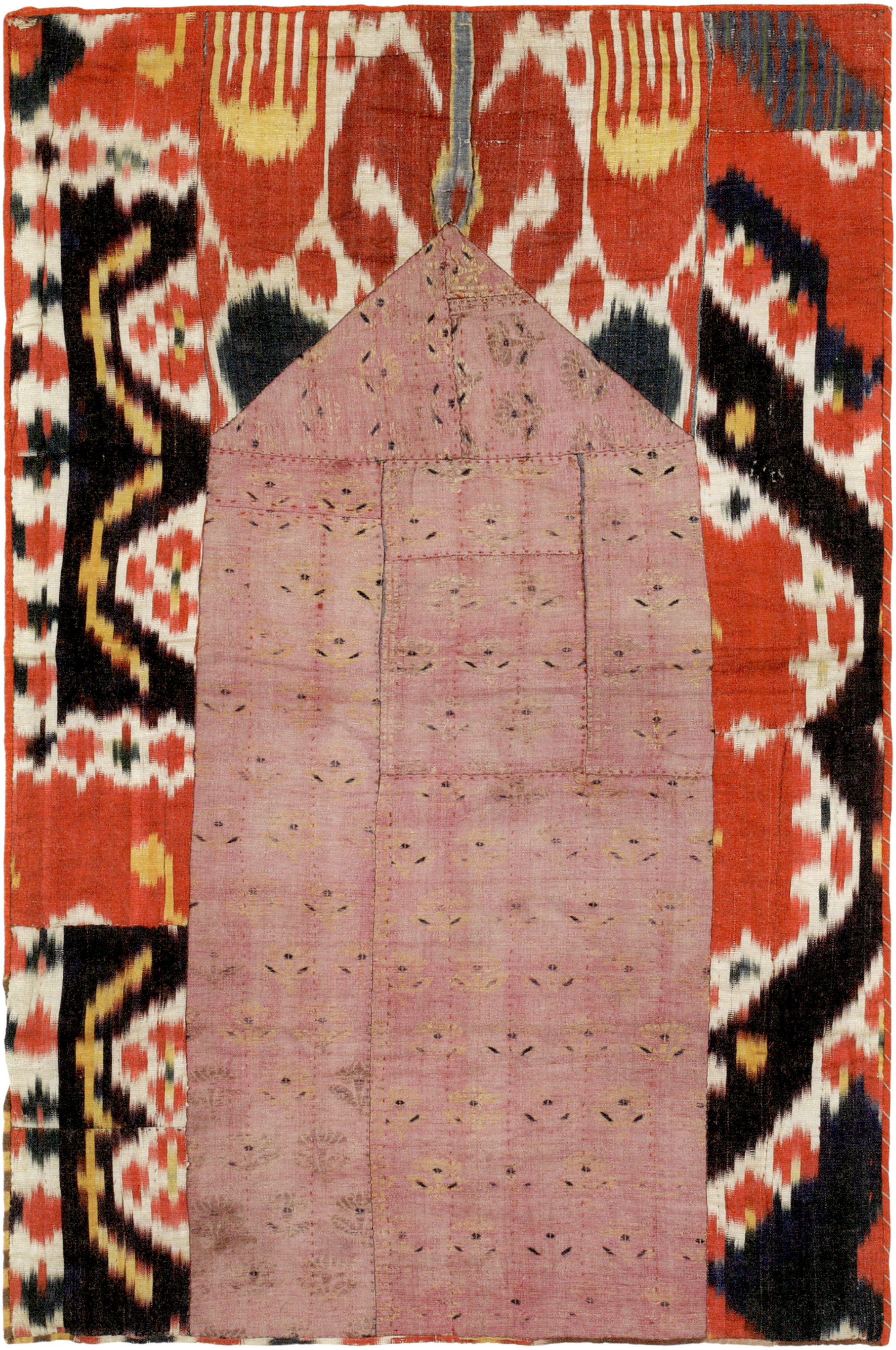

Fig.8

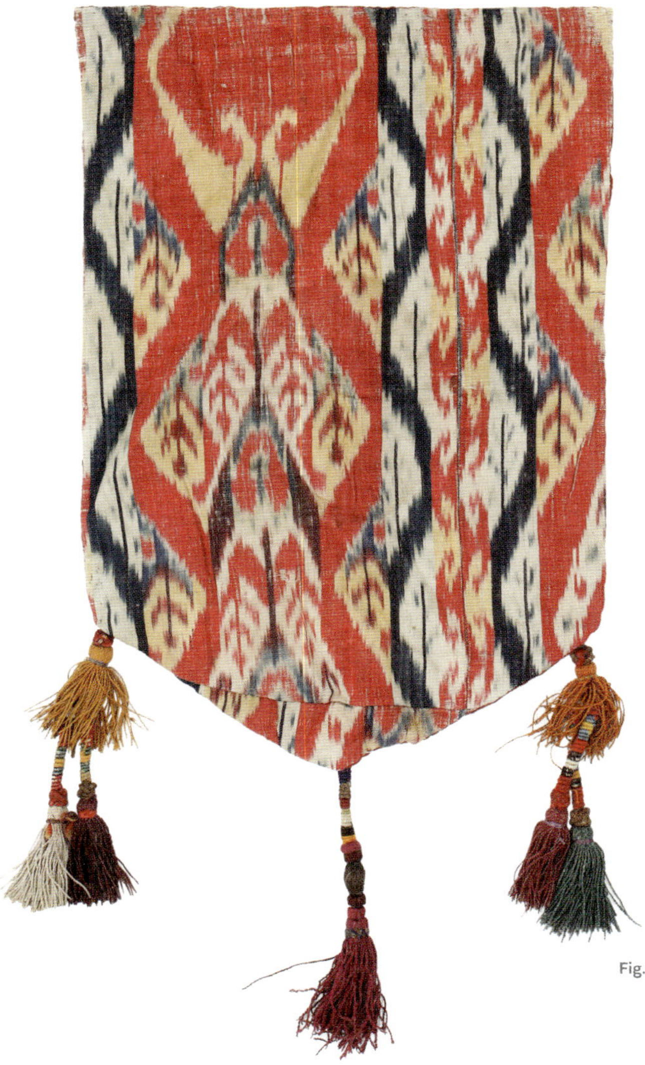

Fig.9

Ikat dyeing and ikat fabrics were undoubtedly known and probably produced in Central Asia in earlier times, but they became fashionable only in the 19th century, possibly after their designs underwent a revolutionary change by becoming vibrantly colorful and elaborate.[12] Whatever its origins, ikat can be seen as a critical 19th-century link in a long chain of sumptuous luxury fabrics produced along the Silk Road over a millennium.

It is likely that the first full-scale commercial production of ikat began in Bukhara in the late 18th century. From there, manufacturing spread northeast to Samarkand and Tashkent by the middle of the 19th century. It continued to thrive further east in the Fergana Valley into the early 20th century.[13]

The history of 19th-century Central Asian ikat production can be told in three stages, based on the design. Early ikats date to the early 19th century and have complex interlacing of small designs and saturated, mottled colors (Fig.9/WCA08, WCA14). These characteristics create visual ambiguity and make it relatively hard to read from a distance. The designs have frequent color changes both in the horizontal and vertical planes, causing the overall composition to "vibrate." The designs also used more intense and saturated primary colors, with fewer pinks or other light colors (WCA14). In the middle period (1860s–80s), there was a rapid increase in the number of new designs. The individual design elements became larger and bolder. The designers became more skilled in creating lighter and plainer backgrounds where design elements were placed to create a foreground (Fig.12/WCA11 and WCA15). The later ikats spanning the period from the 1880s to the 1920s boasted even larger design elements and fewer colors (Fig.10/WCA06 and WCA13).[14]

Fig.10

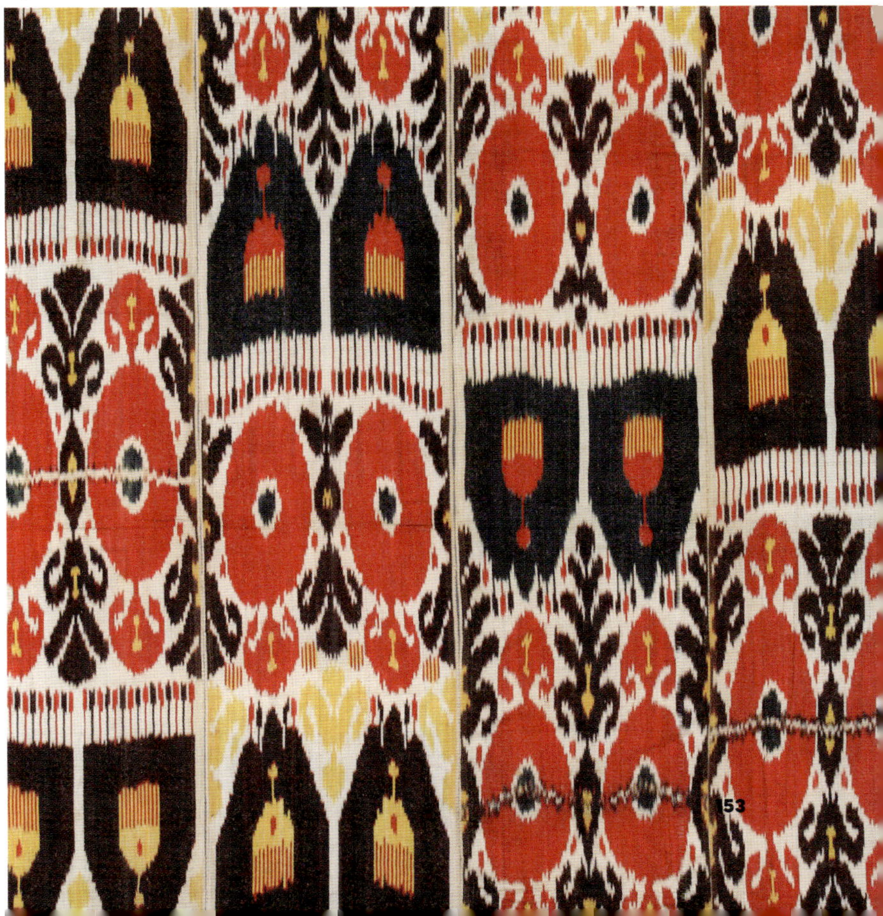

Fig.8
WCA27, prayer cloth

Fig.9
WCA08, bag

Fig.10
Detail of WCA06, hanging, *pardeh*

Fig.11
The reception tent in Samarkand on the day of the great New Year's race. From *A travers le Turkestan Russe*, by Hugues Krafft, published by Hachette & Cie in Paris, 1902

Fig.12
Detail of WCA11, hanging, *pardeh*

Fig.13
WCA24, coat, *chapan*

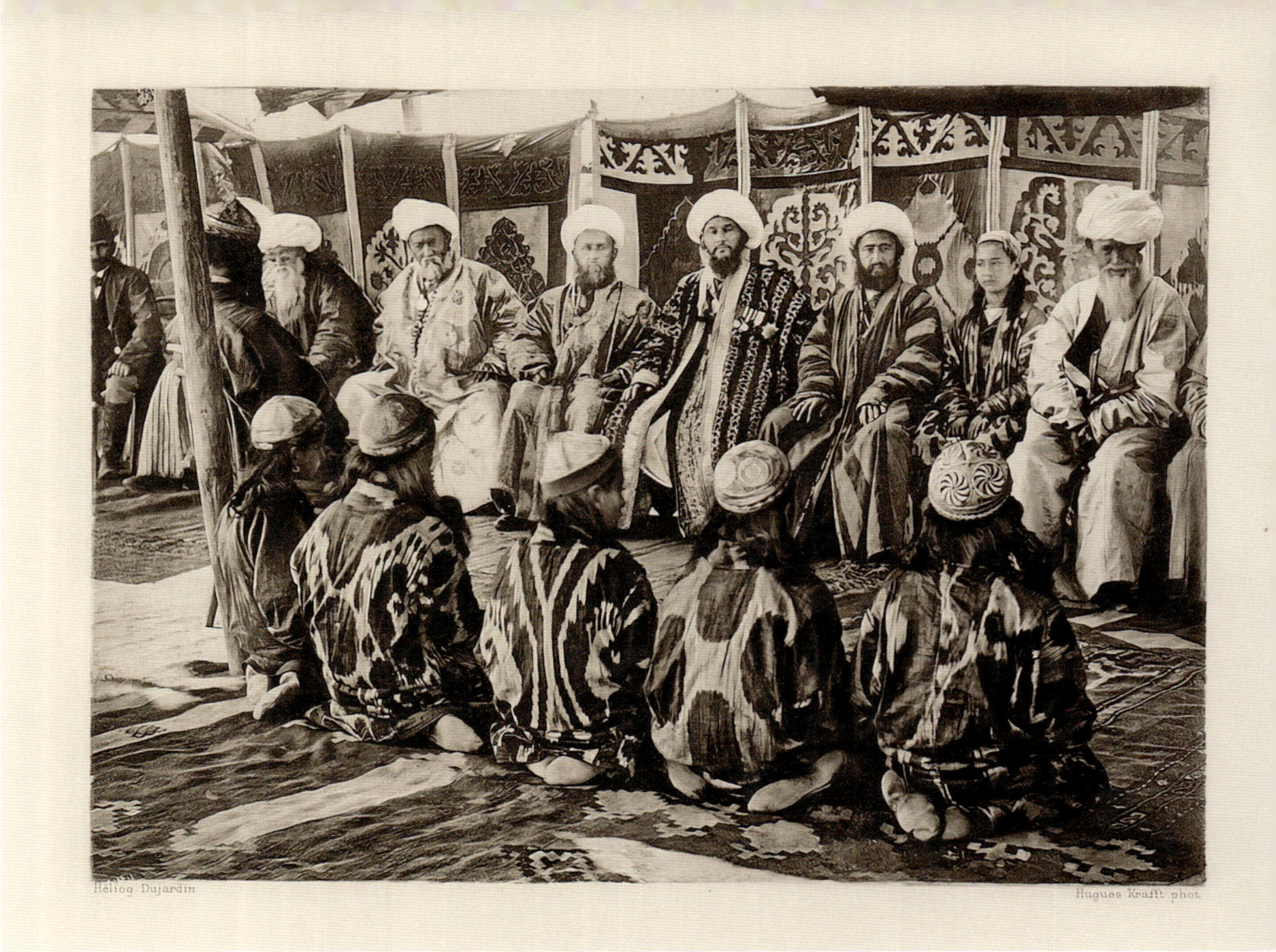

Fig.11

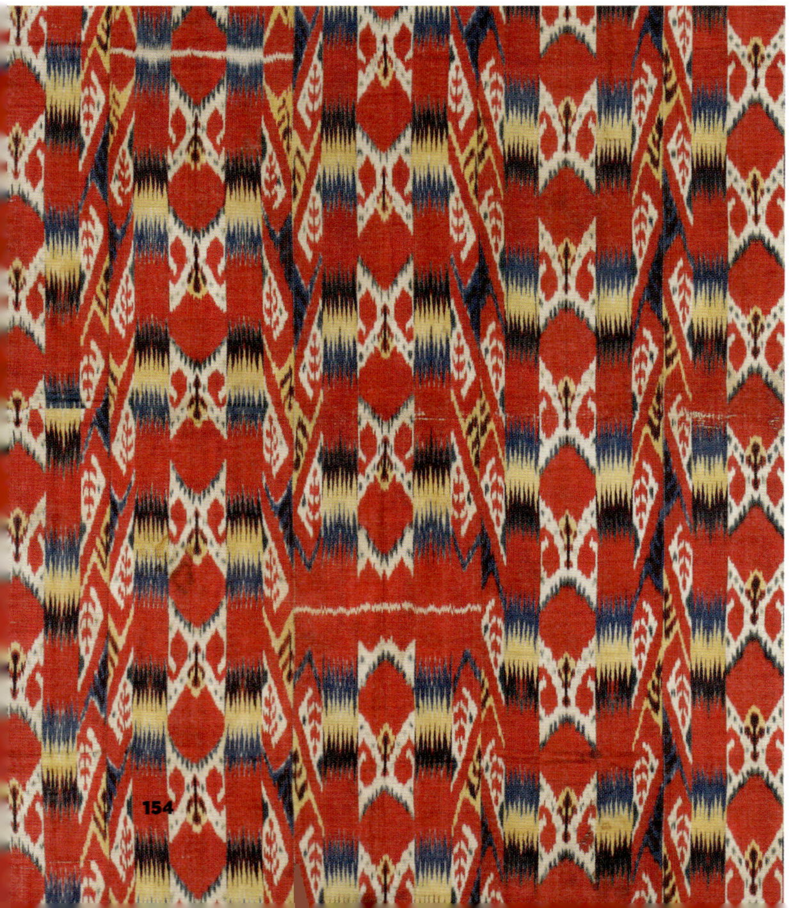

Fig.12

In Central Asia, as in West Asia, the warp yarns are resist dyed and therefore carry the design. The main weave structure favored by the weavers was a warp-faced plain weave with a silk warp and cotton weft. Toward the end of the 19th century, weavers began to experiment with new weave structures; satin weave and velvet were introduced. Weavers began to use red silk yarns for the weft. For those ikats, they chose a warp-predominant, plain-weave structure for the fabric (WCA03). Although designs on Central Asian ikat fabrics are more free-flowing and larger than Syrian and some Iranian examples, they retain their verticality, due to the warp-faced weaves used for their production.

Central Asian ikat fabrics were turned into furnishing fabrics, mostly hangings and covers, or into garments. The hangings or covers were made cut of multiple lengths of the same loom-width fabric, which was cut and attached side by side to create a textile with desirable width. They covered alcoves or were draped over the bedding during the day.[15] When both hangings and garments wore out, they were cut into smaller pieces and turned into other objects, such as bread covers, bags, cradle covers, and linings or facings for other garments or hangings.

Three articles of clothing–a knee- or ankle-length outer robe, a T-shaped, loose-cut, unlined tunic-dress, and trousers–have been the basic costume for men, women, and children in Central Asia for millennia. Outer robes were tailored the same way for men and women (WCA01). The robes had a straight or slightly flaring silhouette.[16]

Aside from the generic robe, often referred to as a *chapan* or *khalat*, worn by men and women, there was a specific women's

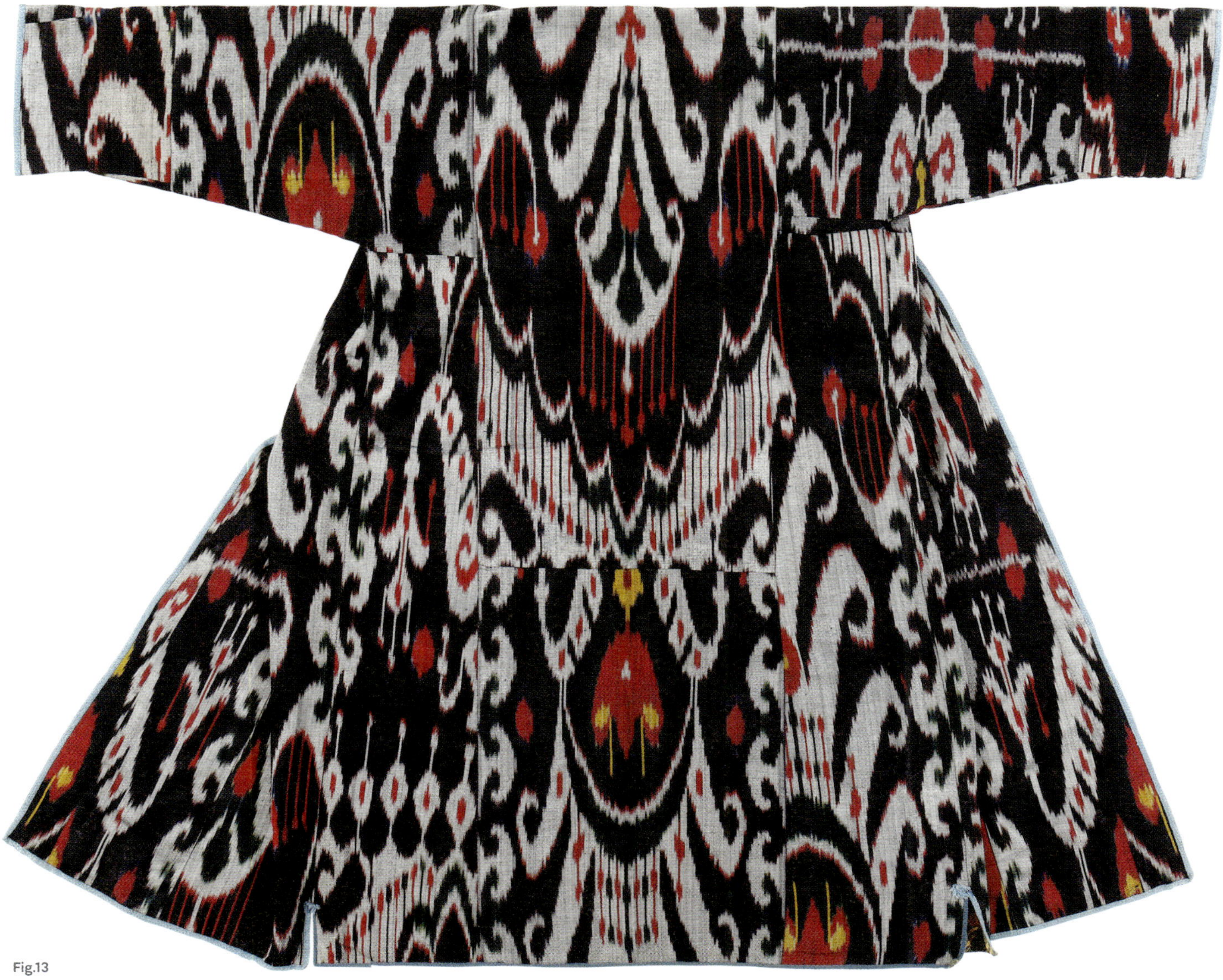

Fig.13

robe called a *munisak*. The *munisak* was worn indoors. It had a wide neck opening and a full skirt that was gathered in small pleats under the arms, creating a more fitted waist (WCA01). Underneath the luxurious ikat robes, women wore a number of T-shaped dresses of ikat fabric reaching to the ankles (WCA23). These tunic-style dresses were referred to as *kurta* in Tajik and *kuylak* in Uzbek. Under the T-shaped dress, women wore bulky trousers that reached to the ankle (WCA09). The cotton fabric formed the top part of the trousers where it was well hidden under the dress. The more precious and colorful ikat fabric was used for the legs, which were more visible.

In any culture within West and Central Asia that produced them, ikat fabrics were considered precious and prestigious. They were expensive due to the high cost of silk and to a sophisticated production sequence that required a large and highly skilled workforce. Other factors affected the importance placed on textiles, especially luxury textiles such as ikat. Centuries of political turmoil and instability in all these regions created an environment that forced people to accumulate and invest their wealth in portable items such as textiles and jewelry. They were light, made with expensive materials, required costly labor to produce, and did not lose their value. Furthermore, we can posit that wearing one's wealth was a lingering vestige of a nomadic past among long-settled societies of West and Central Asia. Today, the visual power of these fabrics has spurred a 21st-century revival of ikat and serves as inspiration for many leading artists around the world. While their visual appeal, artistic attraction, or technical achievement is not denied, our understanding of the ikat textiles is impoverished if we do not also recognize their importance within the history of the cultures that produce them.

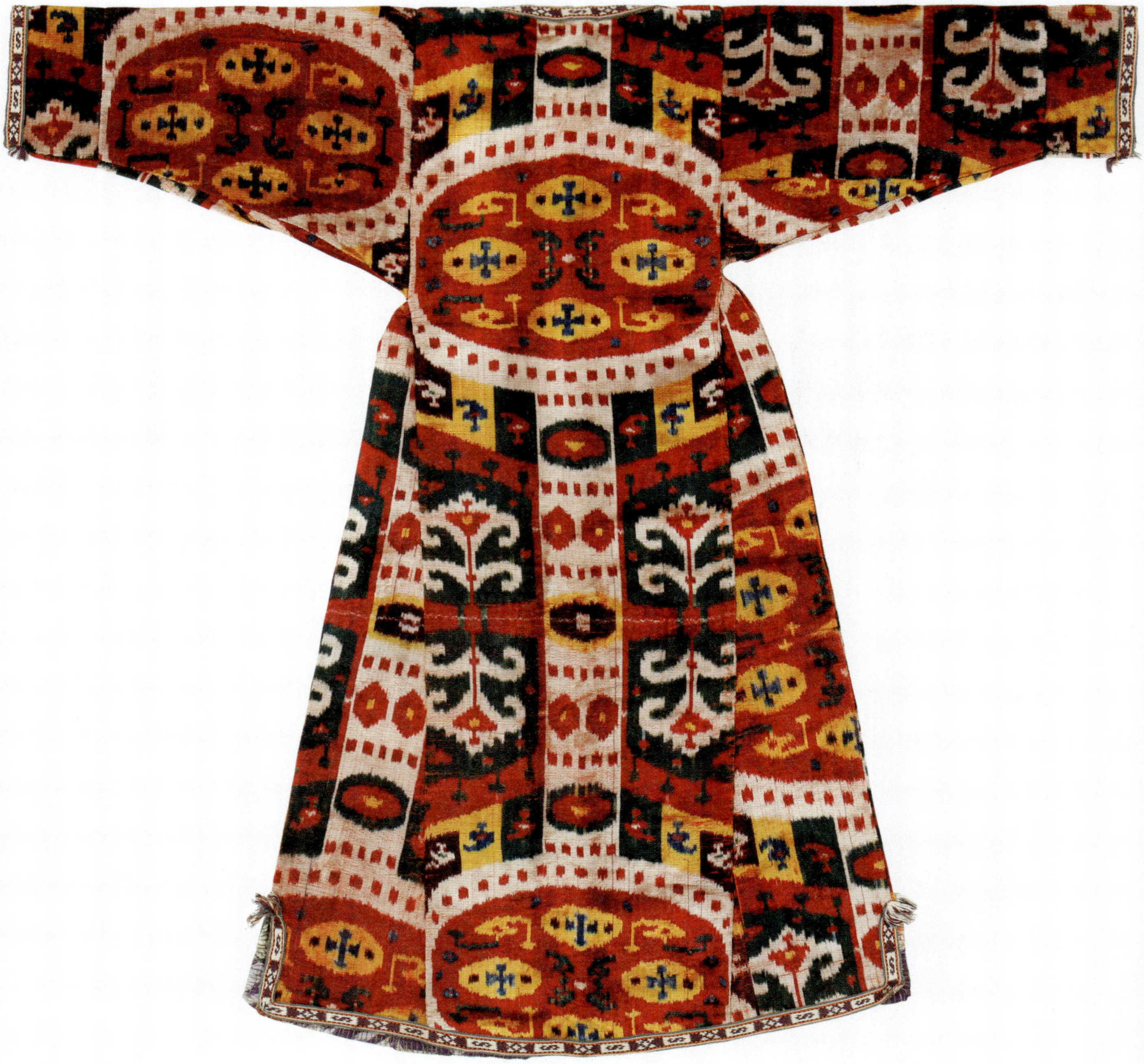

WCA01 Woman's robe, *munisak*, Bukhara, Uzbekistan, fourth quarter 19th century. Silk velvet warp ikat, cotton weft. 50 in x 54 in

Ikat velvet required more yarn, and designers had to adjust their traditional designs considerably to achieve the desired effects when yarns were woven into fabric. As a result, velvet fabric was more expensive for workshops to finance and was woven less frequently than plain-weave ikats. It was produced during a short period from 1850 until around 1910, and only in Bukhara. Silk-ikat velvets were used most often for dowry garments such as this *munisak*. Once they wore out, they were recycled into other functional textiles.

The distinctive look of the *munisak*, an outer robe a woman would wear in her house, was given during the tailoring process by making a few adjustments to the basic construction of a type of robe worn both by men and women. A *munisak* has a wide neck opening and a full skirt that is gathered in small pleats under the arms, creating a more fitted waist. The sleeves are often very long and narrow towards the cuffs. If the family could afford it, the *munisak* was made with ikat fabric, especially velvet ikat. The garment had a special place in a woman's life since it was an item in her trousseau. Depending on the wealth of the family, the bride had one or more *munisak*. The bride wore it during the first day in her husband's home, and afterwards at festive occasions such as weddings as well as more somber events like funerals. Finally, a woman's *munisak* was placed on top of the coffin during her funeral.

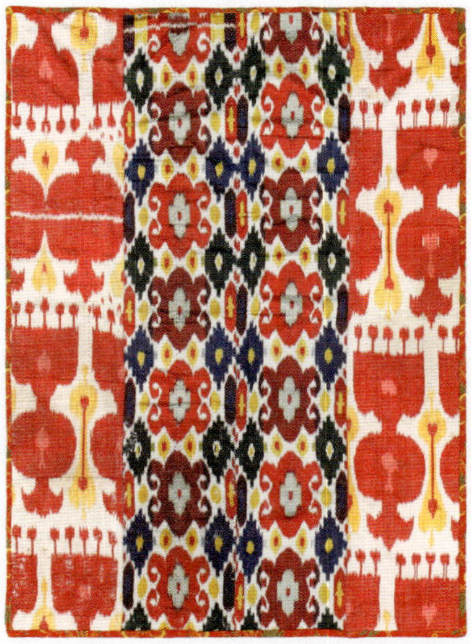

WCA02 Hanging, *pardeh*
Uzbekistan, third quarter 19th century. Silk warp ikat, cotton weft. 90 in x 65 in

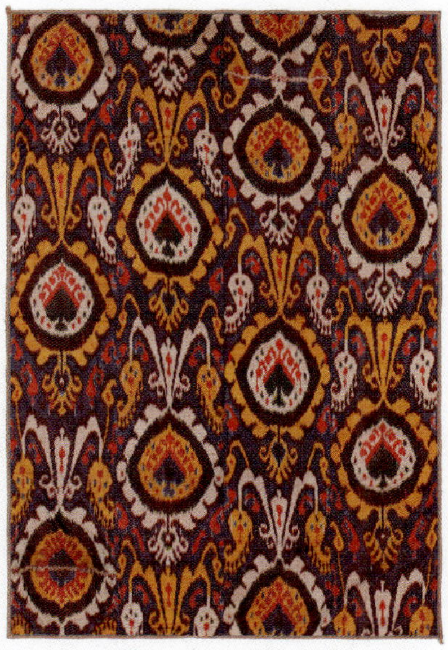

WCA03 Hanging, *pardeh*
Uzbekistan, late 19th century. Silk warp ikat, silk weft. 88 in x 60 in

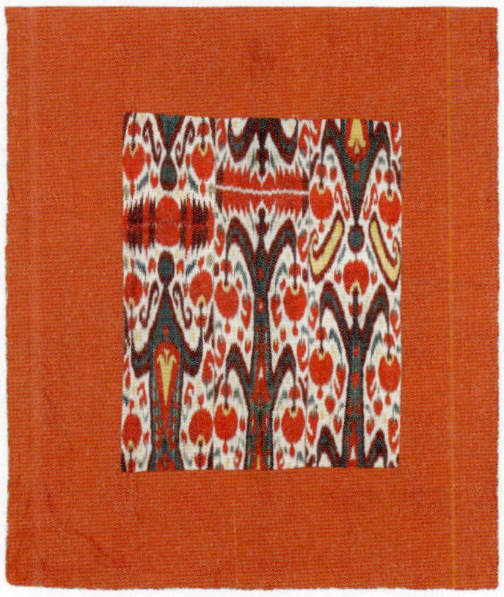

WCA04 Coverlet
Uzbekistan, 19th century. Silk warp ikat, cotton weft, cotton border. 54 in x 50 in. Seattle Art Museum, 2022.38.9

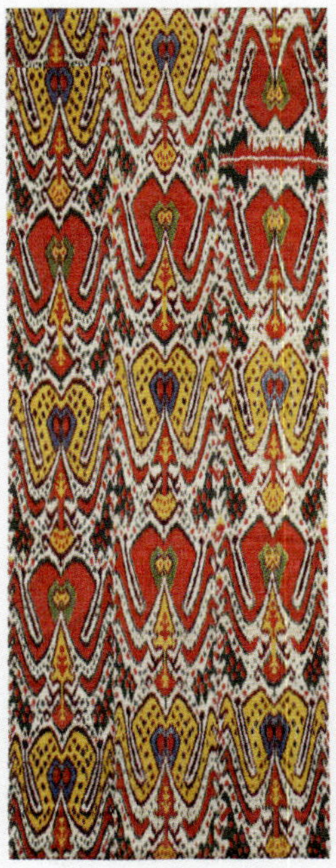

WCA05 Hanging, *pardeh*
Uzbekistan, third quarter 19th century. Silk warp ikat, cotton weft. 33 in x 88 in. Seattle Art Museum, 2022.38.7

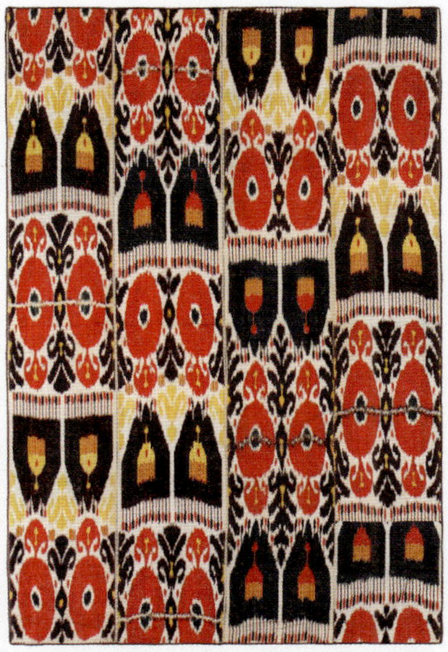

WCA06 Hanging, *pardeh*
Uzbekistan, fourth quarter 19th century. Silk warp ikat, cotton weft, natural dyes. 84 in x 59 in. Seattle Art Museum, 2022.38.5

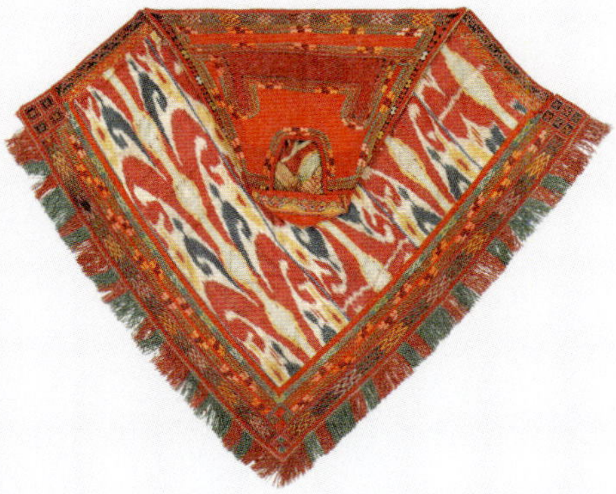

WCA07 Karakalpak woman's cape, *khamiseq*
Uzbekistan, 19th century. Silk warp ikat, embroidery, woven wool felt, cotton fringe. 56 in x 60 in. Seattle Art Museum, 2022.38.13

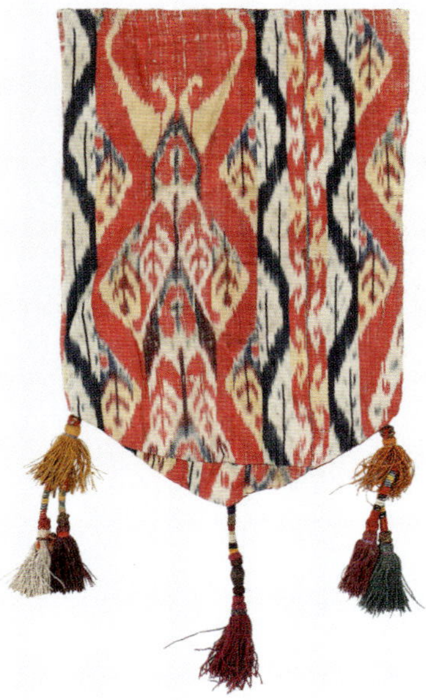

WCA08 Bag
Uzbekistan, early 19th century; hanging itself made in late 19th century. Silk warp ikat, cotton weft. 29 in x 15 in

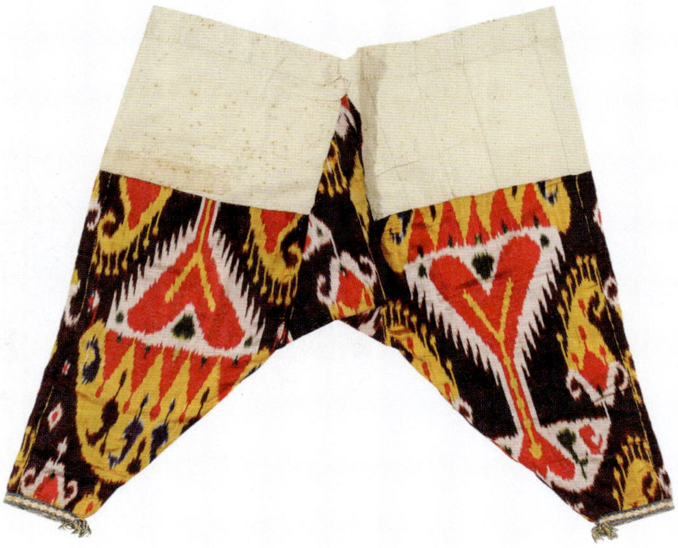

WCA09 Pants
Uzbekistan, late 19th century. Silk warp ikat, silk weft, cotton waistband, silk embroidered cuffs. 35 in x 34 in. Seattle Art Museum, 2022.38.15

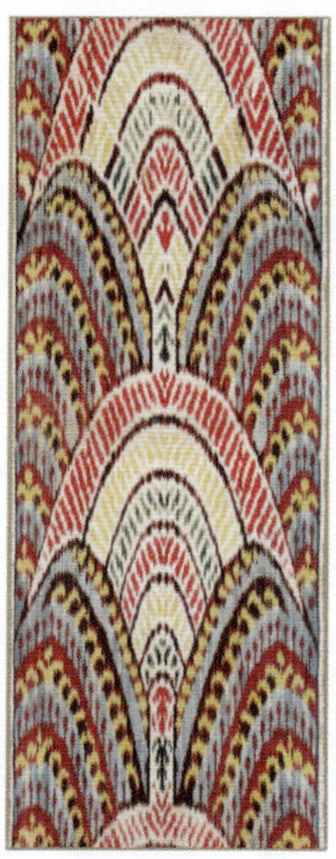

WCA10 Ikat fragment
Uzbekistan, third quarter 19th century. Silk warp ikat, cotton weft. 48 in x 18 in

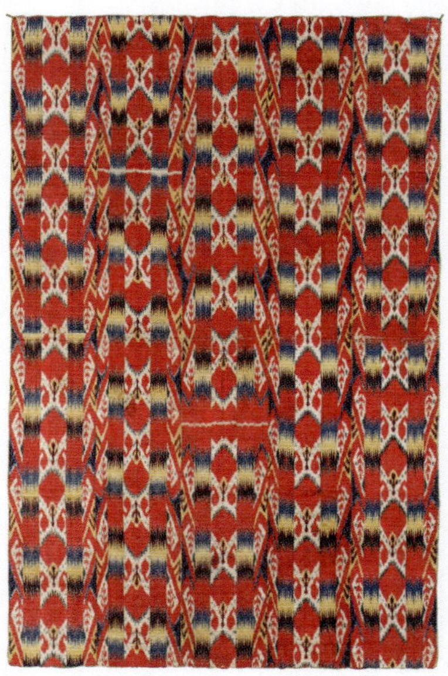

WCA11 Hanging, *pardeh*
Uzbekistan, mid-19th century. Silk warp ikat, cotton weft. 82 in x 54 in

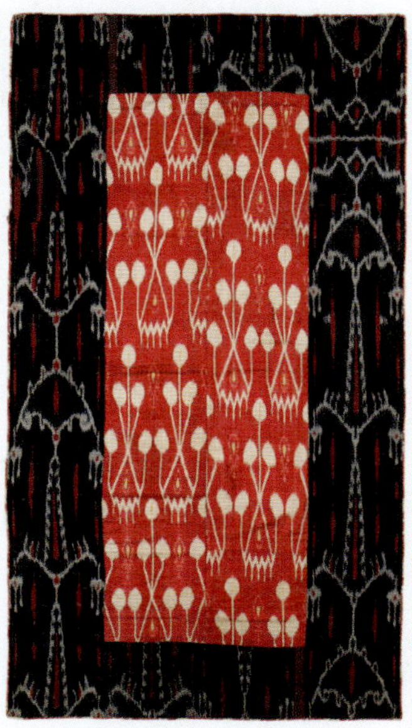

WCA12 Hanging, *pardeh*
Uzbekistan, mid-19th century. Silk warp ikat, cotton weft. 75 in x 43 in. Seattle Art Museum, 2022.38.6

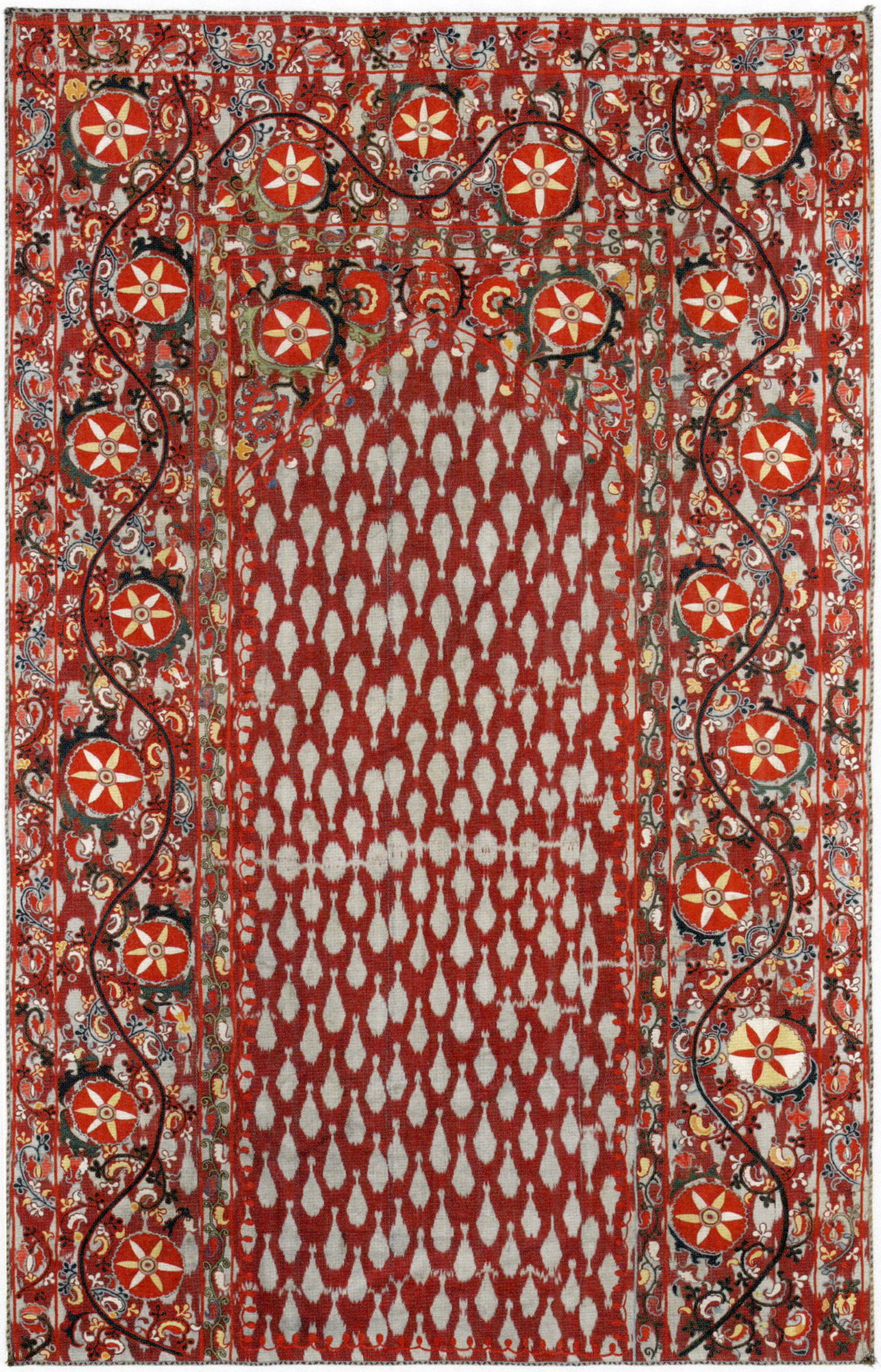

WCA13 Hanging, *pardeh*, Shahrisabz, Uzbekistan, second half 19th century. Silk warp ikat, cotton weft, silk embroidery thread, warp-faced plain weave with chain-stitch embroidery. 105 in x 67 in. Seattle Art Museum, 2022.38.4

The combination of embroidery and an ikat-patterned ground is infrequently seen, perhaps because embroiderers and consumers alike found the clash of the patterns visually jarring. In this relatively harmonious example, though, colorful floral sprays have been embroidered in silk using a chain stitch on an ikat fabric decorated with light-blue teardrop shapes on red ground. The embroidery pattern is familiar from the Central Asian embroidered cover (suzani) tradition, while the pattern used for the ground fabric is found in ikat textiles from the later part of the 19th century. Large covers with niche designs are usually described today as bridal bedsheets, but these normally have a cotton, plain, unpatterned ground fabric within the niche. The presence of a bold pattern in light blue within the niche may preclude such a function in this case.

Central Asian artists have always been more interested in conveying the spirit of nature rather than its actual appearance. The natural forms that inspired ikat and embroidery designs—birds, scorpions, flowers, trees—become decorative, not symbolic, motifs. The tremendous variety and richness of the highly stylized and abstract floral motifs seen on this textile are testament to the embroiderer's ambitious artistic goals, ingenuity, and improvisational skill.

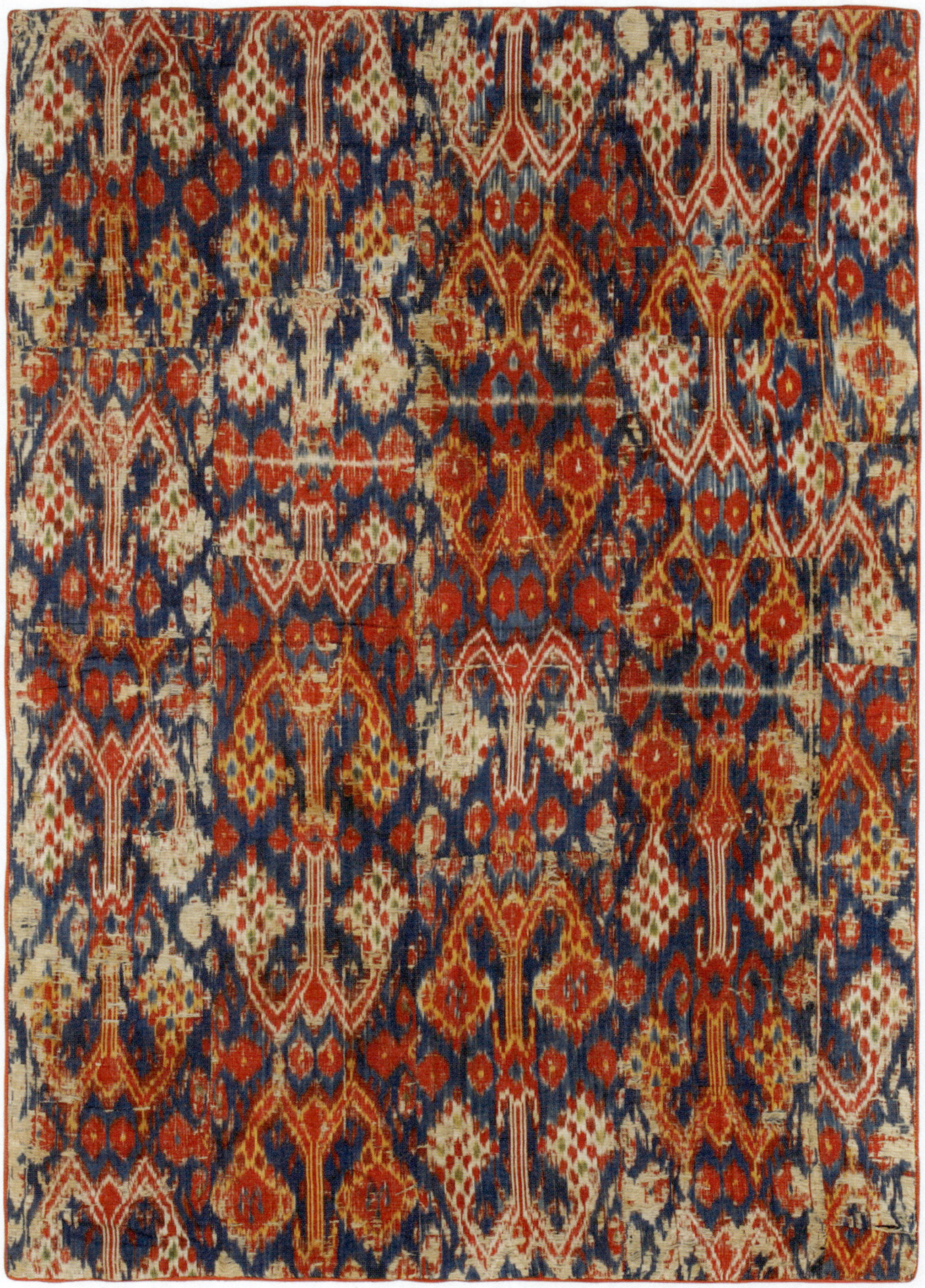

WCA14 Hanging, *pardeh*, Bukhara, Uzbekistan, first quarter 19th century. Silk warp ikat, cotton weft, warp-faced plain weave. 70 in x 50 in

Sometime in the late 18th or early 19th century, the simple ikat designs appear to have undergone a revolutionary change and become vibrantly colorful with elaborately composed designs—aptly illustrated by this early 19th-century hanging. This was a period of experimentation and honing of skills for Central Asian ikat designers and dyers. Earlier ikat designs often are relatively hard to read from a distance. They have frequent color changes both in the horizontal and vertical planes, causing the overall composition to 'vibrate'. This can make it hard to separate the foreground from the background of the design unless it is studied carefully. The colors are also more intense and saturated primary colors, with fewer pinks or other light colors in use. Throughout the century, the ikat-dyeing technique stayed practically the same, as well as the underlying structure of the designs, which were drawn symmetrically on either side of a vertical axis forming a mirror image along the center of each fabric width. However, artists perfected their execution of the dyeing and design features as the century progressed.

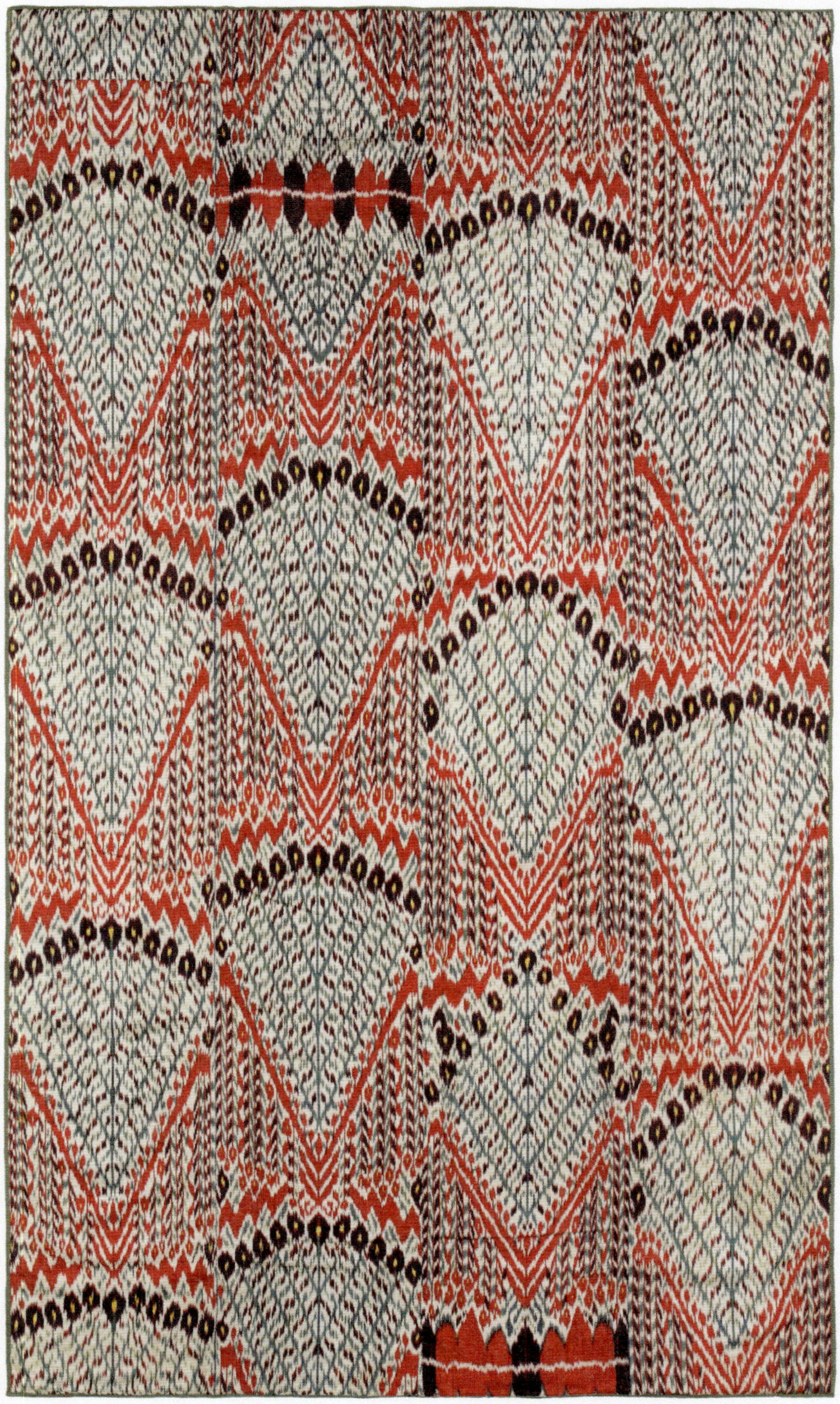

WCA15 Hanging, *pardeh*, Bukhara, Uzbekistan, mid-19th century. Silk warp ikat, cotton weft, warp-faced plain weave. 77 in x 46 in

Bound yarn bundles are the building blocks of ikat design. A design's intricacy results from the number of bundles on the warp rather than the number of yarns in each bundle. To create a complex design with frequent color changes, a dyer had to bind areas of the warp into many small bundles. Then another artisan would submerge the warp in four or more dye baths, drying and rebinding between each different color dye bath. This process was more labor intensive, time consuming, and expensive than binding larger areas of the warp and dyeing it with fewer colors. Thus, complex ikat fabrics—like this example with frequent and multiple color changes in the warp bundles and extensive areas of white—were expensive to produce, making them highly desirable and rare. Covers like this example would have been created by sewing multiple lengths of ikat fabrics together side by side to create a large textile, likely used as a cover for a bedding pile or shelves and niches in a Central Asian urban house.

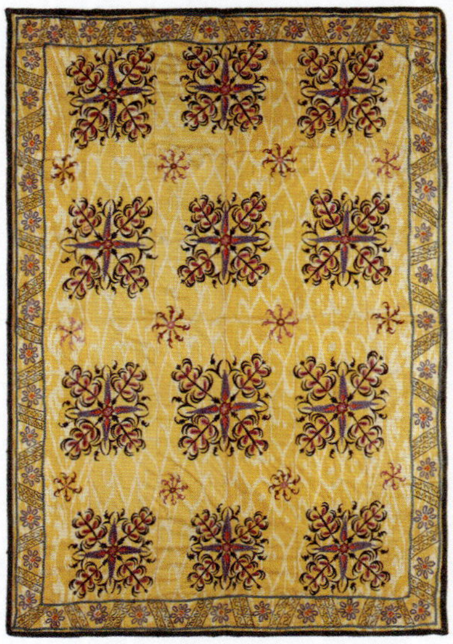

WCA16 Cover, *suzani*
Uzbekistan, late 19th century. Silk warp ikat, silk weft and silk embroidery. 96 in x 52 in

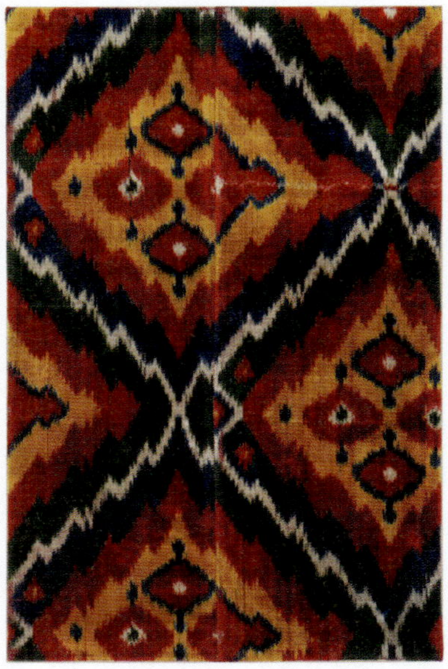

WCA17 Fragment of a coat
Bukhara, Uzbekistan, third quarter 19th century. Silk velvet warp ikat, cotton weft. 24 in x 16 in

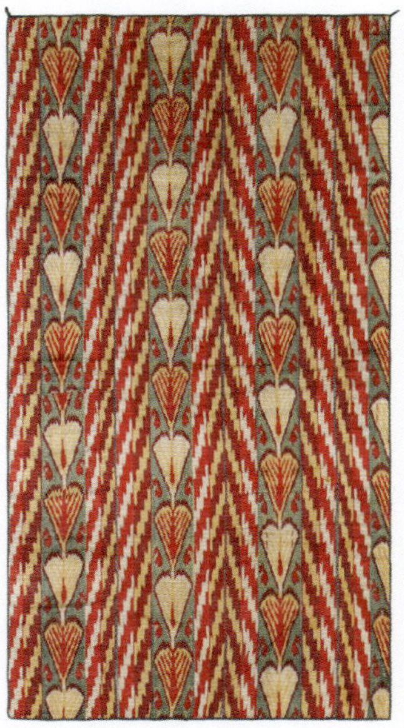

WCA18 Hanging, *pardeh*
Uzbekistan, mid-19th century. Silk warp ikat, cotton weft. 69 in x 38 in. Seattle Art Museum, 2022.38.16

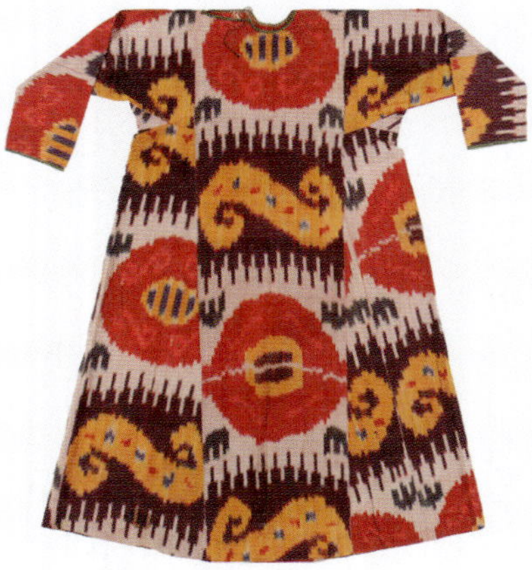

WCA19 Coat, *chapan*
Uzbekistan, late 19th century. Silk warp ikat, silk weft. 57 in x 66 in

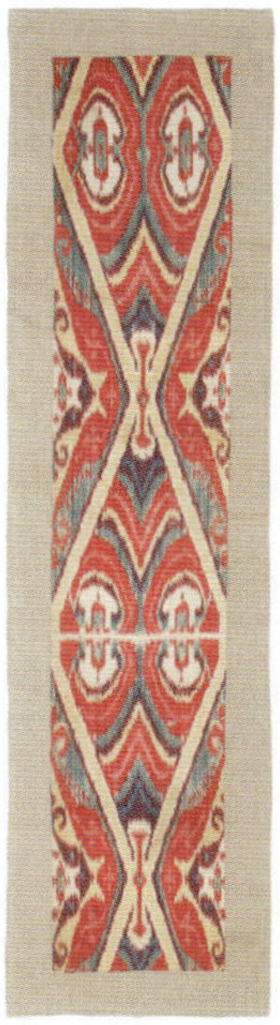

WCA20 Ikat fragment
Uzbekistan, mid-19th century. Silk warp ikat, cotton weft. 78 in x 15.5 in

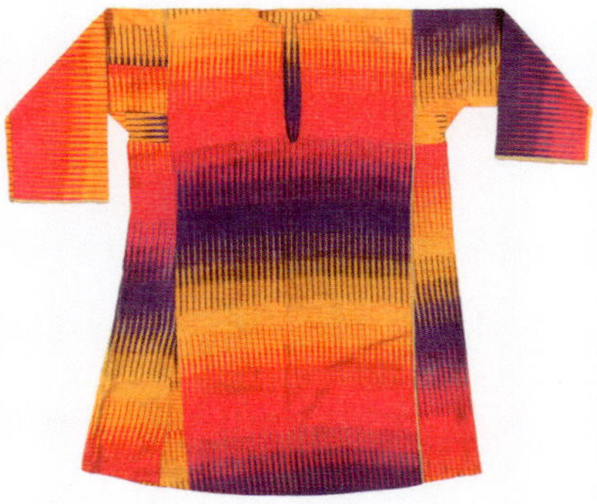

WCA21 Dress
Uzbekistan, early 20th century. Silk warp ikat, silk weft. 48 in x 66 in

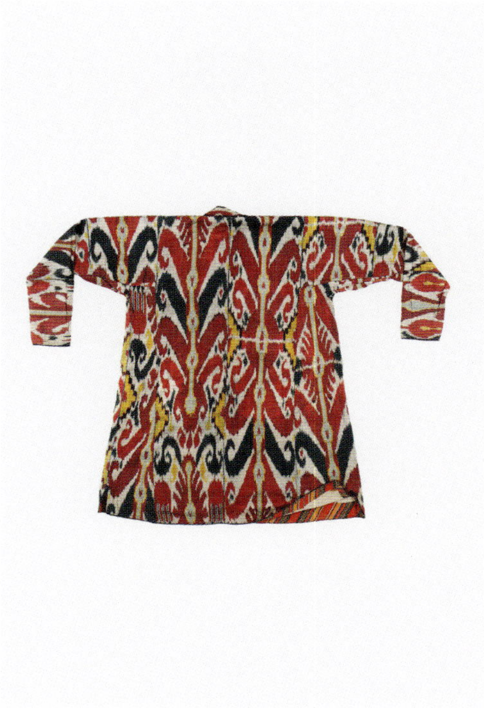

WCA22 Coat, *chapan*
Uzbekistan, third quarter 19th century. Silk warp ikat, cotton weft. 47 in x 66 in. Seattle Art Museum, 2022.38.2

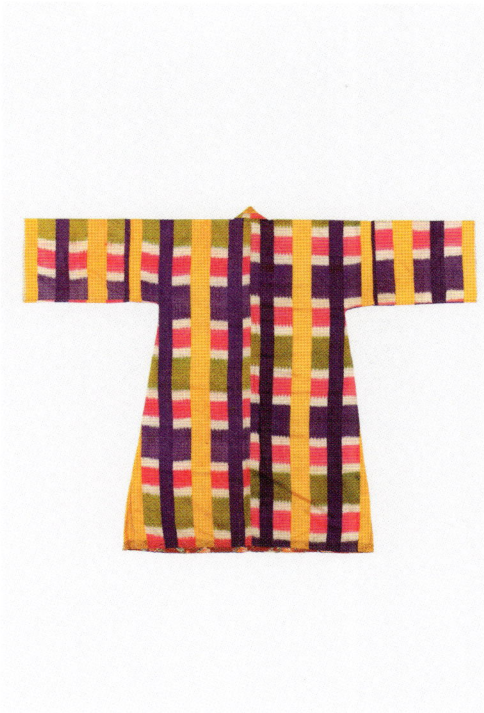

WCA23 Dress
Uzbekistan, early 20th century. Silk warp ikat, silk weft. 44 in x 64 in. Seattle Art Museum, 2022.38.3

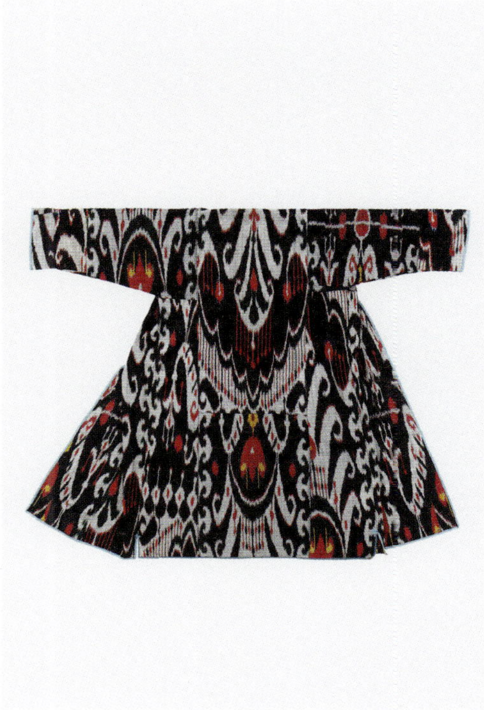

WCA24 Coat, *chapan*
Uzbekistan, late 19th century. Silk warp ikat, cotton weft. 50 in x 60 in. Seattle Art Museum, 2022.38.1

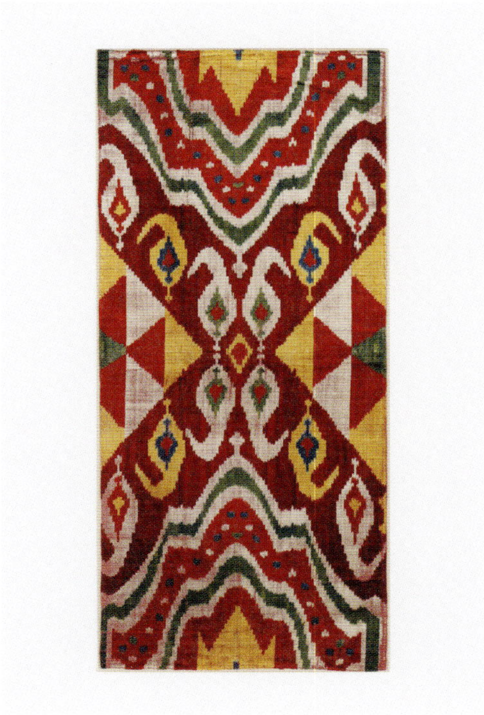

WCA25 Velvet ikat panel
Uzbekistan, late 19th century. Silk velvet warp ikat, silk and cotton weft. 28 in x 13 in. Seattle Art Museum, 2022.38.10

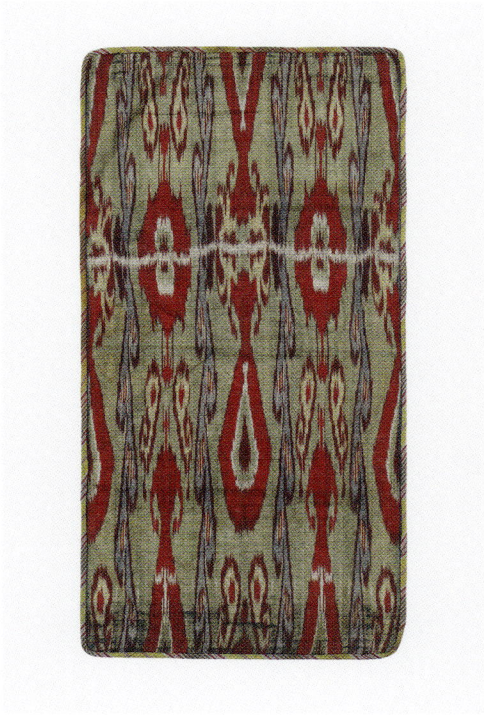

WCA26 Ikat fragment
Uzbekistan, third quarter 19th century. Silk warp ikat, cotton weft. 31 in x 16 in. Seattle Art Museum, 2022.38.14

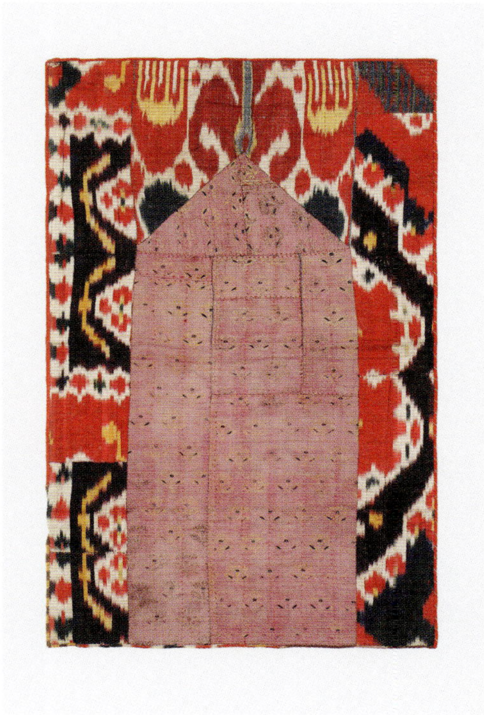

WCA27 Prayer cloth
Uzbekistan, 19th century. Patchwork of cotton wefted silk warp ikat and printed cotton cloths. 29 in x 19 in. Seattle Art Museum, 2022.38.11

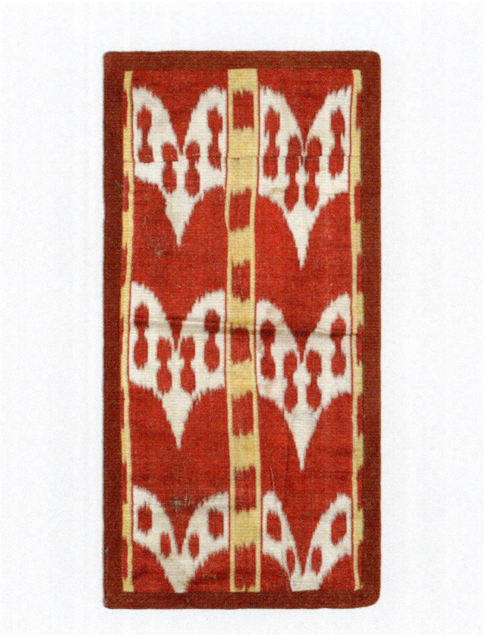

WCA32 Ikat fragment
Uzbekistan, late 19th century. Silk warp ikat, cotton weft. 30 in x 15 in

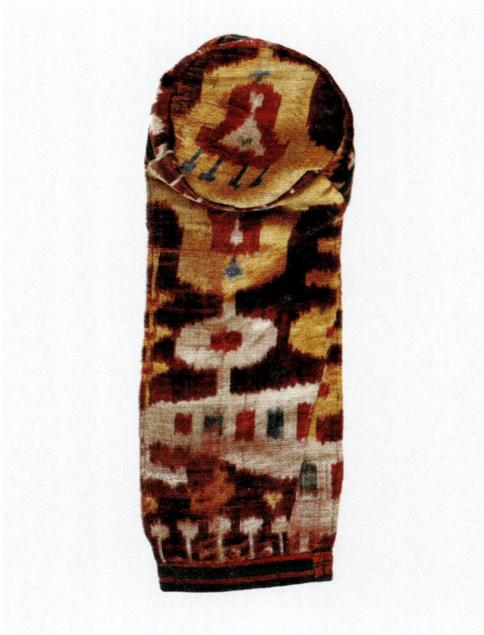

WCA29 Woman's hat
Uzbekistan, late 19th century. Silk velvet warp ikat, cotton weft. 21 in x 7 in. Seattle Art Museum, 2022.38.12

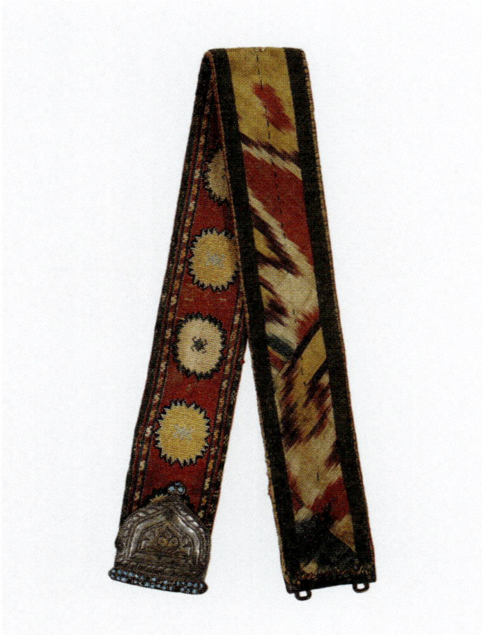

WCA30 Woman's belt
Uzbekistan, 19th century. Silk warp ikat, cotton weft (back), silk embroidery (front), metallic buckle. 33 in x 3.5 in

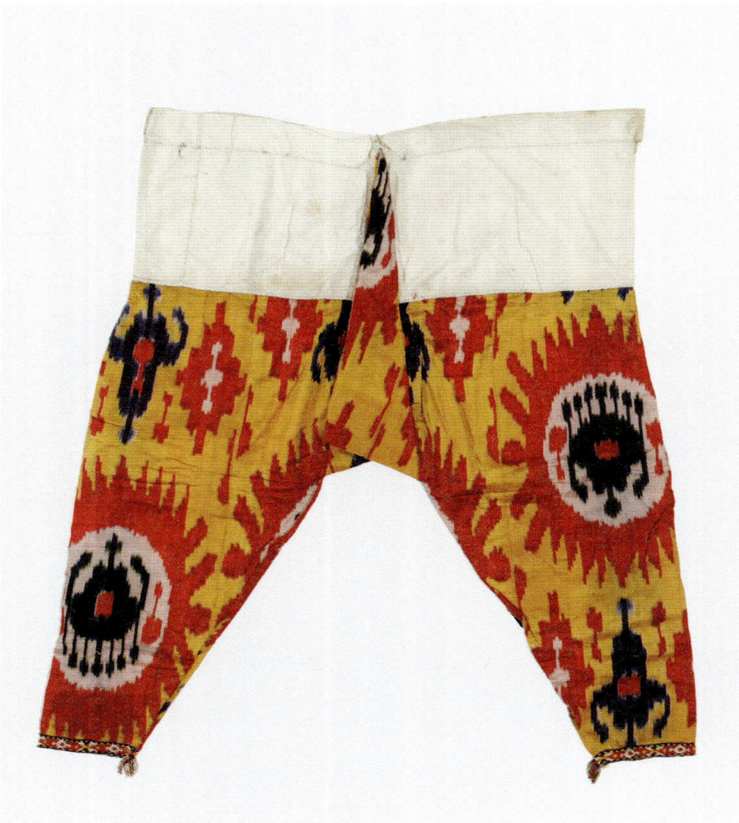

WCA31 Woman's pants
Bukhara, Uzbekistan, 19th century. Silk warp ikat, cotton weft, cotton waistband, silk embroidered edging. 39 in x 42 in

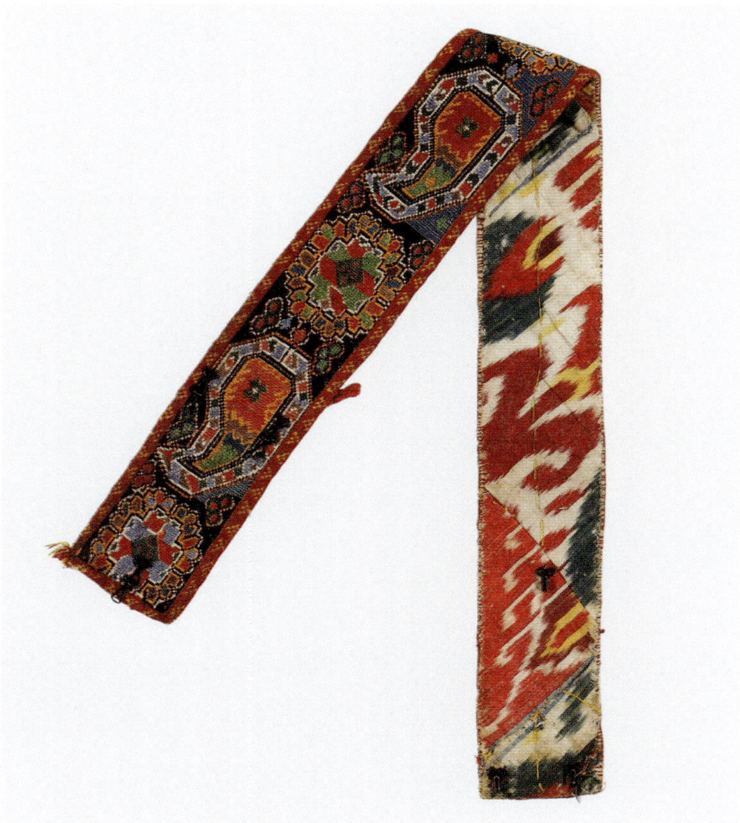

WCA28 Woman's belt
Uzbekistan, 19th century. Silk warp ikat, cotton weft (backing), silk embroidery (front). 38 in x 3.5 in

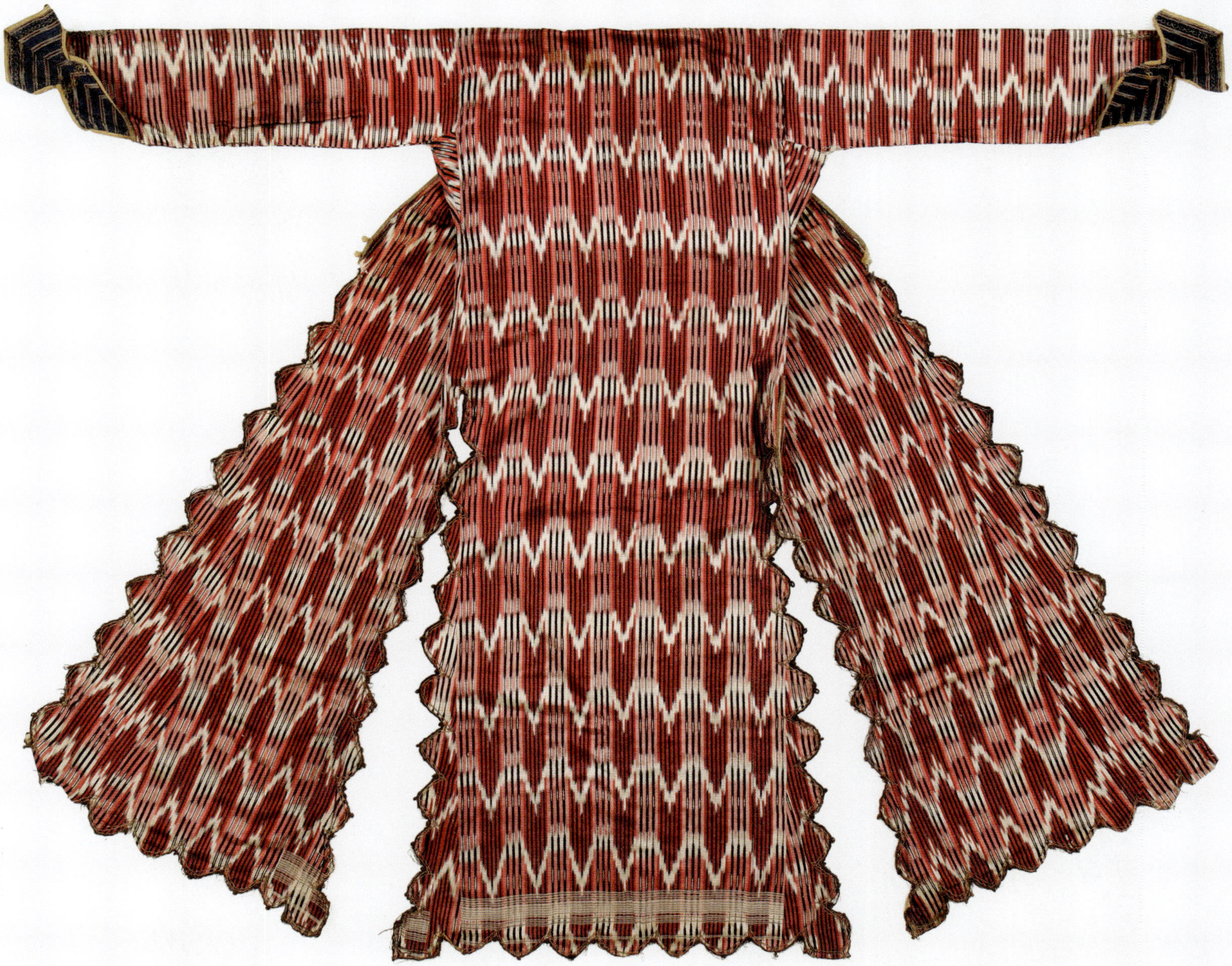

WCA33 Woman's robe, Aleppo or Damascus, Syria, late 19th century. Silk warp ikat, cotton weft, warp-faced plain weave. 53 in x 66 in

An *entari* or *üçetek* was a long, graceful trailing robe worn over the undershirt and baggy pants in many parts of the Ottoman Empire, including Syria. These robes had slender, elegant proportions, like this robe, with a fitted upper part and trailing skirts that had deep slits in both sides up to the hip, creating three separate panels, each with scalloped edges. The long sleeves of this robe have deeply slashed cuffs, which fall back over the wrist revealing the lace-edged sleeves of the undershirt as well as the colorful lining inside the sleeves. A wide range of fabrics was used for the construction of these robes, including Syrian striped-ikat fabrics that were referred to as *aladja*, as seen in this example. The warp-faced, plain-weave structure of the fabric allows the ikat design to come into strong focus, and the arrangement of resist-dyed and plain-color warp yarns on the loom gives the design its futuristic appearance.

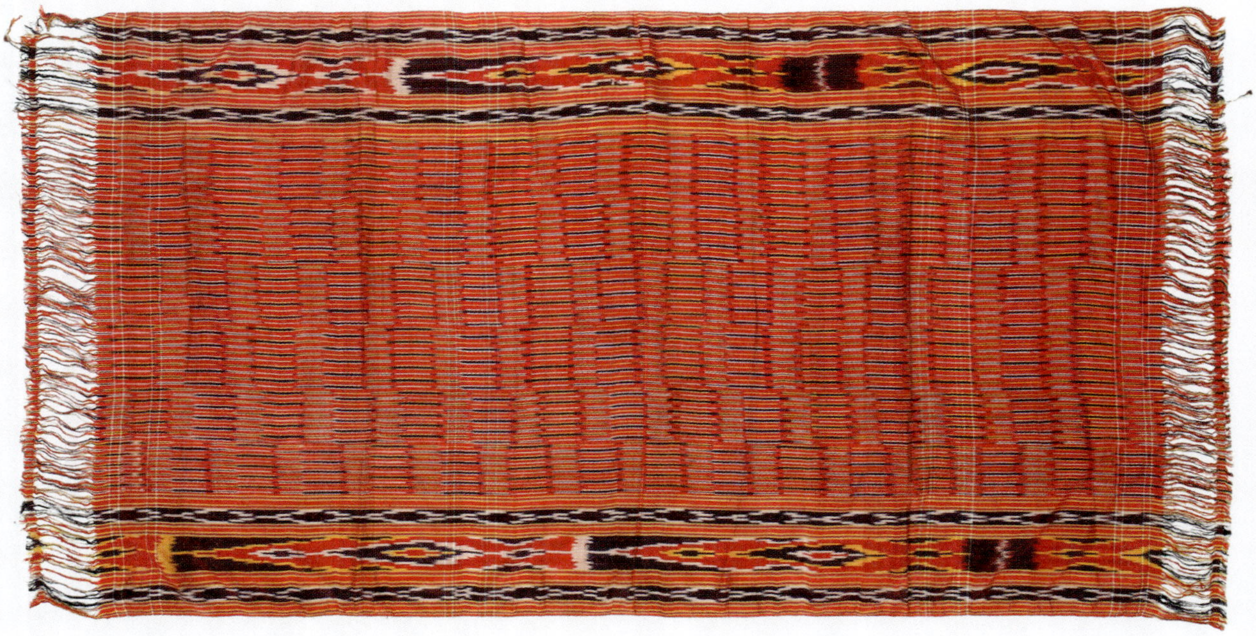

WCA34 Shawl
Aleppo, Syria, 19th or very early 20th century. Silk warp ikat, silk weft. 90 in x 42 in

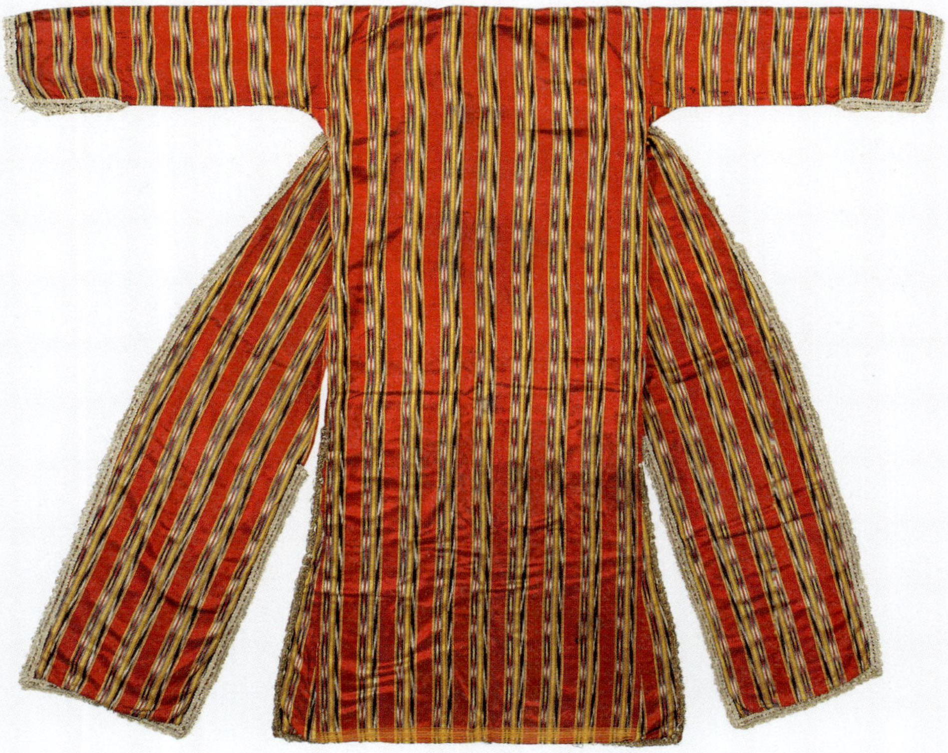

WCA35 Woman's robe
Garment made in Syria (?) from ikat *mashru* cloth made in India, 19th century. Silk warp ikat, cotton weft. 54 in x 64 in

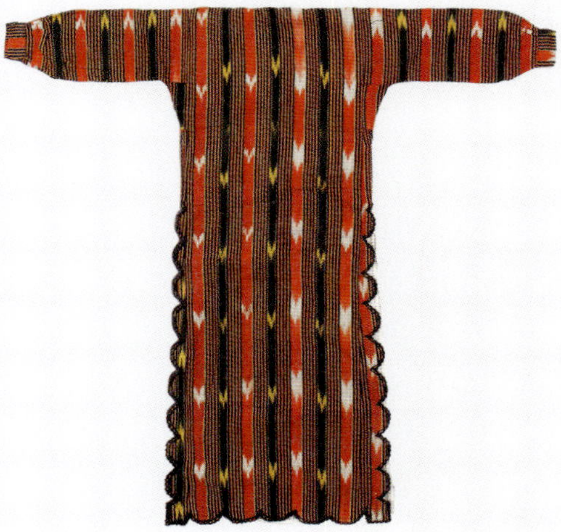

WCA36 Woman's robe
Turkey, late 19th century. Cotton-warp ikat, cotton weft, cotton lining, natural dyes. 50 in x 52 in

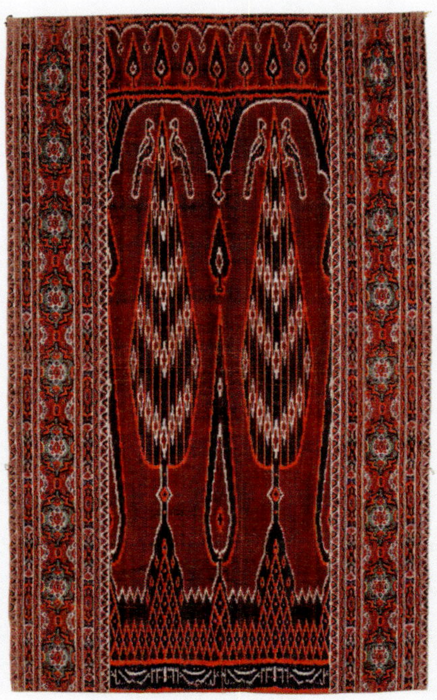

WCA37 Prayer cloth
Yazd, Iran, late 19th century. Silk velvet warp ikat, cotton weft. 73 in x 56 in

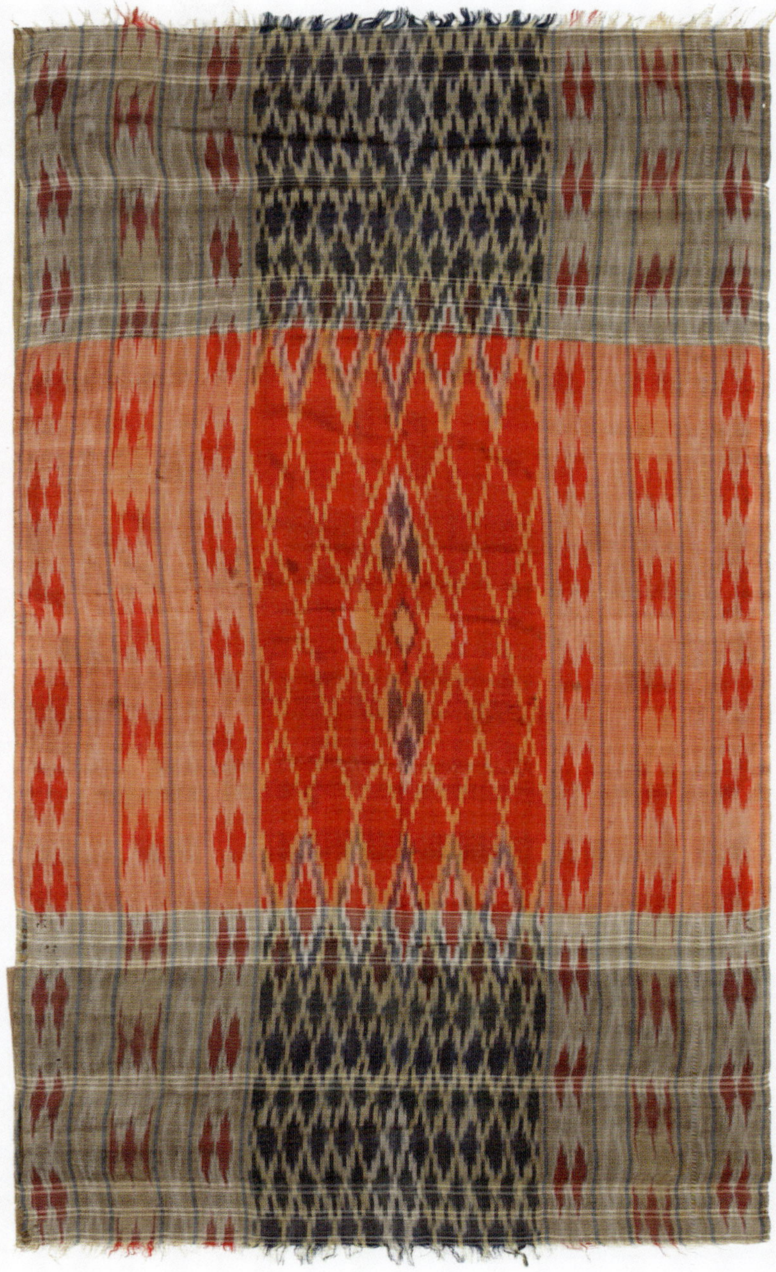

WCA38 Cover or bath wrapper, Yazd, Iran or Aleppo or Damascus, Syria, late 19th century. Silk warp ikat, silk weft, warp-predominant plain weave. 68 in x 42 in

This is a beautiful example of a type of cover known in Syria as *ajami* (i.e., Iranian) towels (*Futa ajamiye*). Their weave structure differs slightly from other Syrian ikat fabrics by being a warp-predominant plain weave, which allows multi-color silk weft yarns to appear on the surface and contribute to the design as horizontal bands. This gives the design a more contained and square appearance. These textiles were used in Syria and in Iran as wrapping cloths in which to store belongings, or as wrappers around bathers' hips in the baths. Future research on Iranian and Syrian ikat traditions and the textile trade between the two countries may reveal where the name comes from, and determine whether these textiles were produced in Iran for the Syrian market, or in Syria for the Iranian market. It could also be a shared tradition.

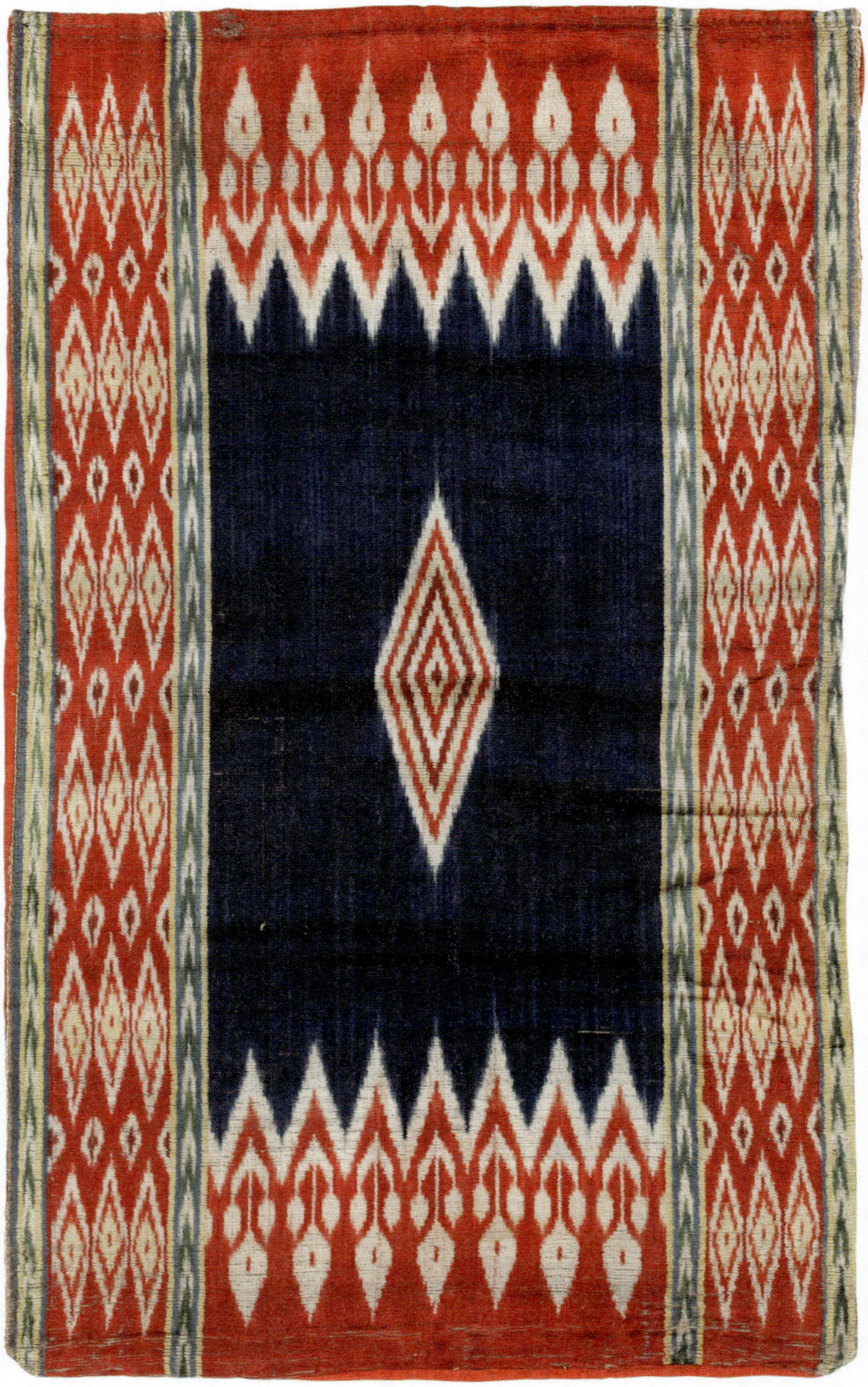

WCA39 Cushion cover, Yazd, Iran, late 19th to early 20th century. Silk velvet warp ikat, cotton weft. 33 in x 14 in

This elegantly designed velvet cushion cover was most likely one from a set which decorated a divan in an Iranian reception room. Aesthetically, it is very different from the well-known hangings with an arch design displaying cypresses and birds. The intense red and dark blue juxtaposed with white create a contrast, while fields of pure colour in the composition calm the eye. As with other ikats from West Asia, the design is based on a manipulation of arrowheads and chevrons and on the warp direction. Velvets such as this cushion cover incorporate supplementary-warp pile in their structure. They were woven following the simple precept of introducing supplemental warp yarns into a foundation weave to produce pile or tuft. Because supplementary-warp yarns were resist dyed in strategic areas beforehand, they created the design during the weaving process when they were pulled to the front at regular intervals.

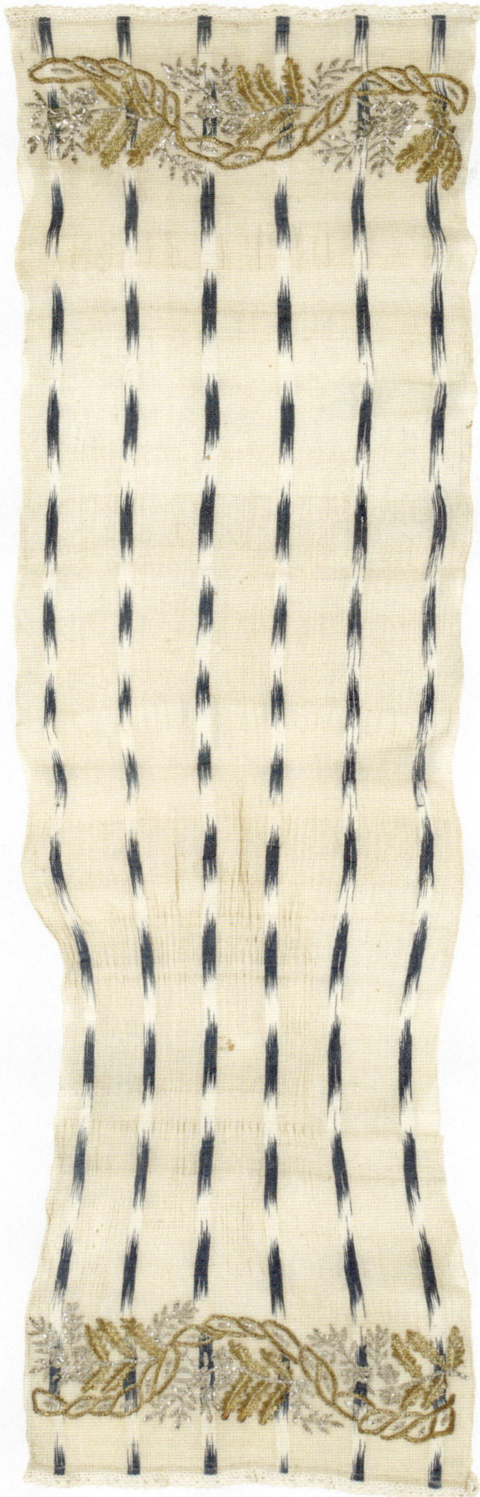

WCA40 Napkin, western Anatolia or Greek Islands, second half 19th century. Linen and cotton (ikat) warp and linen weft, warp-faced plain weave. 54 in x 16 in

Napkins, such as this example, were multifunctional objects, omnipresent in the houses of all subjects of the Ottoman Empire. Primarily they were items to exhibit a woman's good taste and skill in embroidery. They functioned as gifts, decorated the trays of sweets and coffee for guests, or covered small household items in a decorative way.

This napkin has many interesting elements that set it apart. Silver- and gold-color foil is used for the embroidery threads instead of the more frequently seen metallic-wrapped thread with a silk core, although the design executed with these threads is typical of late 19th-century Ottoman style. However, the most interesting part of the napkin is the ground fabric used for the embroidery. It has stripes of blue, resist-dyed cotton warp yarns, while the rest of the warp and weft are linen. This blend of material was commonly used for fabrics in western Anatolia, especially the area of Aydın and Denizli. Although it is hard to pinpoint the exact provenance of the napkin, we can confidently posit that this attractive piece was from the Aegean Sea region, either mainland Anatolia or islands along the coast.

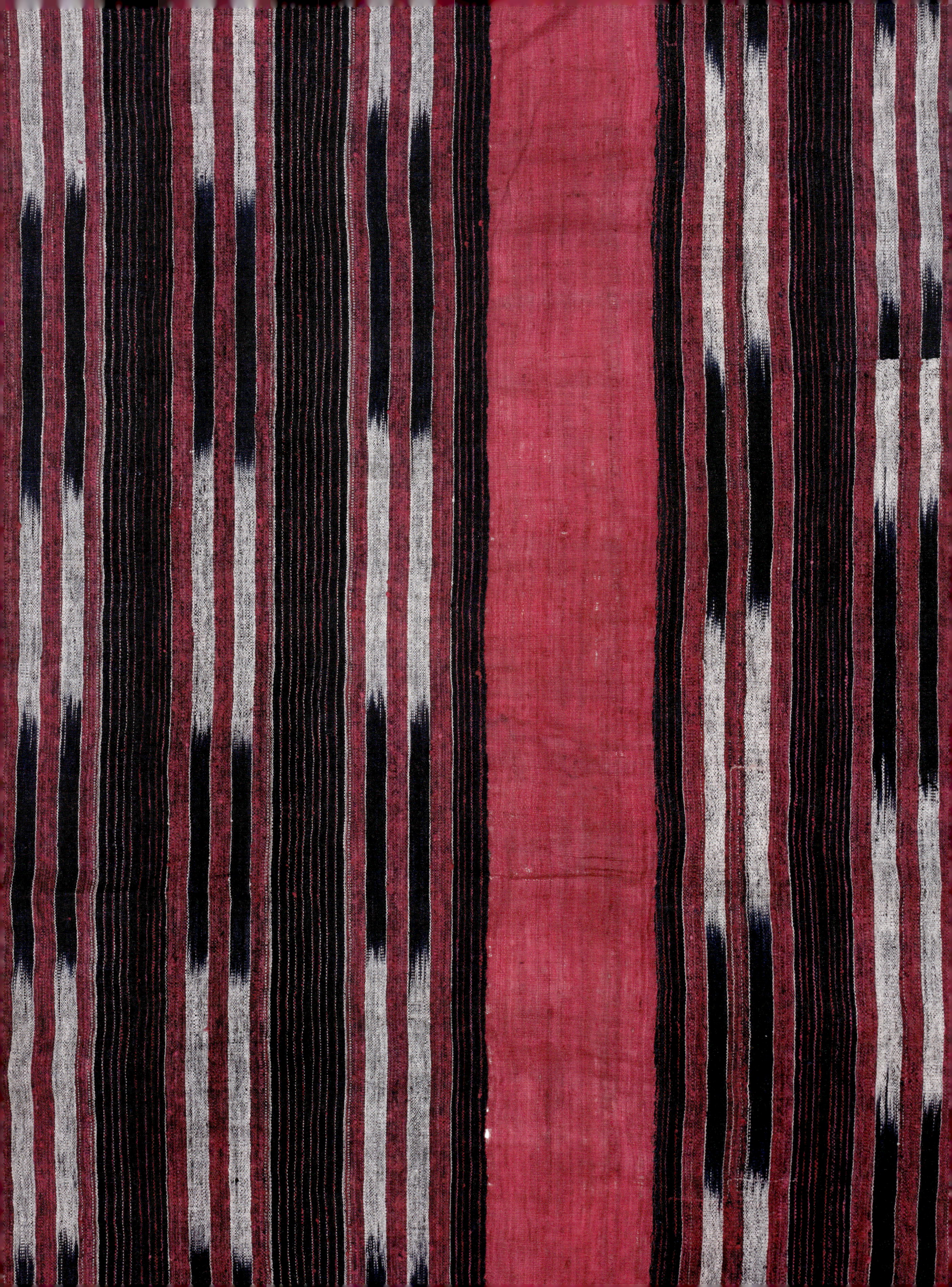

AFRICA

by Duncan Clarke

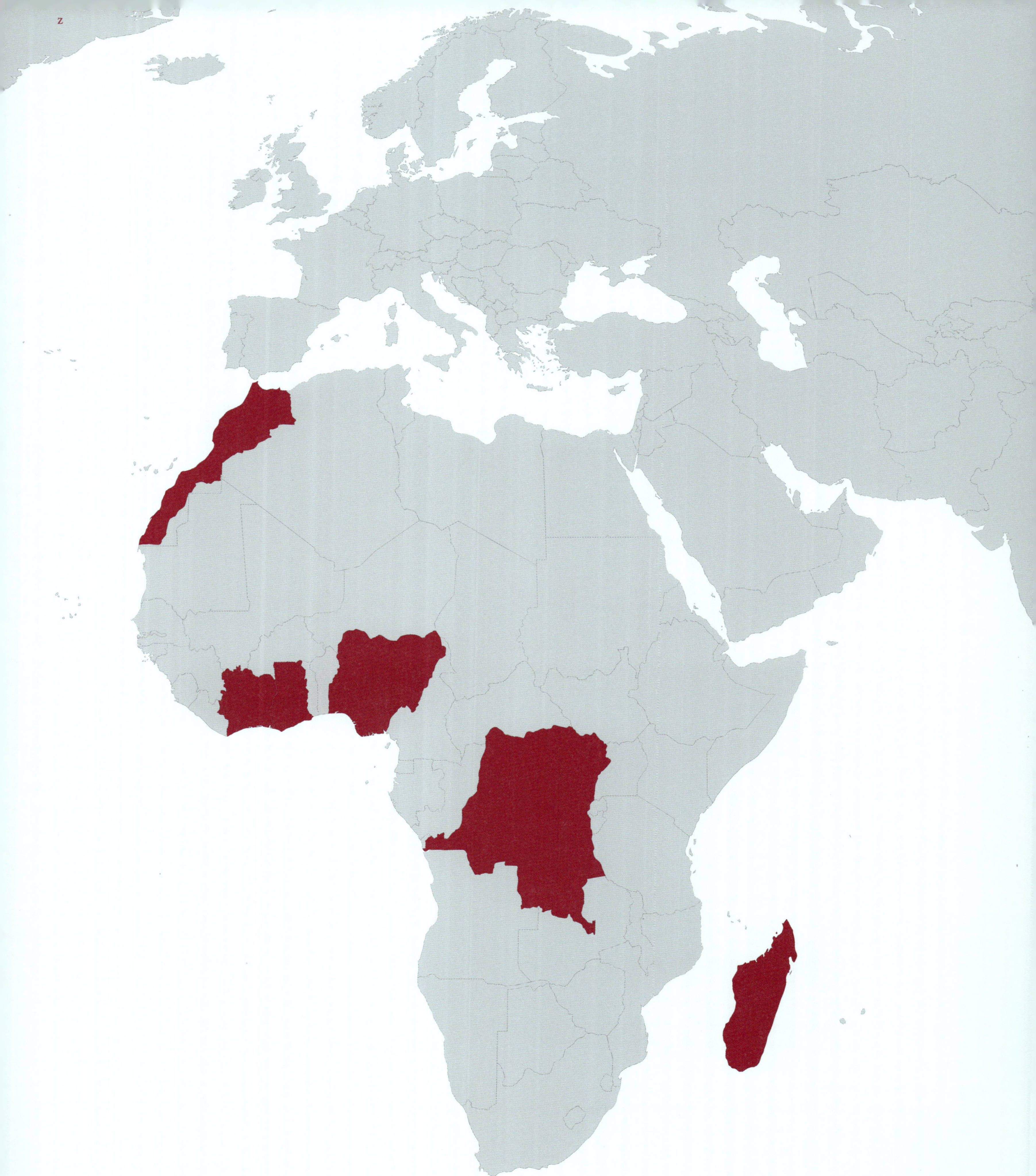

IKAT IN AFRICA

Despite the antiquity of textile weaving in many areas of Africa, the ikat technique was never widespread. In Madagascar, warp ikat raffia prayer mats were woven for Indian patrons in the port town of Mahajanga, while Sakalava women in a few villages wove more elaborate ikats for use as marriage tents. Both traditions were apparently defunct by the middle of the 20th century. Simple warp ikat was used from the 19th century or earlier through to the 1960s, by both male and female weavers on their respective loom types, among some groups of Yoruba people and their neighbours in southwestern Nigeria. One type of ikat does, however, still thrive in West Africa, specifically in central and northern Cote d'Ivoire, as well as adjacent regions of Burkina Faso and northern Ghana.

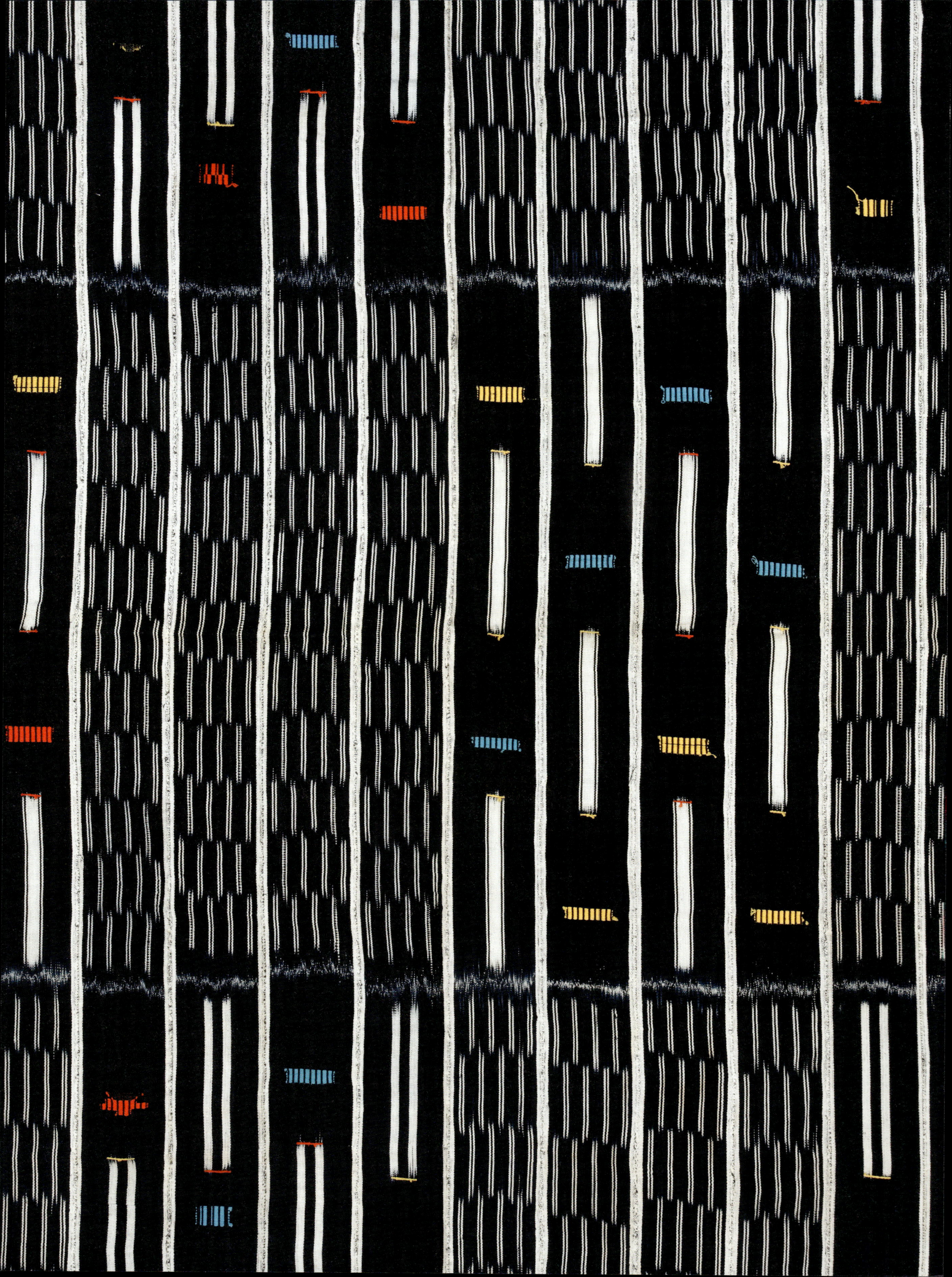

Fig.1
Detail of AF20, mixed ikat pattern man's wrapper cloth, *zaza*

OF EVERY STRIPE

Both weaving and indigo dyeing have a very long history in sub-Saharan Africa. A wide variety of looms and fibers were used over the centuries, the oldest combination most probably being a type of small, single-heddle ground loom used to weave raffia cloth in the rainforest belt of West and Central Africa. Linguistic historians have recently proposed that the use of this weaving technology among Benue-Kwa peoples in what is now Nigeria dates back as far as the 4th millennium BCE.[1] Indigo was used to dye textiles in Meroë; these artifacts have been dated between 300 BCE and 300 CE. However, ikat has played a minor role in the story of African textiles when comparison is made with other areas of the world with a similarly long record of textile production. In West Africa the technique was used in only two quite small regions: among the Yoruba and some neighboring peoples in Southwestern Nigeria, and among the Baule and Dioula peoples in Central and Northern Ivory Coast and southern Burkina Faso. In East Africa the Tanala and Sakalava people of Madagascar wove ikat-patterned raffia cloths.

Two distinct weaving technologies overlap among the Yoruba-speaking peoples in Nigeria: a version of the West African narrow-strip double-heddle loom that was introduced around the 15th or 16th centuries through contacts with Muslim "Wangara" traders from Mali; and a much older vertical single-heddle loom that was confined to Nigeria and neighboring countries. As elsewhere in West Africa weaving on the double-heddle loom was until the past few decades the work of men, while with very few exceptions only women weavers used the vertical single-heddle loom to weave cotton cloths. Yoruba narrow-strip, double-heddle loom cloth, called *aso oke*, was woven in strips around 4 inches (10 cm) wide that were sewn together edge to edge to make tailored men's robes and trousers (Fig.2 and Fig.3/AF04), or women's wrapper cloths, shawls, head wraps, and related garments. Women using the vertical single-heddle loom produced wider panels of cloth, averaging perhaps 24 inches (60 cm) width. A single panel could be used as a woman's head wrap, shawl, or baby tie; two widths sewn together made a woman's wrapper cloth; and three a man's cloth. Blue-and-white warp striped cloths, called *kijiipa*, were produced by virtually all Yoruba women weavers, but there were also numerous much more localized styles, some found only in a single village group.

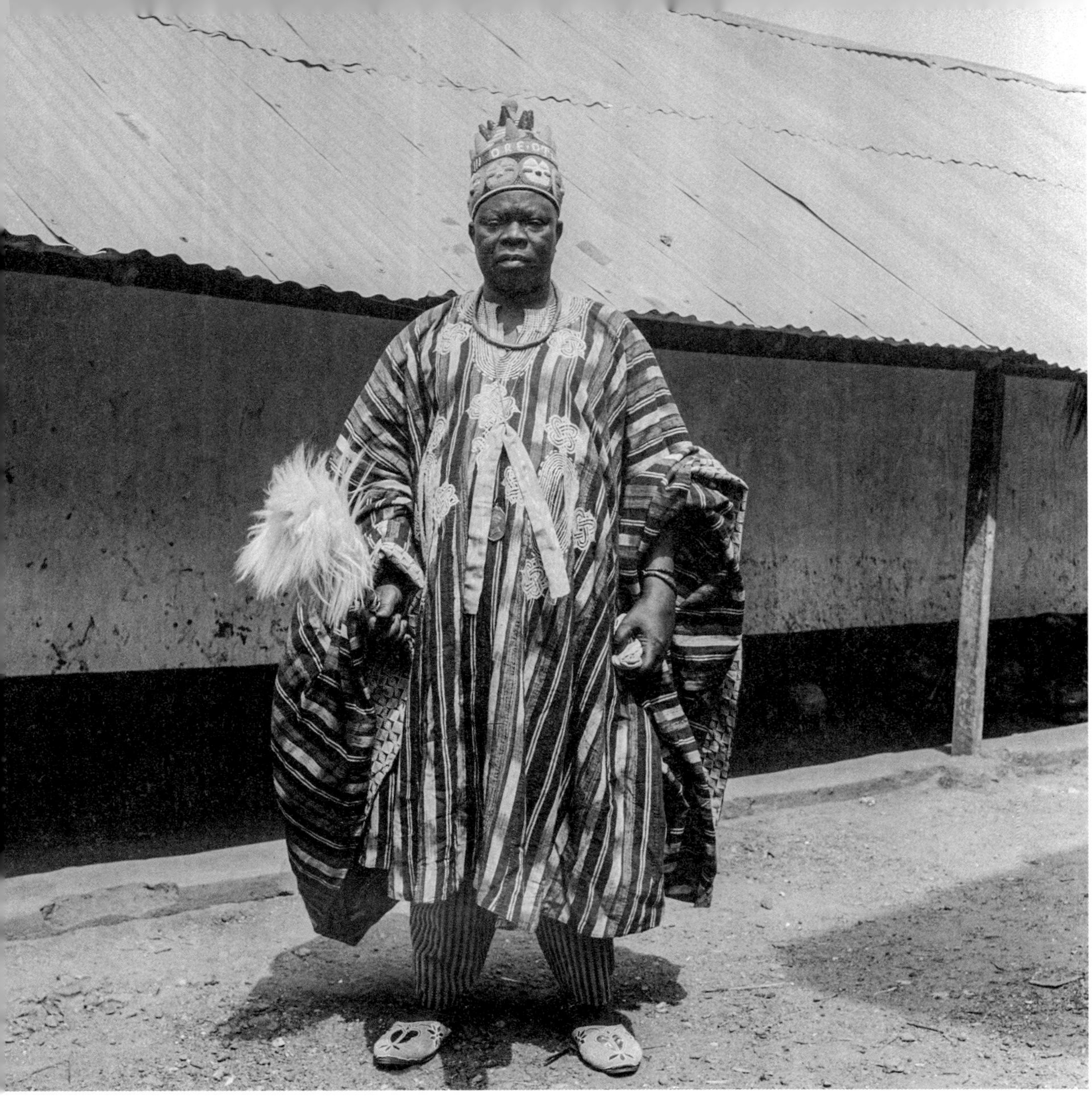

© RAI

Fig.2

Fig.2
Ori of Otun, photograph by William Buller Fagg, Nigeria, 1949–1950. Royal Anthropological Institute London

Fig.3
AF04, Yoruba "Agbada" man's strip-woven *asa oke* tunic

Fig.4
Detail of AF10, Yoruba woman's cloth

Ikat-patterned cloth was woven on both loom types. Indigo was by far the most widely used natural dye in Nigeria (as it was elsewhere in West Africa) and the most common type of *aso oke* strip cloth was blue-and-white warp-faced plain weave with warp stripes of varying widths. Some of these cloths included stripes with warp-ikat patterning in which the warp color alternated between blue and white. A wine-red dye obtained from elephant grass (*Pennisetum purpureum*) was also used, echoing the highly prized red silk *alaari* that reached Nigeria from North Africa via trans-Saharan trade routes. This use of warp ikat was called *waka* in Yoruba. Far rarer than this simple ikat was a more subtle style in which individual warp threads were resist dyed, resulting in a speckled effect that was called *etu*, guineafowl, after the bird's speckled plumage (although more commonly *etu* was a prestigious pattern of blue-and-white check).

Among women weavers ikat was woven only by some groups in the eastern and southeastern areas of the Yoruba-speaking region, including the Ekiti and Owo peoples. Ikat-patterned *aso oke* was simply another design of high-status cloth with no particular significance beyond prestige attire; however, limited documentation suggests some women's weave ikats were restricted to specific functions and occasions in the ancient Yoruba Kingdom of Owo. Nearby Ekiti women wove wrappers with small, white (and later also yellow) ikat. In these a variety of small shapes, including combs, could be discerned within the warp stripes. The same style was woven in larger numbers by women in the northern Edo/Ebira town of Igarra, continuing to be made there using mill-spun cotton at least into the 1990s. A workshop of indigo dyers was active in the small, southeastern Yoruba town of Idanre in the first half of the 20th century. This seems to have been the source of the only Yoruba ikats yet discovered that make a more ambitious use of the technique. Lagos Museum holds two large, three-panel cloths with dramatic patterns of large triangles and diamond shapes in blue-and-white warp ikat. Collection records noted the cloth name as *Ogbingede*.[2] The David Paly Collection

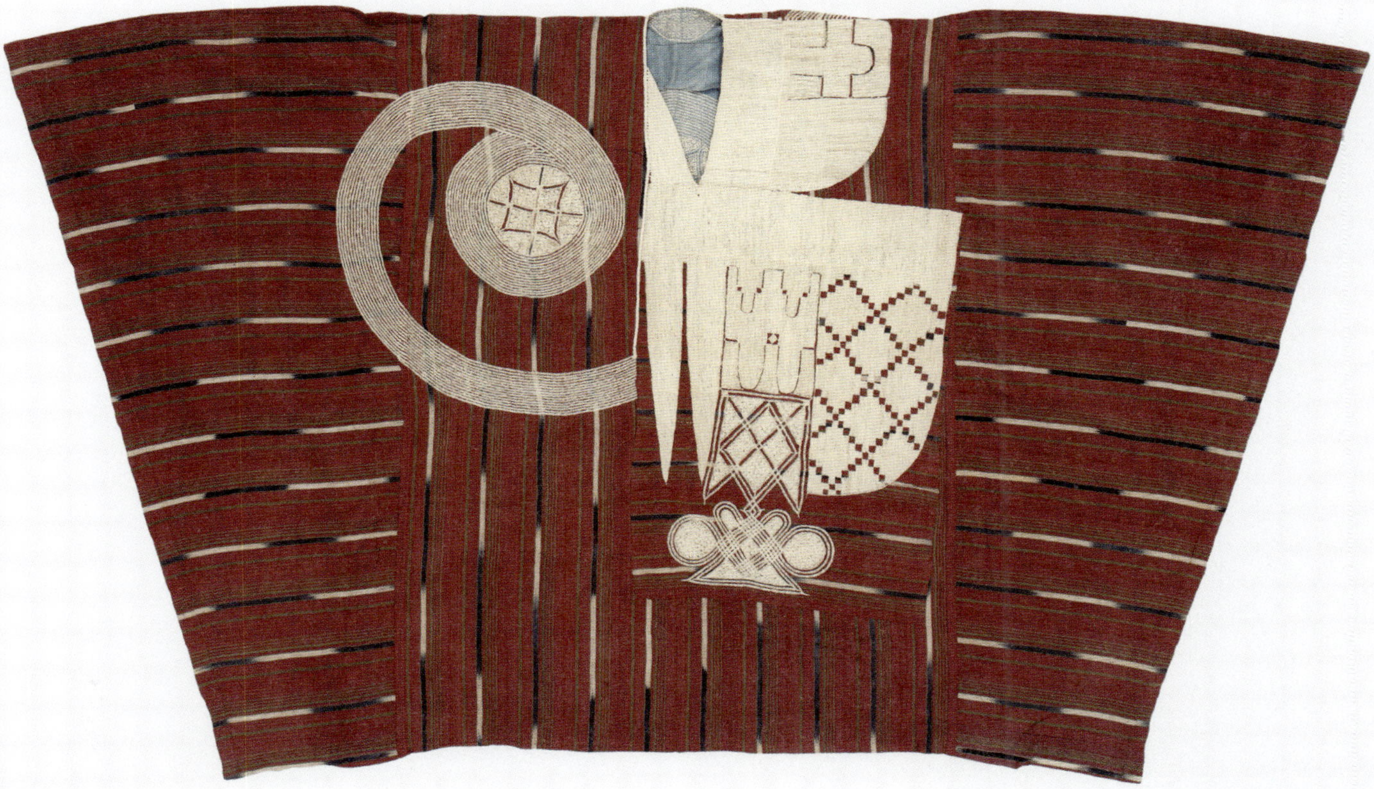

Fig.3

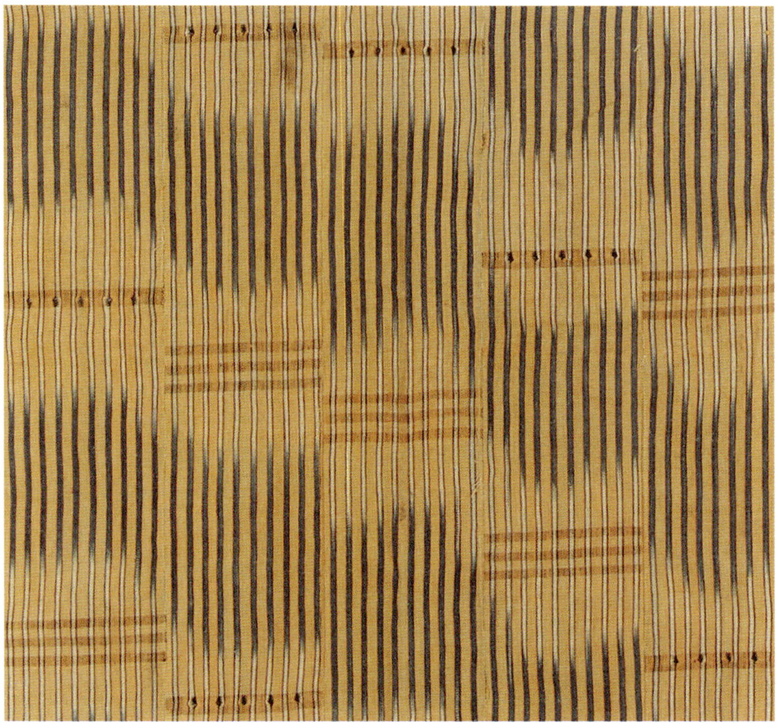

Fig.4

includes one of the two known narrow-loom cloths in the same style (the other is in the British Museum) (AF02).

The earliest known examples of ikat-patterned Yoruba textiles date from the late 19th century, but unfortunately there is no way to establish when the method was first used. Given the simplicity of the technique–as well as the wide range of patterned textiles of many types and origins imported into West Africa over the centuries–we can only speculate as to whether it was a local invention or had an external source.[3] By the end of the 1960s, Yoruba weaving on the women's loom was in drastic decline, and male weavers of narrow-strip cloths had largely adopted imported, mill-spun thread. Very little locally dyed thread was used subsequently, and consequently Yoruba ikat was effectively defunct. A small number of narrow-strip warp-ikat cloths closely similar to *aso oke* examples were woven by Ewe weavers in Ghana and Togo in the middle decades of the 20th century, almost certainly in response to the importation of Yoruba *aso oke*.

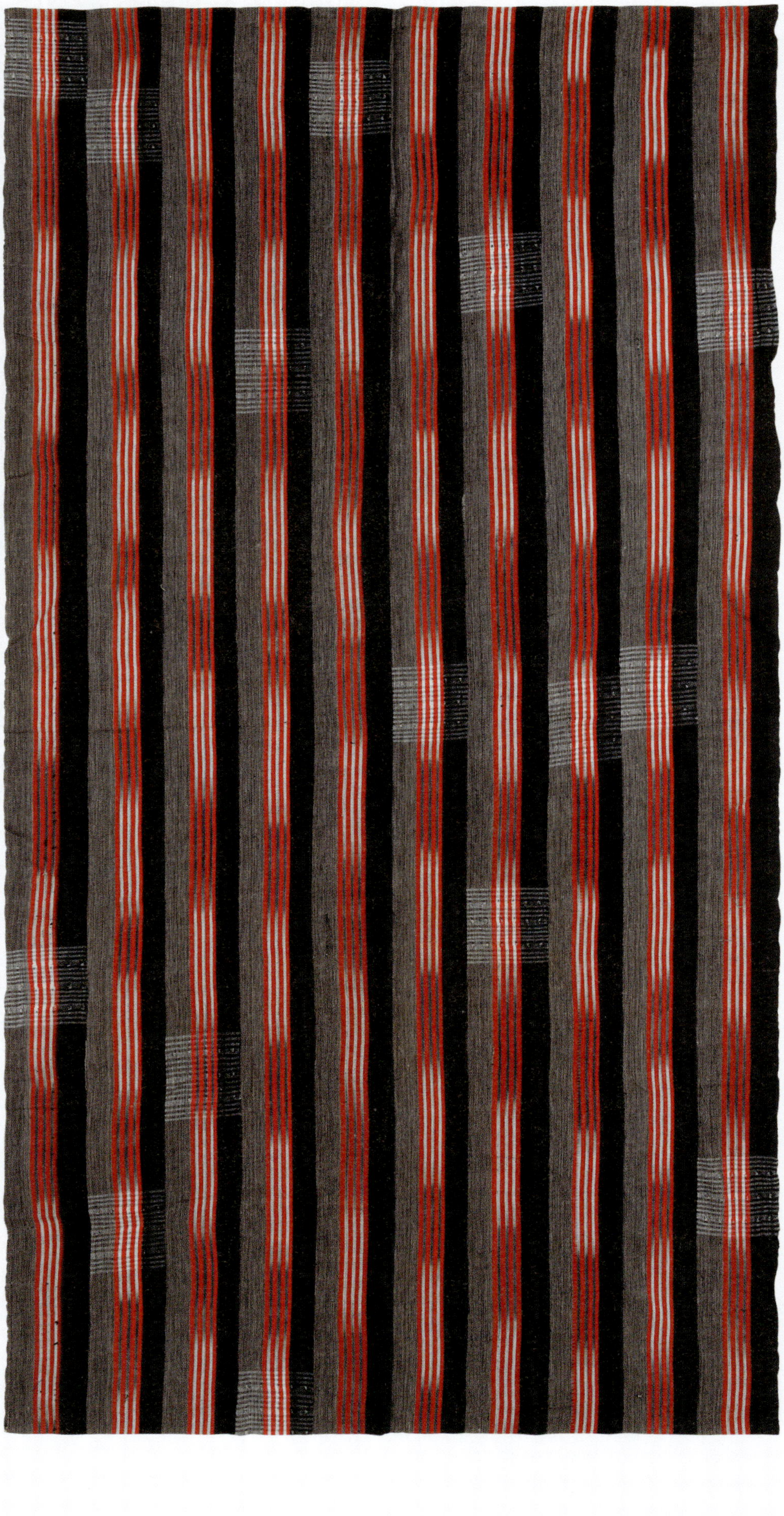

Fig.5

By far the most well-known and widely available ikat-patterned cloths from sub-Saharan Africa are those woven in the second half of the 20th century by male weavers from the Baule people of Southern and Central Cote d'Ivoire. The Baule are an Akan people who were displaced from the forests of southern Ghana by the expansion of the Asante empire in the 17th century. Baule weavers learned both indigo dyeing and ikat patterning from the Dioula, a Muslim trading people of Malian origin who wove strip-weave ikat cloths among a wider repertoire of prestigious textiles. Dioula ikats were typically blue-and-white warp striped cloths that had blocks of simple ikat alternating across the full width of the 4-inch (12 cm) strips. These were known as *suruku kawa*, the "spotted hyena," and were first woven in pre-colonial times in Kong, the most important center of Dioula textile production and trade.[4] Baule weavers began to reproduce these using warps prepared by Dioula indigo dyers during the first half of the 20th century, but by the 1960s had themselves mastered both dyeing and warp ikat. Over the following decades Baule weavers developed a new and more elaborate style of ikat, called *zaza* (AF20), or "mixed patterns," in which the field of the cloth was divided into blocks by alternating sections of two different ikat patterns, often in combination with supplementary-weft float motifs. These dramatic and attractive designs, frequently modified over the years, became popular for women's ceremonial attire throughout much of Cote d'Ivoire (Fig.6). Dioula weavers took the new styles back to their family homes in the north of the country and in Burkina Faso. This contributed to a continuing spread of simple warp ikat into the *Faso dan fani* cloth of Burkina Faso and strip-weave cloth used to make men's gowns in northern Ghana today.

Apart from some simple check-patterned raffia cloths made by Tanala women in the southeast of the country, ikat in Madagascar was a specialty of women weavers belonging to the Sakalava people in a few villages and towns near the northwestern coast. Small raffia prayer mats with a *mihrab* design were made in the port town of Mahajanga for members of the Indian Bohra merchant community. More elaborate warp-ikat-patterned raffia panels, often rather prosaically described as "mosquito nets," were woven by women in the villages of Ambatomainty, Sitampiky, and Kandreho.[5] Some of these may have been hung up as room dividers on ceremonial occasions, but the primary use was to form small tents used for marriage consummation (AF27).

Scholars including Sarah Fee have recently challenged the earlier assumption that the presence of ikat in Madagascar is simply a legacy of the Austronesian origins of the first settlers. Fee noted that the Sakalava term for ikat, *laimasaka*, literally "cooked sails," doesn't have an Austronesian root and that early European travelers did not mention ikat textiles. Instead, she suggests, its origins may lie in the wider Indian Ocean trade networks that circulated cloths from Yemen, Gujarat, and Oman. When Ralph Linton collected several fine raffia ikat panels in 1926 he noted that there were "not over fifteen" women still able to make them.[6]

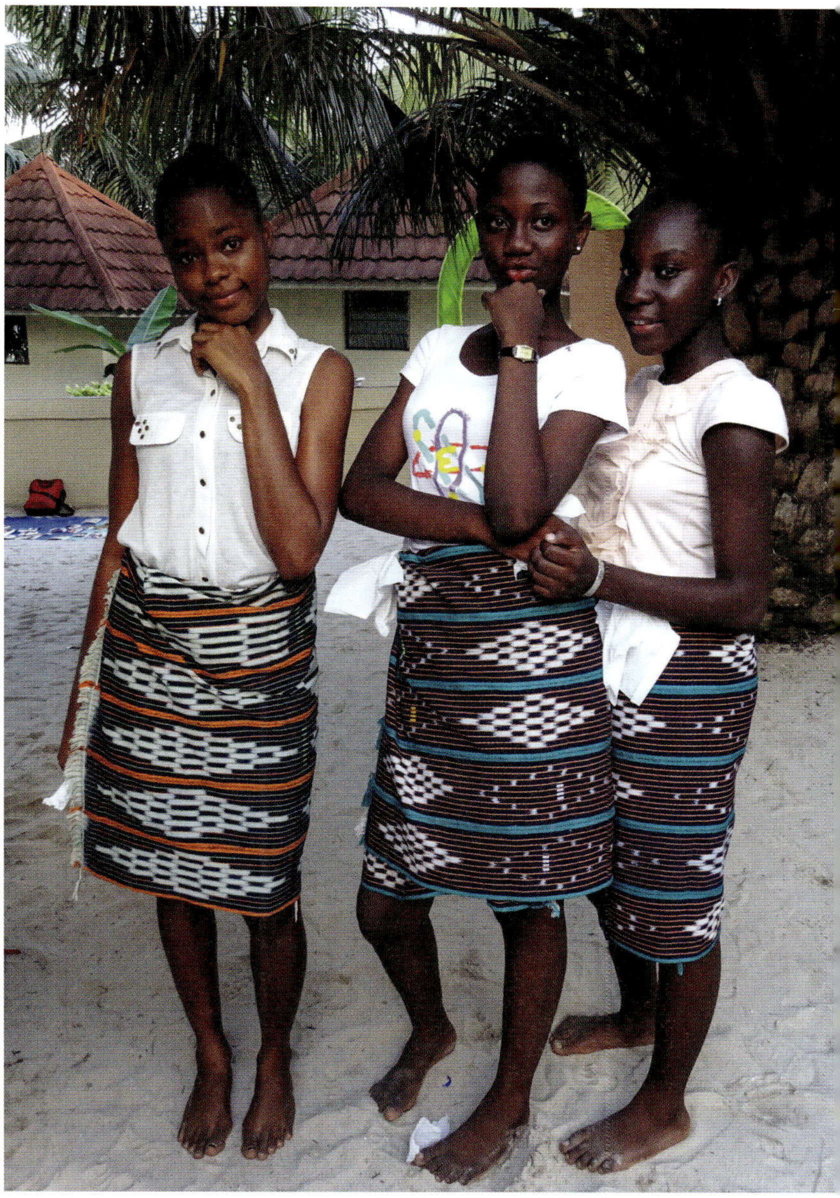

Fig.6

Fig.5
AF09, Yoruba woman's cloth

Fig.6
Three young Baule women wearing ikat-patterned wrapper cloths, photograph by Anne Grosfilley, Cote d'Ivoire, circa 2010

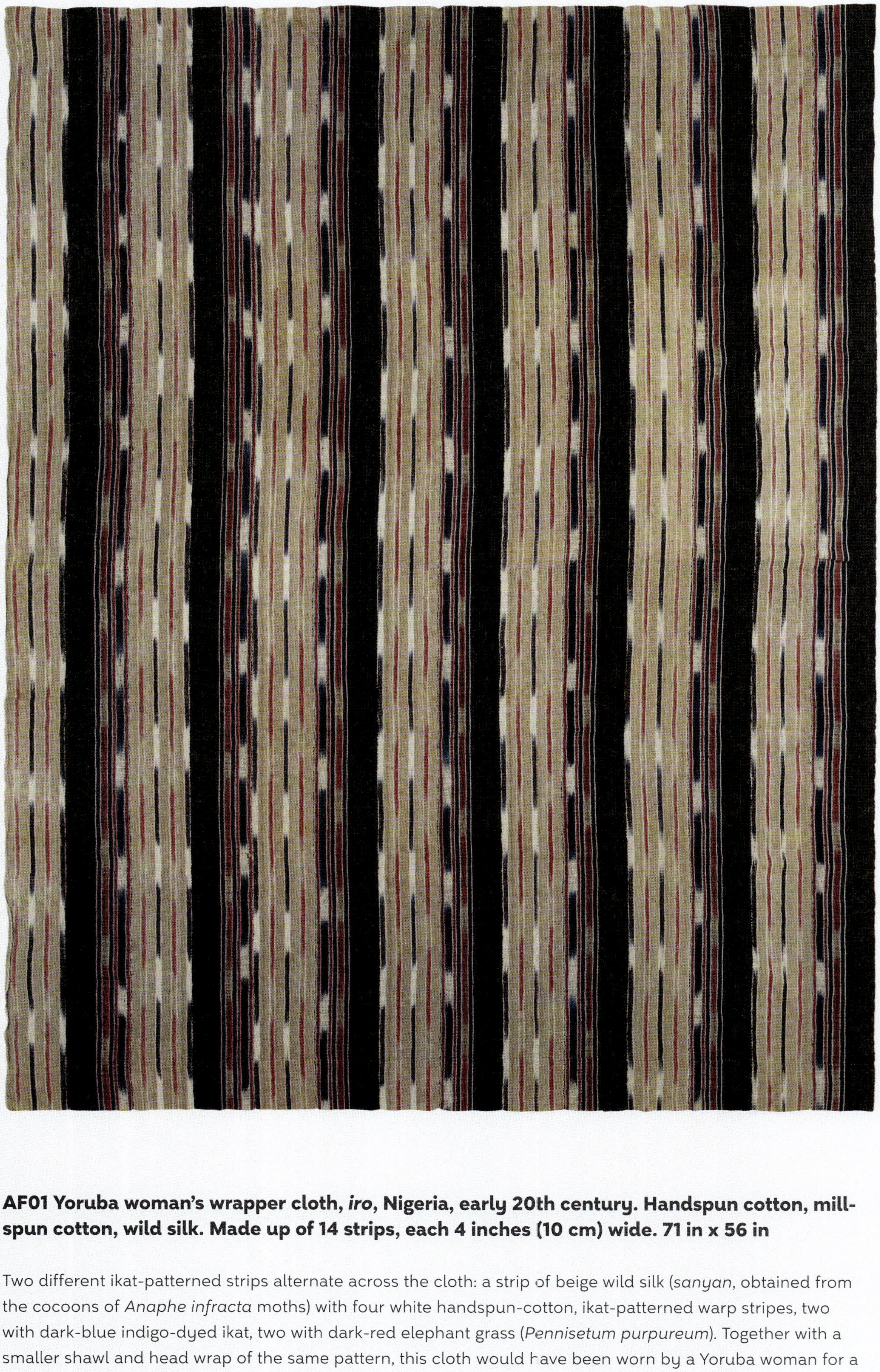

AF01 Yoruba woman's wrapper cloth, *iro*, Nigeria, early 20th century. Handspun cotton, mill-spun cotton, wild silk. Made up of 14 strips, each 4 inches (10 cm) wide. 71 in x 56 in

Two different ikat-patterned strips alternate across the cloth: a strip of beige wild silk (*sanyan*, obtained from the cocoons of *Anaphe infracta* moths) with four white handspun-cotton, ikat-patterned warp stripes, two with dark-blue indigo-dyed ikat, two with dark-red elephant grass (*Pennisetum purpureum*). Together with a smaller shawl and head wrap of the same pattern, this cloth would have been worn by a Yoruba woman for a wedding, funeral, or other life-cycle ceremony.

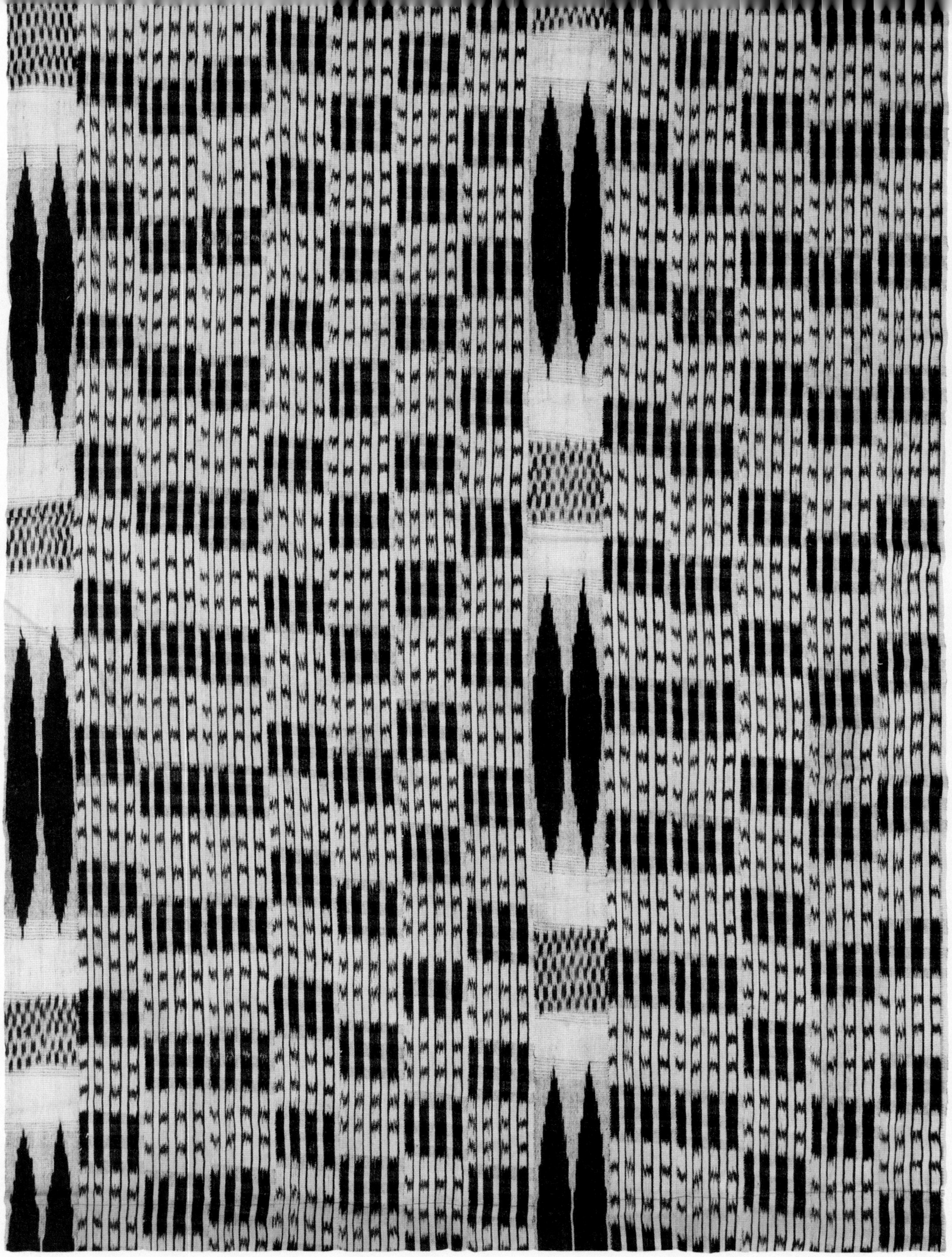

AF02 Woman's wrapper cloth, *Ogbingede*, Idanre, Ondo State, Nigeria, early 20th century. Handspun cotton. Made up of 14 strips across. 83 in x 56 in

On two strips, ikat was used to create pairs of elongated lozenge shapes that alternate with small blocks of blue-and-white ikat. The other twelve strips are made up of alternating sections of ikat and the warp-striped ground. Despite the distinctive use of ikat, this cloth shares an asymmetric layout with many other strip-weave Yoruba cloths of the period, an effort by male weavers to mimic the design favored by women's loom cloth at that time.

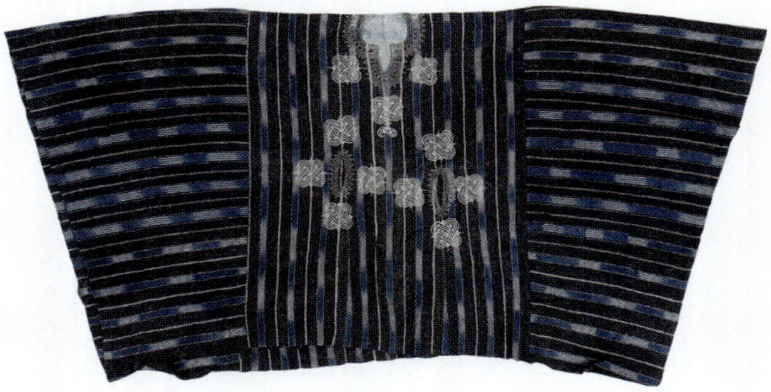

AF03 Yoruba "Agbada" man's strip-woven *asa oke* tunic
Nigeria, early 20th century. Cotton, warp ikat, and cotton embroidery. 45 in x 96 in

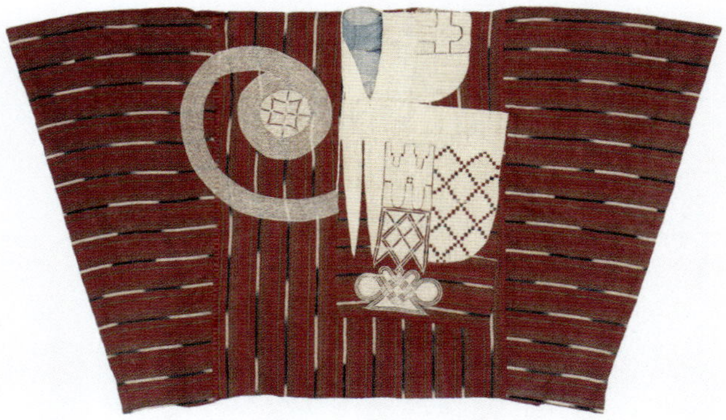

AF04 Yoruba "Agbada" man's strip-woven *asa oke* tunic
Nigeria, mid-20th century. Cotton, warp ikat, and cotton embroidery. 48 in x 105 in

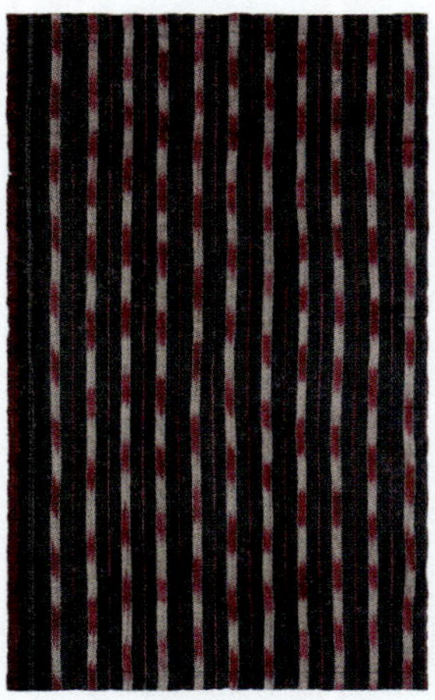

AF05 Yoruba woman's strip-woven *asa oke* cloth
Nigeria, ca. 1920–40. Cotton, warp ikat. 76 in x 46 in

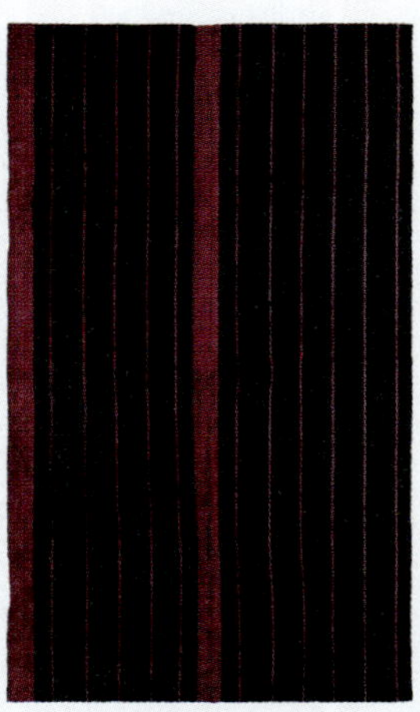

AF06 Yoruba woman's cloth
Nigeria, early 20th century. Cotton, warp ikat, with *alaari* trade silk stripes. 80 in x 48 in

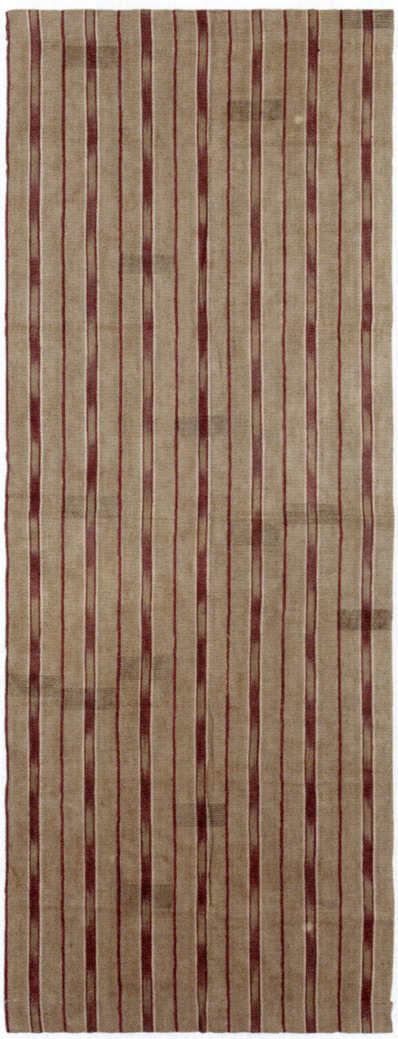

AF07 Yoruba woman's cloth/head wrapper
Nigeria, early 20th century. Wild silk, warp ikat, and cotton weft brocade. 78 in x 29.5 in

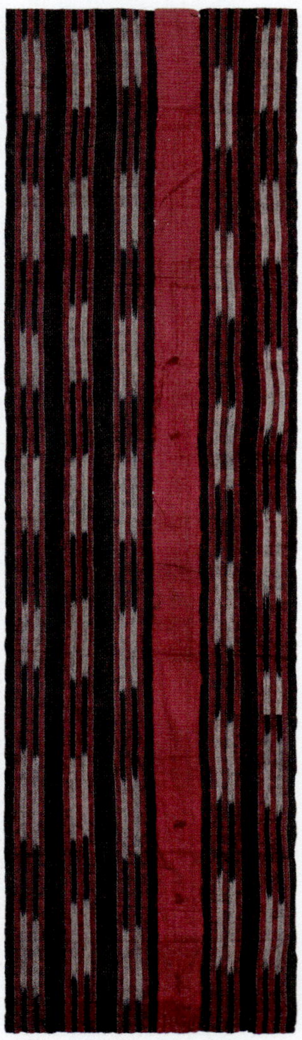

AF08 Yoruba head wrapper
Nigeria, circa 1900. Cotton, warp ikat, with *alaari* trade silk stripes. 88 in x 25 in

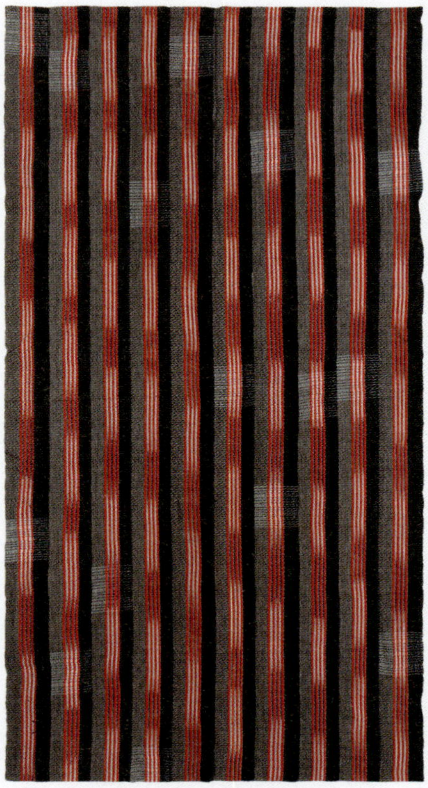

AF09 Yoruba woman's cloth
Nigeria, mid-20th century. Cotton, warp ikat, with cotton weft brocade. 72 in x 48 in

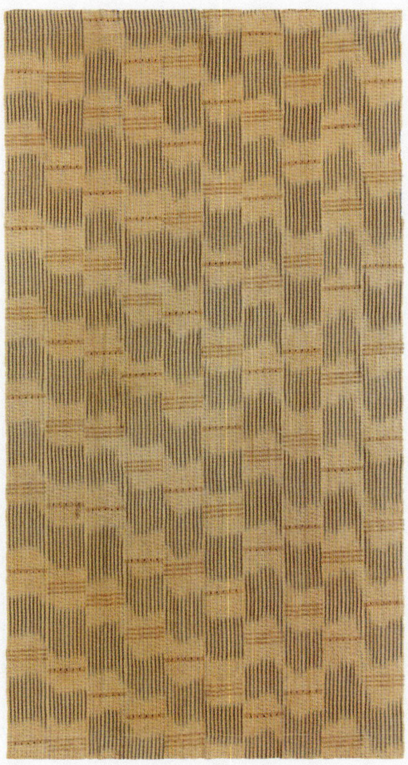

AF10 Yoruba woman's cloth
Nigeria, mid-20th century. Cotton, warp ikat, with cotton weft brocade. 75 in x 40 in

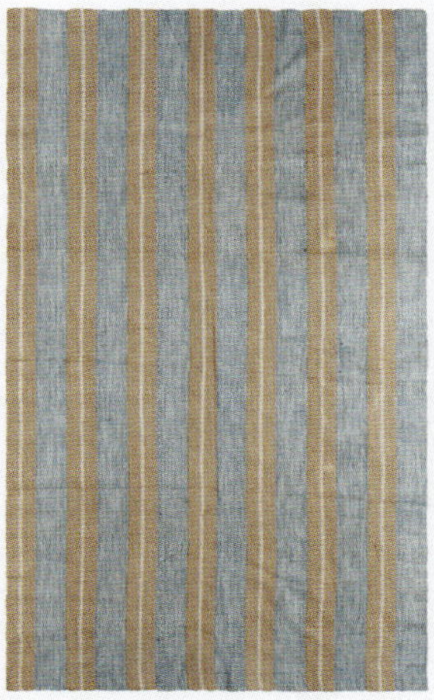

AF11 Yoruba woman's cloth
Nigeria, mid-20th century. Cotton, wild silk, warp ikat. 80 in x 52 in

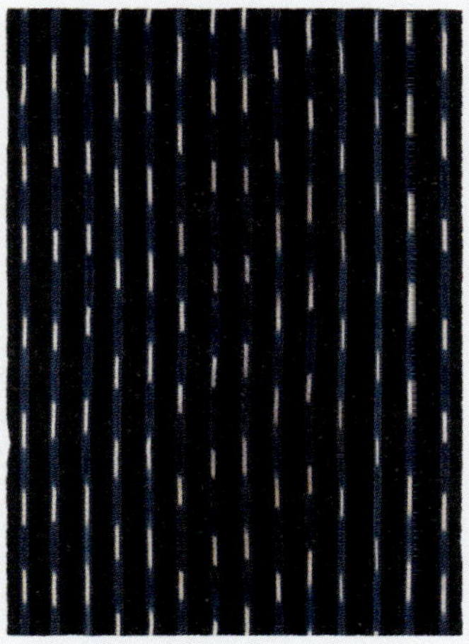

AF12 Yoruba woman's cloth
Nigeria, mid-20th century. Cotton, warp ikat. 73 in x 52 in

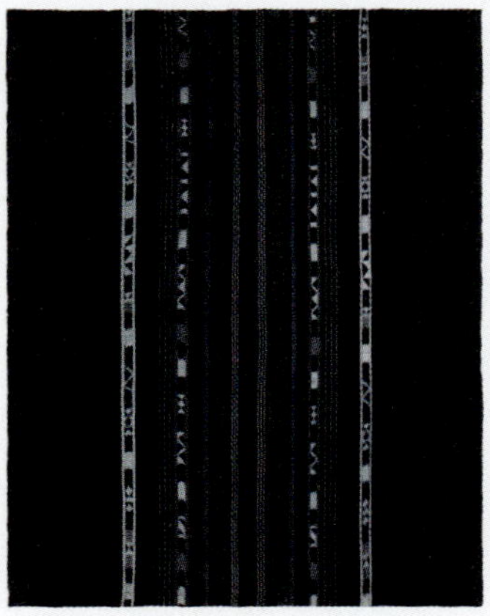

AF13 Edo woman's cloth
Igarra, Nigeria, mid-20th century. Cotton, warp ikat. 71 in x 58 in

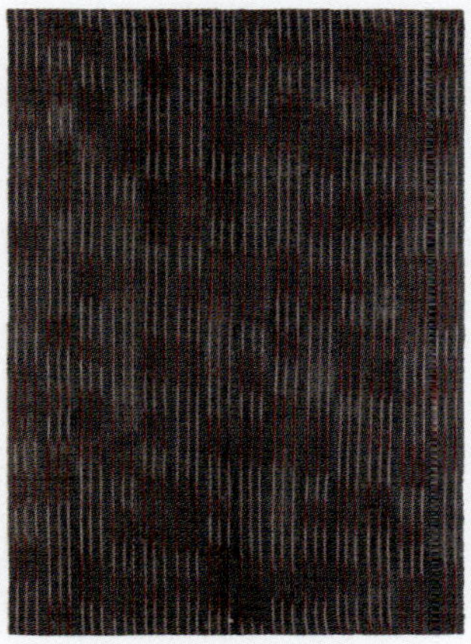

AF14 Yoruba woman's cloth
Nigeria, mid-20th century. Cotton, warp ikat. 69 in x 48 in

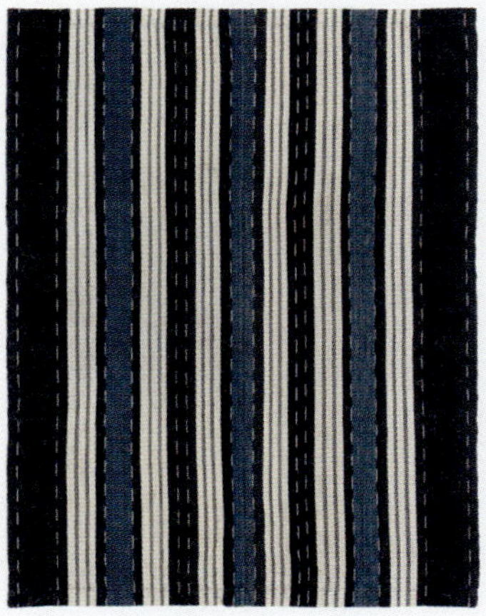

AF15 Edo woman's cloth
Igarra, Nigeria, mid-20th century. Handspun cotton, warp ikat. 64 in x 42 in

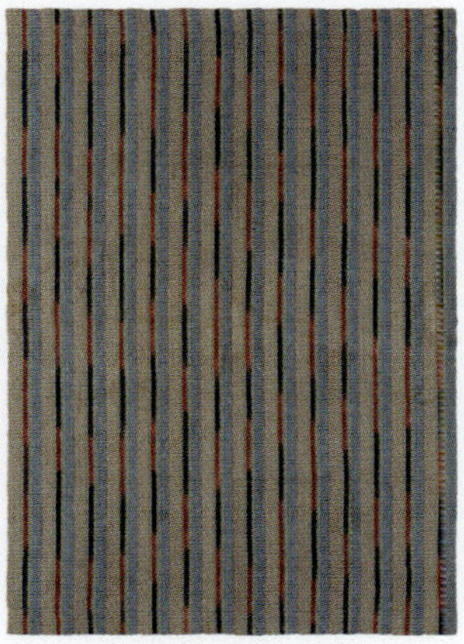

AF16 Yoruba woman's cloth
Nigeria, mid-20th century. Cotton, warp ikat. 71 in x 53 in

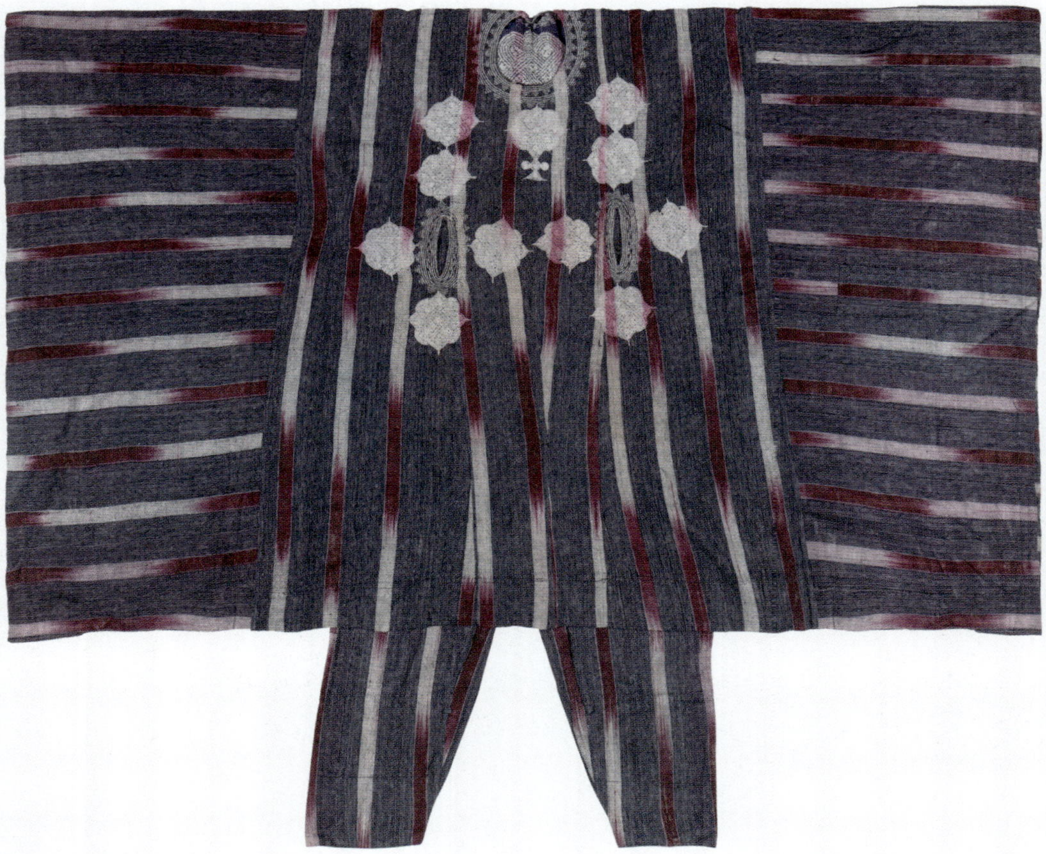

AF17 Yoruba "Agbada" man's strip-woven *asa oke* tunic
Nigeria, mid-20th century. Cotton, warp ikat and cotton embroidery. 97 in x 56 in

AF18 Yoruba woman's strip-woven *asa oke* cloth
Nigeria, early 20th century. Cotton, warp ikat. 72 in x 52 in

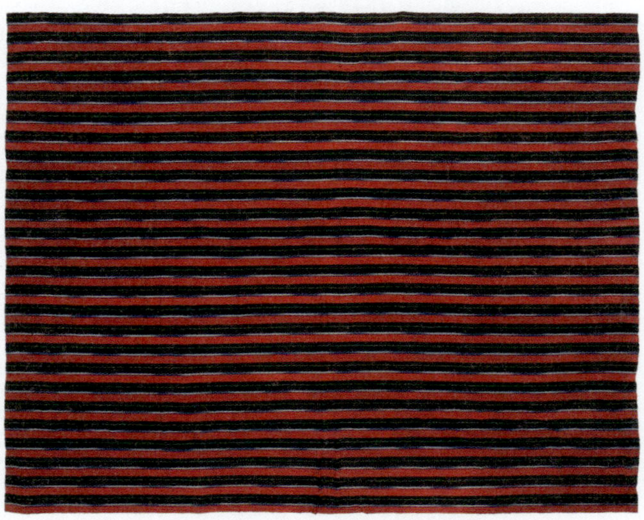

AF19 Man's cloth
Ghana, mid-20th century. Cotton, warp ikat. 129 in x 98 in

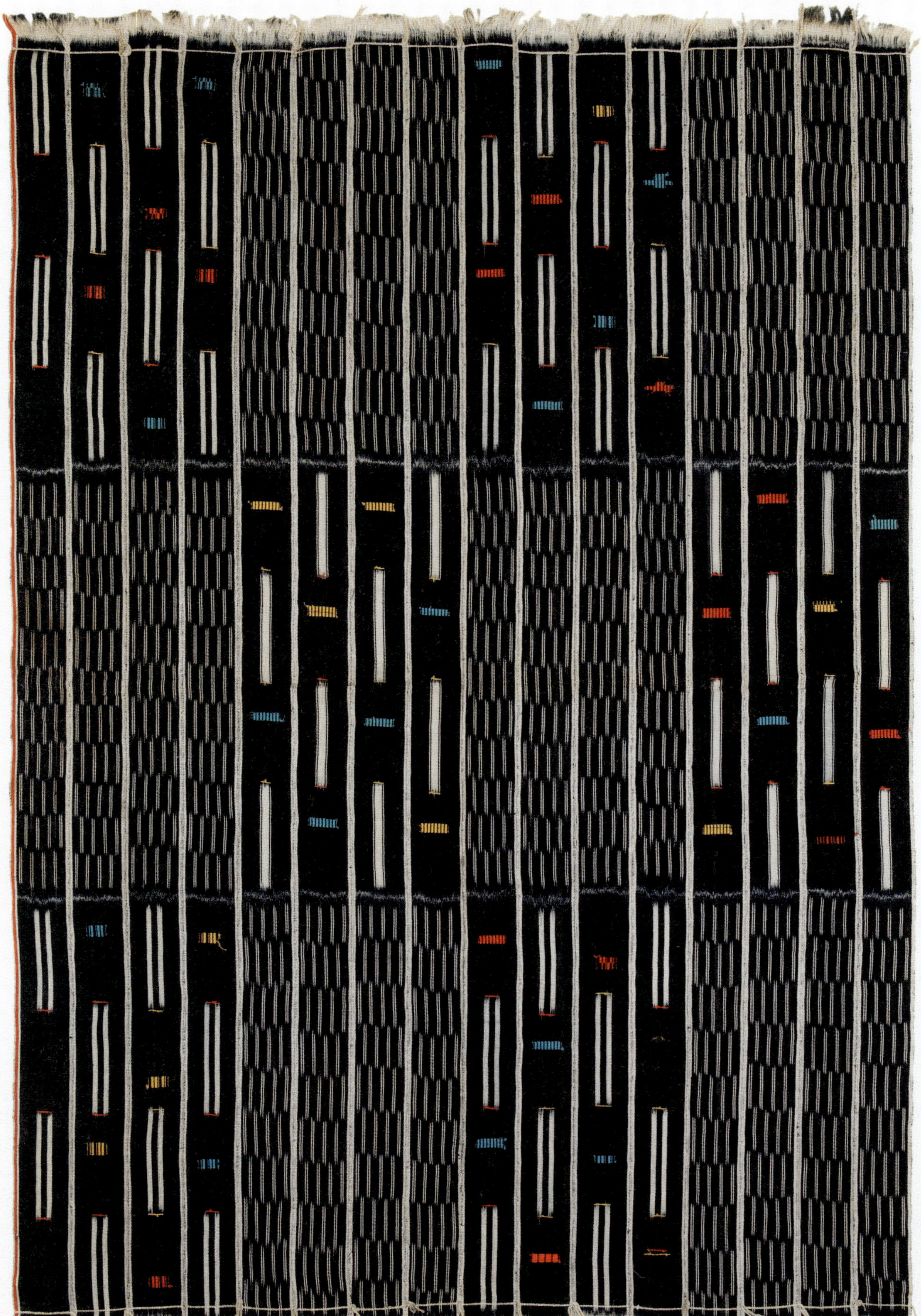

AF20 Mixed ikat pattern man's wrapper cloth, *zaza*, Baule people, Cote d'Ivoire, circa 1970s. Mill-spun cotton. Made up of 16 strips. 92 in x 68 in

Large blocks made up from two different warp-ikat patterns divide the cloth into 16 rectangles. Cloths like this were worn toga fashion by men of the Baule and other ethnic groups in central and southern Cote d'Ivoire, while smaller versions served as wrap-around skirts for women.

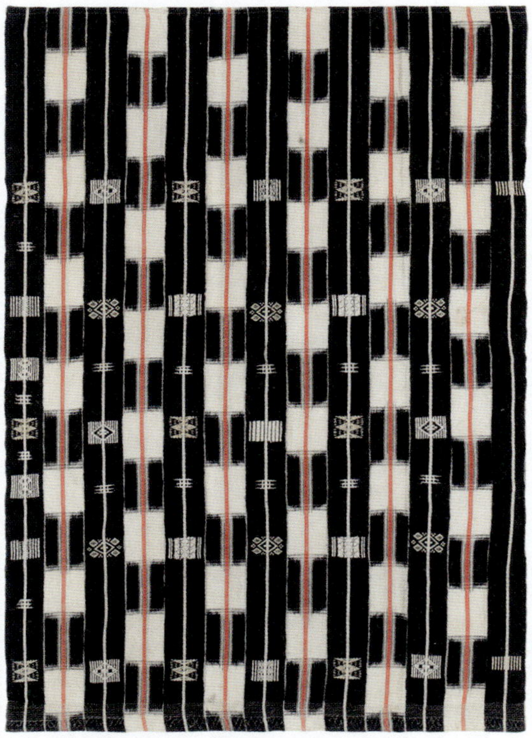

AF21 Dioula woman's strip-woven cloth
Cote d'Ivoire, mid-20th century. Cotton, warp ikat, cotton weft brocade. 80 in x 45 in

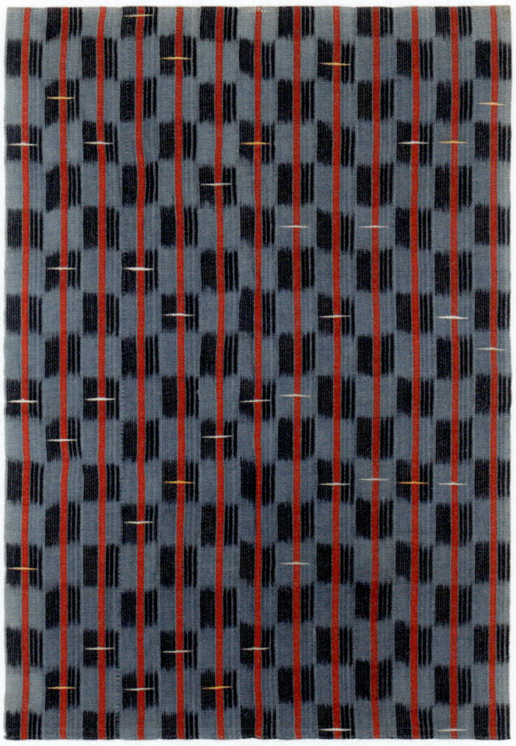

AF22 Dioula woman's strip-woven cloth
Cote d'Ivoire, mid-20th century. Cotton, warp ikat, cotton weft brocade. 64 in x 44 in

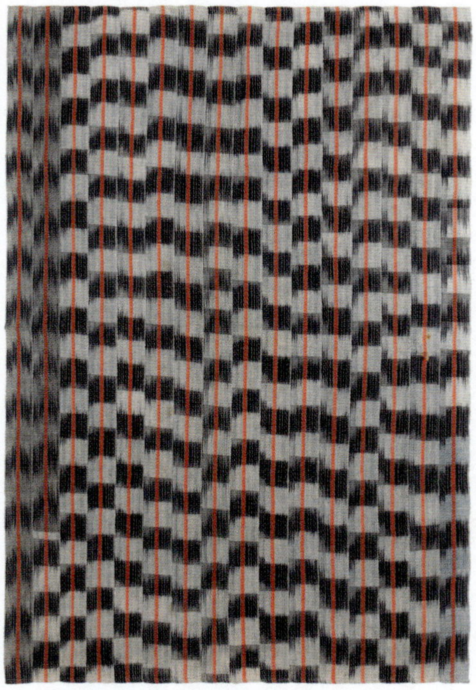

AF23 Dioula woman's strip-woven cloth
Cote d'Ivoire, mid-20th century. Cotton, warp ikat, cotton weft brocade. 72 in x 50 in

AF24 Dioula man's strip-woven cloth
Cote d'Ivoire, mid-20th century. Cotton, warp ikat, cotton weft brocade. 110 in x 76 in

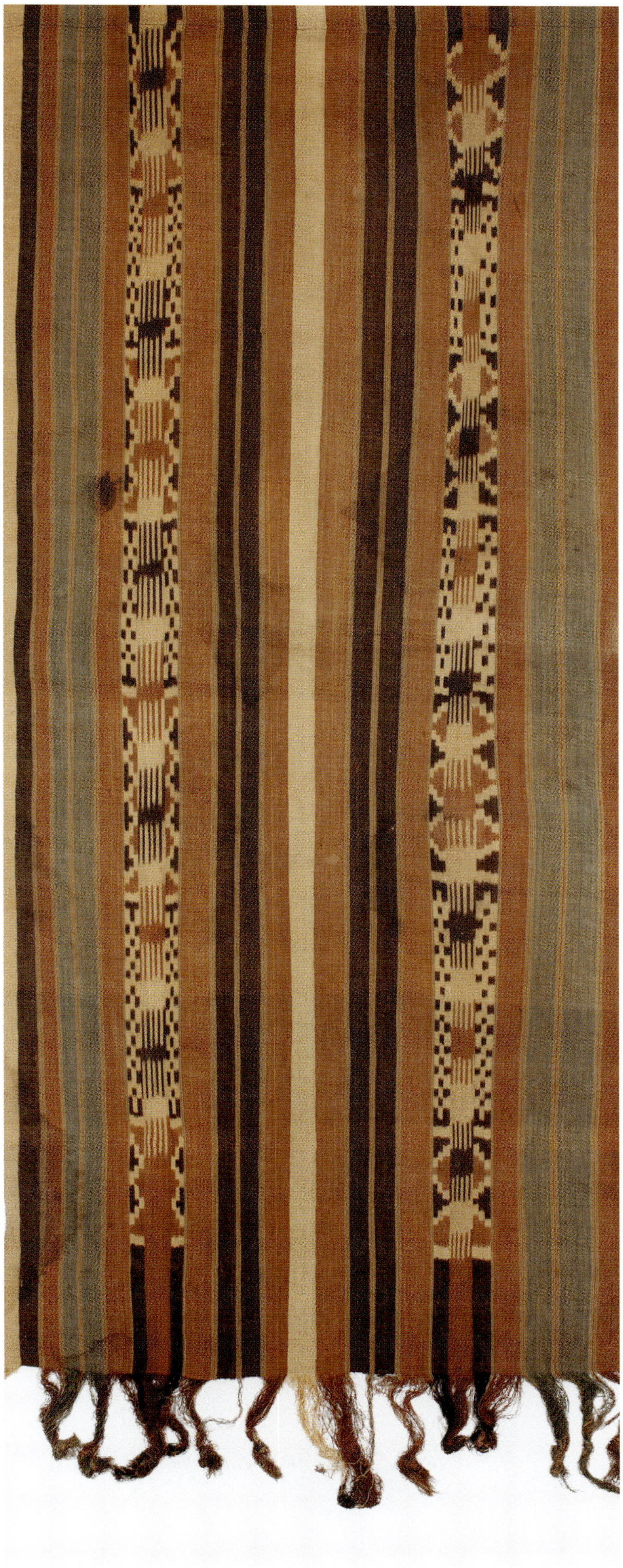

AF25 Sakalava room divider
Madagascar, 19th century. Raffia, warp ikat. 71 in x 24 in

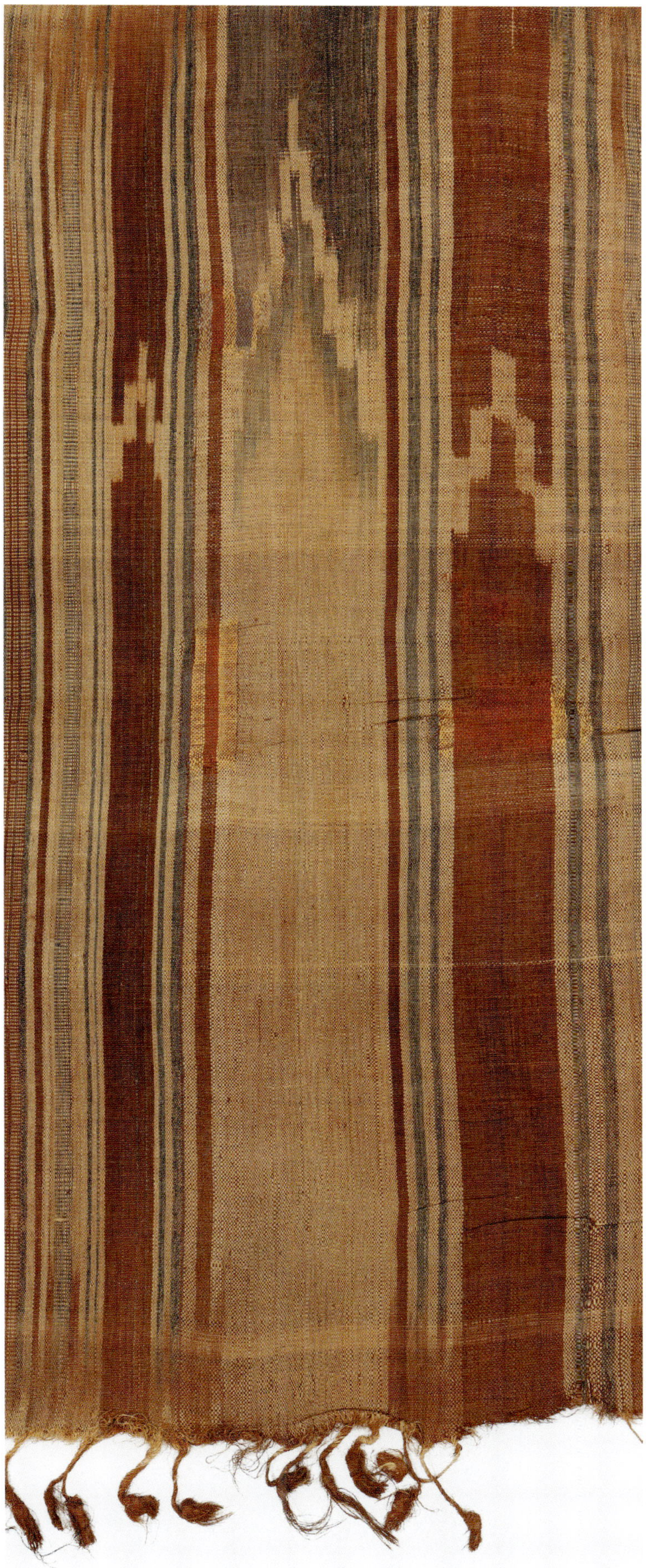

AF26 Sakalava prayer mat
Madagascar, 19th century. Raffia, warp ikat. 41 in x 26 in

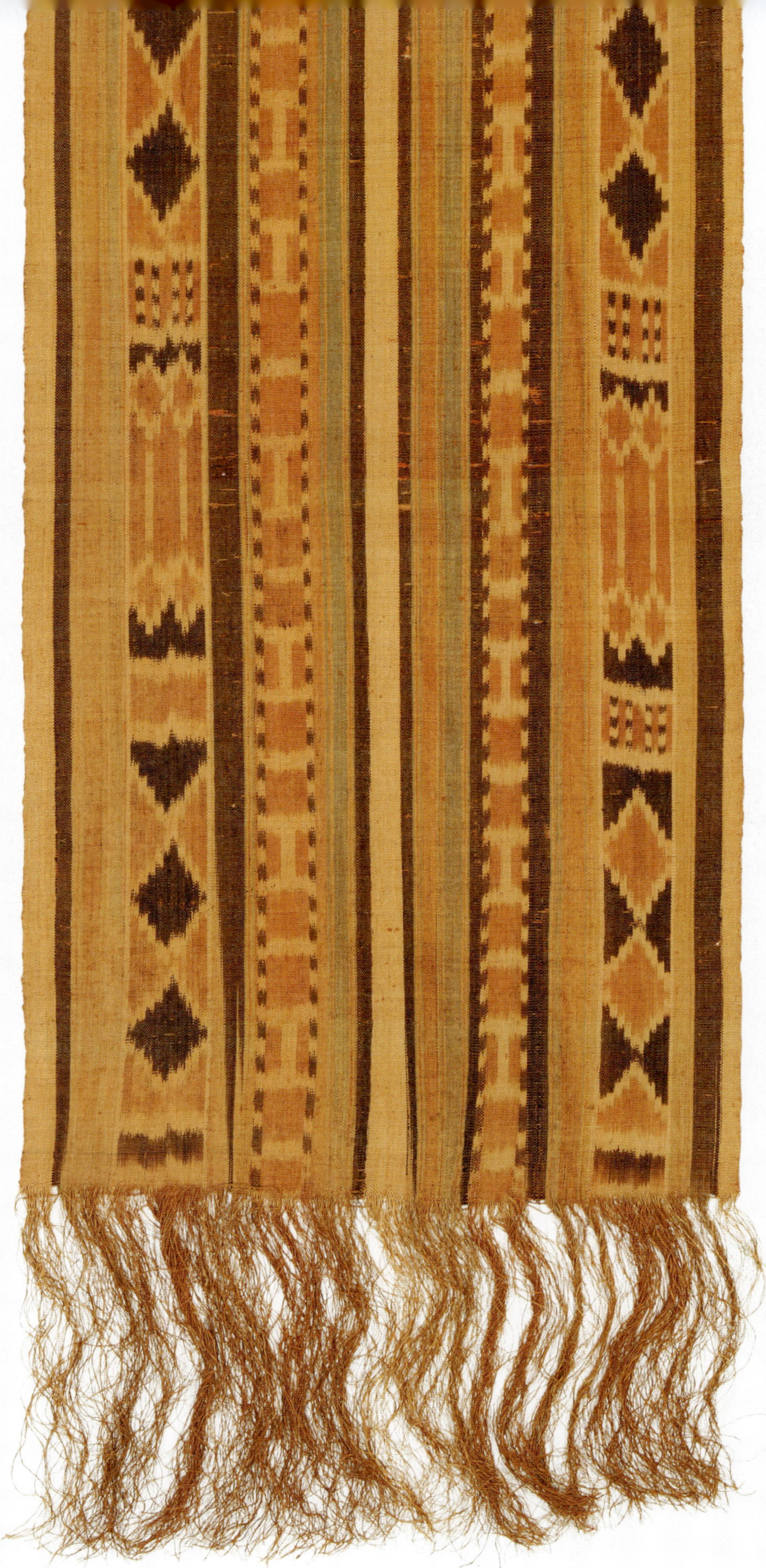

AF27 Tent panel (?), Sakalava people, Madagascar, ca. 1900. Natural-dyed raffia, warp-ikat patterning, primarily lozenge and triangle shapes, set within warp stripes. 71 in x 24 in

The primary use of these cloths, according to early 20th-century missionary accounts, was to form a small, tent-like structure composed of four panels, used on the day of a young woman's wedding.

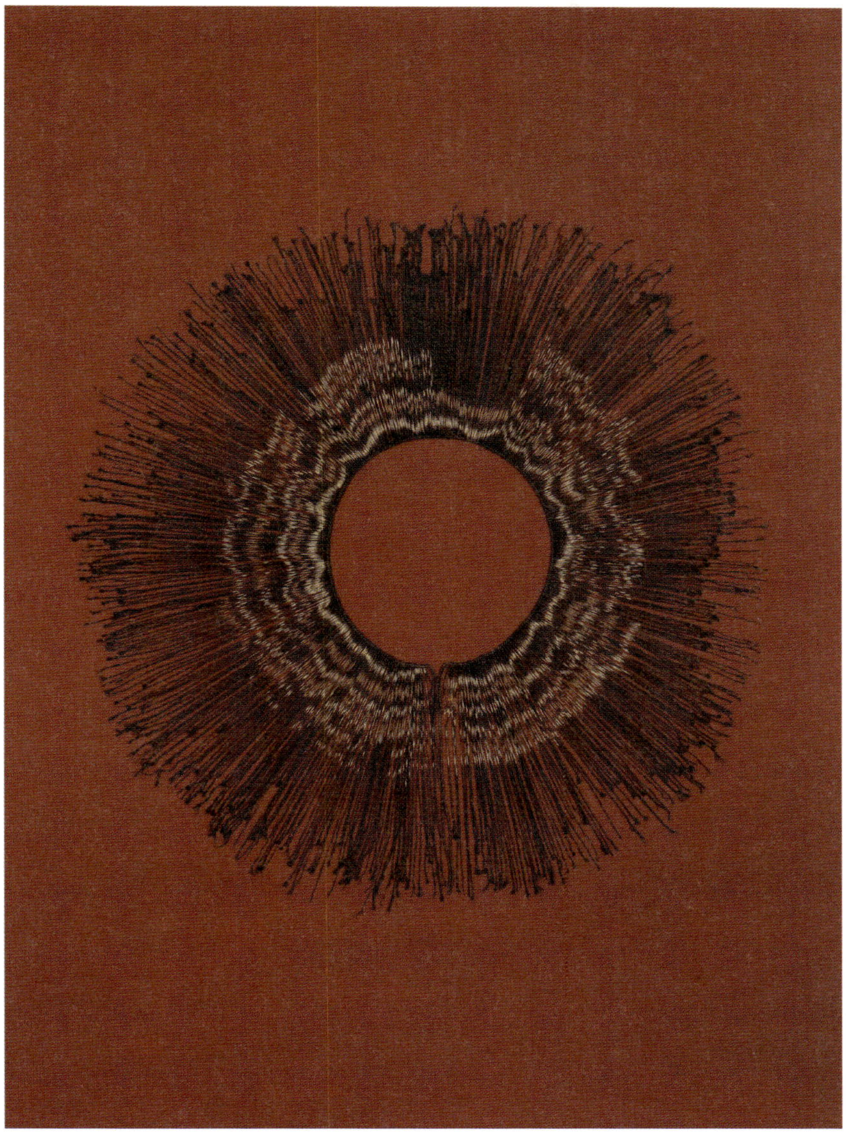

AF28 Ngala woman's skirt
Congo, 20th century. Raffia, proto-ikat. 28 x 27 in

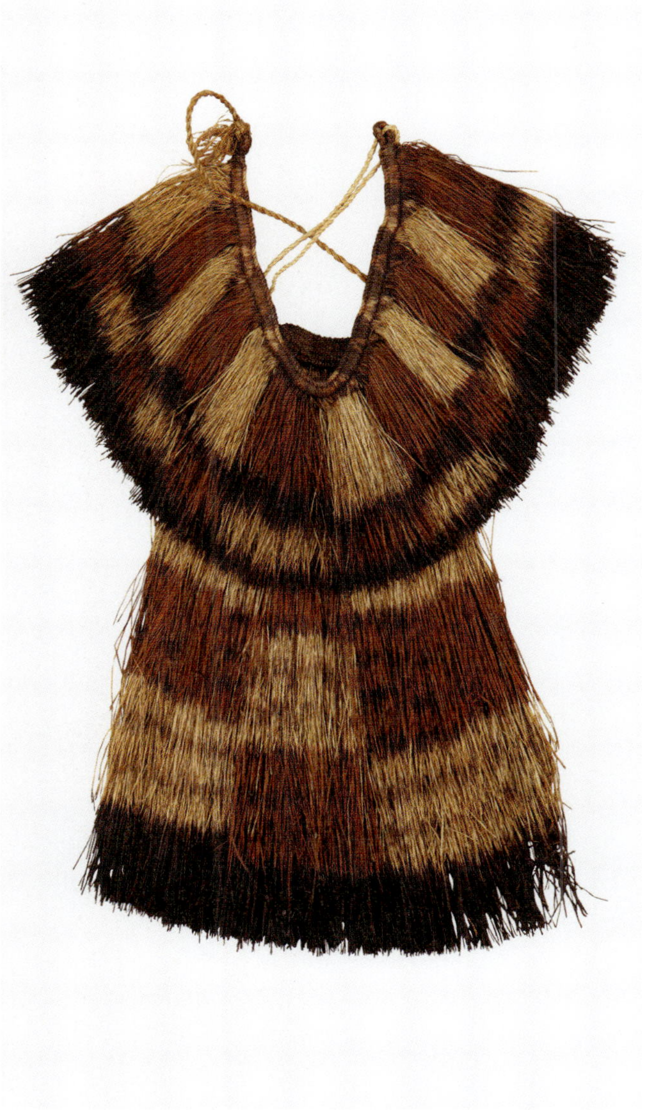

AF29 Mongo dance skirt
Congo, 20th century. Raffia, proto-ikat. 18 x 12 in

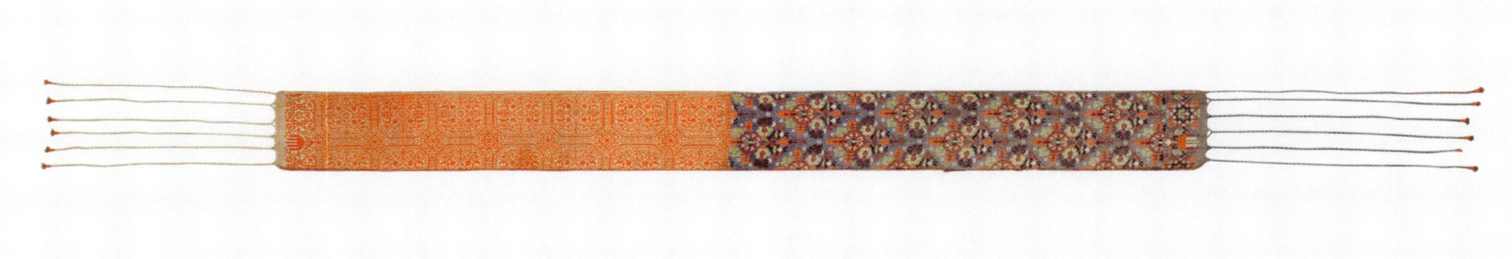

AF30 Woman's wedding belt
Fez, Morocco, late 19th century. Silk warp ikat, silk lampas weave, lined with silk, natural and synthetic dyes. 147 in x 8.5 in

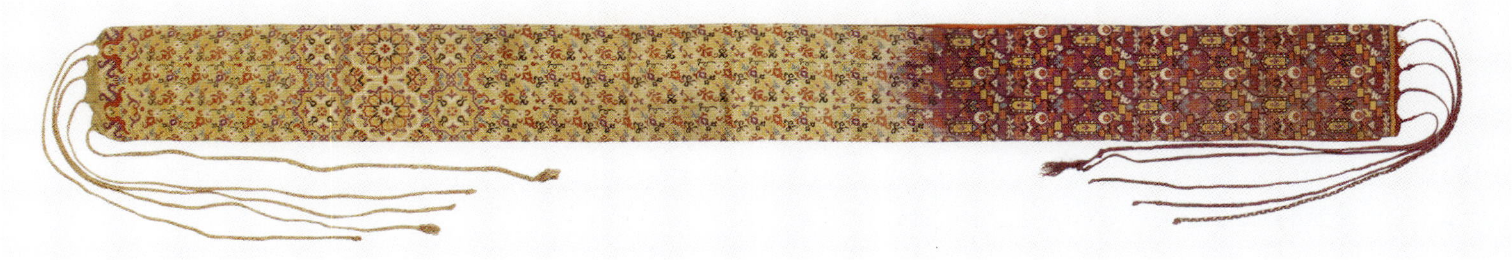

AF31 Woman's wedding belt
Fez, Morocco, late 19th century. Silk warp ikat, silk lampas weave, .ined with silk, natural and synthetic dyes. 120 in x 6 in, including fringes

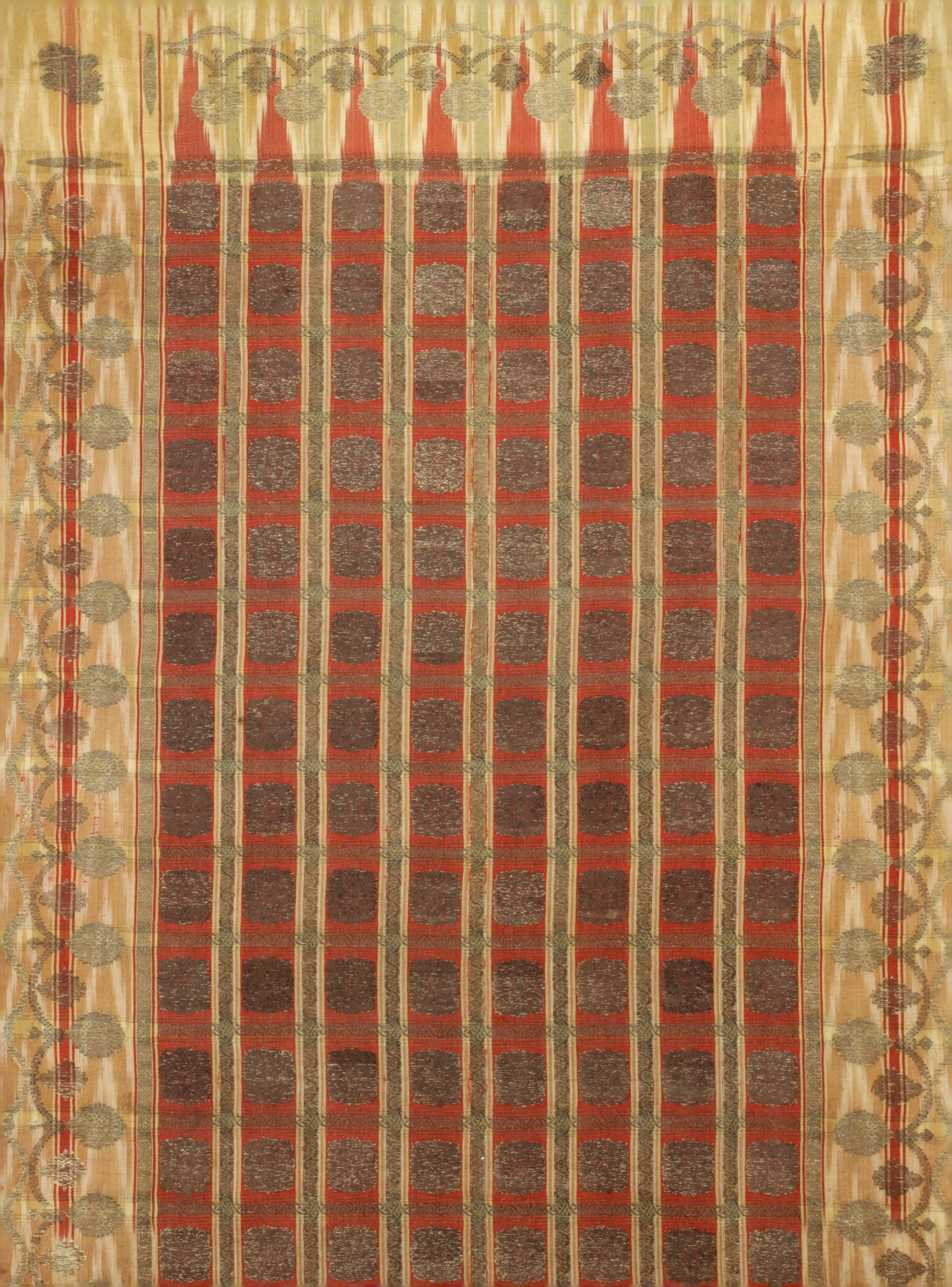

EUROPE

by Martina D'Amato

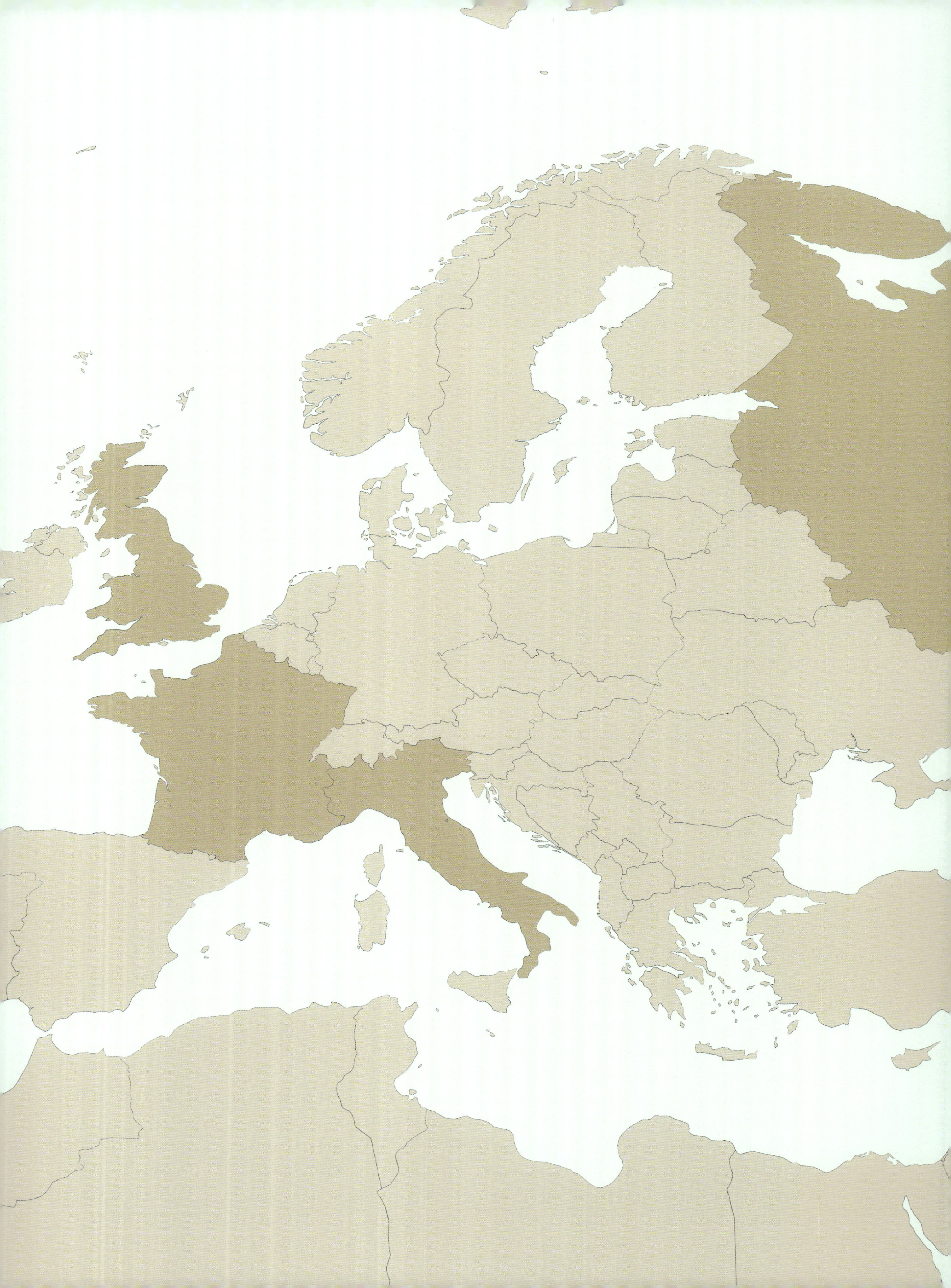

IKAT IN EUROPE

Between about 1650 and 1850, ikat production flourished throughout Europe. Inspired by silks arriving from Western Asia and using the same basic principle of dyeing warps and wefts before weaving, these textiles developed their own distinctive compositions, palettes, and techniques over the course of the 18th and early 19th centuries. The silk-weaving capital of Lyon was renowned for its *chiné à la branche*, which was favored by European nobility and the rising merchant class. Despite the immense popularity of ikat, however, technological advancements nearly wiped out its labor-intensive production by the mid-19th century. Today, the island of Mallorca is the only locale still manufacturing ikats using the traditional method.

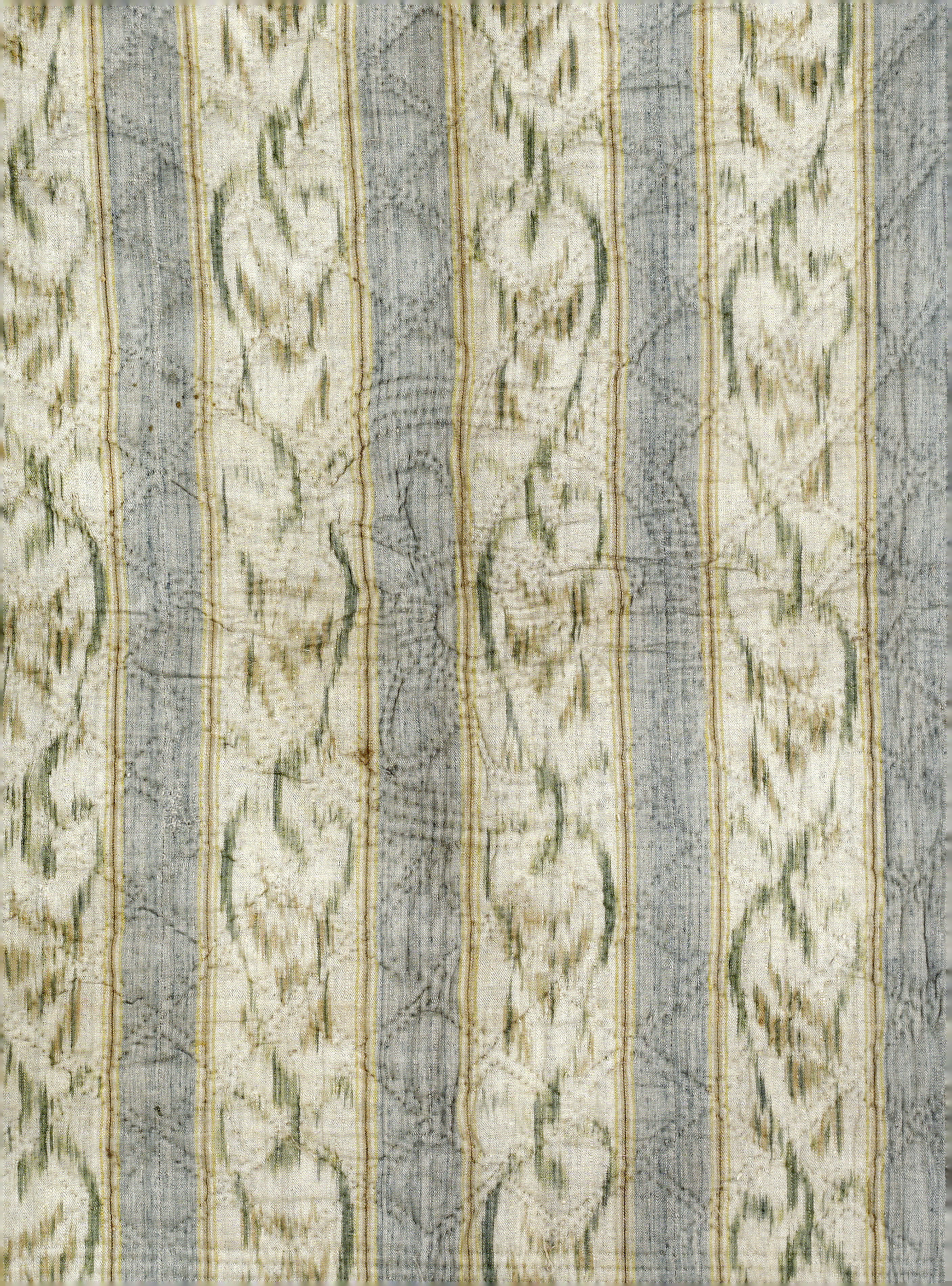

Fig.1
Detail of EU09, counterpane of *chiné à la branche* silk

A TALE OF CLOUDED SILK

Mrs. Brown: That clouded silk becomes you much
I wonder how you meet with such
But you've a charming taste in dress
What might it cost you, madam?

Mrs. Scot: Guess.

– Robert Lloyd, 1762[1]

Chinés, clouded silks, *a fiamma*, *flàmulas*, Pompadour taffetas, *siamoises flammées*, and *telas de lenguas*: Europeans have had a wide and distinctive vocabulary for the warp- and weft-dyed textiles, or ikats, produced across the continent beginning in the 17th century. Though it was certainly the result of Euro-Asian contact, precisely how and when ikat arrived in Europe remains a mystery. Some scholars have suggested, without evidence, a source in Arab-conquered southern Italy or Spain.[2] Others posit that the Dutch East India Company brought Indian *patola* to the West.[3]

Such ambiguities are also manifest in the linguistic influence. Since the early 19th century, *chiné à la branche*, the French term for warp-dyed textiles, has often been mistakenly associated with China, despite the lack of a Chinese ikat-weaving tradition.[4] The verb *chiner* was commonly mistranslated as "to make fabrics in the Chinese manner," with an emphasis on ikat's striping and mottling.[5] This was perhaps due to the indiscriminate use of "Chinese" to describe various Asian imports during the early modern period.[6] More likely, however, *chiné* derived from the French *chaîne* ("warp").[7]

While it remains to be seen whether an agreement will be reached regarding the origins of European ikat weaving or even its terminology, the David Paly Collection sheds vital new light on these understudied traditions. Examples in the collection illuminate the rich and extremely varied history of this technique as it made its way across Europe. European ikats use the same essential method of tying and dyeing before weaving as their Asian forebears, but they feature patterns and practices unique to their regions, from Lyonnais floral *taffetas chiné* to Moscow's brocaded *kanavat*. The following essay offers questions and hypotheses for

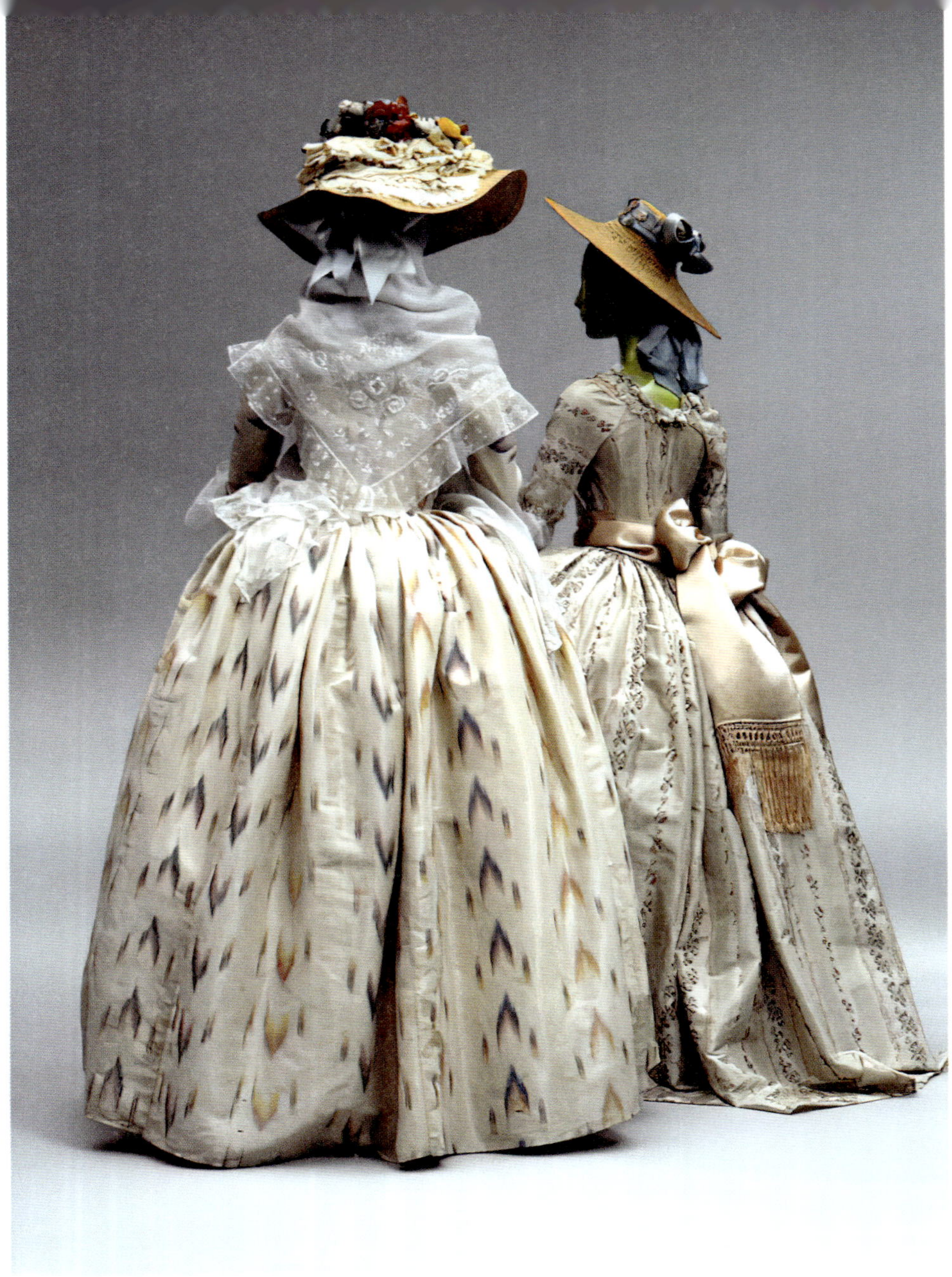

Fig.2

Fig.2
Robe à la Polonaise (left), Britain, ca. 1780. Plain-weave silk taffeta. Metropolitan Museum of Art, 1981.245.2, Gifts from Various Donors Fund, 1981

Fig.3
Detail of EU05, striped furnishing silk

Fig.4
Self-Portrait with his Wife, Giuseppe Baldrighi, 1757. Monumental Complex of the Pilotta, Parma

continued research into ikat's genesis and shortlived preeminence in Europe.

In 1765, Denis Diderot in the *Encyclopédie* and Antoine Nicolas Joubert de l'Hiberderie in *Le dessinateur* (The Textile Designer) offered early technical explanations of *chiné à la branche* as perfected at Lyon.[8] The *chineur* (specialized ikat weaver; "clouder" in English)[9] wound on a drum long warp lengths measured to correspond to the designer's ruled paper pattern. He then unwound, stretched, tied, and numbered the warps in clusters, or *branches*, for dyeing according to the design, tightly wrapping the *branches* with paper or parchment to create areas of resist. The *branches* were delivered to the *teinturier* ("dyer") for dyeing; they were unwrapped and dried, and finally reassembled on a loom for weaving.

Among the earliest dateable warp-dyed fabrics are striped examples produced in Italy and France in the 17th century.[10] The Paly Collection preserves three early, striped *imberlines* or linen-weft satins, all used for drapery and upholstery (EU02, Fig.3/EU05, EU08).[11] Likewise, striped *moquettes* (wool velvets) from Northern Europe covered walls and seating. The secondary pattern on this example (EU06), here embossed over the goat-hair pile using wooden rollers, in imitation of costly cut-silk velvets, is called *velours d'Utrecht*.[12] These textiles, called *a fiamma* for their flame-like motifs,[13] may have taken inspiration from Safavid brocades imported to cities like Venice (Fig.6).[14]

By the second quarter of the 18th century, Lyon was the undisputed capital of *chiné* weaving. The Richelieu collection of fabric samples, compiled in the 1730s and now at the Bibliothèque nationale de France, preserves dozens of *chiné* taffetas, satins, and velvets, many from Lyon and annotated with prices. Just one aune (0.65 meters) could cost 4–6 livres or 80–120 sous, nearly one week's wages for an unskilled laborer.[15] The prohibitive expense meant they were mostly reserved for elites and the merchant class. For the next seventy years, the most luxurious Lyonnais *chinés* were favored by a succession of French royals, from Marie Leszczyńska[16] and Madame de Pompadour

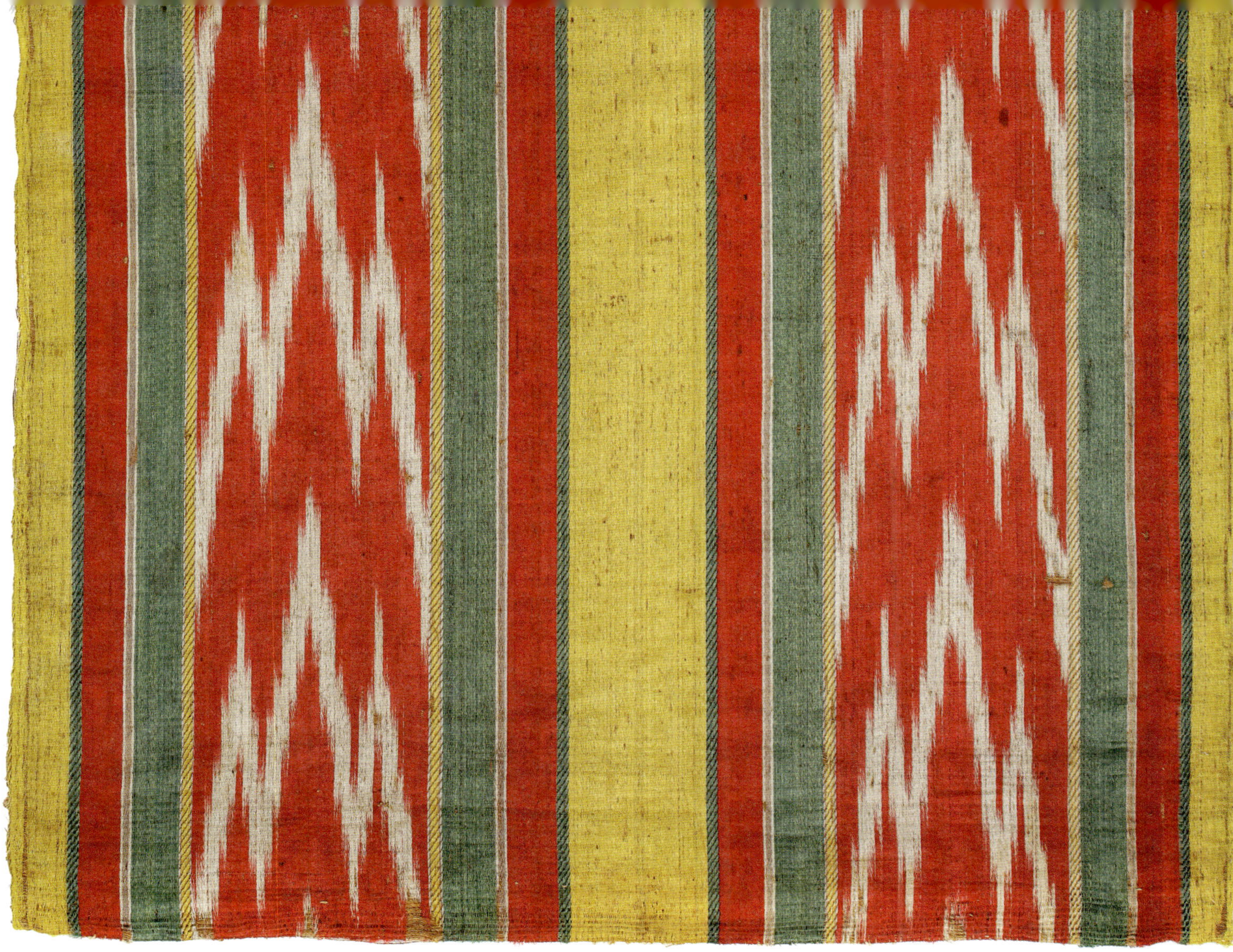

Fig.3

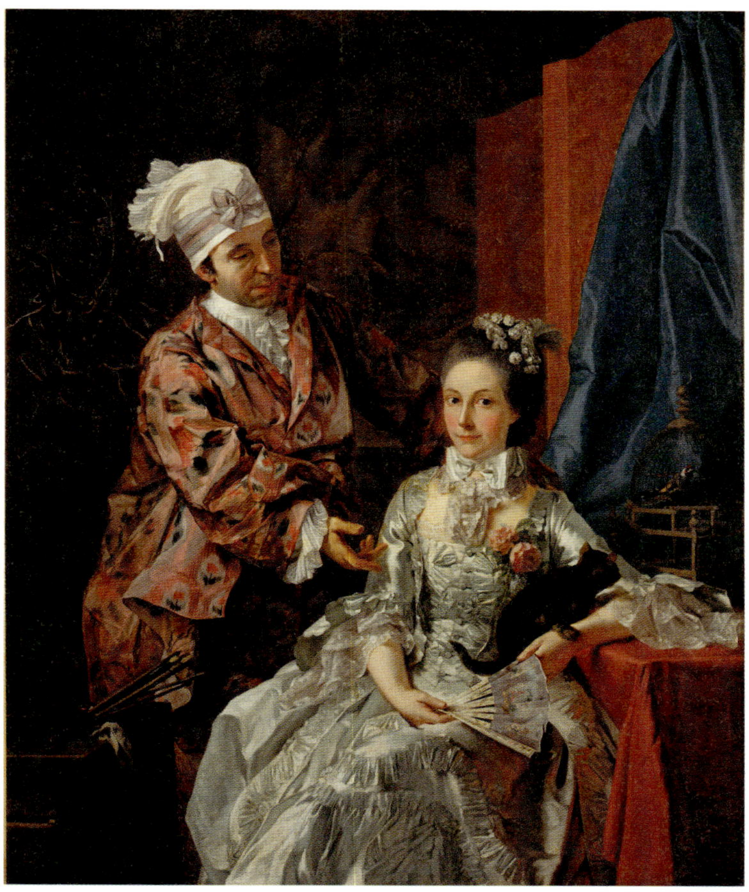

Photo: Scala, Florence – courtesy of the Ministero Beni e Att. Culturali e del Turismo

Fig.4

to Marie Antoinette and Napoleon I.[17] The virtuosity that caught the eye of both Louis XV's queen and mistress is on display in two plain-weave taffetas in characteristically muted pastels with dynamic S-curves of roses and tulips in the Paly Collection (EU03 and Fig.7/EU04). These compositions of so-called "meandering" flowers[18] are typical of mid- to late-18th-century silks for dress and, more rarely, furnishing.[19]

Lyon may have been the most renowned center for *chiné à la branche*, but it was not the only one. Established industries for English "clouded lustrings"[20] and Spanish *flàmulas* also existed by the mid-18th century (Fig.2).[21] A vibrant, meandering floral satin in the Paly Collection, probably also for dress, attests to the technical skills of silk weavers in Lyon's rival textile hubs of Venice and Genoa (EU07). Gesturing to his wife to present her to the viewer in his 1757 double self-portrait, painter Giuseppe Baldrighi instead eclipses her in his *banyan* (dressing gown) of warp-dyed puce silk and a jaunty undress cap (Fig.4).

Elsewhere in France, one might acquire silk *bourettes* or *siamoises flammées*. Members of the working class eager to emulate might have obtained *bourettes*, blended silks made from the waste produced during silk spinning and used for

Fig.5

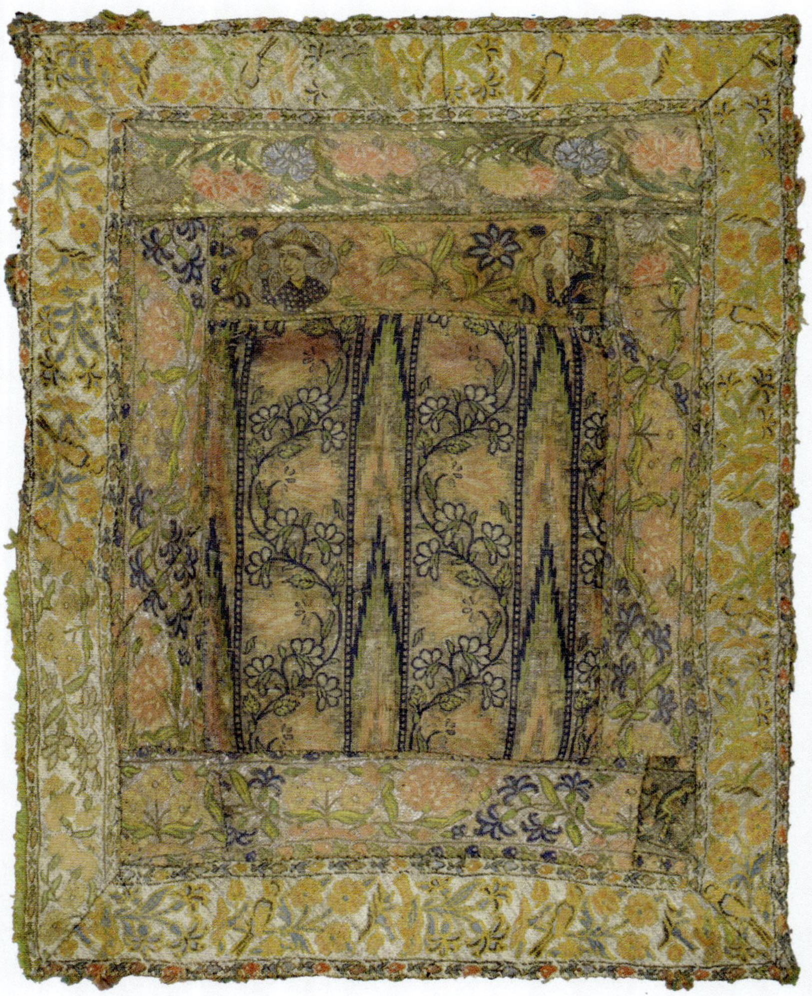

Fig.6

Fig.5
Detail of EU10, counterpane or valance of *siamoise flambée*

Fig.6
Silk mat, Iran, 17th–18th century. Silk brocade with gold- and silver-wrapped thread. Victoria and Albert Museum, T.122-1928

Fig.7
Detail of EU04, *chiné à la branche* silk

Fig.8
Robe à la Française, France, 1760–70. Silk. Metropolitan Museum of Art, C.I.60.40.2a, b, Purchase, Irene Lewisohn Bequest, 1960

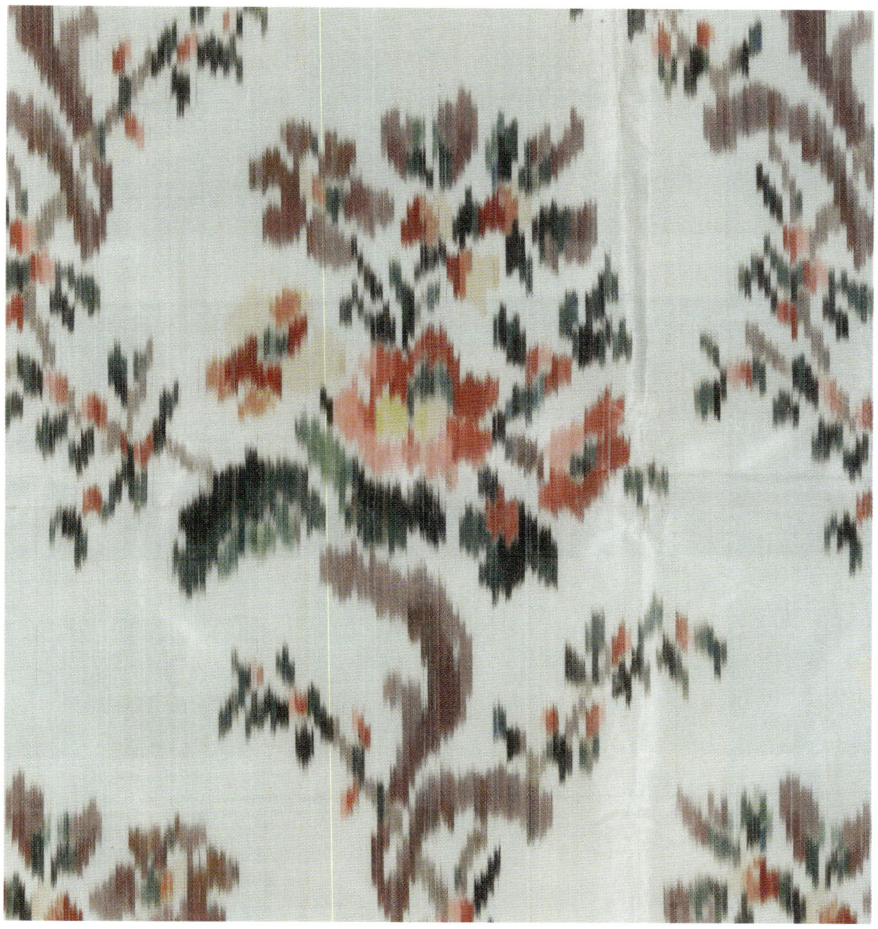

Fig.7

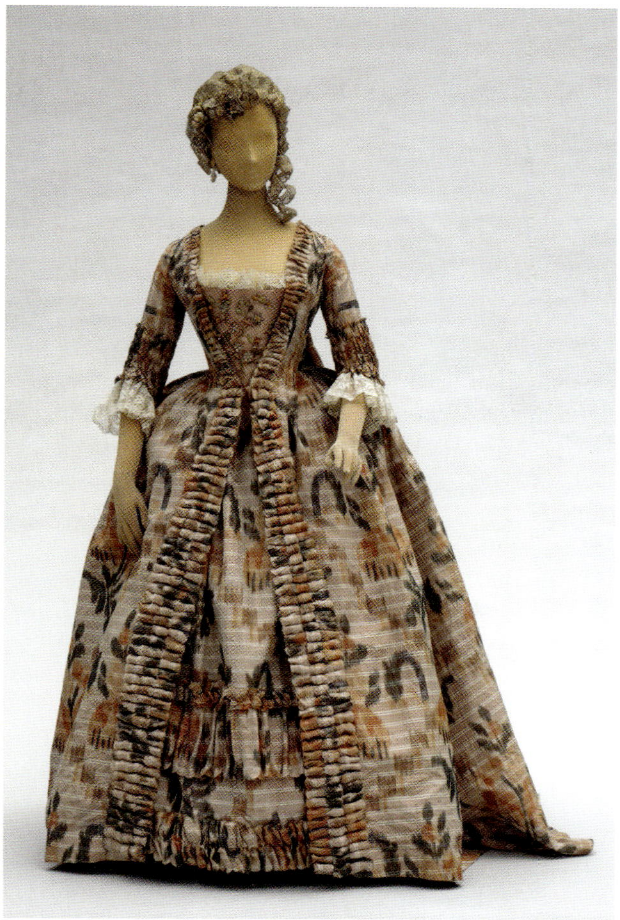

Fig.8

both dress and furnishing. Warp-dyed *bourettes* are recorded as early as the 1730s at a cost of 30 sous per aune, just one-fourth the price of other *chinés*.[22] A 1770s quilted counterpane in the Paly Collection demonstrates the use and reuse, with piecing throughout, of these *bourettes* (Fig.1/EU09).

Northern and western France—particularly Rouen—was known for its *siamoise flammées* or *flambées*, indigo "flamed" ikats of linen and cotton with resist-dyed warps or, more often, wefts.[23] The 1684 and 1686 Siamese Embassies had launched a vogue for *siamoises*, mixed silks, wools, and cottons said to imitate textiles brought by Thai diplomats.[24] Diderot illustrated the weaving of "fiamoife chiné" with a yellow ground and white-and-blue bands, remarkably similar to the Rouennais counterpane in the Paly Collection (Fig.5/EU10).[25] In the wake of the Revolution, *siamoise flammée*, once a favorite of the wealthy elite, was marketed as *toile de Charentes* and *flammé Charentais* to appeal to the wider French public (EU11 and EU12).[26] Mallorcan blue-and-white warp-dyed *telas de lenguas*, so called for the design of flames licking like a tongue, are the only analogous production to these French blue-and-white textiles. It is possible that weavers fleeing France brought *flammés* to Spain.[27]

In the 18th century, a unique silk-weaving tradition developed in western Russia. Worn draped over the head and cascading down the back, the bridal veil known as a *kanavat* blends East and West in its combination of warp dyeing and baroque-style metallic brocade. Rarely can we attribute ikats to known makers but, from the 1780s, the silk mills of Guri Levin and his family near Kolomna, Moscow were famous for their *kanavat*, which were exhibited at industrial expositions and often bear signatures (EU01).[28] Although the patterning is thought to relate to Persian silks (Fig.5),[29] the overall design and color palette much more closely resemble ikats from Ottoman Syria.[30]

The closure of the Levin mills in the mid-19th century coincided with the general disappearance of warp- and weft-dyed textile production in Europe. Despite the popularity of ikat, technological advancements in weaving and printing rendered the laborious resist-dyeing process nearly extinct, save for Scandinavia and Iberia and, by the 1840s, cheaper and easier warp-printing (*imprimer sur chaîne*) all but replaced it.[31] Today, the only remaining weavers of true ikat are on the island of Mallorca, where the tradition of *telas de lenguas* continues, offering a mere glimpse into the last four centuries of European ikat artistry and handwork.

CATALOG

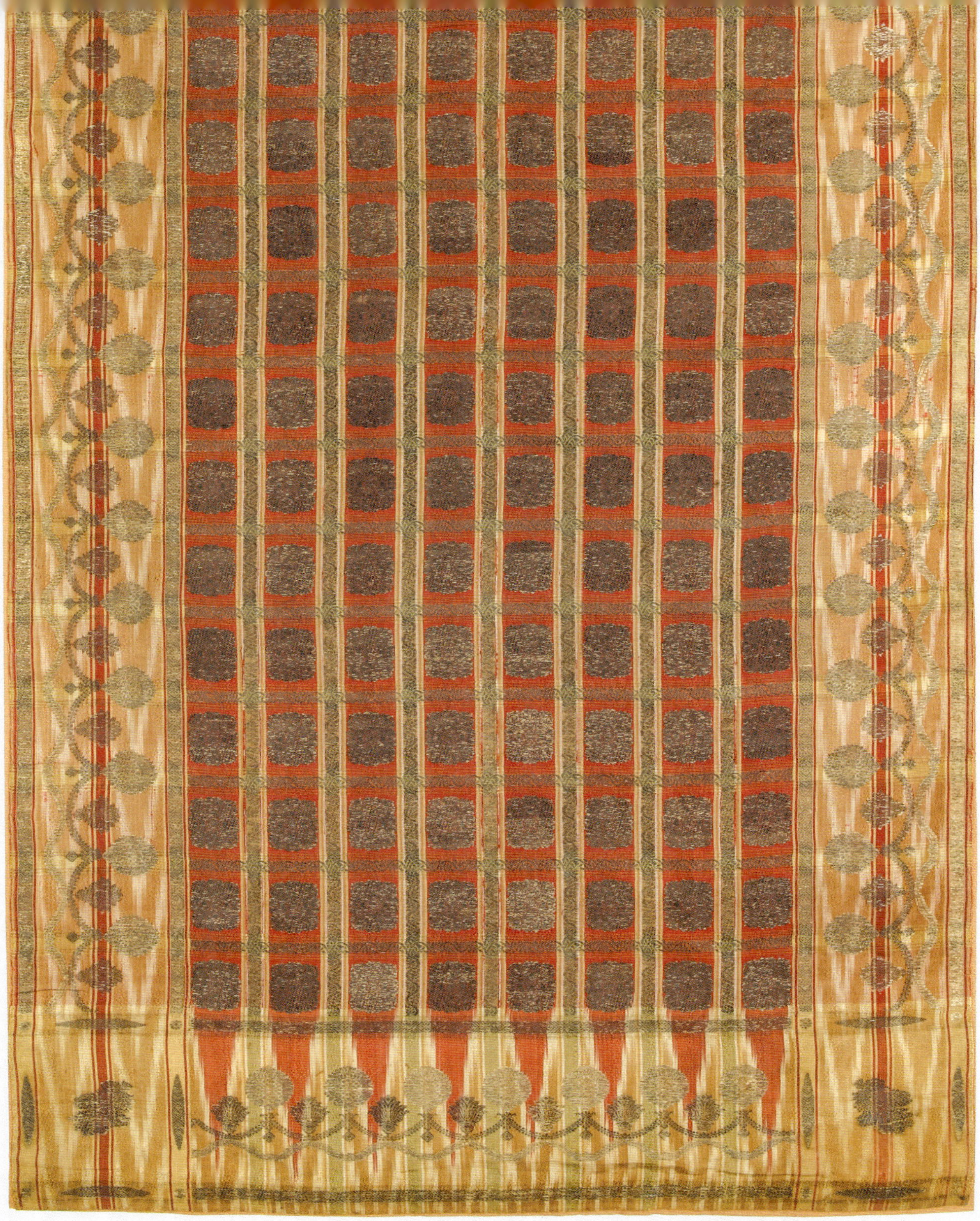

EU01 *Kanavat* bridal veil, the Levin mills, Kolomna, Moscow, Russia, late 18th–early 19th century. Silk warp and cotton weft with metallic-wrapped supplementary weft brocade. 84 in x 48 in

In the early 18th century, the Russian silk-weaving industry found a home in the town of Kolomna outside of Moscow. By the 1780s, the merchant and silk mill owner Guri Levin was well-known for his bridal veils or *kanavat* combining ikat and metallic weft brocade. The term *kanavat* refers to warp-dyed silk shawls worn as veils over traditional hats or *kokoshniks*. While the patterning on *kanavat* is believed to have been influenced by Persian silks imported into Russia, the overall design and palette bear stronger connections to the ikats of Ottoman Syria. The Gurin family's mills continued to produce *kanavat* until the mid-19th century.

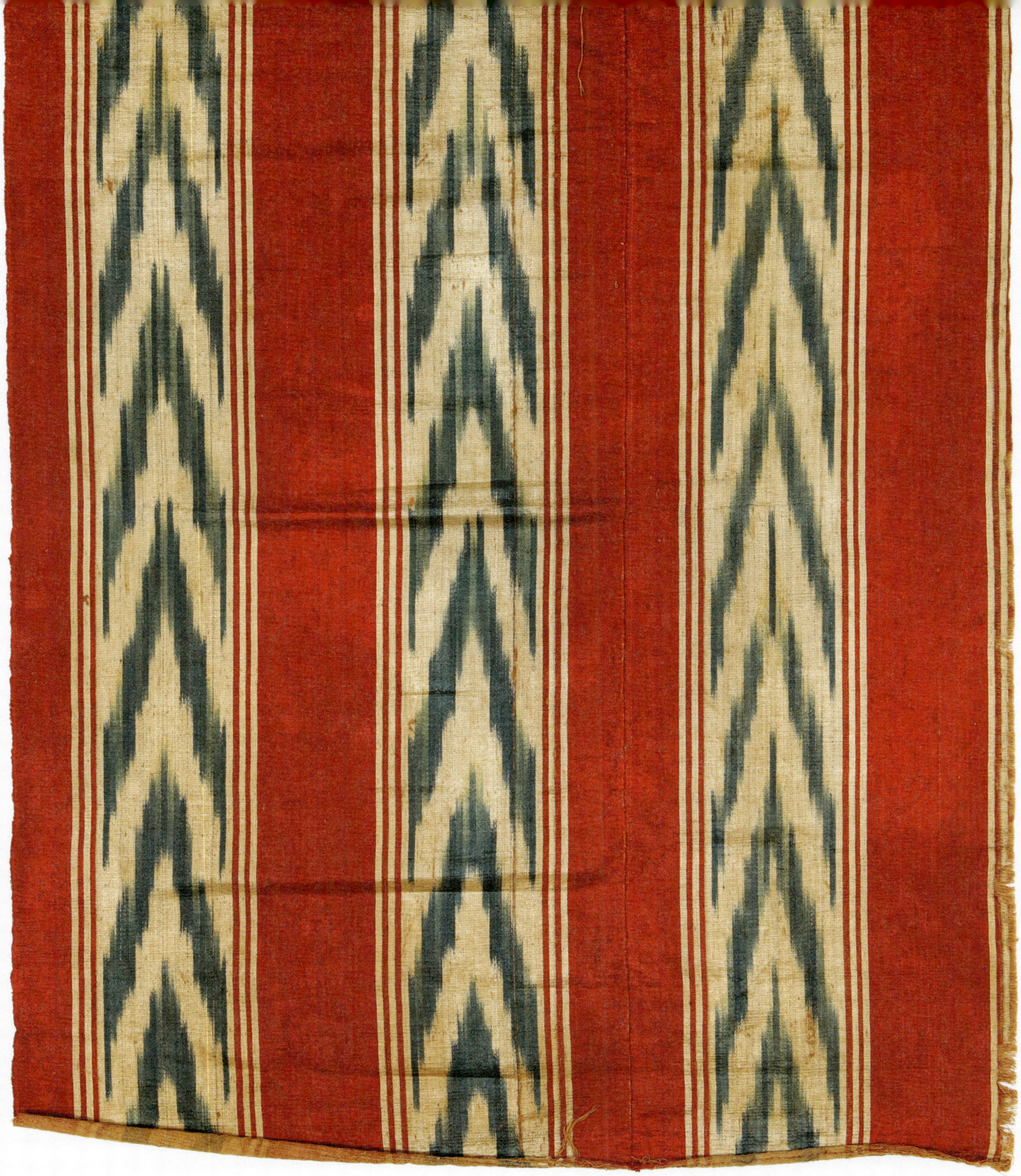

EU02 Striped furnishing silk *imberline*, Florence (?), Italy, second half 17th century. Warp-faced satin weave with silk warp and linen weft. 16 in x 15 in

Warp-dyed silks produced in 17th-century Italy and France, such as this striped linen-weft silk *imberline* in red, white and blue, are possibly the oldest ikats produced in Europe. Typically used for drapery and upholstery, these silks rarely survive as more than fragmentary lengths today. Striped furnishing ikats were sometimes called *a fiamma* in reference to their flame-like motifs. This *imberline* may have been woven in Florence, where silk weaving had flourished since the Middle Ages. The design may be indebted to Safavid brocades entering Europe through trading centers like Venice, which had seen exquisite textiles from China and the Safavid and Ottoman empires pass through its port for centuries.

EU03 *Chiné à la branche* silk
Lyon, France, ca. 1755–65. Plain-weave taffeta with silk warp and weft. 14 in x 24 in

EU04 *Chiné à la branche* silk
Lyon (?), France, ca. 1760–65. Plain-weave taffeta with silk warp and weft. 14 in x 24 in

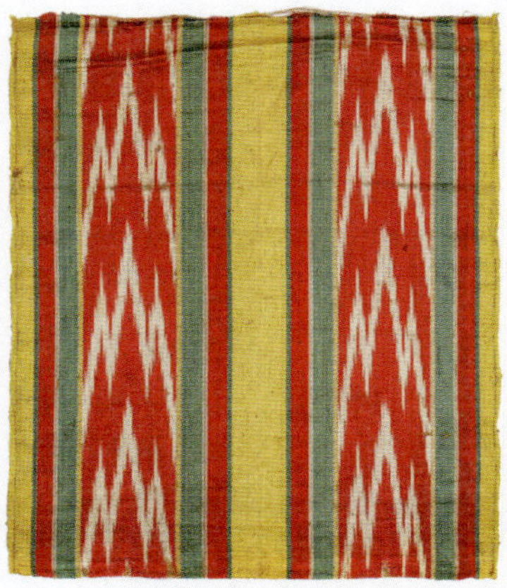

EU05 Striped furnishing silk
Italy or France, early 18th century. Warp-faced satin weave with silk warp and linen weft. 14 in x 12 in

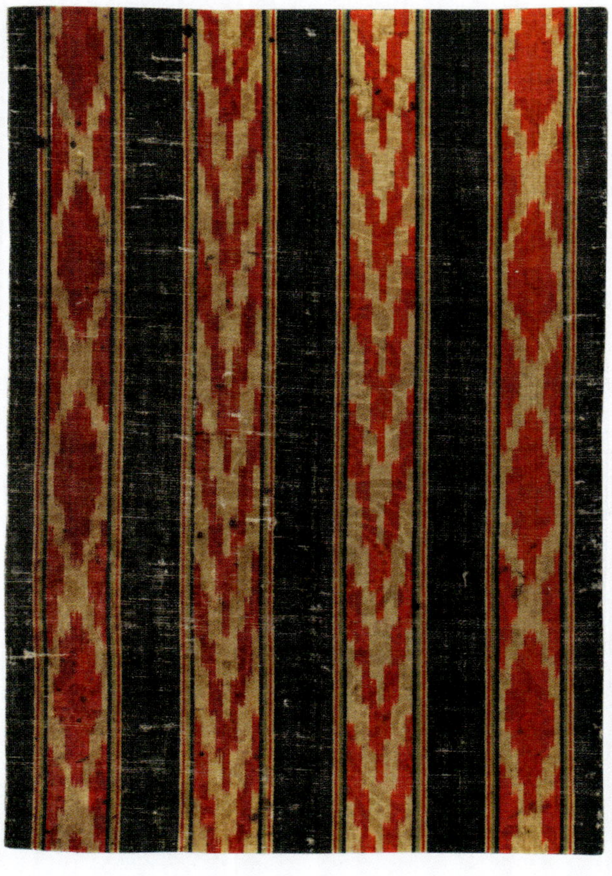

EU06 *Velours d'Utrecht*
Lille (?), France, second half 17th century. Linen warp and wool weft with wool pile, embossed. 28 in x 20 in

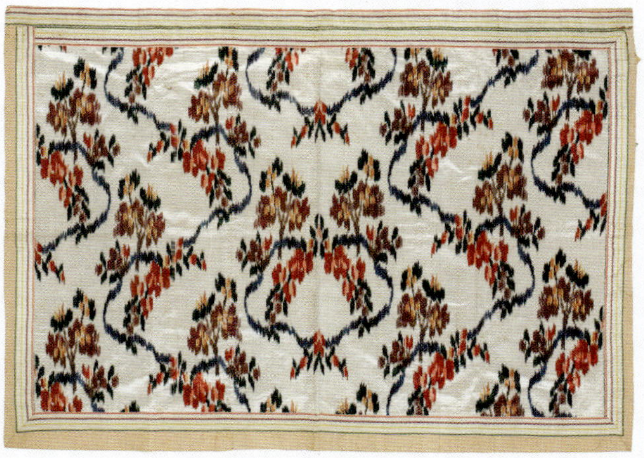

EU07 *Chiné à la branche* silk
Genoa (?), probably Italy, ca. 1755–70. Warp-faced satin weave with silk warp and weft. 32 in x 44 in

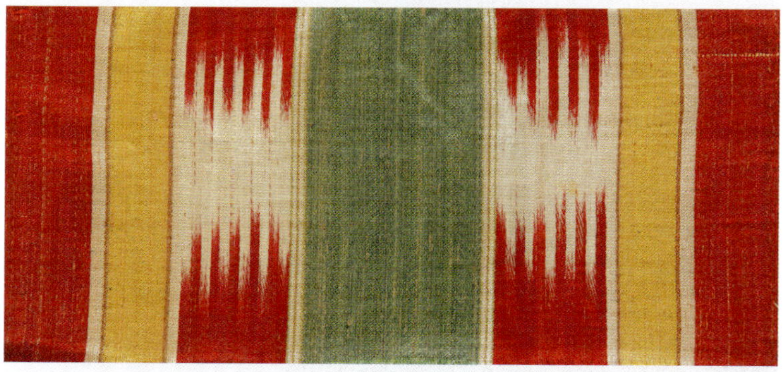

EU08 Striped furnishing silk
Florence (?), Italy, late 17th–early 18th century. Warp-faced satin weave with silk warp and linen weft. 6 in x 9 ir

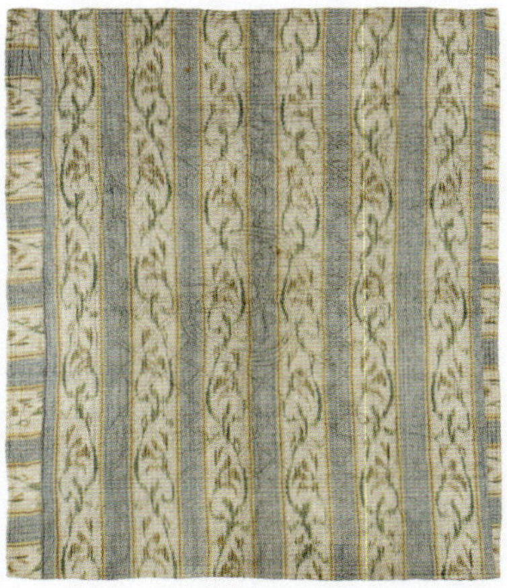

EU09 Counterpane of *chiné à la branche silk*
France, ca. 1770–85. Twilled bourette with silk warp and linen or cotton weft, quilted. 70 in x 80 in

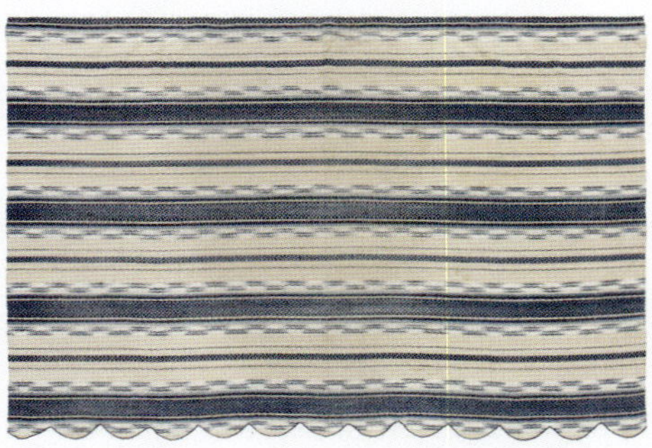

EU10 Counterpane or valance of *siamoise flambée*
Probably Rouen, Normandy, France, second half 18th century. Linen warp and cotton weft. 56 in x 90 in

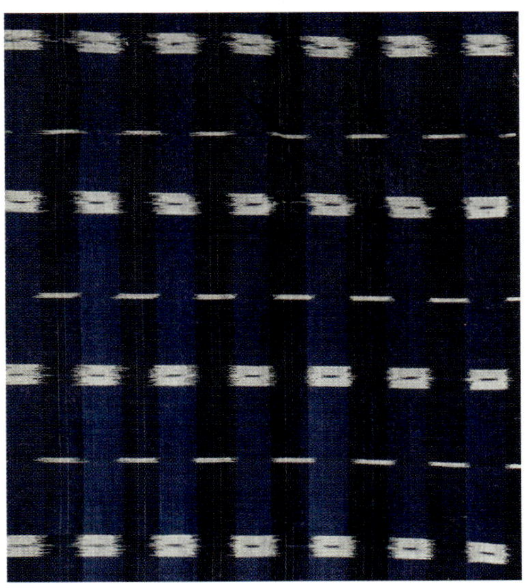

EU11 *Curtain of toile de Charentes*
France, first half 19th century. Cotton warp and weft. 12 in x 58 in

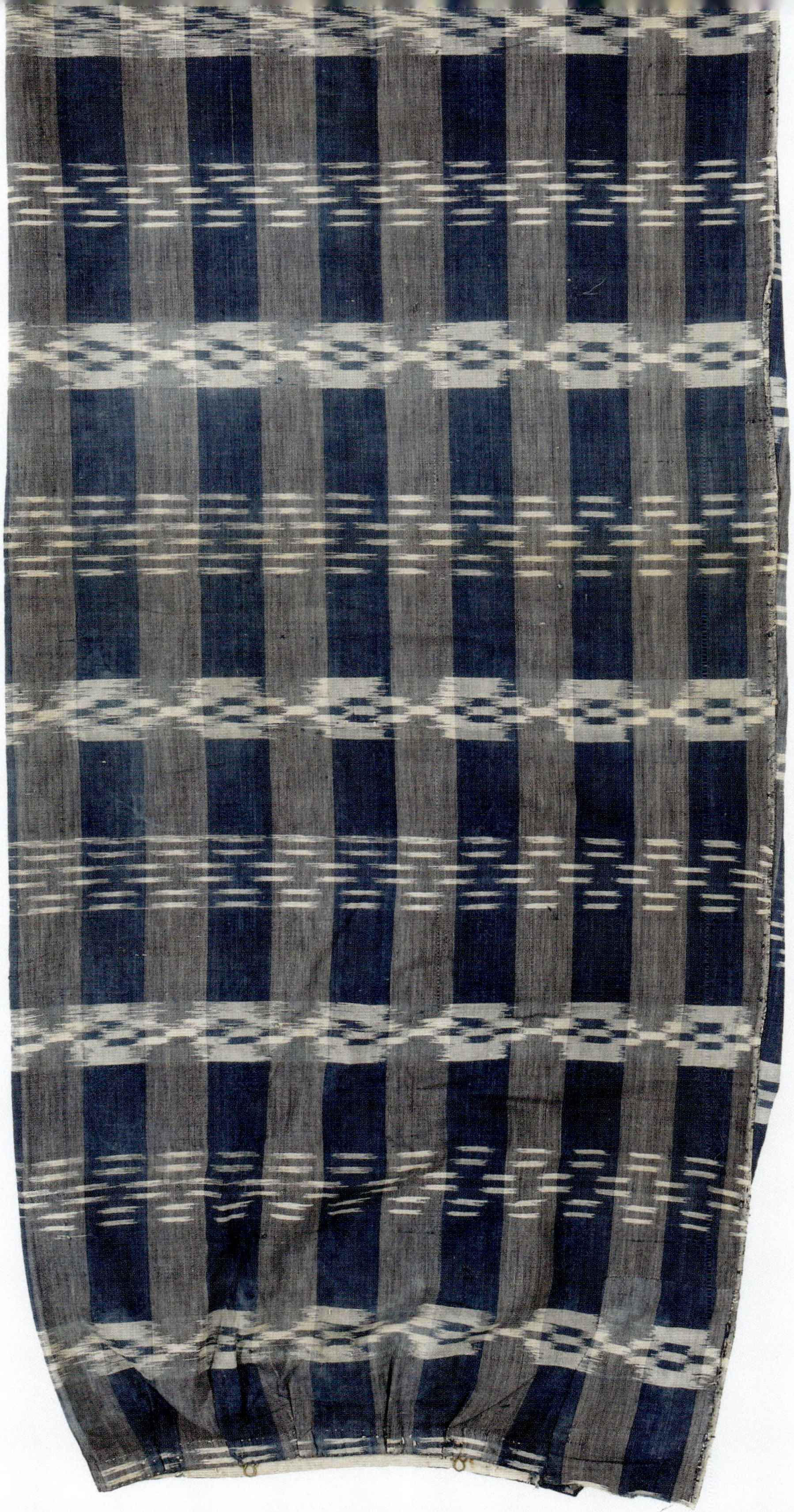

EU12 Bed curtain of *siamoise flambée*, France, late 18th–early 19th century. Linen warp and cotton weft. 12 in x 52 in

Siamoises flammées or *flambées* are "flamed" ikats with resist-dyed warps or wefts made in northern and western France in the 18th and 19th centuries. The Siamese Embassies of 1684 and 1686 had launched a fashion for so-called *siamoises*, mixed silks, wools, and cottons said to imitate the striped cloths brought by the Thai ambassadors. *Siamoises* of linen and cotton, like this complete bedcurtain, were especially popular in the homes of wealthy elites in the provinces. Following the French Revolution, *siamoises*' association with the French nobility led to their rebranding as *toiles de Charentes* and *flammé Charentais* to appeal to the wider populace.

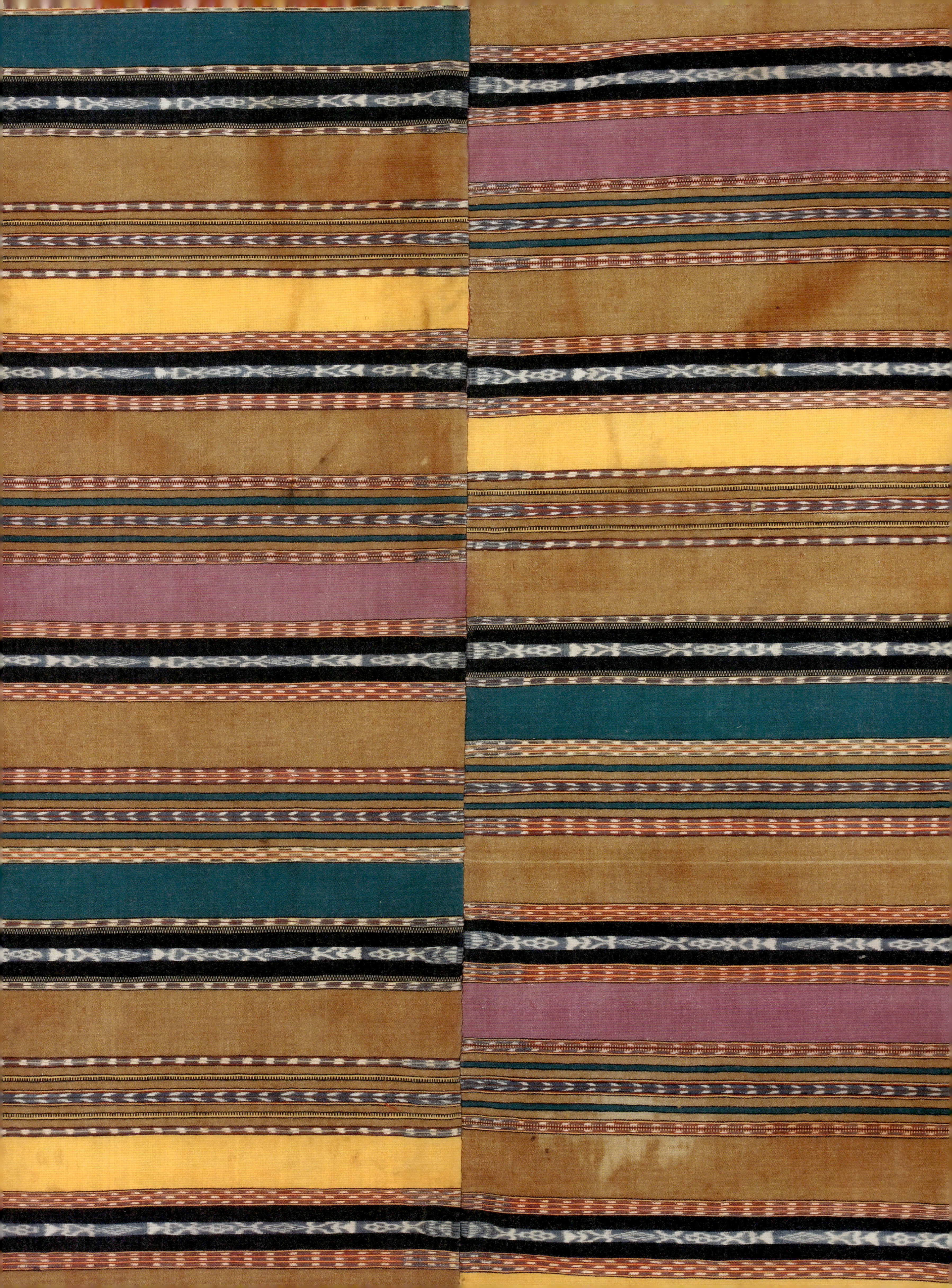

AMERICAS

by Shelley Burian

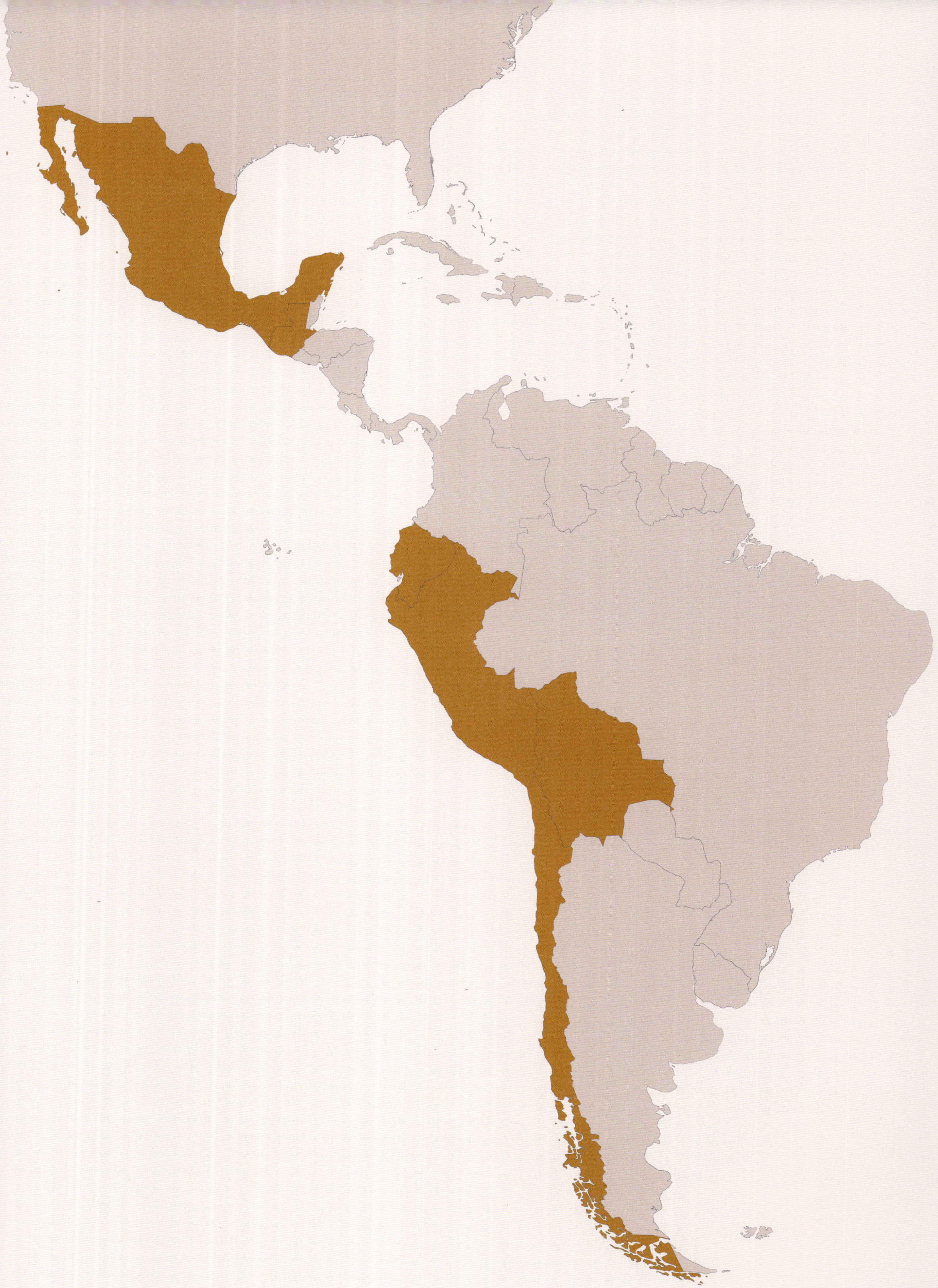

IKAT IN THE AMERICAS

Bound-resist dye techniques were rare among the range of dyeing techniques used in the pre-Hispanic period. After the introduction of textile techniques from other parts of the world through Spanish colonization, variations on the technique were adopted into local repertoires, notably in Guatemala, Chile, Argentina, Mexico, Ecuador, Peru, and Bolivia. In most of these countries, its use was generally limited to certain types of garments and declined after the beginning of the 20th century. In contrast, bound resist has been used across the range of garments worn in Mayan communities in Guatemala and its use has continued to expand.

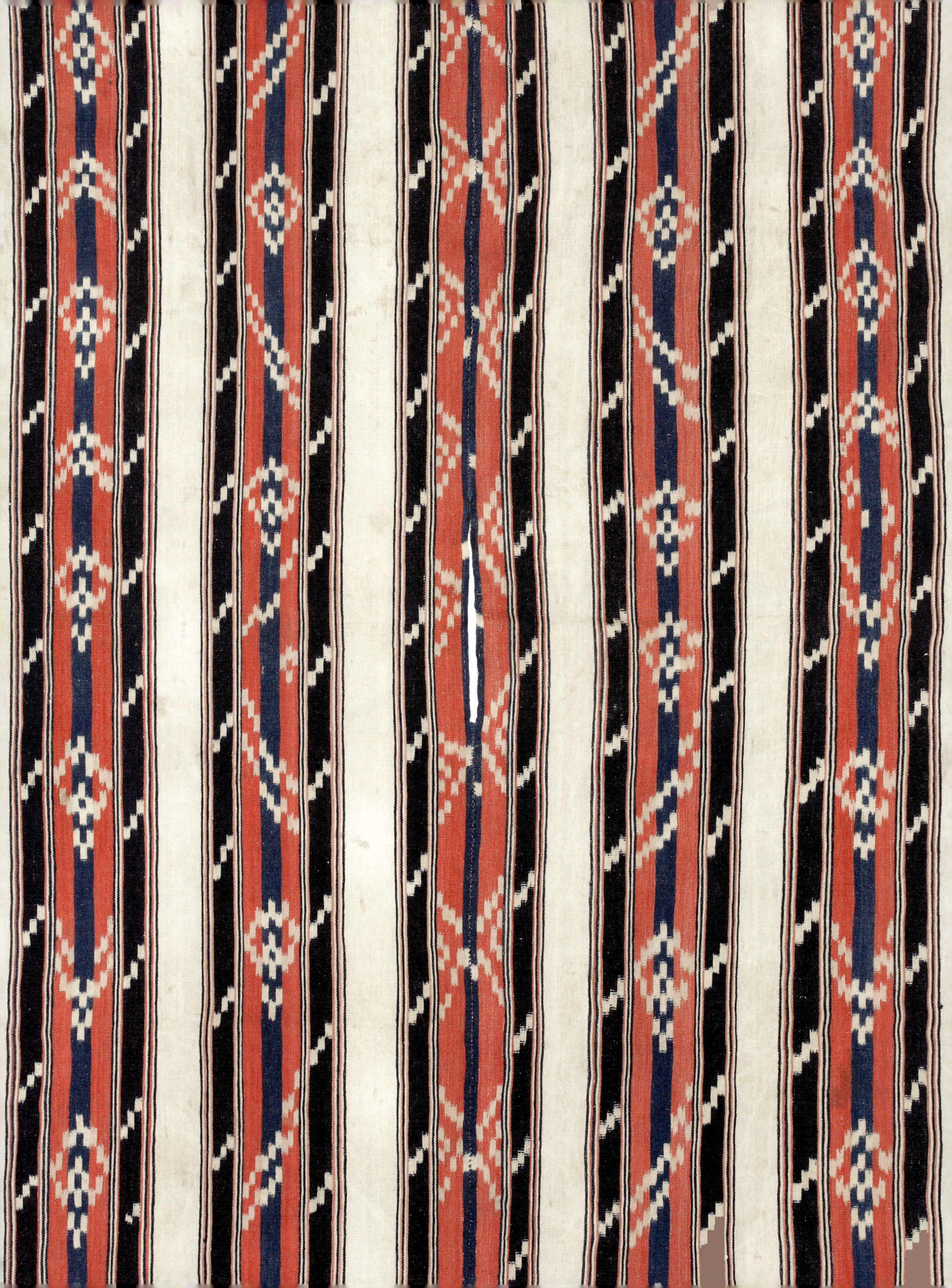

Fig.1
Detail of AM45, poncho

SHROUDED IN MIST

The earliest evidence for bound-resist techniques in Latin America is from pre-Hispanic coastal Peru. Different forms may also have been practiced in pre-Hispanic Mexican and Mayan cultures, but the techniques developed in Mexico during the 18th century and Guatemala at the end of the 19th century are generally thought to be the result of European and Asian influence and trade. The techniques from pre-Hispanic Peru and Ecuador have no recognizable connection with those that appeared in different parts of the Andes beginning in the 19th century. In comparison with other regions in which bound-resist techniques are practiced, those in the Andes are generally used to create relatively straightforward geometric designs. In Mexico, bound-resist dyeing techniques are comparable to the variations used in the Andes, although generally associated with a single garment, the *rebozo*. In Guatemala, bound resist is more common than in other regions in Latin America, used in the compositions of a wide range of garments with a more diverse range of technical and design variations.

Andes: Ecuador, Peru, Bolivia, and Chile

Textiles made with the bound-warp-resist technique in pre-Hispanic Peru can be divided into two groups differentiated by material and geographic/cultural origin. The first and significantly larger group is characterized by the exclusive use of cotton, and by its coastal origin. Examples have been found at different north-coast sites: Barranca in Pacasmayo Valley, Huaca de la Cruz in Virú Valley, and Cao Viejo in Chicama.[1] Some were also found at the site of Pachacámac on the central coast and may have been sent from the north coast as tribute to the oracle located there, as was done with other textiles. The color scheme usually combines brown and white (brown dye on white cotton) or light brown on dark brown, although there are a few rare examples which also feature other dye colors (AM06). In general, the warps are not as tightly packed as they are in other warp-face techniques, with the weave more reminiscent of warp-dominant plain weave than true warp face.[2] The second group is woven entirely with alpaca thread and is associated with Inka textile traditions. There are very few examples of this type known and they are all extremely similar; the warp is tied randomly with no planned pattern and dyed red (AM04).[3] The warps are tighter than that seen in the cotton examples, making the weave a true warp face.

In the 19th century, different communities in the Cuzco region began to use bound-resist techniques, called *watay* or *watado* in Quechua, in ponchos and women's mantles or *lliklla* (Fig.4/ AM03).[4] Modern *watay* in both Peru and Bolivia differ significantly from techniques used in the pre-Hispanic period; all the dyeing is done with animal-fiber thread woven in a tight warp-face weave using a wide range of colors combined with the natural white of the fiber.[5] *Watay* stripes are combined with those woven in other warp-face techniques rather than forming the entire composition of a garment.[6] Although the technique fell out of use in many Cuzco communities during the 20th century, *watay* was recorded as still being in use in Q'atqa-Kauri in the early 21st century and in Ccatcca as of 2017.[7] It has also been revived in Santa Cruz de Sallac.[8]

In 19th-century Bolivia, *watay* patterns began to form part of poncho and *lliklla* compositions in the departments of La Paz and Potosí, and they are still used in some regions today, although the technique is quickly vanishing.[9] In the department

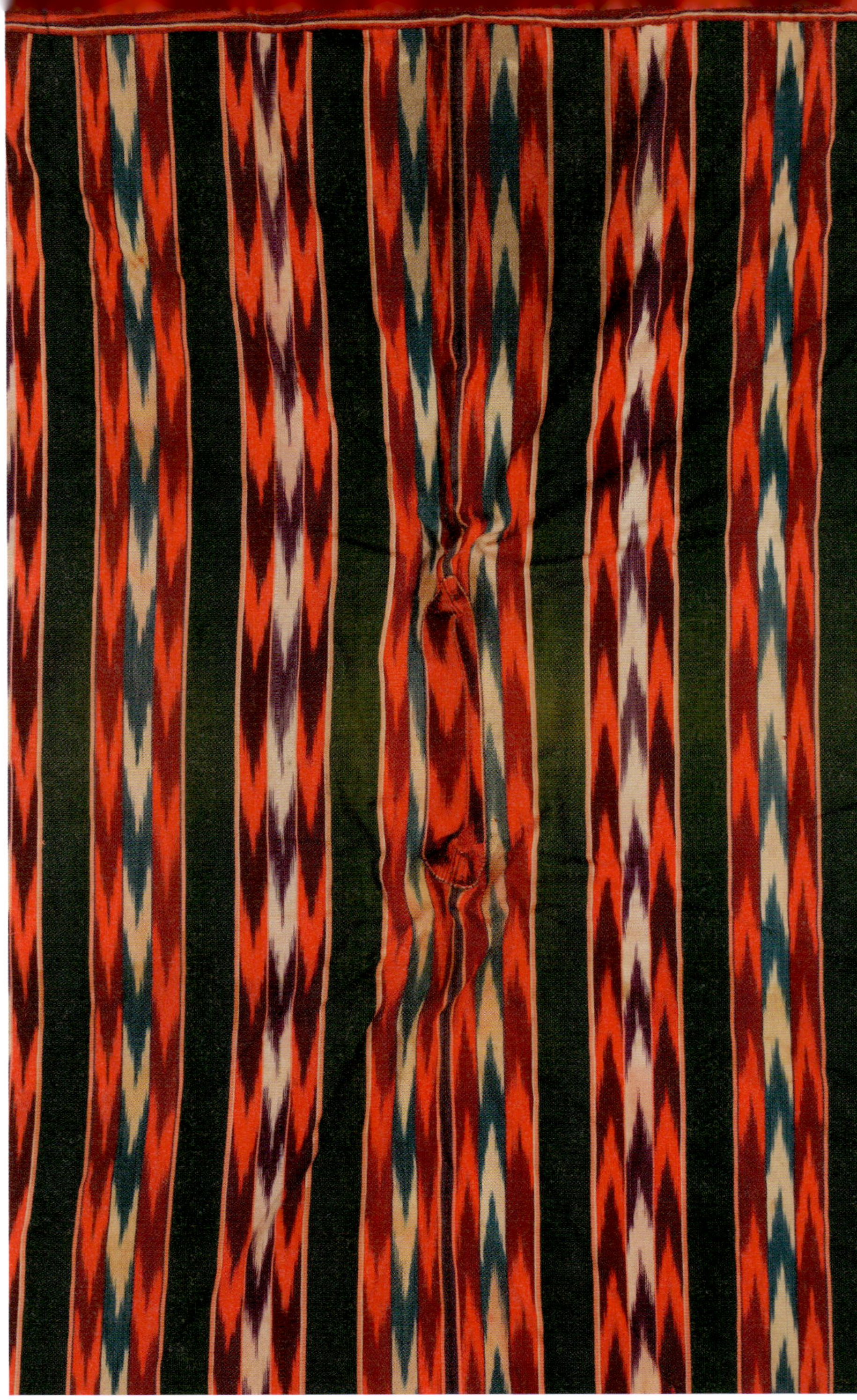

Fig.2

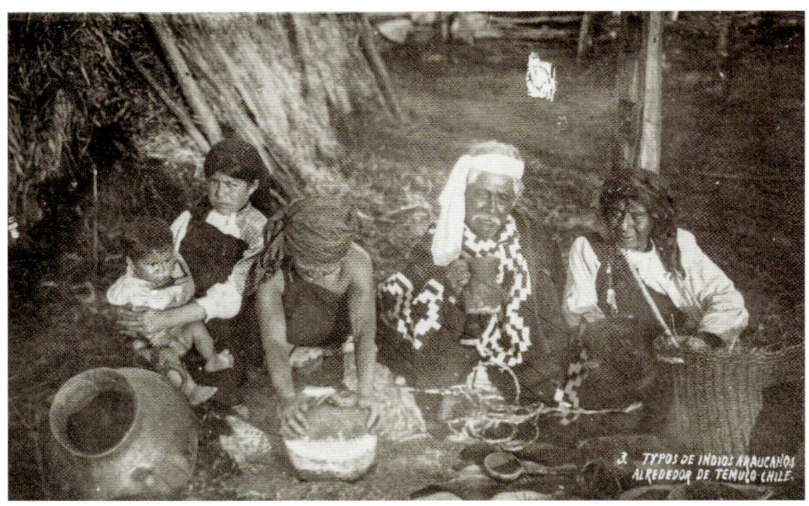

RMN-Grand Palais /Dist. Photo SCALA, Florence

Fig.3

Fig.2
Detail of AM40, poncho

Fig.3
Postcard with photograph depicting a group of indigenous Araucanian (Mapuche) people taken near Temuco, Chile, photograph by Maria L. de Montañez, ca. 1900–1950. Musée du quai-Branly Jacques Chirac, PP0153347

Fig.4
AM03, shoulder cloth, *lliklla*

of La Paz, *wataγ* "zigzag" patterns were used in the province of Bautista Saavedra and the region of Ulla Ulla in the province of Franz Tamayo as part of the compositions of ponchos (Fig.2/AM40), as well as for a form of bag called *capacho* used by indigenous healers.[10] Three distinct styles of *wataγ* patterning were developed for ponchos in the department of Potosí, associated with the Kalcha, Caiza, and Yura regions; the differences lie in the combinations of *wataγ* pattern stripes with those in other techniques, as well as the combination of colors within the *wataγ* patterns (Fig.1/AM45).[11] In Kalcha and Caiza, *wataγ* was used only in ponchos, while in Yura it was also used in *lliklla* and in the modern version of the pre-Hispanic tunic or *unku*.

There are a few textiles which contain warp-bound resist from the pre-Hispanic period in Ecuador (dating from 1200–1500 CE), but the technique differs substantially from that seen in modern Ecuadorian textiles.[12] The weavers used brown rather than indigo dye on the warps, and the weave structure is warp-dominant plain weave with lower thread counts compared with modern textiles.[13] Warp-bound resist dyeing, predominantly with indigo, has a prominent place in modern Ecuadorian dyeing techniques.[14] There is a wider range of variations on bound-resist dyeing in modern Ecuador than in Peru and Bolivia, and the technique is central to the composition of women's shawls and carrying cloths.

The simplest variation of the technique, rectangular blocks pulled by cords into a chevron pattern after dyeing, is found in wool blankets and ponchos, and only a small number of the total warps are bound by comparison with other variations.[15] The blankets are most commonly made in Tungurahua, Chimborazo, and Azuay provinces, while the ponchos are made in the Cuenca region, and in the past possibly in the Imbabura province.[16] A more refined variation of this technique is used in ponchos woven with cotton thread (AM35).

Bound resist is used in women's cotton shawls to create more complex designs. It uses a wider range of colors: indigo dye on undyed white cotton, or two artificial dyes, or black and pink.[17] Variations of these shawls are produced mostly in the Ecuadorian provinces of Cotopaxi (*macana*) and Azuay (*paño*), and in the past possibly in Imbabura, while a closely related variation, called a *pañon*, is worn in northern Peru, near Calamarca.[18] The shawls are similar to Mexican *rebozo*, with a knotted fringe finish on each end, and it is possible they may have a common origin, especially as the bound-resist technique is

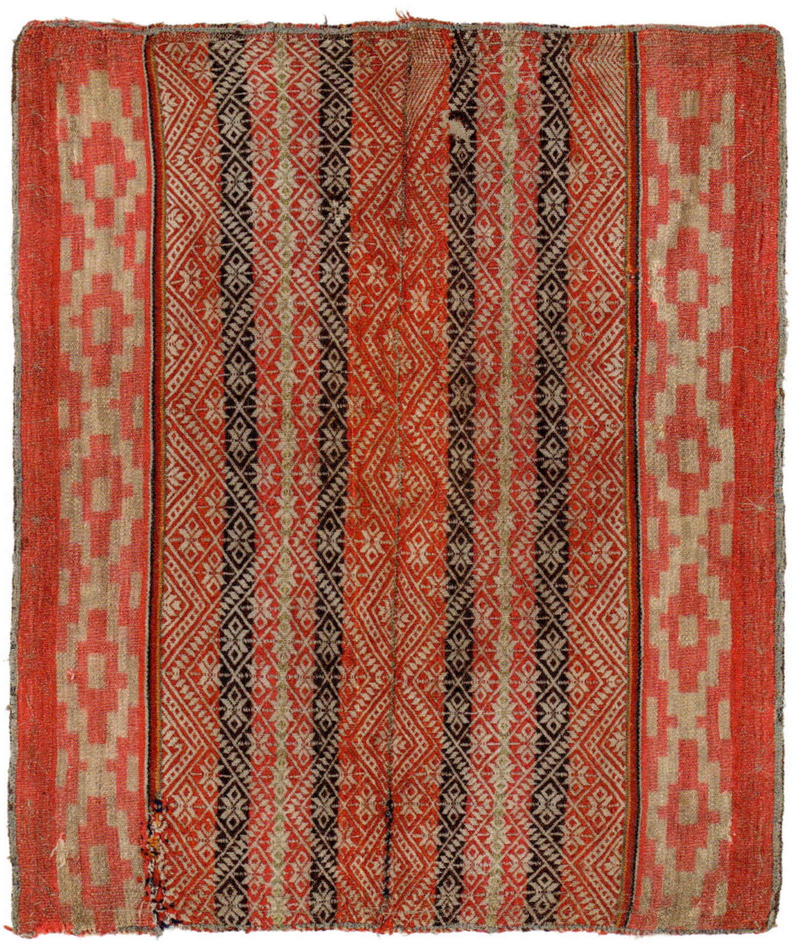

Fig.4

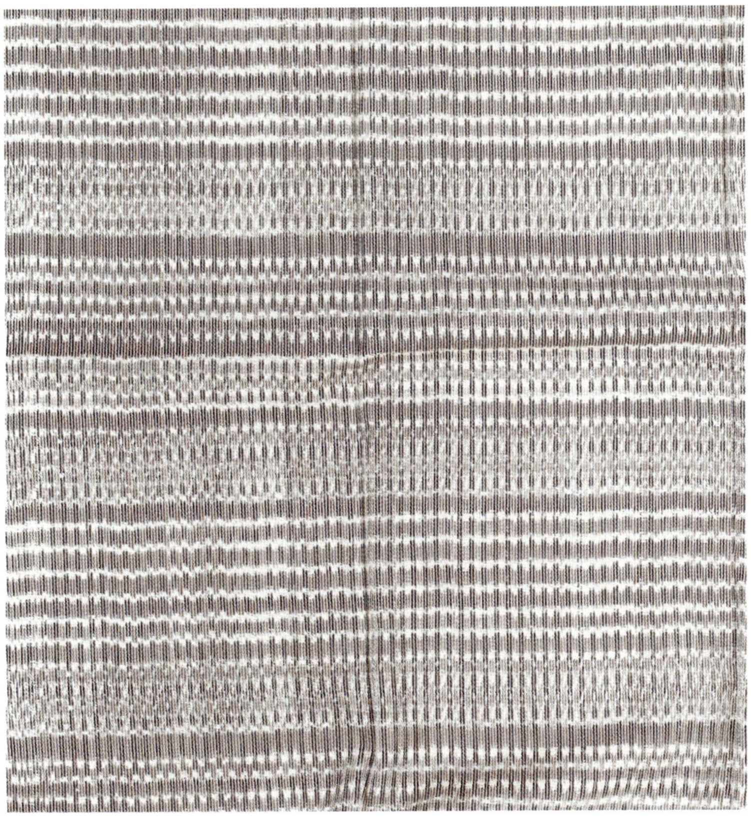

Fig.5

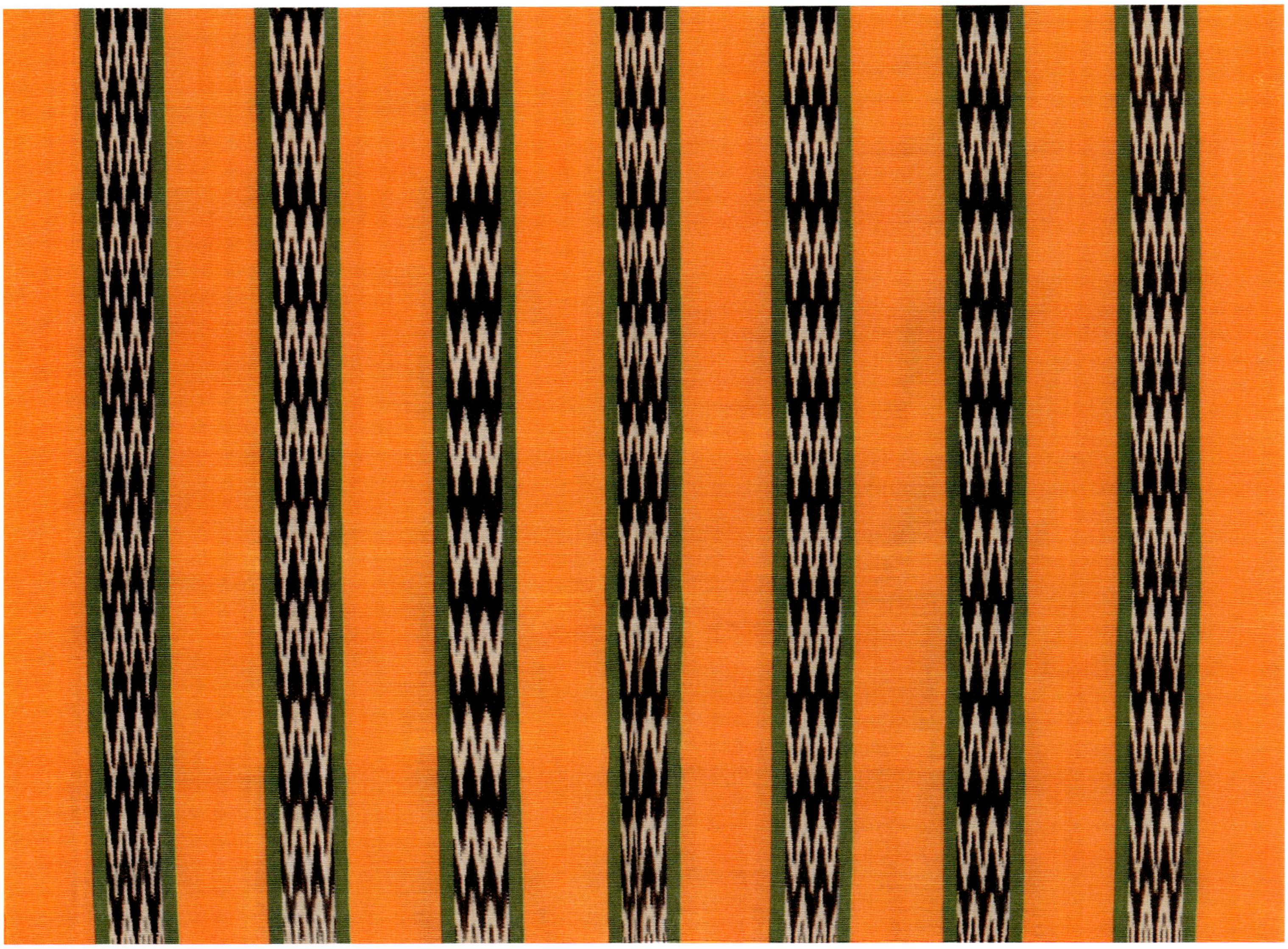

Fig.6

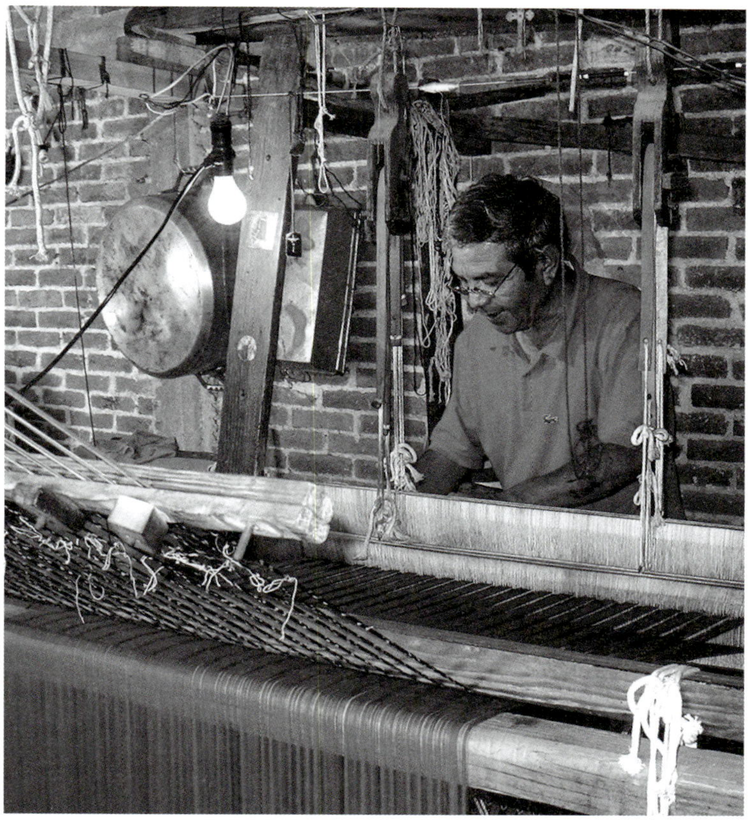

Photo courtesy of Chloe Sayer

Fig.7

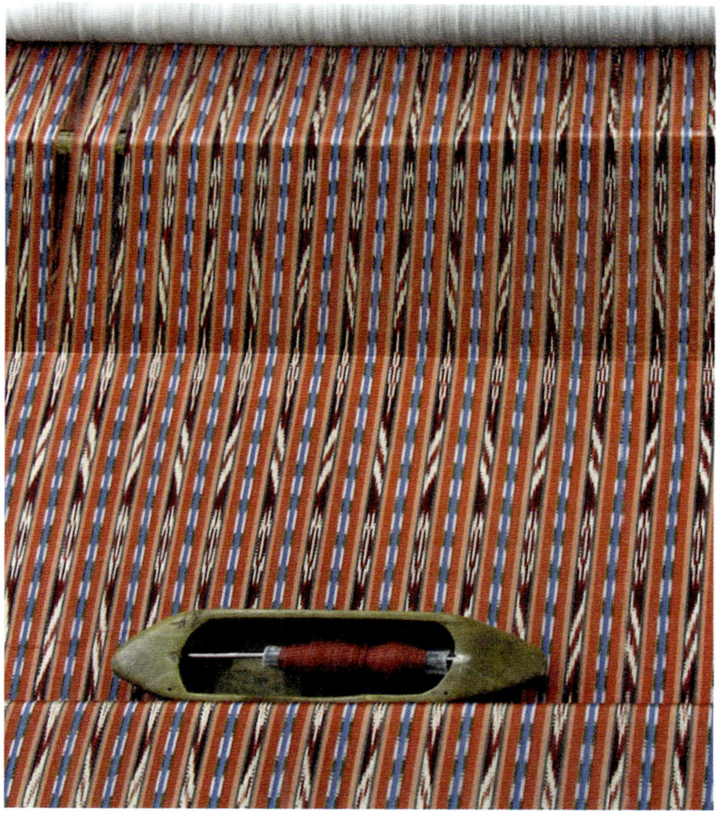

Photo courtesy of Chloe Sayer

Fig.8

Fig.5
Detail of AM07, shoulder cloth, *rebozo*

Fig.6
Detail of AM10, shoulder cloth

Fig.7
Contemporary ikat weaving in Mexico using a treadle loom

Fig.8
A Mexican *rebozo* on the loom

also a prominent feature of the *rebozo*.[19] The majority are composed of small designs which repeat across the entire width of the shawl, with each design containing several components each consisting of a set number of warps.[20] The number of warps in a component determines the order in which they are dyed, with components from different designs with the same number of warps dyed at the same time.

The most well-known of the South American warp-bound resist techniques, possibly because it is arguably the most precise, is found in the ponchos made by the Mapuche indigenous group in South Central Chile (Fig 3) and Argentina pampas (flat grass plains).[21] The ponchos, called *traríñ makíñ* and *trarikán makúñ* in Argentina, are woven with white sheep's wool dyed with deep indigo to form the designs, which is achieved by wrapping the warps with string and maki bark, or applying a white clay earthen paste.[22] The designs are on a larger scale than those in Peruvian and Bolivian ponchos, although they feature the same stepped diamonds and chevron patterns (AM34).[23]

The principle feature distinguishing these ponchos from others in the Andes is the precision of the wrapping and dyeing process; there is so little dye leakage under the covered sections that the designs appear as if they were woven with tapestry weave.[24] Besides the Mapuche, others who live in the same region use this technique in the production of a wider range of textiles: blankets (*jergones*), belts, ponchos, scarves, and saddlebags.[25]

Fig.9

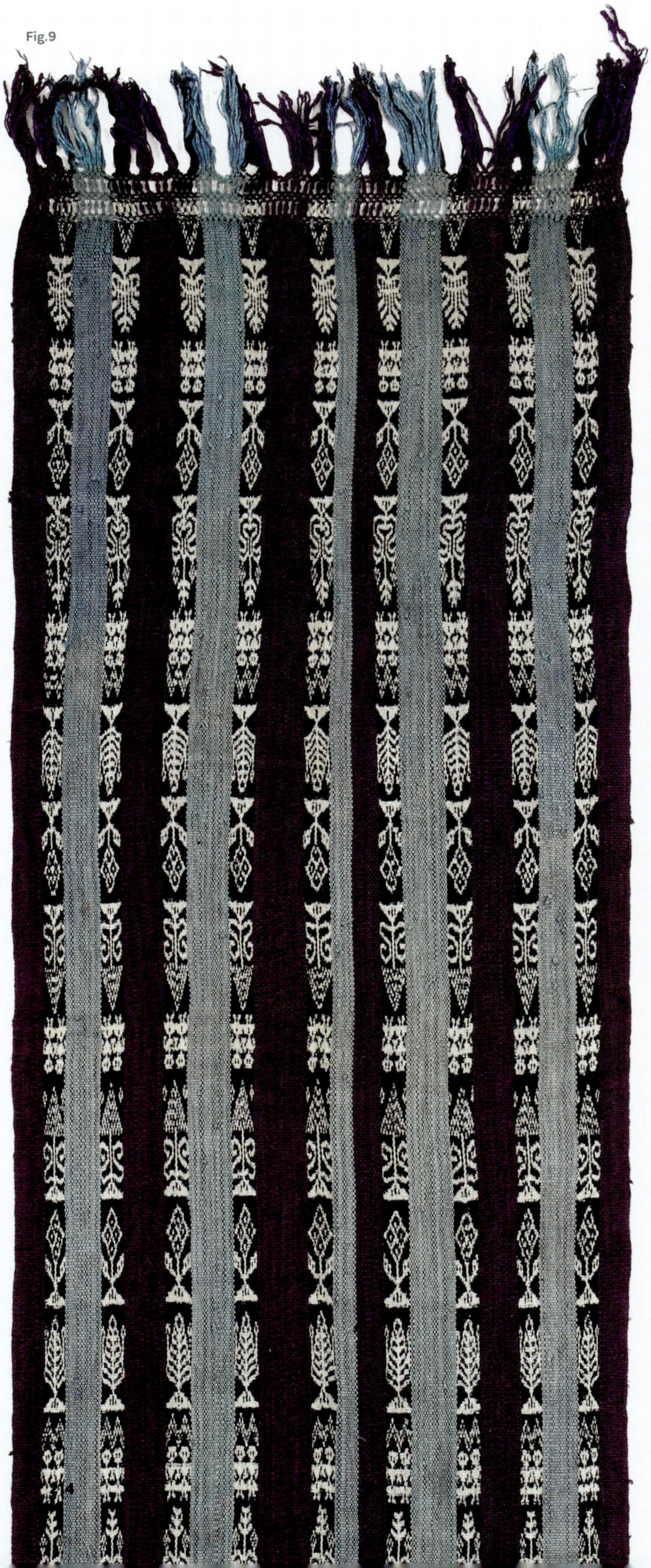

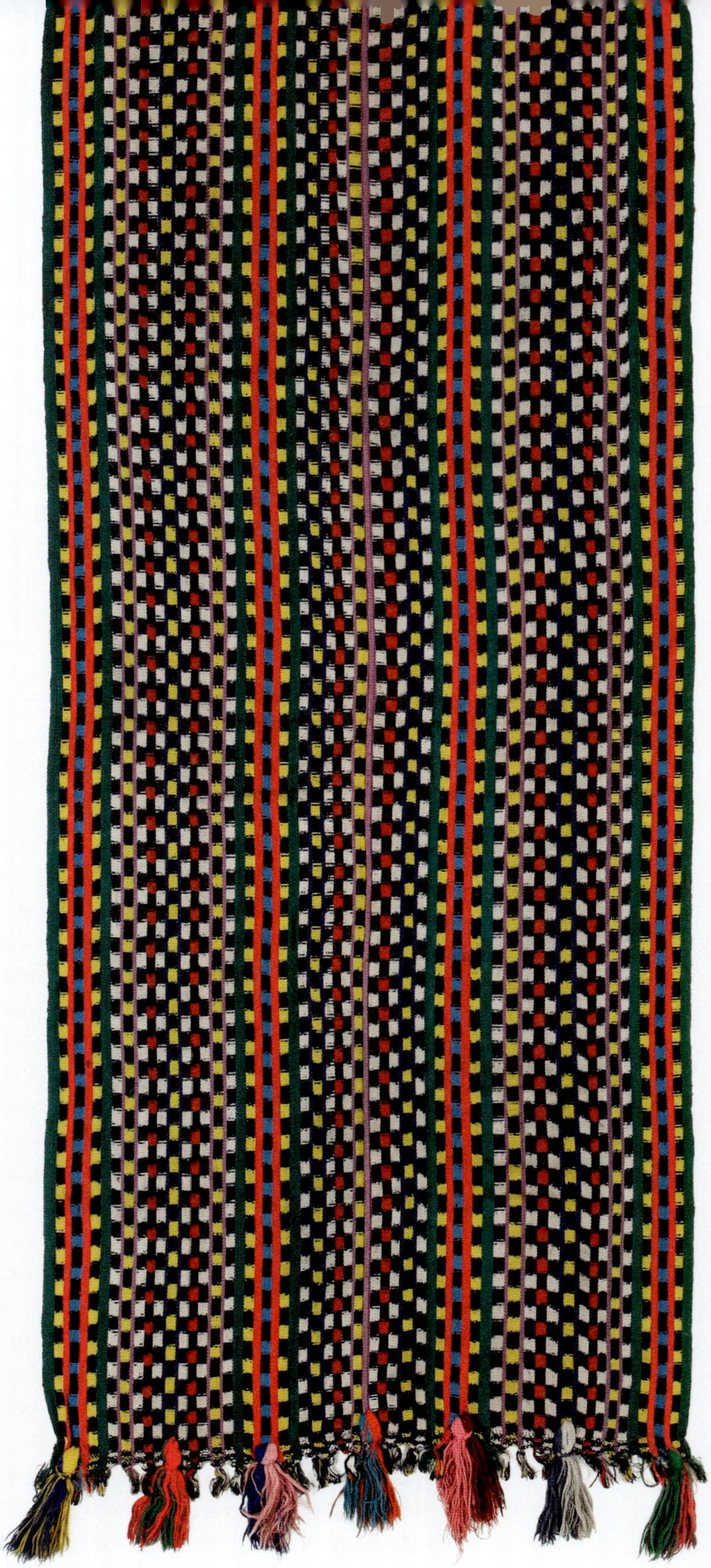

Fig.10

Fig.9
AM23, shoulder cloth

Fig.10
AM28, shoulder cloth

Mexico

In the case of Mexico, the origin of bound-resist dyeing techniques, called *jaspe*, is subject to speculation as there is no known archaeological textile that contains the technique north of the equator.[26] As in the Andes, warp *jaspe* appears to have been the dominant form of the technique, although weft *jaspe* was recorded in Chihuahua in the northwest of Mexico, and the regions of modern New Mexico.[27] The main centers of production from the 18th century through the end of the 20th century were communities in central Mexico: the municipality of Ixmiquilpan in the Mezquital Valley and the mountains east of Santa María del Río in the state of San Luis Potosí.[28] Two groups of garments were produced with warp-face weave compositions containing *jaspe*: ponchos and bags woven of wool spun by hand with the traditional malacate spindle; and the other, more well-known group, *rebozo* (a rectangular shawl with fringe on each end), woven with cotton or silk composed of threads that had been processed in large workshops or by industrial machinery (Fig.5/AM07).[29] The *jaspe* technique itself was similar, with the fiber used to bind the threads being *ixtle* (fiber extracted from agave plants) in both cases.

The use of *jaspe* in *rebozo* was more documented than the other types of garment.[30] A document from 1799 on textile production in the Mezquital Valley contains the earliest description of *jaspe* in Mexico in the section dealing with *rebozo* production.[31] *Jaspe rebozo* generally consist of dyed warps grouped in stripes which alternate with monochrome warp stripes (AM11).[32] The horizontal designs are executed from memory and there are two main types; *llovisna* (a misty pattern) and patterns based on geometric shapes.[33] The technique as it was practiced beginning in the 18th and 19th centuries may have been inspired by ikat-dyed shawls from India worn by people from Malacca, Molucca islands, China, and the Philippines brought to Mexico by the Spanish beginning in the late 16th century.[34] Similarity in motif, technique and size of design in Mexican *rebozo* and the ikat dyeing practiced by the Bagobo tribe from the region of Mindanao in the Philippines suggests that the technique could have been brought from there.[35]

Guatemala

As in the Andes and Mexico, it is difficult to determine exactly when bound-resist techniques, called *jaspe* in Guatemala as in Mexico, were developed, and to trace the cultural origins. Photographs dating from the end of the 19th century include women wearing garments containing *jaspe* designs, indicating that the technique was in use at that time. *Jaspe* production in Mayan communities in Guatemala is unique among the regions of Latin America on several counts. It is the only cultural region in which bound-resist is used in weft patterning as well as in warp; occasionally both sets of threads are dyed (AM12).[36] *Jaspe* patterning is featured in a much wider range of garments than other regions; *cortes* (skirts), different types of shawl such as *rebozos* and *perrajes* (Fig.9/AM23 and Fig.10/AM28); *sábanas*, *tzut*, carrying cloths; *huipiles*, blouses; and some types of belt.[37] The technique is used mostly in the west of the country, with Salcajá and Quetzaltenango (department of Quetzaltenango) as well as Totonicapán (department of Totonicapán) being the most prominent production areas.[38]

The *jaspe* patterns used from the end of the 19th century through the mid-20th were simple (one called *tachones* contains only two threads) and dyed with a limited combination of colors.[39] As in the Andes, combinations of blue and white were the most popular, with more colors having been introduced by the 1930s.[40] While bound-resist techniques in other regions increasingly fell out of use through the 20th century, *jaspe* use in Guatemala grew in the 1960s, with design development increasing drastically after the 1980s.[41]

The process of preparing threads for dyeing depends on whether the threads will form the warp or weft, as well as the type of loom; both treadle looms and backstrap looms are used to weave in Mayan communities.[42] Wefts are arranged in skeins that are the desired width of the finished cloth and sorted into groups called *cordeles* according to the intended designs or *labores*, and tied together to prevent the threads from shifting position. Warps intended to be woven on backstrap looms are prepared in a similar matter, while warps for treadle looms, which are significantly longer, are warped in the order that the individual threads will be woven before being formed into *cordeles*.[43] These differences have caused the knotting process to be specialized; artists who bind the threads work exclusively on one type, either warps for treadle looms, wefts, or warps for backstrap looms.[44]

CATALOG

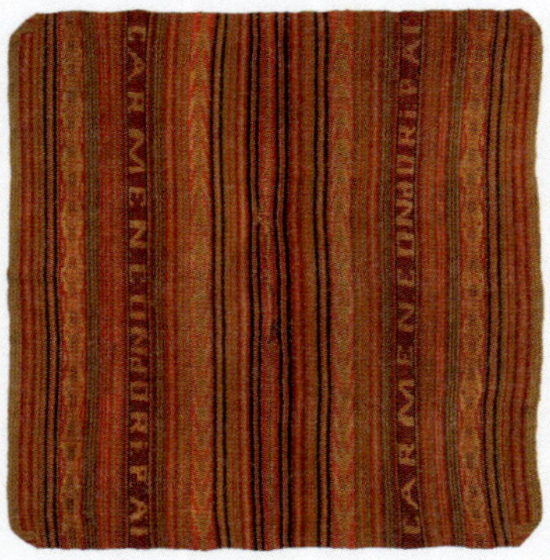

AM01 Poncho
Q'atqa, Cuzco, Peru, 20th century. Sheep's wool, warp ikat, natural and synthetic dyes. 49 in x 48 in

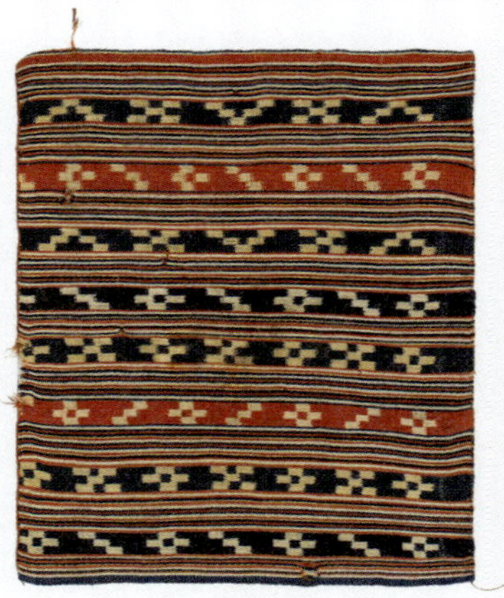

AM02 Ritual coca cloth
Lake Titicaca region, Peru, 20th century. Alpaca, warp ikat. 29 in x 32 in

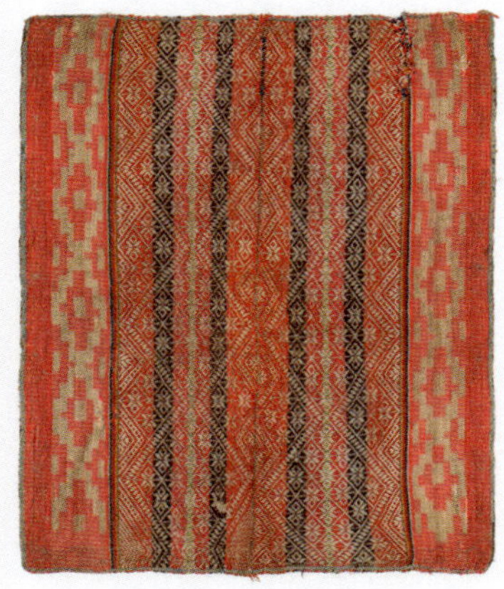

AM03 Shoulder cloth, *lliklla*
Q'atqa, Cuzco, Peru, 20th century. Sheep's wool, warp ikat, wool weft brocade. 27 in x 21 in

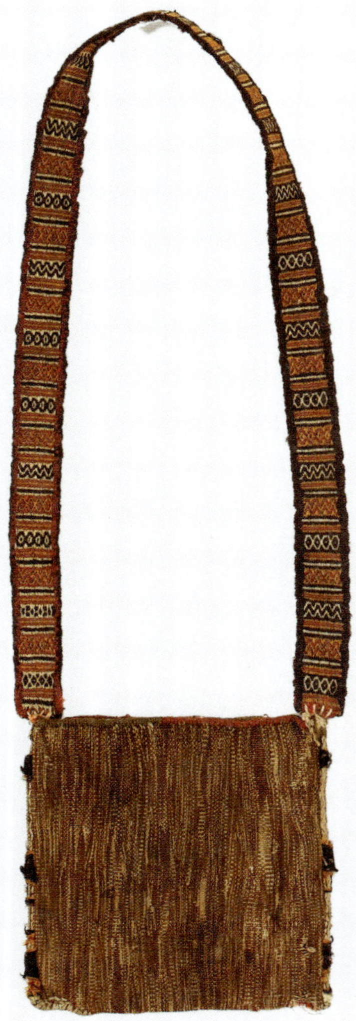

AM04 Coca bag
South Coast, Peru, 15th century. Wool-warp ikat and cotton weft, tablet-woven band of wool and cotton, interrupted tapestry warp. 21 in x 7 in

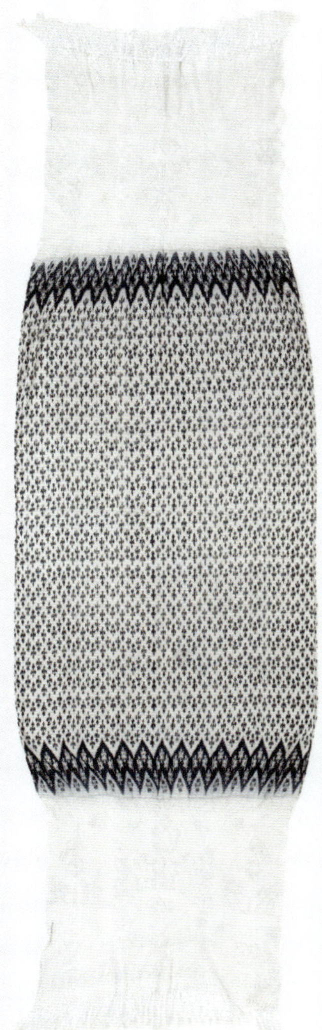

AM05 Shoulder cloth, *rebozo*
Cajamarca region, Peru, 19th century. Cotton, warp ikat with macramé and plantain fiber fringe. 114 in x 35 in

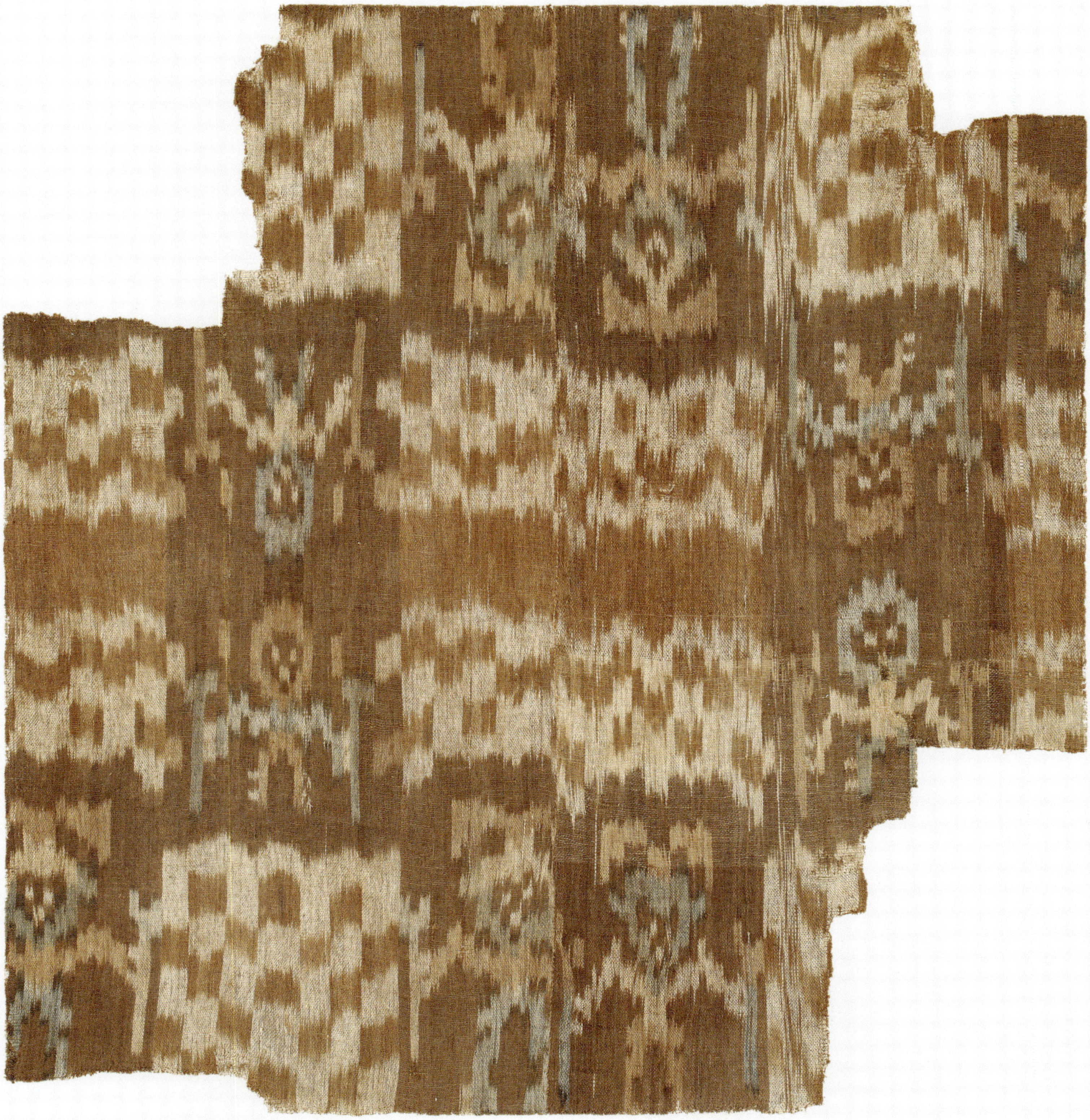

AM06 Burial shroud fragment, Huarmey, Central Coast, Peru, circa 1100. Warp ikat cotton, cotton weft, warp-applied pigment, panel woven. 39 in x 37 in

This burial shroud fragment dating to the Late Intermediate period belongs to the group of cotton-based bound-resist textiles. Based on the find locations, most of the textiles in this group appear to be from the Chimú culture, but staff-holding figures are common in many Andean cultures, which makes their appearance insufficient for identifying a specific culture. The pattern sequence is much more complex than is usual, with a combination of checkerboard squares and four variations of figures. The combinations used for the bound-resist patterns are also rare; pre-Hispanic textiles dyed with this technique usually feature only brown dye on white thread, while this example includes two additional dye layers. After the initial brown dye, certain areas in the figural patterns were unwrapped and dyed indigo or light brown, resulting in light brown/dark brown and indigo/white.

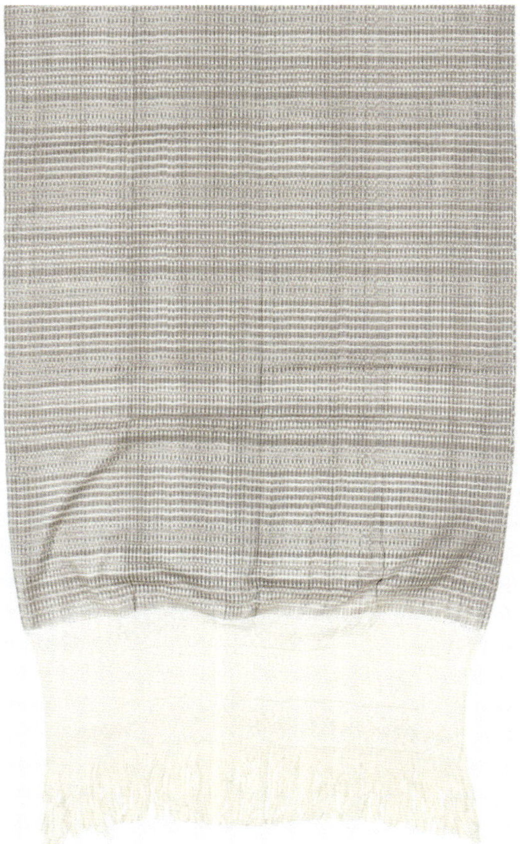

AM07 Shoulder cloth, *rebozo*
San Luis Potosí, Mexico, 21st century. Cotton, warp ikat, macramé fringe. 92 in x 28 in

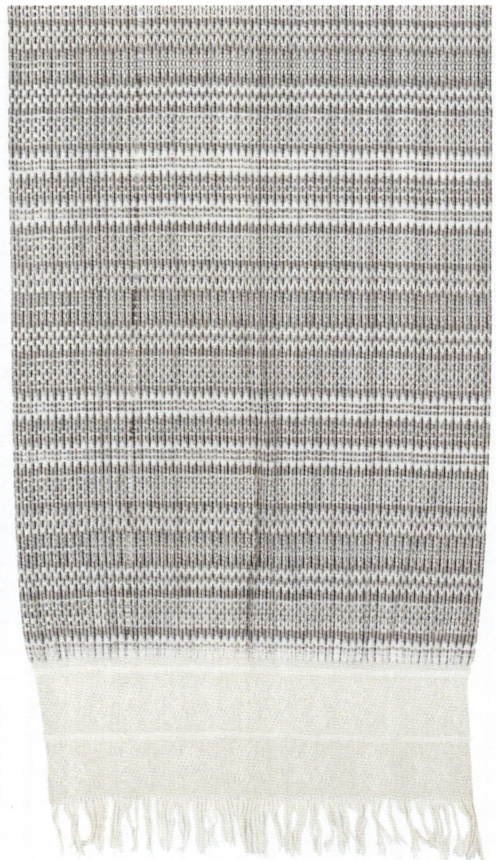

AM08 Shoulder cloth, *rebozo*
San Luis Potosí, Mexico, 1970s. Cotton, warp ikat, macramé fringe. 95 in x 29 in

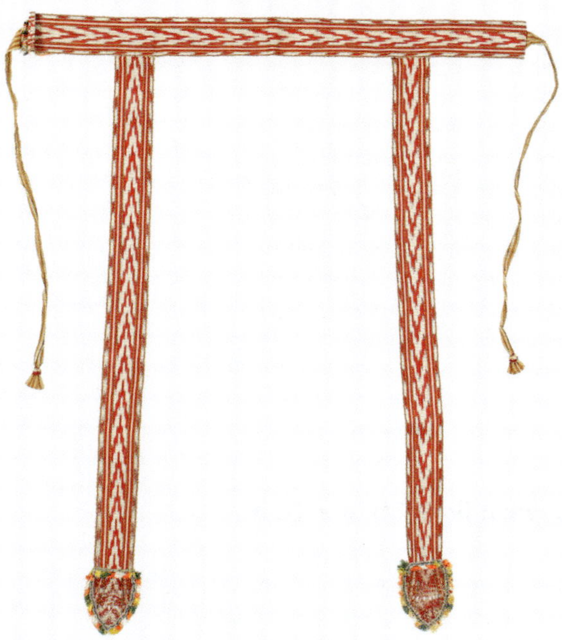

AM09 Ceremonial dance belt
Mexico, 18th century. Tablet-woven warp ikat, linen weft, silk warp with macramé fringe. 31 in x 26 in

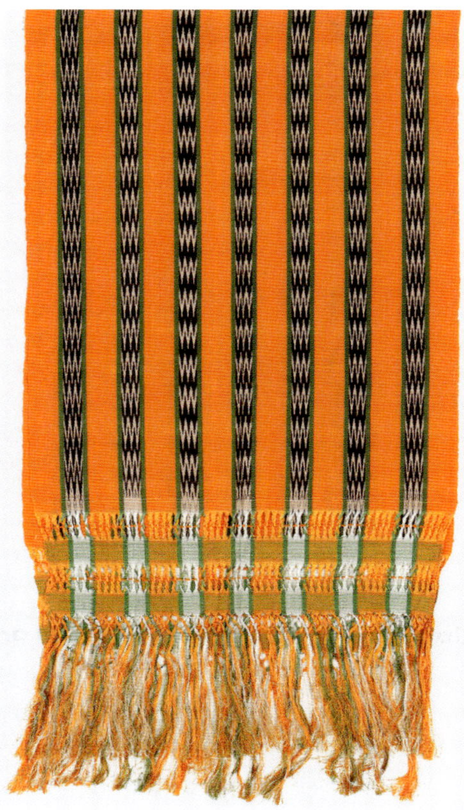

AM10 Shoulder cloth
Yucatán, Mexico, late 20th century. Rayon, warp ikat. 72 in x 22 in

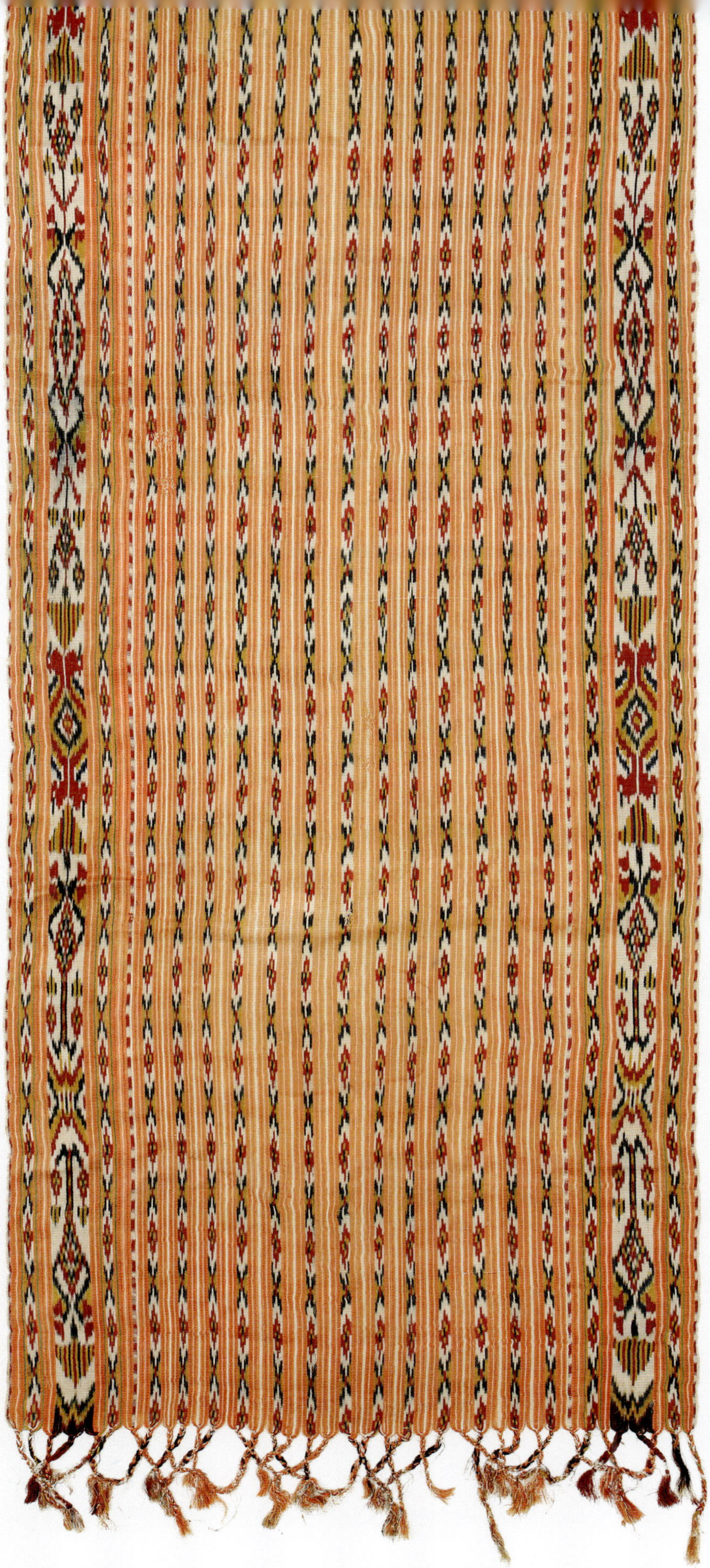

AM11 Shoulder cloth, *rebozo*, Mexico, 18th or 19th century. Silk, warp ikat. 89 in x 28 in

This *rebozo* contains particularly complex *jaspe* patterns, created by dividing warp threads into groups or *juegos* according to the desired patterns, and dyeing each separately. This process requires as many dyeing stages as there are colors. As in the Andes, *rebozos* generally include the natural fiber color as one of the pattern colors; however, the range of other colors is much wider than in Andean bound-resist textiles. This *rebozo* contains shades of red, pink, green, and yellow in addition to natural white. Two wide bands on each long edge feature a sequence of large *jaspe* patterns that combine mist and geometric patterns. In between these wide bands is a repeating series of narrow stripes; light-pink stripes and pinstripes of green and white alternate with *jaspe*-dyed stripes containing simplified versions of the patterns in the wider end bands.

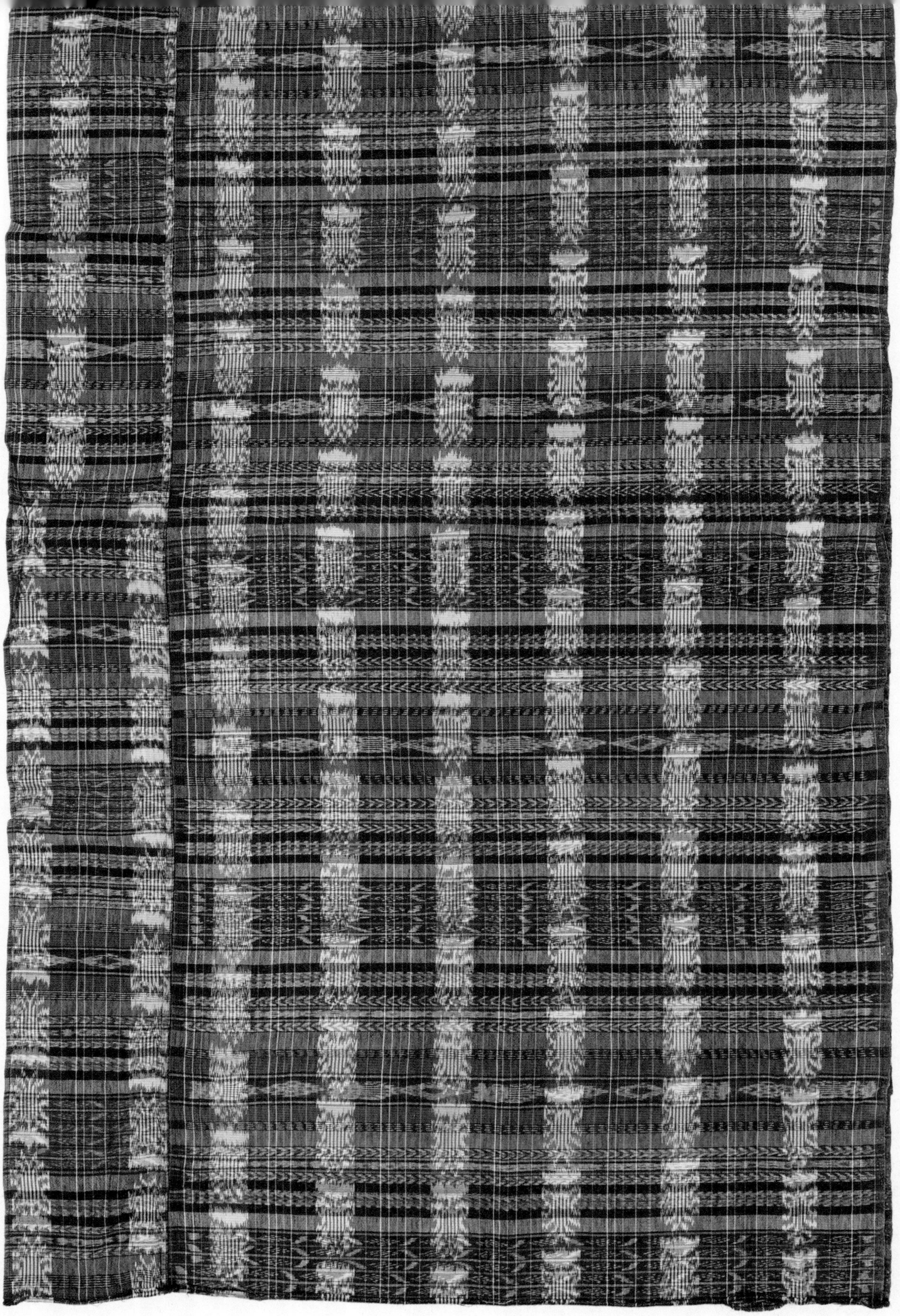

AM12 Woman's skirt cloth, *corte*, Guatemala, 20th century. Cotton, compound ikat. 144 in x 41 in

This treadle-loom-woven *corte* features the technique unique to Guatemala among all the countries in Latin America with bound-resist traditions: double *jaspe*, where both warp and weft threads are bound and dyed to produce intersecting patterns. Both the warp and weft contain several different *jaspe* pattern groups, which are called *contras*. While there is a wide variety of *contras*, they are categorized not by imagery but by the number of *cordele* groups required, usually in odd numbers such as three, five, seven, and nine. This *corte* demonstrates the preference of the blue/white color combination common until the mid-20th century, while hinting at the range of possibilities which came into fashion later with the inclusion of a light-pink shade.

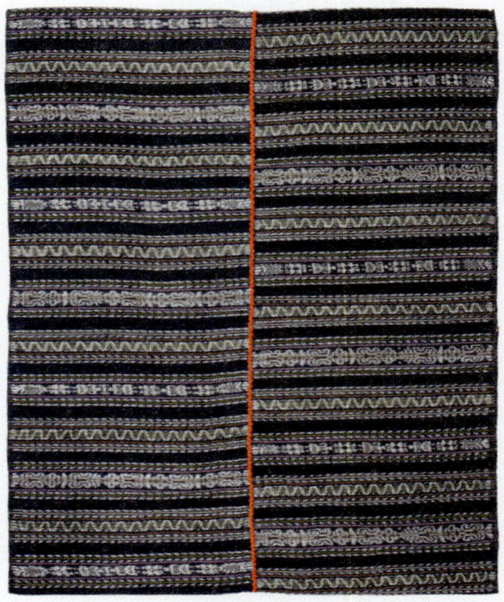

AM13 Woman's skirt cloth
Zunil, Guatemala, 20th century. Cotton, weft ikat.
100 in x 45 in

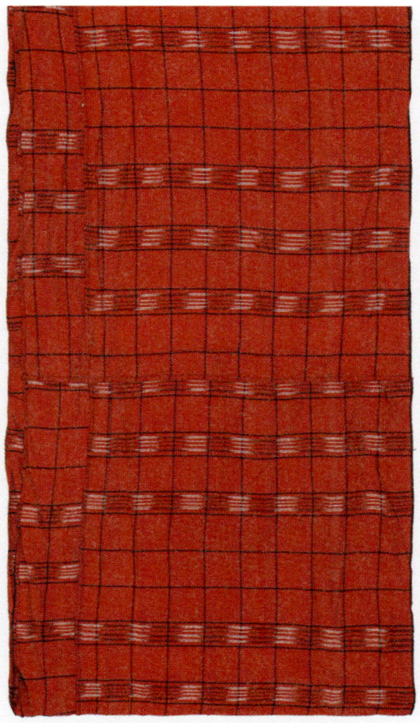

AM14 Woman's skirt cloth
Cajal, Guatemala, 20th century. Cotton, weft ikat.
120 in x 36 in

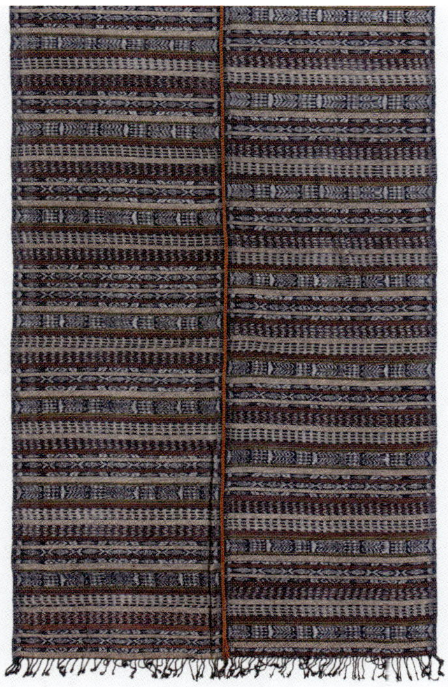

AM15 Woman's skirt cloth
Zunil, Guatemala, 20th century. Cotton, weft ikat.
90 in x 45 in

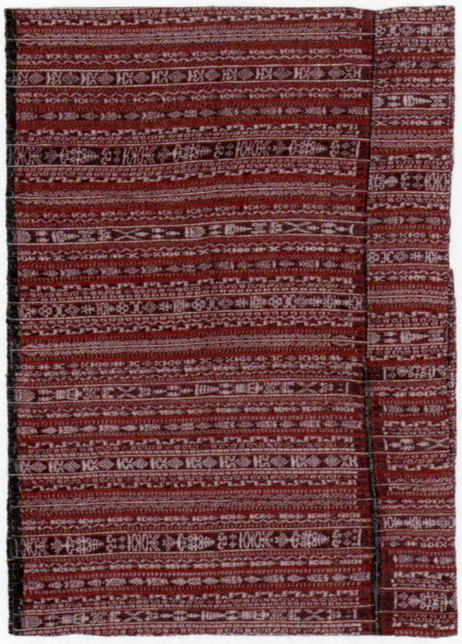

AM16 Woman's skirt cloth
Santiago Atitlán, Guatemala, 20th century. Cotton, weft ikat. 90 in x 47 in

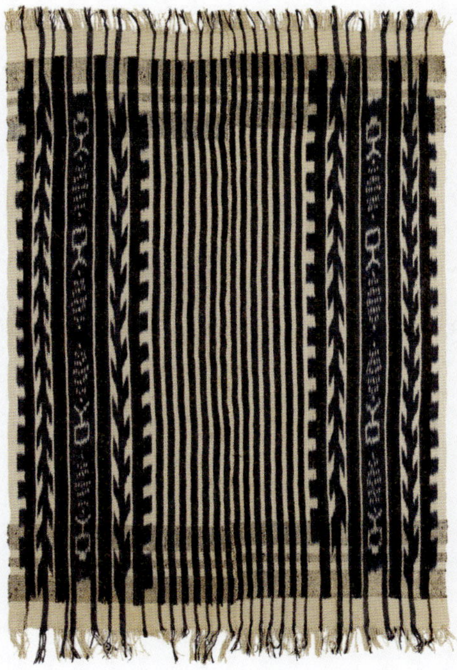

AM17 Blanket
Momostenango, Guatemala, early 20th century. Sheep's wool, warp ikat. 94 in x 60 in

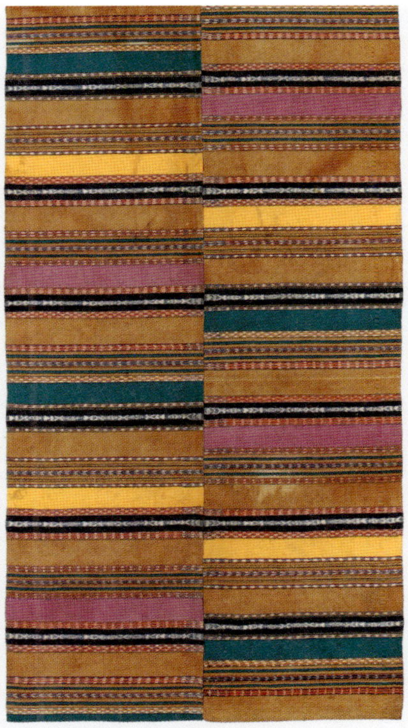

AM18 Table cover
Totonicapán, Guatemala, 20th century. Cotton, weft ikat. 78 in x 37 in

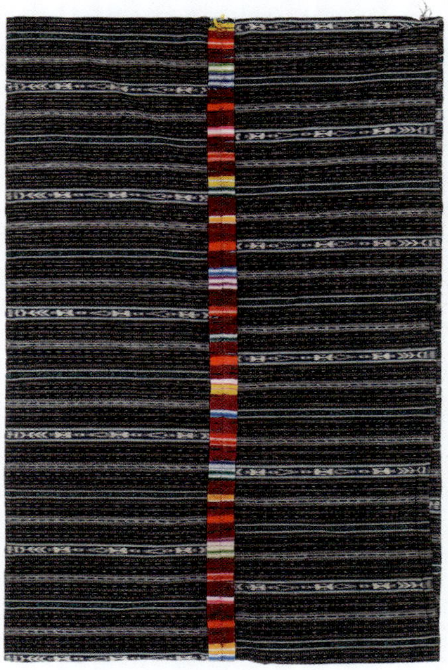

AM19 Woman's skirt cloth
Chichicastenango, Santo Tomas, Guatemala, 20th century. Cotton, weft ikat. 62 in x 31 in

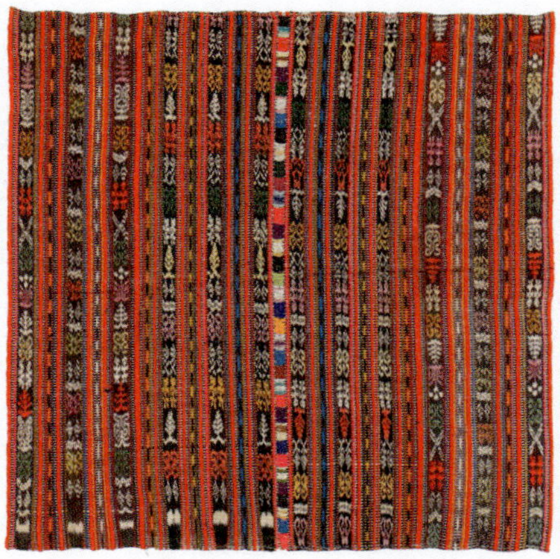

AM20 Woman's shoulder cloth
Sololá, Guatemala, late 20th century. Cotton, warp ikat and lurex fiber. 45 in x 47 in

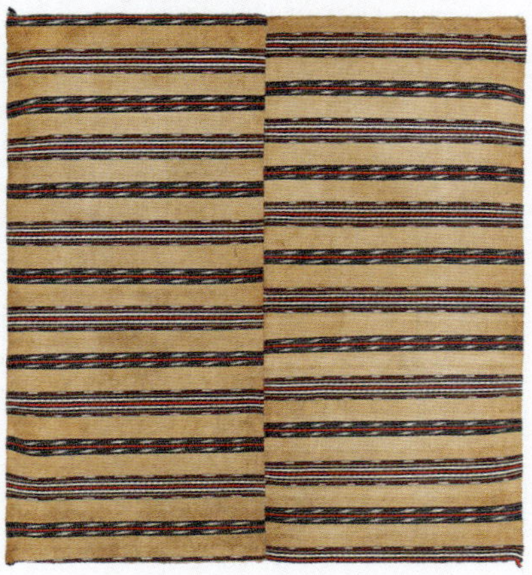

AM21 Woman's shoulder cloth
Totonicapán, Guatemala, early 20th century. Cotton, weft ikat. 45 in x 47 in

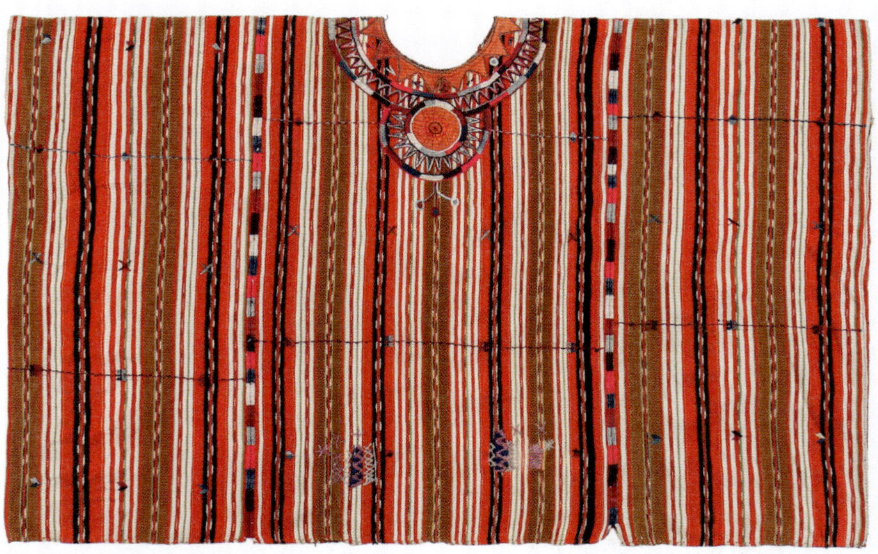

AM22 Tunic, *huipil*
Sololá, Guatemala, 20th century. Cotton, warp ikat. 30 in x 49 in

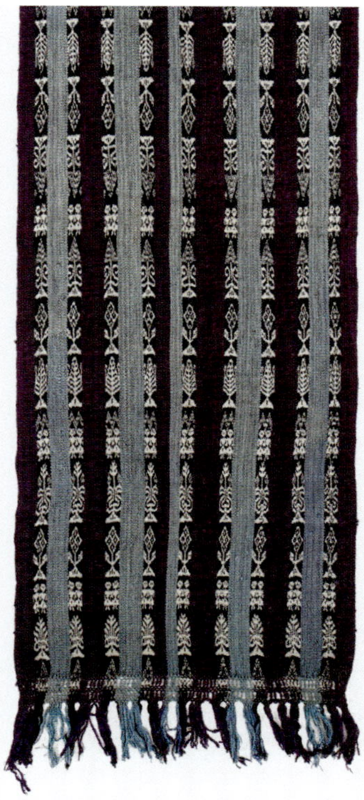

AM23 Shoulder cloth
Totonicapán, Guatemala, late 20th century. Cotton, warp ikat with silk stripes. 30 in x 90 in

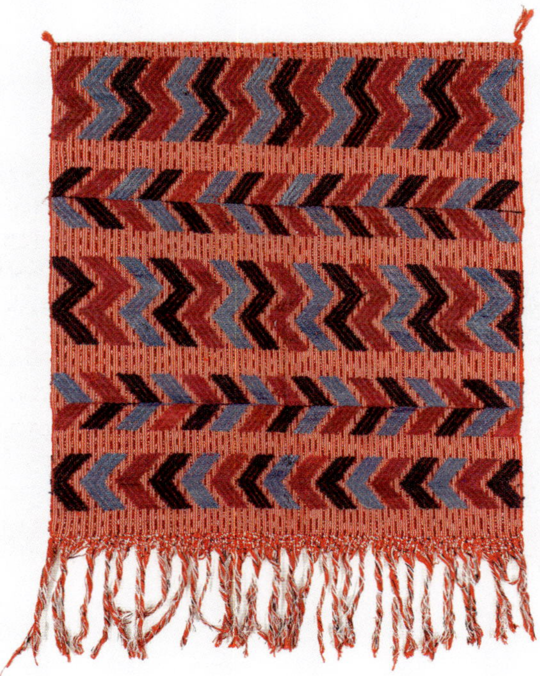

AM24 Man's headscarf, *tsutze* (?)
Guatemala, 1970s–1980s. Cotton-warp ikat, weft float silk, loom brocade. 31 in x 25 in

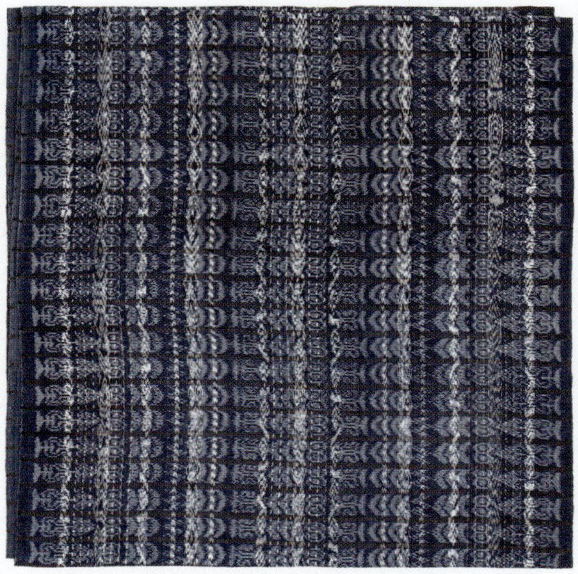

AM25 Skirt, *corte*
Salcajá, Guatemala, 20th century. Cotton compound ikat. 35 in x 140 in

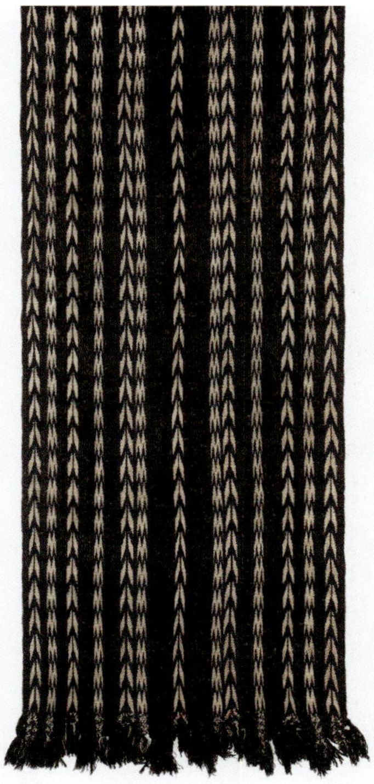

AM26 Woman's shoulder cloth
Totonicapán, Guatemala, 20th century. Cotton, warp ikat with macrame fringe. 29 in x 90 in

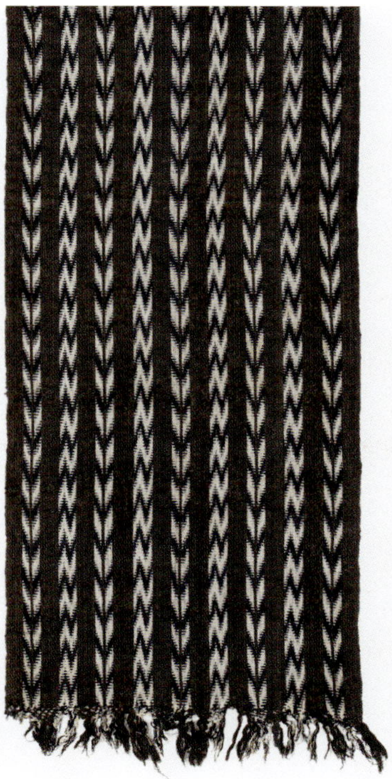

AM27 Woman's shoulder cloth
Totonicapán, Guatemala, 20th century. Cotton, warp ikat with macrame fringe. 29 in x 80 in

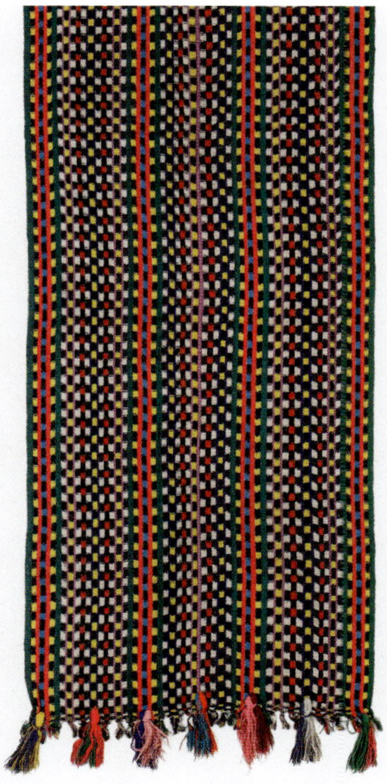

AM28 Shoulder cloth
San Pedro la Laguna, Guatemala, late 20th century. Cotton, warp ikat. 30 in x 80 in

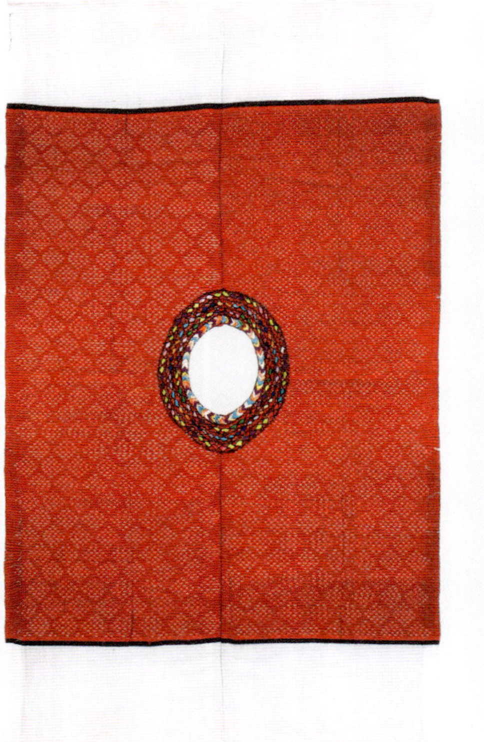

AM29 Tunic, *huipil*
Momostenango, Guatemala, 20th century. Cotton, weft ikat. 30 in x 50 in

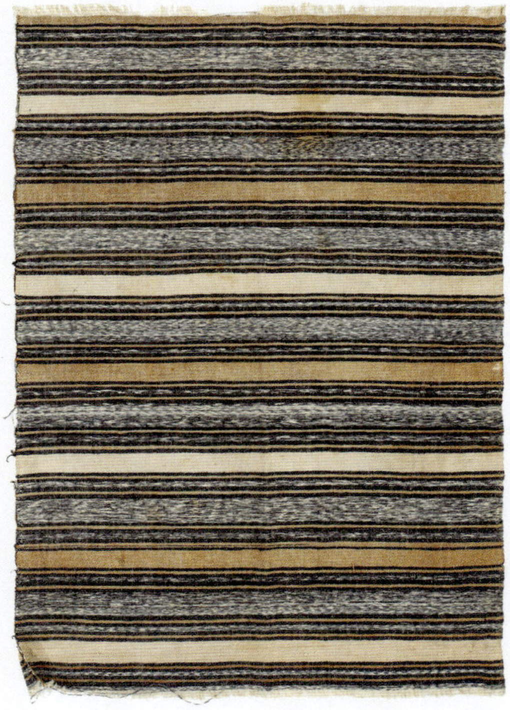

AM30 Altar cloth, *mantilla*
Totonicapán, Guatemala, early 20th century. Cotton, weft ikat. 31 in x 22 in

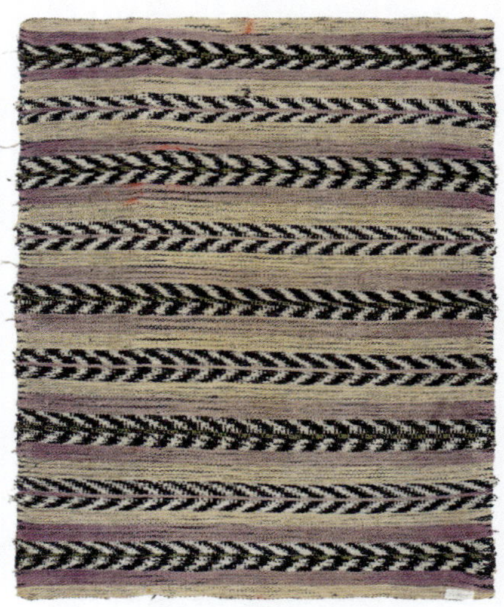

AM31 Man's headscarf, *tsutze*
Coastal Guatemala, early 20th century. Cotton-warp ikat, silk warp stripes with shellfish purple. 22 in x 27 in

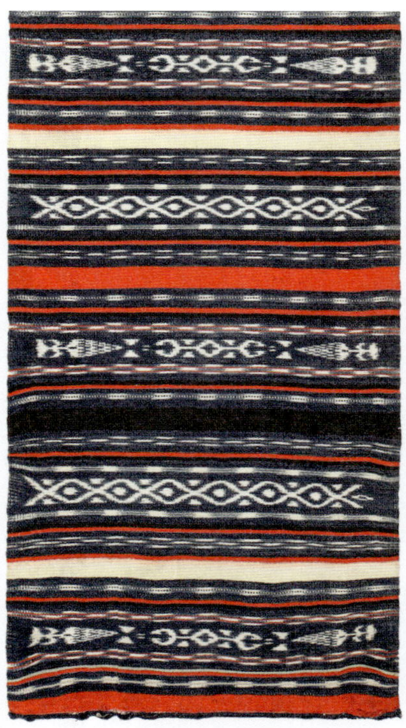

AM32 One panel of a two-panel shawl
Totonicapán, Guatemala, 1950s. Cotton, weft ikat. 31 in x 22 in

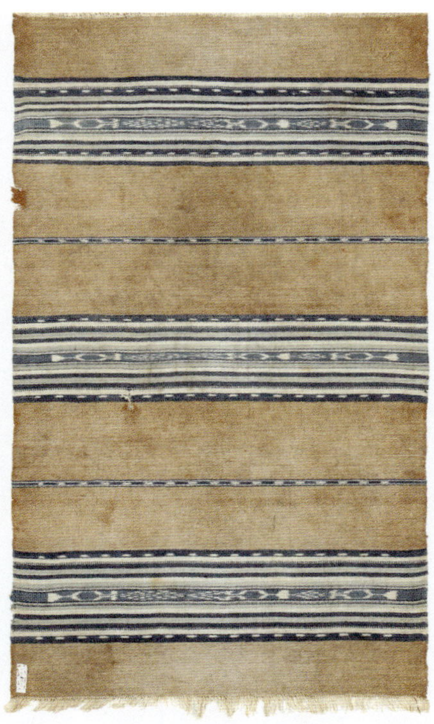

AM33 Altar cloth, *mantilla*
Totonicapán, Guatemala, early 20th century. Cotton, weft ikat, brown indigenous tree cotton. 32 in x 20 in

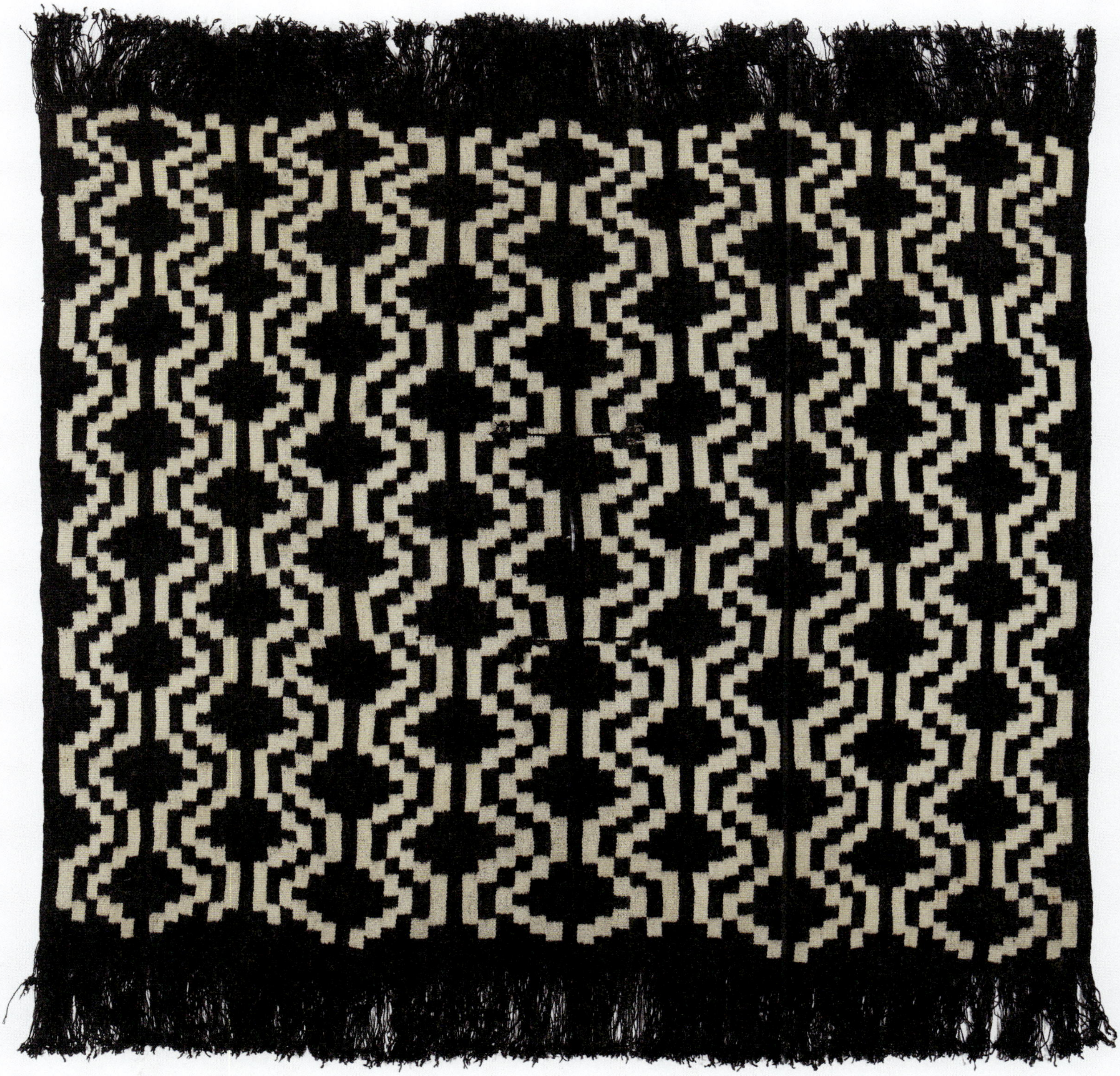

AM34 Poncho, Mapuche, Chile, 19th century. Warp-bound-resist on handspun sheep's wool, twining. 58 in x 59 in

The color contrasts between the white and indigo-dyed sections indicate that this chief or *cacique* poncho was created by a master artisan. In this bound-resist technique, quality is determined by the creator's ability to create as stark a contrast as possible between white and dark sections, and achieve a blue as close as possible to black by multiple dye-bath immersions. In some poncho compositions, the resist-dyed sections are flanked by others such as monochrome stripes (usually red and turquoise) or stripes woven in complementary-warp techniques, and in other ponchos the dyed sections are continuous. This poncho is an example of the latter, with stepped diamond shapes in vertical rows forming a pattern across the garment.

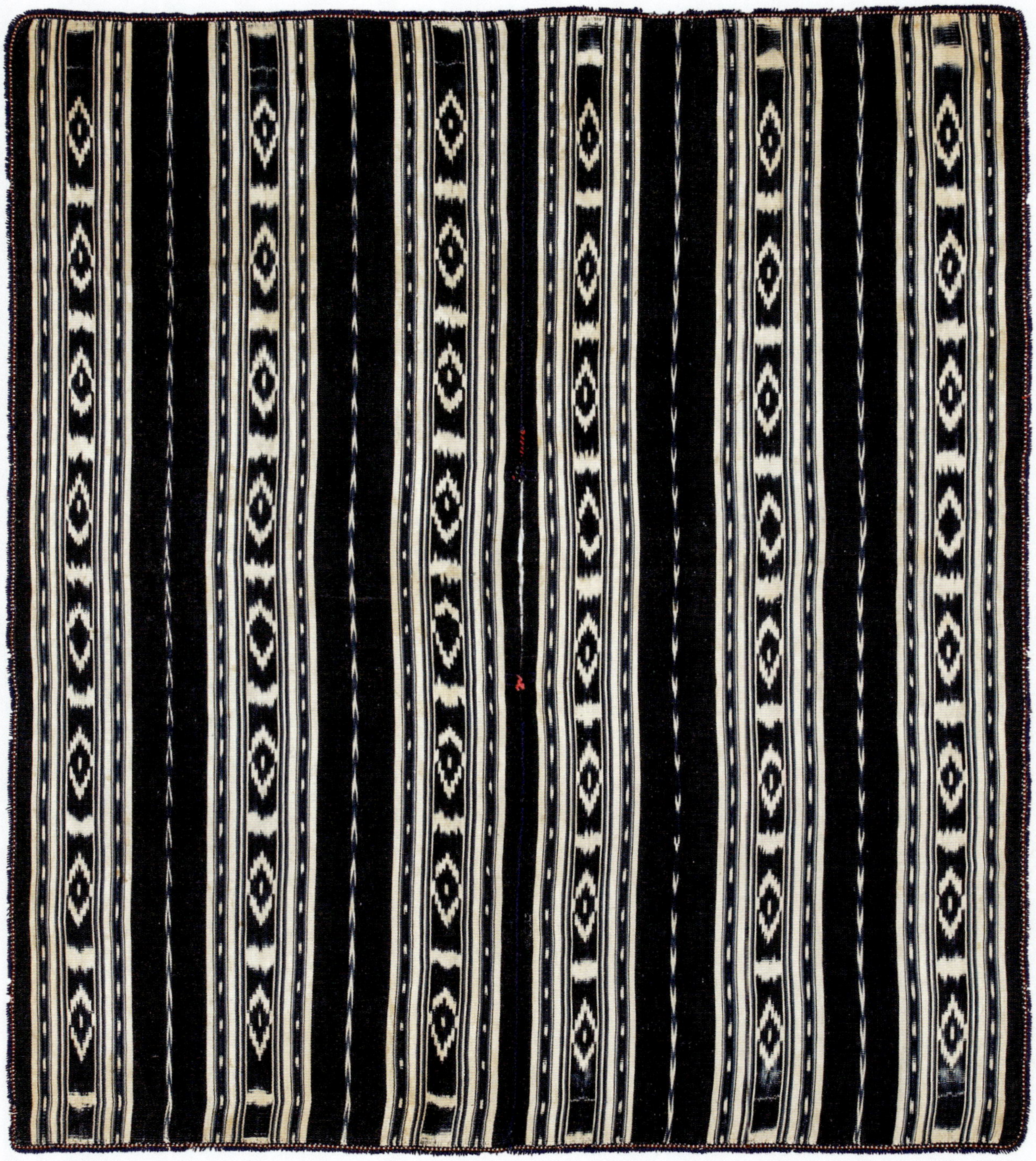

AM35 Poncho, Riobamba, Ecuador, 19th century. Cotton-warp ikat, cotton weft, cotton fringe. 56 in x 50 in

This cotton poncho is woven in the more skillful variation of the technique used in wool ponchos in the Cuenca region. The most common, called *kokomura* in Chimborazo province in the Cacha region and around Riobamba, has a highly standardized composition with eight wide, bound-resist-dyed stripes, four on each half of the garment, containing diamond and chevron designs in white against a blue indigo background. This poncho has a slightly different composition from *kokomura* but shares many of its features. It is smaller, with six vertical bands containing diamond patterns interspersed with horizontal bars. These are flanked on each side by series of narrower white and indigo stripes, and four wide indigo bands. All of the sections with a dark-indigo background also contain small resist patterns in the center.

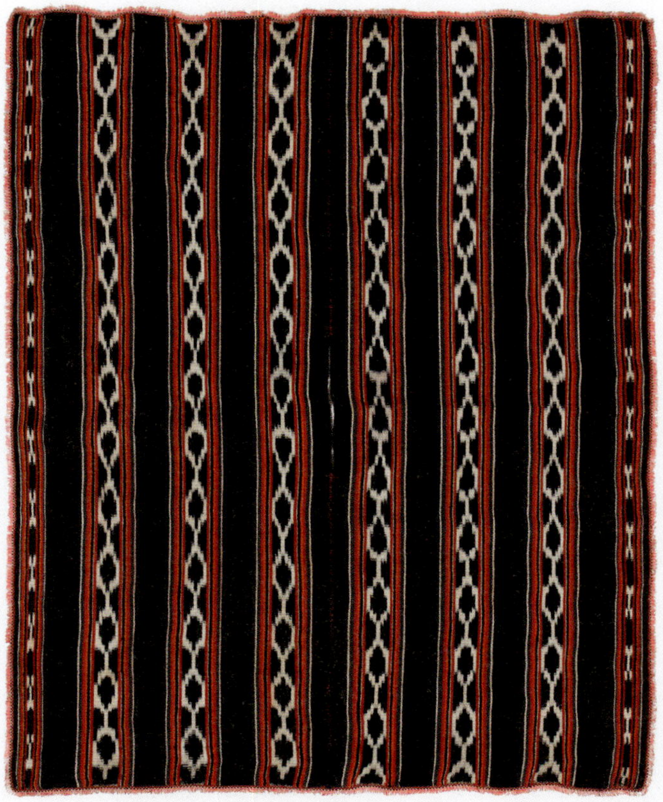

AM36 Poncho
Riobamba, Ecuador, 20th century. Cotton, warp ikat and sheep's wool. 60 in x 49 in

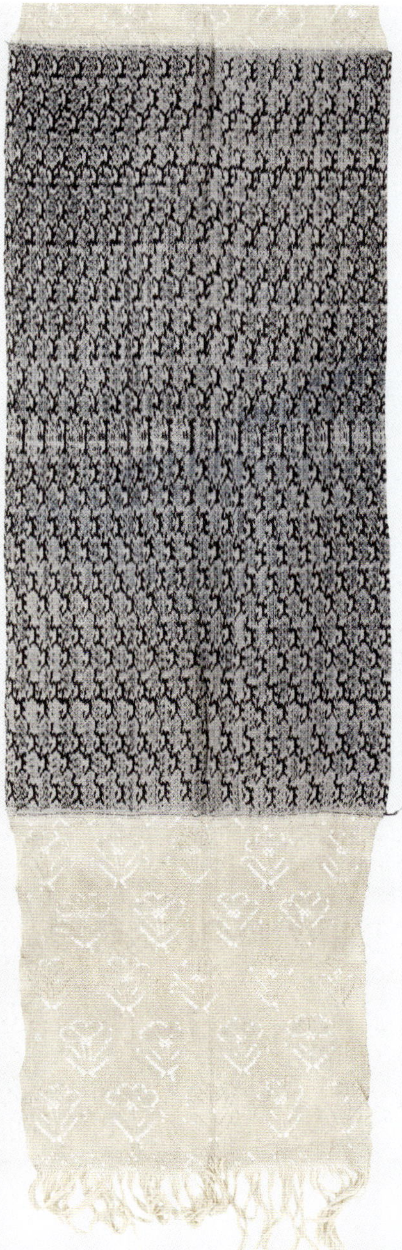

AM37 Shoulder cloth, *rebozo*
Cuenca, Ecuador, 20th century. Cotton-warp ikat with macramé edging and fringe. 29 in x 115 in

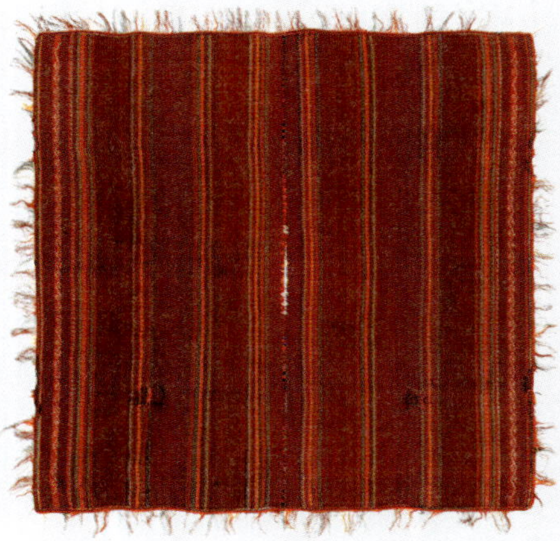

AM38 Poncho
Bolivia, late 19th or early 20th century. Alpaca wool, warp ikat. 50 in x 60 in

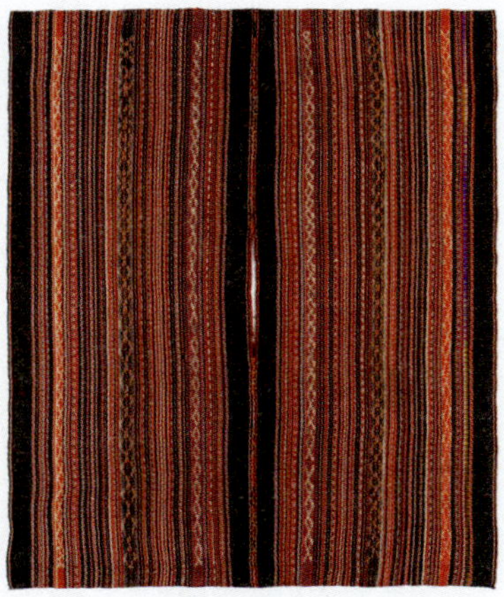

AM39 Poncho
Bolivia, 20th century. Alpaca wool, warp ikat. 70 in x 59 in

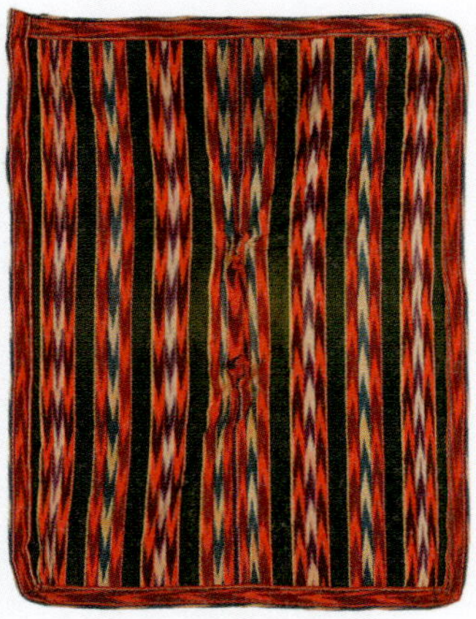

AM40 Poncho
Charazani, Bolivia, 20th century. Sheep's wool, warp ikat. 69 in x 52 in

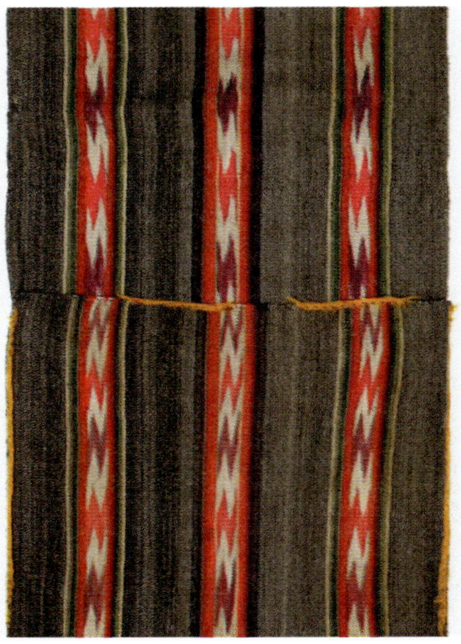

AM41 Shoulder bag
Charazani, Bolivia, 20th century. Sheep's wool, warp ikat. 14 in x 26 in

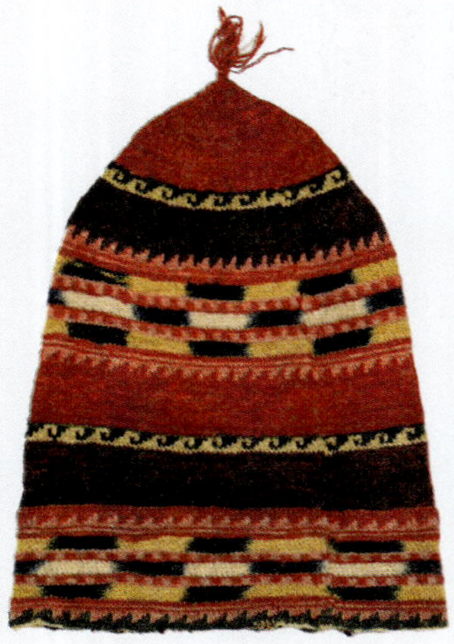

AM42 Hat, *chullo*
Bolivia, 19th century. Alpaca wool, sections of knit ikat. 11 in x 9 in

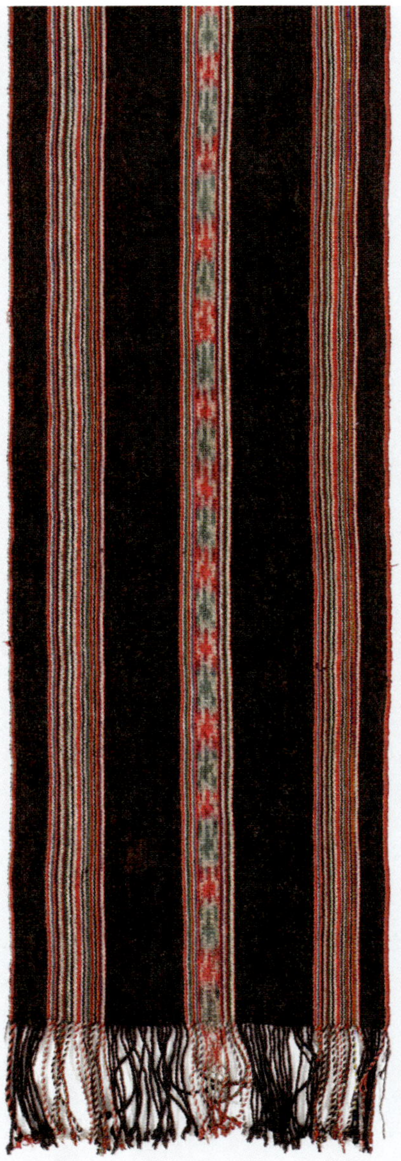

AM43 Scarf
Bolivia, 20th century. Alpaca wool, warp ikat. 36 in x 10 in

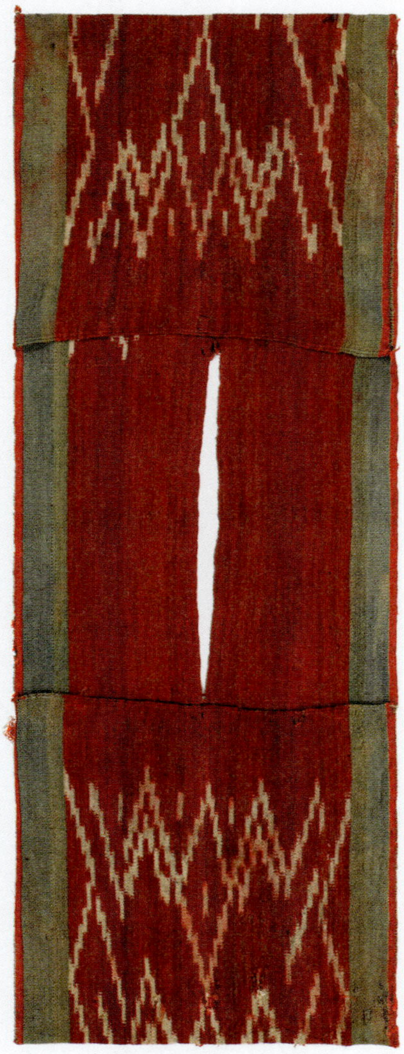

AM44 Shoulder bag
Charazani, Bolivia, 19th century. Wool, warp ikat. 4C in x 16 in

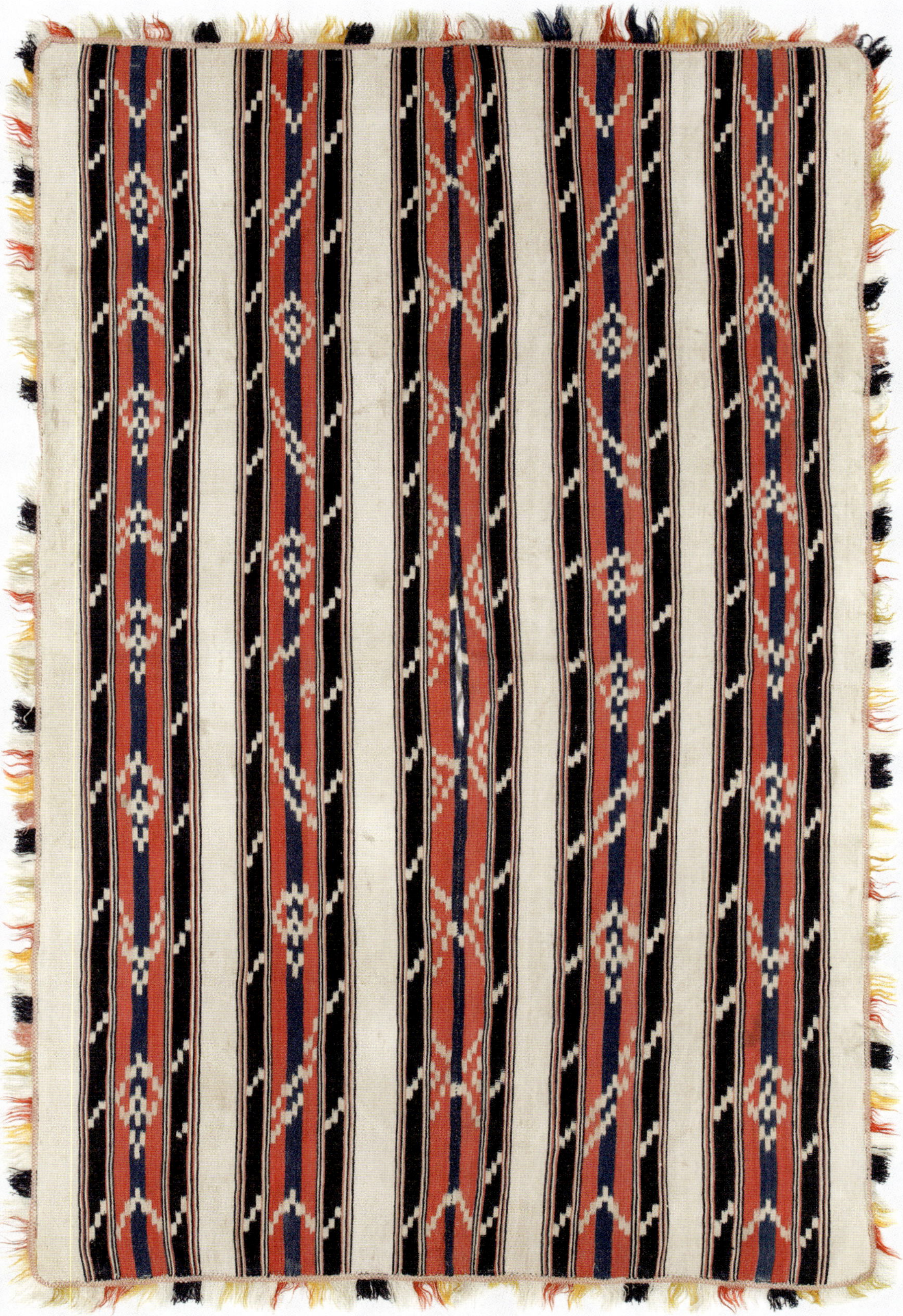

AM45 Poncho, northern Bolivia, early 19th century. Warp *watay* on merino wool, alpaca fringe. 79 in x 54 in

This poncho is an exceptional example of those woven in several regions in Bolivia during the 19th century. The composition features medium-width white monochrome stripes alternating with groups of narrower stripes with *watay* patterns in a continuous repeating pattern across the width of the garment. The use of natural white merino wool provides a contrast with the more vivid pink, light-blue, and dark-blue narrow stripes, while corresponding with the small *watay* patterns formed by small rectangular blocks pulled into diagonal and diamond shapes. This poncho is somewhat unusual in that, instead of being confined to a single stripe, the patterns are formed across multiple stripes of different colors. The alpaca fringe was made separately and attached to the finished garment, containing the same range of colors as in the main body of the poncho with the addition of a bright shade of yellow.

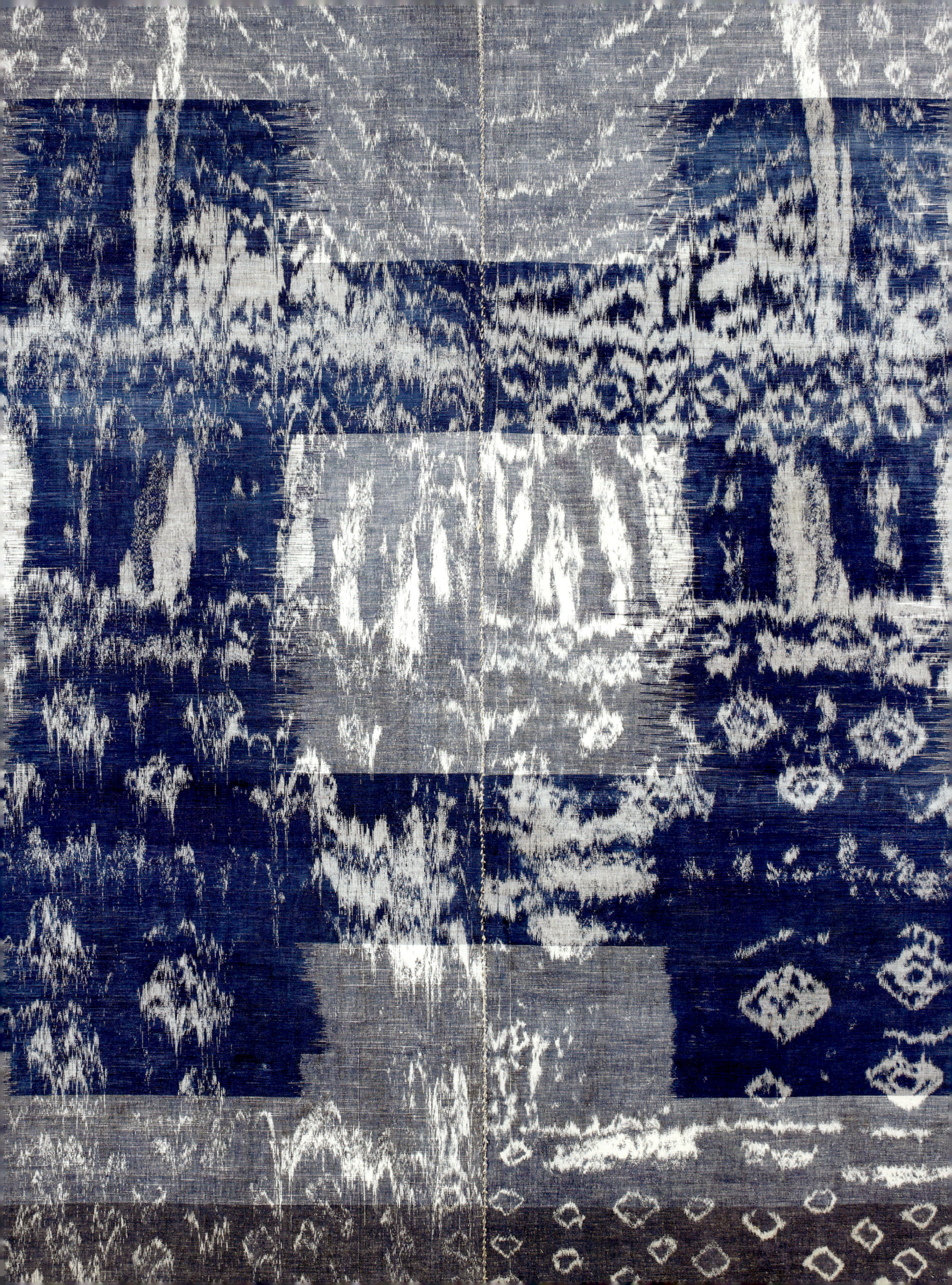

IKAT TODAY

by Polly Barton

In past decades, the centuries-old technique of ikat has taken a new direction through the work of contemporary artists. Since the Fiber Art revolution of the 1960s and 70s, it has been used to create non-functional artworks that push the technique through the incorporation of unconventional materials and new motifs. Alongside this artistic development, ikat, handwoven or emulated through print or machine-made constructions, has become an internationally popular look for soft furnishings. This wealth of present-day expression, a successor to successive ages of textile-making across the globe, demonstrates the extraordinary ability of ikat to continually shapeshift and delight.

THE WARP IS MY CANVAS

Fig.1
IT06, *In Stillness*

The warp is my canvas, the technique of ikat is my paintbrush and the means for my expressive gesture. Colors dyed in rhythmic patterns of ikat along the length of warp become my palette and the surface for weaving ideas.

My work in the studio involves tying, dyeing, weaving, drawing, and painting. I work in layers, and ikat allows for colors and patterns to build within the warp and weft. Working with ikat, I can layer and bundle together the ideas and sketches gathered over time which surround my studio walls–particularly when using double ikat combining ikat in both the warp and weft. I watch the design emerge while weaving: an idea hovering, was embedded and hidden in the tied sections along the length of the warp.

I think often about the idea of resist as ikat's creative potential. On or off the loom, it is in acting with or reacting to the resistance potential of materials (tight or loose ties, types of tie, mordants, type of dye or pigment) that I make my art, find my voice, my gesture, and my way of engaging with the world. Which is to say to lock in a design, encode thread with the memory of an image or a motif, and to push against the need to control the outcome. Ikat as a technique holds secrets as it teaches me that at a certain point it is a team effort–my idea and the technique's possibilities.

Born in New York City, I was trained to weave in Japan forty years ago. I still work on a Japanese kimono loom, and though I have lived in the American Southwest for thirty years, my sensibilities and my work lean in both directions toward the East and West, as I use both of these ancient, traditional patterns while constructing more contemporary artwork. I remember vividly that moment over forty years ago, traveling in a train in Japan with my sensei, master weaver Tomohiko Inoue, and looking out the window at the sun setting behind Fuji-san thinking, "*That* is why I want to learn to weave. I want to paint in silk." When working on *In Stillness* (Fig.1/IT06), I tied bands of the white warp with raffia tape, placed the tied warp in a light-gray dye bath and, using a warp shifter on the back of my loom, created a checkerboard of gray and white. Onto this patterned warp I painted with additional dye the greens and browns which set the mood for the weft ikat to weave in a landscape of space and mystery.

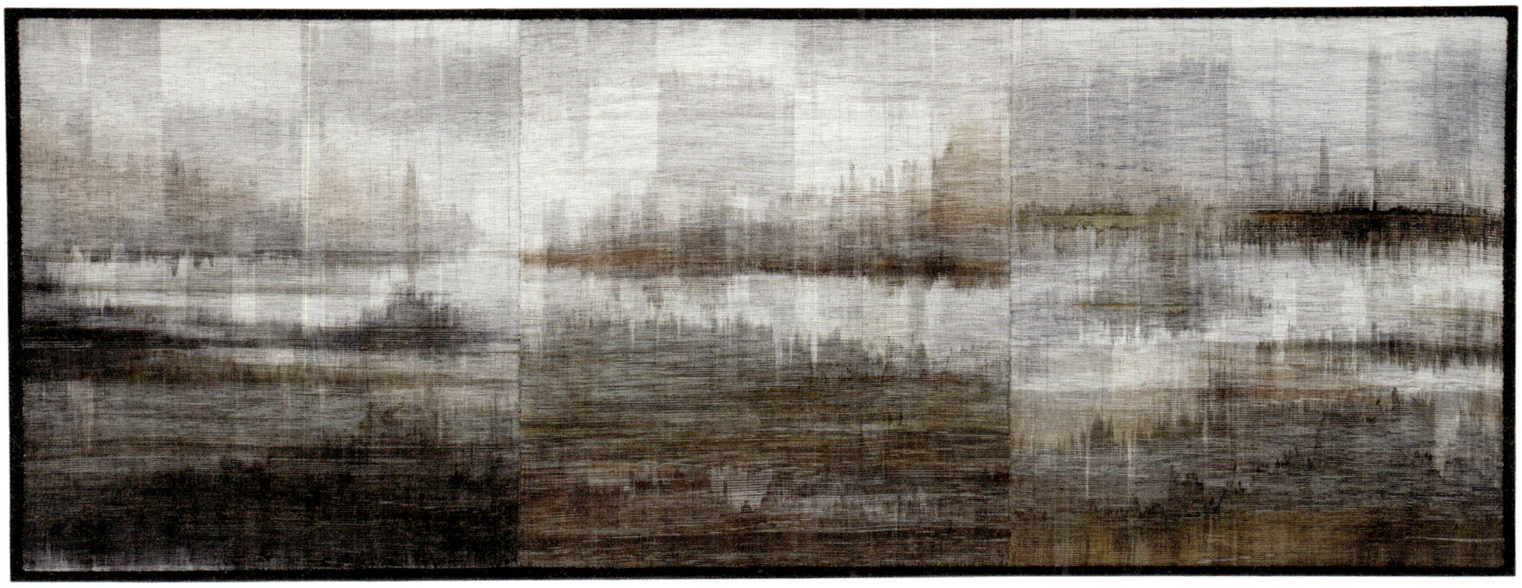

Fig.1

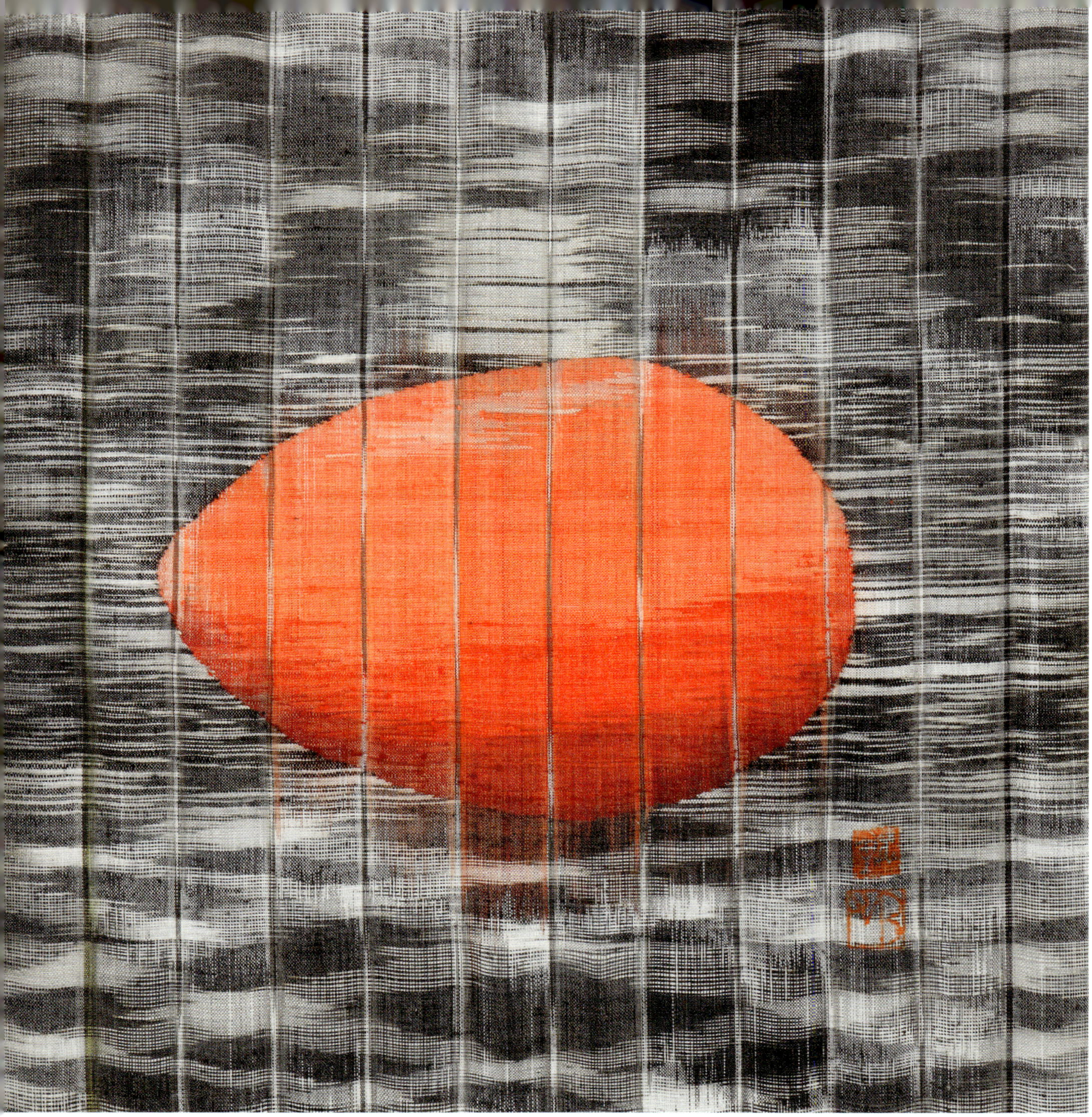

Fig.2

Fig.2
IT05, *Tamago Basada*

Since the work and time in ikat is spent in tying knots–often many knots!–I do not like to weave the same piece twice, and each weaving is a unique work. The appeal and engaging result is flexibility, continual growth as an artist, exploration and problem solving. When tying a knot of resist on thread, this act encodes the thread, locking in the mark of design which carries memory, an historical marker, a global or locally identifiable story which is passed down culturally in the woven membrane or fabric.

My own challenge with ikat is when the threads resist, push back, push me forward as an artist while keeping me connected to the web of woven history. The lines, the graphics, the voice of each piece astonish me with a vitality, a freedom to break rules. Into and onto this surface I paint, stain, rub, let leak and ooze, fuss and finesse with pigment, soy milk, sumi ink, and dye. Embedded messages, unwanted lessons, fading habits, new materials with their surprising results now play in my work as I am tossed time and again up against that hurdle between weaving and painting. I give myself free rein to leap into the unknown.

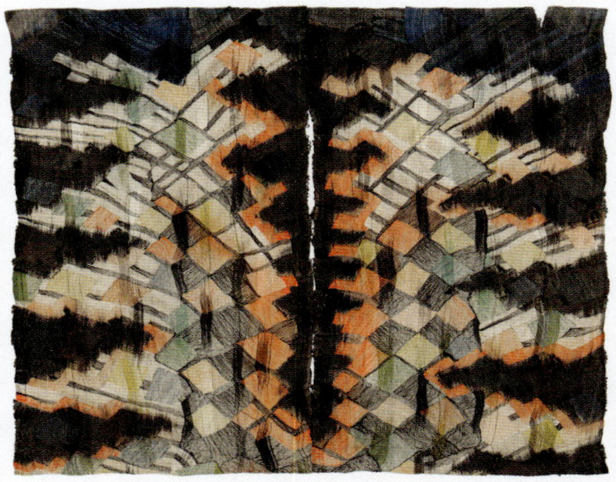

IT01 *Tejido*, James Bassler, 2003. Linen, cotton, silk, nylon, warp ikat and wedge weave. 42 in x 52 in
James Bassler uses ikat to dramatic and majestic effect. The linen warp, tied and dyed with black and indigo, holds the variegated wedge weave weft fibers. Originally woven in 1993 as one nine-foot long piece, *Shroud*, it toured France until 1996. After it was returned to the artist, he cut it and unstitched and rewove the center two selvages together to create *Tejido* in 2003.

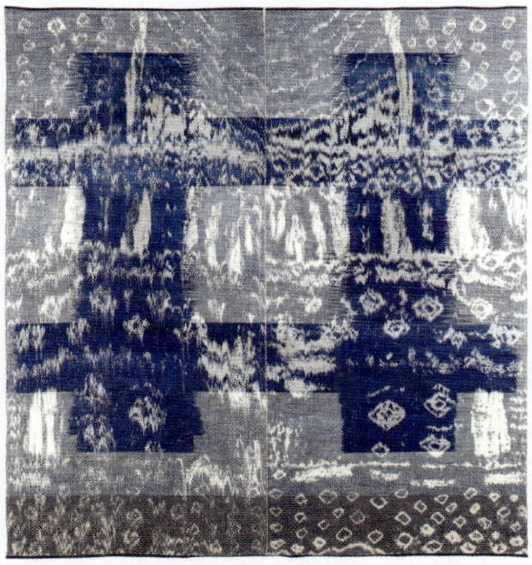

IT02 *Homage to Japan*, Ed Rossbach, 1970s. Linen tie-dye, cotton inserted weft ikat. 90 in x 86.5 in. The Textile Museum, 2019.8.3
This piece illustrates beautifully the fluid nature of ikat; the warp threads sweep downstream. Originally one long piece, the warp was tie-dyed with rocks and sticks and woven with removable wefts which were then replaced with indigo-dyed bands of ikat wefts. These broad ikat bands serve to anchor the design visually. The piece was then cut in half and book matched.

IT03 Untitled, Jun Tomita, 1970s. Cotton, warp ikat, zone-dyed ikat. 16 in x 13 in
It takes a master weaver to control the warp ikat resist ties to line up precisely as Jun Tomita has done in this piece. The artist's hand is present in the variegated colors traveling along the single striped warp threads below the black anchored by the resist ties above. Tomita has used resist as gesture, as a painter might use a brush.

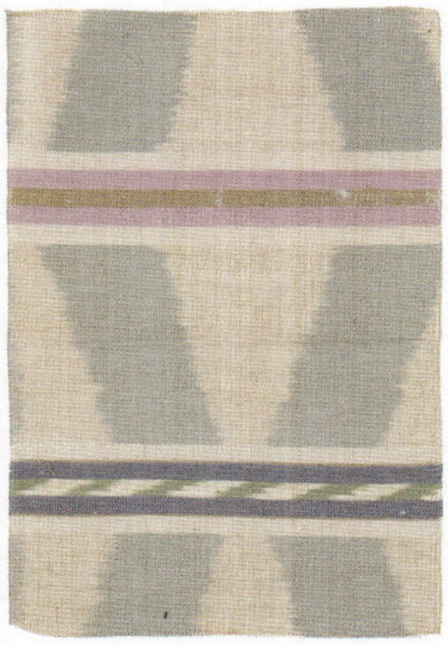

IT04 Sample cloth from Jack Lenor Larsen's studio, 1960s. Silk and linen weft ikat. 22 in x 15 in
Master textile designer Jack Lenor Larsen was brilliant at bringing an East Asian mood into our world, and our living rooms. Refined and elegant, his use of ikat with bands of colors feels borrowed from the East, yet welcome in the West.

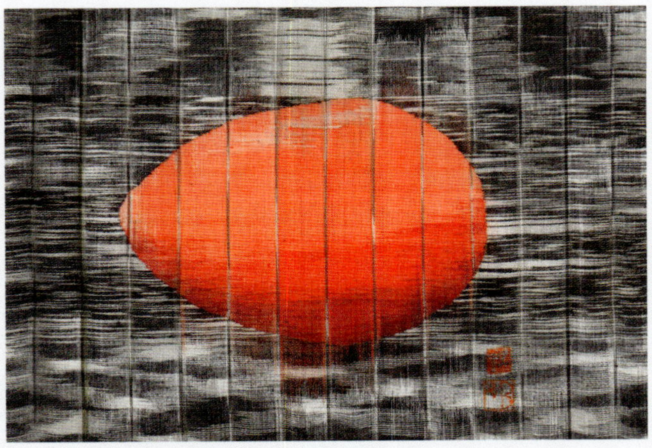

IT05 *Tamago Basada*, Polly Barton, 1996
Silk warp and weft compound ikat, weft tapestry weave. 17 in x 17 in

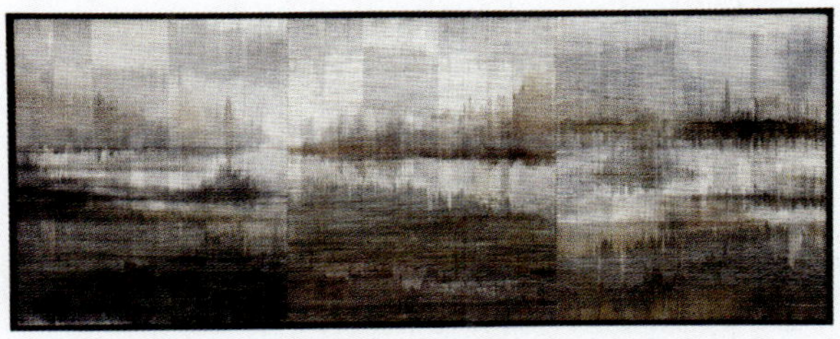

IT06 *In Stillness*, Polly Barton, 2003
Cotton, warp ikat and linen weft painted. 21 in x 54 in

Endnotes

INTRODUCTION

1 Hein.
2 Rouffaer, 1901.
3 Iklé, 1928.
4 See for example Bühler, 1941, 1942, 1972, 1979 & 1980.
5 See Larsen, pp. 21–23 for further examples of proto-ikat.
6 See Crill, 1998, pl. 66.
7 See Fitz Gibbon & Hale, pp. 15, 180.
8 See Fee, p. 423.
9 See Feng, p. 106, cat. No. 42.
10 Bühler, 1972, vol. 3, pp. 157–60, 163.
11 Buckley, p. 26.
12 See ibid, Fig.1 showing "the ikat line."
13 See Dusenbury, p. 60. In view of the broader meaning of *kasuri*, Mary Dusenbury suggests that the term "thread-resist" be used, leaving "ikat" for those produced in Southeast Asia.
14 Serjeant, p. 77.
15 Most of the Yemeni ikats were found in Egypt. See Bühler, 1972, cat. nos. 1–20.
16 Schoff, para. 24, p. 31. See Bier, 2014, pp. 32–40.
17 Serjeant, p. 76.
18 Serjeant, p. 77.
19 See Van Stan, pp. 150–59 and Bird; see also Larsen, pp. 48–50 for early tie-dyed (*plangi*) textiles from Peru.

JAPAN

1 For a discussion of the possible origins of the term "kasuri" see Dusenbury, p. 59.
2 See Nunome; Liu.
3 See Dusenbury, pp. 12–13.
4 See Kobayashi, 2018, pp. 204–17.
5 Ibid, pp. 218–25; Dusenbury, p. 60.
6 See Dusenbury, pp. 61–62.
7 See Stinchecum, pp. 80–82; Kobayashi, 2018, pp. 218–34.
8 Bunka Gakuen Costume Museum, pp. 22–25.
9 Kobayashi, 2018, pp. 289–92.
10 Kobayashi, 2018, p. 254, pp. 265–66
11 Kobayashi, 2001–2002, pp. 3–34.

MONSOON ASIA

1 Reid.
2 Buckley, pp. 22–33.
3 Maxwell, pp. 216–23.
4 Guy, 2009, pp. 129–35.
5 Howard, pp. 3–5.
6 Howard, pp. 126–28, 137–40.
7 Boudot & Buckley, pp. 193–99.
8 McIntosh, 2012, pp. 61–65
9 Fraser-Lu, p. 195.
10 Gittinger & Lefferts, p. 38; Maxwell, pp. 216–23.
11 McIntosh, 2012, pp. 79–89.
12 Gittinger & Lefferts, p. 209.
13 McIntosh, 2012, pp. 46–48, 50, 66–75.
14 Guy, 2009, pp. 121–37.
15 McIntosh, 2012, pp. 168–81.
16 Ibid., pp. 154–55.
17 Ibid., pp. 182–89.
18 Ibid., p. 200.
19 Thanasook, p. 124.
20 Quizon, p. 294.
21 Maxwell, pp. 165, 355–57.
22 Gavin.
23 Buckley, pp. 22–33.
24 McIntosh, 2019, p. 178.
25 McIntosh, 2019, pp. 87–89.
26 Djawanai.
27 McIntosh, 2019, p. 283.

INDIA

1 This dating was first proposed by Walter M. Spink (see Spink, p. 2), and has been followed by most authorities thereafter (e.g. Behl, p. 27).
2 Shamir & Baginski, pp. 65–74. Granger-Taylor, in K. D. Politis et al., Section V10.d, pp. 378–92.
3 Chandra, 1960 & 1961.
4 See Crill, 1998, pp. 64–87; 99–101 and 125–35 for 19th-century South Indian ikats.
5 Crill, 1998, pl. 77.
6 Nabholz-Kartaschoff, 1989, p. 68.
7 Crill, 1998, pls. 83 and 126.
8 Ibid., pls. 84 and 86.
9 Ibid., pl. 90.
10 Ibid., pl. 96–97.
11 Ibid., pls. 46–47.
12 Ibid., pl. 48.
13 Tavernier, vol. II, p. 3.
14 Bühler, Fischer & Nabholz, p.56.
15 See Crill, 1998, pl. 40 for a *tran phul bhat patola* used as a canopy at a wedding in Sulawesi, Indonesia, and Bühler & Fischer (1979), vol. 2, figs. 246–51 and 253 for the same pattern in dress and furnishings in Java.
16 John Ang has suggested a possible connection between the *pan bhat patola* design and that of a *selendang limar* of South Sumatra, with a repeating leaf design (Ang, fig. 1 and pp. 10–11). Ang also reports that a *pan bhat patola* was collected in South Sumatra (ibid., p. 11).
17 See Buhler, Fischer and Nabholz, pls. 18–21; Crill, 1998, pl. 20.
18 Bühler & Fischer (1979), vol. 1, pp. 268–69.
19 See Guy, 1998, pl. 117 for a priestess or shaman from Sulawesi wearing a *patolu* of this design as a waist-sash.
20 See for example V&A IS 149-1984, illustrated in Crill, 1998, pl. 39.
21 See for example Avril, cat. nos. 20–21; Guy & Thakar, pl. 5.
22 Crill, 1998, pl. 43; Guy, 1998, pl. 106–08; Avril, cat. nos. 22–25.
23 Avril, pp. 88–89.
24 See Jain, 2016, pp. 266–71 for examples of striped and ikat *mashru* from the Jaipur royal collection, and Crill, 2021, pl. 83, for a curtain backed with floral striped *mashru*.
25 See Crill, 1998, pls. 107, 108, 110, 112, for 19th-century examples of South Indian ikat *mashru*.
26 Crill, 1998 pl. 114, for a saddlecloth lined with ikat *mashru*.
27 Crill, 1998, pl. 103.
28 Crill, 1998, pl. 102.
29 See Jain, 2016 (acc. no. Tc/F-37), pl. 23B (blue chevrons); Jain, 2009 (acc. no. TNT 219), pp. 148–49, 191 (small-scale repeating tree motif).
30 Jain also points out that the twill-weave foundation of the piece in Jodhpur also suggests an Indian, possibly Gujarati, origin (Jain, 2009, p. 148).
31 See Crill, 1998, pl. 11a (National Museum, acc. no. 59.203/4) and pl. 12 (Calico Museum of Textiles, acc. no. 1364).

WEST & CENTRAL ASIA

1 A small number of these textiles survive in museum collections today, which include The Textile Museum, Metropolitan Museum of Art, Cleveland Museum of Art, Kelsey Museum of Archaeology, and Royal Ontario Museum. See Bier, 2014 and Bier, 2001 for a description of Yemeni ikats, and Shamir & Baginski for newer finds of Yemeni ikat in Eastern Mediterranean archaeological sites.
2 Fieldwork by Dominique Chevallier conducted in the early 1960s, followed by Moser in 1974, is a valuable resource that captured the tradition when there were still a few old masters born during the Ottoman Empire alive to share their knowledge. Chevallier, 1963; Chevallier, 1962; Moser, 1974; Chevallier, 1982.
3 Turpin & Whelan 1993; Kalter et al., pp. 200–01; Moser, 1974; Chevallier, 1962; Chevallier, 1982.
4 Kalter et al., pp. 202–03.
5 Dominique Chevallier mentions that *tarbit* comes from the verb *rabbata*–the intensive form of the root *rabata* (to tie). The man who specializes in this work is called a *rabbat*. Chevallier, 1963, pp. 25–29.
6 Chevallier, 1963, p. 26; Chevallier, 1962, p. 308; Chevallier, 1982, p. 98; Moser, 1974; Turpin & Whelan, p. 25.
7 Turpin & Whelan 1993, p. 31.
8 Chevallier, 1963, p. 28; Chevallier, 1962, p. 312; Chevallier, 1982, pp. 102–03; Moser, 1974.
9 Nabholz-Kartaschoff, 2019, pp. 98–101; Gluck & Gluck, pp. 202–05.
10 Nabholz-Kartaschoff (2019, pp. 98–101) states that "The term means 'reign' or 'ruler' and was derived from the name of King Darius. In contemporary usage it means 'wealth' or 'assets,' and it also appears in lists of the 18th-century Russian customs authority that itemized luxury goods destined for transport to Bukhara by caravan. In those documents, it might possibly be related to the Russian word *dorogoi*, which means 'precious' or 'expensive.'" See also Gluck & Gluck, pp. 202–05.
11 See example presented in Gluck & Gluck, p. 204.
12 See Fitz Gibbon & Hale, pp. 23–111 and Andrew Hale in Krody, pp. 41–51 for the design history of ikat tradition in Central Asia.
13 See Fitz Gibbon & Hale, and Krody, for more detailed information about Central Asian ikat.
14 See Fitz Gibbon & Hale 1997, pp. 23–61; Andrew Hale in Krody, pp. 41–51.
15 Fitz Gibbon & Hale, pp. 237–67.
16 See Fitz Gibbon & Hale, pp. 269–99, and Krody 2010, pp. 53–67, for a detailed description of Central Asian ikat garments.

AFRICA

1 Ehret, p. 63.
2 Plankensteiner & Adediran, p. 37 for a detail of one of the Lagos cloths.
3 Boser-Sarivaxévanis, pp. 188–90.
4 Bauer, p. 138.
5 Fee, p. 423.
6 Mosca, p. 48.

EUROPE

1 Lloyd, p. 300.
2 See Iklé, 1931, p. 48; Nabholz-Kartaschoff, 1968, p. 5; *Flàmules: Les teles de llengües a Mallorca*, p. 38; and Prin, p. 325. See also Nabholz-Kartaschoff, 1969.
3 Rouffaer, 1902, p. 8.

4 The discovery of an ikat fragment at the 4th- to 9th-century site of Astana in Xinjiang Province suggests very early Central Asian production in northwestern China. See Fitz Gibbon & Hale, p. 24, n. 17.
5 "Far i drappi alla cinese … vergare, screziar un drappo alla foggia di quelli della Cina." Di Villanova, p. 119; Scheler, p. 61; Littré, p. 605; and Cordier, pp. 38–39.
6 Rouffaer, 1902, p. 8.
7 Rouffaer, 1902, pp. 6–7.
8 See *Encyclopédie ou Dictionnaire raisonné des sciences, des arts et des métiers*, vol. 3, pp. 339–41; and de l'Hiberderie. See also Miller, L. E., pp. 29–53.
9 Called "clouder" in English; see "Manufactures. Silken Manufacture," p. 461. In the 19th century, the meaning of *chineur* changed entirely, instead referring to a bargain hunter of antiques; see Roland-Gosselin, accessed 11 June 2022, https://www.lefigaro.fr/langue-francaise/actu-des-mots/2018/02/18/37002-20180218ARTFIG00013-mais-d-o-vient-le-mot-chiner.php.
10 A page in the Richelieu collection of fabric samples at the Bibliothèque nationale de France includes striped-and-checked taffetas first woven in the 1660s. "Taffetas. Qui a esté renouvellé en 1734, ci qui avon deja paru il y a plus de 70. ans. Se trouvant encore de ce ancien taffetas de la même façon," [*Échantillons d'étoffes et de rubans recueillis par le Maréchal de Richelieu*], pp. 83–85, accessed 10 August 2022, https://gallica.bnf.fr/ark:/12148/btv1b69364621/f1.item.
11 An identical silk is at the Museum der Kulturen Basel (inv. VI 16512); see Nabholz-Kartaschoff 1968, p. 2; and Nabholz-Kartaschoff 1969, p. 52.
12 Hardouin-Fugier, et al., p. 398.
13 "[Échantillons de tissu]," *Échantillons d'Étoffes des Manufactures étrangères recueillis par le Maréchal de Richelieu*, vol. V (1736), pp. 2810–13, accessed 29 July 2022, https://gallica.bnf.fr/ark:/12148/btv1b6936249g/f1.item. These ikats also resembled another eponymous textile art used in the home: flame-stitch embroidery, also known as *bargello*, *bergamo*, and *point d'Hongrie*.
14 For very similar striped-and-flamed silk brocades and lampas from Persia, see *Persidskie i turetskie tkani XVI-XVIII vekov v sobranii Istoricheskogo muzeia*, pp. 106–07, 109.
15 https://gallica.bnf.fr/ark:/12148/btv1b6936016d/f1.item; and "Étoffes de Lyon / 1736," *Échantillons d'Étoffes et Toiles des Manufactures de France recueillis par le Maréchal de Richelieu*, vol. I, pp. 144–55, Bibliothèque nationale de France, département Estampes et photographie, RESERVE LH-45-BOITE FOL, accessed 11 July 2022, https://gallica.bnf.fr/ark:/12148/btv1b6935848t/f3.item.
16 A 1737 warp-dyed silk-velvet sample in the Richelieu collection is said to have been used for a gown belonging to Marie Leszczyńska. See "[Échantillons de tissus]," *Échantillons d'Étoffes et Toiles des Manufactures de France recueillis par le Maréchal de Richelieu*, vol. III ([1737]), pp. 2087–93, accessed 4 August 2022, https://gallica.bnf.fr/ark:/12148/btv1b6936123w/f1.item.
17 In 1769, painter Joseph Ducreux portrayed Marie Antoinette in a warp-dyed robe à la française (Château de Versailles, inv. DESS 1207).
18 For other meandering silks, see, for instance, Buss.
19 For the use of *chiné* taffetas for furnishing, see Joubert de l'Hiberderie, p. xxv.
20 See, for instance, a pattern book in Rothstein, p. 266ff; and Thornton, p. 185. To encourage the consumption of local English silks, the House of Commons taxed Italian and French "clouds" much like other Continental silks. See Journals of the Board of Trade and Plantations, pp. 229–39, fo. 353, accessed 29 July 2022, https://www.british-history.ac.uk/jrnl-trade-plantations/vol12/pp229-239; and The Journals of the House of Commons, p. 376.
21 Catalonian inventories record *flàmulas* in use from at least 1724; see *Flàmules*, p. 50.
22 See "Étoffes d'Avignon / 1736," *Échantillons d'Étoffes des Manufactures étrangères recueillis par le Maréchal de Richelieu*, vol. V, pp. 2623–27, Bibliothèque nationale de France, département Estampes et photographie, RESERVE LH-45 (D)-BOITE FOL, accessed July 11, 2022, https://gallica.bnf.fr/ark:/12148/btv1b69362074.item.
23 Prin, p. 324; and Rodier, pp. 271–73.
24 See Thépaut-Cabasset, pp. 165–70.
25 See *Encyclopédie ou Dictionnaire raisonné des sciences, des arts et des métiers*, vol. 11, p. 34, pls. CXVI, CXVII.
26 McCabe, pp. 222–23.
27 See *Flàmules*, pp. 38–55.
28 Yefimova, et al., p. 6, cat. no. 15.
29 See Cora Ginsburg 2003, pp. 10–11.
30 See a warp-dyed silk on the reverse of an appliquéd quilt in the International Quilt Study Museum, Lincoln, Nebraska, USA (2015.100.0001). There may be a connection to the Syrian city of Qanawat as well as the area of Russian-controlled Turkestan known as Kanavat.
31 See Kemp, p. 196; and Cox, p. 57.

AMERICAS

1 Rowe, p. 18.
2 Ibid., p. 18.
3 Ibid., p. 18.
4 Ibid., pp. 20 and 22
5 Z. (Waldo Jordán) (Segunda Parte), 15 March 2010, http://textilesandinos.blogspot.com/2010/03/el-watado-tecnica-textil-de-los-andes_15.html; Rowe, pp. 20–22.
6 Rowe & Cohen, p. 99. Rowe, p. 20.
7 Rowe & Cohen, p. 99. Callanaupa Alvarez, p. 59. Rowe (1977), pp. 18–19.
8 Callanaupa Alvarez, p. 59. Rowe & Cohen, p. 99.
9 Z. (Waldo Jordán), (Primera Parte), March 15, 2010, http://textilesandinos.blogspot.com/; (Segunda Parte).
10 Ibid. (Segunda Parte).
11 Ibid. (Primera & Segunda Partes).
12 Two examples are in the collections of the National Museum of Natural History in Washington, DC. Rowe & Meisch, pp. 56 (fig. 1.39) and 59 (fig. 1.42).
13 Rowe & Meisch, p. 58.
14 Rowe, Miller & Meisch, pp. 53, 76, 100.
15 Ibid., pp. 53–54.
16 Ibid., pp. 54–55.
17 Ibid., p. 77. Miller, Laura Martin, pp. 337–58 (337).
18 Rowe, pp. 22–23. Rowe, Miller & Meisch, pp. 78–79, 83–85. Miller, Laura Martin, pp. 337–38, 344.
19 Davis, pp. 309–36. Rowe, pp. 23–24. Rowe, Miller & Meisch, p. 77.
20 Rowe, Miller & Meisch, pp. 77–78.
21 Rowe, pp. 18–19.
22 Rowe, p. 20. Chertudi, p. 158. The term *trarikán makúñ* is also used in Chile, see Mege, pp. 65–93 (86).
23 Rowe, p. 19.
24 Ibid.
25 Ibid., pp. 19–20.
26 de Avila, 2016, p. 3. Weitlaner-Johnson, pp. 27–40 (30).
27 de Avila, n.d., p. 33.
28 de Avila, 2016, pp. 2–3.
29 Ibid., p. 3.
30 Ibid., p. 4; Weitlaner-Johnson, pp. 27, 28, 33. Davis, p. 310.
31 de Avila, n.d., p. 38.
32 Weitlaner-Johnson, p. 33.
33 Ibid; Davis, pp. 315–16.
34 Davis, p. 312.
35 Ibid.
36 Miralbés de Polanco, p. 7. Morales Hidalgo, pp. 10–12.
37 Miralbés de Polanco, p. 12. Morales Hidalgo, pp. 25–34.
38 Miralbés de Polanco, p. 15.
39 Ibid., p. 12.
40 Ibid.
41 Ibid.
42 Ibid., p. 7.
43 Ibid., p. 15.
44 Ibid., p. 9.

Bibliography

Cora Ginsburg 2003. Pressroom, Hong Kong, 2003

Échantillons d'Étoffes et Toiles des Manufactures de France recueillis par le Maréchal de Richelieu, Bibliothèque nationale de France, département Estampes et photographie

Encyclopédie ou Dictionnaire raisonné des sciences, des arts et des métiers, vol. 3. Paris, 1765

Flàmules: Les teles de llengües a Mallorca. Institut d'Innovacio Empresarial de les Illes Balers, Palma de Mallorca, 2009

Journals of the Board of Trade and Plantations: Volume 12, January 1764–December 1767, vol. 72. His Majesty's Stationery Office, London, 1936

Journals of the House of Commons from January the 10th, 1765, in the Fifth Year of the Reign of King George the Third, to September the 16th, 1766, in the Sixth Year of the Reign of King George the Third, The, vol. 30. By Order of the House of Commons, London, 1803

"Manufactures. Silken Manufacture," *The Gentleman's and London Magazine: Or Monthly Chronologer* XLVI, 1776

Persidskie i turet͡skie tkani XVI-XVIII vekov v sobranii Istoricheskogo muze͡ia. Gosudarstvennyĭ istoricheskiĭ muzeĭ, Moscow, 2015

Sekai no Kasuri [Ikat Textiles from the World]. Bunka Gakuen Costume Museum, Tokyo, 2011

"Taffetas. Qui a esté renouvellé en 1734, ci qui avon deja paru il y a plus de70. ans. Se trouvant encore de ce ancien taffetas de la même façon," *Échantillons détoffes et de rubans recueillis par le Maréchal de Richelieu*, 1734

Ang, John, "New Inroads in the Study of Malay Textiles," in *Journal of the Oriental Rug and Textile Society*, vol. 5, no. 2, Summer 2022

Aragon, Lorraine, et al. *Textiles of Indonesia: The Thomas Murray Collection*. Prestel, Munich, 2021.

Avril, Ellen, ed., *Traded Treasure: Indian Textiles for Global Markets*. Ithaca, Reading, 2019

Bauer, Kerstin, in ed. Bernhard Gardi, *Woven Beauty: The Art of West African Textiles*. Christoph Merian Verlag, 2009

Behl, Benoy, *The Ajanta Caves*. Thames & Hudson, London and New York, 1998

Bier, Carol, *A Calligrapher's Art: Inscribed Cotton Ikat from Yemen*. Exhibition Brochure. The Textile Museum, Washington, DC, 2001

Bier, Carol, "Inscribed Cotton Ikat from Yemen in the Tenth Century CE" in *9th International Shibori Symposium, Hangzhou*, 2014 https://www.academia.edu/38477171/Inscribed_Cotton_Ikat_from_Yemen_in_the_Tenth_Century_CE

Bird, Junius, "Pre-Spanish Peruvian Ikat" in *The Bulletin of the Needle and Bobbin Club*, vol. 31, 1947

Boser-Sarivaxévanis, Renée, *Aperçus sur la teinture à l'indigo en Afrique Occidentale*. Birkhäuser, Basel, 1969

Boudot, Eric & Christopher Buckley, *The Roots of Asian Weaving: The He Haiyan Collection of Textiles and Looms from Southwest China*. Oxbow Books, Oxford, 2015

Buckley, Christopher, "First Migrants, First Textiles," in *Textiles of Indonesia: The Thomas Murray Collection*. Prestel, Munich, 2021

Bühler, Alfred, "Ikatten" in *Ciba-Rundschau*, Basel, 1941

Bühler, Alfred, "Ikats" in *Ciba Review*, no. 44, Basel, 1942

Bühler, Alfred, *Ikat, Batik, Plangi*. Pharos Verlag, Basel, 1972

Bühler, Alfred & Eberhard Fischer, *The Patola of Gujarat*. Rock Foundation, New York, and the Museum of Ethnography, Basel, 1979

Bühler, A., Eberhard Fischer & Marie-Louise Nabholz, *Indian Tie-Dyed Fabrics*. Calico Museum, Ahmedabad, 1980

Buss, Chiara, *Silk, Gold and Silver: Eighteenth Century Textiles. Collezione Antonio Ratti*. Fabbri, Milan, 1992

Callañaupa Alvarez, Nilda & Centro de Textiles Tradicionales del Cusco (Peru), *Secrets of Spinning, Weaving, and Knitting in the Peruvian Highlands*. Thrums Books, Loveland, Colorado, 2017

Chandra, Moti, "Indian costumes and textiles from the eighth to the 12th century," in *Journal of Indian Textile History*, vol. V, Ahmedabad, 1960

Chandra, Moti, "Costumes and textiles in the Sultanate Period," in *Journal of Indian Textile History*, vol. VI, Ahmedabad, 1961

Chertudi, Susana, *Tejidos araucanos de la Argentina*. Instituto Nacional de Investigaciones Folklóricas, Buenos Aires, 1961

Chevallier, Dominique, "Un exemple de *résistance* technique de l'artisanat Syrien aux XIXe et XXe siècles: les tissus ikatés d'Alep et de Damas," Extrait de la revue *Syria*, XXXIX, 1962, Fasc. 3-4. Librairie Orientaliste Paul Geuthner, Paris, 1962

Chevallier, Dominique, "A Syrian Craft: The Ikat Weaves," *Middle East Forum* vol. 30, No. 8, Aug–Oct, pp. 25–29. The Alumni Association of the American University of Beirut, Beirut, New York, 1963

Chevallier, Dominique, "Un exemple de résistance technique de l'artisanat Syrien aux XIXe et XXe siecles: les tissus ikatés d'Alep et de Damas", *Villes et Travail en Syrie du XIXe au XXe Siècle*, pp. 89–109. G.-P. Maisonneuve & Larose, Paris, 1982

Cordier, Henri, *La Chine en France au XVIIIe siècle*. Laurens, Paris, 1910

Cox, Raymond, "La 'Grande Fabrique'," *Gazette des beaux-arts : courrier européen de l'art et de la curiosité*, July 1921

Crill, Rosemary, *Indian Ikat Textiles*. V&A Publications, London, 1998

Crill, Rosemary, ed., *Royal Textiles of Mewar*, Noida, 2021

Davis, Virginia, "Resist Dyeing in Mexico: Comments on Its History, Significance, and Prevalence," in ed. Janet Catherine Berlo, Edward Bridgman Dwyer & Margot Schevill, *Textile Traditions of Mesoamerica and the Andes: An Anthology*. 1st University of Texas Press ed. University of Texas Press, Austin, 1996

de Avila, Alejandro B., "Las técnicas textiles y la historia cultural de los pueblos otopames," n.d.

de Avila, Alejandro B., "Mexican Ikat and Transatlantic Trade," in *Textile Society of America Symposium Proceedings (Crosscurrents: Land, Labor, and the Port. Textile Society of America's 15th Biennial Symposium, Savannah, GA)*, 2016

di Villanova, Francesco Alberti. "Far i drappi alla cinese ... vergare, screziar un drappo alla foggia di quelli della Cina," *Grand dictionnaire françois-italien composé sur les dictionnaires* 2. Giuseppe Remondi e Figli, Bassano: 1811

Djawanai, Stephanus, *Ngadha Text Tradition: The Collective Mind of the Ngadha People, Flores (Materials in Languages of Indonesia No. 20)*. Australia National University, Canberra, 1983

Dusenbury, Mary, "Kasuri," in ed. William Jay Rathbun, *Beyond the Tanabata Bridge: Traditional Japanese Textiles*. Thames & Hudson New York, in association with the Seattle Art Museum, 1993

Ehret, Christopher, *The Civilizations of Africa*. University of Virginia, 2016

Fee, Sarah, in Duncan Clarke, Vanessa Drake Moraga, and Sarah Fee, *African Textiles*. Abbeville Press, New York, 2022

Feng, Zhao (ed.), *Recent Excavations of Textiles in China*, China National Silk Museum, Hangzhou, 2002

Fitz Gibbon, Kate & Andrew Hale, *Ikat: Splendid Silks of Central Asia: The Guido Goldman Collection*. Laurence King Publishing, London, 1997

Fraser-Lu, Sylvia, *Textiles in Burman Culture*. Silkworm Books, Chiang Mai, 2021

Gavin, Traude, *The Women's Warpath: Iban Ritual Fabrics from Borneo*. UCLA Fowler Museum of Cultural History, Los Angeles, 1996

Gittinger, Mattiebelle & Leedom H. Lefferts, Jr., *Textiles and the Tai Experience in Southeast Asia*. Textile Museum, Washington DC, 1992

Gluck, Jay & Sumi Hiramoto Gluck, eds., *A Survey of Persian Handicraft*. The Bank Melli Iran, and Survey of Persian Art, Tehran, New York, London, and Ashiya, 1977

Granger-Taylor, Hero, "The Textiles," in K. D. Politis et al., *Sanctuary of Lot in Deir 'Ain 'Abata in Jordan Excavations 1988–2003*. Jordan Distribution Agency, Amman, 2012

Guy, John, *Woven Cargoes*. Thames & Hudson, London, 1998

Guy, John, *Indian Textiles in the East: From Southeast Asia to Japan*. Thames & Hudson, London, 2009

Guy, John & Karun Thakar, *Indian Cotton Textiles*, ACC Art Books, Woodbridge, 2015

Hardouin-Fugier, Elisabeth, Bernard Berthod & Martine Chavent-Fusaro, *Les Etoffes. Dictionnaire historique*. Éditions de l'Amateur, Paris, 1992

Hein, Alois R., *Die Bildenden Künste bei den Dayaks auf Borneo*. Alfred Hölder, Vienna, 1890

Howard, Michael C., *From Dashes to Dragons: The Ikat-Patterned Textiles of Southeast Asia*. White Lotus, Bangkok, 2010

Iklé, Ernest, "Uber Flammentucher" in ed. J. M. Ritz, *Festschrift für Marie Andree-Eysn*. Munich, 1928

Iklé, Ernest, *La broderie mécanique, 1828–1930*. Faucheux, L'Union typographique, Chelles, Villeneuve-Saint-Georges, 1931

Irwin, John & P. R. Schwartz, *Studies in Indo-European Textile History*. Calico Museum of Textiles, Ahmedabad, 1966

Jain, Rahul, *Durbar: Royal Textiles of Jodhpur*. Mehrangarh Museum Trust, Rajasthan, 2009

Jain, Rahul, *Textiles & Garments at the Jaipur Court*. Niyogi Books, New Delhi, 2016

Joubert de l'Hiberderie, Nicolas, *Le dessinateur, pour les fabriques d'etoffes d'or, d'argent et de soie.* Sébastien Jorry, Bauche, Brocas, Paris, 1765

Kalter, Johannes, Margareta Pavaloi, and Maria Zerrnickel, *The Arts and Crafts of Syria.* Thames & Hudson, New York, 1992

Kemp, G. T., Esq., "On the process of printing warps to produce fabrics termed 'clouded' or 'chiné'," *Journal of the Franklin Institute*, March 1844

Kobayashi, Keiko, "The Effect of Western Textile Technology on Japanese *Kasuri*: Development, Innovation, and Competition," in *The Textile Museum Journal*, vol. 40/41, 2001–2002

Kobayashi, Keiko, *Kasuri wo oru: Sekaikakuchi no Kasuri–Nihon no Ukiyo-e ni egakareta Kasuri nado* [Kasuri Weaves: Ikats of the World and Ikats Depicted in Japanese Ukiyo-e]. Japan Publications, Tokyo, 2018

Krody, Sumru Belger, *Colors of the Oasis: Central Asian Ikats*, with contributions by Feza Çakmut, Mary Dusenbury, Kate Fitz Gibbon, Andrew Hale, Sayera Makhkamova, Susan Meller. The Textile Museum, Washington, DC, 2010

Larsen, Jack Lenor, *The Dyer's Art: Ikat, Batik, Plangi.* Van Nostrand Reinhold Company, New York, 1976

Littré, Emile, *Dictionnaire de la langue française* 1, issue 1. Hachette, Paris, 1863

Liu, Da-wei, "Technical Analysis of Ikat from Xuwei No. 1 Ancient Grave in Qinghai 1 Province, China." DOI: https://doi.org/10.21203/rs.3.rs-1689413/v1

Lloyd, Robert, *The St. James's Magazine I.* Flexney, Davies, and Coote, London, 1762

Maxwell, Robyn, *Textiles of Southeast Asia: Tradition, Trade, and Transformation*, rev. ed. Periplus, Singapore, 2014

McCabe, Ina Baghdiantz, *Orientalism in Early Modern France: Eurasian Trade Exoticism and the Ancien Régime.* Bloomsbury, London, 2008

McIntosh, Linda S., *Art of Southeast Asian Textiles: The Tilleke & Gibbins Collection.* Serendia, Bangkok, 2012

McIntosh, Linda S., *Thread and Fire: Textiles and Jewellery from the Isles of Indonesia and Timor.* River Books, Bangkok, 2019

Mege, Pedro R., "Colores en la cultura Mapuche," in ed. Museo Chileno de Arte Precolombino, Francisco Gallardo I. & Luis E. Cornejo B., *Colores de América, 1.* El Museo Chileno de Arte Precolombino, Santiago, Chile, 1992

Miller, Laura Martin, "The Ikat Shawl Traditions of Northern Peru and Southern Ecuador," in ed. Janet Catherine Berlo, Edward Bridgman Dwyer & Margot Schevill, *Textile Traditions of Mesoamerica and the Andes: An Anthology*, 1st University of Texas Press ed., Austin, 1996

Miller, Lesley Ellis, "Representing Silk Design: Nicolas Joubert de l'Hiberderie and Le Dessinateur pour les étoffes d'or, d'argent et de soie (Paris, 1765)," *Journal of Design History 17*, no. 1, 2004

Miralbés de Polanco, Rosario, *Magia y misterio del jaspe: nudos que encierran figuras.* Museo Ixchel del Traje Indígena, Guatemala, 2003

Moraga, Vanessa, "From the Infinite Blue: Mapuche Textiles from Southern Chile," HALI Annual, Hali Publications Ltd., London, 1994

Morales Hidalgo, Italo, *La situación del jaspe en Guatemala*, 1a ed., Colección Tierra adentro 4. Sub-Centro Regional de Artesanías y Artes Populares, Guatemala, 1984

Mosca, Liliana, in Chapurukha M. Kusimba, J. Claire Odland & Bennet Bronson, eds., *Unwrapping the Textile Traditions of Madagascar.* UCLA, Los Angeles, 2004

Moser, Reinhard-Johannes, *Die Ikattechnik in Aleppo.* Pharos-Verlag Hansrudolf Schwabe, Basel, 1974

Nabholz-Kartaschoff, Marie-Louise, *Ikatgewebe aus Südeuropa.* Sandoz, Basel, 1968

Nabholz-Kartaschoff, Marie-Louise, *Ikatgewebe aus Nord- und Südeuropa.* Pharos-Verlag Hansrudolf Schwabe, Basel, 1969

Nabholz-Kartaschoff, Marie-Louise, "From telia rumal to Pochampalli tie and dye: old and new ikats from Andhra Pradesh," in ed. K. Riboud, *In Quest of Themes and Skills: Asian Textiles.* Marg Publications, Mumbai, 1989

Nabholz-Kartaschoff, Marie-Louise, *Pfauen, Blüten & Zypressen: Persische Textilien der Qajaren-Zeit (1788–1925).* Museum Rietberg, Zürich, 2005

Nabholz-Kartaschoff, Marie-Louise, *Persian Textiles: The Ramezani Family Collection.* Verlag Anton Pustet, Salzburg, 2019

Nunome, Junro, *The Archaeology of Fiber Before Your Eyes: A Compilation of Photographs of Fiber Artifacts.* Senshoku to Seikatsu Sha, Kyoto, 1992

Plankensteiner, Barbara & Nath Adediran, *African Lace.* Snoeck, Ghent, 2011

Prin, Rémy, *Ikats, tissus de vie, un voyage de l'Orient à l'Occident.* Parole & Patrimoine, Néré, 2017

Quizon, Cherubim, "Between the Field and the Museum: the Benedict Collection of Bagobo Abaca Textiles," in *Textile Society of America Symposium Proceedings*, 1998

Reid, Anthony, *Southeast Asia in the Age of Commerce, 1450–1680: Volume One: The Lands below the Winds.* Yale University Press, New Haven, 1988

Rodier, Paul, *The Romance of French Weaving.* Tudor, New York, 1936

Roland-Gosselin, Anne-Gabrielle, "Mais d'où vient le mot «chiner» ?" *Le Figaro*, 18 February 2018

Rothstein, Natalie, *Silk Designs of the Eighteenth Century.* Bulfinch Press, London, 1990

Rouffaer, Gerrit Pieter, "Over ikat's, tjinde's, patola's en chine's" in *Kolonial Weekblad*, No. 22. The Hague, 1901

Rouffaer, Gerrit Pieter, *Over ikat's, Tjinde's, Patola's en Chiné's*, Uitgevers-Maatschappij, The Hague, 1902

Rowe, Ann Pollard, *Warp-Patterned Weaves of the Andes.* Textile Museum, Washington, 1977

Rowe, Ann Pollard & John Cohen, *Hidden Threads of Peru: Q'ero Textiles.* Merrell, London, in association with the Textile Museum, Washington, DC, 2002

Rowe, Ann Pollard & Lynn A. Meisch, *Costume and History in Highland Ecuador*, illustrated edition. University of Texas Press, Austin, 2011

Rowe, Ann Pollard, Laura Martin Miller & Lynn A. Meisch, *Weaving and Dyeing in Highland Ecuador*, ed. Ann Pollard Rowe. University of Texas Press, Austin, 2007

Scheler, Jean Auguste Udalric, *Dictionnaire d'étymologie française.* Auguste Schnée, Firmin Didot, Frères, Fils et Cie, Brussels, Paris, 1862

Schoff, Wilfred Harvey, ed., *The Periplus of the Erythrean Sea*, Longmans, New York, 1912 (repr. 1974)

Serjeant, R. B., "Material for a History of Islamic Textiles up to the Mongol Conquest," Chapter XV, "Textiles in the Yemen," *Ars Islamica*, vol. 13, 1948

Shamir, Orit & Alisa Baginski, "The earliest cotton ikat textiles from Nahal 'Omer Israel 650–810 CE," in ed.Marie-LouiseNosch,ZhaoFengand Lotika Varadarajan, *Global Textile Encounters.* Oxbow Books, Oxford and Philadelphia, 2014

Spink, Walter M., *Ajanta: A Brief History and Guide*, Asian Art Archives of the University of Michigan, 1990

Stinchecum, Amanda Mayer, "Textiles of Okinawa" in ed. William Jay Rathbun, *Beyond the Tanabata Bridge: Traditional Japanese Textiles.* Thames & Hudson New York, in association with the Seattle Art Museum, 1993

Tavernier, Jean-Baptiste, *Travels in India* (tr. V. Ball), 2nd edition, ed. W. Crooke. Oxford University Press, 1925

Thanasook, Somboon, "Chuan-tani or Limar Cloth: Cloth in the Lower Region of Southern Thailand," in ed. Jane Puranananda, *Through the Thread of Time: Southeast Asian Textiles.* River Books, Bangkok, 2004

Thépaut-Cabasset, Corinne, 'Fashion Encounters: The 'Siamoise', or the impact of the Great Embassy on textile design in Paris in 1687," in ed. Marie-Louise Nosch, Zhao Feng, and Lotika Varadarajan, *Global Textile Encounters.* Oxbow Books, Oxford, 2011

Thornton, Peter, *Baroque and Rococo Silks.* Taplinger, New York, 1965

Turpin, Deborah Lee and Estelle Whelan, "In Search of Alaja: An Experiment in Matching Text to Text le," *Studies in the Decorative Arts*, Fall, vol. 1, No. 1. The University of Chicago Press on behalf of the Bard Graduate Center, Chicago and New York, 1993

Van Stan, Ina, "A Peruvian Ikat from Pachacamac," in *American Antiquity*, vol. 23, No. 2, 1957

Weir, Shelagh, *Palestinian Costume.* University of Texas Press in co-operation with British Museum Publications, Austin and London, 1989

Weitlaner-Johnson, Irmgard, "Amarres, texturas y flecos: técnicas del rebozo," in ed. Irène Logan and Museo Franz Mayer, 2. ed., *Rebozos de la colección Robert Everts*, Colección Uso y estilo 1. Museo Franz Mayer, México, D.F., 1997

Yefimova, Louisa & Rina Belogorskaya, eds., intro. by Olga Gordeyeva, *Russian Kerchiefs and Shawls.* Aurora Art Publishers, Leningrad, 1985

Z., Waldo Jordán, "El Watado, Técnica Textil de Los Andes Bolivianos (Primera Parte & Segunda Parte)," *Textiles Andinos Bolivianos* (blog), http://textilesandinos.blogspot.com